OUTSIDE IN
Volume II - 1983–2022

OUTSIDE IN

The Oral History of Guido Calabresi

by
NORMAN I. SILBER

Volume II - 1983–2022

OXFORD
UNIVERSITY PRESS

Oxford University Press is a department of the University of Oxford. It furthers the University's objective of excellence in research, scholarship, and education by publishing worldwide. Oxford is a registered trade mark of Oxford University Press in the UK and certain other countries.

Published in the United States of America by Oxford University Press
198 Madison Avenue, New York, NY 10016, United States of America.

© Oxford University Press 2023

All rights reserved. No part of this publication may be reproduced, stored in a retrieval system, or transmitted, in any form or by any means, without the prior permission in writing of Oxford University Press, or as expressly permitted by law, by license, or under terms agreed with the appropriate reproduction rights organization. Inquiries concerning reproduction outside the scope of the above should be sent to the Rights Department, Oxford University Press, at the address above.

You must not circulate this work in any other form
and you must impose this same condition on any acquirer.

CIP data is on file at the Library of Congress

ISBN 978-0-19-763513-1

DOI: 10.1093/oso/9780197635131.001.0001

1 3 5 7 9 8 6 4 2

Printed by Lakeside Book Company, United States of America

Note to Readers
This publication is designed to provide accurate and authoritative information in regard to the subject matter covered. It is based upon sources believed to be accurate and reliable and is intended to be current as of the time it was written. It is sold with the understanding that the publisher is not engaged in rendering legal, accounting, or other professional services. If legal advice or other expert assistance is required, the services of a competent professional person should be sought. Also, to confirm that the information has not been affected or changed by recent developments, traditional legal research techniques should be used, including checking primary sources where appropriate.

(Based on the Declaration of Principles jointly adopted by a Committee of the American Bar Association and a Committee of Publishers and Associations.)

You may order this or any other Oxford University Press publication by visiting the Oxford University Press website at www.oup.com.

Cover Image, Vol. II: Guido Calabresi narrating. Photo Norman I. Silber

Preface to Volume II

In Volume I, Guido tells the story of his growing up. He speaks of his family history, his departure from Italy in the shadow of World War II, his upbringing, and his education in New Haven. Early on, he introduces us to an important distinction between his Italian family and others who also arrived poor, and who also were grateful to have found a refuge and a chance for success in America. Guido's family arrived with an intangible inheritance, a deep awareness that there had been, spread throughout the family's past—and on both sides, and for many generations—considerable wealth, social standing, and intellectual accomplishment. His father, furthermore, had been an anti-Fascist, and both parents harbored liberal political and social views. And so, while many Italian immigrants were "painting themselves red, white, and blue" out of gratitude for their new land, embracing conservative values in politics and religion, the Calabresi family "talked Italian, [and] absorbed our ... history, and unselfconsciously thought of ourselves as being what we always were." This inheritance—and his attachment subsequently to Italy, created a reservoir of confidence, an impetus to achievement, and as a scholar, an unusual lens through which to consider his novel ideas about motivations, incentives, and the ways events and conditions influence choices.

Volume I addresses the educational culture of the schools Guido attended in the 1940s and 1950s—first public schools and then private ones. He distinguished himself academically, always standing at or near the top of class. The challenges to his happiness and success, however, were not purely academic. For worse and sometimes better, he was identifiable clearly as an outsider in the world he had entered, and "not a Yankee." He was Italian American, Jewish by heritage and Catholic by the faith he embraced; this proved at times to be an impediment, and at times to make easier, entering social relationships, clerkships, firms, and even the marriage he wanted, to Anne Gordon Audubon Tyler, most definitely part of a "Yankee" family.

He also reflects on his teaching career and much of his major scholarship in the earlier volume, including the development of his early interest in law and economics. He had written essays as a Rhodes Scholar at Oxford on the negative side effects from some private transactions, and then as a law student began to think about how tort law dealt with them. There ensued pathbreaking articles and books exploring law and economics, including *Some Thoughts about Risk Distribution and the Law of Torts* (1961); THE COST OF ACCIDENTS (1970); *Property Rules Liability Rules and Inalienability: One View of the Cathedral* (1972); and TRAGIC CHOICES (1978).

Another theme running through Guido's scholarship is an appreciation for the complexity of common law statutory interpretation by courts, and the interaction of the common law with legislation. It seemed to Guido, as it did to his former teacher and friend Grant Gilmore, that "the whole background of the common law deserved greater attention by judges as they analyzed statutes." A COMMON LAW FOR THE AGE OF STATUTES (1982) took a deep look at this subject and offered an intrepid justification for interventions to update obsolete statutes and to foster dialogues by courts with legislators. That book stimulated the emergence of statutory interpretation as a field and was for Guido very exciting work which paid "homage both to my teachers and to the common law." Its publication closed a productive early period in his scholarly life and ends this first part of the story.

This volume explores the next phases of Guido's career—his remarkable performance as a dean and as a judge on the United States Court of Appeals.

Table of Contents

VOLUME II

PART THREE: LEADING YALE LAW SCHOOL

18. To Be a Dean	5
19. The Dean's New Day	29
20. Independence	57
21. Restoring the Law School Building	73
22. Almost a Justice: Robert Bork	91
23. Conflict, Community, and Confidence: The Wall	107
24. Clarence, Anita, Catharine, Jack—and Yale	127

PART FOUR: SITTING ON THE SECOND CIRCUIT

25. Bill Wants Him	153
26. Joining the Second Circuit	173
27. The Tort Law Opinions of a Torts Professor	197
28. The Anti-Discrimination Law Reasoning of an Outsider	241
29. The Analytical Reasoning of a Behavioral Economist	269
30. Calabresian Complexities and the Value of Dialogue	281
31. The Immigration Law Decisions of an Immigrant	303
32. An Egalitarian Believer's First Amendment	321
33. Craft, Independence, and Ideology	345
34. Giustizia e Liberta' Recollected: Bad Laws and Injustices	371

CODA

35. Explanations in *The Garden*	423
Image Acknowledgments	439
Index	447

VOLUME II

1983–2022

PART THREE
LEADING YALE LAW SCHOOL

Part Three of the narrative begins near to the moment when Guido has given thought to becoming the dean of Yale Law School. Guido talks about becoming dean and his steps to win financial independence for the school, to redirect the administration of the school, to refresh and revitalize the faculty, to raise funds, and to enhance intellectual discourse. The involvement of several Yale alumni and faculty in national political affairs required Guido to play a part in two historically momentous Supreme Court nominations.

18
To Be a Dean

For most of his life, Guido watched University presidents and deans come and go, succeed and fail—as a Yale college student, a law student, a faculty member, and the child of a graduate student in the French Department (his mother) and a faculty member at the Medical School (his father). He developed strong perspectives about the qualities deans and administrators should have and respect for the ones who did their work well.

His quick rise to prominence as a legal scholar; his interconnectedness with different generations on the Law School faculty; his popularity as a teacher; and his enthusiastic engagement with governance matters provided ample reasons for his colleagues and the University to consider him at several points as a decanal candidate. In 1985, he was selected as dean of the Yale Law School.

My attitude towards being a dean owes a great deal to having known Gene Rostow as a dean. I think back to around 1965 when Gene was finishing one of the great deanships in the history of the Law School. He did less well in the second term than in the first term because, by then, he had made all sorts of people deeply opposed to him; but even his opponents, nonetheless, recognized that his first term was a great one.

He was a great counselor to young faculty members, for instance. Shortly after I started teaching, I was asked to work with the Council of Economic Advisors. I asked Rostow if I was allowed to do it. Rostow said, "Do you want to do it?" I said, "I do not know; I'm asking if it is permitted." Rostow said, "No, you have it backwards." He said, "If you want to do it, of course you can. If you do not want to do it, these are powerful people, and they will resent it if you say no, and that may hurt you sometime. If you do not want to do it, tell them I forbade it." This generosity was part of the greatness of Rostow.

Toward the end of the second term, though, mentor-friend Whitney Griswold was no longer there. He became tired, and the problems grew.

* * *

In 1965, Gene left the Law School to go to work for the Johnson administration. A few years earlier, Kingman Brewster had become president of the University, and this was Kingman's first chance to choose the Law School dean. Coming out of Harvard, he wanted very much to steer the process, and he did. He played different people against each other.

Alex Bickel wanted very much to be the dean, but he found there were those who did not like him and were pushing somebody else. Kingman wanted Lou Pollak, who was very close to him, to be the dean. Rostow, who believed that the faculty should ultimately vote for a dean, was nonetheless not going to stand in the way of Kingman. The whole thing was sufficiently manipulated so that in the end, Kingman was able to name Lou Pollak in a way that made Lou totally dependent on him.

The faculty was completely unhappy with what had happened, and I saw that they were not going to support Lou at all. I saw this coming, and, young punk that I was, I went to see him. You remember he had been my teacher in Constitutional Law. I admired him greatly, and I still do. I told Lou that he should not take the deanship under these circumstances; that he had to tell Kingman Brewster to open up the selection process more.

Various things happened when I did this. What precisely they were, I do not know, but Kingman then called Abe Goldstein back from England—where he was on sabbatical—to run against Lou. But Kingman *still* manipulated the process, and he *still* got Lou as the dean, and the faculty was *still* not happy.

Gene Rostow came to me. He told me that I had done a terrible thing in talking to Lou and that, having done that, I would never be dean of Yale Law School. My immediate reaction was to say to Rostow, "But Gene, what makes you think I want to be Dean of the Law School?"

> *I haven't thought about this until now—but though it was 1965, when I was still very much a kid, Rostow already thought of me as someone who should be Dean of Yale Law School. I'm sure he also thought of Harry Wellington as someone who should be Dean, for very similar reasons: because we were New Haveners and we were Jewish, as was he; and he kind of liked that idea; there were other reasons as well.*

Lou Pollak's deanship was not a success, in considerable part because of inadequate faculty support. Of course, the years Pollak was dean were also very difficult times for deans everywhere. That is all part of the history of the 1960s, of the student unrest and other upheavals during that time.

* * *

After Lou Pollak, Abe Goldstein came on. The most significant part of his deanship was what many have called "the slaughter of the innocents." Abe thought that most of the people who had been named to law faculty positions during Lou's time—and not just at Yale, but across the law school world—were not excelling. In retrospect, he was probably right about this.

It was the time of the great student movement. A lot of good things happened, but it is also the case that just as the people who came on in '56 at Yale outperformed themselves as scholars, the people who started teaching between '65 and '70, by and large, did not. Most schools promoted them anyway, and many of them became, in terms of being scholars, the living dead.

Goldstein, rather brutally, decided to kick out the ones he thought had not produced. He was very program-oriented; he wanted to do things from a curricular, program point of view. He saw that most of these people had not adequately performed. Additionally, he did not like some of them, and his relatively conservative manner may have interfered with appreciating their intelligence.

This callousness he showed toward the hires of the late 1960s was considered by some as a move against the Left. I really do not think it was. Some who were kicked out were conservatives. Abe Goldstein was an equal opportunity tough guy.

He was anti-anarchy and tried to run things in a fairly controlled fashion, which meant that he wasn't able to get much of his positive program through. For instance, his ideas about writing programs never went anywhere; he did do somewhat better beginning an in-house clinical program. Abe brought to mind Henry Wade Rogers, the 1903–1914 dean, whose deanship was not a success because— it was said—he tried to govern by rules, rather than common sense.

I found myself at the center of the "slaughter." I had been secretary of the Appointments Committee—running the whole thing several times under Lou Pollak. Under Abe, I was supposedly leading it again, this time as chair. Abe said that the dean should not be chair of the Appointments Committee—but in reality, of course, he ran everything! On Appointments, he was an extremely strong voice; certainly, strong enough to keep people from getting tenure.

Many of us were upset with this, and an understanding was reached. It was to have people like me, and others, to make sure—whether we voted in favor of tenure or not—that those who were not promoted got good teaching jobs elsewhere. I and others would call schools and say, "You know, Yale is so darn quirky," and "I think this guy's terrific." This had never happened before; those very few who did not get tenure would be on the street. We got all of them good jobs, and they ended up at any number of good places. They did well there, but in retrospect, only a couple of them at most became strong enough so that one could say they really should have been at Yale.

*At that time, getting tenure at the leading law schools was just about automatic— I mean, at Harvard it was three years. And unless you wore the wrong color necktie—and there was one person who did that—you automatically went up. And it did not matter whether you wrote or not! But it was also the case that **not** getting tenure was close to death.*

So the big change that happened in Abe's deanship was this "slaughter of the innocents," if you want to call it that. Abe was responsible for it, and in retrospect, he really should be given credit, along with blame, because it was not a pleasant task. I did not like it much, then, even when I had my doubts about the quality of some.

* * *

What was the effect? There were, as I will mention soon enough, some very good consequences. There were also some negative ones. The first of these is that John Ely, one of the few who had performed in the 1960s, left to go to Harvard. He did that for two reasons, one admirable and the other less so.

The admirable part was Ely found himself in the difficult situation of being a person called on to vote on his friends. He knew that it would violate his own standards to vote for them, because he knew they were not good enough. He believed that Abe was basically right, that these people had not made it. Not through their fault, but through the circumstances. But he did not want to vote either for or against them. By leaving, he could avoid an impossible choice.

The "less-so" was that at Yale he saw, from right to left in Constitutional Law, Bork, Bickel, Pollak, Black, and Emerson, and he said, "Where is there room for me?" He looked at Harvard, and he saw no one. He thought, "I will be the Constitutional Law person at Harvard." But that incredible buzz saw of Larry Tribe came in and turned from what had been his field to Constitutional Law, and being the kind of person that he was, Tribe became the dominant constitutional law star at Harvard. John left again to become dean at Stanford, but, as he said to me and others, it was really this place, Yale, which he continued to love as much as he ever had.

The other negative consequence of failing to promote so many was that the Law School, for many years afterward, had trouble hiring juniors. This problem ended dramatically more than ten years later when I was named dean designate, and we hired as juniors Akhil Amar, Paul Kahn, Harold Koh, and Kate Stith.

* * *

Both Lou Pollak and Abe Goldstein were five-year deans who did not stay as long as might have been expected. After Abe announced that five years was enough for him, a faculty selection committee was appointed to come up with names of possible successors.

> *There's always a faculty committee that comes up with names. The committee somehow gets selected by the University President, the outgoing Dean, and various faculty members. It has a funny job. The President thinks he picks the Dean. The faculty thinks it picks the Dean. They kind of maneuver around each other like an elephant on the land and a whale on the sea. The committee goes back and forth between the President and the faculty and comes up with some amphibian.*

The selection committee focused in on two people—Harry Wellington and me. By this time, Kingman had learned enough about the problems of manipulating a faculty like the Yale Law School that he wasn't going to play the game that he had played before. But he did make it clear that he did not want the faculty to send him only one name; he wanted to be able to choose from at least two.

It was 1975. I did not know if I wanted to be dean at *some* time, but I was in the middle of heavy writing, and I knew I did not want the job *then*. I also thought that anyway—quite correctly, especially in his first term—Harry would be a wonderful dean.

I decided to go see Kingman Brewster. I did it because I knew that Kingman had known Harry at Harvard; I think Harry had been his student, and it was not impossible that Kingman did not want him.

One did not know what the relationship of people like Wellington and Brewster back then was. I did not want Kingman to be in a situation in which the faculty would send him two names, Calabresi and Wellington, and he would decide he did not want Wellington, and come to me and have me say, "Look, I do not want it." I thought that would be terrible, because it might cause a 'constitutional crisis.'

Kingman gave me an appointment at breakfast, at the president's house at 43 Hillhouse Avenue. A great breakfast gets laid out. Kingman is nothing if not elegant! He arrives in a magnificent silken dressing gown. He's about seven feet taller than I am, and after greeting me, we sit down and have breakfast, and over breakfast, I go through my spiel. I tell him, "I know you want two names, but I do not want to be Dean. I do not want to be Dean now, because I'm doing writing that I want to finish. And in any event, I think Harry will be a superb Dean. But because I know that you knew him as a student, I do not want to put you in an awkward position if for any reason you have doubts about him and would like *me* to be Dean."

Kingman listens patiently. When I'm finally finished, he gets up to his full height, gives me his hand, and looking at me directly, he says, "Guido, you have ***nothing*** to worry about."

So I keep my name in the running; two names get sent to him, and Harry gets picked as the dean.

* * *

After the large group of the "innocents" had been "slaughtered," we needed desperately to replenish the faculty. Which is what Harry does in his first term as dean, and even Abe started at the very end of his term, with the appointments of Owen Fiss and Geoff Hazard. Harry, with me back on the Appointments Committee, goes out and looks for those relatively few scholars in each of the other schools, who, despite the distracting times, have succeeded.

We go out and locate wonderful people like Bruce Ackerman, Bo [Robert] Burt; Michael Graetz, Arthur Leff, Jerry Mashaw, and youngsters like Robert Cover, George Priest, Tony Kronman, Lea Brillmayer and Roberta Romano. This group becomes, for decades, the core of the Yale Law School in the same way the class of '56, which Rostow brought in, was the core. The faculty gets rebuilt in a magnificent way, and these scholars become the foundation for much of what makes the Law School great for years to come. This was the extraordinary success of Harry Wellington's deanship, most of it in his first term.

> *Harry said he could not have been as successful as Dean if Alex Bickel had remained alive. They were close, but the shadow that Alex would have probably cast could have been damaging. Alex wanted to be Dean but wasn't suited for it. He may also not have been as brilliant as Harry! Harry had the subtler mind, but not the courage to go out and push his ideas one step further; Alex always did. Alex was immensely hard working. I remember him saying to Ronnie Dworkin and me, partly to push us, "If I was as smart as you, what I could do!" He was saying: "You two get off your duffs and work as hard as I do." Alex died at about the time Harry became Dean, and that freed Harry to do what he wanted.*

At the end of Harry's first term, there were, unfortunately, negative developments. Kingman left. The school's relationship with the University deteriorated. There was a financial tightening. And then, in the hands of Kingman's successor, there was an utter centralization, which put the Law School's finances into bad shape. The University stole almost everything that we got from our alumni or from grants. The Deputy Provost tried to help the Law School, but it was not enough.

> *We were no longer able to cherry-pick the people who had succeeded at other schools as we had done earlier, because we could not offer them decent salaries. The salaries of the Yale Law School when I became Dean were about fourteenth in the top twenty schools. You do not hire people away when you're paying less. You may be able to keep the people you have, but you do not hire people away! Having really top people from outside was closed off to Harry. And the juniors most in demand were unlikely to come to Yale because of Yale's history of firing!*

So in the last five years of Harry's deanship there were real problems with recruitment. Not only were faculty salaries falling way behind, but because of problems with two-career families, we could not keep some very important people, like Bruce Ackerman, because we could not get the Economics Department to take seriously Susan Rose-Ackerman, who was a very good scholar. There were other hits, too. Arthur Leff, at the core of the faculty, died young. Harry was by then too exhausted to react forcefully.

Wellington was also superstitious; he thought that when luck was with him, anything could go. Now, things were turning negative, and he grew passive and fatalistic. He was also a hypochondriac, as I can be sometimes too. They used to call Harry, Ronnie Dworkin, and me, the three Sterling Professors of Medicine, because we would talk about our illnesses!

Toward the end of Harry's deanship, articles start getting written about Yale losing it. You'll find them all over the place. They're "not able to hire," "they're losing their edge," and so on.

* * *

Harry's ten years are about to be up—it's the beginning of his ninth year. The president is now Bart Giamatti, an old friend of mine. Bart's mother had kind of studied Italian literature with my mother, and I had known Bart from the time he had come to Yale as a teacher. He was a remarkable scholar, a remarkable person, with many gifts.

Bart's grandfather had come from a little village in the province of Benevento, three villages over from the people who lived in a cottage on our property in Woodbridge, and who helped us out from the time we bought our house. At a square dance we gave for the junior faculty and Bart when he became President, because he liked to dance, our old farmer welcomed him, and asked him where in Italy he was from. Bart says the name of the village, and then Bart says, "Where are you from?" And this guy says what his village is. Bart says, "Ah, two villages over." This old farmer says, "You are wrong—three villages over. There's this one, this one, and this one." Bart, to his credit, says, "You're absolutely right," and a wonderful relationship was formed between them! The old farmer, Luigi Iannuzi, died years ago. His widow died just four years ago and made soup for me every day, to keep me healthy. Bart was in many ways the epitome of the southern Italian farmer: he was smart, dignified, widely learned, and determined to make it. Bart's grandfather had come at a very young age to New Haven, and then brought over younger brothers and sisters; and there are still cousins of Bart's who run grocery stores and such things all through New Haven. The grandfather got his son to go to Yale. The son became an Italian literature professor at Mount Holyoke. Bart was brought up in that kind of a setting and ended up after high school at Andover for a year, where—by one of those unlikely wild chances—he roomed with Anne's first cousin, Thomas Crosby, who was both a Crosby and Pillsbury. He then came to Yale.

Yale was open to him in the way Yale had become since his father's time. It was now open to a really brilliant person of any sort. Rather than going into an Italian Department, he chooses the English Department, which is the hardest department to make tenure in—and for a while, he acts as if he doesn't even know Italian! He becomes a full professor and, at that point, he shows how much he knows about Italian literature, as well. He was truly wide-ranging and a brilliant writer. His essay on baseball, and why baseball is the epitome of the American game, is fantastic.

But, with all of these qualities, Bart also had a Southern Italian peasant's viewpoint—that you do not trust anybody else. You know how to do it; you can do it, and everybody else has to be treated with suspicion.

* * *

Yale has never really solved the problem of how a great university should be administered. Whitney Griswold was an administrator, but only in a small way—he ran the place by relying on a few friends and a few history professors whom he knew well. And he ran it fine, thank you, by talking to these close friends.

Brewster came in, and he was not an administrator at all. He expanded programs and facilities magnificently, but basically just by spending money! There was no careful planning; there was just the throwing of money at problems. When his presidency ended, Yale was in financial crisis.

In comes this brilliant Italian peasant, Giamatti, who says, "I will take everything under my control. I will run things and get things straight." And he did take control, and it worked pretty well for a while—he got finances into shape. But the other side of this was that he wanted no one who was powerful enough to challenge him or his decisions, anywhere. The deans of the various schools, whom Bart names, are all people who will do what he wants. Bart ultimately picks as provost Bill Brainard, a very good economist and a saint of enormous patience, who was willing to do everything that Bart told him, and able to count pencils and make sure that you do not have one pencil too many.

This control works okay for a while, but as we know, command economies, in the end, collapse. You cannot run things that way for very long.

* * *

When Harry's term was about to end, Bart let it be known that he would not let anybody on the faculty pull out ahead of his making a choice. Obviously, no one *had to* become dean, but no one was allowed to pull out of the running while the process was going on.

Why did Bart do that? Because he knew that I was far from sure that I wanted to be dean, and that I might have pulled out. I probably would not have. But, he doesn't want to take a chance.

The faculty committee has some doubts—I expect proper ones—about me. I do not know if their concerns turned out not to be the right ones that they might have about me, but there were doubts. At that point, it was pretty clear that I am the one whom the faculty prefers, and by a long shot.

When they chose me, they continued the history of choosing somebody who was one of the youngest of the older generation—I was at the younger end of Gene Rostow's appointments and a bridge to the next generation that was there. Tony Kronman was one of Harry Wellington's later appointments. Harold Koh was maybe the last of Harry's appointments or the first of Guido's. The person who becomes Dean at this School, at least, tends to be somebody whom a younger generation identifies with, and who is part of them; but whom an older generation is comfortable with because that person sort of came on with them.

Bart calls me in and says, "Guido, you are the only person on whom the faculty and I can possibly agree. Will you cause a constitutional crisis by saying no?"

He knew me very well. We had walked all day together before he accepted the Presidency. He knew I was a northern Italian, and like all southerners, he was skeptical of northerners. I mean, when he saw Bread and Chocolate, *he saw it with John Wilkinson, his Secretary of the University, and whom I had picked as Headmaster at Hopkins, and so he was a good friend of us both. Bart told him, "Yes, yes, Guido should go see it, but he'll never understand it as I do, because he's from Milan. He's from the North. Mine is a different Italian experience than his." That was both right and wrong. I mean, they're different kinds of backgrounds, but there is much of cultural and spiritual life that is shared.*

Bart knew that what he said about a constitutional crisis was a point I would not take lightly. I said I'd talk to Anne, because there would be some significant sacrifice for her, in terms of her life and her plans. Anne said, "Take it. You may find that you have some skills that you did not think you had." And so I accepted.

* * *

What is interesting is that I did not have the sense to realize what his choice of me meant about Bart. I was sufficiently "Guido-centered" to think that he had picked me because I was his friend, older than him, but close, somebody he really could rely on. If I had noticed that at the same time he picked me, he also named a guy who won the Nobel Prize, a scientist, as dean of Yale College, who was a powerful fellow; and that he picked a dean of the Medical School who was also powerful. If I had noticed the common thread among us, I would have realized that Bart was going to leave. In fact, Bart had decided that at the end of that year, he was going to go. Now that he was leaving, he wanted people there in place who were independent, which, when he was president, he had never wanted. I think if Bart had not decided to go, friendship or not, faculty or not, I would not have been chosen by him to be dean.

But Bart had decided that he was tired of the job. There had been a long and hard strike of the clerical workers, which had brought out the worst in Bart—almost a bunker mentality. He had felt betrayed by the union workers, many of whom were New Haveners like him, who he thought should simply trust him. This brought an odd insistence on loyalty from all concerned—that possessed him; that he really did not understand.

One of the funniest ironies of that strike is that it could only succeed if students were supporting it, but students wanted to be taught. How could the employees succeed in gaining the sympathy of the students? The union brilliantly said, "If people teach off-campus, they are supporting the union." This of course is odd because in most strikes, continuing production off-site is what their employers want to do. The Law School faculty, which had experience in these things, said, "Fine! We'll all go teach off-campus. That way, individual moralities, consciences or not, everything is fine."

Bart was furious with us! And furious with me, because I was one of the people who did that. I tried to explain this to him, but to Bart it was a betrayal. Once again, he needed to be in control. It had to be done his way.

Anyway, the strike was one factor which led him to step down. He also obviously was ill, but he did not know it. He refused to go to doctors; his father had died young of a heart attack, and he had had attacks, which he did not recognize because he did not want to know about them. He ultimately died very young.

* * *

As dean designate, I go to the faculty and I tell them the following: One, that I will always tell them the truth. Two, that I plan to be a five-year dean—I tried to live up to that but did not. Three, that we must make top appointments, and we must make them immediately; and that this will be easy in Law and Economics, because we are so strong there that people will want to come, and my own reputation will not hurt. Four, I said I will push for those, but they should not be fooled into thinking, or suppose, that Law and Economics is what I want the Law School to be all about, because *I do not*. I tell them that I want the Yale Law School to be a place that hires the best across every field, and that just as we're doing hiring in Law and Economics, we will soon enough do it in Law and History, and Law and Philosophy, in all things including straight law. We will spread ourselves across the board. I am going to go after the best people we can get, and we're going to get them, and get them fast! I then say any number of other things about making the place the kind of place that it has always been, emphasizing scholarship, humanity, colleagueship.

I come out of that meeting, and Abe says to me, "Guido, that was a terrible talk. A Dean can, if he is lucky, achieve one narrow thing in his Deanship—*if* he is lucky. You have spread yourself too thin. You want to do everything. It is all going to fail."

I looked at him and I said, "Abe, you may well me right, but that is not me. That just is not me. I have to try to put the Law School's finances in order. I have to fix this building, which is falling apart. I have to hire not just in Law and Economics, but in every other field as well. I have to try to do it all. I may fail, but that's the way it's going to be."

So there we are: to try to do it all.

* * *

The turnover itself was a non-event, because Harry was exhausted. During the spring term, I was running everything, and giving these talks, and telling the faculty what I would do. Today, when the new dean comes in, there is a ceremonial turning over of the maces. Turning them over is part of the good hokum that came after me.

> *The maces belong to me, and they're on permanent loan. One is the walking stick of Morris Tyler, the Mayor of New Haven during the Civil War, and a Lincoln supporter. He was Anne's great-great-grandfather, who gave the Law School its first permanent site in City Hall. The stick represents New Haven in the Law School. The other has always represented the link between the Law School and the whole world.*

The deans before me just walked in the graduation ceremony without a mace.

Portrait of Dean Guido Calabresi, by Philadelphia artist John Nelson Shanks

* * *

I received many letters of congratulations after my appointment was announced, including one from Sister Juliana, who had succeeded my mother teaching at Albertus Magnus when my mother finally retired. Sister Juliana expressed

> sadness that my mother was not alive to see the day. It was sad, because while my father was there, my mother was not.
>
> My mother would have seen this as a sign that the University had finally accepted us. That it no longer treated us as outsiders. My becoming dean of the Law School would have meant a great deal to her. She knew I was highly regarded, but she thought that when it came to be being something like the dean, Yale would always look elsewhere. She would have been pleased.

COMMENTARY

Chapter 18

Eugene Rostow. See Guido's narrative about Rostow's deanship, and accompanying commentary about him, in earlier chapters.

Louis H. Pollak. Louis ("Lou") Pollak served as the dean of the Law School between 1965 and 1970—a period Abe Goldstein referred to as "the Dark Ages," when a generation of students accused the faculty and the dean of racism, sexism, and elitism, and tried to intervene in curricular decisions, admissions decisions, grading decisions, and hiring policies. Laura Kalman concludes that Dean Pollak made laudable, "Herculean" efforts to accommodate change, but that for critics—she among them—these came "too late to pacify students" who saw it as a sign of weakness, and a weakness which strained the dean's relations with the faculty.[1]

Guido's warning. Laura Kalman reports that there was some unhappiness on the faculty when it appeared that Pollak would be chosen as dean, because he was the sort of person who was "too interested in making everybody happy."[2] Guido came, without an appointment, to let him know about his own feelings.[3] In an interview in 2010, Judge Pollak said that he remembered "Guido's coming to talk to me, [making] it clear that he didn't think I was the optimum dean person." Pollak was "a little troubled by that, but not to the point where I [knocks on table] called up Kingman Brewster and said, 'Get somebody else. I don't want to go ahead and do it.'"[4] The selection process was extended. Bittker repeatedly turned Brewster down, and the faculty was presented with the choice of Bickel; Goldstein; Wellington; and Lou Pollak, who was chosen.[5] According to Pollak, Bittker was said to have rebuffed

---

[1] LAURA KALMAN, YALE LAW SCHOOL AND THE SIXTIES: REVOLT AND REVERBERATIONS 156 (2005).
[2] *Id.* at 67.
[3] *Id.*
[4] Interview with Hon. Louis Pollak, Oct. 25, 2010.
[5] *Id.*; KALMAN, *supra* note 1, at 66–67.

him with "No, Kingman, I'm not going to become the dean. I will be the best dean that Yale never had."[6]

In the 2010 interview, Lou was saddened to find their awkward conversation included in Kalman's book—he "intended to classify" it. Guido and Lou continued to be friends until Pollak's death, and, in fact, Guido eulogized Lou with grace and emotion at Lou's memorial. But that earlier encounter affected his relationship with Guido. It was, he said, "a sort of bookmark for me of Guido's lack of confidence."[7] Nevertheless, Pollak had Guido run the Appointments Committee during much of his deanship.

The "Dark Ages." The "Ages" were mainly "dark" from some faculty perspectives; the student perspective has been insufficiently appreciated. To most of the Yale Law School graduates of these years, the "Dark Ages" were years of enlightenment— when students came to appreciate the necessity for active involvement in social change and educational reform, as well as to learn the law. Pollak's liberalism fostered a Law School responsive to student concerns— where student empowerment became, for a time, a reality; where the social distance between students and teachers contracted; and where grading became more humane than at other law schools.[8]

The student-centeredness Pollak established was inherited and, to a considerable degree, sustained by subsequent deans. "Almost everything we did then [referring to Pollak's deanship] has been pretty much maintained in some form or other," Abe Goldstein told an interviewer in 1996. "We still have the same pattern of student participation and governance of the school."[9] Guido certainly furthered, adroitly, the projection of a student-centered school administration.[10]

Pollak left Yale and joined the faculty of the University of Pennsylvania in 1974 and became its dean. In 1977, he became a district court judge who became well known for creative, often liberal, decisions and for demonstratively respecting all the litigants who appeared before him. In an important *habeas* case which arose when he decided to sit as a visitor on the Second Circuit, Guido presided and they decided *Triestman v. U.S.*[11] He died in 2012.[12]

Goldstein and the "slaughter of the innocents." Six teachers with junior appointments were denied permanent appointments between 1970 and 1974: Professors John Griffiths, Robert Hudec, David Trubek, Larry Simon, Richard Abel, and Lee Albert.[13] Guido's discussion of what then were unusual

---

[6] Interview with Hon. Louis Pollak, Oct. 25, 2010.
[7] *Id.*
[8] *Id.*
[9] Bonnie Collier, Interview with Prof. Abraham Goldstein, Oct. 23, 1996, published as YALE LAW SCHOOL ORAL HISTORY SERIES: A CONVERSATION WITH ABRAHAM GOLDSTEIN (2012).
[10] See Guido's discussion in Chapter 18, "To Be a Dean."
[11] 124 F.3d 361 (1997) (enlarging the opportunities for habeas review pursuant to 28 U.S.C. § 2241 when parties raise constitutional questions about the statute).
[12] Dennis Hevesi, *Louis H. Pollak, Civil Rights Advocate and Federal Judge, Dies at 89*, N.Y. TIMES, May 12, 2012; Lincoln Caplan, *Louis Pollak, a "Powerful Heart*," N.Y. TIMES, May 10, 2012.
[13] KALMAN, *supra* note 1.

efforts to find other positions for the victims of the bloodbath is supported by other accounts.[14] David Trubek went to the University of Wisconsin; Richard Abel went to the University of California at Los Angeles; Robert Hudec went to the University of Minnesota; Lee Albert went to the University of Buffalo; and Larry Simon to the University of Southern California. Between the end of 1970 and 1972, only two truly junior faculty members—John Ely and Michael Reisman—were promoted.[15]

The Yale Law Faculty in 1970–1971. Guido was on leave.

Mark Tushnet, a leading Critical Legal Studies scholar, who was a student at Yale between 1967 and 1971, argues against "the Official Story" that the Yale faculty acted as it did to raise the standards for granting tenure.[16] Tushnet frames the dismissals in the context of urban unrest, antiwar protests, and other manifestations of radicalism in New Haven at the time—and fears of the senior Law School faculty of the erosion of their academic authority:

> Though few of the junior faculty had radical politics, they were all substantially more sympathetic to the claims being made by students than were many of the senior faculty. The senior faculty took on the air of a beleaguered garrison, defending the ramparts at all costs against the assaults of the barbarians. Those

---

[14] *Id.*
[15] Jennifer A. Kingson, *Harvard Tenure Battle Puts "Critical Legal Studies" on Trial*, N.Y. TIMES, Aug. 30, 1987.
[16] Mark Tushnet, *Critical Legal Studies: A Political History*, 100 YALE L.J. 1515 (1991).

who suggested even in the mildest way that the students might be on to something were politically unreliable.[17]

Tushnet illustrates with the example of faculty member John Griffiths. Griffiths had helped set up a legal research seminar on problems arising from the draft and was empirically exploring the effectiveness of the Miranda warnings that were given by federal agents who were investigating draft evasion. Such activist interests of the junior faculty demonstrated to many seniors a lack of soundness when taken together with the sympathy shown for the crowds outside the courthouse in New Haven, and for student efforts to have a voice in Law School grading and the curriculum.[18] Many of the faculty involved in the decisions, however, recalled reasons connected to Giffiths's teaching and scholarship, independent of his political sympathies, sufficient to reject him.

Four decades later, Professor Bruce Ackerman regarded the dismissals as "a completely disreputable blot, which stains the history of Yale Law School almost as badly as the ideologically motivated hiring and firing decisions made in the fifties."[19] Several of these actions were justifiable on the basis of scholarly productivity or potential, Ackerman concedes, but "they were right, for the wrong reasons!"[20]

The "slaughter" grayed and darkened the atmosphere. Professor Jerry Mashaw arrived at Yale around 1976. He recalled that while sitting around a table of fifteen or more of the faculty at Mory's, his first impression was "of a very old faculty." There was a palpable sense of a missing generation, and Wellington "was very much in the mode of trying to rejuvenate the faculty."[21]

John Langbein, who was not teaching at Yale at the time, recalled that from a distance, the denials affected perceptions of collegiality and possibly politicization. "There was some sense of political overtones," he said, "because a couple of these folks were active in the sort of nascent Critical Legal Studies movement.... There was [also] the subsequent tenure denial of Bill [William] Nelson, who moved to NYU; and that was a very complicated affair.... These denials left a great deal of ill will. I could detect it even when I came here a dozen years later."[22]

Did the "slaughter" make hiring juniors difficult thereafter? Many, but not all Yale faculty thought that hiring the best junior faculty became a losing proposition for at least a decade afterward. Peter Schuck received an offer from Yale in 1978. Knowledge about the slaughter had spread through the legal academy; he decided to speak with Louise Trubek, the wife of "slaughtered" David Trubek. She warned him that Yale was not a good place for a junior person to go. A member of the clinical faculty warned him, as well, but Schuck accepted his offer because "the period of time that elapsed was sufficiently great that [he] ... just didn't take

---

[17] *Id.*
[18] *Id.*
[19] Interview with Prof. Bruce Ackerman, May 3, 2011.
[20] *Id.*
[21] Interview with Prof. Jerry Mashaw, Apr. 6, 2011.
[22] Interview with Prof. John Langbein, Dec. 12, 2010.

that as a significant factor. [Shuck suspected] that other people wouldn't have as well." Perhaps some people were scared off—but, Shuck believed, "the vast majority would accept that offer, other things being equal. [He] would have thought that they would think that if this happened before, it's not likely to happen again for a while, because Yale doesn't want to have a reputation for eating its young."[23]

Kingman Brewster. Kingman Brewster, Jr., a Yale College and Harvard Law School graduate, was president of Yale from 1963 to 1977; ambassador to Britain from 1977 to 1981; and then the master of University College at Oxford, where he stayed until he died.[24]

During his presidency, Yale began to admit more minority students, and the College began to admit women. Toward the end of his tenure, Brewster faced "widespread ill feeling among alumni, caused largely by a decline in the number of their children admitted to Yale." He also received blame for Yale's financial problems and criticism for his lenience toward antiwar and civil rights protesters at Yale, especially in and around Mayday, 1970. At that time, he was widely quoted as deploring the "racist police action" against the Black Panthers and the "[in]ability of black revolutionaries to achieve a fair trial anywhere in the United States." But at the same time, he won the affection of the student body—when he was awarded a surprise honorary degree at the 1977 graduation, they chanted, "Long live the King!"[25]

Brewster was "a bundle of contradictions."[26] He enjoyed ceremony and prized tradition, but nonetheless was critical of Yale's fraternities and senior societies. "As Yale's President, he was widely considered a dull speaker, although in private he was a deft and irreverent mimic."[27] When Giamatti succeeded Brewster, he praised his "extraordinary sense for the values of the University and for how they meshed with the public good."[28]

A. Bartlett ("Bart") Giamatti. Giamatti, an Italian American, became the youngest Yale president in two hundred years (at forty).[29] "[A] short, stocky man with a beard gone white,"[30] he replaced "[a]n urbane 6-footer from an old New England family."[31] Later, Giamatti, whose bouquet to baseball, *Green Fields of the Mind* (1977) had drawn attention to his love of the sport, went from president of Yale to president of the baseball National League in 1986 and Commissioner of Major League Baseball in 1989. He famously took on baseball star Pete Rose, who was banned from baseball as a result of his gambling, including bets on his own team.

---

[23] Interview with Prof. Peter Schuck, Nov. 29, 2010.
[24] Eric Pace, *Kingman Brewster Jr., 69, Ex-Yale President and U.S. Envoy, Dies*, N.Y. TIMES, Nov. 9, 1988.
[25] *Id.*; Paul Bass & Doug Rae, *The Panther and the Bulldog, The Story of May Day 1970*, YALE ALUMNI MAG., July/Aug. 2006.
[26] *Kingman Brewster Named 17th President of Yale*, THE HARVARD CRIMSON (Oct. 14, 1963), https://www.thecrimson.com/article/1963/10/14/kingman-brewster-named-17th-president-of.
[27] Pace, *supra* note 24.
[28] *Id.*
[29] Robert D. McFadden, *Giamatti, Scholar and Baseball Chief, Dies at 51*, N.Y. TIMES, Sep. 2, 1989.
[30] *Id.*
[31] Pace, *supra* note 24.

Giamatti "was anything but the stuffy blue blood that was the stereotype of Ivy League academic leadership." A colleague was reported to exclaim, "A *human being* as president of a university—my God, what will that be like?" Nevertheless, "in his public and private utterances [he] seemed to exude what made Yale distinctive: a striving for excellence, a devotion to undergraduate education, a love of the humanities and the virtues of learning for its own sake."[32] He emphasized writing and interdisciplinary learning in the curriculum and reinstated a foreign language requirement.[33]

As Guido discusses more fully in a later chapter, Giamatti tightened the central administration's grip on finances and attacked both revenues and expenses to restore "financial equilibrium." He phased out forty senior faculty positions while raising the endowment from $544 million to $1.35 billion.[34]

Brewster's choice of Harry Wellington. After Goldstein announced that he was stepping down, Kingman Brewster interviewed Owen Fiss and asked whether he wanted to be dean; Fiss told Brewster he considered himself too young. As Guido describes, the candidates for the position became Harry Wellington and Guido.

"Not Guido." Notwithstanding Guido's statement that he did not want the position, a number of faculty and students at the time believed he was both interested and under consideration. Students in his Torts class of 1974 remembered entering one day to find the words "NOT GUIDO" written in paint on the classroom wall. The words almost certainly were not painted by a class member, but by an unknown party over the night before.

Guido saw the vandalism on entering. He began to ignore it and to start the lecture as usual, but soon decided to confront the "elephant in the room." Opening himself up, he switched to talking about why these words were incredibly hurtful. By the time he was done, the class had become deeply sympathetic to him, and supportive.

Brewster's decision for Wellington. "Kingman knew a lot about the Law School," Owen Fiss recollected. "He was a lawyer who had been on the Harvard faculty. He had very good friends on the Yale faculty. He had enemies, like the right wing, like Ralph Winter and Bork; Joe Bishop didn't like him at all. But he had good friends on the faculty, too."[35] Fiss offered that Kingman Brewster at the time "could not visualize Guido as dean. He liked Guido, but I don't think he really could visualize himself making Guido dean; so Harry Wellington was appointed."[36]

Lost steam under Wellington. At the time of Guido's selection, President Giamatti predicted that his "intellectual distinction ... will become an even more precious asset to what is doubtless the finest law faculty in the world." The reporter, however, demurred:

---

[32] McFadden, *supra* note 29.
[33] *Id.*
[34] *Id.*
[35] Interview with Prof. Owen Fiss, May 24, 2011.
[36] *Id.*

Not everyone would entirely agree with Mr. Giamatti's description of the Law School. Many say they believe that although Yale continues to attract the best law students in the country, its faculty has been weakened in recent years by the death, retirement or defection of many prized professors, and it has had mixed success in replacing them.[37]

Two years later, in 1987, the *U.S. News and World Report* law school rankings—based on subjective sentiment of other deans—indicated that Harvard and Yale were tied for first place.[38] The next year, Yale ranked first, alone, and has remained there to date.

The choice for Guido in 1984. By the time of the next dean search a decade later, not only was Guido an internationally acclaimed scholar, but from an internal perspective, he was clearly the most willing to immerse himself in the operational aspects of running a law school.[39] He was one of Dean Harry Wellington's closest advisors and had become nearly a de facto dean at the end of Wellington's second term.

For at least a decade, as well, Guido had been the most active, assertive, and among the most effective of faculty members at meetings. His near-complete identification with Yale, and his familiarity with its history "made him a living, breathing version of the institution, which strengthened his hand."[40] He drew on a large repertoire of memories and stories; he would invoke the Law School history frequently to underscore a point or to strengthen his argument. His perspective went back almost thirty years at the School. Such talent and experience gave him "additional credibility, and additional gravitas, in his conduct in meetings and his making of arguments."[41]

When Tony Kronman joined the faculty in 1978, he was instantly impressed:

> How unbelievably quick he was when there was an intellectual question on the table that was being debated! What does this work mean? Does the argument really work? How does this stack up against the work of So-and-so? Where is the field going? What are its chief problems? Is this the kind of person we should be hiring now? He was not always right, but there was no one who was quicker to see the lay of the land than Guido.[42]

Professor Drew Days concurred:

> I don't think I've seen anybody better, in terms of how much he understood the dynamic of the faculty, and the members of the faculty, and who was where on what

---

[37] David Margolick, *"Citizen of Yale" Is Named New Dean of the Law School*, N.Y. TIMES, Jan, 31, 1985.
[38] What the U.S. News Law School Rankings Looked Like in 1987, https://blog.spiveyconsulting.com/1987-u-s-news-rankings.
[39] Interview with Prof. Jerry Mashaw, Apr. 6, 2011.
[40] *Id.*
[41] *Id.*
[42] Interview with Prof. Anthony Kronman, Feb. 4, 2013.

issue. He was good in moving the conversation along. There were some major figures, particularly when I was a younger faculty member, like Leon Lipson, who also had this ability, and did it by turning a phrase like no one I've ever seen. I remember when toward the end of a long discussion about a candidate, Leon Lipson said, 'Oh, now I understand. This fellow is a zircon in the rough.'

He described Guido's ability to argue positions as phenomenal.[43]

By the time of Guido's actual appointment, as well, thousands of alumni had taken Torts or other courses with Guido. Alumni who had not taken his course had met him at functions, or had heard about him, or had read about him. "He was making a big splash in all these different areas of law," said Bill Eskridge.[44] His selection "received an enthusiastic response from all the alumni I know."[45]

By the early 1980s, a broad feeling developed on the faculty that Guido was the obvious best candidate to be the next dean. After Wellington's announcement of resignation, "he was pretty much everybody's choice," especially because "the second term of the Wellington years were "really a deferral of the Calabresi years," because "everybody knew that he would be Dean."[46]

Some faculty members harbored reservations at the time of his initial appointment and his renewal. These mostly stemmed from his indomitable argumentation at faculty meetings. As one faculty member, Jerry Mashaw, put it, they were "daunted by the prospect of riding herd on Guido's enthusiasms."[47] Mashaw considered putting his hat into the ring to be the dean but was deterred, in part, as he recollected, by the prospect of winning and having to debate, at every faculty meeting, a Guido who would have been disappointed![48]

As the Calabresi deanship progressed, the faculty would need to confront a rapid pace of change, and there were quite a few "Guidonian enthusiasms" urged on the faculty. He usually succeeded in gaining their acceptance, and they were usually appreciated with hindsight. Occasionally, he did fail to put one of his proposals though—as when, at the end of the first term and before agreeing to a second, he tried and failed to allow retired faculty to continue to do some teaching at a lower salary as long as there were students interested in taking their courses. "I went too fast and pushed too hard," he said. Nonetheless, defeating Guido when he was convinced of a good idea was not an easy matter.

Subterfuges and redemptive transparency. Although there was no significant opposition to Guido's renewal for a second term in 1990, and there was "widely shared admiration," there also was "resistance, resentment, and criticism of Guido" for

---

[43] Interview with Prof. Drew Days, Mar. 2, 2011.
[44] Interview with Prof. William Eskridge, Mar. 11, 2013.
[45] *Id.*; David Margolick, *"Citizen of Yale" Is Named New Dean Of The Law School*, N.Y. TIMES, Jan. 31, 1985.
[46] Interview with Prof. Peter Schuck, Nov. 29, 2010.
[47] Interview with Prof. Jerry Mashaw, Apr. 6, 2011.
[48] *Id.*

being "extraordinarily, extraordinarily strategic." Several faculty members reported a word that everybody would use. He's "Machiavellian."[49]

Bo Burt endeavored to explain what some faculty members meant. He observed that "every law school faculty believes that it runs the enterprise, and the dean is its nemesis. But, Guido didn't join that fight. I mean, he was very adroit, and told us 'No, I'm just here to facilitate what you wish.'" His smartness and his belief that he could outsmart others wore some people down:

> When he wanted something, he would just maneuver and maneuver and maneuver. We all admired what he had done for the school. He strengthened it immensely! And he was so good for the students. But over the years, his use of subterfuges tried the patience of many of my colleagues.[50]

Furthermore, whereas Guido might have "thought of himself as a master politician and diplomat," Burt (and others) disagreed. "He's a little too transparent for that. He really doesn't do subterfuge *very well*—which is great! There's a kind of stubborn integrity in him. You just know what he's up to. If he were a better Machiavellian, he would be a lesser person."[51]

An early challenge: The 1984 strike by the clerical workers. The start of Guido's deanship nearly coincided with a "tumultuous" period of labor difficulties and major student demonstrations across the University. Arriving in that fall, Professor Robert Ellickson found that the recently formed local union of clerical and technical workers, "C&T-34," had decided to strike, having made no progress negotiating with the University. The low wages of clerical workers and the differential in pay between women and men were central issues. Students and union members wore such buttons as "Yale: Settle" and "59 cents," because women earned, on average, 59 cents on the dollar.[52]

Ellickson believed that at the Law School, Guido added fuel to the conflict.[53] As Guido indicates, he believed that the Union had outsmarted the University administration in characterizing off-campus classes as supportive of the strike; he openly encouraged faculty decisions to teach off-campus as a compromise mode of "neutrality."

The disturbances went on for months and included several different strikes. On these occasions, a faculty member or students would request classes to be moved off campus; there would be divisive votes over the question.[54] The Medical School's second-year class, for example, voted, 53 to 39, not to move off-campus."[55]

---

[49] Interview with Prof. Peter Schuck, Nov. 29, 2010.
[50] Interview with Prof. Robert Burt, Mar. 1, 2012.
[51] *Id.*
[52] *Id.*
[53] Interview with Prof. Robert Ellickson, May 10, 2011.
[54] *Id.*
[55] Margot Hornblower, *Yale Braces for Strike Over Pay*, THE WASH. POST, Sept. 26, 1984.

Picket lines were up outside the building; much of the School population declined to cross the line; and most of the faculty decided to teach at off-campus sites. Guido's new administration helped to identify suitable alternative spaces—the Baptist Church at the corner of Edwards St. and Livingston St., for example, became a main classroom.[56] Guido would come to his office in his capacity as a dean; but, like all faculty members who were honoring the strike, he would teach his classes off-site.[57]

"We did things at the law school that other places didn't do," Dean Mike Thompson recalled. Local 34 went out in cold weather and used fire barrels outside to stay warm. Encouraged by Guido, Thompson made sure the fire barrels were lit every morning and provided the picketers with coffee and hot chocolate. Regardless of the University's displeasure, "we figured these people were members of the Law School community; they were going to come back in here when it was over, so we were taking care of them. They couldn't come in and buy coffee, because they would be crossing the picket line to do that."[58] Conversely, the few clerical-technical workers who wanted to cross the line and go to work, and whom the union therefore called "scabs," were walked through the picket lines by Mike. "I would walk in with them," Thompson said. "That's what we did. We took care of them: At other places around the University there was harassment; at the law school, there was not."[59]

Persuasiveness and authenticity. The Croatian and American law professor, Mirjan Damaska, recalled watching Guido as he dealt with students during the strikes. One day, as he was entering the Law School from Wall Street, he noticed a gaggle of students in the hallway discussing the strike, and in the middle of the gaggle was somebody holding sway:

Guido! I was wondering: "What is going on here? Is Guido striking *against* himself?"

They were against him at first, you know. And as he was talking with them, you had the feeling that he was striking against himself! To me it was amazing, his flexibility, you know, diplomatic skill.

People who don't like him may probably say this is Machiavellian. I like the man, so I would not call him Machiavellian; I think it is some kind of a desire he has to establish harmony. He's capable of temporarily changing his views, adopting the view of someone else, and then leading that someone else, or trying to lead him, to whatever his position is. The way he talked to the students was truly amazing![60]

---

[56] Interview with Mike Thompson, Associate Dean for Building Services, Feb. 6, 2013.
[57] *Id.*
[58] *Id.*
[59] *Id.*
[60] Interview with Prof. Mirjan Damaska, Dec. 15, 2010.

When the strike was over, "people all came back, and they were all part of the community."[61]

Bread and Chocolate and Bart and Guido. The 1978 comedy-drama, *Bread and Chocolate*, follows Nino, an Italian immigrant, to Switzerland from Ciociaria, an area in the South of Italy, in his struggle with Swiss hostility to the southern immigrants. A movie review in the *New York Times* described the opening sequence, which perfectly captures the worlds-colliding premise of this "picaresque tale." As the reviewer describes:

> We could be in Elysium where it's always summer. We watch a boat with a pair of lovers laze its way across sun-bleached water. On shore, a family prepares to picnic on grass whose greenness is absolute....
>
> Everything is perfect until the arrival of an outsider. He is tall and well-built but, close up, he looks most peculiar.... He could be wearing make-up or—and this is the thought that occurred to me—he might possibly be dead ... The fellow sits down to listen to the music while he eats a sandwich.
>
> When he takes a bite, the chamber music group abruptly stops playing. The leader stares at him in disapproval. They can't play if he's going to eat in that fashion. He is clearly a fellow who's never given much thought to his manner of munching.[62]

In the narrative, Guido reflects on Bart's assumption of Guido's likely indifference to the movie, and he emphasizes the social distance between them—treating it as a matter of cultural geography and not simply class.

Turning over the walking-stick maces. At Yale Law School's 2010 graduation ceremony, Dean Post thanked Guido for the Tyler Maces. It was the third time they were handed down to a new dean; the third hand-over, he declared, transformed a nice ceremonial gesture into a tradition:

> In my view ... these maces represent ... the interdependence of our national and international responsibilities. These maces symbolize an authority so capacious that it can transform us into a community that is nevertheless cosmopolitan, and [an authority] that can also shape us into a pedagogical and scholarly enterprise that is both cutting-edge and faithful to its historical roots.

Dean Post reminded the audience that maces are designed to be leaned upon, "just as we lean on the authority that they represent, to help us on our journey."[63]

---

[61] *Id.*

[62] Vincent Canby, *Four Movies, Two for Children and Two From Abroad, Open: Screen: "Bread and Chocolate,"* N.Y. TIMES, July 14, 1978.

[63] Commencement Speech by Dean Robert Post, May 24, 2010.

The Tyler Mace

19
The Dean's New Day

During Guido's leadership as Dean between 1985 and 1994, Yale stayed at the top of the law school rankings, reinvigorated the faculty, and enjoyed continuing positive public attention. Descriptions by students, faculty, alumni, contemporary deans elsewhere, and by subsequent deans at Yale considered the deanship a remarkable success. Among other accomplishments, he did something new at an elite American law school: he redesigned Yale as a student satisfaction-oriented, compassionate, administratively sophisticated place, with a staff designed to address each of the schools' constituencies and to perform necessary functions. Nonetheless, not all the challenges that needed to be addressed when he arrived were resolved by his departure.

Had I ever been an associate dean before I became dean? No, I am an academic. Had I ever made a budget for a major institution, before I became a dean? No, I am an academic! Those sorts of jobs are not what academics care much about, or university presidents for that matter. Others could take care of budgets and so on. In fact, I never did sit down and make a budget, during my entire deanship. What the faculty hoped was that I had qualities that could solve such problems and, in that way, move the school forward.

There were four matters needing attention right away. One was appointments. The matters that had everything to do with establishing what a great law school is about. These other three were the terrible problem of large student loan debts and high tuitions; the fact that faculty salaries were intolerable compared to other top schools; and most immediately, I had the problem of figuring out who among the administrative staff I should keep, and who I should manage to have leave, so that the right tone for my administration would be set.

* * *

While he was still dean, Harry Wellington and I had talked about establishing what became known as COAP, a loan forgiveness program for our graduates who decided to go into public interest work. But, unlike what was being talked about at other schools, we both felt that graduates should be able to get loan forgiveness depending on what they earned, and not on working in what *we* defined as being in the "public interest." I do not recall which of us came up with the idea, but I felt strongly that it was not "Yale" to tell people who were earning much less than they could what was and was not in the public interest.

I actually commit myself to this—to the students, and to the faculty—before I start the deanship. I say that "public interest" is *whatever our great students think is worth earning less money for*. We are the *École Normale Supérieure*, the training place for leaders, I say, and leaders have to set their own agenda, based on their own values.

As an institution, we have our view, and as individual faculty members we have our views, as to what is right, true and just! [Guido pounds the table.] But we are just as proud of the founding of the Federalist Society here, or of a person who becomes a writer and who thinks that the writing work is in the public interest, as we are of what at the time is more conventionally "public interest." Let me say it again: leaders have to decide what leadership is. And if we defined what is worth doing, the Law School would be intruding on the graduate's freedom of conscience.

I speak to the central administration about it. They are fine with it. But then the new administration comes in, and the president is now Benno Schmidt. My proposal goes to the Yale Corporation for its approval while I am in Canada giving a talk, and I get a call while I am there from the provost (or it may have been the deputy provost). The provost says that the corporation has voted it down, because money spent by a Yale faculty, such as the Law School's, to help people after they are out of school for any purpose, is not appropriate.

> *Why did they vote it down? I think they voted it down because some people in the Medical School objected, because they would be under pressure to do something similar. And they had somebody friendly on the Corporation who said, "Oh my goodness, you're causing terrible trouble!" And so it was voted down.*

I can get excited, but I can also play at being calm. And I remember very well what I respond while I'm in Toronto, when the provost says, "Oh, Guido, they voted the loan deferral-loan forgiveness program down."

I say, "Oh, that's interesting. I resign."

He says, "What?" And I say, "I resign." And he says, "What, what?" I say, "No, no, do not get excited. I mean, I'm not going to slam the door tomorrow; but by the end of this year you will need a new Dean."

He asks, "Why?" And I say, "Well, I committed myself to this, and I believe in it. I think it's essential. But more important: you told me that you would back it, that the Administration would back it. And one of two things has happened: either you did not tell me the truth, and then I do not want to be a Dean in your Administration; or else you are so weak that although you are for it, the Corporation can run roughshod over you on something fundamental. I cannot afford to be Dean in an Administration that is so weak. And so, although we will be friends as before, you will need a new Dean." He says, "Well, let's look into it, because they may change their mind." I say, "Of course, if they change their mind, I'd be happy."

And of course, they do. This was the only time I threatened to resign, by the way—the only time during my whole deanship. I'm very proud of the way we did COAP, because it was both crucial, and crucial in *the way we did it*. It was and is very costly, but necessary, if the school was going to be the kind of place that draws people from all over, and then lets them do what they want.

> *Our openness has always been and continues to be a great strength! Deans of most of the top law schools are now from here! There were more people from Yale in H.W. Bush's Justice Department than from any other Law School, even though people say we are the most Left law school. Why? Because we did not pre-define the public interest. Those who were conservatives as well as those on the Left and those who just moved to their own drumbeat could do that defining themselves, and that's as it should be!*

This epitomizes who we are.

* * *

The second immediate concern had to do with salaries. This was a more complicated problem. To get out of what had become an impossible hiring situation, I had to get freedom to hire as many people as I wanted and in the areas I wanted. To do this, I had to get money.

> *I had no experience fundraising. During the interim period when I was dean-designate, I went down to New York because Harry was running a little campaign for the library, which wasn't getting anywhere. He asked me to go see Clifford and Betsy Beinecke Michel, because they had some money. I came back with a hundred thousand dollars, feeling very proud of myself. Harry seemed pleased with me because he was not raising much of anything by then. But I later realized what a total flub that had been! I had no idea whether this was a lot or a little to raise from these graduates.*

When I found out how relatively low our salaries were, I realized that with these levels of pay, we simply could not compete. I determine that somehow or other I would find the necessary money. I wanted to be able to match whatever was being spent by the school that was trying to keep a person we wanted; to match what was being offered by the other dean who was trying to keep the person.

I decided I would not pay more, because I did not want anybody to come to Yale for the money. I specifically did *not want* to *buy* anybody. But I did not want anybody to have to say "no" because of money or costs of living.

> *I announced my policy publicly so that other schools would know that it would not do any good to bid up offers, because I would match what they raise their offers to.*

> *I knew that if they bid things up, they would screw up their salary scale, and make their remaining faculty unhappy. So, my announcement actually acted to keep people from raising salaries in order to try to keep their ablest.*

But then, what does that do with respect to my faculty? How will they feel about what I am doing? Obviously, most of the new people are going to come in and get salaries that are greater than their equivalents already here.

Occasionally there might be a person we wanted who was earning less than those who were their equivalent in ability and seniority already here. In such a case I would pay the person as much as their equivalents on our faculty. I do not want to get anybody cheap, because if you get somebody cheap you get somebody angry.

> *I learned from Gene Rostow that when he hired Charles Black from Columbia, he could have gotten him for very little, but instead he named him the Luce Professor, and announced it as a great event—which it was—and paid him well! This is typical of Gene Rostow's generosity, if you want to call it that. And that generosity is not only the right thing to do—it pays off.*

But most of the new hires would be earning more than their equivalents who were here already. I said to the faculty, "These people will come on earning more than you, and you deserve to be treated as well. You have stayed here and are willing to stay here because you like it here, but you should not be earning less than people who come now. On the other hand, the only way we're going to get good people is to do this. I promise you that within three or four years—as soon as I can—while they will get their appropriate raises, you will have caught up with them. What I'm going to do is hire them that way and write a blank check to you. I will then go to the alums and tell them that I've written that blank check; and they will have to fill it out."

This was my idea. I had to say what I said to the faculty so that they would be happy and join me in doing this this. Of course, they did not know immediately what salaries I was offering because the dean sets them privately. But you know, my Yale colleagues here would soon be able to tell what I was offering because the other schools would inevitably let it be known.

My strategy was to warn the faculty ahead of time, just as I warned them ahead about making appointments in Law and Economics first—and to let them know that their time would be coming. I told them that we would go out and hire at salaries which were higher than theirs were, with the result that in a few years, no school would be paying more than we paid, because if you're hiring the best from the other schools, our salary scale would necessarily have to move to the top. We were going to hire people at what they were getting there and then move our own salaries up. That was a crucially important part of my hiring strategy.

The other part was dealing with the problem of couples with two careers. One of the things that people had been saying was that a reason Yale could not be what it had been was that two-career families would find it easier in big cities like Boston, New York, and Washington than in New Haven. I made finding jobs or compatible travel and living for two-career families a central part of my plan. I managed to get the money I needed with the help of my classmate Tom Barr. He was raising money for what became the Katzenbach Professorship, but he raised a lot more than was needed for the chair, and this was given expressly for me to deal with two-career issues.

Three examples of what we did come to mind. One, and this involved Tony Kronman, was simply getting money so that he and his wife could if they wished live in New York, while he comfortably taught here. Another, which allowed us to hire Alan Schwartz, was to offer to transfer money to the medical School, which desperately wanted to hire his wife but did not have a budget slot for three years. Third was to help some other nearby law schools to have the financing so they could hire the spouses of people we wanted. I told people that I had never been as cold as when I was at Oxford, because it never got below freezing, so they had no central heat, and I froze. And for years, I had been more comfortable in the summers in Washington, where they had air conditioning, than in New Haven, where, because it wasn't all that hot, relatively few people had air conditioning. The schools in big cities did not worry about two-career families. I would put the equivalent of central heating and air conditioning in New Haven and make the two-career families more comfortable here than elsewhere.

It all worked and our hiring—both at the junior level and to an unparalleled extent also, at the lateral level, of tenured professors from other schools—became the envy of every other law school. No one to whom we made an offer while they were visiting at Yale turned us down! At the same time, we were extremely successful in keeping those who were already with us. The next generation of topflight faculty was soon in place.

* * *

I had immediately to create a law school administration that reflected my vision. I had to face immediately the problem of Harry Wellington's associate dean, whose name was Ed Dauer, and who had been his total right hand. Ed had really been running things for Harry, and I think he expected to continue doing that for me. In some ways he was an admirable person, but he could not be my associate dean—he just could not be.

* * *

Ed Dauer was a very smart guy, with a bit of a Napoleon complex—small and determined. Harry originally made him his deputy for financial matters, but his portfolio had expanded until he ran everything! He developed a very special relationship with the deputy provost in charge of the Law School, who would try to ease things for it as much as one could, within Bart's newly centralized system, which I do not think he himself much liked.

The problem for me was that I thought that Ed was the kind of person who got his kicks from being able to say "no"; that he was resentful in some deep psychological way of the fact that he had not gotten tenure as an academic. This shaped everything that he did—his relationship to students, his relationship to faculty. I wanted a different administration. On the other hand, Harry was telling me that this guy was the only one who kept things going! What did one do?

I just took a chance. I told Ed that I was not going to keep him on, and that I was going to help him find another job. I did, in fact, find him a job as the dean at another school.

* * *

My idea of a good administration is one that says "yes" rather than "no." I want everyone in the school to be able to get what they need—that is just a part of me. Some people later call me the "Dean who always said 'yes,'" and think that I never said "no." That's not true! You always try to say "no" so that nobody—even the person you are saying "no" to—notices.

I tell people around me that most people here are asking for things which at some level make sense. This is why in a school like ours—especially in our anarchical school—saying "yes" is the way I want my administration's mission to be understood!

> When I was in Yale College, we quickly learned that there was the big Dean, Dean DeVane, a great figure, and then there was the Associate Dean, a man named Carroll. And then there was an Assistant Dean named Fritz Wiggin. We joked that in Yale College, Fritz Wiggin was the Dean in charge of saying "no." If you could get by him to Dick Carroll, he was the Dean in charge of saying "yes." He wasn't a lawyer, but he tended to want to help people get things done.
>
> Remembering this, what I said to the administrators I hired was "You are here because you want to do this job, not because you're frustrated at something else! What should give you a kick is to make this place better by figuring out ways in which people can get what they are properly asking for in ways that are correct. Figuring out the way is what you can do because you're clever. You're good lawyers, and you're good administrators, and you can figure out ways in which people can get what they need, in ways which will probably give them more than they were asking for; and yet do it in a way which is correct.
>
> This is really no different from being a lawyer, or a judge. When judges have cases where the law is wrong, they try to figure out whether the law really requires it or whether people have really misunderstood the law; so that there is a correct way of looking at the case that permits a desirable result. It's harder as a judge,

because you have less control. But as an administrator, you have much more room even than lawyers for what you can say and what you can do. A good administrator can usually find a way of saying, "you cannot do exactly what you asked for, but here is a way you can do something even better."

I want a staff of people who really want to be civil servants in a law school, and who understand their jobs this way, and I bring in two people at the start to help me assemble such a staff.

* * *

I ask John Simon, already a member of our faculty I know very, very well, to be my deputy dean. I had been here when John was hired in 1961, although he is older than I am. I had seen him through some incredible family crises that he had had, and the way John and his wife handled that moved and impressed me. The main thing about John, that I knew and liked, was that he was, to a fault, a caretaker. He took care of everything and everyone! He did everything with the most *excruciating* care. He was a person who really liked people.

Once there was a woman from Los Angeles who had been my student; when I was judge she came to see me at the court, and I went to see her. She said, "I was in town arguing a case, and I wanted to come by because when I was your student, my grandmother died, and you were so warm and kind, and you do not know what it meant to me, and so on. You did so much to make law school humane and wonderful. And I love you more than anyone—except of course, John Simon." He had been her small group teacher! This is the kind of person John is.

I knew that John wrote beautifully, so that he would edit me, and nothing went out of my office, of significance, that John did not look to. He had been a practicing lawyer, who knew what it was like to be an academic, because he had created a whole new field: "not-for-profit law." He was modest to a *fault*, but he had my back in everything he did.

* * *

I of course needed pros for specialized work—finances, fundraising, admissions, etc. At the very end of his term, Harry had hired this rather remarkable young woman, Jamienne Studley, who really wanted to be an academic civil servant. She came out of the law school placement operation at the Association of American Law Schools and had done very well. With Jamie and John as a foundation, we set out to hire other people.

The Associate Dean for Admissions, Jim Thomas, I knew I wanted to keep. I had known him for years, and he was a remarkable Dean of Admissions! He'd done well here as a student and had been a very good football player at Wesleyan. There's a marvelous picture of him as quarterback, behind Dominic Squatrito at

Wesleyan, who also came to the Law School and became a Federal District Judge. It is a picture of this huge Squatrito rump, and this very elegant Jim Thomas quarterback behind him—which kind of told it all! Jim understood the Law School, and what it meant to be here, and he could sell the Law School wherever he went and convince people that they really wanted to come here: minorities were affected by his very presence; but everybody else was impressed, too!

> *Jim and Jamie Studley did not always get along, because Jamie was brusque, and Jim had his limits, and he did not always do things in ways which were [pause] you know, well-done in a traditional administrative way. Jamie occasionally let him know her displeasure. With a white woman dealing with a black man—it was not always an easy situation. But in time they came to like and respect each other.*

I wanted to keep Jim in his position because he was also somebody who had chosen to do *this* job, and he was loving it. Also, he was significantly responsible for the fact that the one thing that had never failed, even during the weaker moments, at the end of Harry's deanship, was the high quality of the students we were getting.

* * *

What to do about the Registrar's Office? The registrar, classically, had been the most important person in the school. In the old days, when I was a student, you had a dean and he had an associate dean, Jack Tate, who was an *extraordinary* human being, who taught me a lot about running things. He was the author of *The Tate Letter in International Law*. He was a remarkable man; he was the associate dean of *everything*! But there was also Elsa Wolf, the registrar, and she ran *everything*, too! Elsa Wolf was a super-secretary who'd grown up. Elsa did it for decades.

> *At the very time Anne and I were married, in 1961, students in my Estate and Gift Tax course were taking their exams, which then had to be graded. Jan Deutsch, who later joined the faculty and was a close friend from college, was invited to the wedding. He was also a student in the class. Elsa said, "You're taking the exam this morning, but you are going out to the wedding reception. Bring these suitcases full of a hundred and one exams and give them to Guido when he goes off, so that he can grade them before he takes off on his honeymoon!" At the reception, Jan appears with two suitcases of exams. He puts them in the trunk of our car, and off we go! Can you imagine a school where the Registrar would give a student in the class all the exams? By the way, I've never given such good grades in my life!*

This was the flavor of the registrar in that era. Registrars were very powerful people! People like Elsa had a proprietary feeling about the school and few qualms about telling the faculty and the dean about how it should be run.

> *At my very first faculty meeting we were going over admissions. Gene Rostow was Dean. Elsa came in and said to the faculty, "Do not you realize that you've admitted too many Jewish students? If you keep doing this nice Jewish boys won't want to come!" Elsa was just as Jewish as could be, but she said that! And she said, "Start to watch out!" Charles Black literally picked her up, and took her out of the room, while saying, in his deep Southern accent, "Elsa, get the hell out of here! That is not us!"*

The registrar under Harry Wellington was very good, but again, too rule-oriented. She was known as "Madame Mao," and was very rule-bound. She did not seem right to me, because in terms of *students*, this was the person they dealt with most—more, in a way, than with somebody like Jamie, although Jamie was the associate dean for students.

* * *

I had to find a registrar, and the problem was that the person who was most qualified had been a secretary who did not have a college degree; and the registrar had become a sort of higher figure over all the secretaries. Together with the rest of the new administration, we decided that that person, Zina Shaffer, was nonetheless the right one. Zina was a refugee—she spoke with something of an accent, but she was just as smart as could be; she saw everything and knew when to let students get away with things, and she knew when not to. She was very grandmotherly—a wonderful Jewish grandmother who knows what's going on, and lets you know it, and says, "This time you're okay, even though your paper is late, but be careful because you'll get into trouble if you keep doing things like that." She became a *beloved* registrar, and actually, nobody got away with too much! Yes, they got away with a lot, but not things that mattered, because she was careful about that.

We needed a new finance person because of the complicated financial relationship with the University, and because I wasn't going to keep Ed Dauer. We also needed a fundraiser.

For finance we found Stephen Yandle, who had gone to Northwestern and there helped build the American Bar Association buildings which became part of Northwestern Law School. He became the dean for finance at Northwestern. He came from Virginia Law School, was very elegant, but had not forgotten the "Lefty" kind of ideas of his law school days, and yet he looked utterly perfect for his role! Jamie knew him. She said, "This is somebody who decided he *wanted* this kind of job."

He also understood what struck me as unlikely given his rather Left background: the importance of incentives. Like me, he knew the advantage of creating independence with incentives rather than commands. Which is what we did when he and I persuaded the University to give us independence. We then turned around and did the same with organizations in the law school, with tremendous success!

> *Steve and I gave increased independence to all sorts of student organizations, starting with the Law Journal, which had been draining money from the school. Once they were independent, they started making money, hand over fist! They always had ways of making money, and now they had reasons to do it! The Law Journal has now been giving very good gifts to the Law School! Our policy with all the organizations was to give them a good financial starting point and then say, "The rest is up to you." Steve understood that, really well.*

He also knew about buildings; and early on my obsession in terms of finances, became the doing of something about our decaying building. This included negotiating with the University.

Steven became my key person in the administration for dealing with the University. The central administration—other parts of it—did not like him, but he and Chip Long, the deputy provost, hit it off, and understood each other. I wanted Steve to help me get the University to give us what we needed and then get out of our way.

When I came in, the Law School was nominally running a very significant deficit. If you looked at our budget—the budget had us overspending. But this was a *fraud*, in the sense that what were pluses and what were minuses were completely arbitrary.

> *For instance, on the plus side of the budget there was a $40,000 figure for maintenance of the Sterling Law Buildings. What was this $40,000? It was the income from a million dollars from the Sterling Trust that had been given when the buildings were built. This donation was still valued at a million dollars, and the income from it at $40,000. Now, the University, for years, invested terribly! The bonds and stocks may not have grown the forty thousand into more; or maybe they had. If you looked at the figures over the years, though, you would see that depending on the strength of the dean; the relationship between the dean and administration; and the strength of the administration, each had stolen from the other! There might be more Sterling Professors who were paid out of university funds than there should be, or less. It was really difficult to tell.*

It was obvious that the policy of the University was to keep the Law School in debt because, to the extent that the Law School was in debt, they could control it! They could say, "This is what you can spend on, and this is what you do not spend on." This might not have mattered when you had an administration like Kingman Brewster's, which said, "Spend anything"—although Lou Pollak was so dependent on Kingman that Lou and his associate dean, Ralph Brown, actually had been very, very tight—and so our relationship with the University did not hurt us much. It also did not hurt us when Harry first came on with Kingman. Harry was ebullient and Chip Long wanted to help, and money was there to be spent! But, as I said earlier, everything became disastrous when Bart became president and tightened everything up, in Harry's second term.

> *I do not think the University was trying to make money from the Law School, the way many, many universities do because you can run law schools on the cheap. I think Bart wanted everything in his hands and once you have control, it is tempting, if you need money and see a place where you can squeeze, to get some money. It was the temptation—and it's still there—of saying, "Gee, we're short. Why don't we raise the amount that they have to pay for Central Administration as a way of getting some money from somebody who is relatively rich?" It would have been far better if they decided how much they had to tax us at the start, and then let us alone.*

The administration was saying "you say we've got to keep up with the other schools, but what does *that* mean? You are already paying your professors more than most other Yale faculties are." It was a situation where people could say, "You are in debt, that debt is growing, and we want you to reduce that debt." It made for an impossible situation! That was how things were at the end of Harry's deanship—what we were talking about before, when as I said, Yale Law School salaries were fourteenth among the top twenty; when we did not give enough for summer stipends; you know, all of which were viewed as indications of a school in trouble.

We had to get out of that, and that would ultimately involve negotiating for independence; but it also meant that we to raise outside money on our own, because the University was not going to provide what we needed. So, after hiring Yandle, we needed to find somebody to be a fundraiser. Steve and Jamie Studley suggested Carroll Stevens, who, on the face of it, looked the most unlikely person for the Law School. He was a Southern Baptist—very broad in his views of religion but from a deeply religious school and background.

I talked to him, and he was the most intelligent fundraiser I'd ever met! Most fundraisers are not very smart—you know, they do things in a bureaucratic way. But this was a guy full of ideas. Harry told me (because I asked him to look at the people I was considering) that he was doubtful about Carroll, because he said, you know, "given who Yale Law School graduates are: kind of New York, frequently Jewish—this guy just won't go." My feeling was that they would be so surprised to have somebody who is *smart*—and also loves people—that it would work. I thought I'd take a chance on him. He was the riskiest pick of all, but it turned out to be a superb choice.

We also kept the guy who was doing the Annual Fund, Ralph Burr; and together with the new people, this was the whole fundraising operation: Ralph Burr, who had done the Fund Drive; Carroll Stevens, as associate dean and general fundraiser; and me. We did not have a huge bureaucracy, and we did not need it! [Sighs]

> *Even though our salary structure in general became our own decision, on the question of compensating my administrators, it was a constant fight with the University. The University tended to hire ten people, pretty much all of whom are no good, for very little money. I would say "I do not need ten people. I need two people, each of whom is great, but I've got to pay them enough. It will cost me less, and I will get more out of it. Keep out!" This was a long-term struggle. I ended up getting them their salaries most of the time, but every year it was a fight.*

* * *

Once the civil service was in place everybody worked well together. It turned out to be a team of people who really liked each other.

Of course, John Simon was not an administrator by nature—he was an academic and a lawyer—but he fit in very, very well with the team. We were friends and have remained friends. John did his work with me for five years, and when I took a break at the end of my first term, he became the acting dean for a little while, and then he stepped down.

> *For his party when he went back to full-time teaching, I wrote a bit of doggerel about him with many verses. Each stanza ended with: "John Simon, Acting Dean; John Simon, Acting King; John Simon, Acting "Iff". I remember one line: "When Guido from afar spewed fumets and catarrh; Who calmed him down without a frown? John Simon, Acting Czar."*

Having done five years as the deputy dean, which is more than anybody can possibly do in that position, I knew I could never find somebody like him for all the years left in my second term, and so I thought the best thing to do was to pick three people who thought of themselves as possible deans and have them be deputy deans so that they would learn the underside to deaning, and have them each do it for a year.

* * *

That is what I did. I picked three people—Bob Ellickson, Tony Kronman, and Peter Schuck, and, for what was scheduled to be my last year, asked a fourth whom I knew would be very, very good, and whom I would have been delighted to have had as deputy dean for five years, Al Klevorick, who had been my student. Al was an economist and did not have a law degree; he knew he was unlikely to be picked by a law faculty to be Law School dean, and so he had no incentive to use that last year of deputy deaning as a springboard to the deanship. I knew that if I named these four and told them at the beginning that they would each do a year, and that the last year it would be Al, that in effect I would have a group of people, each of whom would care about leaving that job in very good shape for the next person. I wouldn't have John Simon—but I would have as close to that as I could get.

It is interesting that these people, who had very strong views as faculty members, understood their role as deans. For example, Bob Ellickson, a marvelous teacher and great scholar, had very strong ideas, even about such questions as appointments! But during his year as Deputy Dean, he was immensely supportive in every area.

It worked out pretty much as I hoped—very well.

* * *

How do you integrate old ways with the new ones? Think about the Annual Fund, run by Ralph Burr, and the new people he needed to work with—Carroll Stevens and me. Ralph had come out of University Fundraising. I knew him because at one time he had dealt on with Anne's aunt and her husband, who were very wealthy, did not have children, and were very elegant people and who could only be dealt with by a true gentleman. Ralph was wonderful with them, and they loved him. He was a truly old-fashioned kind of a person, who never pushed people. How he came over to the Law School originally, I do not know. At the Law School he had a very good secretary who became kind of his assistant, with a slightly higher title. The only thing is, that all the two of them did for the Alumni Fund, was to send things short little letters out. That's it. I thought that we could do things better if we just got them more organized and energized.

The key to that part of the operation was one question. I asked, "Do we have a reunion gift drive?" Ralph said, "Oh, we do indeed! It's tremendously successful. Twenty-one percent of the Annual Fund comes from reunion classes." I said, "Twenty-one percent? There is a reunion class every five years. If we did nothing, it would be twenty percent."

In other words, we did *not* have a reunion gift drive separate from the Annual Fund and I immediately knew we could raise a lot more money from annual giving if we had both, and that any school that does not have a reunion gift drive has an upside fundraising potential that is enormous. Ralph understood, and we put together a reunion gift program that was both "gentlemanly" and effective. We went from raising $1.5 million a year in the annual fund to $11 million by the end of my deanship.

Carroll was in charge of all fundraising, including the Annual Fund Drive, but mainly he went after capital gifts. He would be involved in all of the meetings connected with the Annual Fund, but he knew enough to let the administration of the Annual Fund be in Ralph's hands. He let Ralph do whatever he wanted. It was typical Yale Law School anarchy!

> *Anarchy works if people are responsible. It does not work if people are not responsible. My theme was: "we do not need rules; we can do things in an entirely personal way if each of you is responsible. And if you see that somebody is taking advantage, be sure that I am seeing it, too. And understand that the Dean has a powerful memory; the Dean sees everything and does not forget." This did not mean I would stop it, but I was thinking of Pope John XXIII, that very great Pope, who said, "The Pope should see everything and do very little. Let people who are on the spot take care of all the problems. Be pastoral; be loving."*
>
> My view was that this school was small enough so that it could run in an anarchical way.
>
> * * *
>
> I was dealing with people who liked each other and were attuned to my vision of a place which was "to be excellent but humane." They reflected this vision in everything that they did, and they were people who were fun to be with, and whom I could trust. Carroll would come up with ideas. He was the Bruce Ackerman of fundraisers: some false positives, maybe. At times, he would suggest things which were not exactly realistic: "Jeepers, if we could only do this, it would be just wonderful!" Sometimes it did not work. But in fundraising as with Bruce in constitutional theory, you know, when it *does* work, it really is quite something!
>
> *What I said before—about how most people are asking for things which at some level make sense—is important in fundraising. If you see the people you're trying to get money from as people who have interesting ideas, you will respect them more, even if their viewpoints are very different from yours. And they will come to like you more, much more than people who may share their viewpoints, but do not respect them.*
>
> This was the key staff, and this whole civil service remained in place through Tony Kronman's deanship, which is a really long time.

COMMENTARY

Chapter 19

Administrative changes. "The Dean's Office seemed pretty penniless in the 1970s, and pretty much lacking in energy," recalled Bill Eskridge.[1] Dean Wellington in his second term appeared unmotivated to address keeping the school clean or the heat

---

[1] Interview with Professor William Eskridge, Mar. 11, 2013.

set at the proper temperature, much less transforming the curriculum, improving overall student satisfaction, or improving faculty morale.[2] But "If Yale has indeed slowed down a bit in recent years," the *New York Times* ventured, Guido "may be the best equipped to arouse it anew."[3]

Taking over, Guido surprised many of his colleagues by disrupting the bureaucratic "dean and assistants" model. Like most other law schools, administrative staff were preoccupied with minimizing expenses, holding students at bay, and enforcing academic custom. Guido took the helm and to a very considerable degree, "reinvented the Office of the Dean and became an aspirational model for future law deans everywhere."[4]

Decades later, the faculty would recall new and grand expectations that he fostered from the outset: that the dean would make possible almost anything that faculty members and students reasonably desired. As the narrative describes, he began by revising the mission of the staff, converting the school administrators into a service-oriented corps who understood their main responsibility as almost "white glove" nurturing and catering to the wants and even the whims of faculty and students. The climate changed almost immediately, but many decisions required spending money. This became easier, when, a few years into the deanship, Guido succeeded at increasing alumni giving and establishing independence from University control over spending decisions.

Getting to "yes." Carroll Stevens and Stephen Yandle were charged with implementing a vision Guido had formed in his head. "We didn't need to help him with the vision," Stevens explained, "we needed to understand it well, to buy into it, and see its efficacy for ourselves, so that in our own way we could contribute not just in support of him, but organically in other ways as well, because it was a whole set of maneuvers, and a lot had to be done in a very long arc."[5]

At so bureaucratic a university, where school endowments did not keep pace with expenses, and where the need for approvals from the central administration never entirely vanished, saying "yes" became an art in itself. The team needed to "keep a strategy in mind, and our story straight ... because you never knew where you're going to have a chance to advance arguments [for new spending] or have to defend them. The 'learned behavior' around all of Yale in those days was, 'No.'"[6] Guido needed to change the learned behavior.

Faculty perspectives. "The law school pre-and post-Guido are two different law schools," said Dennis [Denny] Curtis, who joined the faculty in fall 1969 as a supervising attorney and instructor in law and who continued at Yale as a Professor Emeritus in 2011. "There were a lot more possibilities than there had been before under anybody else. There were a lot more answers of "yes," and a lot more

---

[2] *Id.*
[3] David Margolick, *"Citizen Of Yale" Is Named New Dean Of The Law School*, N.Y. TIMES, Jan. 31, 1985.
[4] *Id.*
[5] Interview with Carroll Stevens, Dec. 13, 2011.
[6] *Id.*

interesting things that people thought about to do and got the money to do."[7] An illustration standing out to Peter Schuck was the ease with which the *Yale Journal of Law and Feminism* could be created. "After a casual conversation with some of my friends to determine if there was any interest," said Sherrie Nachman, "I approached then-Dean Calabresi with a list of all the things that we would need to start our journal—an office, a computer, and a budget. I was prepared for the hard sell, but Guido simply said 'yes.'"[8] The *Journal* was founded in 1987.[9]

Dean of Admissions James A. [Jim] Thomas. Thomas graduated from Wesleyan University, and then from Yale Law School in 1964. As Guido says, one reason that he retained Thomas was because his ability to find, recruit, and support students who matriculated, especially minorities. He helped to address racial divisions and diminish alienation from an overwhelmingly white and privileged law school environment.

Professor Drew Days illustrated the camaraderie Jim engendered. Days, an African American graduate of the law school who became a member of its faculty in 1981, taught courses including federal jurisdiction and antidiscrimination law, and directed the International Center for Human Rights. In 1993, at a private home in Washington, African American students from the law school class of 1973 held a party in Jim's honor and invited the newly elected "Yalie First Family"—the Clintons—to the party. Days had temporarily relocated to Washington, D.C., to become Solicitor General in the new administration and was invited to the event. He assumed that the Clintons would never attend, but when he and his wife arrived, they saw a magnetometer on the front lawn—Bill and Hillary had come to honor Jim Thomas.

Professor Drew Days

As Days described it, they ended up staying for two and a half hours, during which time they had "a ball."

---

[7] Interview with Professor Dennis Curtis, May 31, 2011.
[8] Interview with Professor Peter Shuck, op. cit. Sherrie Nachman, *The Yale Journal of Law and Feminism Twenty Years Ago: Reflections from Our Founding Members*, 20 YALE J. OF L. & FEMINISM 247 (2008).
[9] Id.

They were burlesqued by their classmates, ten or twelve African American graduates of Yale Law School. They did things like giving Hillary, before she became the 'source of all evil' in the administration, a long witch's hat. Bill Clinton was given a rubber arm with a hand that he could shake when he was all alone in the White House. Harlon Dalton gave him a toy tank, so that he could play with that instead of declaring war. It went like this for two and a half hours.

There was no question in Days's mind that Jim Thomas was "really a critical figure for all of these former students."[10]

In 1989, Guido established, and personally funded, anonymously, the James A. Thomas Lecture, to honor him and address the legal problems of marginalized groups.

Listening to Justice Sotomayor at the James A. Thomas Lecture in 2014. Left to right: Robert Post, Reva Siegel, James Thomas, and Deborah Thomas

A liberal approach. Embracing new ideas truly was not a matter of financial capacity but of outlook. Arriving in 1993 as Guido was completing his deanship, Jack Balkin was struck by the spirit of "classic liberalism" that Guido embodied; he was "supremely pragmatic, in every sense, *in all the best senses* of the word, 'pragmatism.'"

> Guido wants things to work. He wants to win. He wants things to go well. He wants everything he's associated with to be grander, and bigger, and better. *This* is his ideology. He will make deals. He will make fabulous arguments in any direction that's necessary, for the thing to happen. He will do somersaults and curlycues, and he'll be dazzling! But you know, at the end of the day, that it's about pragmatism.
>
> I always saw that thing in him. Maybe, in fact, that *isn't* him and *I just saw it in him*; but I honestly think that *is* him. He has that very sunny view about the

---

[10] Interview with Professor Drew Days, Oct. 12, 2012.

world. He also understands that what's very important, at the end of the day, is not standing on principle, but making things *better*—which is also a view that I share.

Remember, [that as a Dean] he is politician as well, and a politician who has to get things done. Sometimes he can't make the deal work, or he says the thing in a way that doesn't sound convincing to some people, and people don't trust him, and so they're angry at him. This happened, too. It didn't happen to me, but I saw.[11]

Guido's sunny disposition and liberal pragmatism accounted for much and explained why the two clicked.

There were large manifestations—the student loan forgiveness policy Guido speaks about—and small ones. At one point, a faculty member needed to hospitalize his son immediately, but his health insurer refused to cover the substantial expense. Guido advanced law school funds without hesitation, conveying that, "If you get it back from the insurer that's fine. If you don't get it back, we'll deal with it." The faculty member fought with the insurance company, recovered the money, and wrote a check back to the University, immensely appreciative for Guido's immediate willingness to help.

Fundraising to support faculty hiring and programs. Tony Kronman marveled at Guido's "sheer cleverness" at diagnosing and attacking problems, "an uncanny, quick instinct for the nerve of a practical problem." These included fundraising. If a donor wanted to give money—but for the wrong purpose—and a faculty member was not really interested in that purpose but might be persuaded to do something, "Guido would [snaps his fingers] just like that, see it, and fiddle, and work it from both ends, and make a match."

Partly, these successes were accomplished by persuasive charm; but partly, Kronman stressed, it was because of his enormous desire to please faculty members. "He always made the point to me that a Dean possesses a great deal of power, and can exercise great power, but only [when he is] the instrument of the faculty. The Dean serves the faculty, not the other way around."[12]

Communication and administration. Michael Thompson developed an interest in law school administration while a student at Georgetown. In 1990, he became the Associate Dean for Building Services at Yale and has continued in that role for more than thirty years. "Guido thinks very closely about how he's going to convey something, and about the way he is going to communicate about what he wants you to do," Mike said. "You understand why he wants you to do it that way, and you have time to voice your criticism, when you talk with Guido. It was *not* like, 'you do it or else.'" "I learned the most from Guido about being a dean."[13]

---

[11] Interview with Professor Jack Balkin, June 1, 2011.
[12] Interview with Professor Anthony Kronman, Feb. 4, 2013.
[13] Interview with Associate Dean Mike Thompson, Feb. 6, 2013.

Associate Dean Mike Thompson

Birthday wishes. From the time that his deanship began Guido personally has called many people—*hundreds* of people—on their birthdays and sung to them. The distinguished American and Croatian Professor of Law Mirjan Damaška was introduced to Guido's custom and smitten by its thoughtfulness. "He calls you and sings to you. I thought for a while he did it only for me, but then it turned out he did it to everybody! And then, that has continued year after year. He will always say to me, '*Cento di questi giorni*,' which means in Italian: 'a hundred of these days.' It is always touching. And he sings well."[14]

Cynics considered these calls part of a decanal charm offensive—but most colleagues accepted them as stalwart efforts to spread joy and friendship and maintain communication. "I love Guido to pieces," Damaška said a quarter-century after Guido's deanship ended. "He still calls me up on my birthday and sings 'Happy Birthday' to me. He's just the dearest man! There is a child-like humanity to Guido. He is so special! Some people, I think, misunderstand that."[15]

Listening to complaints. Even faculty with whom Guido often disagreed found that the lines of communication were open. Professor Owen Fiss conceded being an aggravation to the dean. Coming between them most often were differences over the appointments Guido wanted to make, which included an increasing number of "podium" visits proposed to increase coverage and sometimes to placate the Law School's "Barons."[16]

To press his views, Fiss took advantage of the fact that Guido had adopted a personal rule of answering every faculty communication immediately:

> You see, this was a whole new policy of faculty attentiveness. He would answer every faculty call or memo within thirty seconds of him receiving it. I don't even

---

[14] Interview with Professor Mirjan Damaška, Dec. 15, 2010.
[15] *Id.*
[16] Interview with Professor Owen Fiss, May 24, 2011.

know, now, what I was crazed about, but my office on the second floor was at the top of the stairwell leading down to the Dean's office on the ground floor, and Guido came up to see me quite a bit.

The new instant access policy had its drawbacks, too, and after a while, Fiss recalled, the likelihood of so quick and so personal an answer probably deterred him from complaining as often as he might have!

Professor Owen Fiss

Hiring. Replenishment of the faculty ranks with great scholars would be among the most significant results of Guido's deanship. The Law School faculty long had been celebrated as among the greatest assemblies of talent when Guido became the dean; but, as he recounts, along several dimensions, Yale was less attractive than it had been to top scholars at other major law schools. Few appointments were made in the early 1980s, and a few of the senior faculty seriously entertained offers from other law schools.

When Guido became dean, "from the very start, people had the sense that 'We're back in the game—we're going to be able to hire who[m]ever we want! This is the Yale Law School!'" Tony Kronman remembered that "Guido just embodied such confidence about the place that everybody began to share it."[17]

"Humanity and Excellence." Harold Koh, who would become a Yale Law School dean after Tony Kronman, pointed to the mantra, "humanity and excellence," which Guido coined and repeated often. The mantra emanated naturally—unselfconsciously—and it encompassed a general theme, a fundraising motif, and a specific criterion for the new scholars they wanted to hire. His rhetoric, and its earnestness—together with the new changes in financial autonomy, motivated donors to make gifts which allowed making new hires

---

[17] Interview with Professor Anthony Kronman, Feb. 4, 2013.

and increasing the salaries of the existing faculty.[18] "Our salaries went back to the levels they had been," Koh recounted, and Guido began to do substantial, aggressive lateral recruiting.[19]

Appointments and professional judgment. In hiring, Guido proved himself "an impeccable judge of academic horseflesh" whose "highly intuitive approach" involved evaluating a combination of intelligence, personality, character, and drive, leading him to decide whether or not to make a bet. "I think he makes that assessment in a microsecond," a faculty member speculated. Having picked someone, Guido was "all for that person for the rest of their life."[20]

The judgments he made about the quality of someone's academic work were "incredibly sure, and often very severe."[21] Guido has, Kronman asserted, "an aristocrat's nose for greatness in all domains, including intellectual work," and possesses "confidence that he knows what's good and he knows what's shit."[22]

> So there is Guido, the Man of the People, the champion of democratic values, the one who carries the banner on behalf of diversity, who is easily approachable by the least among us, whose gown you can touch. All of that is true, and it is an incredibly important part of the charisma of the man. But it goes along with a great aristocratic reserve of judgment, a fierceness.... He is very politic, and he avoids cruelties, and incivilities, but he's not shy about thinking—and if need be, saying—'This is just not good. The person is a second-rate person. That's it.' He might say, 'Their candle flickers. Others burn more brightly.'[23]

Professor Anthony Kronman

---

[18] Interview with Professor Harold Koh, Aug. 26, 2013.
[19] *Id.* See interview with Stephen Wizner, Nov. 30, 2010.
[20] Interview with Harold Koh, Aug. 26, 2013.
[21] Interview with Anthony Kronman, Feb. 4, 2013.
[22] *Id.*
[23] Interview with Anthony Kronman, Ms=arch. 4, 2013.

Guido "landed" all the lateral hires to whom offers were extended. This was attributable partly to Guido's skills, and partly also to the fortuity of the timing of the hunt for lateral talent. At Stanford—where many of the laterals came from—there were divisions over matters that were ideological, pedagogical, and political.[24] These also were years of trouble on the faculty at Harvard, when the Critical Legal Studies movement created fissures. David Trubek, who had been denied tenure at Yale and moved to the University of Wisconsin, where he was granted tenure, visited at Harvard and found that his tenure bid was blocked.[25] He referred to Harvard Law School at that time as "the Beirut of legal education."[26] Asked in later years why Yale was not similarly afflicted by rifts over CLS, Guido drew attention to the decades-long dominance of the Legal Realists at Yale—and quipped that "those with Cow Pox don't get Small Pox."[27]

Stanford emigres Robert Ellickson, Roberta Romano, Robert Gordon, Ian Ayres, and John Donohue. Robert Ellickson and Roberta Romano visited Yale from Stanford and both received offers and decided to come. Robert Gordon, Ian Ayres, and later, John Donohue came after visiting and received offers—all of them received their offers before they left town. "Guido had the view that if he gave an offer while somebody was in New Haven during a visit, they would accept it; [but] if you waited a year till they went back to Palo Alto or whatever, they would not accept it, because the thought of New Haven was okay when you were in New Haven, but it was unthinkable that you would go to New Haven from elsewhere!"[28]

Bringing back the Ackermans. In 1971, Bruce and Susan Rose Ackerman were young assistant professors at the University of Pennsylvania. Guido got them to visit at Yale when Susan had difficulties succeeding in a Penn economics department that was conventional, conservative, and male.[29] The Ackermans joined the university on a longer-term basis in 1974 when the Yale Economics Department offered Susan a position. Back at the law school at that time, Bruce Ackerman and Owen Fiss joined the regular faculty. The appointment of Fiss was shepherded by Abe Goldstein; Ackerman's selection by Guido.[30]

In 1982, however, difficulties Susan encountered in the Yale Economics Department led her to accept a position at Columbia Law School directing a Center

---

[24] David Margolick, *The Trouble with America's Law Schools*, N.Y. TIMES, May 22, 1983; Jennifer A. Kingson, *Harvard Tenure Battle Puts "Critical Legal Studies" on Trial*, N.Y. TIMES, Aug. 30, 1987; interview with Professor Robert Ellickson, May 10, 2011.

[25] Kingson, Harvard Tenure Battle Puts "Critical Legal Studies" on Trial, *supra* note 24.

[26] *Id.*

[27] Richard Michael Fischl, *The Epidemiology of Critique*, 57 MIAMI L. REV. 475, 478 (2003) (quoting letter from Guido).

[28] Interview with Professor Robert Ellickson, May 10, 2011.

[29] The Penn economics department (whose tenured members were entirely males) emphasized theoretical work, especially microeconomics; *see* John Tschirhart, *Ranking Economics Departments in Areas of Expertise*, 20 J. ECON. ED. 199, 212; *see also* 29 U. Pa. Almanac No. 30, Women Among the Full-Time Faculty of the University (1983) (overall percentage of tenured standing faculty overall rose from 8.6–9.8 between 1978 and 1982).

[30] Interview with Professor Bruce Ackerman, May 3, 2011.

for Law and Economics. Bruce moved with her, in a jump that did not go unnoticed in the Academy.[31]

Guido believed that Bruce's departure struck a reputational blow such that the school needed to do whatever was necessary to get him back. "I wouldn't say that Guido thought of Bruce as indispensable," Kronman recalled, "but pretty close to that. This was someone we absolutely had to have!"[32] Guido engineered for Susan a jointly funded offer of a dual appointment at the Law School and the Political Science Department, and both Ackermans returned; Guido was the moving force.[33]

Bringing in Alan Schwartz and John Langbein. As Guido indicates, he was determined to bring East from the University of Southern California his former student, Alan Schwartz. Schwartz was already making extraordinary, prolific contributions to the theory of contract law. In order to make the move possible, Guido needed to situate Alan's spouse Ilsa, who was a highly accomplished Ph.D. neurochemist and neurobiologist. The Medical School coveted her but could not immediately make her an offer—they did not have a slot available for two or three years. Guido arranged a budget transfer allowing the Medical School to hire Ilsa when the Law School hired Alan.[34]

Recognizing that he faced significant recruiting impediments to bringing two-career families to New Haven, Guido added raising money for this purpose to his fundraising appeals.

Bringing John Langbein. Guido and his appointments chairman Tony Kronman would meet, discuss directions to take, and—to some extent—consider existing weaknesses in essential areas of the curriculum. "Who is really good out there? Whom would we love to appoint?"[35] John Langbein fit the bill. At the University of Chicago, he had become an outstanding authority on trust, probate, pension, investment law, as well as a as a superb legal historian. Although Langbein loved the University of Chicago, several of his Chicago friends had moved to Yale, including Owen Fiss and Tony Kronman, and former students George Priest and Carol Rose. Langbein also had become fond of Robert Ellickson, who had visited at Chicago.[36] Kronman was especially instrumental in helping to bring him to Yale.

Recruiting Heather Gerken. "There is probably no better recruiter in the Universe than Guido," declared Dean Heather Gerken, recalling the toast to her he had made at a dinner in 2006 (after Guido had left the deanship). At the time, Heather was an accomplished Harvard scholar whom the faculty determined that it wanted.

> I did not meet Guido until I came to visit, when I had a sort of extraordinary dinner with him. He was in full recruiting mode at the time. We had this long discussion, and he told me what he thought made Yale special.

---

[31] David Margolick, *Two Schools of Thought Divide Two Schools of Law*, N.Y. TIMES, Oct. 9, 1983.
[32] Interview with Anthony Kronman, Feb. 4, 2013.
[33] *Id.*
[34] Interview with Guido Calabresi; interview with Alan Schwartz, Feb. 9, 2011.
[35] Interview with Professor Anthony Kronman, Feb. 4, 2013.
[36] Interview with Professor John Langbein, Dec. 12, 2010.

> Sometime later, after the faculty voted me an offer, there was a party—there always is—and people give these very nice toasts. Everyone else would give a toast praising you and saying nice things. It kind of makes you want to break out in hives.
>
> The thing that was amazing to me was that Guido gave a very different toast. Instead of the 'what makes you special' toast, Guido gave 'are you ready for us?' toast.

Instead of flattering her directly, he tested her resolve. He asked if she was "ready to give the school everything she had to be great." Did she want to be stronger? Was she willing to do better work than she ever had? Would she be willing to "go up the wall" with him? There was an edginess to these challenges—they would have repelled many others—but they primed Heather to accept the offer, on the spot. And after the event, David Simon, her husband, asked Heather if Guido only had one dinner with her—*really*? "That was the only dinner," Heather confirmed. How, David wanted to know, could Guido possibly figure her out so perfectly? Heather did not know. "That was my introduction to the magic of Guido," she said.[37]

Dean Heather Gerken

Reeling in Jack Balkin. Professor Balkin began his writing career at the University of Missouri-Kansas City and earned renown for writing about jurisprudence and constitutional theory—particularly among progressives in the Academy. Visiting in 1992–1993, Guido made him his offer. Bruce Ackerman was the chair of Appointments, but as customary the offer was made by Guido:

> He wouldn't tell you what was going on—but you kind of knew. He would give you a call, and he would say, 'Come and meet me in my office.' You would toddle down to the Dean's office, which is this magnificent structure, very impressive. He would sit you on a couch next to him. I don't know whether he would pat your hand or something, but in any case, he would sit very close to you, and he would say, 'We

---

[37] Interview with Professor Heather Gerken, May 28, 2014.

really very much want you to be a member of the Yale faculty.' It was a very effective, a very emotionally filled sort of experience. He's so good at it, and he's just so warm. How could you say no at this point? It was very thrilling.[38]

Professor Jack Balkin

Critics asserted that Guido "*talked* Left but *appointed* Right."[39] Indeed, there were conservative arrivals, including John Langbein, Robert Ellickson, and Alan Schwartz. As Langbein put it, however, "Guido had a nose for what he thought might be quality, and he couldn't care less about ideology. He wanted to build a lively law school."[40] His hiring in fact also included moderates like Akhil Amar, Paul Kahn, Carol Rose, and Jed Rubenfeld; and left-progressives Jack Balkin, Robert Gordon, the Ackermans, Harold Koh, Paul Kahn, and Ian Ayres.

Professor John Langbein

---

[38] Interview with Professor Jack Balkin, June 1, 2011.
[39] Interview with Professor John Langbein, Dec. 12, 2010; LAURA KALMAN, YALE LAW SCHOOL AND THE SIXTIES: REVOLT AND REVERBERATIONS 326 (2006).
[40] Interview with John Langbein, Dec. 12, 2010.

Nurturing excellence. Guido called Vicki Schultz from Italy while he was on sabbatical and she was deciding whether to leave The University of Wisconsin (which she loved), or take an offer from Harvard Law School, (from which she graduated).[41] When he called, she said, "You just had the feeling that at the moment he was talking to you, you were the most important thing in the world to him."[42] He told her to write telling him everything she could possibly want in order to do her best work and be happy at the Law School and to "put absolutely everything on the table," being "incredibly generous to herself."[43] Vicki wrote a long letter with a specific request to hire other Law & Society scholars and people interested in gender studies.[44] Guido responded with his personal promise to do everything he could, a promise he honored.[45] In contrast to her recruitment by the dean at Wisconsin, and to what she knew about subsequent Yale deans, she came away "feeling marvelous and highly valued."[46] Throughout the whole process she "never experienced Guido as ungenuine in any respect." It set a model for subsequent deans to live up to, and deviations were noticed.[47]

A wealth of resources. Blair Kauffman directed the Law Library at the University of Wisconsin-Madison when he interviewed for a position as head of Yale's Goldman Law Library prior to its renovation. He let Guido know that the classification system was archaic; and that it was impossible to find a book efficiently unless one had worked with the collection for years.[48] Blair ventured that a major new reclassification effort would be needed. He "guesstimated" that it would cost a million dollars. Would the law school be willing to do that?

"A million dollars is a lot of money," Guido replied, "it's not a punch in the nose."[49] When the interview closed, Guido took Blair with him to call on Steve Yandle, whom he referred to as his "Dean for Dollars":

> Guido goes, 'Steve, could we afford a million dollars for a reclassification project in the law library?' It was *obvious* that the answer he was supposed to give was 'yes'! [Laughs] And so Steve took the hint and said, 'Yes, we probably could. Yes.' So Guido said, 'You've got it.'
>
> And I thought, Wow! What a nice place to come to! Such receptiveness to ideas![50]

Impressed, Kauffman moved to Yale.[51]

---

[41] Interview with Prof. Vicki Schultz, June 4, 2013.
[42] *Id.*
[43] *Id.*
[44] *Id.*
[45] *Id.*
[46] *Id.*
[47] *Id.*
[48] Interview with Blair Kauffman, Mar. 24, 2011.
[49] *Id.*
[50] *Id.*
[51] *Id.* The collection was modernized to be readily accessible in print and digital form; the physical space was renewed. See Message from the Director, Annual Report of the Goldman Library, 2015–2016, https://library.law.yale.edu/sites/default/files/yale_law_library_annual_report_2015-2016_0.pdf.

The clinical programs. Prior Yale deans supported live-client clinics to a greater degree than at most other schools; Guido built on the earlier efforts, raising their stature, improving their physical facilities, and diversifying their faculty.

In ways he intended, the renovation of Ruttenberg Hall compelled many academic teachers who wanted renovated offices to be neighbors of the clinic. The increased financial support he received from alumni, together with his new independent decision-making authority, made it possible to raise salaries and to change leave policies to bring clinicians and academics into closer parity. He raised funds for a William O. Douglas Distinguished Clinical Professorship and awarded the first chair in clinical legal education at Yale to Stephen Wizner, in 1991.

As had been occurring at other schools, Guido re-designated clinicians as "clinical" professors of law, rather than as "adjunct" professors. He encouraged gender diversity and essentially achieved gender parity, supporting the clinical tenure of Mary A. McCarthy (Senator Eugene McCarthy's daughter) and of Jean Koh Peters (the sister of Professor Harold Hongju Koh). Two other women, Brett Dignam and Kathleen Sullivan, also joined the clinical faculty in those years. "He was absolutely intentionally diversifying the clinic for gender," reflected Jean Koh Peters. "Up until then, men tended to hold the higher-status jobs, and there were women who were instructors, who did a lot of work, but did not hold those status jobs."[52]

Recharge. Before his second five-year round, Guido took a semester off—not to rest up, but to work on scholarship. At Yale, a drop-off in the productivity, even of a busy dean, might be a disappointment to himself and to others. "Look, this is a tough place," said Ian Ayres, who became a tenured and distinguished professor:

> I feel pressure all the time. What's my next article? What can I do to hold my head up with these amazing people that are my colleagues? This position is not a gift. You're supposed to keep doing something, and at some point, if you can't do it anymore, you should get out of the way. Guido exemplified this [ethos, and] in this break between the first five years and the second five years of his deanship, he negotiated for a semester off, and actually wrote a *Yale Law Journal* and a *Harvard Law Review* article during that period. Just amazing!"[53]

Finessing the selection of the second-term Deputy Deans. When John Simon stepped down at the end of Guido's first term, Guido "asked a ton of people to be deputy dean." For some reasons which any faculty member would understand, and others peculiar to the new vision and pace that Guido had brought with him, nobody

---

[52] Stephen Wizner, *The Law School Clinic: Legal Education in the Interests of Justice*, 70 FORDHAM L. REV. 1929 2001–2002; interview with Professor Jean Koh Peters, May 30, 2013; interview with Professor Dennis Curtis, May 31, 2011; Laura Holland, *Invading the Ivory Tower*, 49 J. LEG. ED. 504 (1999).
[53] Interview with Professor Ian Ayres, Jan. 3, 2012; Calabresi, *Foreword: Antidiscrimination and Constitutional Accountability (What the Bork-Brennan Debate Ignores)*, 105 HARV. L. REV. 90 (1991); Calabresi, *The Pointlessness of Pareto: Carrying Coase Further*, 100 YALE L.J. 1211 (1990–1991).

wanted the job. Furthermore, as Guido says, nobody wanted to serve for five years, which had been the model.

A possible solution was obvious: divide up the length of the obligation and reduce their teaching requirements. Even so, to engage already busy academics required the sort of finesse Guido might have used to win a trick at bridge. Robert Ellickson described Guido's play:

> Guido called five of us down to the Dean's Office. The five of us were, in order of our actual service, Jerry Mashaw, me, Tony Kronman, Peter Schuck, and Al Klevorick... Guido says "Well, I'm thinking about how to fill this deputy deanship position, so here's my idea. I think all of you would make excellent deputy deans. I understand that nobody wants to take it for a long term, and I have worked it out so that one year would be enough. And a really good way to work it would be [that] you do it in the following order, and then this will take care of this problem that I have. But of course, if any of you don't want to do this, you can just raise your hand.

We all kind of scratched our heads.

Had any had been asked privately, all would very likely have said "no." But he had boxed them in. "It was just impossible," said Ellickson, "for any of us to be the one who caused the thing to unravel, at that point! We were hooked into it. And that's how I was recruited to be deputy dean!"[54]

Professor Robert Ellickson

[54] Interview with Professor Robert Ellickson, May 10, 2011.

20
Independence

Large private nonprofit universities are complicated, and their trustees, presidents, and provosts routinely address hard budgetary challenges and policy choices. The resource allocations and employment decisions they make reveal their priorities for scholarship and research, as well as their management philosophy about the distribution of administrative power. Among the large organizational problems is calibrating the allowable degree of professional autonomy and financial decentralization.

The primary business model in most of legal education long has been relatively straightforward: large classes are taught by relatively small faculties; access to the Bar is regulated through accreditation and examinations; high tuition charges are assessed and are tolerated by students due to the availability of loans and substantial market value of law degrees. At many institutions, this model has generated substantial profits, which can be either retained or redistributed to other parts of the school.

From the perspective of a law school faculty, placing a heavy central hand on employment policies and maintaining control over spending decisions appears counterproductive and confiscatory. On the other hand, if a law school suffers a secular reputational decline, or if legal education as a whole falters, a law school would suppose that interdependence and reciprocity may have a positive, stabilizing effect.

On becoming Dean, Guido found a confusing situation which, at least on paper, indicated the least desirable mix of both worlds—minimal profit, minimal financial support, and maximal interference from the central administration.

Working for autonomy from the central University was the riskiest—and also the most necessary—gamble that I took in all my years as the dean. Yale was not inclined to grant schools independence, because Yale does not accept —and I'm very glad that they do not—Harvard's notion of "every tub on its own bottom." Yale has never been that way; moreover, under Bart Giamatti, it had moved very far in the opposite direction.

There were at the time some leading law schools that were independent, like Harvard, and some like Stanford that chose to be dependent, with the University backing them very strongly. Harvard's notion, supposedly, was: every part of Harvard fends for itself; if it cannot raise the money, tough! This can be very hard on schools with little fundraising capacity. Very good for schools with wealthy alumni—it's amazing, in that context, that the Harvard Law School doesn't pay

> *salaries which are fifty times higher than anybody else! I do not know what they do with their money. But you know, with the size of that student body, and if they really are a tub on their own bottom, I just do not understand their finances.*

Yale always thought that the central University should protect, and help finance, parts of the University that are less well off.

When I stepped in, we were treated like one of the "less well-off" parts, for there was a yearly deficit, which we supposedly needed to have the University meet. As a result, I found myself in a situation where the Law School was barred from doing anything—hiring, starting new programs, fixing the building, *anything*—without getting permission.

If we raised money, unless it was raised for a specific purpose—and hence was not available to be used for anything else—that was used for reduction of the supposed deficit. The University wasn't intrusive in issues of hiring in the sense that they did not say whom we could hire or not, but they certainly were suggesting, "You cannot hire many, and you cannot pay them adequately, because you're in deficit, and you cannot afford it."

I found myself arguing about how many pencils I could have, when I did not want pencils. I wanted a renovated building, a better salary structure, new faculty, and new programs! The building was crumbling, full of rats, with many leaks, with poor heat, and dirty as could be. It was a genuine impediment to hiring. Where could I put the people I was courting when in other schools they had offices that were nice? We had a library with no lights and no room. The building catastrophe was technically the University's responsibility; but the *whole University* was physically falling apart. Fixing the Law School was *way* down on *its* list of priorities!

> *I did not even like the way they had started fixing the other buildings, because they were doing it on the cheap. When you do things on the cheap, you get things that are cheap. Abe Goldstein did some fixing here on the cheap and the fixes all had to be destroyed! He had two seminar rooms with sound that bled each the other, so that neither could be used; but they were cheap! That's what the University led him to do.*

From my perspective, if we remained dependent, and supposedly had a deficit of a million-five, a million-eight a year—a deficit, which would balloon if I were to hire anybody good—we were done for. The phony deficit would keep growing, and any money we brought in from alums would have to be used to try to reduce it! What could we do about the building, then?

I wasn't going to put up with this! You know, I come from an economics background! There are times when investing more in the underlying framework of a place, not less, is what is financially wise. I could not help remembering that my grandfather Ettore, at twenty-one, was the Chief Financial Officer of the textile mills he had started working at the bottom of; and by the time he was twenty-eight, he was running the whole operation. I would like to think I inherited just a tiny bit of that capacity to see a financial picture in its breadth.

* * *

Bart left shortly after I arrived, and Benno Schmidt became the new president. In him, I found a president who was much more understanding of the problems of the graduate schools and the Law School, because Benno had been dean of the Columbia Law School.

Many have given Benno poor marks as Yale president because of his dealings with the college, his situation with his wife, and some other things, which happened. But in terms of the professional schools—and I do not mean just the Law School—Benno was a great President.

With him as president, I thought it might be possible to become independent. And so I asked myself, "Okay, what risks am I taking if I take the Law School independent?" I asked myself how big the risk was that the Law School would not be able to raise enough money to run on its own. I wondered, if we reached an agreement for independence, if we could, in annual fundraising, generate enough money so that I could meet the blank check that I told you that I wrote and start paying the salaries to the new hires and the existing faculty that I was promising. It scared me that the Law School's endowment at that point was very small.

I do not remember what it was; the endowment then made up forty million, sixty million, something of that sort; as against nearly $1.2 billion now!

But because I did not think the Law School would ever be able to compete with other schools if it was not independent, I decided to bet that we could raise much more money. I thought we were not raising money anywhere near what we could in annual giving, and I also bet that in terms of *capital giving*, much more money could come in, too, *probably* even if I did not do anything! I was not sure of myself as a fundraiser, and I did not have any expectations that I would do anything exceptional, but I bet we could do these things nevertheless.

Why? Because of demographics and because of the effect of independence on our alums. My gamble was based entirely on a financier's view of the market, and of what was going on. You see—and I never said this to the University when I was negotiating—I thought that Yale Law School alums, both in annual giving and in capital giving, would give a lot more if I assured them that the Law School was keeping their donated money and that their gifts were not helping Yale University. I thought that there were many people who were wealthy alums, from colleges that they liked, who did not like Yale University—but loved Yale Law School.

> *The model there is the Princeton or Dartmouth person, devoted to their colleges. Many of our best graduates came from Princeton or Dartmouth, like Jack Danforth and Oscar Ruebhausen. They did not care about helping Yale University, but they cared a lot about the Law School. I mean, I do not really want to help Harvard. But when Radcliffe was separate, we loved to give to it. Radcliffe was a wonderful place when my wife was there, and when it was independent we both wanted to support it.*

Another extremely important group I thought would be more inclined to giving was the group who liked the Law School because it was liberal and freely admitted Jews, Catholics, minorities of every sort, and admitted women long before the rest of the University. The Law School had an openness that Yale University as a whole, and certainly the Yale College of earlier years, did not have! There were older alums of this sort who remembered a Yale which pre-Whitney Griswold was, pre-Kingman Brewster: the Yale of Charles Seymour and James Rowland Angell. They remembered a Yale University they did not like, and a Law School they did. I thought that by announcing a separation and independence, I could get people to give who wouldn't otherwise do so.

* * *

I thought about purely demographic changes that had occurred. The Law School, for many years, was a local, Connecticut school. It became more of a New York, and then finally became a great national, school. The Annual Fund had grown, even though we had done nothing to make it grow, simply because more of our graduates had become major wealthy lawyers, or very wealthy non-lawyers. Without *anybody doing anything*, the Annual Fund kept going up. The demographics were that people from the "great" national school period were now getting old enough to die, or to make end-of-life capital gifts. Sounds brutal! Still, I thought that even if we did not do anything, the Law School was going to start getting capital gifts in larger amounts.

> *You do not become a partner in Cravath, or Sullivan, or whatever, without accumulating the kind of estate where, if you have no children, you can give a huge amount. And even if you have children, a million dollars is something you probably can do!*

My bargaining advantage in the negotiations as I entered into them was my willingness to bet that this money would be coming in. I saw these sources of potential surpluses if the University did not eat them away; the University was focused on the fear that the deficits, even if somewhat phony, were growing and might well become real.

***

Not long after Benno became the president, I started negotiations with Bill Nordhaus, the provost, and his deputy, Chip Long. I found in Benno a president who was potentially open to a new relationship, and in the provost, someone who was difficult to deal with on a day-to-day basis—some have described him as "weaned on a dill pickle"—and someone who found me just as difficult.

I do not want to seem negative about Bill, though. He is brilliant, and as many brilliant scholars do, he wanted things done his way. But as an economist, he saw independence as probably a good idea. He saw a situation in which the Law School was demanding more and more and more and more. He knew this to be a recipe for more and more conflict with the University. He also did not want the Law School to go down. Also, his father and his brother were Yale Law School graduates—both remarkable people; and Bill may have had feelings for this place.

Additionally, he found *me* difficult to deal with for the same reason I found *him* difficult to deal with! *I'm* not an *easy* person! He and I shared some of the same characteristics. He really did not want to have to get into a fight with me, either. Whether this is because he was worried that if that happened, I would try to go over his head to Benno, who had been my student, or whether basically he liked me, I do not know.

The University knew that if these talks fell apart, and we did not reach an agreement, and I wasn't the dean, we would go back to the old ways. That meant that sooner or later they would have to deal with the problem of the Law School building that was falling apart. (The ABA Accreditation Committee, perhaps, not totally accidentally, had described the building as a disaster which had to be fixed, and soon.) The pressure to fix the building was certainly something, which they were very, very glad to have off their backs!

I told the University that although it was its obligation to fix up the building, I would take that obligation over. I said, [sighs] "I am going to do it."

***

We came to agree that the Law School should be independent, and that going independent should be "revenue-neutral." That is, we agreed that independence was not going to be a way in which the University got money from the Law School, or the Law School got money from the University. It was supposed to be just an arrangement in which both sides agreed that it was better for the Law School to be independent than not! Now, that's a very easy thing to *say*, but what does "revenue-neutral" *mean*? We had to figure out what that meant.

What did that mean in terms of paying part of the University's administrative costs? How much should we pay for that? How many Sterling Professors—paid out of University funds derived from a donor who was especially interested in the Law School—do we get? And issues concerning other contributions from the University. There were times when we were really very far away.

At a certain point, I actually said, "Let's bring in accountants, and go back to the beginning, and see how much you stole from us, and how much we stole from you. And let's just see!" And they said, "How can we possibly do this? *Absolutely not!*" I said, "I do not want to do it! But you know, if we've got no other way, this is what we've got to do."

* * *

In the end, the deal was made because I was willing to take over the obligation of fixing the building, which would cost a huge amount of money, and because I chose to bet on the interest rate. What I said was, "Okay, the Law School is getting a million dollars from the University each year. I am willing to forget about inflation, to forget about the fact that this 'deficit' is increasing. But I'm not willing to start out without that million dollars; I cannot do it. That clearly is not 'revenue-neutral.' I'm willing to leave your support at a million dollars a year and no more. And if there is inflation, we lose." I did not say, "If there is not inflation, we win."

I did not want the million considered as a subsidy, because I did not want anybody to be saying the University is subsidizing this rich law school. As I saw it, the million dollars were "liquidated damages." That is, when we looked over the whole history of the financial relationship, and who had taken what from whom, a million dollars a year, fixed, was what we were owed.

* * *

As it turned out, my bet on the interest rate turned out to be right. In the remaining years of the agreement to pay the million, rates moved in a direction so that paying us a million dollars flat turned out to be advantageous to us. This became something that, by the next deanship, some people in the rest of the University were starting to complain about. Even though I had called it liquidated damages, they said, "Why are they getting this amount?" I believe the matter was settled by transferring a lump sum to the Law School's part of the University's very well managed endowment, and by no longer making yearly payments.

Nordhaus, who by then was fully on board, was able to say to the Yale Corporation, "Look, this is a good deal," because everybody believed in inflation. "The Law School is now capped at a million dollars, and they're off our back! They've taken responsibility for the building, which is an enormous undertaking. We do not need to worry about them. The million dollars is something that will disappear, in a while. We would have had to pay something like it anyway." He could describe it, not improperly, as a good deal for the University—which, in many ways, it was!

> On the other hand, it was also a wonderful deal for us! It freed us. It allowed us to do what needed to be done for the building, which is another very important part of my deanship, because [sighs] I'm a great believer that things happen in places, not abstractly. Just like anarchy exists in a place where people are responsive to it, there are places where learning occurs.
>
> The faculty was not particularly involved in any of this, at the time. I told them about the negotiations afterward, but while they were going on, I just said, "This is what is going to happen. It lets me do what I promised you I would do when I said I would hire many people and fix the building."
>
> After it was final, and all agreed to, Steve and I went out to dinner, and we celebrated.

COMMENTARY

Chapter 20

"Every tub on its own bottom." President John T. Kirkland of Harvard applied this phrase to the University's funding model in the early nineteenth century; the term developed out of John Bunyan's *The Pilgrim's Progress*.[1] When asked about his efforts to find a location to build the Divinity School, Kirkland responded that, "It is our rule here for every tub to stand on its own bottom."[2]

Now known as "Responsibility Centered Management," or RCM, this model requires each unit within the University to be responsible for its own bottom line. Proponents of this model are often concerned about the free-rider problem that results otherwise—that different schools or components of a university would not contribute their fair share to recruitment and fundraising.[3] Critics of RCM worry about dramatic inequalities between the fundraising abilities of different units. At Harvard, for example, the Faculty of Arts and Sciences and the Graduate School of Arts and Sciences had a combined endowment of $8 billion, greatly overshadowing the School of Education and the School of Design, which each had access to endowments of less than $500 million.[4]

Negotiations. In conversations Guido had with Bart Giamatti in anticipation of his deanship, Guido seems already to have contemplated financial independence, but not to have requested it—probably because the suggestion would have gone

---

[1] JOHN BUNYAN, PILGRIM'S PROGRESS 43 (1678)("*Presumption said, Every Fat must stand upon its own bottom.*").
[2] Dominic A. Hood, *Harvard Explained*, THE CRIMSON, Oct. 24, 2002.
[3] Leroy W. Dubcek, *Beware Higher Ed's Newest Budget Twist*, 13 NEA HIGHER EDUC. J. 81, 81 (1997).
[4] Hood, *supra* note 2.

nowhere with Giamatti. He actually affirmed that, "So long as the School is able to meet its needs ... then the fact that other parts of the University may benefit more from general University endowments can only be viewed as a fine thing."[5] But the needs of the School were "very great" in light of dire competition, University charges against the School were egregious, and the contribution of the University to the Law School from the general University unrestricted endowment was "especially low" compared to other schools.[6]

When Benno Schmidt took over, Guido pressed him and the new provost more emphatically. He emphasized his predicament, asking the provost to stand in his shoes, and to see that his constituencies "expected great things, and visible ones."

He told the provost that on assuming the deanship, he had written to the alumni that he found himself "dreaming of what we could do if ... the Yale Law School Fund were suddenly to double," and that these words had become dangerous because the fund chairman had written to the alumni, on his own, in 1987, that the doubling of the fund had become a reality.[7]

If donors did not see improvements, Guido wrote, they would not keep giving. And if the faculty did not see better compensation and additional faculty slots filled, Guido said, he would "have a mutiny" on his hands. His projections of the gap between the University's commitments of support and the existing and projected operational expenses would not make it possible to fulfill the expectations of donors.[8]

In 1986, as Guido recounts, he reached with the provost a general understanding or an agreement in principle according to which the independence and financial autonomy of the Law School would be accomplished on terms of "fiscal neutrality." Neutrality was understood to mean that the University's historical contribution to the cost of running of the Law School would be maintained "without adding or subtracting to the support the University [historically] gave or received from the School."[9]

Guido asserted that a "zero base-line" for the law school—with four deans, forty-four full-time faculty, and visitors, "confidential salary" commitments, and contingent liabilities—would mean a commitment to ongoing university support of about $1,800,000; but the provost calculated the number at $800,000.[10] The University's low calculation depended partly on recent unilateral accounting changes, which squeezed schools and departments across the University by off-loading prior commitments.

---

[5] Letter from Guido Calabresi to President Bart Giamatti, Jan. 18, 1985.
[6] Id.
[7] Memorandum Letter from Guido Calabresi to the Provost, July 27, 1987, Dean Guido Calabresi—Chron. Corres. Files, Bound, 1985-1987, RU 846 Series Accession 2001-A-040, Yale University Library.
[8] Id.
[9] Id.
[10] Id. Adjusted for inflation, the difference in their calculations would be approximately $2.4 million in 2020 dollars.

William Dawbney Nordhaus. Nordhaus graduated from Yale College and received his Ph.D. in Economics in 1967 from the Massachusetts Institute of Technology. He joined the Yale faculty in 1967 with appointments in the Economics Department and the School of Forestry and Environmental Studies. His work explores the economics of climate change, resource constraints on economic growth, and economic approaches to addressing global warming. In 2018, he won the Nobel Prize in Economics.[11]

Provost and Professor William Dawbney Nordhaus

He served as the provost of the University between 1986 to 1988—a very short term—which occurred during a period of difficulties for the central administration, among them the financial challenges and labor actions by clerical workers and graduate assistants, which Guido discusses.[12]

Guido's assumption that the Law School's progressive admissions policies would spur fundraising if the Law School were independent. Like some other elite law schools, Yale Law School abjured discriminatory hiring and admissions practices well before undergraduate colleges did. Yale Law School appointed many more Jewish faculty members by the 1950s than the College and, beginning in 1948, it implemented an admissions policy to increase African American enrollment, which made Yale "the first elite, predominantly white law school" to implement

---

[11] Coral Davenport, *After Nobel in Economics, William Nordhaus Talks About Who's Getting His Pollution-Tax Ideas Right*, N.Y. TIMES, Oct. 13, 2018.

[12] Department of Economics, Yale U., https://economics.yale.edu/people/faculty/william-d-dnordhaus; Jesus I. Ramirez, *To Teach or to Strike: Yale Grad Students May Withhold Grades*, HARVARD CRIMSON, Apr. 16, 1988; *Clarification*, HARVARD CRIMSON, Apr. 20, 1988.

any kind of affirmative action program.[13] The Law School also began admitting women well before most other law schools and long before the College, which only acquiesced in 1968.[14]

Annual giving. At law schools everywhere during the later 1990s, annual alumni giving campaigns became more important sources of income than previously, especially at elite institutions. Most often the campaigns emphasized the need for alumni to support need-based financial aid.[15] In 2001, University of Alabama Dean Kenneth C. Randall provided a helpful guide to fundraising for law school deans, indicating that other law deans began to use alumni annual giving appeals for a substantial percentage of their revenue close to a decade later than Guido.[16] Randall pointed to the general incompetence of law school deans at fundraising, because scholarly pursuits seldom prepared them for conducting major fundraising campaigns. From this perspective, Guido's early decision to communicate as he did is remarkable.

Reconceptualizing communications with alumni. Guido's annual letters to alumni—typically three or four, but sometimes as long as eight dense, single-spaced pages—broke the conventional mold in their rich detail about events and changes, arrivals and deaths, and about the dean's dreams for the future. Judged by recollections of alumni, and by the financial support that came in increasing amounts, they helped engender a new sense of excitement about what was going on at the Law School and what Guido's plans were.

In his first letters, he emphasized the ways diversity and the encouragement of public interest work would be priorities. He mentioned student activities including the founding of First Generation Professionals, a conference on Women of Color in Law, and explained his Career Options and Assistance Program (COAP) and student loan initiatives.[17] Diversity and progress were important themes; the overarching narrative, however, was his determination to cement the status of the Law School as unquestionably the best in the nation—a feat which could only be accomplished with "generous help."[18]

Guido made it clear that he would not think small: "In the next five years," he wrote in his first letter, "we will ... seek to give everyone at the School the sense that decency, civility, and caring are not only in competition with rigor and originality, but feed them and are fed by them."[19] Yale would "continue to try to be the nearest thing the United States has to an E'cole Normale Sup'erieure, a training place for leaders in the public service."[20] He emphasized how much needed to be done to "truly ... be the center of humane studies in law" and recruit a world-class faculty,

---

[13] See generally Chapter 7; LAURA KALMAN, YALE LAW SCHOOL AND THE SIXTIES: REVOLT AND REVERBERATIONS, 47, 102, 104 (2006).

[14] Judith Schiff, *Yale's First Female Graduate*, YALE ALUMNI MAG. (Sept./Oct. 2013), https://yalealumnimagazine.com/articles/3742-yales-first-female-graduate; Kate Heinzelman, *Yale's First Classes of Women Look Back*, YALE DAILY NEWS (Feb. 20, 2002), http://yaledailynews.com/blog/2002/02/20/yales-first-classes-of-women-look-back.

[15] C. T. Clotfelter, *Alumni Giving to Elite Private Colleges and Universities*, 22 ECON. OF EDUC. REV. 109, 110 (2001).

[16] Kenneth C. Randall, THE DEAN AS FUNDRAISER, 33 U. TOL L. REV. 149, 149 (2001).

[17] Guido Calabresi, Letter to Friends and Graduates, Sept. 27, 1985.

[18] *Id.*

[19] *Id.*

[20] *Id.*

including "the problem of retaining and attracting to New Haven faculty members whose husbands and wives also wish to work."[21] "Excellence and decency are all too scarce in our society," he repeated in virtually every one of his letters.

He also reported on unpleasant controversies—trying, as best he could, to place them in a favorable light. When the nomination of Robert Bork to the Court divided the Law School community, Guido told alumni about the difficult experience, but emphasized the "close friendship and intellectual and personal comradery that clearly existed among these faculty members who had just finished taking opposite positions...."[22]

He presented personal views about incidents of race hatred and bigotry that had taken place at the School, and contextualized an unfortunate analogy he had drawn to Hitlerian racism, explaining that he could not hope that "evil can be turned into good," but believed that it was possible, "by unambiguously bearing witness to those values we hold most dear, [to] draw some good out of such hateful occurrences." He felt that at the Law School "just this [was] ... happening."[23]

After reaching the understanding about financial independence, he wrote to alumni about the implications for the law school.[24] "Independence," explained Guido, "means that in spending our moneys we now have the freedom (and responsibility) that are essential to our remaining a leader and innovator in legal education."[25]

Captivation and embarrassment. As a fundraiser, Guido wielded a potent combination of effortless charm and strategic behavior. He cultivated personal relationships with potential donors—not all graduates of the Law School—that eventuated in multimillion-dollar gifts and pledges, including from the Ruttenberg family, Lillian Goldman, and Oscar M. Ruebhausen, that were copacetic to their desires. He raised dedicated funds for distinguished chairs and scholarships, among others the Florence Rogatz Professorship, the Alfred M. Rankin Professorship, the Klagsbrunn Scholarship, and the J. Skelly Wright Professorship. There were dramatic increases in the reunion and annual giving efforts. In the last year of his deanship alone (1993–1994), the total of cash receipts and pledges were calculated at $37,587,908, a number which exceeded all expectations.[26]

There were also stumbles. The YLS class of 1964 did very well for itself, financially. When the twenty-fifth reunion came up, according to Professor Robert Burt, its campaign goal was to raise $1 million and to become the first class anywhere to raise $1 million. "Guido communicated to all of us, that if we raised $1 million, that he would name the auditorium, which was about to be rebuilt, 'The Class of 1964 Auditorium.'"

His class raised the $1 million, but found that the entrance to the auditorium was emblazoned with the name *"Levinson,"* and not *"The Class of 1964"*:

---

[21] Letter to Friends and Graduates, Sept. 30, 1986.
[22] Letter to Friends and Graduates, Nov. 2, 1987.
[23] Letter to Friends and Graduates, Nov. 5, 1990.
[24] Guido Calabresi, Letter to Friends and Graduates, Oct. 31, 1988.
[25] *Id.*
[26] Memorandum from Leslie West to Carroll Stevens, Updated Figures, Summary of 1993–1994 Law School Capital and Annual Gifts and Pledges, Nov. 2, 1994.

What happened? Well, we heard that he got $3 million from a bigger bidder—that's what we heard. I think he just thought, well, we would understand. You don't turn away $3 million just to keep a promise that you've made to the Class of 1964. But there was an eruption of outrage!

At our next reunion after the renaming—non-naming—Guido was no longer the Dean at that point—there was a cocktail party in the library. And when we went into the *'Lillian Goldman Library'* (which Guido was responsible for, of course—and it is fabulous) we could see that the reading room was now the *'Class of 1964 Reading Room,'* which he offered to our class as a gesture of peace.

Guido arranged for a cocktail party at which he commissioned a cake in the shape of a crow. Guido ate it, acknowledging that he was "eating crow." As Burt recalled, "'And well you should,' everybody said."[27]

President Benno Charles Schmidt. Benno Schmidt's tenure as president of Yale University is remarkable in at least two respects: for the amount of money he raised (growing the university endowment from $1.7 billion to $3 billion); and for his abrupt resignation in 1992, which made for an unusually short six-year term as president.[28]

A graduate of Yale College and Yale Law School and a law clerk to Chief Justice Earl Warren, Schmidt became president of Yale University in 1986 after a short stint as dean of Columbia Law School. At his inauguration as president, Schmidt was described as "pleasant and personable, but also strong-willed and ambitious."[29]

President Benno C. Schmidt

---

[27] Interview with Robert Burt, Mar. 1, 2012; ROBERT BURT, TWO JEWISH JUSTICES: OUTCASTS IN THE PROMISED LAND (1989).
[28] Richard Bernstein, *The Yale Schmidt Leaves Behind*, N.Y. TIMES, June 14 1992.
[29] Craig W. Baggott, *Yale President Announces He Will Resign*, HARTFORD COURANT, May 26, 1992.

Although Guido asserts that Schmidt was good for the graduate schools, Schmidt was broadly criticized for his plans to reduce faculty by 11 percent across the faculty of arts and sciences and slash programs; to reduce the autonomy of faculties and schools that were not performing well financially—including the School of Management; and for failing to fix many of the buildings that were in disrepair.[30] In a letter personally responding to one alumnus donor, Guido wrote that the best thing that Benno had done for the Law School was to finally agree to the independence—ironically insulating the Law School from the uncertainty and instability that Benno's *own tenure* as president had brought to the university:

> I can well understand that the news of Benno Schmidt's departure as well as the way the whole thing was done could be troubling to you. We all were quite surprised and, frankly, shocked. Happily, though, his leaving will have essentially no effect on the Law School or on the appropriate treatment of pledges such as yours.[31]

Although supporters praised Benno's business acumen and steadfastness in the face of financial pressure, detractors complained that he was not in tune with the intellectual needs of a university. The frustration felt by much of the faculty and many of the students is captured by a tune that could be heard around campus toward the end of his presidency: "Benno doesn't listen, and when he listens, he doesn't hear; and when he hears he doesn't understand; and when he understands, he's against it."[32] The University community hoped to be led by a president whose talents and experience did not force a choice between "an administrator, or a scholar—that is, by someone who can raise money, or someone who can raise an institution's sights," but it was not clear that in Benno they had gotten either.[33] On his resignation, the *Yale Daily News* noted that from the beginning, "Schmidt drew fire with a brusque leadership style, a non-academic agenda, unpopular appointments, and a low campus profile."[34] Many were disappointed and puzzled, moreover, when Schmidt then left public nonprofit education to pursue a career in the private, for-profit school industry.[35]

Independence in hindsight. Three decades later, Dean Robert Post reflected on the autonomy that Guido obtained and the degree to which the Law School had held onto it after Guido's deanship.[36] By the time that Post became the dean in 2009, there were six other "self-support schools" at Yale in addition to the Law

---

[30] Nick Ravo, *"Where's Benno?" New Refrain at Yale Belies Record*, N.Y. TIMES, May 26, 1989; Bernstein, *supra* note 28.
[31] Letter from Guido Calabresi to Julien Cornell, June 8, 1992 (on file with author).
[32] Bernstein, *supra* note 28.
[33] Anthony DePalma, *Schmidt's Exit Creates Worry and Hope at Yale*, N.Y. TIMES, May 27, 1992.
[34] Joshua P. Galper, *Schmidt's Term Earned Funds, Not Popularity*, YALE DAILY NEWS, Sept. 11, 1992.
[35] Id.
[36] Interview with Robert Post, Oct. 23, 2017.

School—schools required to live with what they earned. Only the Medical School and the Law School stood out as truly free from having most of their academic programs and expense allocations reviewed by the University. Subsequent deans used this freedom for expansions and programmatic innovations, some of which created deficits and required borrowing. For several years, the University continued to provide the million-dollar subsidies that Guido negotiated, but the University ended them in exchange of an endowment augmentation. Thereafter, the Law School budget depended entirely on income from endowments, contributions from donors, tuition payments, grants, and other tuition or fee-based sources.

The University and Law School endowments over these decades grew phenomenally. In negotiations with the University shortly after Guido became Dean, he reported a University contribution to the Law School, which would indicate an endowment of about $6.8 million.[37] This growth permitted fundamental fiscal security that almost every other institution of legal education could envy. Nonetheless, control over the endowment—and access to the use of endowment funds—remained in the hands of the University. Despite endowment growth, there was not nearly as much financial freedom as Guido hoped for.[38]

The building indebtedness. As Guido relates more fully in the next chapter, he took up the complete renovation of the Sterling Law Building and, with it, the challenge of raising money to pay for it. By Guido's reckoning (and the reckoning of others at the Law School), he raised enough money in outright gifts and pledges to cover its estimated cost.[39]

During Anthony Kronman's deanship, however, the University apparently changed its general rule for capital withdrawals, which affected the Law School's ability to tap past unrestricted endowment funds that Guido intended for reconstruction and remodeling while new multi-year pledges were coming in.

The University treated draws for the reconstruction of the building as ordinary loans to the Law School. As a result, the University billed the Law School unexpectedly large amounts for rebuilding and remodeling expenses. To cover these construction costs, the Law School incurred approximately $120 million in interest-bearing loans from the University.

Over the next three decades, consequently, the Law School budget included large debt payments to the University. The effect of this was magnified by the financial collapse of 2008, when, during Robert Post's deanship, Yale's endowments,

---

[37] Memorandum Letter from Guido Calabresi to the Provost, *supra* note 7. The University did not and does not confirm the precise size of the Law School's endowment. In his 1987 letter to the Provost, Guido described the University's contribution to Law School operations in the previous year as $343,000—an amount that would correspond—assuming a 5 percent payout—to an endowment of approximately $6.8 million. *Id.* Published University budget reporting indicates that by 2014, the Law School's endowment income had risen to $52.3 million. Fiscal 2018 Operating Budget, *Yale U. Budget Book: FY 2018*, 1, 66 (2018). Assuming a 5 percent return on a rolling average of its endowment, this would indicate an endowment that year of roughly $1 billion. By the above reckoning the Law School endowment increased in constant dollars roughly 6,000 percent over these years.

[38] *Id.*; Memorandum Letter from Guido Calabresi to the Provost, *supra* note 7.

[39] See Chapter 21, "Restoring the Law School Building."

including the Law School's, fell by nearly 25 percent from the previous fiscal year. This reduced endowment contributions to Law School income dramatically.

Moreover, the Yale Corporation also put a hold on all University projects in their planning stages, many of which involved the Law School.[40] It also charged the Law School for University services, for example, computer support and public safety protection. Further, notwithstanding the understanding that had been reached, important matters of finance remained with the central administration: over investments and the timing for withdrawal of unrestricted gifts temporarily invested in the endowment; over union-related pay questions; and over other decisions with a University-wide impact. Indeed, at times Guido described what had been accomplished as "quasi-independence."

But thanks to Guido, the Law School was "on its own bottom." It was substantially independent in making spending decisions, large and small. Building on the considerable autonomy prior deans had established in many non-financial areas, Guido achieved "an extraordinary amount of independence, on all the core issues."[41] If he went to the University, it was "for help, and not for permission" on most matters—what hires to make, what areas to hire in, and what salaries to pay. The faculty decided on its own what JD curricular innovations to embrace, what tuition to charge, and how big the entering class would be. The size and salaries of the administrative staff became within the Law School's power to establish.

The agreement provided the school unrivaled freedom for its time. As news spread to other places, the relationship to the central University became an aspirational model for deans at other institutions.[42] Without this freedom, Yale Law School would not have been as nimble as it needed to be to adapt to the external legal academic culture, build its reputation, and preserve its unusual character.

---

[40] Jingyi Cui, *Robert Post Leaves a Flourishing Yale Law School*, YALE DAILY NEWS, Apr. 27, 2017.
[41] Telephone interview with Ian Solomon, Dec. 11, 2019. Solomon served as Associate Dean for Finance at the Law School during the Kronman Deanship (2002–2005); and later became Dean of the Frank Batten School of Leadership and Public Policy at the University of Virginia.
[42] *Id.*

21
Restoring the Law School Building

Craftsmen and first-class designers built the Sterling Law School building between 1929 and 1931. Constructed in the Collegiate Gothic style and at great expense, the academic quarters mirrored the English Inns of Court, while the library resembled the sixteenth-century King's College Chapel at Cambridge. Masons embellished the stonework with sculptures. Stained glass medallions depicted historic symbols of law and justice. Carved wood paneling surrounded the lecture halls. Archways exhibited tableaus of crime and justice. Heavy tables and ornate fireplaces incorporated sometimes humorous and ironic references that contributed to a winning sense of sophistication. The overall success of the architecture helped to elevate the school's reputation and connect Yale to elite English legal and educational traditions. Over the years that followed, however, satisfaction with everyday living conditions inside the building diminished. As Guido described in the previous chapter, the University spent little on upkeep and on modernization. Design and space limitations emerged. Fifty years after its original completion, occupants and visitors came to regard the building as ill-kept, dingy, and outmoded.

The Sterling Law Building under construction, 1930[1]

I am a great believer that people behave better in civilized places; that where they are, what is around them, *if it is beautiful,* if it is made to bring

---
[1] Credit: Sterling Manuscripts and Archives, Yale U.

them together, helps them to do that. Having had the advantage of living in Italy, of studying at Oxford, and also seeing the Yale College system, I had a very strong feeling that if you have the right place, it helps you be what you want to be.

I remember coming back from England and Italy to a New Haven that then was very shabby. I said to my father, "I guess I'll get used to it." My father said, "That is *exactly* the problem. You will get used to it, and you won't notice it." He was right. If you're in a place that you're used to, you just do not notice. But when you are in someplace beautiful, and you wake up feeling gloomy and down, you only need to step outside. There you see things which are lovely, and your spirit rises.

An exterior ornamental detail, Sterling Law Building

This Yale Law School building had a great deal that worked for it. There were any number of places where people would come together, and there were some beautiful elements.

The problems with it, though, were many; and they were not only technical problems—such as that the heat did not work, so that you either froze or it was hot all the time. The problems included difficulties that had *always* been problems.

There wasn't sufficient light in the library, so that one couldn't comfortably work there. I had this very much in mind when I became dean, because I remembered when I was a student, and Arthur Corbin, in his eighties, used to come and carry a lamp with him. He would get down on his hands and knees and try to plug the lamp in! If we took the lamp from him and asked, "May we do it?," he'd be offended—because in his eighties he still thought that he could do everything. So several of us would distract Corbin when he came in. One of us would start asking him a question about contracts, and while he was completely engaged in his answer, somebody else would take the lamp and plug it in. I was determined that there would be enough light in the library.

One of the places which did not work was the Second Floor. On the Ground Floor, it was lively—everybody was there. And on the Third Floor, there was the library, the bathrooms, and a number of faculty offices. Students would go out from the library, or come back from the bathrooms, and they might see a light on in a professor's room. They'd knock, and they'd meet there, and they'd talk.

But on the Second Floor, there was a problem. That was where the library work was done *inside* the library, so that on the Second Floor there was no reason for students ever to go *outside* of it. Yet that was where most of the faculty offices were. That was one problem to address.

Another was that the building had to be, if we did fix it, handicapped accessible. I did not want the handicapped accessibility to be ugly or demeaning in any way. So, I was willing to spend money.

There had been developed a little kind of a mechanical device that you could get on if you were in a wheelchair to go up or down. We could have used this for each of the classrooms to be directly accessible. But this was not what I had in mind, and *cleverly*, the architects solved the problem. They made the entrances to the different classrooms so that at every one there is a perfectly *natural* entrance, without having to feel that if you're handicapped that you have to do something special. If the elevators had to make more stops to produce the same natural effect, then that had to be.

The central hall on the First Floor was, and had to be, completely a meeting place. If it was possible, I wanted this to remain the Law School's "hot house." I was determined that this vision of a place where everybody was "at" each other, which the original architects had, would be maintained. So in picking the new architect, I wanted somebody who was in love with the original architect, James Gamble Rogers.

Rogers was the person whom Harkness picked to do, first, Harkness Tower, and then the colleges he financed at Yale. He was the person whom Harkness took with him to England to see the colleges there. He was a Twentieth century kind of Gothic Revival enthusiast, although he also did the New Haven Courthouse on Greek Revival style.

There's a story, involving my wife's family, about how Edward "Ned" Harkness came to give the money for the colleges to be built. Harkness was a very shy person, and very, very wealthy. He had gone to Yale but had not really liked the fraternity side of Yale. And then he had gone to Cambridge and fallen in love with the college system. At a certain point in the 1920s he decided he wanted to give money to Yale to have every student be in a residential college, in the same way that they were and are in England.

He went to the president, Angell, who, as I've said before, was not a very nice man. He was smart, but not very nice. Angell was the first non-Yale graduate to be president since the very beginning, and Angell was afraid of what the fraternity alums would say about this idea. So he diddled and daddled.

Finally, Harkness got annoyed and he went to Harvard. Lowell, the president of Harvard—who was also a nasty man but who on this was a step ahead—wasn't worried about what Harvard people would think because he was very much a Harvard guy. Lowell opened his drawer and showed him plans for the Harvard houses. Harkness gave, I believe, ten million dollars then, which was a *huge* amount of money, to build the houses at Harvard.

Well, you can imagine that when that happened, all Yale exploded! They had botched it! So, Angell and others said, "Well, we will build colleges. It will take somewhat longer. They may not be quite so fancy, but we'll have a fundraising drive to do it." Then somebody said, "We should try to get Harkness back involved, because it just doesn't look right."

But how do you do that? Harkness was very suspicious of people asking him for money and was a very shy kind of person.

Well, probably his closest friend was my wife Anne's grandfather, Franklin Muzzy Crosby. They had been at school and at Yale together. Anne's grandfather was the family that had started General Mills, so that they were wealthy themselves. Light years apart from Harkness, because Harkness was *immensely* wealthy. The Harknesses originally were partners of Rockefeller, but they had gone into railroads in the southwest, his father had. Ned Harkness and his wife had no children.

But the Harknesses used to vacation all the time with Anne's grandparents because they were such good friends. We have family movies of Mrs. Harkness, who was *very* funny, and Anne's grandmother, who also was. You know, there they are in a zoo making believe they were penguins. There are any number of other stories about them. They were just very close friends. So somebody from Yale asked Anne's grandfather if he could say something to Harkness, and Anne's grandfather said, "Yes."

The next time these two were fishing, which they used to do all the time, as they were casting, Crosby says, "Ned?" and Harkness says, "Yup?" Crosby says, "Think Yale's changed its mind." Harkness says, "Thought they would."

That was the whole conversation! Harkness went back to Angell and said, "I will give you *fourteen* million because I want the colleges at Yale to be better than the houses at Harvard."

That's the background. The next part of the story that involves Anne is that, after Anne's aunt died, we were going through her papers and we saw a little journal that she kept during a trip to England, when she was around twenty. In her journal there is this note: "Saw Uncle Ned [Harkness] in London with some architect named Rogers. They're on their way to Oxford. They look like the cats that have eaten the canary. I wonder what they're up to?" It was Harkness, taking Rogers—or Rogers taking Harkness—to see Oxford and to think about what they wanted to do about Yale.

So that's the kind of architect Rogers was. I wanted someone like him, and that's who we found. We found architects who were in love with James Gamble Rogers. They were Canadian American. Interesting people. *Interesting people.* I said to them that I wanted to increase the number of places in which people came in accidental contact with each other.

Look at how the architects responded. First, they made the classrooms different from each other, so that teachers who like to teach in different ways in relation to their students could have a different-type classroom. There are some classrooms which are flatbed; there are some that are round. There's one that looks like a Padua operating room—you know, everything down like this. There's one which kind of wraps around. But they designed it so that each teacher could find the right space—because I'm *very conscious* of teaching styles being different—being able to do that matters to me. So that's one of the things that they did. All these different rooms coming off this main hall, so that people come in and out, and into contact with each other.

I wanted the rooms on High Street that had been made into administrative offices brought back to being seminars. That's what they had been when I was a student, and they were *perfect*. They were *made* to be seminar rooms, and the idea was to bring them back, and there was no reason not to. The administrators had sort of eaten them up along the way, because they were near the dean, and it made sense for them to be near the dean. But it made much more sense for them to be seminar rooms, because that's what they were designed for originally, and they're *wonderful* seminar rooms, and they are much more needed now with small group teaching, which did not exist when I was a student. But they had been eaten up; and so that that was another thing that I wanted.

The question then was, Where do you put the administrators? The answer to that was that the administrators would fit very well just right above the Dean's Office, because there was a stairway which went right upstairs from that office. The question was then: How do you get the faculty members who kind of like those old offices up there and would rather not move, to go somewhere else? You have to make *new* faculty offices which are *as* attractive, or *more* attractive, than the old ones; so that faculty members with seniority will move into those and move out on their own.

The original faculty offices were designed for particular members of the faculty when this building was built. The office that was at the corner of High and Wall was the one that was made for Roscoe Steffen. The one that was made for

> *Corbin was on the second floor. Nobody knows this particularly, but they were made so that some had closets; some had a wash basin. When the building was built, each office was made to suit a particular professor. I wanted to do it again. I couldn't do quite that—but I could talk to a senior member of faculty and say, you know, "We're converting what were student rooms into offices. Can we make it in some way that would be an office that would really fit you?" And then we could get that person to move there. That took a certain amount of time, but it worked.*

As I say, the Second Floor was a problem. I did not know what to do about it. But the architects themselves came up with this wonderful idea of having the student deposits, mailboxes, carrels, and bathrooms there. So the Second Floor became the place where students go *all the time*. To get their mail, to leave their coats, and so many other things. So that at every floor, this kind of accidental meeting, arguing and discussing, would take place.

Another goal which I had in mind, but took longer, was related to faculty and to the school's clinical program: it was how to make the clinical program both be in spaces and places which were as good, as comfortable, and as attractive, as other faculty offices, and yet also be available to people who came in off of the street so that clients did not feel they had to go through where students were. They might want privacy because they were going to see lawyers. The clinical space had to be somehow something that had its own entrance for the clients and yet was directly a part of the building.

Exterior restoration work, including redesign of clinic entrance, mid-1990s[2]

---

[2] Photo credit: Robert Lisak, courtesy of Yale Law School.

That worked out because on Wall Street there was a place that looked as though it *demanded* an entrance. [Laughs] It was *made* to be an entrance. And so, we made it into an exterior entrance, but it was completely connected with the rest of the offices and with the courtyard.

It had always seemed to me *odd* (though handy for portraits) that across from the great windows in the library, there were some closed-off areas that looked like windows with closed arches, which made all that side, two floors above the library—lifeless. They were then just stacks, just stacks and of no interest—with little windows looking out over the courtyard.

There again, I thought, and I said, "You know, that's *odd*," and the architect said, "Why do not we open them? Why do not we make that a space which *completes* the library, gives more light both to the library and spreads it from the library to this other place, and has the people who are studying in the stacks and the people who are studying in the library, be part of the same space, a space large enough so that everybody in the library, every student could have a place to work on their own?" That's what we did.

Another problem was: How do you deal with all the code requirements, many of which were going to make the building uglier? What do you do? You make somebody like Bob Ellickson our representative on the project for code compliance and such things. Bob Ellickson is a staunch libertarian, who cannot stand many code ideas, but who knows he has to follow the law—because he's a very much a law-abider. He figured out what needed to be done, whether the signs for "EXIT" or this and that, really needed to be ugly, what the requirements were for handicapped accessibility. And then, when those requirements were met, he figured out what we could do what we *wanted* to do, which was *better* than the requirements, and not ugly. It worked. Took a long time.

A final problem was this: How do you do all the work and keep the Law School running? That took a lot of sacrifice from some of the classes. We would do a lot during the summer. There would be parts of the building which just were not used at a certain amount of time. They've forgotten now, but they sacrificed.

Compare the inconvenience from what we did, in the time we did it, with the six or seven years of total closure of a building of the same age, which is the Second Circuit Court Building in New York! The architect who did that building also did the Supreme Court, and was another great architect of that period. You know, it makes me laugh, the amount of money that they spent, and the amount of time that it took, even with a complete closure! They did a wonderful job, but it makes me laugh.

* * *

Very few law schools have a tradition of students living in the very same law school classroom building, but it was part of the Oxford-Cambridge College idea. It is one of the good things that got lost in growth. By the time of the rebuilding, space for students to live had already been cut down, and cut down further, almost to nothing as faculty size, student activities, number of classes, all of that, library, all of that, increased. It became increasingly difficult to have students here. More and more space was taken. The problem was—and is—that if we were going to stay *here*, there wasn't really any room for student housing.

The original space set aside for expansion for the Law School was where the Beinecke Rare Book Library is. That space was supposed to be for the Law School to expand. It disappeared way back in Gene Rostow's time.

There is a story about that. The University Librarian was a man named James Babb. Running a library wasn't "his thing" originally. He was a lawyer. He graduated from the Law School but had gotten interested in rare books. He was an odd guy, from Idaho. He had married some old New Haven-Branford type. He had become, in those odd ways of a Yale of then—I do not know if it was through his Senior Society or what—he had become the University Librarian.

It happened that Babb was a good friend of mine. He was older, but his children had been at school with me and we got to know each other very, very well. I was just a young faculty member when this great gift from the Beineckes, to build that building, came in. I learned that it was going to be there. I had lunch, as I frequently did, with Babb, and I said to him, "Jim, how could you do this? How could you take this space, which was destined for the Law School? And how did you do it?" He looked at me and he said, "Where is your Dean?"

In the middle of his Deanship, Gene Rostow went on sabbatical. This was about 1960. He was the Dean from 1955 to '65, and he was taking a term or a year off in Cambridge. Babb looked at me and he said, "Gene Rostow is in Cambridge dining at high table, and I have been having dinner with the Beineckes for fifteen years."

That was the lesson, you know! In a university, as in anything else, if you are able to come in with the money at the right time, you may very well be able to get space that is "not available"!

Now, not having that space that led me to think: Is there something that the Law School *can* do? Well, we could go under part of High Street and expand the law library with space there. And this was done, and I think done quite *beautifully*.

View of expansion space to the east of the law school, circa 1960–1963, before construction of the Beinicke Rare Book Library.[3]

There was method in my madness in going there, because one of the things one did not know—*doesn't know*—is how much space for books is going to be needed in the future. I thought that if in expanding the space for books we expanded it in a way that connected to *the one category of books which can never be replaced by computers*, which is *rare* books; then we would be able to sell that space to the University, if space for ordinary books would not be needed. So that it seemed to me in terms of *library* expansion, doing something which was beautiful—even though underground—but which *connected* to the Beinecke's rare books, was a sensible way of doing things. I still think that that's true.

＊＊＊

My hope was to find living space for students which would be connected to the building. I do not think it can ever happen, now—that is, I do not think we can get space for students to live as part of the Law School, as they did originally; but if you go back to alums, that is the one thing that they come back to again and again. They say, "This is something which you *really* ought to work on." They say it to every dean. They've said it to every dean since.

They say, "You've got to get space back so that the students are *living* there. They say, "Living in the Crown Towers," where so many of them do, "that's fine." "We know it's a substitute. But one of the things that made *our* experience in law school special was *living there*."

---

[3] Credit: Yale Manuscripts and Archives.

People started cutting this space down even when I was a student—but when you go back further, the older alums say, "we *all* lived there, and argued there late into the night, not just ate there."

* * *

My dream for accomplishing their desires was, and would still be, to get space by straightening out the Tower Parkway, which, as you know, curves around past Grove Street. That originally was straight. It ran along the cemetery—through where the power plant is. I wanted to straighten it, but I just have never been in the position of authority to do it.

You see, this area is one part of the original "Nine Squares" that were New Haven, that were in the *original* colonial design laid out by Eaton and Davenport as the *New Jerusalem*. But that "Square" is not square anymore. It got cut because at the beginning of the twentieth century, a mayor named Tower wanted to make this fancy drive.

My dream was to tear *down* the power plant; to go *straight* on back there and then connect with a new boulevard—and not a super highway—which would come around in back of that, and to get rid of all that *awful* area, that *terrible* crossing, over by the end of the Payne-Whitney Gym. This would have won the University a *huge* amount of space around the gym. It would also bring into the University complex everything, including the hotel that is there, and it would open room for a shopping area. The straightening-out plan would also have accomplished something meaningful because you could say to the historians: "it brings back the original Nine Squares design."

From the standpoint of the Law School, it would mean that that nearby triangle of land—which is a park that was given to the city and is maintained by Yale—would have become available to the Law School for expansion and directly connected to it. I knew the person after whom the little park was named, Mrs. Pope, who was the wife of an English professor. I got her husband, who survived her, to tell me that he would say it was okay with him if the park was moved someplace else, on other University property.

And even more: that corner of Grove Street and York, which would become part of this, was the *one* part that, at least in the eighteenth century, quite early, was a corner that was owned by a freed slave. His name, Blackman—whether that was a pseudonym I do not know. One could bring back this fact, and memorialize it, so that in all parts of the community I thought, this idea of restoring the Square was something that could be sold.

The *problem*, however, is the University Power Plant. It is an ABSURDITY! An *absolute* absurdity! The Power Plant needed to be completely redone!

But come back to the historical situation sometime after I became dean. Bill Nordhaus had become—temporarily—kind of Yale's business manager. Benno Schmidt had gone as president of Yale. It's an Interregnum. Nordhaus correctly understands that there is going to be a problem with the environmental authorities if you move a power plant, because the towers of a power plant have to be *taller* by a certain amount than *any* building. This would mean that if you built a new power plant, the towers would have to be taller than the Kline Science Building.

Now, I'm *sure* they could have gotten an exemption. Even apart from that, I am sure that if they had thought about it, they could have left the towers there and then rebuilt the rest of the power plant and made believe it was the same one! They in fact rebuilt everything in the power plant on the Grove Street side; had they done the same thing on the other side, down Ashmun Street, what I wanted could have been accomplished. But I couldn't get anybody to listen to me!

Howard Lamar was the Acting President of Yale. He was very interested in making everybody feel good, after people in the College hadn't felt so good. Unfortunately, I think one of the things that they kept saying to me is, "You're doing this because you want that land for the Law School." That *was indeed* a part of it, but *not* the most important. I had no one with me, and it never happened!

* * *

Another hope was instead to take over part of the Hall of Graduate Studies, and to promise that we'd redo the part that was *directly* across from us and make that into a Law School space and connect it in a way that could be nicely done. A problem with that is that, again, it would look like the Law School was *grabbing* something else.

Oh, and one other of my dreams was to try to convince Yale—and I got about as far on that as my others—that they should sell us Berkeley College, or one of the *parts* of Berkeley, the part of Berkeley that is directly across the ground from us, which would have been nice, because then you could also have what was then called a "Master's House." You could have an associate dean who lived there and was kind of the Head of the College, and have the students live there and be connected to the Law School with a tunnel. I mean, it would be right there! But I think the problem with *that* is even *worse* than going for the graduate school. In Berkeley, you have graduates who are associated with that college, and would not like a new Berkeley College to be built someplace else.

It's too bad none of these hopes came true—because it does mean that when the Law School went back to having living-in facilities, it had to be in the "Swing Dorm," which *is* very near. It has been done very nicely—Baker Hall-- but it is not *quite* the same as having the living space be right here.

* * *

When I started to fix up the law school building, there were some people who thought that there ought to be whole new law campus somewhere; and the University on various occasions suggested that we should let them have this building as another college. Make it into a new college and in return *build* us a *whole* new building. Somewhere!

I vetoed that *right* from the start because the old building is beautiful and works, and thus could not really be replaced. I also did it because it seemed to me that one of the things that made this Law School, that characterized this Law School, that made it what it is, was how much it is part of the University. That is, the connection of the Yale Law School to Economics, Philosophy, Sociology, to the Sterling Library, has been crucial from the very start.

The symbolism of being here, rather than being, like the Harvard School of Management, off somewhere, is fundamental. Think about what happened to other law schools that were at the center—like Virginia, which was in the original Jefferson plan and then gets built a beautiful new campus, *beautiful*, but someplace else. They all become disconnected.

When I was Dean, the symbolism of being here, and being the best academic show in town, seemed to me just too important, both as symbol and as reality. For, as I said, if you're off someplace else, people aren't going to come!

If Yale Law is the *école normale supérieure, the* training place for leaders, the *academic* law school, then *its* seminars, *its* faculty workshops—all of its happenings—are things that people should come easily from all over the University to hear. At a recent workshop the dean of the Divinity School was there. The university chaplain was there; the Catholic chaplain, along with an alumnus of the Law School from Rome, whom he knew, was there; and there are *almost always* members of Political Science faculty, and so forth.

This goes back to the Yale approach which to some extent came out of necessity in the nineteenth century. John Langbein has written that when the Law School was poor and used practitioners in the nineteenth century, it still had the vision that Ezra Stiles had given it in the eighteenth century, when Stiles said—actually well before the appointment of the first Professor of Law in 1801—that law should be taught not merely as a profession but as the basis of a free society. And Woolsey in 1848 had reiterated that we taught law not just in its professional sense. How did the Law School do this? It was by having people from the Arts and Sciences teach at the law school. So William Graham Sumner, who's known as a founder of sociology, taught economics at the law school in the nineteenth century. Others taught philosophy and history.

To some extent this came out of necessity in the nineteenth century. Since the law school was short of money, it used practitioners to do much of the teaching. But by adding non-legal scholars to its faculty, it made a virtue out of the necessity. They did not have money to have "academic" law scholars, and so they used these other people. This is the time when the great law school was Columbia, even more than Harvard. Then came Langdell with his pseudoscientific notion of the case method and so on. People said, "Yale is all very fuzzy." Looking back on it, "You know, this was fuzzy. This wasn't that good." But even then, it was something those at Yale were very proud of.

The idea of moving somewhere never even *went* to the faculty; I ruled that out. The faculty never even *thought* about it. I just said, "That's just *not* going to happen!" How much cheaper would it have been for a new school building? Ha ha! Maybe seventy million dollars cheaper? I mean, I do not know! You could build a mighty nice law school in those days for thirty million dollars, and it cost about a hundred million to fix this thing up! I do not know the exact number. I do not remember the exact cost; but it was not inexpensive.

I was guided by what I had learned from Whitney Griswold. One should always do the luxuries first, the things that make a building beautiful. For then you will always find the money for the necessities. If you do the necessities first you will get a fine functional building, but you will never raise the money to make it excellent and beautiful. The first thing I did was raise money to bring back the beautiful ceiling of the library. The next was to find the craftsmen who would bring back the woodwork and the stained-glass windows to their previous glory. Fixing the heating, the air conditioning, the plumbing—all the necessities—came later and were done magnificently, too. The result is a building that not only works and works well, but is a joy to be in. This required a lot of money to be raised, but somehow, it was.

The Law School stayed right where it has been for so long. The fact is that Yale Law School is still just across the street from Sterling Library!

Yale Law School's location with respect to Sterling Library.[4]

---

[4] Credit: Google Maps, https://www.google.com/maps/@41.3138432,-72.9278188,279a,35y,180h,39.44t/data=!3m1!1e3.

COMMENTARY

Chapter 21

Guido's dream to straighten out Tower Parkway and relocate the power plant. The dream never did come to fruition; the Parkway remained an awkward back door used mainly for racing to other parts of the city. The odious fossil fuel power plant also survived, albeit with some cosmetic—but no doubt expensive—efforts at concealment. It remained very much a "pig with lipstick."

Yale's Central Power Plant, located on the corner opposite the Sterling Law School

How bad was the condition of the law building, really? Guido describes a Sterling Law School Building in nearly complete disrepair—a physical wreck which cast a specter that his entire deanship would be soured by the unpleasant physical living environment—regardless of whether he effectively revived the intellectual climate.

In truth, the law school was dilapidated. But it was not in worse shape than many other buildings at Yale. For example, the undergraduate halls were described by college alumni as "ill-lit and poorly maintained ... a warren of confusing public spaces, shabby offices, and uninviting classrooms."[5] The Hall of Graduate Studies, across the street from the Law School, consisted of virtually unteachable classrooms and roach-infested dormitory rooms, with leaky ceilings and bad plumbing. Nonetheless, shared misery was no consolation.

The disrepair inspired contemptuous condemnation from law students who needed to be at the law building every day. William Eskridge, a student there near to the peak of the building's degradation, recalls the "lamentable, deplorable condition." The office at the *Yale Law Journal* was filled with dust and mold, and it had

---

[5] Philip Langdon, *Renovating a Classic Campus*, YALE ALUMNI MAGAZINE, Nov. 1998.

"a bad odor." To Eskridge, "Yale Law School smelled like it was in decline," literally.[6] Visiting faculty, considering whether they wanted to remain, noticed dilapidation. "People had water dripping from the roof onto their desks," Vicki Schultz remembered.[7]

By the time Guido took the helm, the University had begun to address the decay at some other buildings, which it chalked up to "deferred maintenance," which others labeled the "favored euphemism for neglect."[8] The University acknowledged the need to redo the Law School but made no commitments about a time frame. It was highly doubtful that it would have gotten around to making repairs soon, or with adequate capital to rejuvenate the space according to high standards. Indeed, work to renovate the Hall of Graduate Studies, across the street, had just begun in 2019.

Accreditation as a tool in negotiation. Guido put on something of a show about burdensome ABA oversight. He deployed the ABA's negative criticism of the facilities strategically, to persuade the University that the law school building needed to be renovated; that it would be expensive; and that the University would be better off allowing the law school to become independent and assume financial responsibility for the renovations.

A letter to Guido from A. Kenneth Pye, the former Dean of Duke Law School and then President of Southern Methodist University, is informative in this regard. It makes it evident that Guido had a working relationship with Pye dating back to his membership on an ABA Accreditation Committee.

Pye commiserated with Guido's tight walk. Guido had an interest in providing detailed descriptions of deficiencies in the physical plant in order to elicit negative criticism from the ABA that would help to persuade the central administration of the need for additional financial support. He balanced this against the risk, in doing so, of excessively alarming some members of the Accreditation Committee, who might presume that the conditions *actually* were so intolerable as to be worthy of sanctions.

He wrote that at his own institution, he too had "been engaged in a similar charade." It was "one of the most frustrating experiences I have encountered in legal education." He described the ABA accreditation committee as "a committee of persons who know little about legal education and less about university financing."

Their correspondence did not amount to collusion to arrive at a helpful University response, but the ongoing tussle with the accreditors surely boosted Guido in his quest for financial independence for the law school. It was convenient to have a friend in a position to "tango."[9]

---

[6] Interview with Prof. William Eskridge, Mar. 11, 2013.
[7] Interview with Prof. Vicki Schultz, June 4, 2013.
[8] *Id.*
[9] Letter from Southern Methodist University President A. Kenneth Pye to Yale Law Dean Guido Calabresi, Feb. 22, 1994, Yale University Archives.

Building codes and new standards. Apart from standard ABA compliance, the renovations were badly needed to bring the building into compliance with mandates from the fire marshal and with new requirements for compliance with the accessibility standards imposed—during the course of the renovation—by the Americans with Disabilities Act of 1990.[10]

Spatial limitations. Renovation of the building did not add significant new space to the law school. As the law school population grew significantly—not the J.D. student body but staff, administrators, graduate students and faculty—the need for additional space became apparent.

Plans to construct a new law school mixed-use building were developed and implemented during the deanships of Harold Koh and Robert Post, with $25 million in funds raised from alumni Robert C. Baker and his wife Christina. Baker Hall, located along Tower Parkway, adjacent to the Power Plant, added 137,000 square feet to the Law School campus, with residential suites, a student center, lecture hall, and rooms for seminars and programs. The building was remodeled from one originally constructed as a "swing dorm" to house students temporarily while undergraduate colleges were being renovated. It was inexpensively constructed and poorly finished; converting it to an adequate law school facility cost the law school a significant amount. But it was done well. Construction was completed in August 2018.

Guido and Robert C. Baker embrace at the ribbon-cutting ceremony for Baker Hall, Sept. 20, 2018[11]

Why renovate rather than move? The rundown state of Sterling Law Building, combined with the immense cost of renovation begs the question—why not either

---

[10] *Id.*
[11] Photo credit: Peter Hvizdak/Hearst Connecticut Media (obtain permission).

relocate or tear the building down and start anew? Harold Koh, who became the dean in 2004, observes that the University would have preferred to turn the law school into a residential college; there was "a serious proposal on the table for the law school to move near the Divinity School, way up Prospect Street."[12] Furthermore, as Guido says and is indicated in the previous chapter, the cost of reconstruction turned out to be higher than expected.[13]

As Professor Robert Ellickson put it, "if you know Guido, this was never an option. Guido has so much personhood, if you will, tied in with this building, that that was *absolutely never* an option."[14] Mike Thompson, the Associate Dean of Building Services, emphasizes that Guido's reputation as a "hands-on Dean" extended to walking the floor every morning, when "he would look at the posters and things that were up there." He took care to make sure that the posters were hung using the correct tape, so as not to damage the walls.

His identification with the law school included its physical well-being as well as its mission and its morale. Renovation of the physical space laid the needed foundation for more general renewal.

Vaulted and light-filled ceiling of the library after the renovation

---

[12] Interview with Prof. Harold Koh, Aug. 26, 2013.
[13] See the previous chapter, "Independence."
[14] Interview with Prof. Robert Ellickson, May 10, 2011.

22

Almost a Justice: Robert Bork

> *In July 1987—two years into Guido's deanship—Robert H. Bork was nominated by President Ronald Reagan to replace retiring Justice Lewis Powell as Associate Justice of the Supreme Court. At the time, Bork had a prominent but controversial reputation as a legal scholar and a conservative public servant. The nomination provoked the most ferocious conflict over a Supreme Court nomination in modern history of judicial appointments.*
>
> *Both sides solicited Guido's participation and support, and he had competing perspectives to consider—as a dean, as a colleague, as a friend, as a legal scholar, and as a progressive.*

Robert Bork came to teach at Yale as one of three important appointments late in Gene Rostow's administration: John Simon, Ronald Dworkin, and Bork.

Not bad! Bob came from the University of Chicago with tremendous grades and recommendations, and it was odd that Chicago hadn't gone after him, which made some people suspicious.

> *He had written a quite wonderful article about anti-trust. I disagreed with much of it—anti-trust was a field I knew—but his discussion of why courts should read anti-trust law as being only about protecting competition, rather than competitors, is an*
>
> *extraordinarily brilliant and interesting reaction to originalism—profoundly anti-anti-originalist and well worth taking into account! But totally wrong! [Clangs cup].*
>
> *Over time his scholarship re-did much of anti-trust law! What he's written in constitutional law may be interesting; may be right; may be wrong—I think it's wrong. What he wrote in anti-trust showed that he was a really first-rate scholar!*

Bob comes for interviews and—I know this from conversations with him afterwards—people had told him that Yale is this "Leftie" place, where if you really come out as you are, nobody will appoint you. This is *terrible* information to give, but it is the kind of thing that people might well say to somebody whose views were tough enough so that, even in Chicago, he caused some concerns.

He comes through and has interviews with people. In those days, you do not present a paper. You just go from office to office; you have lunch; and it's a question of how smart and argumentative people think you are. He comes through and basically people think, "This guy is too bland! He may be smart, but there's nothing to him!" He was headed towards defeat.

What got him his appointment here was the fact that Bickel, Wellington, and I had read this paper with care, and we said, "This is an *extraordinarily* important paper." Each of us, independently and then together—because we are very close—come to the same conclusion: there is just *too much* of a disconnect between this paper and Bork's demeanor, and these interviews simply have to be ignored, because the person who gave those interviews cannot be the same person who wrote the article. We urged the committee to let him go to the faculty, which voted him an offer.

I told him my version of his appointment many times, and he always said, "Yah, yah, yah, you say you're the one who's responsible for my whole career." We joked about it because in a way it's true, but in a way it's not! It was his article.

He came and *immediately* became an extraordinarily important member of the faculty. He became very close to Charles Black and Alex Bickel; they were the "Three B's," and they taught constitutional law seminars together. They had three *totally different* positions, but they liked each other; it was very interesting to watch their interplay. Bickel, using Harvard legal process ideas, moved Bork from some rigid positions, extreme ones, to which he later slipped back. But these three worked off each other: the kind of legal *realism* that Black brought; the legal *process* that Bickel brought; and the Chicago viewpoint that Bork brought—this was a wonderful kind of spectrum of viewpoints!

He had an incredible sense of humor. He was funny and sharp to a degree that was outstanding. When he was interviewed to be Solicitor General, either Erlichman or Haldeman was talking with Nixon, and Nixon said to them, with Bork in the room, "Yes, he's very good, but isn't he too smart?" and Bork shot back, "For the right job, I could have a prefrontal lobotomy." You know, he was always right on top of things!

Their *families* liked each other. Bob at the time was married to a woman, Claire Davidson, who was Jewish, of a liberal background, and *utterly loyal* to Bork. I mean, she just stood behind him in everything and backed him up totally, but softened him. She made him see what there was to be seen in other sides.

Claire developed cancer, and it was incurable, not operable, and she was sick many years. She then became a ship in full sail. I mean, the little things that had made this quite remarkable, very intelligent lady a little bit whiny, just did not matter anymore! The focus was always on the important things, and Bob took care of her in a way that was utterly admirable. I mean, he was with her every moment. He was as wonderful a husband in that situation as one could imagine. Since everybody loved her, it made him very much part of the faculty.

In addition, with us was Arthur Leff, who was a remarkable human being. Arthur thought that one of the things that you could do here was have more than just workshops—you could have a lot of informal conversation among faculty. We were smaller then, and Arthur—in part because he liked it, in part because he thought it was the thing to do—not only arranged with deans to have coffee and donuts in the faculty lounge, but he would go there and sit in the faculty lounge for a couple of hours every morning, from ten to eleven-thirty and so on.

Robert Bork in his office at Yale Law School, 1970.
Yale Law Reporter.

Bob and Ralph Winter, both of whom worked hard—but you know, a little bit of laziness was there—enjoyed taking a break! They would be there and talking, along with Arthur, and so people would be attracted there, and the conversations were quite remarkable! Arthur had *very* different views from Yale conservative Winter and Chicago Bork.

So, while there were *strong* differences on issues of faculty policies—homosexuality, particularly—Bob was *very much* a member of the faculty, and very much well regarded and loved. When we talked about affirmative action in getting Black students, and from poorer backgrounds, Bob was for it! He was not the kind of caricature of many of the accusations made later. What he became after he was turned down for the Supreme Court, sadly, is another story.

A great debate on our faculty was whether to add to the non-discrimination requirements we made of employers recruiting here, "sexual orientation." Bob talked about the small law firm in the South that had Christian values; could we really discriminate against it? I made an argument the other way, which was, "I take it Bob, that you're not saying that "orientation" is a ground for discrimination, but actions. If the firm in Charleston prohibits anyone who engages in oral or anal sex in sex out of marriage, whether in homosexual or heterosexual relationships, from being hired by that firm, that firm might not be discriminating." We were making technical points, which I do not think convinced anybody, really! Joe Goldstein got the floor—he did not have much of a voice— and he croaked, "All of this is all very well and good, but the real issue is that these are our students. What do we owe to them?" This was Joe at his absolute best! The addition went through, Bork voting against.

When Bork becomes Solicitor General, there is great joy in the faculty! You know, everybody thinks that this is something which is exactly what he should do! When he went down to Washington to take the job, everybody thought that this was a good thing.

We had fun, for a while, after he went to DC. When the Yale DC Alumni group asked me to one of their dinner meetings, Bob Bork was the toastmaster and I was the speaker. I talked about what I was working on, which was ownership of bodies, and transplants, and who got a right to get a kidney transplant, and so on. Everybody loved it! It may have gone on somewhat longer than an after-dinner talk should have, although, the audience seemed quite interested. When I finished, Bob got up and said, "This was a magnificent talk. I have never been made as aware of my kidneys as now," and he rushed out to go to the bathroom!

* * *

Then came the *slaughter*, the "Saturday Night Massacre," when Nixon went back on his promise to allow the investigation of the Watergate scandal to take its course. Elliot Richardson and William Ruckleshaus resigned: first the Attorney General and then the Deputy Attorney General; and the third person in line was Bob Bork.

He stayed and followed the order to fire the Special Prosecutor, Archibald Cox. This was something for which Bork was pilloried. But many of us who talked with Bob at the time know that what he did then was done from the best of motives.

According to what Bob Bork told me at around the time it happened, Richardson and Ruckleshaus had promised the Senate Judiciary Committee at the time they were appointed that they would resign if there was interference with the Special Counsel. Bork had not been asked, so he had made no equivalent promise. He was, however, planning to resign. But Richardson and Ruckelshaus said to him, "Do not resign, because if you resign, one of two things will happen: either everybody will resign, and the government will fall by resignation," which is not the American way, The President is President, he is not the Prime Minister.

Causing the government to fall would be wrong. Alternatively, if the government doesn't fall, after you resign, somebody who is a hack underneath you will stay; and the investigation will be stopped."

Richardson and Ruckelshaus urged Bob to fire Cox but to continue the investigation seriously. And remember that after he stayed, Leon Jaworski was appointed as Special Prosecutor. He continued the investigation responsibly, and ultimately the threat of impeachment and Nixon's resignation followed.

Richardson and Ruckelshaus had said to Bob, "We will defend you when you are condemned for this." But Richardson did not, and I never had respect for Richardson after that.

* * *

Nixon Fires Cox

Bork's relationship to Yale Law School after the Saturday Night Massacre got complicated. In part, this was because the students, in particular, tended to buy the criticism of his not resigning—but there were other reasons why. After he joined the DC Circuit, he found it *much* less comfortable to come back to New Haven. The reasons were not simply ideological.

Pastdaily.com

Several sad things had happened. Alex Bickel died in 1974. Bork's wife Claire died in 1980. Charles Black retired in 1986 and moved to New York where his wife Barbara became dean of Columbia Law School. The people he was *closest* to were no longer here, and he said to me, "When I come to New Haven, if I go to the Grove Street Cemetery, there is my wife. I look around, and where is Alex? He is dead, not here. Where is Charles? Also, not here. I cannot stand it." So it was as much this *personal* thing, this loss of connection, as much as anything that distanced him from the school.

* * *

In July of 1987, Bob is nominated for the Supreme Court. It is not obvious that he will have difficulty with the process: A year before, in June 1986, Nino Scalia was nominated by Ronald Reagan and was quickly approved by the Senate, unanimously. Remember, he was not in any way a swing vote.

Scalia had asked me to write something to the Judiciary Committee. I wrote a letter saying that I disagreed with a lot of things about him, but his First Amendment positions were important and rather interesting. In any event, I said that somebody like Scalia is a perfectly appropriate appointment to the Supreme Court. Five Scalias are not, but one certainly is.

If the Republicans had been more intelligent, they would have nominated Bork first and Scalia later, because the fact that Nino was Italian would have made it more difficult for Democrats to oppose him. There had never been an Italian. And the fact that he was Catholic also, politically, would have cost the opposition more. Besides, Scalia was a less known person. His opinions on the DC Court were actually more extreme than Bork's, but he did not have the public persona that one could attack. In any event, Bork gets nominated second.

* * *

At the time of the Bork nomination, I recently had become the dean, and I was asked for my views. I made it clear that although I would *never* appoint Bork to any court—that he would be *among the last people* that I would appoint, just as I would expect to be the last person he would appoint—this was a fine nomination. It's a different thing to support a person for a position and to agree with his views! You cannot understand me if you do not understand that difference. You know, I can say I disagree *totally* with Bob and I would not appoint him and still endorse him when somebody who has the authority to do so chooses him for a judgeship.

I have had to say I disagreed with Bob again and again, because there are people— and I think of Steve Reinhardt—who say, "Either you were wrong about what you thought he would do, or you must have agreed with him more than you say." But that is wrong and not me.

I was also not at all sure that Bob raised as much concern as other conservatives who were being considered, in part because he would want to distinguish himself from Scalia, and in part because he really did, still under the influence of Bickel, I thought, have this Legal Process outlook—that *precedents* were important; that you do not unsettle settled law.

In one speech to the Federalist Society, in particular, he said that he certainly would not go back on the New Deal. He emphasized that those who were pushing to ignore the whole line of Commerce Clause cases, and trying to go back to originalist versions, were wrong. He and Scalia had not by any means always gotten along on the DC Circuit! They were very much in opposition to each other on some things! Each wanted to be the leader, so there was some egotism involved.

I also thought that from an institutional perspective, the nomination of somebody who was a Yale faculty member was a *good* thing for Yale. The fact that his views might be different from the faculty—so what? Here was a Yale professor who was going to the United States Supreme Court, and I'm sure there were plenty of people who thought that William O. Douglas was a pain when he was there—but he was very much linked to Yale!

For a dean either strongly to oppose Bork, or strongly to favor him, would also raise institutional questions. For the dean also is the school, and all of its students and alums, as well as himself! So when he was nominated, I said, "I disagree with him, but this is a fine choice." I decided not to testify on his behalf, but I praised the choice.

Some people criticized me because of the position I took. I might have just stayed out of the fray, but that wasn't me. You know, that wasn't me. Another dean would have, but that just is not my personality.

At the hearing, many people from Yale went down to Washington. Burke Marshall testified against Bork; Joe Goldstein testified in favor of him. Why? Again, [laughs] it was different views of the merits of the appointment. I remember people saying to me, "What will happen when they come back to New Haven?" Burke and Joe were *extremely* close friends. Reporters asked, "Will they speak to each other after this? What will happen to your faculty when you've got people going down and speaking so much against each other?" I said, "Did you happen to follow them after the hearing and see where they went?," and these newspaper people said, "No." I said, "Well, if you had, you would have found they'd gone to some bar together and started drinking and talking happily about what they had done." The press did not really understand that.

* * *

The crucial moments of the hearings were those when Bob testified. Unfortunately, [sighs] while he was very funny and extremely smart, he also had a high opinion of himself, and he believed he could get by on his intellect alone and be approved because he was brilliant. Bob, also, always was a little lazy—a bit unprepared as a teacher. Sadly, that side of him came through in the hearings.

He talked down to the Senators, and he wasn't politically smart in the sense that others—I think Scalia—would have been. Others in that position have been much less honest perhaps, but when Bob was asked why he wanted to go on the Supreme Court, he gave a completely academic answer, which was totally wrong at the human level, about it being "an intellectual feast."

> *I remember thinking at the time that if I was there and somebody asked me a question of that same sort, I would have said, "I'm a refugee. I'm an immigrant. This country has done great things for me. If the President of the United States thinks I can be of service to this country, of course I'd go!" This would be true, but would also connect with people.*

At the hearing, Bob persistently gave the wrong answers, and so he could be defeated.

* * *

The whole thing became: "Bork is an evil man! Bork is a racist! Bork is this; Bork is that!" They looked at Bork's and his children's parking tickets! They looked into his garbage and his video rentals! You know, they did all sorts of things, which politicians *do*, because it's so much easier to attack the person than the ideas. It was very unfair, and it would have been, *even* if they had found anything of importance, which they did not.

I wrote a letter critical of the Judiciary Committee after they were attacking him brutally, making personal attacks.

> *I said, "Look, the Senate has a right to confirm or not confirm, advise and consent. If you say honestly that you do not want Bork on the Court because his views are too different from yours, Democratic Senate, you can do it honestly. By and large, when Senates have tried to do that, they haven't really succeeded, but you have a right to do it. What you should not do is what you are doing, which is attacking him as a racist, which he is not; attacking him in any number of personal ways, which are totally unfair! Because if you do it this way, you may well defeat him and feel very good about it, but you will make the Administration very angry, and the Republicans will say, 'We will not forget it,' and it will come back and haunt you later." This certainly is what happened. "The result will be," I said, "that all you will get is somebody who is younger, dumber, with much the same views, who hasn't written as much."*

I think what I said was right then. I think personal attacks like that are contaminating the nominating process today. When it was over, it looked to the world as though his defeat in the Senate vote on his nomination was a statement about him as a person. So it was a disaster. A total disaster in the way that a rejection of his political philosophy would not have been.

One thing they did not go after him for was his homophobia, because that wasn't an issue then! On that, I would have been hard put to defend him. One should remember, though, that there were plenty of real liberals of my parents' generation, for whom discrimination based on sexual orientation was different from racism! Fortunately, generations change.

* * *

After his nomination was rejected, he resigned from the DC Circuit entirely, and in many ways he became a different person. Some of the positions he took in the later years were, I think, very silly. My nephew Steven clerked for Judges Winter, Bork, and Scalia, and then went into Ed Meese's White House. He thought his clerkship for Bork was a great experience, and years later helped Bork with some of his books. He tried with limited success to make them more scholarly. Bork's last writings, frankly, are often just sour. How much of this came from the bitterness of the nomination episode and how unfairly he felt he was treated, I do not know.

Bork at his September 15, 1987, hearing with former President Gerald Ford and then-Senator Robert Dole (Charles Tasnadi / Associated Press)

* * *

Who is to say what would have happened if he had gone on the Court? I have no doubt that in the Flag Burning case, he would have voted to uphold the law along with (oddly) Justice Stevens, and in opposition to Scalia and Kennedy. In the Gay Rights cases, Kennedy has certainly taken positions, which are very

> different from the ones that Bob would have taken. As to *other* issues, if he had gone straight on the Court without the bitterness, he probably would have *stayed* with the New Deal "constitutional moment," as Bruce Ackerman would put it, in the Commerce Clause cases, the regulation and antitrust cases, and so on. He would have said that it is there, and it is not for us to change it. This would have gotten him into disagreement with Scalia, and he would have become a third *pole*.
>
> The whole Court might well have been different because of it. Who is to know?

COMMENTARY

Chapter 22

Bork's early antitrust scholarship. Guido recalls that Bork was appointed to the faculty at Yale in 1962 because he had written an article so important that it offset his less-than-stellar interview performance. While Bork had published a few articles before his appointment,[1] his first work that really started to "re-do" antitrust law, as Guido puts it, was actually published in *Fortune magazine*, in 1963—a year after he joined the Yale faculty.[2] It was probably a draft of this article to which Guido refers. The central argument that Bork developed over these years is that antitrust law was designed to protect competition to the benefit of consumers and not to protect competitors.

Bork's homophobia. Guido describes Bork's opposition to amending the Law School's anti-discrimination policy to include discrimination on the basis of sexual orientation as firm and civil—asserting a concern for small religious law firms. William N. Eskridge, Jr., at the time a closeted Yale Law student, who later would become outstanding as a scholar in the field of gender and sexuality law, remembers Bork's point of view quite differently. "Some of the faculty were resistant. Some of them were opposed. One member of the faculty, and maybe no more, made this a personal crusade," he recalls. "Probably the most strident anti-homosexual judge I can name in American history was Robert Bork."[3] Indeed, to try to garner more opposition to the change in policy, Bork wrote a memo to the faculty, arguing that "homosexuality is obviously not an unchangeable condition like race or gender.... Societies can have very small or very great

---

[1] *See, e.g.*, Robert H. Bork, *Vertical Integration and the Sherman Act: The Legal History of an Economic Misconception*, 22 U. CHICAGO L. REV. 157 (1954).
[2] Robert H. Bork & Ward S. Bowman, Jr., *The Crisis in Antitrust*, FORTUNE MAG., Dec. 1963.
[3] Interview with Prof. William Eskridge, Mar. 11, 2013.

amounts of homosexual behavior, depending upon the degrees of moral disapproval or tolerance shown."[4] Like Eskridge, many of Bork's colleagues found his position untenable.

Bork's hostility to civil rights legislation. Although defenders argued that Bork's views about civil rights put him in the mainstream of conservative constitutional interpretive thinking, he had a record that included vocal opposition to of the 1964 Civil Rights Act, asserting that "justifiable abhorrence of racial discrimination [might well] result in legislation by which the morals of the majority are self righteously imposed upon a minority.... If it is permissible to tell a barber or a rooming house owner that he must deal with all who come to him regardless of race or religion, then it is impossible to see why a doctor, lawyer, accountant, or any other professional or business man should have the right to discriminate."[5]

The "Saturday Night Massacre." Following inexorably from revelations of what occurred at the Watergate Hotel on June 17, 1972, President Nixon, under immense public and political pressure, appointed a special (and independent) prosecutor, Archibald Cox, to investigate these and other irregularities during the 1972 presidential campaign.[6] Only eight days after the special prosecutor succeeded in getting the D.C. Circuit Court of Appeals to order Nixon to "hand over the tapes," the president ordered the Attorney General, Elliot Richardson, to fire Cox.[7] The Attorney General refused to follow this command and so resigned, as did his deputy, William Ruckelshaus. Robert Bork, as Solicitor General, was the next one in line. In this way Mr. Bork became Attorney General of the United States.

Bork fired Cox.[8] As Cox left his position, he warned that "whether we shall continue to be a government of laws and not of men is now for Congress and ultimately the American people" to decide.[9] This "massacre" set the stage for the impeachment of President Richard Nixon.[10]

During Bork's confirmation for appointment to the D.C. Circuit in 1982, Richardson and Ruckelshaus stated that they had encouraged Bork to follow the president's orders and stay on, to steady the ship.[11] But Robert Bork also

---

[4] ETHAN BRONNER, BATTLE FOR JUSTICE: HOW THE BORK NOMINATION SHOOK AMERICA 72 (2007); *see also* WILLIAM ESKRIDGE, DISHONORABLE PASSIONS: SODOMY LAWS IN AMERICA, 1861–2003 ch. 9 (2008).

[5] Robert Bork, Civil Rights—A Challenge, New Republic, Aug. 31, 1963.

[6] ROBERT H. BORK, SAVING JUSTICE: WATERGATE, THE SATURDAY NIGHT MASSACRE, AND OTHER ADVENTURES OF A SOLICITOR GENERAL xii (2013).

[7] John A. Farrell, WITH THE SATURDAY NIGHT MASSACRE, NIXON MISCALCULATED. WILL TRUMP?, *Politico* (Feb. 3, 2018), https://www.politico.com/magazine/story/2018/02/03/nixon-trump-saturday-night-massacre-216929.

[8] Dylan Matthews, *Richard Nixon Also Fired the Person Investigating His Presidential Campaign*, VOX (May 10, 2017), https://www.vox.com/policy-and-politics/2017/5/10/15603886/saturday-night-massacre-explained-nixon-watergate-archibald-cox.

[9] Jeffrey Frank, *Comey's Firing Is—and Isn't—Like Nixon's Saturday Night Massacre*, NEW YORKER (May 9, 2017), https://www.newyorker.com/news/daily-comment/comeys-firing-is-and-isnt-like-nixons-saturday-night-massacre.

[10] Kenneth B. Noble, *Bork Irked by Emphasis on His Role in Watergate*, N.Y. TIMES, July 2, 2017.

[11] BRONNER, *supra* note 4, at 66.

controversially believed, as a matter of interpreting the constitutional power of the Executive, that the president had the right to fire Cox.[12]

The relevance of the "Saturday Night Massacre" to the legal status of Special Counsel Robert Mueller. The post-Watergate Independent Counsel Law expired in 1999, and in the absence of congressional reauthorization, regulations regarding the appointment and authority of "Special Counsel" were developed by the Justice Department.[13] When in 2018 former FBI Director Robert Mueller was appointed by the acting Attorney General, renewed legal and constitutional questions surfaced about whether President Trump could fire or otherwise control Mueller if the investigation came too close to him for his comfort. These problems reinvigorated the debate about whether Robert Bork courageously "steadied the Justice Department amid a constitutional crisis," or obsequiously "acquiesced to a president caught in the vice of Watergate."[14]

Guido's difficulty in deciding what to do. Robert Bork was on everyone's list of possible nominees. In a pre-nomination interview, Guido called him "a person of enormous ability and integrity and great humor," and estimated that "of all the conservative constitutional law scholars around, Bob Bork is the most distinguished."[15] When the choice became official, a story in the *New York Times* referred to Guido as "a close friend of Judge Bork's."[16] The article quoted a distinctly mixed message: Guido "cringe[d]" at Bork's views on some civil liberties issues and at his ignorance of the significance of discrimination in America. But he expected to support Bork "because of his personal integrity, because of his professional quality," and because, while Guido had "very strong disagreements with him," he had "no reason to believe that anybody else that this Administration would nominate and get confirmed would be any better ... and would probably be worse."[17]

Adamant opposition to Bork quickly emerged; battle lines had formed by the time of the committee hearings, which began in mid-September. Friends and law school alumni urged Guido either to testify in support or else to amplify his disagreements. To such exhortations, he typically replied with a letter exposing his conflicted self. "After much thought, I have decided not to testify in the Bork hearings."[18] If he did appear, he said he thought at first it would be in support for a friend and colleague; but "unfortunately, testifying would require me to wear a badge, in simplistic terms to be classified as 'pro-Bork.'" But he cared too much about lending that much

---

[12] See BORK, *supra* note 6.

[13] Isaac Chotiner, *Neal Katyal Has One More Question for Robert Mueller After His Testimony*, NEW YORKER, July 24, 2019.

[14] Joan Biskupic, *Another Saturday Night Massacre? Washington May Be Ready This Time*, CNN (Aug. 12, 2017), https://www.cnn.com/2017/08/12/politics/robert-bork-mueller-trump/index.html.

[15] *Legal Scholars: Bork's Nomination Would Have Great Impact*, UPI ARCHIVES (July 1, 1987), https://www.upi.com/Archives/1987/07/01/Legal-scholars-Borks-would-have-great-impact/5263552110400.

[16] Stuart Taylor, *Bork at Yale: Colleagues Recall a Friend but a Philosophical Foe*, N.Y. TIMES, July 27, 1987.

[17] *Id.*

[18] Letter from Guido Calabresi to Roberta G. Gordon, Esq., Sept. 23, 1987 (Calabresi Records, Yale Manuscripts and Archives); see also Guido Calabresi to Hon. Steven Reinhardt, Sept. 16, 1987 ("I thought long and hard about your letter and I finally decided not to testify.").

pro-Bork support, "given the number of people and causes that I care about [on] the other side." And if he did appear, he went on, he would have divided his comments into "what I thought about Bork as an individual (which is very positive); [and] what I thought of his judicial philosophy (which is very negative)." He wrote that if he decided to comment for the record, it would be in the form of a letter to the Judiciary, laying out his complicated thinking.[19]

Guido did write a lengthy letter to senators, taking a decidedly mixed position.[20] Bork, repeated Guido, is a person of the highest integrity, but a person with whom he frequently differed on matters of faculty policies and judicial opinions. Bork was likely to hold to an underlying, rigid approach to legal analysis: the key to reaching Justice Powell was a sense of fairness, but to reach Bork it would be necessary to fit an outcome into his predetermined theories. And even Guido's personal praise could be discounted because he opened his letter by reminding members of his close personal ties to Judge/Professor Bork, and of the fact that his nephew, Steven G. Calabresi, was Judge Bork's law clerk.[21] The letter offered hardly any cover to those who supported Bork's appointment—without unambiguously supporting those who opposed it.

Bill Clinton's opposition. Bill Clinton filed testimony against Bork that focused on Bork's conservative judicial activism.[22] Bork's opponents believed that Clinton's public opposition would be important because of his Southern background and working-class support. He disliked Bork's "conservative judicial activism," encountered at first hand while a student in Professor Bork's constitutional law class at Yale. And as the Governor of Arkansas, he was affected directly by a case Judge Bork decided against him at the time of the nomination:

> When he was on the DC Court of Appeals, I lost a case in Bork's court involving whether a multi-state utility could override my state's public service commission and

---

[19] Letter from Guido Calabresi to Hon. Steven Reinhardt, Sept. 16, 1987.
[20] Letter from Calabresi to Members of the Senate Judiciary Committee, Sept. 28, 1987 (Calabresi Records, Yale Manuscripts and Archives).
[21] *Id.* Steven, the son of Guido's brother Paul, graduated from Yale College and then from its Law School in 1983. He developed conservative political views early in college, and as a law student, played a leading role convening a three-day symposium that was nominally about federalism, but largely about theories of originalism; Bork was a featured speaker. The symposium gave birth to the Federalist Society, a group of conservatives and libertarians in which Steven took a leadership role. Michael Kruse, *The Weekend at Yale That Changed American Politics*, POLITICO, Sept. 1, 2018. Steven became Judge Ralph Winter's law clerk in 1983–1984 and Judge Bork's law clerk during 1984–1985. In 1988, he became a research associate at the American Enterprise Institute, where he helped Bork write THE TEMPTING OF AMERICA: THE POLITICAL SEDUCTION OF THE LAW (1990). He joined the faculty at Northwestern University in 2013. Their different political views did not keep Guido from supporting Steven's career or interfere with a close uncle-nephew relationship over decades, during which they conversed often and debated opposing views about the law and the Constitution. When Guido was nominated by President Clinton for the Second Circuit Court of Appeals, Steven called his former classmate Brent Hatch (son of Senator Orin Hatch) to encourage his father to vote for Guido, which was "as close as I've ever come to fulfilling my promise as a five-year-old (see Chapter 25, "Bill Wants Him":) to get elected president, and appoint [my uncle] to the Supreme Court." Interview with Prof. Steven G. Calabresi, Nov. 18, 2013.
[22] Additional Submission, Statement of Governor Bill Clinton on The Nomination of Judge Robert Bork, NOMINATION OF ROBERT H. BORK TO BE ASSOCIATE JUSTICE OF THE SUPREME COURT OF THE UNITED STATES, SEPTEMBER 15–30, 1987 Part 4 (1987) 4320; Miss. Indus. v. Ferc, 257 U.S. App. D.C. 244, 808 F.2d 1525 (1987) (per curiam).

require Arkansas to pay costs of a big nuclear power plant being built in Mississippi. And our 'conservative, originalist, state's rights' Judge, Bork, said they could, [require it, without even] finding that we needed the power. Anyway, I believed Bork told the truth in class; and so I thought he would be to the right of where I think it is appropriate for a Supreme Court to be. But then I got really mad [and almost retracted my opposition statement] when the [Judiciary] committee started looking into the movies Bork rented. I called [Biden], and I said "if you want my testimony, you got to stop this, otherwise I'm going to withdraw it." That's how I knew Biden, anyway.

Clinton maintained a relationship of friendly communication with Senator Biden which began during the Bork hearings.[23]

Bork's sense of humor. Guido recalls Bork's quick, barbed, and witty sense of humor; others who share this recollection have also pointed out that it was not always well received or well timed. While preparing him for his Supreme Court confirmation hearing, for example, White House Counsel Arthur B. Culvahouse had Bork practice answers to what he thought could be controversial questions—including the "John Fedders question," named for the former head of the SEC investigative branch who had been in the news at the time for beating his wife.[24] When Culvahouse practiced the question on Bork: "Mr. Bork, did you ever beat your wives?" Bork responded, in an attempt at humor, "No, but don't ask them."[25]

Marriages. Guido mentions Bork's first wife, Claire Davidson and Guido's fondness for her, and doubts about Bork's second wife (Mary Ellen Pohl) who was married to him at the time of his nomination. Others concur with Guido that they could scarcely have been more different. Bork met Claire as an undergraduate at the University of Chicago and they married in 1952.[26] Claire was the "daughter of working-class European Jews," and was known as a "New Deal enthusiast."[27] She was not particularly interested in religion, and during their marriage, neither of them practiced either Judaism or Bork's "generic" Protestantism.[28] This all changed after Bork married Mary Ellen in 1982, only two years after Claire's death. Mary Ellen spent fifteen years as a Catholic nun who eventually convinced Bork to officially convert in 2002.[29] As Bork recalls, when he did convert, Father Richard John Neuhaus sent a note saying that St. Jude, the patron saint of impossible cases, could now get some rest from Mary Ellen's importuning.[30] Mary

---

[23] Interview with President Bill Clinton, Oct. 20, 2020; according to the president, his communication with Senator Biden in 1993–94 did not include discussing the possible choice of Guido for Attorney General. *Id.* See Chapter, 25 "Bill Wants Him."

[24] Georgia Dullea, *A Battered Wife's Fight, In and Out of Court*, N.Y. TIMES, Nov. 9, 1987.

[25] BRONNER, *supra* note 4, at 81.

[26] *Id.* at 46.

[27] *Id.*

[28] *Id.*

[29] Sophia Mason, *Judge Robert Bork, Conservative Icon and Catholic Convert, R.I.P.*, NAT'L CATHOLIC REGISTER (Dec. 20, 2012), http://www.ncregister.com/daily-news/judge-robert-bork-conservative-icon-and-catholic-convert-r.i.p.

[30] *Id.*, Tim Drake, *Judge Bork Converts to the Catholic Faith*, CATHOLIC EDUCATION RESOURCE CENTER (2003), https://www.catholiceducation.org/en/faith-and-character/faith-and-character/judge-bork-converts-to-the-catholic-faith.html.

Ellen continued to work as a freelance writer and lecturer on Catholic life and culture, and serves on the Board of the School of Philosophy, Catholic University of America, and Christendom College.[31]

Aftermath of the Bork nomination and confirmation. The vote on the confirmation occurred on October 24, 1987. The Senate, by a vote of 58 to 42, denied Bork approval.[32] The battle and its outcome marked a turning point in the history of the Supreme Court nomination process.

Changing everything, maybe forever. The nomination and the events surrounding it enraged many Republicans. Bork's name "became a symbol of conservative grievance."[33] Notwithstanding Guido's accurate correction of the historical record by noting that Democrats decried the defamation of Abe Fortas, the name "bork" gained currency as a verb, defined in the Oxford Dictionary as "to defame or vilify a person systematically."[34]

After the defeat of Judge Bork, President Reagan turned to Douglas H. Ginsburg, who could be described as the "even more radical" nominee that Guido feared—younger, less able, and with views further away from Guido than Bork's. His nomination collapsed because of allegations that he smoked marijuana with his students, and the nominations that followed—of Anthony Kennedy by President Reagan and David Souter by George H.W. Bush—went forward consistently with historic norms for consensus. The degree of circumspection displayed by the nominees in hearings, however, led to the revelation of a bare minimum of illumination of judicial philosophies and approaches.

With the nomination of Clarence Thomas by George H.W. Bush, hopes for a bipartisan consensus vote again fell apart. Guido takes up the Thomas nomination later on in his narrative.[35]

Robert Bork, post-rejection. In his years on the District of Columbia Court of Appeals prior to his nomination contest, Bork had developed ideas about originalism and constitutional interpretation that gained him not just conservative support, but respect more broadly within the academic community.[36] After the nomination was rejected, he stepped down from the D.C. Circuit Court. He spent less time on writing scholarly work and more time on screeds explicating the moral decay of America. With provocative and nearly apocalyptic titles like *Slouching Toward Gomorrah: Modern Liberalism and American Decline* and *The Tempting of America: The Political Seduction of the Law*, he catered to his own bitterness rather than to continue to seek to be relevant to the legal academy.[37]

---

[31] Mary Ellen Bork, Crisis Mag., https://www.crisismagazine.com/author/mebork

[32] *Linda Greenhouse, Bork's Nomination Is Rejected, 58–42; Reagan Saddened,* N.Y. TIMES, Oct. 24, 1987.

[33] Nina Totenberg, *Robert Bork's Supreme Court Nomination "Changed Everything, Maybe Forever,"* All Things Considered, NPR (Dec. 19, 2012), https://www.npr.org/sections/itsallpolitics/2012/12/19/167645600/robert-borks-supreme-court-nomination-changed-everything-maybe-forever.

[34] *Id.*

[35] See Chapter 24, "Clarence, Anita, Catharine, Jack—and Yale."

[36] *See, e.g.,* Ernest Young, *Rediscovering Conservatism: Burkean Political Theory and Constitutional Interpretation,* 72 N.C.L. REV. 619 (1994); Steven G. Calabresi & Lauren Pope, *Judge Robert H. Bork and Constitutional Change: An Essay on Olman v Evans,* 80 U. OF CHICAGO L. REV. ONLINE 155 (2013).

[37] ROBERT H. BORK, SLOUCHING TOWARD GOMORRAH: MODERN LIBERALISM AND AMERICAN DECLINE (1996); ROBERT H. BORK, THE TEMPTING OF AMERICA: THE POLITICAL SEDUCTION OF THE LAW (1990).

As Guido indicates, Bork was invited back to the Law School on several occasions during this period in an effort to mend feelings. In 1994, his portrait was unveiled and placed in a prominent location at a fitting ceremony he attended.[38] Wounds proved difficult to heal, however. In 2005, he told a reporter that although he did not "fault the Law School as such," the behavior of some former colleagues had been "vicious."[39] In 2006, he fell while ascending to the dais at an event at the Yale Club of New York City, and was seriously injured. He brought suit for $1 million plus punitive damages—an action some considered remarkable given his strenuous opposition to abusive tort claims.[40] Signs pointed to "a ruptured relationship" with Yale.[41]

---

[38] *See* George Priest, *The Abiding Influence of the Antitrust Paradox: An Essay in Honor of Robert H. Bork*, 31 HARV. JL. L. & PUB. POL. 455 (2008) ("[O]n the back wall [in Room 120] directly facing the instructor, and looking over the shoulders of every student, is a large portrait of Judge Bork. It is an excellent portrait, though perhaps emphasizing Judge Bork's sternness and seriousness more than his wonderful sense of humor.").

[39] Adam Liptak, *Yale Law Frets Over Court Choices It Knows Best*, N.Y. TIMES, Nov. 13, 2005.

[40] Peter Lattman, *Robert Bork Files Slip-and-Fall Lawsuit Against Yale Club*, WALL ST. J., June 7, 2007; Isaac Arnsdorf, *Robert Bork Settles $1 Million Lawsuit with Yale Club*, YALE DAILY NEWS, May 12, 2008.

[41] Arnsdorf, *Robert Bork Settles $1 Million Lawsuit with Yale Club*.

23

Conflict, Community, and Confidence

The Wall

> *The political and social climate at Yale Law School in 1985 was shaped by two previous decades during which student rights and a willingness to engage in social protest expanded greatly. The environment at the Law School reflected events outside its doors, including a contest between progressive and conservative elements that found expression in differences over women's rights, gay rights, affirmative action, AIDS, natural food, criminal justice, and corporate power—to name only some of the more prominent. An issue that cut across all of these conflicts was locating the boundary between permissible and unacceptable speech and expression.*

After I became dean, the Federalist Society invited somebody named Pendleton, who was Black, to come speak. A student, I think, put up an open message on the wall of the long corridor on the main floor. It described Pendleton as an "Oreo"— Black on the outside, white on the inside.

This set off a terrible fuss between the people who thought that it was wrong for Pendleton to come at all, and the ones who were furious that somebody who might well not have been Black described this visitor in that way. Some people were urging me to throw the visitor out! Other people were urging me to discipline the people who had insulted him! This incident raised the issue of what one does about free expression when it comes home to roost in a place that talks about free speech. Inevitably it also made me think about how to make this a teaching moment.

At this time there was a great deal of pressure from the Left to stop speech that was hateful. This was a time—perhaps oddly, in view of their positions some years earlier—when the defenders of unbridled speech tended to be those of the Right. They were then, as to some extent they say they are now, those who fought against making a set of rules to control speech that is too awful to be allowed.

In that context, I decided that the person involved, and those who put up the "Oreo" sign, had a right to speak, and that I wouldn't permit anybody to stop him from speaking and others from putting the sign up on the wall. And that everybody else had the right to say anything that *they* wanted, in response. But I also made clear that I, as much as anybody else, could speak my mind about it. I could and did make my own view known, which was that I thought the speaker's position was despicable but that it was offensive to slur him in a racist way.

That morphed into the Wall, a place where people in the Law School were allowed to say anything they wanted, however scurrilous or obscene. I was quite explicit that what was permitted went beyond even the protections of the First Amendment. (The First Amendment has been interpreted not fully to protect certain sorts of speech—for example pornography, incitements to violence and other sorts.) I did not want to get into a lawyer's fight over where the line was between what was allowed and what was not allowed; I did not want some technical dispute over whether something was on this side or that side of the First Amendment. I thought that would be a *hopeless* discussion.

I did draw one bright line. I said, "Anything goes, so long as the people who put something on the Wall are part of the Law School community and so long as they identify themselves. They will be protected, that is, they can be attacked by anyone else in speech, but what they say has total immunity."

The only things that they *do not* need to sign their names on, I said, are any criticisms of the dean and faculty. I just did not want the rule to look as if it were devised to protect *us*. As an actual matter—and I was kind of glad of what it said about the place—they all signed their names anyway.

* * *

When these rules came out, Bob Cover, the author of some of the most thoughtful essays ever written about the ways law shapes the normative structure of the world, took the position that I was right not to make restrictions about speech, but that *requiring people to sign* was wrong. He said that anonymity of criticism was important, and that there would be more speech if I did not require people to sign.

Bob and I had a kind of open debate in the hallways. I argued that he was right in theory, and in practice, too, in the world as a whole, where you couldn't protect people who signed their names. There anonymity was necessary. But in a smaller place like the school, signing was not dangerous, because you could protect people. And allowing the "Wallsters" not to sign would actually chill speech. If something came up unsigned, people would often attribute that statement incorrectly to a particular group. They'd say, "Oh, these are the Federalists doing this," or "These are the Lefties," or "These are the Catholics." That would tend to keep people from joining that group. In a small society it was too easy to *assign* responsibility to a particular group without a real basis. This would tend to chill membership in less popular organizations and would hurt speech.

This aspect was actually quite controversial, in a funny way. Donald Kagan, a very conservative historian, met me on the street one day and said something the opposite of what conservatives would say later: "Who is this nut, Cover, who says that you should allow anonymous speech?" I remember telling him, "Listen, Don, he is taking a very powerful position. I think mine is the right position; but if he were Dean and I were not, I'm not sure if I wouldn't be taking his position and he wouldn't be taking mine!"

> *Jeffrey Rosen, YLS class of 1991, at the same time, was opposing me from the Left while Kagan was against me from the Right. He called my policy almost as bad as that in place at the schools that, out of political correctness, clamped down on what some deemed offensive speech. Rosen, who has had quite a remarkable career since, was wrong, I think, just as Kagan was. In the context of the time, what I had come up with turned out to be very conducive to free expression.*

It is true that the requirement of signing probably did have an effect on some extreme speech. It may have kept people from saying some things that would be *way* beyond First Amendment protections—although, as we shall see, not by much. People wouldn't write something too disgusting for words and sign it. And that did make life easier for me as dean; but that is not the point. Still, I was glad that Bob Cover made his point, for anonymity does have a great deal to be said for it.

Political Protest on the Wall (undated, early 1990s)

In fact, the Wall liberated people to say all sorts of things. So much so that occasionally it became a little difficult for me to defend my rule, though I never regretted it. What appeared on the Wall was sometimes truly offensive, yet that in itself demonstrated that people were not afraid to speak out. One of the great joys was that at a third-year class dinner, the class decided to call up and honor two people, one from the far Left, one from the far Right, who had been the most aggressive "Wallsters."

* * *

What should one do when people say or write things that are pretty awful?

Bob Cover, at the time that he died, was defending, before the Executive Committee of Yale College, a twerp who during GLAD Awareness Days—which is something that Gay-Lesbian activists organized—had put out folders called "BAD Awareness Days," "Bestiality Awareness Days." In these folders he made references to various students and professors who were gay, joking about bestiality and such things. It was toward the end of Giamatti's administration, and the kid was hauled up before the Executive Committee and put on probation—so that if he breathed, he'd be out.

Bob thought this was totally wrong. He thought that this kid's actions were disgusting, but were protected by free speech traditions, as well as by the *Woodward Committee Report* about free speech at Yale. He brought the case back to a new Executive Committee at the beginning of Benno Schmidt's administration, to try to get the probation lifted.

C. Vann Woodward was a great historian, who was asked to come up with a Report stating the university's position on freedom of expression at Yale—on speech that might be offensive and what people would be allowed and not allowed to do. It was written in the context of the Vietnam War and of an invitation to General Westmoreland, who had been shouted down. The Report was very libertarian, very sensible, very pro-speech; but written at a very abstract level! Harry Wellington and Eli Clark from the Law School were part of the group that helped Woodward write it. The theoretical set of principles in the Report pretty much allowed me to do whatever I wanted.

Bob Cover died while this was going on, and more out of respect for Bob than anything else, I took the case on. I got people who had been involved in the *Woodward Report*, like Harry Wellington, to affirm that what this guy had done, however disgusting, was protected.

We won. I was there when the Executive Committee dropped his probation. This kid was overjoyed. At that point, I turned to him and said, "Listen, you won, and you had a right to win because free speech is important; but what you did was detestable." I then lectured him! I said, "I'll defend your right to do all that; but if you do not realize that what you did was something which was hurtful to other people and *wrong*, then you are not going to grow up! You're not going to become a decent person!"

My lecturing him had happened quite un-self-consciously. I had defended him because I believed in free expression and because Bob was a friend for whom I felt I had to take on the matter. But I lectured the kid, letting him know my fierce view of his behavior. And doing it taught *me* something about *my* role: you can, if you are teaching, speak strongly for the position that you believe in, and turn any number of events into teaching moments.

> *Before I became Dean, while I was the head of the Board of Trustees at Hopkins School, somebody's jacket was taken from a kid's locker; and there was some strong suggestion that this was done because the kid was black. The Headmaster, John Wilkinson, who later became Giamatti's Secretary of the University, got the school together, to talk about it; he used the incident as a teaching experience. I'm not sure he was quite aware of how unusual that was in schools of that sort. I thought, "Isn't that interesting?" and I remembered, later, the way the Headmaster had turned a bad event into a teaching experience for kids in the school. In retrospect I think this was the beginning of my understanding of the importance of looking for teaching moments.*

There were plenty of other situations during my deanship that tested the limits I might put on free expression. Somebody wrote a letter to Black first-year students which implied that they were all rapists. I thought right from the beginning that this was likely to be somebody from outside the school, because some of the people who received letters, although they were not Black, looked Black in their pictures in the Facebook. And some who were Black, but whose pictures did not readily identify them as such, were not written to. This suggested to me that the letter was written by somebody who wasn't really part of the school.

I thought that the letter was a violation of libel laws. I was determined to find out who had written it. I had handwriting experts look at the letter, and after they checked it against writing samples of everyone at the school, the experts told me that nobody in our community had written it.

But I also said something about the incident that caused a huge stir: I described what the letter had said as "the sort of thing that Hitler said." It has often been said that "whenever you compare something to what Hitler did, you lose." Certainly, what I said upset some people. For example, some of the Jewish students said, "How can you describe this in terms of Hitler and the Holocaust?"

We had a school meeting about it. I explained that I was not comparing this to the Holocaust at all. I said that what was Hitler-like about this statement was that it cast slurs on a particular ethnic or racial group in a totally undifferentiated way. No matter what you did, no matter your history, you were linked to the speaker's hateful stereotype of that group. This was what made Hitler's racism different from so many other quite awful types of racism. To Hitler, if you were linked in some racial genetic group, then no matter what you did, you were scum! And that's what I was trying to emphasize. That Hitler's statements led to the Holocaust made the result incomparable to anything else. But the starting stereotype was the same kind.

What I said caused a stir at that moment. I did not really mind that it did. It created a teaching moment in which I could explain that there are differences even among awful racist statements.

* * *

The Film Society in Yale College had the right to use the Law School to show its films. During the exam period, to make a lot of money, the Society decided to show a porn film. The name of the film was *Wanda Whips Wall Street*. I did not and do not know what it was about, for of course, I did not watch it.

Various groups at the Law School, primarily women's groups, were very upset by this. I told them that under the University rules, this was permitted. The Film Society had reserved space and could show the film. I told the protesters that I would not stop the Film Society, but I would happily join a picket line attacking the showing. I invited them to *join me* when I would be picketing this film, which was advertised as "hard-core porn." I told them I would carry a sign that said, "Porn Peddlers are Scum." The protesters were surprised, pleased, and said they would join me.

As a judge I never call anybody scum, because ultimately what do I know? When you say, "porn peddlers," you're not talking about individuals; I was making a statement about a certain form of communication. I wasn't making a transcendental statement about the individual human beings who were doing this.

I was criticized by some faculty members for acting in this way—Peter Schuck, in particular, said that I was chilling speech. He thought I was wrong, as a dean, not to remain neutral. I answered him, "Yes, of course. I am chilling, in the way that anyone who speaks chills. That is what free speech is about! I have a right to speak; I know I am dean, but everyone knows that I am not going to use my deanship to punish anyone for their views. Being Dean doesn't cause me to lose the right to say how I feel! This is what the law of free expression is about."

* * *

A whole mass of undergraduates, mainly freshmen, came into the main corridor of the Law School on their way to watch *Wanda Whips Wall Street*. Some had been drinking. Some of them were wearing raincoats! A lot of nasty remarks were being made to me and the other protesters as people walked in, suggesting in rude terms that anybody who would oppose the movie was gay. It was a fairly rowdy crowd of youngsters in the middle of exams; here was a porn movie, and they were going to see it!

The movie was scheduled to start at eight o'clock. At this point the people who put on the movie were embarrassed, because they hadn't meant to do anything quite this controversial. They were just trying to raise money. So they came over to the protesters and asked if anyone wanted to say something before the movie began. The group that was with me on the picket line asked me to speak. Under the circumstances, I couldn't say no.

I walk into the auditorium, which is jammed. At five minutes of eight I go up to the stage.

There is a lot of noise. I shout in my most Dean's Marine Sergeant voice, "SHUT UP!" I tell them that I am going to talk to them for five minutes. I say that the movie is scheduled to go on at eight o'clock, and if they let me talk now, it will go on then, otherwise it will be delayed. They shut up!

I say, "Tonight you've decided to act *like animals*. You have *a right* to act like animals, under our rules, and so we're not stopping you." "But be aware," I say, "the reason we allow speech of any sort is not because it is not hurtful. Do not think that speech is harmless; do not think that it is cotton candy." "Speech can hurt; it can do harm; it can cause people to do bad things. Do not believe any of this stuff that speech is okay because it doesn't do anything. That's nonsense!" "That's not why we allow it."

I talk about Paolo and Francesca in Dante's *Inferno:* "They are reading a French novel before they go to bed with each other! [laughs], because the novel had the power to arouse them! "That's always been known!," I say. I add, "The notion that, oh, television doesn't really lead to violence—that's silly! *Of course* people are moved by speech!"

"The reason we allow it," I tell them, "is because it is so difficult to distinguish what should be permitted, that is, what is important or useful, from what is not. Drawing appropriate lines is *virtually impossible* and will always be used to stop ideas that ought not to be stopped. That is why we protect freedom of speech!"

"But the people who through speech do hurtful things"—and this is what was on my mind—"should be aware that they are hurting others." I looked at them and I said, "What you're looking at tonight is hurtful to any number of people. Really, *deeply* hurtful. If you do not think it hurts you, if you think that you're so tough that there's nothing in speech that can hurt you, then think about whether the speech will hurt somebody you love—a parent, a sibling. Think of speech that would really hurt them."

I repeated, "Think about what you are watching, and realize how speech here hurts people deeply; and understand that that is what you are doing tonight. That is why you are acting like animals: you're not caring that you hurt others."

I stopped. The place had fallen completely silent. And then, the house bursts into *huge* applause! Just huge, and these rowdy Yale freshmen are applauding as I leave!

Then the lights dim. *Wanda Whips Wall Street* begins. Of course, nobody *else* leaves!

> But I received many letters afterwards from kids who were there. They said, "You know, I'd never watched a movie of that sort. I come from Oshkosh or whatever, and I wanted to see what it's like. But you really taught me something."

I told this story to people. The people who had protested with me have also told the story to others, and so on. Another teaching moment.

* * *

Benno Schmidt told me, one day, that he was not going to stop the military service branches from recruiting in Yale College, in spite of the fact that the military barred gay persons from service, because he thought that they had a First Amendment right to do so.

I said, "I can understand that. But then what you must do is not just say that you think they're wrong. When they come to recruit, you should go on the picket line!" He said, "That's not my style."

I said to him, "Then you have a problem. While you're saying that they have a First Amendment right to recruit here, the kids who are being hurt by that First Amendment right are not going to feel that you're really willing to put yourself on the line for them. If you do picket, then the kids will recognize why you let the recruiters come and understand that the first amendment can hurt the recruiters as much as it hurts them. But if that's not your style, then the whole thing rings hollow."

* * *

I had the military recruiting situation in mind when some rather dramatic events occurred. First, some students invited a "Lieutenant" of Louis Farrakhan, the leader of the Nation of Islam, to speak.

> *At the time, I said, "He has a very high title in this organization, but I'm not sure if that title signifies more than the title of a "Vice President" of a bank would—in those days every loan officer was called "Vice President" —or an "Assistant Dean" at the Harvard Law School! [laughs] There were so many of them; you give those titles out!*

More important, he himself had made some very strong anti-Semitic statements.

Well, there was going to be picketing by the students opposed to his coming to the Law School, and the speech was going to get a huge amount of attention. I was more interested in teaching my students, than in dealing with the publicity. Once again, I decided to join the picket line. I did think the fact that I would be out there on the picket line would make the Law School's position evident. I said to reporters, "He has a right to speak. And anybody, including me, has a right to protest so long as they do not interfere with this person speaking."

> *Some people have said to me, "but did not you think that some important alumni might be offended by your picketing? My answer was that at one level I did not care, but at another level I was confident that graduates of the Law School, no*

matter their politics, if I explained to them why I was doing what I did, would understand. I became extremely close to graduates whose views were very different from mine, because I took their views seriously and asked them to do the same about mine. It always worked.

The Lieutenant came, and he had these goons next to him, very big bodyguards, dressed in suits—very elegant. One of them headed toward the balcony, where a little Asian American student was carrying a sign saying that this guy was trash, or something like that. I anticipated that confrontations like this might happen, and I had various people—staff members—placed around the hall. This goon was going to an area where Barbara Safriet, *a very strong* woman, who was a great associate dean, was patrolling.

The scene was marvelous: this great big, fierce looking fellow, approaching this little Asian American with his sign. Barbara goes up to the bodyguard and calmly says, "This is the Yale Law School. You are here because we believe in speech. *Get the hell away from this kid!*" The goon looks at her, and walks away, sheepishly. That became a kind of local legend!

Outside the building, in the meantime, I was on the picket line with a sign that said, "*Racism is Garbage, No Matter Who Spews It.*" *The New Haven Register* ran a big picture saying, "Yale Dean Pickets Own School." It was another teaching moment—an opportunity to say to the students, "We allow this for all the free speech reasons, but I'm going to put myself on the picket line to say how I feel and let people attack me for it."

After this, I began to be approached by any number of people to picket for all kinds of causes. That is the danger of speaking—you then almost automatically become in demand to speak more.

Some of the requests in themselves you can use as teaching moments, explaining that there are many things that are wrong in the world and that you feel you are wrong. But one must always remember that one is playing a role, and in each of your roles one can speak to some things but not to others. If you speak to all of them, if one speaks to all of them, one weakens the role one is in.

I told those who asked me to picket that I had resigned from the board of the Institute of Medicine when it passed a resolution against the Vietnam War. I had said, "Why are you doing this?" This was a group of people, mainly doctors but also with a couple of lawyers and economists, whose job was improving medical care. They said, "Oh, we're doing it because the Vietnam War is killing people, and medical care is about saving people." I said, "Yes, but that is not what your role here is! That is not what we should be talking about in particular, and if we start talking about this, what we have to say with respect to medical care gets diminished! I do not think there's anybody here who's more against the Vietnam War than I am, but I think we are not doing our job, and we are weakening our role. If you want to do it, then do it without me!"

In the cases of *Wanda Whips Wall Street* and the Farrakhan Lieutenant it was appropriate for me to act because the film and the speaker were dividing the Law School. I saved speaking up for those occasions. My reluctance to do it more than I did may have taught people that it is not worthwhile to demonstrate about *everything*; you cannot make a scene about *everything*, just as you cannot write a separate concurring or dissenting opinion about *everything*!

But you cannot let a concern about being excessive become an excuse for not speaking up when it's necessary or just appropriate. It must never become a reason not to speak in the very situations where it's most dangerous and potentially most embarrassing to do so, because those are likely to be the situations where no one else will.

* * *

Act Up was a gay rights group advocating for people to behave more responsibly with respect to AIDS. Some people from Act Up put up a *huge* erect phallus, a picture of a very large penis, on the Wall, and signed it.

I did not usually put things on the Wall myself, but this time I wrote a letter and I put it on the Wall. It said that I thought this was disgusting and self-indulgent. My letter immediately caused a big fuss. You know, "Why is Calabresi so excited about this?" A graduate student, a woman, said, ". . . he must be especially interested because it's a very attractive penis!" I do not know; I suppose it probably was! [Laughs]

I stood in front of the Wall and talked with a whole lot of people there, including the very able, interesting, thoughtful woman who was the leader of the group that had put the picture up. I kept asking them, in this afternoon-long discussion, "Why *do* you think I spoke about *this* one? What do you think it is about this case that has caused me to get involved in a way that I usually do not?" Some said, "Because the Federalists complained," and I said "Oh, give me a break!" [Laughs] "No, Federalists and the others did not complain! Or they said, "Because you're Catholic and the whole business of sex bothers the Church." I said, "Come on now, it doesn't bother me!"

I kept pushing them and then asked, "Why do you think I said you were self-indulgent?" I got them slowly to understand that this picture was so *big*, that anybody who worked in the Law School, in the Registrar's Office, any secretary, or anyone, could not avoid it!

The Wall, and the culture of the Wall, was expressly open to anybody in the school or who worked in the school, not just students. So it was perfectly possible for somebody such as a secretary in the Registrar's Office, who objected to something on the Wall, to write on the Wall how awful that picture was, or how much it bothered them. But how likely was it that a secretary or a cleaner would feel comfortable doing that?

I was willing to make the students a mandatory part of the Wall culture because becoming a lawyer means being able to deal with issues that you do not like and having to speak about them. The students may not like what is on the Wall, but I do not need to defend them. They can and should use their speech to defend themselves if they find something offensive. But that is not true of the people who work in the school.

It was the first time I got the sense that some employees were upset by something on the Wall. I realized that some people who worked in the Law School were disgusted by the picture of the phallus but did not feel that they could or should say something. The picture was so large that they could not help but see it! I thought it was my responsibility because I'm dean of the Law School to speak for them. I thought, "I'm the Dean of the Law School. I'm not Dean of Students. I'm not Dean of Faculty. I'm Dean of the whole place."

And so when the students asked me why I called them self-indulgent, I said to them, "By the very fact that you're a student here, whether you like it or not, you're in a different category from the people who work here, and you're saying to them, 'You have to live up to my standards, perhaps to my cultural progressivism, and argue with me if you don't like it.'" "That is the essence of self-indulgence." That of course just caused a stir because these were by and large left-leaning students, and the one thing they did not want to be told was that they were thoughtless radicals inconsiderate of the relatively poor people who worked here. I had hit them with something they *really* cared about. Not the penis, [laughs] but being upper class!

The woman who put up the penis poster *then* understood immediately. She said, "Oh, my God, you're right!" The group took the *large* penis down and put back a *very small* one!

Interestingly, the woman was a typical, good Yale Law School student. She approached me right after and said, "I'd like to have a session in Room 127 on ways of dealing with AIDS and what people should do. Will you join me in that?" I said, "Absolutely, I'll be there, and I'll be with you." Yet another teaching moment.

* * *

It is also important, however, often, to be friendly to the people you have criticized. In terms of teaching, it is crucial that the culture should be understood as respectful and civil. Peter Schuck is willing to say, "Your picketing is chilling." You must welcome Peter's perspective while then telling him, "You do not know what you're talking about!" He too is very much part of this whole wonderful Yale Law School experience, of culture, and even architecture which encourages everyone to argue with each other. It does not mean you should be nice when you allow Fascists to talk, but you should be careful about who you call Fascists.

* * *

Once, students were protesting and saying the school was doing something or other wrong—I do not remember what, but I think it had to do with the upcoming tenure votes of popular junior faculty.

I was standing there listening, and arguing with them, when who comes walking through the hallway but Benno, the president of the University. A good First Amendment lawyer himself, Benno sees his dean being attacked and jumps up, and starts to tell the students about how really wonderful the dean is! At that point, the students start to laugh and say, "Mr. President, get off there! We love Guido! We know exactly what we're doing, and he knows exactly what we are doing. We do not need *you* to tell us that he's okay! This is what it is all about!" Benno is surprised, but understands, and goes off happily.

* * *

So that's the story of the Wall. It was a real space then. Later, because of the Internet, it became a digital space. It was a wonderful way of teaching students about law, about being in a law school, about being lawyers, about taking responsibility for your views and being willing to speak out for them.

Whether real or virtual, the freedom to speak out and the taking of responsibility for your views remain essential to a great law school.

Public interest appeals and announcements on the physical Wall (undated, ca.1985)

COMMENTARY

Chapter 23

Teaching moments. Guido relished "teaching" or "teachable" moments, which, as discussed in pedagogical literature, occur when "a unique, high interest situation arises that lends itself to discussion of a particular topic."[1] Educator Robert Havighurst popularized the idea in the 1950s; John Wilkinson, the Hopkins Headmaster, may have encountered the idea through Havighurst or others who were developing the concept.[2]

Instrumentalizing a teachable moment involves timing and trust. As Havighurst explained, "It is important to keep in mind that unless the time is right, learning will not occur."[3] The other essential element is the generation of perceived trust:

> Psychologists emphasize the epistemic trust created in the learner when the learner sees her teacher understand the learner's mind. This trust facilitates learning: the teacher's understanding mind becomes an accessible source of information which the learner is willing to generalize.[4]

Capitalizing on a teachable moment requires the teacher to display calculated manifestations of perceived trust in combination with genuine empathy and love.

It cannot surprise the reader who has come this far to know that Guido used teachable moments instinctively. His management of the "penis on the wall" affair exemplified his ability to persuade people by stepping into their shoes and offering perceived choices rather than proscriptions. He objected to the penis on grounds the student would empathize with, instead of compelling her to embrace an opposite, unpalatable ideology. He changed her mind on her own terms.

The strike of clerical workers. The strike was discussed in an earlier chapter.[5] Professor Robert Ellickson, then one of Guido's deputy deans, describes Guido's deployment of his "teachable moments" approach in the context of the clerical workers' strike:

> Guido loved this. He just absolutely loved this! He thought these [campus conflicts] were pedagogical moments—that students had to think about what their values were, what appropriate conduct was. Whenever Guido had a chance—whenever there was disquiet—Guido would "pour a match on the gasoline" in order to get the educational moments. If you had a picket line and students didn't go to class, it

---

[1] FREDRIC B. LOZO, SEQUENTIAL PROBLEM SOLVING (2005).
[2] ROBERT J. HAVIGHURST, HUMAN DEVELOPMENT AND EDUCATION (1953).
[3] *Id.* at 7.
[4] *See* Gergely Csibra & Gyorgy Gergely, *Natural Pedagogy as Evolutionary Adaptation*, 366 PHIL. TRANS. R. SOC. B. 1149 (2011); Peter Fonagy & Elizabeth Allison, *The Role of Mentalizing and Epistemic Trust in the Therapeutic Relationship*, 51 PSYCHOTHERAPY 372 (2014).
[5] See Chapter 18, "To Be a Dean."

seemed to *me* to be pedagogically destructive ... but in Guido's spin, this was much more pedagogically informative. Perhaps.[6]

Ellickson believed that other alternatives would have been less incendiary—for example, debates in the auditorium between both sides. This did not occur, he thought, because Guido did not think that they would have "worked" to teach the larger lessons as effectively.[7]

As divisions about supporting the strike and instances of race bigotry occupied students, Professor Drew Days spoke to them in front of the Wall (undated, ca. 1984).

Free speech and pornography. An undergraduate Film Society scheduled a showing of *Wanda Whips Wall Street* as part of what wags dubbed the "Potter Stewart Festival," in honor of the famed Justice who "knew porn when he saw it."[8] Members of Yale Law Women, led by Jennifer Coberly and Maria Testa, organized a protest which included an antipornography film clip before the feature, the distribution of educational literature, and picketing. According to the *Yale Daily News*, the Society's Director, Bill Broderick, anticipated the protests and "was resolved to sit through the storm."[9]

---

[6] See text and commentary in Chapter 18, "To Be A Dean."
[7] Interview with Prof. Robert Ellickson, May 10, 2011.
[8] Jacobellis v. Ohio, 378 U.S. 184, 197 (1964) ("I know [pornography] when I see it, and the motion picture involved in this case is not that.").
[9] Andrew Fish, *Law Students to Protest Porn Film*, YALE DAILY NEWS, Sept. 22, 1987 (misidentifying the college Society as a Law School Society).

The audience was mainly undergraduates and the protesters were mainly law students holding signs, including "Porn is War on Women" and "Our Bodies Are Not 'Speech,'" along with Guido, whose sign indeed read "Porn Peddlers Are Scum."[10] Guido spoke impressively, distinguishing eroticism from pornography, recognizing it as speech but emphasizing that "Speech isn't cotton candy."[11] The *Yale Daily News* reported that "the audience of over 500 people responded to Calabresi's remarks with loud applause."[12] While Jennifer Coberly of Yale Law Women strongly believed he had not sufficiently distinguished pornography from protected free speech, others felt he had described the matter just right.[13] It was the kind of teachable moment Guido enjoyed—bringing to life sharp differences about the intrinsic harms of pornography and trying to mediate conflict with discourse.

Robert [Bob] Cover. Cover graduated from Columbia University Law School in 1968 and taught there from 1968 to 1971. He joined the Yale Law School faculty and soon found a place at the heart of the community.

His writings about legal history and jurisprudence were crucially affected by the free speech movement, the civil rights movement, and the anti-Vietnam war movement of his early adulthood. His writing explored jurisprudence and legal history in sophisticated ways that earned him respect from traditional progressive scholars, while it exposed flaws in contemporary legal process scholarship that established his place among the newer Realists and Critical Legal Scholars.[14] In his essay, "Violence and the Word," Cover characterized Law as a form of violence:

> Legal interpretation takes place in a field of pain and death.... A judge articulates her understanding of a text, and as a result, somebody loses his freedom, his property, his children, even his life.... When interpreters have finished their work, they frequently leave behind victims whose lives have been torn apart by these organized, social practices of violence. Neither legal interpretation nor the violence it occasions may be properly understood apart from one another.[15]

In *The Left, The Right and the First Amendment, 1918–1928*, for example, he identified conservative jurists with "the militant politics of the street."[16]

---

[10] Andrew Fish, *Students Criticize Porn Film Showing*, YALE DAILY NEWS, Sept. 29, 1987.
[11] *Id.*
[12] *Id.*
[13] Matthew Klein, *Porn Censors Beware—Someday You May Find Your Speech Stifled*, YALE DAILY NEWS, Oct. 1, 1987.
[14] ROBERT M. COVER, JUSTICE ACCUSED: ANTISLAVERY AND THE JUDICIAL PROCESS (1975); Cover, *The Supreme Court, 1982 Term—Foreword: Nomos and Narrative* 97 HARV. L. REV. 5 (1983); Cover, *The Origins of Judicial Activism in the Protection of Minorities*, 91 YALE L.J. 1287 (1982); Cover, *Violence and the Word*, 95 YALE L.J. 1601 (1986); Robert M. *Cover Dies; Legal Scholar at Yale*, N.Y. TIMES, Jul. 20, 1986.
[15] Cover, *Violence and the Word*, supra note 17; Cover, *The Left, the Right and the First Amendment: 1918–1928*, 40 MD. L. REV. 345 (1981).
[16] Cover, *The Left, the Right, and the First Amendment*, supra note 18, at 388.

Bob Cover died unexpectedly from a heart attack at the age of 46 in 1986.[17]

The penis on the wall, continued. Professor Peter Schuck had a particularly public disagreement with Guido over his problem with the depiction of the penis, which Guido describes. Peter notes that it happened "at a time when the campaign against AIDS had reached a fever pitch," and that it was one of Peter's students, Cathy Bowman, who put the poster up on the Wall, depicting "an erect penis, quite graphic, with veins and all that." Guido denounced it for the reasons he describes. Peter posted doggerel in which he "criticized his view, mockingly—but in good spirit."[18]

Professor Peter Schuck

He disagreed with Guido's position about the cowardice of anonymity, contending that he stood with Bob Cover in supporting "a role for anonymity, [because] not everybody is as courageous as you would like people to be in identifying themselves with certain points of view."[19] Professor Vicki Schultz, who taught discrimination law, advised Bowen that she also disagreed with Guido's position on a different ground, because she opposed the suppression of sexualized speech; but she did not press her position publicly at the time.[20]

---

[17] *Robert M. Cover Dies; Legal Scholar at Yale, supra* note 17.

[18] Interview with Prof. Peter Schuck, Nov. 29, 2010. During the interview, Professor Shuck shared his limerick, "Up Against the Wall," which read in part: "There once was a Yale dean named Guido/ Who often sent students a screed-o/Containing his thoughts, his 'ises' and 'oughts'—A Scholar's form of libido. One day while patrolling the hall/His gaze found Democracy Wall/ And what did he see? A stiff—oh, dear me—A thingamajig thick and tall/ ... So Lest the Dean be in doubt of what Cathy Bowman's about/ I'm sure she'd respect/ The penis erect/ If condem-ed—so Guido CHILL OUT."

[19] Interview with Peter Schuck, Nov. 29, 2010; Memo from Schuck to Guido Calabresi, Sept. 21, 1990 (reiterating position in favor of protecting anonymous speech in the context of the "Yale Students for Racism" letter).

[20] Interview with Prof. Vicki Schultz, June 4, 2013; *see generally* Vicki Schultz, *The Sanitized Workplace*, 112 YALE L.J. 2061 (2003).

Yale Daily News, Dec. 2, 1992.

Racist Acts. On September 18, 1990, Black law students received a letter signed by "Yale Students for Racism." It referred to "two black men" who assertedly assaulted a female student. The letter ended with "Now do you know why we call you N*****s?"[21]

The letter came two weeks after racial and anti-Semitic slurs were spread across several carrels in the undergraduate library, which compounded concern at the law school. Guido sent a memo to faculty, immediately, condemning the unattributed letter and reiterating his position on the importance of being willing to take responsibility for speech. He invited investigation by the New Haven Police and the F.B.I. About half the faculty honored a student moratorium the next day, "calling attention to intolerance."[22]

Tape on the wall. Guido, said Associate Dean Mike Thompson, was "a hands-on Dean, who listened and knew everything that was going on. He walked the floor every morning. He would look at the Wall; he would look at the posters and things that were up, and he would note something. You cannot use Scotch tape in this building for hanging posters, because it literally eats the stone walls, and one of the few rules here is that you cannot use Scotch tape on them, only masking tape. If Guido saw a poster that was up with Scotch tape, he would take it down. It would be sitting on my chair or on my desk when I got in."[23]

---

[21] *Yale Students to Protest Racist Acts on Campus*, N.Y. TIMES, Oct. 10, 1990.
[22] *Id.*
[23] Interview with Associate Dean Mike Thompson, Feb. 6, 2013.

Taped posters on the Wall, 1994

Reappointments and teachable moments. Guido framed continuing for a second term as dean as necessary to honor the moral commitments he made to four young faculty members he played a part in recruiting in 1984 and 1985: Akhil Amar, Paul Kahn, Harold Koh, and Kate Stith. He felt obligated to help them as only a dean could—and also to help Harlon Dalton, who had been appointed shortly before Guido became dean—to be promoted to tenure.

No "slaughter" on Guido's watch. Guido's sense of obligation grew as he came to believe that all five of them deserved promotion and realized that faculty sentiment did not run toward promoting them all. Furthermore, the damage done by the earlier "slaughter of the innocents" under Abe Goldstein was not lost on him.

Lateral tenured appointments had been made earlier, but internal promotions remained an issue. During Guido's first term, two potential candidates for tenure who had been hired during Wellington's deanship were rejected: after eight years at Yale, Perry Dane was voted down; Guido called on Lucinda Finley before the actual voting happened to let her know that the tenure process was likely not going to work in her favor. Dane went on to Rutgers Law School, remained a friend of Guido, and continued to work in constitutional theory; Finley went to the University of Buffalo. Their departures depressed several of the junior faculty.[24]

During the spring of 1989, many law students boycotted classes as part of a nationwide protest against lack of diversity on the faculty, and in particular to pressure the law school to grant tenure to Harlon Dalton and to make a permanent tenured offer to visiting professor Catherine MacKinnon.[25]

---

[24] Interview with Prof. Kate Stith, Apr. 4, 2011.
[25] Andrew Wilson, *Law Students Stage Boycott*, YALE DAILY NEWS, Apr. 7, 1989. When the faculty did not bring up a permanent offer with tenure, MacKinnon accepted a tenured professorship at the University of Michigan.

For the five internal candidates who came up, Guido played a critical role in determining how the reappointment process would work. All five would come up at the same time, seriatim; and the order in which they were to be considered would be drawn by lot to avoid any semblance of favoritism. Unlike the procedure when promotions were made during Rostow's deanship, in Guido's deanship each vote had been taken separately.

The fall of 1990 was a tense period around the law school, as "one by one, our heads were on the block, to be chopped or not to be chopped."[26] Rumors spread that some candidates were facing a distinct possibility of rejection, and students organized and lobbied for retention. To the chagrin and dismay of some faculty who opposed granting tenure to one or more of them, Guido seemed not to be interested in discouraging the lobbying. One faculty member offered that Guido's posture was "perhaps" consistent with his approach to "teachable moments," but observed that it was also consistent with getting all five of them tenured.[27]

Guido participated assertively. A colleague attributed his inspired argumentation to the "humanistic, warm, familiar quality to Guido, that didn't lead him to say no on promotions ... he has always been able to find some good in people, and the cases that he made for some of them were convincing." Because of Guido's persuasion, said one faculty member, "I probably voted for some who turned out to be very weak..."

The outcome was the one that Guido wanted—and by December, the faculty had voted to promote them all.[28]

---

[26] *Id.*

[27] Interview with Prof. Robert Ellickson, May 10, 2011; *see* LAURA KALMAN, YALE LAW SCHOOL AND THE SIXTIES: REVOLT AND REVERBERATIONS 338–41 (2014).

[28] KALMAN, *supra* note 31.

24

Clarence, Anita, Catharine, Jack—and Yale

Guido was in the start of his second term as dean when, in the summer of 1991, President George H.W. Bush nominated Clarence Thomas to replace Thurgood Marshall as a Justice of the Supreme Court. The choice of Thomas was immediately controversial, especially because Thomas, an African American 1974 graduate of Yale Law School, had, as chair of the Equal Employment Opportunity Commission, opposed affirmative action, racial quotas, and timetables for progress in achieving racial diversity. Thomas was also a Catholic who many liberals believed held anti-abortion views.

President Bush announced that his appointment was entirely based on merit, but news media widely reported that political calculation had motivated the choice of Thomas much more than estimations of his legal talent. Personal attacks had lowered the level of discourse during Robert Bork's nomination process and started to do the same after the Thomas nomination. Guido knew Clarence Thomas, viewed developments with concern, and accepted an invitation from Senator John Danforth to testify to Thomas's intellectual ability.

Along with everyone else, however, he did not anticipate that Anita Hill, YLS '80, would soon report that Thomas engaged in inappropriate conversations of a sexual nature with Anita while she worked for him. Anita had been one of Guido's students. As the drama unfolded, Guido responded to requests to react publicly in the moment. In this chapter, Guido considers in retrospect the conduct of those involved, the meaning of what happened, and his own role.

Clarence Thomas was not my student in law school—I did not even know him until his last year. That is when Jack Danforth, who had been my student and was Class of 1963, contacted me. In the more than fifty years I've been at the Yale Law School, Jack and Bill Clinton are among the very smartest students I have known who have gone into politics. Plenty are very, very good—Hillary Clinton, Gary Hart, and others, but Bill and Jack are at a level above. Totally different kinds of mind from each other, but topflight.

Jack has remained a close friend. He and I have been friends for a long time and he continues from time to time to seek my advice on things. He wrote the report on the government's siege of the Waco, Texas, compound, and before he put it out, he asked me to look at it and to go over it with him. He spent the night at our house. We have a continuing relationship that goes way back.

Jack became Attorney General of Missouri in 1968. A few years later, he told me that it was disgraceful that no one had been on the staff of the Attorney General of Missouri who was a person of color. He wanted to rectify that. He wanted to hire a person who was very able, because it was a job that required a great deal, and clearly it was important that whoever broke the color barrier in a state like that be somebody who was very smart. Did I know anybody?

I said I knew a person in the graduating class who I thought was immensely able, and who would be just terrific! His name was Rufus Cormier; he was from Southern Methodist University, had been an All-American football player, and was as smart as they come. He was very well put together and had been my student. I asked Rufus if he was interested. He said no.

Rufus was going to go back to Texas; he was going to become the first black partner in a major firm, and then he would do civil rights work. You know, he had his life all set up, and that's what he did!

He then said, "But I know somebody who is extremely smart and who doesn't have a job yet."

* * *

It was Clarence Thomas. This was the fall of the third year for Clarence, and he did not yet have a job. I do not know *exactly* why, but there were plenty of possible reasons. He walked around wearing dungarees, you know—not Levis, but bib-type dungarees, which in effect said, "I'm a farmer from Georgia!" He was also very far to the Radical Left. He was not playing by the conventions, in his quirky dressing and politics, in a way that would make you likely to get hired by your standard firm at the time.

Rufus told me Clarence was very smart and that I should meet him. So I did. We had a conversation about law and many other things.

I asked him who his favorite teacher was, and it was Tommy Emerson, 'Tommy the Commie,' whom he had had in the course in which Tom was planning all the strategy for privacy for bringing what would ultimately be Roe v. Wade. *Which is why when Clarence was asked, what did he think about* Roe v. Wade *in his hearing and he said, "I hadn't thought about those things," I laughed. That was as "inaccurate" as Abe Fortas or John Roberts, or anybody else in such hearings saying, "Oh, no, I have not thought about those things. I do not know anything about them."*

I saw that he *was* very smart and very strong, as well as very Left. He had no job. He said he was interested.

I called Jack Danforth and said, "There's somebody I can suggest." Jack was interested. I said, "I cannot say I know him well. He wasn't my student; but Rufus, whom I trust in judgment and in everything else, tells me that he is as 'smart as seeing,'" which was Rufus's way of indicating he was even smarter than Rufus. I added, "And judging by my conversation, he is indeed smart. He is also very Left." Jack, in his wonderful Missouri drawl, said, "I'm not worried about his politics. If he is smart enough, and if he wants to work for me, all that will work itself out."

I did not know then of his relationship with Quintin Johnstone. Clarence received one bad grade and it was from Quintin in Property I. He went to find out what he'd done wrong, and Quintin told him; Quintin could be very tough (Quintin gave me my worst class grade in law school). Clarence said, "Fine," and went back and took another course with Quintin. This was almost unheard of! So he goes back and takes another class with Quintin—who grades things, by the way, totally anonymously—and Clarence got an "Honors," which Quintin reserved for the best in the class. This was not his only excellent grade; he had a fine record.

It says something about Clarence. There's a tough-mindedness—maybe a self-destructiveness, some people would say—a willingness to go back into the lion's mouth. He wasn't going to let Quintin or anybody else hold him in low esteem if he could help it. They became and remained good friends despite their later ideological differences. When Quintin turned ninety, Clarence wrote him a lovely birthday message.

Clarence goes to work for Danforth, in Missouri, and moves more and more to the Right! I kind of lose track of him, except that every once in a while, his name comes up, and he seems to be more conservative than he was before.

* * *

Danforth helped him all the way through the rest of his career; Jack was responsible for his becoming head of the Equal Employment Opportunity Commission. I do not know the workings of the Republican system for placements. But Clarence continued in close touch with Jack, who very much became a father figure to him, and was his primary mentor and sponsor. Jack had let me know how pleased he was with this guy and with my sending Clarence to him.

In due course, Clarence gets nominated to the DC Circuit, and then he gets nominated to the Supreme Court!

Democrats had been offended by the treatment of people they had nominated who Republicans turned down in the past. Republicans were furious at the treatment given to Bork. It was a continuing game of tit-for-tat. Any number of people started attacking Clarence, and supposedly for being *stupid*, when obviously what they were attacking him for was that they thought he was much too conservative.

On the EEOC, especially, as he had moved more and more to the Right, he had taken positions against affirmative action and so on. Moreover, many liberals were offended by the fact that he was taking the place of Thurgood Marshall. After all, who *was* this guy to fill those shoes?

This drumbeat about his being dumb made me mad, just as it made Judge Gibbons mad. John Gibbons, a Third Circuit Judge, was quite liberal. He had known Clarence at Holy Cross. He had the same reaction, independently, as I did, and he also testified for Clarence.

* * *

Why did I testify? I was mad! It seemed to me that many liberals were playing the same kind of stereotype game that the conservatives do, especially with Black males to defeat them. Many conservatives stereotyped every Black male with references to people like Willie Horton, the convict who Michael Dukakis supposedly let out on a furlough to kill again—you know, the rapist, the hidden danger, and so on—and they used that stereotype to defeat them.

But to liberals, too often, the Black male conservative they want to beat is tagged as dumb. And that seemed to me horribly offensive, as well as wrong in the instant case, both because of what I knew of him and what Jack had said about him! And I certainly did not think that my position as dean or professor required me to shut up.

I must also admit that, perhaps, I thought Clarence had become more and more conservative out of opportunism. You can like that or not, but that is no different from what any number of people who have gotten on the Supreme Court had done to get there.

> *When I talk about opportunism, I remember an article that Lewis Powell wrote, an op-ed piece. When I'd read it—about being tough on crime—I laughed out loud because I said, "This guy's written it because it echoes the Nixon line, and there is a Southern seat on the Court he is aiming for." Later when they were looking for an Italian for that Court, I smiled and said to myself, had I written an article of that sort, I would have put myself in line. I did not, but lots of people have done similar things. Powell on the Court was very different from what the Powell who had written the article looked like.*

Clarence had been picked up by the Republicans—by Danforth. That made him toward the Center, then. Then the Republicans with Reagan had moved much to the Right, even of Danforth. It was not surprising that somebody who was ambitious and now in the Republican camp, would move in that direction. Such people later, if they do get on a court, sometimes rethink their positions. Who knows where they ultimately come out? I did not think there was any particular reason to assume that Clarence Thomas would inevitably be a far-Right figure on the Court.

His background and what he was like in law school undoubtedly influenced me in this, and I said as much in a letter. I wrote in the *New York Times*, saying, "Do not forget that people's background matters. Remember that this person came from an impoverished community in Georgia." I knew, too, that one of Clarence's closest friends in school, Eric Clay, had gone on to the Sixth Circuit where he is a powerful, quite Left, liberal judge. They remained friends.

What I missed in predicting where he would come out politically was his remarriage; that he had been married to an African-American woman from his own background, but he had broken up long before his appointment, and had married an extremely conservative white woman from the Middle West.

I thought that appointing Clarence Thomas might surprise the Republican administration that nominated him, just as the appointment of David Souter did.

* * *

My testimony was near the start of the hearings. Joe Biden was Chairman of the Committee. He put together a panel of witnesses trying to be even-handed. He balanced Erwin Griswold against Clarence Thomas, with me, in favor. It was mid-September 1991, many days before the Anita Hill revelation.

Anita talked with congressional staffers about Clarence a week before my testimony. But it was confidential, and I had no idea that this was in the wings. Besides, I wasn't testifying about his behavior at the EEOC. I was testifying about what I knew.

When I testified, I did not speak about his political positions or things of that sort. My aim was simply to say, "If you want to go after this guy because you do not like his views, okay, and then people can argue about that; but do not call him dumb."

Guido (with his back to the camera) answers questions from Senator Biden about Clarence Thomas, Sept. 18, 1991.

A couple of weeks later, the Anita Hill memo comes out into the open. When it does, Democrats and Republicans on the Committee are at each other's throat.

In the hearings, in his attacks, Jack Danforth behaved in a way different from how I have ever seen him act. Well, it was the *only* time I have ever seen him be vicious. It was very un-Danforth, and his wife still thinks he was wrong, and criticized him for it. But Jack was like a father whose child is being attacked. In terms of his family or of people he is supposed to look after, he can be really quite amazing in their defense! Still, I thought that he had overdone it.

Anita says in a memoir, "Rumor has it that Calabresi called Danforth during the hearing and tried to dissuade him from smearing me." I do not remember that, and think it is unlikely, because I remember being surprised at the viciousness of Jack's attack—it wasn't like Jack. It would have been unlikely for me to call ahead of time to tell him something I would not have expected him to do. It is quite possible that when Jack behaved that way, I said to various people, "Gee, he should not do that," and perhaps, I even called him because I really thought he had not behaved well. But I do not now remember doing that.

Jack and I have never really talked directly about his treatment of Anita.

* * *

As the hearings go on, it seems that almost everybody involved is a Yalie—a Yale Law School graduate! The people who testified: there was a crazy guy from the South who testified for Clarence who was a Yalie; there was the guy named Jim Brudney, who was accused of leaking the memo—a Yalie; there were the Senators: Jack Danforth, a Yalie; Arlen Spector, who was one of the most vicious, was a Yalie and a great law school friend of Jon Newman. And of course, there were the principals themselves: Anita Hill and Clarence Thomas. All of them Yalies!

Because there were all these Yale graduates, the press was then all over New Haven; and this was happening in the middle of Alumni Weekend, just before and during the time when the dean is busiest! On Alumni Weekend, I would give something like forty different speeches: every reunion class, every affinity group, and everything else! One thing that I did not have time to do, literally and physically, in the middle of all that, was to read what the precise accusations were, what was being said, and what the allegations really were. And so I hesitated to get involved in the conflict and to take a clear side without knowing everything there was to know. And I really did not have the time—but I've got to say, I did not mind, in one way, not having the time!

* * *

I knew and know Anita Hill well. She'd been my student, and I knew her in a way that I did not know Clarence. I liked, and still like, Anita. She is as trustworthy a person as there can be. My instinct was certainly not to disbelieve what she was saying, because I thought it was extraordinarily unlikely she would be lying. On the other hand, I was not ready to say where that fit in with Clarence. I was not going to take back what I'd said about his being smart. Anita's accusations did not make me think that he was less smart, which is what I had testified on.

I did ask my own Senator Lieberman, who was not only my representative but had been my student, to remember that my testimony for Clarence happened before the Anita Hill explosion. I was not in a position to say whom I believed without looking into it much more. I wrote, called, and left a message for Senator Lieberman to say that as to the recent accusation, I was not in a position to say anything without looking into it much more.

People have said of me that I wanted to have it both ways at the time, and there is some truth to that. I told the *New York Times* that I respected both of them and could conceive of a situation in which Clarence "thought he was doing nothing abusive, but Anita thought that what he did was terribly threatening." But right at the moment, I did not really know. The whole thing seemed puzzling. Too many things were odd, including Jack's behavior. I had to try to find an explanation that seemed reasonable in terms of my knowledge of the people.

*   *   *

What do I now think was going on? I will tell you.

Let's assume for the moment that the memo describing her encounters with Clarence never got leaked. In it, she described a series of conversations, events, vulgar remarks, and so on that she said he had made. Remember, when she wrote it, she did not want it to be leaked. It was a private memo to the Committee. People had convinced her that she should let the Committee know of her dealings with him, and in that memo, as I recall it, she did not make any allegations of physical harassment or that he was actually trying to have sex with her. Okay? So, assume that this confidential memo had not been leaked.

Assume that the Judiciary Committee had to ask a group of people to look into it and see what happened, *privatim*, and to give the Committee a report. Suppose they asked somebody like Jack Danforth on one side, and a Democrat from the Committee, somebody like Joe Biden on the other; and somebody like me as a third. What would Clarence Thomas and Anita Hill have said to us privately?

I think in that setting, Clarence might have said, "Yes, I talked dirty to her. Why? Well, she was from my background and from the Yale Law School, and that's the way we talked at the Yale Law School when I was there!"

> *I remember at the time when Clarence was at the Law School, I was going to my office near the balcony of the auditorium—the office that is right at the balcony, Paul Kahn's office now. I was working there, and there was some noise outside— late one evening, ten, eleven, something. I came out and there were a whole group of students, black, white, men, women, who were part of the group that Clarence hung around with. I do not remember if Clarence was there; I did not know Clarence as a student. It was before I had recommended him, so I probably would not have even noticed if he was there. But they were certainly his friends, and I can give you the names of people who were there, many of whom have become very distinguished lawyers. I said, "What's going on?" And they said, "We're showing a porn movie. Want to join us?" And I said, "No thanks," and went back to my office.*

Remember what the "sex for everybody" 1970s environment was like—for men, women, including Black women as well as Black men. Among many feminists at the time, women's liberation meant sexual liberation, including acceptance of what, to me, seemed very crude verbal and physical expression. But much of the Law School student body seemed to think that way and did not find vulgar sex talk to be out of bounds. So, I think Clarence would have said, "That's why we talked that way." And given his time in law school, that might even have been correct.

Anita, on the other hand, would have said, "That wasn't me, and that wasn't my Yale Law School." And she would have been completely correct, too.

They both would have been correct, because the difference between YLS 1972 and YLS 1980 was enormous! In between Clarence Thomas and Anita Hill's years at Yale, Catharine MacKinnon had come roaring through the Law School. Unless you know about her or were there, you can have no idea how she redefined feminism and changed the conversation about sexuality and sex relations.

It was like Girolamo Savonarola going through Florence. After Savonarola, Botticelli stopping painting nudes and starting to paint religious figures! People have no idea how a world changes!

In my hypothetical conversation, Anita would have said, "That wasn't me, and it wasn't my Yale Law School." And Clarence would have said, "Why did not you tell me to stop!?" And she would have said, "I tried, but you did not hear me!" You know, "I tried, but you did not hear me. And you were my boss. What can you do with your boss?"

He might then have said something like, "You must have hated me." And she would have said, "No, I really did not like what you were saying, but I did not hate you! In fact, in many ways I respected you! You had done amazing things. You had come from a poor background as I did, and you were here and doing a lot that I admired! I just did not like *that*!"

He might then have mused, "Oh, that's why when you got to Texas, you would write me to ask me for advice?" She would have said, "Sure," for this was completely consistent with disliking the crude language.

***

If that had been the conversation, it would not be too complicated for the Committee in my hypothetical to consider whether Clarence, as head of the EEOC, had done something which he should not have done, and therefore should not go on the Supreme Court.

It would have been of the same order as—but less important than—the questions of whether Douglas Ginsburg should have gone to the Court given that he smoked pot with his students. Remember that what Ginsburg did was illegal, and it didn't lead to the conclusion that he could not be on the DC Circuit. Like Ginsburg, Clarence was on the DC Circuit already; and whatever might have been the effect on his Supreme Court nomination, in the ethos of the time, no committee such as the one in my hypothetical would have said, "What happened means you have to get off of the Circuit Court."

In other words, the Committee might have said, "Mr. Thomas, you were offensive and insensitive, and that is enough to keep you from being confirmed for the Supreme Court. But even so, it would not have said, "You must resign from the Circuit." Alternatively, in the mood of that time, the Committee might have said, "Let's drop the whole thing and confirm him." In any event, the episode would have been reduced to a human scale: human beings reacting in ways which are regrettable, but understandable.

But of course, my hypothetical is fictional in every way. Anita's memo is leaked. It is now out all over the papers. "Black man behaves in a sexually predatory fashion." Remember, we now know that white men were behaving that way, and worse, all the time without serious repercussions. But a Black man? I think you can understand why Clarence Thomas described the events as a "high-tech lynching."

Fortunately, things now might be changing, and today people have been forced to resign for engaging in verbal harassment. But even now, to force a resignation, such allegations have been repeated and forcefully asserted by many complainants.

In his hearing, Clarence denies it entirely: "Nothing ever took place. Absolutely not." If my hypothetical is correct, did he convince himself that it was not so, or was he consciously misstating? I do not know.

Many people have lied to get onto the Supreme Court, surely, but most of those lies would not have injured another person. On the other hand, in that context, if you are in such a position, how much do you minimize that injury and focus instead on having done something which, at the time, might offend some people, but which, when it was done, was no big deal, *you* thought. A misstatement does not seem like such a big deal.

If you were to ask classmates of Anita whether Anita was capable of lying, they would all have said no. Anita had the reputation of being the straightest person

> *in the world. Was she fantasizing, as others suggested? One of her teachers said to me, "No, no, she's a very good student, but she doesn't have the far-out imagination that leads to fantasizing." The view of Anita among her contemporaries was, "No fantasies, quite able, and absolutely rock-straight."*

The moment Clarence denies that anything occurred, all the people who had urged Anita to write her confidential memo say to her, "You see? We told you that he was a scum bag, and he wasn't only doing those things because that was the way they talked back at Yale when he was there, and all of that; he *was* coming on to you; he was assaulting you sexually." At that point, it is not surprising that she believes them. She starts to fight back and says things, which by then she believes, recharacterizing what was motivating his talk. And the whole thing explodes.

I do not know whether what I have described is in fact what happened. It is a speculation, a guess, an opinion. Who can ever really know? But it is the best I can do given what I know of the people involved.

I have asked myself, of course, if my hypothetical is correct, what I would have done were I in Clarence's situation. I hope I would have the strength to tell the full story, to try to explain it, even though I knew it would lead me to going down in flames, even though I would be thrown out on the street. I hope I would have that strength.

> *I have this feeling that before you throw a stone, ask yourself what you would do in that same situation. I am, maybe, vain enough to think that I would behave right and go down in flames. That is a bit of vanity. I am not somebody who came from nothing and would go back to nothing. It's all very well to say, "Oh, I would be the martyr," but some people can afford to be martyrs!*

I say this because if my hypothetical is correct, what Clarence did was wrong. But before you judge him, you'd better be mighty sure about how *you* would behave in a situation like that. Would you tell the truth or not? Remember, if you denied everything, you might get to the Supreme Court and safety; while if you admitted it, you would likely be out in the street, without a penny, and with all the negative stereotypes attributed to you.

That is my take on it. I have no way of knowing if my hypothetical is an accurate one. I have not asked Justice Thomas. I have not asked Jack Danforth—I am not sure Jack would know. I have not asked, because I really do not know how I would ask.

* * *

My relationship with Anita remains wonderful. We rarely speak or see each other, but when we do, it is a very friendly thing. And Clarence will always take a call from me. He is always very friendly. When I asked him to speak to my college classmates, who were holding a mini-reunion in DC, he was happy to do it! When he swore in Jack Danforth as UN Ambassador, I went down. Clarence swore him in and I was there, and he was very friendly and warm. That said, he will never take a law clerk from me. It is a warm but complicated relationship.

Yet, Justice Thomas cannot deny that I was one of those who went out and backed him, and that I did it at very considerable cost. Any number of alums were furious at me for that; they thought that he was to the right of Goldwater. And the fact that he has turned out to be so conservative as a Justice has made them even angrier. "What the heck were you doing going and testifying for him?" The vote to confirm him was very close, and these people continue to think that I played a large part in getting him through. I think that is nonsense. My testimony was well before Anita's accusations became known. And by the time the vote was taken, I do not think my testimony mattered at all.

Some have said that I should have, at the last minute, taken my testimony back and attacked him. I was not prepared to do that. Many have suggested my sense of loyalty to Yale might have been the reason. Perhaps, but I doubt it. I am immensely loyal to Yale. But my loyalty is an institutional duty and not a raccoon coat or "Rah, rah!" loyalty. It is not "my country, right or wrong!" And remember, there were Yalies on every side of this fight!

* * *

If I had reached the conclusions then that I have reached now, would I have testified for him then? [Sighs] Suppose my testimony was scheduled at the *end* of the hearings instead of the beginning, would I have gone ahead and testified? Probably not. As much as I can understand his being driven to say what he did, from a human point of view, it did hurt another graduate, and as dean, I couldn't affirmatively support him. Would that have caused me to go and testify *against* him? Again, probably not.

If Anita's memo had remained secret, and I was on the hypothetical committee I described, and I came to the feeling that what had happened was as I described it, in the context of the time, I might have said, "That's really irrelevant to his going on the Court." I mean, there were plenty of reasons against his confirmation, and plenty for, but *given the ethos of the time*, I think I would have concluded that talking dirty was really not that relevant. It is interesting how much that ethos has changed, and for the better.

* * *

Toward the end of my deanship, I invited Anita to come back for a visit. I did this because I wanted it to be very clear that I thought her behavior was both courageous and above reproach; and that I could understand how once Clarence denied that anything had happened, she might come to believe the more

> disturbing version of what had gone on. I wanted her to know that she was an important part of the Yale Law School.
>
> And what do I think of Clarence now? Exploring his decisions is for another time, as is discussing the disconnect between his current, highly praised personal behavior and those opinions. I think his opinions reveal originality and notable intelligence. In other words, I still think he is very smart.

COMMENTARY

Chapter 24

Guido's testimony. Guido describes his objective in testifying on behalf of Clarence Thomas as having been to dispel the notion then circulating—which he believes was racially exploitative—that Clarence Thomas was not smart enough to serve on the Supreme Court. Guido characterizes his testimony as focused on Thomas's intellectual ability, rather than his political positions or his character.[1] Prior to his testimony, indeed, Guido published an op-ed in the *New York Times*, defining himself as a progressive liberal who had chosen to endorse "a decent human being who cares profoundly for his fellows," and who "does know the deep need of the poor and especially of poor blacks."[2]

Guarded praise. Reviewing the testimony, one can see why Thomas might have understood it as faint praise. Guido asserted that Thomas was likely the best nominee that the Democrats would see proposed to them in the current political moment. Guido was forthright in his defense of Thomas's intellect—and the message that Guido seemed to want Senator Biden and the Judiciary Committee to take away was that Clarence Thomas kept an open mind, was not on the unmovable "far right," and could be persuaded by rational argument to depart from his most controversial and extreme conservative stances. Guido repeatedly stated that he disagreed with Thomas's position about affirmative action and hoped that he would change his mind on this and other matters.

Guido conceded that the Bush administration was not making a good faith effort to nominate a moderate whom Democrats could accept as a centrist. He tried to convince the senators that since it was inevitable that the president would nominate someone extreme, they should prefer someone with a capacity for growth and change—a capacity that Guido attributed to Thomas.

Omission of his principal motivation. His testimony did not state or imply what the oral history indicates was his principal motivation for appearing: his concern

---

[1] A video recording of Guido's testimony on Sept. 18, 1991, is available at https://www.c-span.org/video/?21699-1/thomas-confirmation-hearing-day-6-part-3.

[2] Guido Calabresi, *What Clarence Thomas Knows*, N.Y. TIMES, July 28, 1991.

that Clarence Thomas was being treated unfairly; that his intelligence was being undermined by exploiting racial stereotypes. To the contrary, one commentator reported that Guido's remarks amounted to no more than a declaration that "a man of Judge Thomas's background, independence and skin color was likely to be better than any other candidate President Bush ... was likely to select."[3] When Guido finished his prepared remarks, Senator Biden declared that he prayed that Guido was right—that Thomas would, in fact, change his mind about many of his views.

The exposure of Anita Hill's harassment. Guido testified in support of Clarence Thomas on September 17, 1991. On October 6, the story broke that Anita Hill had filed an affidavit with the Senate Judiciary Committee, affirming that Clarence Thomas sexually harassed her when she worked for him at the Department of Education and then the EEOC. On October 11, she delivered public testimony.

Anita Hill's testimony. Ms. Hill declared that she declined to go out socially with Thomas when he invited her, explaining that she did not want to jeopardize her working relationship. Nevertheless, Thomas continued to ask her out and began "to use work situations to discuss sex." Some of his conversations were "vivid" in describing pornography that he watched, including films of women having sex with animals, group sex, and rape scenes. Ms. Hill made it known to Thomas that she had no interest in discussing these matters, but "her apparent disgust only urged him on."[4] When the harassment subsided temporarily, Ms. Hill, under the impression that Thomas's involvement with a new girlfriend signaled the end of this verbal abuse, felt that she would be able to continue to work for him when he moved to the EEOC. After some months there, however, he resumed the sexual harassment.[5] The stress of working for him became so disabling that she was hospitalized for stomach pains and resigned from her job at the EEOC. She took up a teaching post at Oral Roberts Law School in Oklahoma.[6]

Hesitation. Following the leaked affidavit, Guido stayed publicly silent for two days. On October 8, he published a short statement of opinion in the *Los Angeles Times* arguing that the Senate Judiciary Committee had no good choices left. "To go forward with the confirmation vote as scheduled seems to say that sexual harassment is a trivial matter," Guido wrote. "To delay the vote, however," he added, "inevitably plays into the hands of those who having willfully failed to investigate the data in timely fashion when it was put before them, now use it—without investigation—to besmirch Thomas."[7]

---

[3] Calabresi, *supra* note 2 David Margolick, *At the Bar; In a Confirmation Battle W with Yalies, The Law School's Dean is Caught in the Crossfire*, N.Y. TIMES, Oct. 11, 1991.

[4] ANITA HILL, SPEAKING TRUTH TO POWER 69 (1997).

[5] THE COMPLETE TRANSCRIPTS OF THE CLARENCE THOMAS—ANITA HILL HEARINGS OCT. 11, 12, 13, 1991 23–24 (1994).

[6] *Transcript of Nina Totenberg's NPR Report on Anita Hill's Charges of Sexual Harassment by Clarence Thomas*, JEWISH WOMEN'S ARCHIVE (Oct. 6, 1991), https://www.jwa.org/node/18888.

[7] Guido Calabresi, *Whatever the Next Step Is, The Scoundrels Win*, L.A. TIMES, Oct. 8, 1991.

The opinion statement was criticized as too late in coming to support Hill when it could have been most helpful, and saying too little when it appeared.[8] Guido replied that he had at first been occupied, when everything erupted, with events of Law School Reunion Weekend, and that he privately defended Ms. Hill "at the place where it really mattered," by telephoning Senator Jack Danforth and urging him to moderate his criticism of her.[9]

Anita Hill testifies, October, 1991.

The Anita Hill revelations changed everything, of course. A nomination which was surely going to succeed suddenly became doubtful. It actually might have been withdrawn under a threat of a Democratic filibuster given this new and sensational development.[10] In the end, the Committee sent the nomination to the Senate without a recommendation, and on October 15, the Senate approved the nomination by the narrowest margin in a century, 52–48.[11] Senator Lieberman, who Guido contacted personally after the Hill affidavit became public, changed his previously announced 'yes' vote to a 'no'.

---

[8] Margolick, *At the Bar*; N.Y. TIMES, Oct. 11, 1991.

[9] *Id.* Many years later, Guido could add no further details to the *New York Times* story; nor could Senator Danforth recall a specific conversation in which Guido counseled him about his treatment of Ms. Hill. Telephone Interview with Sen. John Danforth, June 19, 2013. Anita Hill refers to reports of the conversation in her autobiography, SPEAKING TRUTH TO POWER. HILL, *supra* note 4, at 264 ("Rumor has it that he called Danforth during the hearing and tried to dissuade him from smearing me."). In the roughly contemporaneous memoir, RESURRECTION: THE CONFIRMATION OF CLARENCE THOMAS (1994), Senator Danforth, while defending many of his actions, acknowledges having gone to extreme lengths to destroy Ms. Hill's credibility by searching high and low for evidence of "delusions" and "erotomania" and "fighting dirty in a fight with no rules." He also expresses remorse for some of his conduct. *Id* at 207.

[10] R. W. Apple, Jr., *The Thomas Confirmation; Senate Confirms Thomas, 52–48, Ending Week of Bitter Battle; 'Time For Healing,' Judge Says*, N.Y. TIMES, Oct. 16, 1991; Adam Clymer, *The Thomas Confirmation, Senate's Futile Search for Safe Ground*, N.Y. TIMES, Oct. 16, 1991.

[11] R.W. Apple, Jr., *The Thomas Confirmation*.

Clarence Thomas is sworn in by Justice Byron White as Virginia Thomas, Barbara Bush, and President George Herbert Walker Bush look on, October 18, 1991.

Did Guido make a difference? Guido thinks that his testimony, early in the hearings, did not matter at all in the end. He might well be wrong. Senator Biden emphasized that of all the testimony in favor of Clarence Thomas up to that time, he had found Guido's "by far" the most persuasive. A scholar who testified against Thomas noted that Guido's testimony "was pivotal because ... he was someone from the intellectual community standing behind a candidate whose qualifications were shaky."[12] If Guido had never testified—or if he had explicitly revoked his testimony after the allegations of Thomas's sexual harassment of Guido's former student came to light—events might have unfolded differently.[13]

Guido's theory of the case. In the contemporaneous *L.A. Times* op-ed, and also in response to *New York Times* reporter David Margolick, Guido in broad strokes sketched the theory he elaborates in this oral history—that both Anita Hill and Clarence Thomas could have been telling the truth, as each of them knew it. His hypothesis was that she had genuinely felt pressured and harassed, although he did not intend to harass, nor did he perceive that he was doing so—and that a group of reasonable "third party" objective observers could disagree as to who was right or to be believed. Faculty colleagues recalled reading this assertion at the time and concluding that, having placed himself in a very difficult position, Guido was trying to have it both ways.

In his own account of the Thomas nomination, Senator Jack Danforth recalls privately suggesting to Thomas that "the simplest explanation was that it was

---

[12] *Id.*

[13] Thomas Confirmation Hearing, Day 6, Part 3. Available at https://www.c-span.org/video/?21699-1/thomas-confirmation-hearing-day-6-part-3.

a question of mistaken intentions, but that just wasn't an explanation that was available."[14] In a later interview Danforth said, "That was what I kind of wanted it to be, because it was understandable. But she really totally denied that, and it could not have been."[15]

Guido's explanation provides a historical foundation for this "mistaken intentions" explanation that "could not have been." Guido says it "could not have been" because Clarence Thomas denied flatly and unequivocally that any of the events Hill described took place. Referring to the proceedings as a "high-tech lynching," Thomas claimed that Hill fabricated everything—and that none of her described conversations ever took place.[16] Senator Danforth indicated that Thomas might have been willing to go in a different direction, if only Anita Hill had been willing.[17] As a result of the missing "mistaken intentions" approach, Thomas and Hill appeared to have mutually exclusive points of view.

The decisions of the Senate Judiciary Committee, which Senator Biden chaired, also fostered the appearance of the necessity of believing that one or the other must be lying, and these appearances were "neither wholly accurate nor accidental."[18] Reporters Jill Abramson and Jane Mayer concluded that the Judiciary Committee failed to follow up leads on several other allegations.[19] If there had been additional witnesses, the "it never happened" position might have been untenable.[20]

Although the procession of events undermined Guido's sophisticated theory of miscommunication almost from the outset, it had the comfortable virtue of explaining Hill's version of events in terms other than by choosing between his deviance and her prudishness, or between his mendacity and her complicity in an attempted political assassination. And as a general matter of cultural history, his hypothesis reflects what was happening at Yale and harmonizes with broader changes.

Perspectives at Yale in the 1970s. There is disagreement about the wholesomeness of student culture and discourse about sex, at Yale and other male-dominated elite universities, and at their law schools. It is clear, though, that before the mid-1970s understandings about "sexual liberation: the meaning of sex discrimination, the nature of harassment, the implications of new forms of contraception, toleration for

---

[14] DANFORTH, *supra* note 9.
[15] Telephone Interview with Sen. John Danforth, *supra* note 9.
[16] Flashback: Clarence Thomas Responds to Anita Hill, *YouTube* (Oct. 11, 1991), https://www.youtube.com/watch?v=ZURHD5BU1o8.
[17] *Id.*; Other women who were willing to testify about being harassed by Thomas; one, Angela Wright, was willing to testify publicly; a transcript of a phone interview with her was released instead. JILL ABRAMSON & JANE MAYER, STRANGE JUSTICE: THE SELLING OF CLARENCE THOMAS 46 (1994).
[18] David A. Graham, *The Clarence Thomas Exception*, THE ATLANTIC, Dec. 20, 2017.
[19] ABRAMSON & MAYER, *supra* note 19, at 55.
[20] *Id.*

sexually charged language by men, and the acceptability of pornography were quite different than subsequently.[21]

Insensitivity to the objectification of women was institutional. When women were first being considered for admission to Yale's undergraduate college in 1969, for example, jokes about the relevance of their looks were popular and widely perceived to be innocuous.[22] Asked whether the looks of the women applicants were being considered as a factor in admissions, the undergraduate Dean of Admissions replied that physical attractiveness was not important except as it "contributes to the 'attractiveness' of the applicant as a whole."[23]

Nationally, and at Yale, liberal support for the First Amendment included condemning censorship of pornography and sexually charged words in politics, art, and literature, and between consenting adults as repressive reflections of conservative values.[24] Sex researchers William Masters and Virginia Johnson described sexualized conversation and pornography as normal and useful tools to foster attraction and arousal—their books became bestsellers.[25] Freudian psychoanalytic theory asserted that women could be liberated from "crippling repressions" by open discussions of sexual desire.[26]

Enter Thomas. Clarence Thomas started at the Law School in 1971, shortly after the Yale Law Women Association was founded in 1969.[27] He was among male students who joined women students who advocated for real changes in the status of women, as these were prioritized by the Association at that time. Students then were principally taking up issues connected to increasing the numbers of women and equalizing their treatment. They were insisting on the teaching of a class about women and the law, demanding that there should be more than the single woman faculty member, and pressing the Law School to "affirmative[ly] recruit" women students.[28]

---

[21] December 1978; A Timeline of Women at Yale, *Yale Daily News*, https://www.celebratewomen.yale.edu/history/timeline-women-yale. In 1971, for example, a committee of students and faculty distributed, university-wide, an unofficial, illustrated booklet, *Sex and the Yale Student*, which approached casual consensual sex as part of women's liberation. The booklet directed readers to campus groups concerned with sexual issues "including the women's liberation movement and a homosexual discussion group." *See* Joseph B. Treaster, *Unofficial Sex Booklet Draws Mixed Notices at Yale*, N.Y. TIMES, Sept. 17, 1970.

[22] *Id.*

[23] A Timeline of Women at Yale, *supra* note 21.

[24] *See, e.g.*, Pacifica Foundation v. FCC, 556 F.2d 9 (D.C. Cir. 1977), cert. granted 438 U.S. 726 (1978) (upholding power to regulate patently offensive words); Richard Halloran, *Federal Commission on Pornography Is Now Divided on the Easing of Legal Controls*, N.Y. TIMES, Sept. 6, 1970; Irving Kristol, *Pornography, Obscenity and the Case for Censorship*, N.Y. TIMES, March 28, 1971; Emanuel Goldman, *Defending Pornography on Its Merits*, HARV. CRIMSON, Jan. 22, 1974.

[25] WILLIAM MASTERS & VIRGINIA JOHNSON, HUMAN SEXUAL RESPONSE (1966); WILLIAM MASTERS & VIRGINIA JOHNSON, HUMAN SEXUAL INADEQUACY (1970); WILLIAM MASTERS & VIRGINIA JOHNSON, THE PLEASURE BOND (1974); *see also Sex and the Married Couple*, THE ATLANTIC, Dec. 1970. ("Masters and Johnson consider *Playboy* a good outlet for sex information. 'There are millions of men reading it, eighteen to twenty-eight years old, who parade as knowledgeable about sex but who have the same old misconceptions about mutual orgasms being a necessity and penis size being important,' says Gini Johnson. 'Men read the magazine predisposed to reading about sex, and we want them to have good information.'").

[26] SHULAMETH FIRESTONE, THE DIALECTIC OF SEX 41 (1970).

[27] Laura Kalman, YALE LAW SCHOOL AND THE SIXTIES: REVOLT AND REVERBERATIONS 195 (2005).

[28] *Id.* at 196–98.

Clarence Thomas, Yale Law School Facebook photo

Yale Law Women also called out incivility and disrespect in class and outside. They spoke to the sexual politics of the Law School, describing the conduct of some faculty as "a blatant overstatement of the transfer of sexual desires into the drive for power," which led professors to either ignore women students or to "pick[] them off," as if the professors were "on the prowl."[29] Pornography and conversational sexual vulgarity, however, were not perceived as problems feminists or others at Yale at that time were sufficiently concerned about to try to moderate or eradicate from the Law School's culture.

Nonetheless, several portraits of Thomas report that his preoccupations reached and exceeded the bounds of the day.[30] "By the time he reached Yale Law School," Jane Mayer and Jill Abramson state, "Thomas was known not only for the extreme crudity of his sexual banter, but also for avidly watching pornographic films and reading pornographic magazines, which he would describe to friends in lurid detail ... [and that] his detailed descriptions of the movies and magazines he had seen were an open form of socializing during these years that seemed funny to some, offensive to others, and odd to many."[31]

Departures and arrivals. Thomas graduated from Yale in 1974, the same year that Catharine MacKinnon began to pursue graduate studies in political science at Yale. She enrolled in the Master of Studies in Law program at the Law School, too, and while she was there, she began developing a legal argument that would let women sue for sexual harassment.[32] MacKinnon eventually entered the J.D. program and graduated in 1977.[33] During her time at Yale, she made revolutionary contributions

---

[29] *Id.* at 199.
[30] *Id.*
[31] ABRAMSON & MEYER, *supra* note 19, at 59; *see also* KEVIN MERIDA & MICHAEL FLETCHER, SUPREME DISCOMFORT: THE DIVIDED SOUL OF CLARENCE THOMAS 129 (2007).
[32] Debora Dinner, *A Firebrand Flickers*, LEGAL AFFAIRS, Mar.-Apr. 2006.
[33] OWEN FISS, PILLARS OF JUSTICE: LAWYERS AND THE LIBERAL TRADITION 119–20 (2017).

to feminism—especially by connecting sexual harassment to discrimination, and pornography to gender oppression.³⁴

The characterization of pornography as anti-feminist. Guido omits mentioning feminists beside Catharine MacKinnon, but he is correct that the outpouring of popular and academic secular literature condemning pornography and the rhetoric of "sexual liberation" as anti-feminist, dates after 1973.³⁵

Anita Hill, Yale Law School Facebook photo

Anita Hill enters. Ms. Hill entered the Law School in 1977. By that time, the fissure between anti-pornography feminists and free speech/sexual freedom proponents had surfaced in many places, including Yale. One manifestation surfaced in December 1978 when a *Yale Daily News* editorial board rejected a *Playboy Magazine* advertisement, which solicited women to a casting call

---

³⁴ Guido compares Catharine MacKinnon to Girolamo Savonarola, the Renaissance Dominican Friar who briefly enraptured the city of Florence with his "gospel of republican liberty, civic empire, and universal Christian renewal," destroying priceless 'secular' art in the politico-religious whirlwind he created, before being publicly hanged and burned to death in the spring of 1498. *See* DONALD WEINSTEIN, SAVONAROLA: THE RISE AND FALL OF A RENAISSANCE PROPHET, 1–2 (2011).

³⁵ Catharine MacKinnon provided, as of 1984, an "illustrative, not exhaustive" list of the body of work that she termed the "feminist critique of pornography." Her list did not include any work published before 1973: George Steiner, *Night Words, in* THE CASE AGAINST PORNOGRAPHY 227 (Holbrook ed. 1973); SUSAN BROWNMILLER, AGAINST OUR WILL: MEN, WOMEN AND RAPE 394 (1975); ROBIN MORGAN, GOING TOO FAR: THE PERSONAL CHRONICLE OF A FEMINIST (1977); KATHLEEN BARRY, FEMALE SEXUAL SLAVERY (1979); ANDREA DWORKIN, PORNOGRAPHY: MEN POSSESSING WOMEN (1981); RUTH LINDEN ET. AL., AGAINST SADOMASOCHISM: A RADICAL FEMINIST ANALYSIS (1982); Robin Dorchen Leidholdt, *Where Pornography Meets Fascism*, WIN 18 (1983); *see* MacKinnon, *Not a Moral Issue*, 2 YALE L.& POL. REV. 321, 324 n. 10 (1984); *see also* Ellen Willis, *Hard to Swallow*, N.Y. REV. OF BOOKS, Jan 25, 1973 (reviewing the widely viewed and financially successful, and to a considerable extent, socially acceptable pornographic movie *Deep Throat*, concluding that "today's porn is based on the conceit that taboos are outdated, that the sexual revolution has made us free and innocent—a fiction that can be maintained, even for the time span of a movie, only at the cost of an aggressive assault on all feeling."). By 1979, feminism and anti-pornography, including the use of pornographic vocabularies, had been fused; *see, e.g.,* Barbara Basler, *5,000 Join Feminist Group's Rally in Times Sq. Against Pornography*, N.Y. TIMES, Oct. 21, 1979.

for the magazine's "Girls of the Ivy League" issue. Two days later, the business board of the newspaper decided to run the ad on principles of free speech. Then, the editorial board responded with an editorial that discouraged woman from modeling for the magazine and encouraged a boycott of the Ivy League Issue.[36]

At the same time, MacKinnon was elevating the discussion of feminism at the University through her writing, popular lectures, and litigation. While Hill was a law student, MacKinnon was helping students in the College to bring *Alexander v. Yale*, the groundbreaking lawsuit establishing that sexual harassment was a form of sex discrimination, and therefore prohibited by Title IX.[37] The case was decided in 1980, the same year that Anita Hill graduated. Four years later, MacKinnon, in law review scholarship, described the rhetoric of "de-repression" and "sexual liberation" as anti-feminist from the perspective of the feminist community as a whole.[38]

Do you believe Anita Hill now? In recent years, and especially subsequent to the "Me Too" movement of 2017–2018, conversations around and about sexual violence and harassment in the workplace reached ever-greater public attention. Prominent men in a variety of industries and professions—from Harvey Weinstein to Judge Alex Kozinski—departed or were removed from positions of power, and some faced punishment by law for their unacceptable behavior. Justice Brett Kavanaugh survived accusations of sexual assault on Christine Blasey Ford thirty-six years prior which were made in the course of the hearings on his nomination. In 2018, he was confirmed, 50-48.

Revisiting Anita Hill. In the wake of this grassroots movement of, and on behalf of, victims of sexual abuse, Anita Hill returned to the public eye. In 2017, she was selected to lead the Commission on Sexual Harassment and Advancing Equality in the Workplace to address sexual harassment in the entertainment industry.[39] Her personal story gained renewed attention as well, including in work by journalist and advocate Jill Abramson.[40] Abramson urged the impeachment of Justice Clarence Thomas based on what she said was evidence of his harassment of Anita

---

[36] Basler, supra.

[37] 631 F.2d 178 (1980); Diane Henry, *Yale Faculty Members Charged with Sexual Harassment in Suit*, N.Y. TIMES, Aug. 22, 1977.

[38] Catharine A. MacKinnon, *Not a Moral Issue*, 2 YALE L. & POL. REV. 321, 327 (1984). ("In this analysis, the liberal defense of pornography as human sexual liberation, as de-repression—whether by feminists, lawyers, or 'neoFreudians'—is a defense not only of force and sexual terrorism, but of the subordination of women. Sexual liberation in the liberal sense frees male sexual aggression in the feminist sense."). A decade later, however, a survey at Yale found that 79% of women and 88% of men believed that pornography should be protected; 65% of women and 28% of men agreed that pornography "made them uncomfortable." Jennifer Vanderbes, Pornography debate raises free speech issue, *Yale Daily News*, Weekend Section, Mar. 24, 1995.

[39] Ellen McCarthy, *Anita Hill Chosen to Lead Hollywood Sexual Harassment Commission*, THE WASH. POST, Dec. 16, 2017.

[40] Jill Abramson is the co-author, along with Jane Meyer, of STRANGE JUSTICE: THE SELLING OF CLARENCE THOMAS, documenting the campaign of misinformation that the Bush administration conducted in the wake of the Hill revelations to ensure that Thomas would be confirmed.

Hill and others, and of lies he allegedly told about this harassment to win appointment to the Supreme Court.[41]

Anita on Guido. In connection with Guido's reflections here, Professor Hill—in lieu of a lengthier response—said that she has thought of him, since law school, as "a supportive and genuine person [who] has contributed greatly to my intellectual growth and understanding the law."[42]

The judicial legacy of Justice Clarence Thomas. As a Justice, Thomas remained a riddle. Supporters considered him very able—Professor Akhil Amar concluded that if the success of a Justice is measured by new ideas launched into the constitutional conversation that eventually prevail, "well, then Thomas is way high in the pecking order."[43] Those who worked at the Court described him as decent a person as could be with everyone working there and others in need.[44] And yet, in no way did he make the sort of shift in views that Guido had hoped for and believed was possible. His positions were as out-of-step with progressive jurisprudence as his detractors had forecast.

* * *

Larger Perspectives about Guido's deanship. One colleague referred to Dean Calabresi as a "super-enzyme," who jet-propelled a school which was "going where it was going." Harold Koh, Yale's dean between 2004 and 2009, believed that Guido's accomplishment was more impressive: Guido, was "without question the greatest dean in the history of the law school," and "only someone who's been a dean can say that with so much confidence." Without Guido's talent as a dean, Koh asserted, "we would probably be the 20th best law school in America today, if we were lucky . . . I mean, Steve Jobs—just think of Jobs and other people who are thought to have been, sort of, turnaround artists. They've got nothing on Guido."[45]

Reorientation of scholarship throughout the legal academy. Guido's decanal success can be understood not only in terms of his internal accomplishments, but as an exporter of the cosmopolitan, interdisciplinary approach to scholarship which he himself pursued as a scholar and promoted in many ways while he was dean. "The fact of the matter is that if we look at number twenty-five in law schools today, compared to number twenty-five when Guido Calabresi was beginning his Deanship," said Professor Bruce Ackerman, "the twenty-fifth in the country was a provincial place, responding to the perceived imperatives of Minnesota law or

---

[41] Jill Abramson, *Do You Believe Her Now: The Case for Impeaching Clarence Thomas*, N.Y. MAG., Feb. 18, 2018; Julia Jacobs, *Anita Hill's Testimony and Other Key Moments From the Clarence Thomas Hearings*, N.Y. TIMES, Sept. 20, 2018.

[42] Prof. Anita Hill to Norman I. Silber, by email, Sept. 16, 2020 (on file).

[43] Nina Totenberg, *Clarence Thomas: From "Black Panther Type" to Supreme Court's Conservative Beacon*, NPR (July 14, 2019), https://www.npr.org/2019/07/14/740027295/clarence-thomas-from-black-panther-type-to-supreme-court-s-most-conservative-mem.

[44] Michael O'Donnell, *Deconstructing Clarence Thomas*, THE ATLANTIC, Sept. 2019.

[45] Interview with Prof. Harold Koh, Aug. 26, 2013.

Missouri law or wherever." Today, Ackerman argues, Yale is part of—indeed is in the leadership of—a nationwide intellectual community that Guido Calabresi was instrumental in building. "He's this sort of Christopher Columbus Langdell figure, really, in this interdisciplinary revolution in legal thinking."[46]

Yale personified in Guido. Over the course of his deanship Guido became the personification of the Yale Law School. "It's a real phenomenon," said Tony Kronman. "What explains it is very complicated."

One factor was his "omnipresence." Guido was "out and about, and everywhere, and he was up and down the halls, and into faculty offices, and he was constantly on the road, meeting with alumni." He was "physically there, to a degree that no dean in the history of the Law School ever had been."[47]

Another factor, alluded to earlier in a different context, was Guido's ability to express his view of the ethos of the school, continually, with a very simple mantra about "excellence and humanity." It corresponded to a mission statement. As a subsequent dean explained, it fit easily into historic standards:

The phrase brilliantly communicated ... the Realist history of the place ... We're not going to be stymied by blinkers, by established ways of studying the law. We're going to throw all of that aside, and with a kind of breathtaking audacity, chart an entirely new course for the sake of the truth—the truth for its own sake."[48] Guido made this case "not in a way that a lawyer makes an argument, but by embodying, in his behavior and personality, these two strands, so that he came to seem to be excellence and decency himself, joined in a single living human being."[49]

Because he conveyed all of that with such energy, and so omnipresently, he personified the school—a fact that the faculty largely admired. As Dean Kronman reflected, "maybe it's not so surprising that his identity and that of the institution came to be fused to a degree that had never been true before ... [he became] part of the lore of the school, and part of its personality."[50]

Deanship as a calling. Professor Robert Ellickson placed Guido's devotion to Yale in religious terms. "I remember telling people that Guido is a religious man. I think that he had the view that higher powers had ordained that the Yale Law School would be the great law school in the United States, and the world, and he conveyed it. When I give my talk on New Haven at 1L orientation, which I do most years, I say, 'I should tell you at the outset that it is not my view that New Haven is the center of the universe. That's a view I associate with one of your Torts teachers!' "[51]

---

[46] Interview with Prof. Bruce Ackerman, May 3, 2011.
[47] Interview with Prof. Anthony Kronman, Feb. 4, 2013.
[48] *Id.*
[49] *Id.*
[50] *Id.*
[51] Interview with Prof. Robert Ellickson, May 10, 2011.

Comparisons to John Sexton. The roughly contemporaneous accomplishments of the dean of N.Y.U. Law School between 1988 and 2002 invite comparisons. Guido observed, in a tribute to John Sexton in 2004, that Sexton, too played a part in the reorientation of the legal Academy toward cosmopolitanism during this period, and that he was "a master builder, a wonderful scholar, and a true friend."[52]

An N.Y.U. faculty colleague described Sexton in terms applicable to Guido as well—"loyal and generous, counseling colleagues and doing them favors," and "good at placating different factions of faculty..."[53] Like Guido, Sexton was praised for the fresh sense of intellectual vitality and excitement he had brought with him, for attracting some of the finest faculty anywhere, and for catapulting NYU Law School into the ranks of elite law schools.

Sexton's success, however, differed in its origins and outcomes. The sale in 1977 of the Mueller Pasta Co., which had been donated to the Law School decades earlier, along with Sexton's cultivation of a small group of wealthy donors, allowed him a platform of wealth to use to increase student scholarships, to innovate in JD and graduate programs, and expand fundraising and public relations. He spent lavishly on conferences, programs, and publications to rebrand the school. He leveraged the school's Manhattan location to lure faculty away from other institutions:

He [invited] some of the best legal scholars in the country ... to move into eight spacious dorm rooms ... for free. [He] began recruiting permanent faculty from this elite group ... professors who [he decided] could have taught anywhere in the country. N.Y.U. gave some of them personal loans every year, on top of their salaries [and] if they stayed for a decade or more, the loans would be forgiven.

Sexton also created what he called the "first Global Law School," a group of scholars visiting from other countries.[54] The sums spent on advertising NYU's accomplishments were extraordinary by the standards of the day—millions of dollars, cumulatively—on expensive glossy reports and magazines. Admirers called it sophisticated marketing, but critics branded the tactic as "Sextonism" or "law porn."[55]

Like Guido willing to take risks, Sexton succeeded in his quest to move his school up where other deans with comparable resources were less successful. During the Sexton deanship, N.Y.U Law School moved from ninth place in the *U.S. News* Rankings in 1988, to fifth by 2002, the year Sexton became New York University's president. Perhaps unsurprisingly he thereafter argued the case for strong centralized administration and law school "subsidiarity" and against independence.[56]

---

[52] Calabresi, *Tribute to John Sexton*, 60 NYU ANN. SURV. AM. L. 2 (2004).
[53] *Id.*
[54] Rachel Aviv, *The Imperial Presidency. John Sexton has a vision for N.Y.U.'s future. His faculty aren't buying it*, NEW YORKER, Sept. 2, 2013.
[55] Stephen Bainbridge, Law Porn Morphs into Law Spam, ProfessorBainbridge.com, Nov. 14, 2011. https://www.professorbainbridge.com/professorbainbridgecom/2011/11/law-porn-morphs-into-law-spam.html; Brian Leiter, *Sextonism Watch*, BRIAN LEITER'S LAW SCHOOL REPORTS, Aug. 5, 2005.
[56] *See* John Sexton, *Subsidiarity and Federalism: The Relationship Between Law Schools and Their Universities*, 87 FORDHAM L. REV. 911 (2018)(including a colloquy with Guido).

Guido began with a school that had almost nowhere to go but down; his challenge and his success was accordingly different. Guido got the legal academic community—colleagues, faculty at peer institutions, the media (including, especially, *U.S. News*), and a large number of law school applicants, to conclude that this school, which always had been outstanding, had reinvented itself—that it had become an even better and more exciting place.[57]

---

[57] Compare Ellen Simon, *How Outgoing Dean of Yale Law School Coaxes Millions of Dollars Out of its Alumni*, CONN. L. TRIB., May 24, 1994 ("... the school has been on a real high [in recent years] because of the obvious quality of the school itself and the success of so many of its graduates.") with David Margolick (1985), David Margolick, *"Citizen of Yale" Is Named New Dean of the Law School*, N.Y. TIMES, Jan, 31, 1985 ("Many say they believe that although Yale continues to attract the best law students in the country, its faculty has been weakened [during Wellington's second term]....").

PART FOUR

SITTING ON THE SECOND CIRCUIT

The path from an elite academic teaching position to the federal judiciary is well-travelled. Guido was sixty-one years of age when in 1993 the Clinton White House raised the possibility of a federal Court of Appeals judgeship. Deciding to pursue it, but without leaving teaching behind entirely, he became an appellate court judge in the following year.

This chapters in this Part explore ways Guido's life experiences and academic background color the fabric of his jurisprudence. His narrative illuminates, for example, his approach to torts law and ways his opinions emerge in part from a life spent teaching and writing about torts; ways his immigration decisions are connected to his immigrant experience; ways in which his complicated religious heritage and his escape from fascism inform his views of first amendment religious and expression; and so on. As well, the narrative tells a story about interpersonal dynamics on multi-judge tribunals and the challenges judges face when they disagree.

25

Bill Wants Him

> *During the 1992 presidential campaign, Bill Clinton promised to reshape the character of the Federal courts and reverse the shift to the conservative Right that had been orchestrated during the Reagan and Bush administrations. During his first several years as president, Clinton had that chance—The* New York Times *reported that he chose more judges than any president before him, and that almost 60 percent were women or from minority groups, a much higher proportion than predecessors.*
>
> *The ideological composition of the bench did not move very far from where it had been, however. In part this happened because most of the judgeships that opened were to replace liberal judges; and in part, news accounts suggested, because Clinton had been "burned" by failed nominations of younger and more radical appointments for Department of Justice spots during his first few days in office. A Clinton White House deputy counsel told reporters that "All that a young academic brings is ideology untested by experience." The president's White House counsel recalled in his own oral history that when he wanted to appoint ideal judges, he "was looking for people who were 55 years old and over ... people who had lived, people with broad experience; [and] the President was of like mind. I wanted to appoint at least some liberals. He wanted moderates. We were not ideological—almost to a fault."*

I was in my eighth year as dean and going to finish my deanship, when I got a call from someone in the White House saying, "There's going to be a vacancy on the Second Circuit. If you want it, Guido, you should start lining up senators and build up support." I said, "Thank you very much, but I like to finish what I am doing. I've got two years still, as Dean. That's what I'm going to do."

Earlier that year—shortly after the 1992 presidential election—I was called down to Washington by Bernard Nussbaum, Bill Clinton's first White House Counsel, to give the Clinton administration my advice about the Solicitor Generalship. I suggested Drew Days, who I said was a person of wisdom.

> *I think I knew that they were also looking at me when they asked for my advice, but there were obvious reasons not to hire me for the position of SG. One was that I had never set foot in a courtroom; another was that I had written a letter to the* New York Times *which began "I despise the Supreme Court," [laughs] or something of that sort. Shortly after my visit, the* Washington Post *published something saying, "Guido Calabresi is being considered for Solicitor*

General, but this is absurd because he has said he despised the Court, and he has never been in a courtroom." Or somebody quoting some unknown person who probably wanted the job, saying it was absurd. In any event, I think when I suggested Drew, they said, "Oh gee. That's an interesting idea," and they went with him.

I heard that there was some discussion that I might be the Attorney General. Bill Clinton went through one woman, after another woman, trying to fill that position, but none of them turned out right.

He wanted Pat Wald, but she said no. He then went after Paul Gerwitz's wife, Zoe Baird, and that exploded because of her hiring of an undocumented worker; then he went after Kimba Wood, and that exploded, too.

I was told by a friend of Joe Biden's that at that point Biden went up to Bill and said, "Bill, you've got to stop this. I know you want a woman, but it just is not going to work. And the only way out of it is to name somebody outside of politics. Somebody like Gerald Ford's naming of Ed Levy." I was told that Bill said, "I know. I agree, and I'm going to name Guido. What do you think?" And Biden said, "Terrific." But he met Janet Reno and he liked her.

Given everything that Clinton's AGs had to deal with, including the Waco Siege and the various Clinton scandals and impeachment, I guess I'm darn lucky not to have gotten it. It's not a job I would have liked. I've often mused about what might have happened in judiciary policy, in the Department of Justice if I had been there.

* * *

The White House staffer who first told me about the opening on the Second Circuit called back, a month or two later, and he said, "Well, Guido, if you're interested in ever being a judge you'd better act on it now, because there won't be another Connecticut vacancy for six to eight years." (That turned out to be wrong, because people die, and there were other ways to name people from Connecticut.) I assumed that was right, and I said jokingly, "And you think I'll be too old." They said, "No. No. No." But you know: "Yes." "Yes." I said, "Look, I told you. I like to finish what I'm doing."

I had no idea if I wanted to be a judge. Certainly not a Federal Court of Appeals judge. At about the same time, Lowell Weicker, who was then Connecticut's governor, suggested that I might in a year or two become Chief Justice of Connecticut. That interested me because I'm a common lawyer—a tort teacher. But I just said no, because Connecticut had a 70-year retirement age. It would have taken me two or three years to learn my job, and by then I would have been a lame duck.

The staffer then said something odd. He said, "Are there any conditions in which you would accept?" I sort of sighed and said, "Look, I'm an immigrant. I'm a refugee. If the President of the United States asks me to do something which I am capable of doing, and which is honorable—I do not care what it is— I will never say no." I'm a patriot, you know. It is just what you do. "But that's the only condition in which I'll take anything. I want to finish. If something comes up after I've finished, I'll think about it."

Kate Stith was my younger colleague whose husband was José Cabranes. He had been Yale's General Counsel until he became a district court judge in Connecticut, and by then was the chief judge. I told Kate, "José has nothing to worry about." José, perfectly properly, was lining up people to support his appointment to the Court of Appeals. He was and is very powerful, Hispanic, and very smart; he was doing exactly what he should have been doing.

I wanted to be sure that they weren't going after me to block José Cabranes. There were rumors that José played a role in keeping me from being appointed President of Yale in 1992, at the time Benno left. Those were groundless, as far as I know.

The President of the University is chosen in an odd sort of way by the trustees of the Yale Corporation, and the trustees are elected for different terms. José and Ellen Peters were appointed as trustees at the same time, and if it had happened that Ellen Peters had been the "successor trustee" for twelve years, and the "alumni trustee" with a shorter term had been José—then he wouldn't have been on the Corporation and Ellen Peters would have been.

If she had been on the Corporation, Ellen surely would have been chair of the committee to look for a president, because she was the only one who had experience doing it. If so, I think Ellen would have pushed for me to be president very strongly; and I might have gotten the job. It would have been a horrible thing to have happened to me—I would have done it, but it would have been a horrible thing! Instead, she wasn't there, and José was.

The person who became head of the search committee was some clergyman who had come on relatively recently. I was certainly a candidate, as having been a very successful dean. Against it was the fact that the last president had been another law dean, Benno Schmidt, who had been hated. Not fairly, but he had left the job suddenly, leaving the University in something of a lurch.

The key man who was on the Corporation at the time was Senator David Boren from Oklahoma. He called me and said there were two people he thought could be Interim President after Benno had left so suddenly. I was one, and Harold Lamar, who was his teacher and whom he loved, was the other. He told me that he was pushing—successfully as it turned out—for Lamar, because Lamar was too old to become President, while he thought I was somebody who could be.

Clearly there were people on the Corporation like Boren who were thinking of me. But he, like Ellen Peters, had left by the time the choice was made. And, for reasons that I do not understand, the committee also included, for the first time, a faculty member. That faculty member was Abe Goldstein, from the Law School. I've told you about some of Abe's reactions to my deanship earlier. We kind of respected each other, but he clearly was against me as President. And, as I said, this turned out a great blessing.

In any event, Abe was far more important to my not becoming the University President than José, who I do not think had anything much to do with that. The most that can be said about José in this regard is that he was not Ellen, who would have been pushing for me.

[Sighs] Kate told José what I told her, and I'm told he thought, "I'm glad." Kate, who in some ways has more distance, told me afterwards, "I heard your story and thought, 'I do not want to tell José, but I think he is dead, because they do not say something like that unless they have something specific in mind.'" That turned out to be true; but it also turned out that José wasn't dead at all.

José was close to Senator Patrick Moynihan, who arranged to have him be appointed from New York. The White House was perfectly happy to appoint him. It all worked out [laughs], in a complicated way!

*   *   *

Some months later, in the fall of my ninth year, I get a call from the president's counsel, who says, "Bill wants you to go on the Second Circuit. Will you do it?" I said, "Look, I told you, if he wants me I will do it. I do not know what being a federal appellate judge is all about, but I will. The answer is: Yes. But it has to be him wanting me for whatever reasons, and not you guys wanting me to block somebody else."

He said, "No. No. No. It is not that. He wants you. May we start the FBI check?" I say, "Sure. But Bill Clinton is coming up to Yale in two weeks for some event. I'm going to ask him if he really wants me, and if it really is Bill who does, *then* your starting the FBI check will be fine. If it's not, you will have wasted your time."

In a couple of weeks, Bill comes up to Yale, and I ask him, "What's up? Is it that you need me or am I part of some complicated political maneuver?" He immediately says all sorts of nice—I do not think accurate—reasons why he needs me. But apart from the reasons he gave, it was clear that *he* wanted me.

Although I never taught either Bill or Hillary, I knew them well in school, because it's a small place. But neither of them were students of mine, in part because their first year was the year I visited at Harvard, and so didn't teach Torts that fall.

I think what was going on was that Bill wanted his first group of appointments to include distinguished district judges, practicing lawyers, really good politicians, and someone who would stand out as a scholar. The scholars who came to mind to him were Walter Dellinger and me. But Walt comes from North Carolina, and Senator Jesse Helms would have done everything he could to block him. My appointment instead would be easy. That was why he "needed" me.

And he turned out to be right in thinking that my appointment would be easy. Senator Joe Lieberman is very close to José and had been pushing him very strongly; but from the moment I was nominated, Joe became a strong supporter, and testified for me—his professor, and his son's dean—and so on. Senator Christopher Dodd immediately came on the bandwagon. Harry Wellington, who had committed himself to support José, now said, "Of course I support you." Everything fell into place. None of it was to block José and as it turned out he was soon enough appointed; but at the time he was angry. He felt betrayed, and it's understandable.

* * *

I was nominated in January, after the FBI had done its work. But I wasn't confirmed until July, so I continued to be dean. I only missed one year of my deanship.

I chose the following September for my formal swearing in. The day was the sixteenth of the month, fifty-five years to the day from when I had landed in America. At my swearing in, I talked about all the people who had helped this immigrant on his way. I mentioned them by name, and I said that America had done great things for me, and I was grateful. But there were other people in this country whom America had not helped, and I said I was dedicating my judgeship to them, and to trying to give them the opportunities I had been given.

Justice David Souter, who swore me in, had tears in his eyes.

Upon being sworn in by Justice Souter, Sept. 16, 1994

COMMENTARY

Chapter 25

Serving out the second term. The initial invitations to cut short the second term of his deanship to take a judgeship or another federal office placed institutional loyalty in some tension with Guido's other aspirations.

Departing from Yale mid-term would have derogated from accomplishment of a completed and highly successful two-term deanship. The perception of a premature departure could have been accentuated because, as readers of a previous chapter will recall, Guido breached statements that he would serve for only one term, primarily to secure the promotion of junior faculty members he had brought into the law school. Violating his commitment to serve out a second term soon after bringing all these new members of the tenured faculty on board might have been poorly received.

Furthermore, as Guido observes, the positions that were suggested to him—as Solicitor General or as a Court of Appeals Judge, or as Attorney General—were not offers—they were possibilities. These were highly coveted jobs sought by many ambitious aspirants. To make a serious bid for them would require nearly all-consuming attention, with uncertain prospects for success and the complete likelihood of distraction from deaning. He would need to place himself in the running by lining up support mid-stream.

Return to the faculty at the end of a second term? Langbein's Law. Returning to the regular faculty at the end of a decade of deaning would be possible. But while returning to teaching may be simple, returning to scholarship is much harder. As John Langbein offers, "Deans never come back to scholarship":

> If you spend five or ten years doing deaning, you are spending them in a different career. You are into labor relations, student relations, student recruitment, faculty recruitment, therapy for all of the above, and getting the building fixed up.
>
> The first day Tony Kronman took office here there was a plumbing failure, and the first memo he had to send out was about where you could go to use the toilets! He then put at the bottom of that: 'I think I'm coming to understand what this job may be about!'
>
> Do that for ten years, and you have lost touch with the frontier of your field, and you are not going to get it back.[1]

Some colleagues detected that during many years of deaning, Guido was not reading the major journal literature; and that, while he still loved teaching, his successful deanship was leading him away from scholarship and toward a larger role in academic administration—president.[2]

---

[1] Interview with Prof. John Langbein, Dec. 12, 2010.
[2] Interview with Prof. Robert Ellickson, May 10, 2011.

Becoming the president of Yale would have been well-suited to his deep attachment to the University; it would have been a logical and realistic next step. For the reasons Guido states here, however—including the opposition he himself fomented while fighting for the school's financial autonomy—that door did not open.³

Discussing the state of the American Judiciary, Jan. 22, 1987

Bill Clinton's approach to making judicial appointments. The proposition that "it is important to put somebody in place who is *really* qualified seems almost quaint, today," President Clinton reflected in 2020.⁴ "The Federalist Society did [President Trump's] vetting, and they used a different standard, ideological purity." Mr. Clinton reflected his determination to appoint judges who were "smart, experienced, fair, and would do a good job," and who would raise up public support for government, which had been driven down by twelve years "of 'trickle-down economics' and the theory that the government was a source of all evil, which were the two real anchors of the Reagan philosophy." "I wasn't concerned about moving the courts way to the left," he stated, "I just wanted to make sure they were fair and open and to get rid of the right-wing bias so far as my appointments allowed."⁵

Nor did Clinton believe that "the only place to go for judges of the Court of Appeals was people who had been district court judges, which had become "too much of a pattern" because "that sort of legal background is not the only experience you want on the higher courts." President Obama may have "bested him a bit" on bringing diversity to the bench, but Mr. Clinton took pride in stating that his appointments had the highest rankings for the ABA.⁶

---

³ See Chapter 20, "Independence."
⁴ Interview with William Jefferson Clinton, Oct. 20, 2020.
⁵ *Id.*
⁶ *Id.*

President Bill Clinton

Clinton's czar for judicial appointments. In 1993 Bernard Nussbaum left the firm of Wachtell, Lipton, Rosen and Katz to become counsel to the president of the United States.[7] Along with Bruce Lindsey, who had been Clinton's National Campaign Director, Nussbaum handled the selection of nearly one hundred federal judges for the appellate federal courts, including the selection of Justice Ruth Bader Ginsburg as nominee to the Supreme Court, and the new Attorney General, Janet Reno.[8]

Although Mr. Nussbaum's White House committee was responsible for initially identifying most of the potential judicial appointees and then presenting them to the president, Guido Calabresi was an uncommon exception.

Their personal relationship. Clinton, a graduate of the class of 1973, knew Guido by his scholarship and teaching reputation as a law student, and by conversing with him in the law school hallways—although he did not study with him. A decade or more later as dean, Guido honored both Bill and Hillary as successful alumni—inviting visits while Bill was the governor of Arkansas, prior to his becoming a presidential candidate, and then when he became president.[9] According to Nussbaum, Guido's name was proposed first by Bill Clinton as somebody he wanted to appoint.[10]

---

[7] Margolick, *At the Bar;* Ruth Marcus, *The Man Behind the President*, WASH. POST, July 1, 1993.

[8] Russell L. Riley, oral history interview with Bernard Nussbaum, *UVA Miller Center* (Sept. 24, 2002), https://millercenter.org/the-presidency/presidential-oral-histories/bernard-nussbaum-oral-history-2002-white-house-counsel.

[9] See, e.g., invitation from Guido Calabresi to Governor Bill Clinton, June 18, 1987; Governor Clinton to Guido Calabresi, Oct. 29, 1987 Dean's file, Yale Manuscripts and Archives.

[10] Telephone interview with Bernard Nussbaum (unrecorded) 2017.

Guido unveils President Bill Clinton's Law School portrait at Clinton's twentieth reunion, Oct. 9, 1993

President Clinton's motivation. Clinton elaborated on his reasons for folding Guido into the appointments mix. "I liked him," President Clinton said.[11] "I thought he had a really good reputation as a professor, even though when I could have taken Torts with him he was somewhere else." Clinton recalled that he "hung around the law school a lot and had chances to talk to him [and] just thought he'd be a good judge because he seemed connected to the scholarship of the law and to the experience of real people in their lives, and I thought his experience would be helpful. And I was intrigued by the story of his life. I thought that if he was half as smart at writing opinions as he was carrying on conversations, he would be a great judge. And when I became President, he had been Dean of the Law School, and was very successful."[12] As well, Clinton reflected, if the nomination did not succeed, Guido would return to his professorship.

Consistent with the president's sentiment, Nussbaum recalled that Bill was intent to elevate several illustrious professors from the academy whose stature fit into the overall design for the composition of the appellate bench. Guido's Italian ethnicity and reputation as a centrist—as a liberal progressive but not an extremist—added to his attractiveness.[13]

Rumors in Washington—did Bill consider Guido for the position of attorney general? Guido says that a friend of Senator Biden's told him that President Clinton thought of him as a future Attorney General if his current plans did not work out. Without casting any doubt that Guido heard what he said that he heard, the president rejected the suggestion that he had had any conversation with Biden about Guido occupying that role. It was true that Clinton had formed a relationship with Biden which solidified "during the 1980s when [Joe] was doing the Bork hearings," and that Clinton became "very friendly

---

[11] Interview with President William J. Clinton, Oct. 20, 2020.
[12] *Id.*
[13] Interview with Bernard Nussbaum, *supra* note 10.

with him," working very closely together on the Crime Bill.[14] Still, he said, "I know I never told Joe Biden any such thing ... One of the things I learned about Washington is ... that Democrats, even more than Republicans, try to figure out what the press [or somebody else] wants to hear and then tells them. Republicans [on the other hand, more than Democrats,] try to figure out something damaging because they think that's what the press wants more than even the real storyline."[15]

Judge José Cabranes is blind-sided. Professor Kate Stith, a scholar and professor at Yale Law School, as well as the wife of Hon. José Cabranes, recalled that Senators Lieberman and Dodd already had announced publicly that they would be supporting José Cabranes to fill the one available open Connecticut seat on the Second Circuit, on the day that Guido called her down to his office:

> Guido said he had been thinking that after being dean he wanted to be on the Court of Appeals.
>
> I told him it is a different Court of Appeals than it was when Learned Hand was there. We discussed the merits.
>
> Then I said, 'There's a problem, Guido. There's no opening, because there's the [Thomas] Meskill opening, and the next one's not till [Ralph] Winter retires. I don't think that's going to be for some years. You could ask Ralph.'
>
> Guido said, 'Oh.' That was that.[16]

But sometime later, returning from a family vacation, José and Kate received a disappointing message from Senator Lieberman: Bill very much wanted Guido.[17] And at that point, Kate understood that the support they had gathered was going to evaporate; indeed, Senators Dodd and Lieberman retreated from José.

Professor Kate Stith

[14] *Id.*; see also Mr. Clinton's discussion of Senator Biden in Chapter 22, "Almost a Justice: Robert Bork."
[15] Interview with President Clinton, Oct. 20, 2020.
[16] Interview with Prof. Kate Stith, Mar. 11, 2013.
[17] Appellate Seats Sought for Calabresi, Cabranes, *Hartford Courant*, Jan. 27, 1994.

As a matter of necessity, Nussbaum had been alert to the ever-present danger of stoking local Democratic rivalries or of embarrassing senators, judges, or other political allies. Surprise maneuvers could lead allies to have to retract earlier commitments or abandon well-laid plans. In this case, however, bruised feelings were unavoidable.

Nussbaum categorically rejected assertions that Bill's preference was strategically motivated by a desire to thwart Cabranes.[18] The problem for the White House was how to appease José Cabranes and his community of support in light of Bill's revealed preference for Guido.

Senators Lieberman and Dodd announced, as they switched to Guido for the Connecticut position, that they were intent on finding a way to elevate Judge Cabranes. With help from Senators Dodd, Lieberman, and Moynihan, and with pressure applied by many Cabranes supporters, Kate and José secured a New York seat for him; Judge Cabranes would not have to wait for a Connecticut seat to open up. And so, the following summer, both Guido and José Cabranes were confirmed. Guido was confirmed a couple of weeks ahead, and so he became the more senior judge.[19]

Public reactions. Some press responses to these events as they unfolded during the fall were uncharitable to Bill Clinton and to Guido, in the extreme. A *New York Times* article derided the selection process and lambasted Guido for his flattery, manipulation, hyperbole, effusiveness, ambition, and blind loyalty to Yale alumni.[20] The *Times* reported that Hispanic rights advocates had been "deeply disappointed."[21] Together with the cartoon that accompanied it, it raised questions about the domination of two branches of government by the Yale Law School and ridiculed the spectacle of internecine warfare. It mocked the Yale Law School's First Couple—for "anointing" the dean of same law school; in favor of a previously favored graduate

---

[18] Telephone interview (unrecorded) with Bernard Nussbaum, Dec. 2017.
[19] *Id.*
[20] *See* David Margolick, *At the Bar: For President Clinton, Old-School Ties Take Precedence Over Senators' Wishes in a Search for a Judge,* N.Y. TIMES, Oct. 29, 1993.

Margolick's column was laced with notes of comedy and satire at Guido's expense. Mentioning that Guido had said he believed both Clarence Thomas and Anita Hill, Margolick ventured that "[i]f the four protagonists in Rashomon had also been Yalies, he would undoubtedly have believed all of them." He lampooned Guido's attribution to the Clintons of "Walt Whitmanesque" virtues that had grown in proportion to the couples' rising fortunes.

According to Margolick, Guido had jumped on the Clinton bandwagon early and cleverly. He recounted that when Guido learned that Bill Clinton was driving by the law school during a campaign stop in New Haven, he lay in wait for the motorcade. "Having caught the candidate's eye, Mr. Calabresi hugged him, kissed him, then persuaded him to attend a law school picnic."

When discussing the possibility of a judicial appointment, Margolick wrote, Guido sounded "at times like William T. Sherman, uninterested under any circumstances [and at other times more like] Cincinnatus at the plow, waiting for his countrymen to call." *Id.*

Years later, Margolick reflected on his reporting about Guido. He considered Guido "one of the few characters in the legal world whose persona was so large—and so charismatic." He felt that Guido "could handle that article, and would actually enjoy the piece, which was snide, but affectionate." Telephone interview with David Margolick, Jan. 17, 2020. Margolick had no involvement in the cartoonish pen-sketch which accompanied the column.

Why did Margolick cover Guido as extensively as he did? "Because the *Times* had an elitist bias back then, and law deans at elite schools were prominent people; and because he was an important and intriguing person, larger than life." Margolick genuinely liked him, a lot. *Id.*

[21] Margolick, *supra* note 23.

of the same law school; who was himself married to another professor of the same law school!²²

Sketch accompanying David Margolick's "Old School Ties" column

Vetting inside the White House. However intensely Bill Clinton was interested in appointing him, Guido needed to go through an internal vetting process at the White House. An undated, unattributed discussion memorandum, prepared by an intern for discussion by the White House selection committee, identified the benefits and drawbacks to his nomination.²³ The memo appears to have been drafted by a person or persons antagonistic to the appointment.

It reported that as a dean, Guido received great credit for reinvigorating the leadership of Yale Law School and recruiting "a new crop of superstars." But he also sparked student protests: he had "tangled" with women's groups and resigned from the all-male Century Club in New York only after what the memo described, without further description, as "intense pressure." Guido allegedly told a feminist scholar "that feminist thinking was 'not interesting, important, or worthwhile,'" without attributing or questioning the source. He had, the memo continued, been attacked for showing "insufficient support for gay rights, affirmative action, or feminist-oriented classes ...," which occurred in the context of progress in these areas albeit not as quickly as Guido himself wished.²⁴

---

²² *Id.*

²³ An incomplete, undated, and unsigned copy of the memorandum—longer than seven single-spaced pages in length—is located in "Doug Band's files" in the Clinton Archives. Clinton Archives, File Unit: Guido Calabresi [2nd Circuit Court of Appeals] [3], Rec. 26083550. Band was then a student at Georgetown who became an unpaid intern in the White House in 1995. He served in the counsel's office for four years afterward, and then in the Oval Office as the president's aide. Entry, Doug Band, Georgetown Univ. Alum. Database, https://alumni.georgetown.edu/news/doug-band. After the Clinton presidency he remained a Clinton business and legal associate. *See* Russell Berman, *The Man at the Center of "Bill Clinton Inc.",* THE ATLANTIC, Oct. 28, 2016.

²⁴ Id. See Chapter 19, "The Dean's New Day."

On the other hand, the evaluation curtly conceded, he had been reappointed for a second five-year term, and on the whole "won high marks for his tenure."[25]

In the political arena, Guido's involvement in the Bork and Thomas Supreme Court nomination controversies revealed, according to the memo, an awkward political actor who made some unnecessary enemies:

> [H]e came to the strong defense of long-time friend and colleague Robert Bork. [F]ew doubted the sincerity or loyalty involved [, but] some of Bork's opponents were put off by the ferocity with which Calabresi attacked them.

With reference to the Thomas nomination, the memo repeated the *New York Times* accusation that Guido had allowed his "blind Old Blue boosterism" to permit himself to be "used by the right wing to help legitimize Judge Thomas." Criticism of Guido's congressional testimony was magnified, it said, because while "lauding Thomas, [he] also heaped criticism on the existing members of the Court, calling Justice Souter and Kennedy "grey" and "mediocre," and describing the Court as a whole as "despicable" and "statist."[26] Criticism escalated again, the memo reported, when Anita Hill came forward. Guido "declined to withdraw his support ... and instead urged a delay in the hearings while decrying the harm done to 'both of these fine people.'" Guido, per the memo, allowed himself to "blow with the wind."[27]

The memo went on to credit Guido's attachment to Bill and his laudable support during the primary season. Guido had defended both of the Clintons against attacks by Mario Cuomo, Jerry Brown, and the Christian Right. He had hosted a reception at Yale Law School for Hillary; after Bill's election, Guido defended the young administration—but the memo chortled that he had done it "in a back-handed way," telling reporters 'the mistakes they've made don't seem to me to amount to a hill of beans *compared to the Bay of Pigs.*'"[28] It is hard to miss the suggestion in the memo that his loyalty was commendable, but that he had been naïve or clumsy.

Bill wanted to appoint somebody with liberal views about the law, but the memo observed that even Guido's revolutionary tort theories, concededly progressive and brilliant, could not be "pigeon-holed" as liberal, because his writings in the field of tort law "paved the way for the most powerful movement of contemporary legal conservatives—the school of "law and economics."[29] Those who vetted him worried that he could be attacked by consumer groups because he had been compensated by the utility industry for testimony which urged Congress to place the cost of the

---

[25] *Id.*

[26] *Id.* The memo was referring to Guido's opinion op-ed in support of the Thomas nomination, *What Clarence Thomas Knows*, N.Y. TIMES, July 28, 1991 ("I despise the current Supreme Court and find its aggressive, willful, statist behavior disgusting—the very opposite of what a judicious moderate, or even conservative, judicial body should do.").

[27] *Id.*; see Chapter 24, "Clarence, Anita, Catharine, Jack—and Yale."

[28] *Id.*

[29] *Id.*

meltdown at the Three Mile Island nuclear plant on consumers, rather than utility company shareholders.[30] It was also possible that even the Torts Bar would find his views about cost allocation objectionable!

Of all the reservations stated or implied by these White House deliberators, however, the concerns that loomed largest appear to have been those about Guido's stance on abortion and privacy rights.[31] The possibility that he would have difficulties with pro-choice segments of the Democratic coalition had already become visible when Guido's name had surfaced as a possible Solicitor General. By the time he was considered for the Court of Appeals he had been criticized by some women's groups who were suspicious of him for his critique of the rationale used by the Court in *Roe v. Wade*.

As Guido discusses elsewhere, he denounced the rationale of the majority opinion in *Roe* because it denied any value at all to fetal life and based its reasoning on a right to privacy rather than equality.[32] As summarized by the memo, Guido's difficulty with that rationale was that it alienated the views of pro-life Americans by "denying that fetuses are people...."[33] It was not that Guido might oppose judicial protection for abortion rights, the memo stated; indeed, he had written that he might find a fundamental right for married couples to use contraception.[34] The problem, the memo said, was that he would not say just how much protection of reproductive rights he would provide. Guido, furthermore, had made provocative statements in this area. Without providing any context, the memo asserted that he had written that "if men could become pregnant, anti-abortion laws would be clearly valid," which it asserted engendered hostility in the pro-choice community.[35] All these were concerns about whether Guido was sufficiently progressive. These seem ironic now, considering the subsequent judicial record.[36]

---

[30] *Id.* As part of his confirmation process, Guido submitted a public biographical information questionnaire, where he described his consultation relating to distributing the costs attached to Three Mile Island. Hearings before the Committee on the Judiciary United States Senate, June 21, 29, 30; July 21; August 3 and 11, 1994, Part 4, Serial No. J-103-28, p. 251 at 13. In *In the matter of Jersey Central Power & Light Co.*, and *In the matter of Metropolitan Edison Co.*, before the New Jersey Department of Energy and the Pennsylvania Public Utilities Commission 1980, "it appeared that both General Public Utilities and also the Public Advocate" might rely on *The Cost of Accidents* to try to persuade the tribunal deciding whether or not to place the cleanup costs of the accident on ratepayers or on shareholders. Examining the way regulators had been treating unanticipated windfalls and risks, and the disincentives to continuing to invest if it came out differently, he "concluded that the costs were appropriately part of the cost base." *Id.* In our conversations, Guido elaborated that his invitation to testify was arranged so that whatever side Guido thought had the better case, he would testify either for the defendant utility or the plaintiff consumer groups and receive the same fee.

[31] See Chapter 15, "Subterfuges and Tragic Choices"; see Chapter 31, "Immigration Law Decisions of an Immigrant."

[32] CALABRESI, IDEALS, BELIEFS, ATTITUDES, AND THE LAW 87–114 (1985).

[33] *See* Ann Scales, book review, *Tragic Voices*, 4 YALE L. & POL'Y REV. 283, 295 (1985); see Chapter 15, "Subterfuges and Tragic Choices."

[34] CALABRESI, *supra* note 35.

[35] The memo likely referred to Calabresi, *Do We Own Our Bodies?*, 1 HEALTH MATRIX 5, 12 (1991), where Guido created a hypothetical supposing that a nuclear fallout accident led to the passage of a law compelling bone marrow donations from *everyone*. He analyzed such a law as being constitutional; and analogously he hypothesized that "if men [also] became pregnant, anti-abortion laws would be constitutional." In the very next sentence he continued, "men can't become pregnant, and such laws hence must inevitably be suspect." *Id.*

[36] See generally Part IV, Sitting on the Second Circuit (see, e.g., characterizations as progressive of Guido's jurisprudence reviewing deportations and asylum in immigration law; reviewing workplace harassment and

Take, for example, the memo's concern that Guido might not be deeply committed to affirmative action.[37] The memo directed attention to his criticism of the rationale for the *Bakke* decision (which upheld the use of race as a factor in admission decisions). It characterized his views as "generally supportive," but warned that his critique of the decision (indicating problems with the delegation of a power to discriminate) raised questions about the depth of his support for civil rights. His subsequent jurisprudence in this area and the others suggests the memo writers had no crystal ball.[38]

Sign-off. Notwithstanding concerns expressed in the extant portion of the memorandum, the committee deliberations led, ultimately, to the committee's recommendation in favor of appointment. The one-paragraph "sign-off" message characterized Guido as a nominee who would be hailed by the legal academy and by leaders of the bar.[39] It alerted the president to the elusiveness of Guido's politics, and the fact that he had said and done enough to displease elements of the Left and the Right. In its entirety, it reads:

> You know Calabresi well: he has been a professor at Yale Law School since 1959, and the Dean there since 1985. He is one of the nation's most prominent and well-respected legal scholars. Calabresi, 61, has been criticized by some women's groups and other liberals for his support of Supreme Court nominees Robert Bork and Clarence Thomas; conservatives resent his subsequent support for Anita Hill. Nevertheless, his selection will be hailed by academics and bar leaders as our most distinguished nominee to date. A majority at the ABA rated Calabresi "qualified," and he received some "well qualified" votes.[40]

However equivocal the discussion memo, the final report diminished most concerns and would not possibly deter the president from going ahead with the nomination he wanted to make. Bill knew about Guido's qualities, and he wanted him. Bill had already determined that he would govern from the Center; this appointment would reflect his determination.

What about the Supreme Court? Dreams of ascending to the Supreme Court occur to nearly every law student; Guido was no exception. Steven G. Calabresi

---

sex discrimination; reviewing campaign finance regulation; reviewing claims of racial profiling; reviewing complaints in financial and pharmaceutical tort actions; assessing claims of violations of fourth amendment search and seizure complaints; and reviewing claims of religious separation clause violations).

[37] See Chapter 28, "The Anti-Discrimination Law Reasoning of an Outsider."
[38] See generally supra Part III, On the Second Circuit.
[39] Bernard Nussbaum, Bruce Lindsey, Jack Quinn, Melanne Verveer, Susan Brophy, Eleanor Acheson, & Ron Klain, Memorandum for the President, Feb. 4, 1994, Clinton Archives, Rec. 061726SS, available at https://catalog.archives.gov/search?q=%222015-0195-F%22&sort = naIdSort%20asc; Todd S. Purdum, *Yale Law Dean Is Nominated To 2d Circuit Appeals Court*, N.Y. TIMES, Feb. 10, 1994.
[40] Bernard Nussbaum, Bruce Lindsey, Jack Quinn, Melanne Verveer, Susan Brophy, Eleanor Acheson, & Ron Klain, Memorandum for the President, Feb. 4, 1994, Clinton Archives, Rec. 061726SS. The American Bar Association report downgraded him significantly because he had negligible courtroom experience and very little experience with litigation. *Id.*

recalls being five or six years old (1955 or 1956) when Uncle Guido—a law student at the time—took a walk with him in the Woodbridge neighborhood:

> I told him, "Uncle Guido, I've just learned that I was born in Madison, Wisconsin." My uncle replied, "Yes, that's true. It means that you're the first member of the Calabresi family who will ever be eligible to run for President."
>
> At that point, I expressed surprise. I said, "Uncle Guido, does that mean that you and Daddy can't be President?" "That's right," he said. Your father and I were born in Milan, Italy, so we're not eligible to be President." Then he paused, and with a twinkle in his eye, said, "But I *am* eligible to be appointed to the Supreme Court."
>
> So then I asked, as any five-year-old would do, "Well, how do you get appointed to the Supreme Court?" My uncle replied, "Well, it's sort of complicated, but basically the President picks you." I paused, and I said, "Well, then I'll run for President, and appoint you to the Supreme Court."
>
> At which point, my uncle replied, "That would be nepotism ... No, that would be the reverse of nepotism, because in Latin, nepotism means *an uncle preferring his nephews*. And your appointing me to the Supreme Court would be the case of the *nephew preferring his uncle!*"[41]

Steven said that his uncle treated him "with respect and warmth and earnestness—and very much as an adult, even in childhood.[42]

A real opening. In March 1993, Justice Byron White announced his retirement; Guido's name appeared on many lists of persons being considered.[43] Guido's friend and former student, the senior Republican member of the Senate, John Danforth, wrote to Bill that "the best possible nominee for the Supreme Court would be a man very well known to you: Guido Calabresi." Danforth continued:

> Probably there is nothing I could say about Guido that would add to your knowledge of him.... Guido is a decent, kind and caring person. In a word, he has soul. I am not sure that the advice of a Republican senator is at all appropriate with respect to Supreme Court nominees.
>
> I did want you to know that I think Guido would be a splendid choice and that if he is selected, I would do everything in my power to support his nomination.
>
> Sincerely,
> Jack[44]

Bernard Nussbaum confirmed that Guido was qualified and neither too young nor too old to be considered. He had a file of support letters. But, in the view of the only

---

[41] Interview with Prof. Steven Calabresi, Nov. 18, 2013.
[42] *Id.*
[43] Thomas L. Friedman, *Clinton Expected to Pick Moderate for High Court*, N.Y. TIMES, Mar. 20, 1993; GEORGE STEPHANOPOLOUS, ALL TOO HUMAN: A POLITICAL EDUCATION (1999).
[44] Sen John Danforth to President Clinton, May 20, 1993, Clinton Archives Rec. 082923.

person who ultimately counted, as Nussbaum recollected, Guido was not the proper choice for the moment. Although Bill assured Jack that he would "take Guido into consideration during [his] review process," as the process went forward, Guido did not fit Bill's criteria.[45] Clinton recalled years later that the Republican Senator's endorsement certainly did not hurt him in light of his estimation of Senator Danforth, but that Bill had not been giving thought to Supreme Court potential when he made his appointments to the Circuit Courts.[46] "I wasn't thinking about it because I just had this one case, this one appointment. I didn't know that I would get another one."[47]

President Clinton "either wanted somebody with a political as well as legal background, or somebody who was otherwise groundbreaking, to make it clear that the Supreme Court—at least on my watch—was not going to be known for moving hard to the right or having nothing but ideological fights."[48] He first offered the seat formerly occupied by Justice White to politicians—to Governor Mario Cuomo and Senator George Mitchell; and both declined. "It is true that I considered both George Mitchell and Mario Cuomo," Clinton recalled, "and George Mitchell said, 'look, I'm married. I'm going to have another child, or he did have a young child, and am going to start a new life, I just can't do this.' Governor Cuomo literally did not want to leave New York ... I thought they would both have been exceptionally good."

Then he offered it to other political actors; Governor Richard Riley of South Carolina declined. Secretary of Interior Bruce Babbitt, "would have been brilliant," but it was "the only time in my life that I have ever received an overwhelming plea: 'Please don't take him out of Interior, we need him!' It was his friends who did him in."[49] Clinton disputed that declining to nominate him had anything to do with the opposition of Senator Orrin Hatch and other senators from western states, or from the "New Right Judicial Selection Monitoring Project" which had been set up by Robert Bork.[50]

Clinton then turned serious attention to appellate judges. There were many reports about the brilliance of Arkansas Judge Richard S. Arnold in the Eighth Circuit—including from Hillary who early in her career had heard from the illustrious Judge Gerhard Gesell that Arnold was "the most brilliant person he had ever met." "I thought," said Clinton, "just on the merits, you know, Brandeis, Frankfurter ... he would be in the Pantheon."[51] But Clinton decided not to nominate him. There were concerns related to Arnold's rulings in abortion cases, an earlier divorce, and about the perception of cronyism.[52] President Clinton reflected that

---

[45] President Clinton to Senator Danforth, May 27, 1993. Clinton Archives Rec. 082923.
[46] Interview with Bill Clinton, Oct. 20, 2020.
[47] *Id.*
[48] *Id.*
[49] *Id.*
[50] *Id.*
[51] *Id.*
[52] POLLY J. PRICE, JUDGE RICHARD S. ARNOLD: A LEGACY OF JUSTICE ON THE FEDERAl BENCH 333, 341 (2009).

Arnold's lack of clarity on abortion was of some concern, but it was, he said mainly that it "could almost have been considered nepotism" if he had chosen him. Their friendship had begun in the 1970s, when Dale Bumpers was governor of Arkansas and Arnold was his chief counsel.[53] They remained good friends, and continued to play golf together even after Bill left the White House."[54]

Clinton interviewed Stephen Breyer—who was recovering from an accident. "I knew he'd been sick, and we didn't have a bad interview—[but] meanwhile, Hillary and several other people mentioned [Circuit Judge Ruth Bader] Ginsburg to me, and I started reading about her." Ginsburg had spent a considerable part of her career arguing for gender equality and women's rights, and it was her litigation strategies more than her judicial record that impressed him. "I said let's get her in here, and we snuck her in on a Saturday; and I thought, Ginsburg is unique." Getting past some genuine concerns about her age—she was sixty, the same age as Guido—he selected her. Ginsburg accepted the nomination in June 1993 and was confirmed that August.[55]

The second Supreme Court opportunity. In April 1994, Justice Blackmun announced his retirement. This was after Guido had been nominated for the Second Circuit and shortly before his confirmation. By this time, the president's counsel was no longer Nussbaum, but Lloyd Cutler, who was particularly close to Steven Breyer. Bill Clinton and Hillary's first choice likely would have been Richard Arnold. Arnold, as indicated earlier, was extraordinarily popular within the judiciary because of the power and depth of his opinions, and his support may also in part have been due—according to Guido—to the fact that Arnold had been first in his Harvard class in the same year that Scalia was third, "and both knew it." But Arnold was passed over this time too; perhaps because of opposition from women's groups concerned about his position on abortion, and more immediately because of concerns about the current state of his long-standing leukemia, which, it was suggested, had become acute.[56] "I knew I had to consider his condition and his bout with cancer. I thought a lot about it ... made a real study of it. I thought it was highly likely that he would not survive the first eight or ten years after I left office."[57]

With Arnold's nomination failing, Cutler was able to press successfully for Breyer.[58] President Clinton nominated Breyer, who had been an assistant special prosecutor during Watergate, who was expert in administrative law matters, who worked closely with Senator Edward Kennedy—and who he had considered and rejected for the earlier vacancy.[59] Chances Guido might become a nominee to the

---

[53] Interview with Bill Clinton, Oct. 20, 2020.
[54] *Id.*
[55] JOHN ANTHONY MALTESE, THE SELLING OF SUPREME COURT NOMINEES 151 (1995); JANE SHERRON DE HART, RUTH BADER GINSBURG: A LIFE 304 (2018); Bill Mears, *Memo reveals Clinton's difficulty over Supreme Court choice*, CNN POLITICS, Apr. 15, 2014.
[56] PRICE, *supra* note 55.
[57] *Id.*
[58] *Id.*
[59] *See* Gwen Ifill, *White House Memo; Mitchell's Rebuff Touches Off Scramble for Court Nominee*, N.Y. TIMES, Apr. 16, 1994; GEORGE STEPHANOPOLOUS, ALL TOO HUMAN: A POLITICAL EDUCATION (1999).

Supreme Court effectively disappeared when the last of the Clinton vacancies was filled.

Guido's judicial career. President Clinton nominated Guido Calabresi on February 9, 1994; the Senate confirmed him on July 18. As he says, he was sworn in by Justice David Souter in the Levinson Auditorium of the law school on September 16, 1994, fifty-five years to the day he and his brother and parents arrived in America as "refugees from a hated dictatorship, literally without a penny or family or friends, yet strangely excited, full of hope that this new life in a new land would bring rewards in freedom..."[60]

In his speech on that occasion, he turned back to childhood to remember some of the teachers and mentors in New Haven who had identified him as a child of promise and who along with "the good fortune of his parents and his background," helped him to transcend anti-Jewish, anti-Catholic, and anti-Italian prejudices. He believed himself the beneficiary of benevolent "affirmative action," in his day.

Nor did Guido miss this opportunity to identify a central lesson from American legal history that would guide him:

> Our tragic moments—for which we are still paying and will long pay—are those times when our laws furthered bigotry and discrimination... *Dred Scott, Plessy, Korematsu*, we know them and many others all too well.
>
> Our moments of glory have been those times when our laws and our courts have made the fight against discrimination and bigotry a central part of our legal system. As lawyers we know these cases, those great moments, by heart too.

He intended to question any logic or reasoning that might lead to endorsing the tragic moments or undermining the great ones.[61]

---

[60] Public Swearing in of Guido Calabresi, Yale Law School, Sept. 16, 1994 (Judge's file).
[61] *Id.*

26
Joining the Second Circuit

The U.S. Courts of Appeals, along with other lower federal courts, were enlarged in size and jurisdiction early in the twentieth century. Afterwards, as Edward Purcell writes, they grew in stature and "found ways to exercise great authority." The limited docket of the U.S. Supreme Court guaranteed that the Courts of Appeals were for most litigants the final opportunity for appellate review. As the national market grew, and as the role of government expanded during wars and depressions, public law litigation—involving the federal government and citizens seeking to protect themselves from government—became an increasingly large part of the business of these Courts.

Over the remainder of the twentieth century, the Second Circuit developed an exceedingly fine reputation for judicial innovation, craftspersonship, and integrity—notwithstanding the 1939 bribery conviction of Judge Martin Thomas Manton, as Guido mentioned earlier. Brilliant majority opinions and dissents by judges including Learned and Augustus Hand, Jerome Frank, Henry Friendly, Charles Clark, and others, led Circuit decisions to be cited frequently and often followed by other jurisdictions.

In 2016, on the 125th anniversary of the Circuit Court, historian John Witt described it as "a great court for a very long time ... a court of superlatives ... first among peers."

The reputation for excellence grew through formal and implicit norms for group behavior—including standards for civility, persuasive written memoranda, and norms for participation that established a "vital tradition of adjudication." Joining the Second Circuit in 1994, Guido soon recognized that skills and talents needed to become a great judge differed from those he had honed becoming a great scholar and a great dean.

I had no idea what was involved in being a judge on the Court of Appeals. I had never looked for the job; and as a torts scholar, I mainly read cases decided in state courts. I obviously was interested in federal cases and I had developed views about the role of federal courts that I laid out in various writings—for example, *A Common Law for the Age of Statutes*. And having been a Supreme Court clerk, I had a vision of what the Supreme Court was like. But I really did not know what a Court of Appeals, and specifically the Court of Appeals for the Second Circuit, was like; or how it really worked.

I felt that I had a lot to learn, which actually made me quite humble coming on the Court, although, I do not think many of the people there thought so. People did not expect humility of me. People always have their expectations.

I had acknowledged my gaps to Burns, the chairman of the ABA Committee on the Federal Judiciary. He said, "You've never practiced law." I told him that was true, and it made me humble, but that I thought I could bring something from the Academy.

There were people who were already on the Court who very much had that sense of me and so were not particularly worried. Jon Newman, who had just become Chief Judge when I came on—and who had known me for a very long time—also knew what I might bring that might be kind of special. He also knew what I knew I did not know. He had no worries about me at all.

Jon had just become Chief Judge, but in some ways he had been doing the job for a while because a typical Second Circuit thing had happened: Jim Oakes had gotten off a bit early as Chief Judge to let somebody whose views were completely different from his, Tom Meskill, have a shot at being Chief Judge, which Tom wanted to do before he retired. Meskill, whose place on the Court I took, served as Chief for a year, but Jon was already at his right hand. Contrast that with what may have happened recently in the Sixth Circuit, where it was said that somebody got off early so that a very conservative judge would be able to step in and block somebody who was not. The camaraderie on our Circuit was and is quite lovely, and very clear.

The first thing that happened when I came on was that Jon said that I should start working right away. "You won't be hearing cases until the fall, but we need you to take motions, and sit on a motions panel right now." I did, before my formal swearing in. Also, before the summer was over, he summoned Fred Parker, and José Cabranes, along with me—who had each been confirmed within weeks of each other—to Hartford, and he talked to us about the traditions of the Second Circuit. He told us we were not an ideological circuit; that we were collegial, that we did have strong disagreements, but despite that, we should be very reluctant to go *en banc*.

He told this to the three of us. We were very different people: Fred was very much a Vermont Republican, with tremendous experience as a district court judge and incredibly good sense. He was slow in his work, but he "ground exceedingly fine." José, a very powerful, brilliant, conservative, and self-assertive person, had been Chief Judge for many years of the Connecticut District Court and was determined to be recognized as a force on our Court by everyone, and perhaps especially also by me—this academic—right from the start.

* * *

I should have known, however, that inevitably there would be a suspicious reaction to the arrival of somebody who came as the previous dean of the Yale Law School, who was senior in age to many of the most senior active judges, some of whom had essentially been my students, and whom I had helped in their own careers.

One of these was Ralph Winter, of course. He was a few years younger than I but had been on the Court for more than a dozen years before I arrived. In many ways, he, Amalya Kearse, and Jon Newman—politically very different but close friends who had gone on the Court at the same time—ran the Court. All the time that he was a judge, Ralph had wanted to continue teaching where he had been a distinguished professor. As dean, I made sure that happened and protected him from people on the Left who wanted to get rid of him. His teaching was not as successful as it had been, and so there were reasons to say he shouldn't teach. He was, for example, giving almost everybody "Honors" grades. Nevertheless, I protected him, and he knew it.

Ralph might have been elevated to the Supreme Court if Reagan had been a different sort. It is said that he was both James Baker's and Ed Meese's second choice after Robert Bork fell. If, around 1987, Reagan had asked them who their second choice was, he might well have named Ralph. Instead, Reagan liked to play people against each other, and so he went to Meese and came up with Douglas Ginsburg, Meese's first choice. When Ginsburg failed, he went to Baker whose first choice was Anthony Kennedy. But Ralph had been very much in the works and when this was happening, I said, "How can we make this financially and logistically feasible for you?" Because I knew there were family reasons that might make it hard for him to go to Washington.

But when I came to the Circuit, Ralph did not do the equivalent for me. I do not really know why. Perhaps my expectations were wrong because courts are different from law faculties. Perhaps it was that he did not want to be seen as closer to me than José, who was a close friend. Perhaps it was that he did not want to be viewed as an academic like me. I do not know, but I had counted on him, kind of to teach me and to mentor me, and in doing so, to explain me to those who might not understand me.

We've remained good friends, and you know, we were fine, but this coldness at the time was part of my learning to be a judge.

* * *

I did not know José Cabranes before I joined the Court. He had never been a faculty colleague. I believe he had been a student of mine in Torts, but frankly, I did not remember *Joe Cabrains*, as Ralph has said that he pronounced his name then.

> *How he did in my class, I still do not know, because when he was on the Yale Corporation, he had the Corporation pass something which said that the records of people who were significant in public life should be taken from the school and kept in the president's office, so that his transcript here at the law school is not here. Not just his, but others were removed for that reason.*

I really did not know him but—as I told you earlier—José was unhappy about how I had been named to the Court from Connecticut when he thought the place was his. And because we both came on at the same time and I was perhaps better known. I wouldn't be surprised if he thought he felt he had to, kind of, "put me in my place."

* * *

There were also other judges of the Circuit who did not know me before I came. I should have known they were going to be worried that I would try to lord it over them in the way Charles E. Clark—the last Yale Law School dean on the Second Circuit—had when he came on. Having been a dean and a great scholar, Clark's attitude was very much, "What have you been doing, just wasting your time while I have been doing great things as a scholar and a dean? Now I'm retiring to this judgeship, and I will tell you what to do!"

> *I was totally different from Charles Clark, who [pounds fist repeatedly] wanted to establish federal procedure! Who wanted to demonstrate that judges could be liberal and powerful! So he and Frankfurter created the myth of Holmes the liberal! Clark, who wanted to be far tougher in criminal cases, where he and Jerome Frank and others disagreed! Clark had very definite ideas about what he wanted to do.*

Learned Hand was furious at Clark's attitude. He couldn't stand it and always referred to him to the other judges as "the GLAPP"—the "Greatest Living Authority on Practice and Procedure."

I did not realize how much there would be of this kind of worry about somebody like me. If I had been more perceptive, I would have realized it just by looking at Dick Posner's reception in the Seventh Circuit. Dick became much loved by his colleagues and a great Chief Judge and all of that, and respected much in the way that I would like to think I am, now, on this Court. I mean, a very senior person, and mentor to many, and so on. But when Dick came on— and for years and years after—the Seventh Circuit thought him to be a real pain in the neck, whether he was one or not.

> *Dick has gotten off the Court and rather angrily. It makes me wonder if some memory of his earlier reception still lingers. I hope when I leave those early concerns have disappeared.*

I guess that when I came on, I thought that I would be understood differently, because I was not like Charles E. Clark—a rather difficult fellow—or Dick, who was inclined to push his own theories aggressively from the outset. But in courts where seniority is a very important thing, bright "juniors" have to realize it, I now recognize that some people did not see me as very different from Clark and Posner.

All who join a court like this come eager to bring certain things, which they think they understand better than others. But all are "new kids on the block," and patiently have to learn the customs and dynamics. I sort of understood that I was the new kid—but I did not fully understand the expectations that I wouldn't behave as a new kid should. And my new colleagues found that some things I did seemed to confirm their expectations.

* * *

Let me give you two examples, one silly and one less so. Early on, John Walker sent around a little limerick, which his law clerk had written about a case, because he thought it was fun and good. It wasn't very good.

I'm a doggerel writer, not as good as John Simon, but I'm a doggerel writer, so I wrote a quite long doggerel about this case and I sent it around. *Not a word*, from anybody, of recognition that it had been sent around!

I did not realize until later that a junior judge *doesn't do that*. You know, it did not strike me as being anything out of line. It wasn't talking about the judge; it wasn't that I was criticizing the clerk's limerick.

> *Now, Dennis Jacobs and I frequently write limericks, sharp ones, back to each other. When I said "dubitante," in a case that I concurred, he wrote, "When you say you're dubitante, are you really pro or ante? . . . I think there's some of that in Dante. . . ." In Dante, there are people in Limbo—ones whom T.S. Eliot refers to—who do not pick sides. Dennis taught literature before he went on the Court. He knew I would recognize the reference immediately. That kind of thing.*

So there it was. I mean, I would not have done it if Walker had written the limerick—this was his law clerk, for heaven's sakes! But it *was* his chambers. I should have known better. Perhaps I should have learned this lesson as a young faculty member, but faculties are different, and at least Yale has never treated junior faculty that way. In any event, I was never really a junior faculty member because I became a full professor so fast.

* * *

Much more significant was my seemingly presumptuous behavior in a case that came up very early. It involved the terrible Lockerbie, Scotland, Pan Am plane crash ultimately attributed to Libyan terrorists. A suit was brought claiming that the airline engaged in "wilful misconduct" and that therefore, damages against *Pan Am* were not limited by the Warsaw Convention and the Montreal Accord.

The panel that heard the appeal was Richard Cardamone, Frank Altimari, and Ellsworth Van Graafeiland. Cardamone tended to be sensitive to injustices. Altimari was very smart, conservative, and did not have a judicial temperament. He was opinionated; he had been a politician on Long Island; Cardamone, also with a political background, may not have been as smart, but he had that concern for injustice that makes for a good judge.

The district court ruled for the airline and the panel reversed, two-to-one. One may speculate why. Altimari may have been affected by the fact that he came from Long Island, where the passengers were from. Cardamone may have been moved by what he viewed as the very low damages that the Convention and Accord would give. In any event, the panel held that there was "wilful misconduct" by the airline under the Warsaw Convention and the Montreal Accord.

Van Graafeiland dissented, violently, saying that this was terrible. He thought that they had ignored an opinion by Meskill in an earlier case which defined what "wilful misconduct" was. He asked for the case to be reconsidered.

Van Graafeiland [Van] was quite a character. He was deaf as a post and became a judge when he got too deaf to be a practicing lawyer. He got John Van Voorhis, who was a great judge on the New York Court of Appeals, to support him. Van Voorhis was of an ancient, and very wealthy, New York Dutch family and he was very much taken with Van Graafeiland, who, although also of Dutch origin, was poor and made his way. Van Voorhis used his considerable political influence to get Van Graafeiland on the Court of Appeals.

Van was immensely aggressive. There's a story that once, after he had gone after a lawyer extremely hard, the other judges said to him when he got back to chambers, "Van, you were really too rough on this man." He said, "Yes, I guess I was. I should apologize." He goes out and sees the lawyer and runs after him. The lawyer sees him coming and thinks Van Graafeiland is still going after him—and he takes off as fast as he can!

He did not use a hearing aid up on the bench. One time the calendar had stated, as the first case on the docket, a discrimination case in which somebody had been fired who claimed that it was for racial reasons; but where the defense was that he had been fired because he was gay, which in those days was not protected. The second case on the docket was a big securities case with lots of big lawyers from New York and Boston and Washington arguing.

As sometimes happens, the order of cases was reversed. This securities lawyer is up there arguing and Van Graafeiland cannot hear a thing. He does not realize the order had been reversed, and a few minutes into the securities lawyer's argument, Van interrupts and says, "All right, all right counsel, but tell me honestly: Is your client a homosexual?" The whole place just comes apart.

Van asked for *Pan Am* to go *en banc*.

There followed any number of memos. Some judges wanted to go *en banc* because they thought the panel ruling was against what Meskill's earlier opinion had held. Others did not want to go *en banc* either because they liked the result or because of our Court's historic reluctance to go *en banc*. Altimari, of course, was fiercely defending the panel opinion and opposing *en banc* reconsideration.

My view was, "This is torts. I know more about this than almost anybody." So I wrote a memo which said, "The panel's opinion does run counter to what Meskill's earlier opinion held." It clearly did. I said, "But Meskill's opinion misunderstands the Convention and the Accord." Which it did; I knew them. My memo concluded that we should go *en banc* to overturn Meskill's opinion and should come out the way the panel did, even though the panel should not have come out that way on its own.

* * *

Well, you can imagine that that memo pleased no one! Altimari was furious because I had said, "You did not respect Meskill's opinion." Well, he was trying very hard *not to follow it* without being obvious about it! I think his reaction was something like [pounds fist repeatedly] "Well, that's just what you'd expect from some Northern Italian rich guy who thinks that people like me, from the South, do not know from beans! Who does this academic intellectual think he is, this fellow in an ivory tower, whose path to the top was paved for him while I've had to work my way up?" And so on. At the same time, Meskill, and all the people on that side were furious, saying, "Who is this kid telling his seniors that their considered judgments were out and out wrong?"

From a technical point of view, I still think my memo was perfectly appropriate. But it was certainly not something which would make my new colleagues think that I was doing anything *but* coming on strong. Both Charles Clark and Learned Hand would have smiled knowingly.

> *I think that Fred Parker, who was junior to me but was a very experienced judge, did not mind ... Nor did Richard Cardamone have problems. He was somebody who liked intellectuals—people teased him because he often began his opinions with quotations from Shakespeare, or Dickens, and his opinions were fuzzy—but he was very concerned with a sense of right and liked people who, because they had ideas, could further it.*

Others, like Pierre Leval, also could appreciate what I brought. He knew what he, as somebody who had been a longtime district judge, could bring to the table, and expected those who were senior on our Court to respect him for that; analogously I think he appreciated what I might know from having been an academic and an expert in a particular field like torts.

Still, others thought that what I was saying was interesting, but that after all, I should really "know my place." Perhaps they were thinking, "'True Americans' would know instinctively," and "Guido is an outsider. We know how to behave."

What about José, who was junior to me? I think he thought that this episode gave him a way, as would another way not long after, in *Taber v. Maine*, to assert himself in relation to me.

> *From the beginning, there came to be a supposition, that now finally is fading, that José didn't like me and that we were kind of enemies. It was more complicated. I think it simply was a person who understandably wanted to be respected and recognized as the powerhouse that he was, wanting to be sure that someone else, like me, who was powerful, did not overshadow him.*

There may have been more going on psychologically than even he knew.

* * *

In any event, my involvement in the *Pan Am en banc* disagreements was an experience that helped entrench in some people the feeling that I was being aggressive and trying to do too much too soon. As a long-standing judge now, I could do what I did then perfectly well, although I would probably express myself more politely. As a junior judge, I shouldn't give a party for the whole Court, but now I can give a party. As a junior judge, the appropriate thing might have been to talk informally to some of the other judges, and say, "Here is the problem. What is the best way of handling it?" Then, very senior judges, like Jon Newman, would have found a way to say what needed to be said without offending anyone.

* * *

The *Pan Am* episode reflects something of the reactions to me that surfaced in the next few years. These varied from person to person. There was never a problem with somebody like Dennis Jacobs, who was senior to me but not at all defensive. He was smart, brash, had been appointed as the last Bush appointee, in part, when my nephew Steven was helping the administration make appointments. Jacobs knew this and thought it was kind of fun. He was also an outsider in the sense that he did not come with judicial or prosecutorial experience. He came from practice.

Others, like Dan Mahoney, worried about me moving the Court to the Left, because he was so conservative; he had been the head of the Conservative Party in New York. Roger Miner worried a bit. He wasn't aggressive about it,. They sort of wondered about me. An early opinion I wrote said something about foreign law, about which Roger thought of himself an expert. I got the message from him suggesting I should pay more attention to what senior judges had said about the topic. And it's not surprising, if you think of Learned Hand and Charles Clark, and the ethos of the Second Circuit. As I said, the same thing happened to Posner in the Seventh Circuit, without that history.

* * *

But these initial suspicions of me washed out, in time—some sooner and some later. With Frank Altimari, it happened not in the first year or second year, but shortly after that. We were talking, and I learned that he came from Calabria. I knew that he was a sculptor, and I asked about his family, and what they did. He said his father was a stone mason, and his grandfather had also been a stone mason. I said, "Oh, Frank, now I understand why you're a sculptor. You're just carrying on the family tradition." He got tears in his eyes and hugged me, and we became very good friends. Toward the end of his life, I would get him stone in Italy, from Carrara, and also, at the very end, when he could not work marble, pumice from Volterra. He then even had me come to speak in Long Island where his home was. It had taken a little while for him to understand that I was not a northern snob, but eventually he understood.

With others who had been uncomfortable with me initially, it took time. And, just as with Posner, my getting greater seniority. But in every case of the people who were my senior, things occurred that led them to understand me better, and even to like me. For instance, Tom Meskill and I were involved in a torts case, which came out as it did, as he wanted it to, and should have, because I showed him that I understood its complexity. Jon Newman, of course, was never a problem, in part because he had no qualms about telling me off—no, not telling me *off*, but telling me what he thought I should do to be a judge and not only an academic.

And, over time, some of my most senior colleagues, like Jim Oakes and Bill Feinberg, came to view me as an intellectual ally. It is interesting, even when much later, in the upstate New York racial stereotyping case, *Brown v. City of Oneonta*, where Oakes was on the wrong side, he not only didn't mind, but told me he appreciated someone taking that position.

It may have taken somewhat longer with Amalya Kearse. It wasn't that she was concerned about my being smart. She is smarter than anyone—amazingly intelligent—and knows it. She wanted to be very sure that I respected her, which of course I did, but it might not have been obvious from the get-go. This was in part because I tended to talk a lot during argument and she instead is very brief and to the point. When she realized that my talking was not disrespectful—it was just me—and that I knew that she, as much as anybody, represented what our Court was, we became good friends.

Amalya, Ralph, and Jon were very close friends who had come on together. Jon was more senior, she next, then Ralph. Politically, they were very different: Jon a Democrat, she a moderate Democrat, and Ralph very conservative. But they liked each other, and, as I said earlier, from the mid-1990s until they all went senior, they really ran the Court.

People who do not know how a court like ours works might misunderstand what it means to "run the Court." The Chief Judge has administrative, but very limited substantive power. That means that leadership is as much symbolic as anything. And so it was with these three. They set the tone, gently but firmly indicating displeasure if anyone was not collegial or in other ways got out of line. By their agreement and their force, they pretty well controlled whether—almost never—we might go *en banc*. By their friendship, despite their ideological differences, they taught us all that ideology was secondary to doing our job as judges.

The last one of the older group to become a good friend, actually, was Ellsworth Van Graafeiland. That didn't happen until we'd had any number of fights. He fought with everybody, of course, but at least once, he *really* got mad at me. When he had a heart attack, however, I sent him flowers and wrote him an affectionate note, and ultimately, he came around.

* * *

Thinking about it now, the person who could have kept me from some of my early mistakes, but whom I would never blame for his not doing so, would be Jon Newman. Jon could have called me in separately and said, "You know, there is this history. You should not do this and the other … You need to understand that this Court operates cautiously and incrementally and with great respect for seniority." I would have understood. Jon did not do that, I think, in part because he kind of liked me to bring "outside-the-box" thinking to the Court. He wasn't threatened by my rather wild hypotheticals. He knew, perfectly well that to the extent my behavior was causing problems for me, I would overcome it. I think he thought, "In time, he'll handle it. So he has a rough time for a bit? That's the way life is."

> *Part of the problem was that from time to time I came up with arguments and issues that the parties had not thought of. This can be troublesome for the other judges on the panel, as well as for the parties. At first, I tended to act as if I expected the parties, and perhaps even the other judges, to react to my unexpected notion right then and there. That is what an academic does. In time, I realized that on the bench, instead, one should always suggest that this may be new and unusual and that further briefing on the matter would be very helpful to us. That is both instrumentally wise and shows respect for all concerned. Having unusual ideas is something useful an academic judge can bring to the Court, but doing it right is part of an academic learning to be a judge.*

Jon did protect me when I needed it—not in terms of keeping me from doing things that troubled others, but by dealing with the consequences. He was strong and aware enough to know that he could be successful in doing that.

* * *

> Now it is totally different. Life with my colleagues has come to be very comfortable. In this funny, gradual way, my colleagues have come to understand me better.
>
> I have also learned.

COMMENTARY

Chapter 26

The U.S. Court of Appeals for the Second Circuit. The Second Circuit is headquartered at the Thurgood Marshall U.S. Courthouse in Lower Manhattan, although its jurisdiction also extends to Connecticut and Vermont. It was established by the Evarts Act in 1891, at first, as a court of three judges. It grew to six seats by 1938, nine by 1961, eleven by 1978, and thirteen by 1984.[1]

The magnitude of New York's maritime activity and its strength as a financial center required New York Courts to decide important admiralty actions and commercial disputes from the beginning. "After the Civil War, no circuit was busier than the Second, no district busier than the Southern District of New York."[2] Especially during the 1920s, 1930s, and 1940s when Learned Hand, Augustus Hand, and Jerome Frank served on the bench, the Supreme Court held the decisions of the Circuit in very high regard, finding them on the whole well-reasoned, practical, and erudite. The Second Circuit opinions in these decades enjoyed an unrivaled reputation.[3]

In most important fields of legal doctrine, Second Circuit jurisprudence has played an important and often leading role. It is "renowned for its landmark rulings in ... white collar crime and securities law."[4] It has "a long tradition of breaking

---

[1] U.S. COURT OF APPEALS FOR THE SECOND CIRCUIT, THE JUDGES OF THE SECOND CIRCUIT (2016); Robert A. Katzmann, *Preface: One Hundred Twenty-Five Years of the U.S. Court of Appeals for the Second Circuit: A Brief Project Overview*, 85 FORDHAM L. REV. 1 (2016); Irving R. Kaufman, *The Second Circuit: Reputation for Excellence*, 63 A.B.A. J. 200 (1977); JEFFREY B. MORRIS, FEDERAL JUSTICE IN THE SECOND CIRCUIT (1987).

[2] MORRIS, *supra* note 1, at 70.

[3] In the second half of the twentieth century, other circuits, especially the U.S. Circuit Court of Appeals for the District of Columbia, became as eminent. Michael E. Solimine, *Judicial Stratification and the Reputations of the United States Courts of Appeals*, 32 FLA ST. U. L. REV. 1331, 1341–42 (2005)("Over much of the twentieth century, the conventional wisdom ... ranked the Second and District of Columbia Circuits highest with regard to prestige and influence.") (citing MARVIN SCHICK, LEARNED HAND'S COURT 5 (1970), referring to it as "one of the top appellate courts in the history of the country," and stating that the Second Circuit was, during the 1940s, judicially reviewed the most and reversed the second least). But see Robert Anderson IV, *Distinguishing Judges: An Empirical Ranking of Judicial Quality in the United States Courts of Appeals*, 76 MO. L. REV. 315, 360 (finding that in recent decades "the Second Circuit and D.C. Circuit judges have no higher outside-circuit ratings on average than judges in most other circuits.").

[4] Kaufman, *supra* note 1, at 201; Karen Patton Seymour, *Securities and Financial Regulation in the Second Circuit*, 85 FORD. L. REV. 225 (2016).

new ground on issues of social justice."⁵ Intellectual property law, especially copyright and patent law, has been forged by leading Second Circuit precedents.⁶ In free expression and civil liberties matters, "the Second Circuit predated the Supreme Court's protective First Amendment rulings," and in the field of libel law, it moved toward the protection of free speech "long before English courts."⁷ For better than a century, it has been a "leading force" in drawing lines to balance individual liberty and national security.⁸

In so many areas of law, as John Fabian Witt has written, the Circuit has demonstrated "remarkable doctrinal innovation given the constraints under which it operates."⁹ The Circuit also became well known for its collegial atmosphere and for the respect it showed to litigants, as well as for the high expectations it set for the appellate bar.

As noted, the Circuit has been composed of great jurists including Billings Learned Hand and Augustus Noble Hand; also Henry Jacob Friendly; the legal realist Jerome New Frank; the Federal Rules architect Charles Edward Clark; and the controversial Irving Robert Kaufman. The Circuit's honored position endured notwithstanding the tarnish caused by the resignation in 1939 of the corrupt Judge Martin Thomas Manton; nor did it lose luster even as other circuits demonstrated their own excellence. Three judges have been elevated to the Supreme Court—John Marshall Harlan II, Thurgood Marshall, and Sonia Maria Sotomayor.

En banc (or in banc). Nearly every chief judge of the Circuit has offered the desire to maintain peer collegiality as a principal reason for rarely hearing cases *en banc (or "in bank")*.[10] It appears that this bias against *en banc* hearings has not noticeably diminished the Circuit's attractiveness as a forum for litigants, nor the Supreme Court's readiness to grant certiorari to hear Second Circuit panel decisions.[11]

In part to maintain collegiality among peers when *en banc* proceedings are convened, and perhaps to encourage more of them, Chief Judge Dennis Jacobs asked Judge Jon Newman to chair a committee to set internal protocols affecting

---

⁵ Matthew Diller & Alexander A. Reinert, *The Second Circuit And Social Justice*, 85 FORDHAM L. REV. 73 (2016).

⁶ Kenneth A. Plevan, *The Second Circuit And The Development Of Intellectual Property Law: The First 125 Years*, 85 FORD. L. REV. 143 (2016).

⁷ Floyd Abrams, *Free Speech and Civil Liberties in the Second Circuit*, 85 FORD. L. REV. 11 (2016).

⁸ David Raskin, *Threats Against America: The Second Circuit as Arbiter Of National Security Law*, 85 FORD. L. REV. 183 (2016).

⁹ John Fabian Witt, *Constraint, Authority, and the Rule of Law in a Federal Circuit Court of Appeals*, 85 FORD. L. REV. 3, 6 (2016).

[10] Michael B. de Leeuw & Samuel P. Groner, *En Banc Review in the Second Circuit*, N.Y. L.J., Dec. 18, 2009 (noting that the Second Circuit heard fewer than forty cases over thirty years and the Ninth Circuit heard fifty-two cases over three years); Jon O. Newman, *In Banc Practice in the Second Circuit: The Virtues of Restraint*, 50 BROOK. L. REV. 365 (1984); Martin Flumenbaum & Brad S. Karp, *The Rarity of En Banc Review In the Second Circuit*, N.Y. L.J., Aug. 24, 2016; Jon O. Newman, *Foreword—In Banc Practice in the Second Circuit, 1984-1988*, 55 BROOK. L. REV. 355 (1989); Jon O. Newman, *In Banc Practice in the Second Circuit*, 60 BROOK. L. REV. 491 (1994). Judge Newman uses the English spelling *in banc* in preference to the French *en banc*. See also Mario Lucero, *The Second Circuit's En Banc Crisis*, 2013 CARDOZO L. REV. DE•NOVO 32 (2013) (arguing for greater use of *en banc* tribunals).

[11] Newman, *supra* note 10, at 368.

how Judges should proceed in them. Jacobs also named Guido and Judge Richard C. Wesley to the committee.

Judge Wesley said he knew he was chosen because he had spent years on a tribunal which heard its cases *en banc*, the New York Court of Appeals[12] And he thought that Guido was there because he had been the Dean of a Law School and dealt successfully with competing views of faculty all the time; he "had the sensitivity to know the way people need to express themselves."

> We put together a set of protocols. The protocols we came up with are very detailed—right down to the number of days that a party has to call for an *en banc*, and who speaks first at the conference after the oral argument. They have made the process far more pleasant in the sense that there is no argument about *how* we do our work.

Guido, said Judge Wesley, is not only very bright and inquisitive, but "understands everybody's temperature."[13]

Jon Ormond Newman. Newman, a clerk to Earl Warren and D.C. Circuit Judge George Thomas Washington, served as the United States Attorney for the District of Connecticut before becoming a district judge in that state. Named to the trial court by Nixon, he was appointed to the Second Circuit by Jimmy Carter.

During his first year as a district judge, Newman wrote for the three-judge panels convened to assess whether Connecticut's abortion ban violated the constitution, producing opinions that anticipated *Roe v. Wade*.[14] In his memoir, *Benched*, Newman described these cases as "most likely the ones for which I am best known."[15] As a district judge, he also presided over prisoner rights litigation led by Watergate Burglar G. Gordon Liddy, who was then incarcerated in Danbury.[16]

As an appellate judge, Newman wrote the first Second Circuit opinion, deciding a case based on a certified question of state law.[17] He became universally revered by colleagues as the Circuit's "honest broker," and the "keeper of the flame."[18] A sign he placed in his office read "Jon Newman=God."

A non-ideological Circuit? Guido contends that the Circuit has not been "ideological." His statement implies that some other Circuits *are* ideological—as has commonly been asserted. A reporter for the *New York Times* described the Fourth Circuit, based in Virginia, as "the shrewdest, most aggressively conservative federal

---

[12] Interview with Hon. Richard C. Wesley, Aug. 13, 2020.
[13] *Id.*
[14] *See generally* Andrew D. Hurwitz, *Jon Newman and the Abortion Decisions: A Remarkable First Year*, 46 N.Y. L. SCHOOL L.R. 231 (2002).
[15] JON O. NEWMAN, BENCHED 5 (2017).
[16] See NEWMAN, supra note 15, at 123; *see also* G. Gordon Liddy, WILL: THE AUTOBIOGRAPHY OF G. GORDON LIDDY 346–47; Stover v. Carlson, 413 F. Supp. 718 (D. Conn. 1976); Liddy v. Wilkinson, 413 F. Supp. 724 (D. Conn. 1976).
[17] Kidney by Kidney v. Kolmar Laboratories, Inc., 798 F.2d 467 (1986); 68 N.Y.2d 343 (1986); 808 F.2d 955 (1987); see Chapter 30, "Calabresian Complexities and the Value of Dialogue."
[18] Interview with Hon. Richard C. Wesley, Aug. 13, 2020.

appeals court in the nation."[19] A reporter for the *Washington Times* accused the Ninth Circuit, based in San Francisco, of "manipulative judging at its worst."[20]

The Second Circuit has not as often been characterized so definitively, but it has been commonly described as "liberal," based in part on some of its rulings and in part on the large number of appointments made during Democratic administrations. A considerable number of the Circuit's historic "liberal" or "progressive" decisions, however, were written by Republican appointees, notably James Oakes, and in an earlier era, Learned Hand and Henry Friendly.[21]

There is some empirical support for Guido's assertion that the Court's institutional and collegial tradition has to a significant extent constrained ideological behavior: it appears true that the odds of getting a panel of "liberal" rather than "conservative" judges during the period between 1993 and 2000 were somewhat greater than in several other circuits. Efforts to quantify ideological leaning indicate that institutional constraints in the Second Circuit (and in the First, Fifth, Seventh, and Eighth Circuits) produced decisions "more conservative than what one would expect if considering only the panel and circuit preferences."[22]

Fred I. Parker. The Boston-born son of a plumber and a homemaker, Parker attended trade school before entering college at the University of Massachusetts. He received his law degree from Georgetown, where he became friends with Patrick Leahy, the future senator of Vermont. Over his period as a judge, he became known as an "independent, moderate" Republican.[23] Parker was selected for the district court by Republican George Bush, and for the Second Circuit by Democrat Bill Clinton.[24] He died prematurely in 2003.[25]

Dennis Jacobs. Jacobs received a B.A. from Queens College in 1964, pursued graduate studies in English Literature at New York University, and received an M.A. in 1965. After teaching, he entered New York University Law School and graduated there in 1973. He worked as a partner at Simpson, Thacher & Bartlett until President Reagan appointed him to the bench in 1992. His thoughtful opinions in areas of civil liberties, civil rights, and surveillance generally have upheld government power in matters of immigration and national security. His opinions in matters of criminal procedures have generally, but not uniformly, supported law enforcement; and he has been more progressive on some social issues.[26] He served as Chief Judge of the

---

[19] Andreas Broscheid, *Comparing Circuits: Are Some U.S. Courts of Appeals More Liberal or Conservative Than Others?*, 45 L. & SOC. REV. 171 (2011).
[20] *Id.*
[21] *Id.*; *see also* CASS SUNSTEIN ET AL., ARE JUDGES POLITICAL? AN EMPIRICAL ANALYSIS OF THE FEDERAL JUDICIARY (2006).
[22] Broscheid, *supra* note 20, at 186.
[23] Wolfgang Saxon, *Judge Fred I. Parker, 65; Served on Second Circuit*, N.Y. TIMES, Aug. 14, 2003.
[24] *Id.*
[25] *Judge Fred I. Parker, 65*, N.Y. TIMES, Aug 14, 2003.
[26] *See, e.g.*, Scott Horton, *Injudicious Judge*, THE ATLANTIC, Sept. 23, 2011 (castigating *en banc* opinion against a Freedom of Information Act Request for documents regarding the government's interpretation of FISA amendments); Ian Milheiser, *Federal Appeals Court Strikes Down DOMA in Opinion by Republican-Appointed Judge*, THINK PROGRESS (Oct. 18, 2012), https://thinkprogress.org/breaking-federal-appeals-court-strikes-down-doma-in-opinion-by-republican-appointed-judge-c85e323b0a5b.

Circuit between 2006 and 2013, during which period he oversaw the rehabilitation of the Thurgood Marshall Federal Courthouse.

The relevance of literature to judging. Judge Jacobs has written about the different ways that his love of literature has shaped his professional and personal experience. Liberal arts education provided ideas about "what to read next, to hear next, and to look at," while his voracious reading during years of graduate study and teaching shaped his approach to appellate judging.[27] As a judge, he came to think of himself "as a graduate student with a terrific fellowship (and a modest stipend) that lasts for life," whose interest in poetry has helped "to be able to weigh words, to hear their resonance, and to pay attention to sound and rhythm."[28] As Guido alludes to here and later in his story, Jacobs enjoys allusions to literature in memos to his colleagues.[29] He does not, however, make reference to them often in his published judicial writings.[30]

José Alberto Cabranes. José's parents, Carmen and Manuel Cabranes, were born and educated in Puerto Rico. José was born in Mayaguez, Puerto Rico, in 1940. Near to the outset of the "great migration" in 1946, they moved to the South Bronx where Carmen became the executive director, and Manuel the director, of the Melrose Settlement House. Manuel came to hold significant positions in New York City government; he was also a probation officer at one time. He and Carmen were successful advocates for Puerto Ricans in economic, cultural, and political life.[31]

José grew up in Queens. He graduated from Columbia University in 1961; from Yale Law School in 1965. After law school, he engaged in practice, taught law, and also took up Puerto Rican causes, including the founding of the Puerto Rican Legal Defense and Education Fund. He left a teaching position at Rutgers Law School in 1973 to head what became the Puerto Rico Federal Affairs Administration in Washington, D.C.[32]

In 1975 Cabranes moved to New Haven to become Yale University's first general counsel. President Carter nominated him four years later to a Connecticut district court seat.[33] In 1984, he married Kate Stith Pressman, then an associate professor at the law school.[34] As Guido has recounted, Judge Cabranes assumed a seat on the

---

[27] Dennis Jacobs, *Aye Birds Tune, A Federal Judge Considers Poetry From the Bench*, POETRY MAG. (Sept. 2009), https://www.poetryfoundation.org/poets/dennis-jacobs.

[28] *Id.*

[29] See Guido's quotation of verse sent by Judge Jacobs, in Chapter 28, "The Anti-Discrimination Law Reasoning of an Outsider."

[30] But see Fisher v. Vassar Coll., 114 F.3d 1332, 1351 n. 7 (2d Cir. 1997) (Jacobs, J., concurring) ("How fascinating is that class/ Whose only member is Me!" W. H. Auden, *Islands*, 24 THE SHIELD OF ACHILLES (1955)).

[31] Congressional Confirmation Hearing on José Cabranes, Statement of Hon. Robert Garcia to Sen. Edward Kennedy, Chair: Hearing Before the Committee, 72, Nov. 29, 1979; Information Services on Latin America, 10 *ISLA* 173 (1975); *see also* LUIS ANTONIO CARDONA, HISTORY OF THE PUERTO RICANS IN THE UNITED STATES OF AMERICA 393 (1995).

[32] Congressional Confirmation Hearing, supra note 31. Among his academic publications is JOSÉ CABRANES, CITIZENSHIP AND THE AMERICAN EMPIRE: NOTES ON THE LEGISLATIVE HISTORY OF THE UNITED STATES CITIZENSHIP OF PUERTO RICANS (1979).

[33] JOAN BISKUPIC, BREAKING IN: THE RISE OF SONIA SOTOMAYOR AND THE POLITICS OF JUSTICE 85–86 (2014).

[34] *Jose Cabranes & Kate Pressman Wed*, N.Y. TIMES, Sept. 16, 1984.

Second Circuit in 1994, just weeks after Guido began his service. He assumed the New York seat, which Richard Cardamone had occupied.[35]

Although President Carter chose Judge Cabranes for the district court with the aid of civil liberties and progressive groups—and of especially Puerto Rican organizations— and furthermore was selected for the Second Circuit by Bill Clinton, his judicial opinions revealed many conservative views. In fact, during the George H.W. Bush presidency and the presidency of his son George W. Bush, commentators speculated he might be elevated to the Supreme Court.[36] When Chief Justice Roberts named him to the three-judge Foreign Intelligence Surveillance Court of Review in 2013, the *New York Times* described him as "a Democrat, but not a liberal."[37]

Ralph Winter. Like Guido, Ralph Winter taught at Yale Law School before his appointment to the bench, ultimately teaching in seven different substantive fields.[38] He gained respect for writings about corporate law and labor issues; he argued with his mentor Harry Wellington that public sector unions could lead to dangerous concentrations of power.[39] Winter was also involved in the litigation that became *Buckley v. Valeo*,[40] where he argued against campaign finance restrictions in the Supreme Court on behalf of the plaintiffs.

Amalya Lyle Kearse. Kearse grew up in New Jersey, the daughter of a physician and a postmaster. She graduated from Wellesley and then from the University of Michigan Law School in 1962. She was the first Black woman appointed to a federal appellate court; by then she had already broken barriers—the first Black woman hired by a Wall Street law firm, Hughes Hubbard and Reed. It is an indication of the existing prejudice that on her selection for the Second Circuit, a Hughes Hubbard partner felt that it was important to state that she became a partner "not because she is a woman, not because she is a black, but because she is just so damned good."[41]

Her tenure has been marked by cautiously progressive rulings in civil rights and civil liberties that garnered acclaim from practicing lawyers and her fellow judges. Amid the controversy surrounding the nomination of Clarence Thomas, Jon Newman argued that she should have been named to the Supreme Court.[42] Outside of the Second Circuit, she became well known as a World Bridge Federation World Life Master and an author of books on the subject.[43]

---

[35] See Chapter 25, "Bill Wants Him."
[36] JOAN BISKUPIC, BREAKING IN: THE RISE OF SONIA SOTOMAYOR AND THE POLITICS OF JUSTICE 86 (2014).
[37] Charlie Savage, *Newest Spy Court Pick Is a Democrat but Not a Liberal*, N.Y. TIMES, Aug. 20, 2013.
[38] Paul Frisman, Conservative Nominee to Appeals Court Criticizes Activist Judges, *Hartford Courant*, Dec. 6, 1981, at B1.
[39] Harry H. Wellington & Ralph K. Winter, Jr., *An Imbalance of Power*, N.Y. TIMES, June 12, 1972 at 35.
[40] 424 U.S. 1 (1976).
[41] Tom Goldstein, *City Lawyer and Connecticut Judge Joining Circuit Court*, N.Y. TIMES, June 25, 1979; *Wall Street Firm Hires Negro Woman Lawyer*, N.Y. TIMES, Apr. 12, 1962.
[42] *See generally* Jonathan M. Moses, *Kearse Is Lawyers' Pick for High Court*, WALL ST. J., Jun 14, 1993; Jon O. Newman, *A Replacement for Thomas*, N.Y. TIMES, Oct. 10, 1991.
[43] *See, e.g.*, AMALYA LYLE KEARSE, BRIDGE AT YOUR FINGERTIPS (1979); KEARSE, OFFICIAL ENCYCLOPEDIA OF BRIDGE (3d ed. 1977); KEARSE, BRIDGE CONVENTIONS COMPLETE (1977).

Charles Edward Clark and his truculence. Illustrative of the behavior that colleagues found difficult to take is *Puddu v. Royal Netherlands Steamship Co.*[44] A longshoreman who had been injured by a falling boom contended that the vessel was not seaworthy. The panel, agreeing with the defendants, found that the accident was caused by the stevedores' negligence. *Puddu*'s outcome, on its face, appeared neither complex nor controversial—the original opinion took up barely two pages in the *Federal Reporter*.

Charles Clark would not accept it. The longshoreman petitioned for rehearing *en banc*; Clark was the only judge to vote in favor; he wrote a dissent to the denial of the rehearing, after the denial he requested reconsideration of the denial; then he again dissented, at length, from the denial of the reconsideration. When he did, by the way, he turned to Guido's new article *Some Thoughts on Risk Distribution and the Law of Torts* for the proposition that the shipowner was "best situated to distribute the loss broadly amongst the beneficiaries of the industry.... [T]o make the burden fall on seamen or longshoremen is to require them to subsidize the shipping business."[45]

Clark's truculence made him "the person you would want in a fight against long odds and rough opposition."[46] It was he who stood up first, alone in the Second Circuit, in opposition to repressive postwar "loyalty" and "security" measures during "McCarthyism."[47]

In an earlier chapter, Guido also portrayed Clark's strategic effort to obtain Guido as a law clerk.[48]

Billings Learned Hand. Hand graduated from Harvard Law School in 1896 and started working for his uncle's law firm in Albany. He became a United States District Judge in the Southern District of New York from 1909 to 1924, where his reputation grew, particularly in the areas of civil liberty. His reputation was such that by 1923, Justice Holmes wanted him on the Supreme Court; in 1924, President Coolidge appointed Hand to the Second Circuit. The Circuit was further strengthened in the next few years by the appointments of Thomas Walter Swan and Hand's cousin, Augustus Noble Hand.[49]

Becoming accustomed to the external norms of judicial behavior—comparisons with Judge Richard Posner. Guido discusses difficulties becoming accustomed to the interior norms of the Court. As discussed in the extended comment below, both judges at times encountered criticism for their outspokenness as judges in public life.

One should never compare anyone to Hitler. In June 2004, Guido made comments about *Bush v. Gore* to the American Constitution Society, a group of progressive lawyers that reached a wider public. He described *Bush v. Gore* as a case in

---

[44] 303 F.2d 752 (1962).
[45] *Id.* at 758.
[46] Fred Rodell, *For Charles E. Clark: A Brief and Belated but Fond Farewell*, 65 COL. L. REV. 1323, 1328 (1965).
[47] *Id.* (first citing United States v. Josephson, 165 F.2d 82, 93 (1950); and then citing United States v. Sacher, 182 F.2d 416, 463 (1953)).
[48] See the discussion in Chapter 10, "A Law Student at Mid-Century."
[49] GERALD GUNTHER, LEARNED HAND: THE MAN AND THE JUDGE (1994); Richard Posner, *The Learned Hand Biography and the Question of Judicial Greatness*, 104 YALE L.J. 104 511 (1994).

which a legitimate institution—the Supreme Court—had acted illegitimately to clear the way for Mr. Bush to claim victory in the 2000 election. This was, he had said, analogous to what happened when Mussolini was installed by the king of Italy, and "what happened when Hindenburg put Hitler in."[50] He had made clear in his original statement that he was not comparing Bush to either Mussolini or Hitler—but the press did not report it that way.[51] Several Republican congresspersons pressed Justice Breyer to investigate Guido, alleging inappropriate political activity. Justice Breyer referred the matter to the Judicial Council of the Second Circuit.

In retrospect, and notwithstanding his statement that he was "not suggesting for a moment that Bush is Hitler," Guido realized that his remarks in some respects bordered on the political. He drew attention to a subtle political remark that did not receive much notice at the time of the episode, to the effect that in democracies, after an illegitimate use of legitimate power, it was important to "put that person out" at the next opportunity, to protect against the reassertion of power.[52] This, he said, led him to apologize to the Circuit in a letter to the Chief Judge. He expressed "profound regret" for remarks that "in hindsight, reasonably could be—and indeed have been—understood to do something which I did not intend, that is, take a partisan position."[53]

After the apology, a hearing took place. The Council cleared Guido of any violation, determining that the American Constitution Society was a legal-education group and not a "political organization." Guido's remarks, the Council reported, could well be interpreted as partisan, but they took place in the context of a panel directed to understanding and improving the legal system, a lecture of the sort encouraged by the ethical canons. It would not be appropriate to chill participation in such activities further. But it also noted that however academic the remarks had been, it presented an unfortunate appearance of partisanship. Nonetheless, since Guido had already apologized and had been publicly admonished, no further sanction would be necessary.[54]

Judge Posner's intemperance. Judge Posner had made statements that expressed conservative "political" views, which were never charged against him.[55] However, in 2016, he too found himself in hot water near the end of his judicial life for demeaning the Supreme Court and a departed conservative Justice. He asserted that the Court was "at a nadir," that posthumous effusive praise for Justice Scalia was "absurd," and that there was "absolutely no value to a judge of spending decades, years, months, weeks, day, hours, minutes, or seconds studying the Constitution."[56] The next year,

---

[50] Julia Preston, U.S. Judge Apologizes for Equating Victories of Bush and Hitler, N.Y. TIMES, June 25, 2004.
[51] *Id.*
[52] In re Charges of Judicial Misconduct, 404 F.3d 688 (2005).
[53] *Id.*
[54] *Id.*; Josh Gerstein, *Judge Scolded for Advocating Bush's Defeat*, N.Y. SUN, Apr. 11, 2005; Robert M. Howard, *The Limitations on Judicial Free Speech*, 27 JUST. SYS. J. 350 (2006).
[55] *See, e.g., "An Affair of State": An Exchange Richard Posner, reply by Ronald Dworkin*, N.Y. REV. OF BOOKS, Apr. 27, 2000.
[56] Richard A. Posner, *Law School Professors Need More Practical Experience*, SLATE, June 24, 2016.

he called legal technicalities "antiquated crap" and forcefully advocated a mandatory retirement age for judges.[57] In the predictable storm of criticism that followed his remarks, Judge Posner resigned from the bench—completely. He told reporters that he had become tired of long quarrels with his Seventh Circuit colleagues about the treatment of pro se litigants, that he was having other difficulties with his colleagues, and that it was appropriate for him to retire at his age.[58]

Richard Cardamone. Cardamone's father owned a wholesale food and liquor business. He graduated from Harvard College and from Syracuse University Law School in 1952, and practiced in Utica. In 1962, he began his judicial career by gaining election to the New York State Supreme Court. In 1981, President Ronald Reagan nominated him to the seat that had been vacated by Judge William Hughes Mulligan. Cardamone prided himself on his pragmatism and open-mindedness, which he attributed to raising ten children; he was "the epitome of collegiality and kindness." He often anguished over his decisions, in one case reflecting that "one wishes to decide a case comes lightly to mind, on a wing; but often how one must decide it comes arduously, weighed down by somber thought."[59] He died on October 16, 2015.[60]

The Pan Am Case.[61] A few days before Christmas in 1988, Pan American flight 103 blew up over Lockerbie, Scotland, with 259 Americans aboard. At the trial of the consolidated cases brought by passengers' and crews' survivors, the jury needed to determine whether Pan American World Airways and Alert Management Systems were guilty of misconduct that caused the explosion and the crash.[62]

The parties agreed that the Warsaw Convention on international air transportation, which limited recovery by passengers to $75,000, governed the dispute unless "willful misconduct" caused the damages, and in an earlier ruling, the Second Circuit established that punitive damages were unavailable.[63] The jury concluded that Pan Am did act with willful misconduct by disregarding passenger safety with knowledge of the probable consequences.

On appeal, the defendants raised questions about the sufficiency of the evidence, the disallowance of testimony, and the legal basis for damage awards. As Guido discusses, the majority opinion on the panel upheld the district court and remanded for a determination of damages. Van Graafeiland dissented at great length. "My name will be anathema to the hundreds of people who are seeking

---

[57] Joel Cohen et al., *Should There Be Age Limits for Federal Judges?*, SLATE, July 5, 2017.
[58] Debra Cassens Weiss, *Why Did Posner Retire?*, ABA J., Sept. 7, 2017; Adam Liptak, *An Exit Interview with Richard Posner, Judicial Provocateur*, N.Y. TIMES, Sept. 11, 2017.
[59] Letelier v. Republic of Chile, 748 F.2d 790, 791 (1984).
[60] Sam Roberts, Richard Cardamone, Judge, Dies at 90; N.Y. TIMES, Oct. 23, 2015.
[61] In re Air Disaster at Lockerbie Scot., 37 F.3d 804 (1994). The original opinion, In re Air Disaster at Lockerbie Scot., 38 Fed. R. Evid. Serv. (CBC) 953 (1994), with a dissent by Judge Van Graafeiland, was followed by a petition for rehearing. The panel withdrew the original opinion and replaced it by the one at 37 F. 3d. 804, which contained a new majority opinion and a revised dissent.
[62] In re Air Disaster at Lockerbie Scot., 37 F.3d at 811.
[63] In re Air Disaster at Lockerbie, Scot. on Dec. 21, 1988 ("Lockerbie I"), 928 F.2d 1267, cert. denied, 112 S. Ct. 331 (1991).

recoveries probably in excess of $ 1 billion," he wrote, "and my long-time friendship with Judge Platt may suffer some stress."[64] In his opinion, however, the district court proceeding had been unlawfully unfair.[65]

Ellsworth Van Graafeiland. Van Graafeiland studied agriculture at Cornell and the University of Rochester, graduating in 1937, and returned to Cornell Law School for his LL.B. degree. He practiced in Rochester until President Ford appointed him to the seat previously occupied by Henry Friendly in 1974.

His opinions and reactions to novel issues were invariably protective of upstate New York Republican cultural values. He was among the first federal jurists to challenge the constitutionality of racially based quotas.[66] He dissented from cases establishing judicial power to fashion a common law remedy for constitutional violations.[67] He disallowed various claims against the United States brought by the veterans, their families, and the defendant chemical companies in Agent Orange litigation.[68] He voted to uphold the severe Rockefeller drug sentencing laws.[69]

Van Graafeiland stayed on the bench until November 2004, when he died at age eighty-nine.

J. Daniel [Dan] Mahoney. Mahoney Graduated from Columbia Law School in 1955, served in the Coast Guard, and then entered private practice in New York City. He helped to found, and became the State Chairman of, the New York Conservative Party, representing conservative causes and clients including the *National Review* and its editor, William F. Buckley, Jr. President Reagan appointed him to the United States Court of Appeals for the Second Circuit in 1986. He died in 1996.[70]

Roger J. Miner. Miner graduated from SUNY-Albany and New York Law School in 1956, and began a career in law, politics, and teaching, in Columbia County, New York. He was elected as a state supreme court justice in 1976; President Reagan chose him for the United States District Court in 1981. In 1985 he was appointed to the Second Circuit.[71]

Miner gained a reputation for his attachment to neutral ethical norms.[72] He was mentioned as a possible nominee for the Supreme Court in 1987 following the defeat of Robert Bork, but encountered opposition from anti-abortion groups because he had not chosen an anti-abortion activist to replace biological parents who declined to allow corrective surgery on a newborn that, they were told, would only live a matter of weeks.[73] In 1996, as Guido discusses in a later chapter, he also wrote

---

[64] In re Air Disaster at Lockerbie Scot., 37 F.3d at 830.
[65] *Id.*
[66] Charles K. Whitehead, *Hon. Ellsworth A. Van Graafeiland*, 97 CORNELL L. REV. 5 (2012).
[67] *See* 579 F.2d 152, 155 (1978), vacated and remanded on other grounds sub nom. City of West Haven v. Turpin, 439 U.S. 974 (1978), modified, 591 F.2d 426 (1979).
[68] *See* Stencel Aero Eng'g Corp. v. United States, 431 U.S. 666 (1977); Feres v. United States, 340 U.S. 135 (1950); Peter Schuck, *The Role of Judges in Settling Complex Cases: The Agent Orange Example*, 53 U. CHI. L. REV. 337, 342 (1986).
[69] Wolfgang Saxon, *Ellsworth Van Graafeiland, 89, Appellate Judge, Dies*, N.Y. TIMES, Nov. 25, 2004.
[70] Lawrence Van Gelder, *Judge J. Daniel Mahoney, 65, Founder of Conservative Party*, N.Y. TIMES, Oct. 26, 1996.
[71] Douglas Martin, *Roger J. Miner, 77, Dies; Judge Valued Neutrality*, N.Y. TIMES, Feb. 20, 2012.
[72] *See, e.g.,* Roger J. Miner, *Judicial Ethics in the Twenty-First Century: Tracing the Trends*, 32 HOFSTRA L. REV. 1107 (2004).
[73] Martin, Roger J. Miner, 77, Dies, NEW YORK TIMES, Feb. 20, 2012.

the opinion for a majority of the Court of Appeals which endorsed a doctor's right to help terminally ill patients to commit suicide.[74] Miner died in 2012.[75]

Thomas [Tom] Meskill. Meskill was born in New Britain, Connecticut, in 1928. He graduated from Trinity College in 1950 and in 1956 received a law degree from the University of Connecticut. While practicing law in New Britain, he made losing Republican political bids for Congress and finally won a seat in 1966. In 1970, after two terms in Congress, Meskill was elected governor. During his governorship, the state's 1860 law banning abortions was struck down by the Court of Appeals, provoking a major political battle in the state.[76] Meskill served for a single term and then chose not to seek re-election. President Ford named him to the Second Circuit in 1975. He served as Chief Judge in 1992 and 1993 and died in 2007.[77]

James Lowell Oakes. Born in 1924 in Springfield, Illinois, Oakes graduated from Harvard College and Harvard Law School. He spent two decades practicing law and working in the state government in Vermont. President Nixon chose Oakes to become a federal district judge in Vermont in 1970 and elevated him to the appeals court in 1971, but, as the *New York Times* reported, Oakes was not proud about this. After the Watergate scandal, "he used adhesive tape to cover the signatures of President Nixon and Attorney General John N. Mitchell on the judicial commission that hung in his chambers."[78] He soon became one of the Circuit's leading liberal voices—his name became "synonymous in some circles with liberal jurisprudence."[79]

Oakes embraced legal realism. Reviewing a book on the craft of judging, he emphasized how much it ought to depend on living life in the world as much as knowing the formal law. He considered it "imperative that a judge keep abreast of the day's news: social, cultural and economic trends, scientific and environmental affairs," and said that he spent, conservatively, "30–35 hours a week on top of the regular workload" doing so." He served as Chief Judge from 1988 to 1992.

Wilfred [Bill] Feinberg. Judge Feinberg was born on June 22, 1920, in Manhattan, and graduated from Columbia College in 1940. After service in the Second World War, he attended Columbia Law School, graduating in 1946 and practicing in New York before President Kennedy appointed him to the Southern District in 1965. President Johnson picked him (rather than Judge Edward Weinfeld, of greater stature, but who was older and without as much political support) for the Second Circuit to fill the seat being vacated by Judge Thurgood Marshall, who had been named solicitor general. The views he took were generally progressive; for example, he dissented from an *en banc* majority opinion, which delayed (temporarily) the

---

[74] Quill v. Vacco, 80 F.3d 716 (1996); see chapter, Calabresian Complexities and the Value of Dialogue.
[75] Martin, Roger J. Miner, 77, Dies, N.Y. Times, Feb. 20, 2012.
[76] *Id.*; see Chapter 30, "Calabresian Complexities and the Value of Dialogue."
[77] Dennis Hevesi, *Thomas J. Meskill Dies at 79; Ex-Congressman, Connecticut Governor and Federal Judge*, N.Y. TIMES, Oct. 30, 2007.
[78] Adam Liptak, *James L. Oakes Dies at 83; Nixon Choice for Federal Bench*, N.Y. TIMES, Oct. 16, 2007.
[79] *Id.*

publication of the Pentagon Papers in the *New York Times*, and ruled in several cases permitting employees to pursue efforts to unionize.[80] Whatever questions there were about his appointment, they were overcome during a career universally considered distinguished. Feinberg served forty-five years at the Second Circuit, eight of them as Chief Judge. He died at the age of ninety-four in 2014.[81]

Guido's own clerks. From the outset, law students perceived that obtaining a clerkship with Guido would be an extraordinary prize that would reflect the estimation of a renowned academic and dean of ability, intellectual resilience, and integrity. More, it reflected Guido's judgment about creativity and about the student's potential to make a difference in the world. Guido's connections in the legal profession, and his ebullient personality were also quite visible. Guido also made a conscious effort to add racial, gender, and sexual orientation diversity to his own deliberative process.

As other Circuit Court Judges did, Guido left clerks alone in offices in his New Haven chambers for much of their days, working on the cases. They ate lunch together, debated lines of argument with them when clerks wanted, or when Guido corresponded with other judges. Guido prepared exceptionally detailed, handwritten notes about each case, taking them into oral arguments and post-argument conferences. The clerks usually accompanied him from New Haven chambers to his Manhattan Courthouse for scheduled sittings; once a panel reached a decision, clerks helped to execute and articulate Guido's positions.

He chose more than ninety clerks between 1994 and 2020. More pursued academic careers or public service occupations than went into private practice—in fact, no judge helped more law clerks into academia than he did.[82] He "fed" more clerks to the Supreme Court than all but a few other judges.[83]

Guido sustained relationships with most of his clerks after they finished. He helped them along their career paths and treated them as members of a judicial "family." He and Anne hosted annual picnics for them at their Woodbridge home.

His law clerks are listed by year below, with an asterisk to indicate those who pursued academic careers:

1994–1995: Daniel S. Alter, Douglas A. Berman*, Jeffrey O. Cooper*; 1995–1996: Melissa R. Hart*, Neal K. Katyal*, William J. Nardini; 1996–1997: Thomas B. Colby*, Rachel A. Harmon*, Kenji Yoshino*; 1997–1998: Richard B Katskee, Jennifer S. Martinez*, John A.E. Pottow*, Catherine M. Sharkey*; 1998–1999: Todd

---

[80] William Yardley, *Wilfred Feinberg, Federal Appeals Court Judge and Mentor, Dies at 94*, N.Y. TIMES, Aug. 4, 2014.

[81] *Id.*

[82] Howard Wasserman, Academic Feeder Judges, Florida International University Legal Studies Research Paper No. 20-02 7 (2020) ("The clear 'winner' in this study is Guido Calabresi, ... Forty-two former Calabresi clerks are in the legal academy, 27 at top-25 law schools."); Karen Sloan, *Want to Be a Law Prof? Clerk for these Judges*, NAT. L. J., Feb. 4. 2020.

[83] Thirty-two of his clerks went to the U.S. Supreme Court during the period 1985–2014, ranking him high among top "feeder judges." *See* Alexandra G. Hess, *The Collapse of the House That Ruth Built: The Impact of the Feeder System on Female Judges and the Federal Judiciary, 1970–2014*, 24 J. GENDER, SOC. POL. & L. 61, 80 (2015).

S. Aagard*, Gerard N. Magliocca*, Richard A. Primus*, Amanda L. Tyler*; 1999–2000: Linda C. Y. Lye, Eduardo M. Peñalver*, Danielle M.Spinelli, Amy J. Wildermuth*; 2000–2001: Risa L. Goluboff*, Daniel S. Markovits*, Gil Seinfeld*, Noah D. Zatz*; 2001–2002: Gitanjali S Gutierrez, Christine Lehmann, Maritza U.B. Okata, Anne K. Small; 2002–2003: Christopher S. Elmendorf*, Gregory M. Klass*, Elizabeth A. Olson, Christian M. Turner*; 2003–2004: Roberto J. Gonzalez, Amy N. Kapczynski*, Serena K. Mayeri*, Jacob J. Sullivan; 2004–2005: Patrick D. Curran, Katie R. Eyer*, Jennifer E. Laurin*, Jon D. Michaels*; 2005–2006: Michelle W. Anderson*, Jamal K. Greene*, Jud Mathews*, Thiruvendran Vignarajah; 2006–2007: Rebecca J. Charnas Grant, Seth Grossman*, Kevin S. Schwartz, Micah W.J. Smith; 2007–2008: Joshua A. Chafetz*, Erin P. Delaney*, Paul MacMahon*, Karen M. Tani*; 2008–2009: Joseph Blocher*, Rachel Bloomekatz, Adam Jed, Natalie Ram*; 2009–2010: Brian T. Burgess, Jeffrey Dubner, Michael H. Page, Benjamin J. Rogers; 2010–2011: Anya Bernstein*, Michael Coenen*, Sonja R. Ralston; 2011–2012: Sparkle L. Alexander Sooknanan, John F. Muller*, Thomas Wolf; 2012–2013: Justin Collings*, Farah Peterson*, Brian Soucek*; 2013–2014: Catherine Itaya, Luke Norris*, David Wishnick*; 2014–2015: Nathaniel Cullerton, Eric S. Fish*, Kevin Lamb; 2015–2016: Andrew T. Davis; Shayak Sarkar*, Brooke J. Willig; 2016–2017: Travis Pantin*, Caitlin Tully, Allison Whelan*; 2017–2018: John Boeglin, Courtney Elgart, Sam Thypin-Bermeo, David Maners-Weber; 2018–2019: Alison D. Gocke*, Diana Li, Noah Rosenblum*, Matteo Godi; 2019–2020: Whitney Brown, Sean Colenso-Semple, Adam Davidson*, Skylar Albertson; 2020–2021: Kate Redburn*, Joyce Dela Pena, Spencer D. Smith*, José E. Argueta Funes*.

Clerks at an annual reunion in Woodbridge.

27

The Tort Law Opinions of a Torts Professor

> *Judicial decision-making requires that laws be applied to facts according to theories about how and why they should be applied. Writing about the interrelationship between theory and application, Cass Sunstein has illustrated the point with an easy example drawn from torts cases: judgments about tort causation intrinsically depend on theories of moral responsibility.*
>
> *As we have seen, Guido came to the bench from academia, having spent much of his career evaluating traditional tort theories and developing novel ones. While he has been on the bench, by a special arrangement with Yale, he has continued to teach. Under these circumstances the inclination of a scholar—teacher-judge to emphasize approaches that he championed as an academic have colored his judicial approach. Theories appealing to an academic, however, might fail in the face of discrete facts and particularized circumstances.*
>
> *Guido knew that there would be a long learning curve as he came to understand the workings of the Court—he was also confident that even while he was learning he could bring his own strengths as a torts scholar to the appellate court.*

Taber v. Maine, my first significant opinion, came to me by random assignment, in my first sitting as a Court of Appeals judge. It involved an off-duty seaman named Taber who was hit by a drunk driver named Maine, another seaman. Taber sued both Maine and the U.S. government, which meant that the opinion needed to deal in part with whether the government was liable under the "master-servant" doctrine for the willful or intentional acts of its servant; and also to deal with the "*Feres* doctrine," the odd doctrine that prevents people who are in the military from suing the government.

* * *

The master-servant question is historically interesting. At the end of the nineteenth century, courts started seeing two sorts of suits. One set of cases was brought against bill collectors who in collecting a bill, did not just put pressure on a debtor, but punched him. There was another group of suits by women who were working in department stores, and were raped by their supervisors. Department stores were a relatively new development. They had enormously long corridors that were dark, and there were a number of rape cases.

When courts first looked at these they saw no cases imposing master's liability where servants behaved intentionally wrongly. Not knowing why, they made up reasons. Some said, "Well, when it is the intentional conduct of the servant, it is not really in pursuit of the business of the master." Others said, "the master did not want the servant to do what was intentionally wrongful." But *negligent* behavior by the servant was not often in the pursuit of the business of the master *either*, and often not desired by the master; and yet employers *were* liable in many such cases! Nonsensical distinctions! Some courts just said, "no precedents, no recovery."

In time, many states came around to saying that where the tort benefits the business directly, then we will allow the plaintiff to recover from the master. So, in the bill collector cases, "Yes," but the rape cases, "No."

Notice that that distinction was not drawn in negligent master-servant situations. The master was liable when a gas station attendant carelessly lit a cigarette which caused an explosion even though the servant's smoking (which was "a detour") did not benefit the master directly.

By the late 1960s, some state courts began to treat intentional torts in the same way they did negligent torts; that is, as a practical matter they placed liability on the master when that would lead to risk reduction because the conduct of the servant was part of the cost of the employer's output. This may have been in part because of my articles; it certainly was influenced by an important opinion by Judge Henry Friendly in *Bushey v. U.S.* (which in passing discussed my analysis). Courts began to decide master-servant questions by placing liability on the master when that would lead to risk reduction by the master, or when the conduct of the servant was part of the cost of the employer's output. Among the states that did this was California, and for complicated reasons, the law of California was the guiding law as to master-servant liability in our Second Circuit case, even though the accident had actually happened in Guam.

* * *

So come back to *Taber*. This case in 1994 about the drunken sailor and the government's responsibility for the sailor's actions comes to me. My ideas apply directly. The master-servant part relates directly to "Some Thoughts . . . and the Law of Torts," "The Decision for Accidents," and of course my first book, *The Cost of Accidents*.

I write an opinion which essentially says that the focus of the master-servant analysis, even in an intentional wrong case, should properly be on the relationship between the serviceman's behavior and the costs of military enterprise. I wrote that drinking was a harm which was a risk of the enterprise.

A fair number of states now follow this broader view of master-servant liability in intentional torts cases. Some stayed with the old distinction based on whether the intentional wrong "directly furthered" the business of the employer. Not surprisingly, the states that hold to that old distinction often stretch the meaning of what "directly furthers" the employer. Is a resort employer, who encourages "dirty dancing" by employees, liable when an employee goes further and sexually harasses? There are, however, situations where even "stretching" the meaning of "directly furthers" is not available.

> *This has come up in Connecticut, which holds to the narrow view of intentional torts, in suits against the Catholic Church for sexual abuse by priests. Connecticut courts have said, "That isn't helping the Church, so it has no liability on master-servant grounds," even though abuse certainly is a risk of going to see a priest at a Church.*
>
> *But again, not surprisingly, states like Connecticut make it much easier in such situations, to prove negligence directly on the part of a master—negligence in hiring, in training the intentionally wrongful servant. Such ways of reaching the same result are what you would expect when the door is closed to master liability for intentional torts that arise in the scope of employment.*

So I wrote that liability should fall on the government—that is, if the government could be sued under the *Feres* doctrine.

* * *

The part about the *Feres* doctrine is directly connected to the discussion in *The Common Law for the Age of Statutes*. The doctrine is a clear example of courts reading limitations on suing into the Federal Torts Claims Act, limitations that were not in the statute. They did it in order to make the rules for injuries to someone in the *military* be like the rules for employees under workers' compensation. When employees are covered by workers' compensation, the statute establishing worker's compensation prevents them from suing their employers in torts.

Originally the *Feres* doctrine did no more than this, because soldiers were already covered for their injuries arising out of their military service. In time, however, courts started applying the *Feres* doctrine more broadly, and giving military employers more protection than private employers. They found reasons such as preserving military discipline and promoting sound military decision-making. The original *Feres* decision, right or wrong, is a very good example of courts making statutes fit the legal topography, which I wrote about in *A Common Law for the Age of Statutes*. The later decisions do not make much sense.

* * *

So I tried to bring the *Feres* doctrine back to its original meaning in *Taber*, saying, "Look, I don't know if they were *right* to try to change the meaning of that law to make it fit together with the rest of employer liability; but that is what they *did*.

That is the meaning we should understand." Therefore, I said that because the plaintiff in *Taber* was more like an employee who was covered by voluntary insurance than like an employee subject to workers' compensation, the *Feres* doctrine with its original intent to mirror the workers' compensation scheme should not apply to bar recovery in this case.

The discussion was complicated and sophisticated.

When the case first was assigned to my panel, I did something that used to be done all the time in the Second Circuit, especially by Henry Friendly. I circulated a memo before the oral argument to explain aspects of the case which the others might not immediately see. Here was a case that I had written two books on, so I wrote a long bench memo explaining why it had to come out the way that it ultimately did come out.

Pierre Leval—who had clerked for Henry Friendly—was presiding, and he seemed to me to be a very senior and wise judge. He was both, but in fact he had just come on the Second Circuit and this was his first time presiding. The memo I wrote explaining my view of the case evidently convinced him. He understood, and he went along with me. The third judge on our panel, Judge Pratt, was about to retire. He didn't want to get into it. He agreed with the result and that was enough.

[Judge Pratt] didn't want to spend enough time trying to figure out whether to write a dissent, so he did something quite unusual. He concurred in the result without a comment. He just didn't want to get into it. It was too hard.

After we released the opinion, some of the other judges felt, I think, that this was Guido showing off his erudition. Certainly it was a much broader, very different kind of opinion than is usually issued. But it was a complicated case, and it made sense to me to explain the reasoning at length. Van Graafeiland could not understand a thing in it, and he was unhappy. His daughter had been the U.S. Attorney bringing the case. He was very proud of her, understandably, and she lost. He thought that the result was wrong and he may even have taken it as a personal affront.

One of the other judges of the Circuit asked that *Taber* be taken *en banc*. I do not know what moved him [Sighs], but maybe it was because he was being protective of the military and of government. There were some things in the opinion which might have seemed really quite hard on the government, and on the Navy. That might have tempted some judges to say "Guido is making the government pay too much." Remember, we can be a very conservative, pro-government, Circuit.

Some judges may have thought that I should have paid more attention to what the district judge in Guam had said. Their memories of when they had been district judges, or their links to the states, etc., that they identified with, may have led them to feel that more deference was due to them, and that courts of appeals should be more respectful of their knowledge of local law—in this case, Guam.

The only problem with that is that it turned out that if there was any mistake in *Taber v. Maine*, it was that I gave *too much* deference to the Guam court's reading of the law of Guam, because I hadn't picked up—and nobody talking about it picked up—that the Supreme Court in *Salve Regina v. Russell* very recently had made it clear that one should not give deference to federal district judges' supposed knowledge of local state law. So, if anything, I gave too much deference to the district judge's view of what Guam Law was.

I do not know whether some of them wanted just a bit to put me in my place. But fortunately of course all this flew in the face of our tendency not to take cases *en banc*.

Whatever. Jon Newman quickly got into the act, as he was wont to do in these things. He suggested some changes in language that toned down the master-servant discussion—offering a way I could limit a little bit what I was saying about the Navy and still come out the same way. In effect, he said, "We're not going to go *en banc* on this if Guido makes some changes." Leval and I made changes along those lines, and released an amended opinion. That was enough to defeat the *en banc* request.

> *Amusingly, as soon as the opinion was released I received a note from Dick Posner telling me how wonderful he thought the opinion was, and what fun it was occasionally to be able to make one's views the law. I didn't think I had done that—I thought I had just clarified the law!*

Twenty-five years later, I still like the approach I took in *Taber v. Maine*. The length and the style may be a mite too academic; I do not know whether it is or not. But it untangles the master-servant problem, and the *Feres* doctrine in useful ways, and it helps everyone understand the recurring issues. Subsequent cases and the torts literature has been favorable to it; I do not think that there is any case that has undercut it. It has found its way into casebooks. I am not sure if this is because *Taber* explains the *Feres* doctrine, or the master-servant problem, but it did deal with both.

* * *

Soon after came another torts case, *Stagl v. Delta*. It began after a plane arrived late to LaGuardia airport and everybody rushed to the baggage carousels. Luggage was pouring out. There was absolute chaos! Somebody pulled a suitcase off, and in the process knocked down an elderly lady—injuring her—and took off.

The lady sued Delta. Her case raised a pretty standard, straightforward torts question: Did Delta have a duty of care to the lady that was breached? Did the disappearing wrongdoer break the chain of causation? The "intervening wrongdoer," was not likely to get caught. If caught, he might have funds to compensate the lady, but he is not likely to be found. If he *can* be found, Delta can go after him for reimbursement or a contribution. But ought Delta bear the burden of going after him? Or should it be the plaintiff?

These are standard torts questions. But I mention the case because it taught me something about restraining the inclination that I certainly then had to write opinions as though they are law review articles. Jon Newman was the presider on the panel, and when I started to write a treatise, or at least an article, about "last wrong-doer," "intervening causes," and other fun things, Jon said to me in a nice way, "You're a judge. Decide *this* case." He added, "You'll have plenty of time when other cases come up to say the other things, both directly and in talking to other people on the court. And, of course, you can always write articles. Sometimes it is necessary and useful to write an "article" in an opinion, but, as a general matter, you do not do that." I took his advice, and opinion in *Stagl* is a nice, efficient, and even elegant opinion sending the case back to the trial court for a determination of whether the act of the intervening wrongdoer was the foreseeable consequence of the situation created by Delta.

I use this case in talking about intervening causes in my Torts classes. Lots of teachers do. It is not the kind of opinion that torts scholars would write an article about—they would wait for a much bigger and more complicated set of facts to come along. But that's why *Stagl* is worth mentioning. It is a useful opinion. It helped me to learn my job and to think about whom one writes for.

You see, all judges write for the Law. We decide cases, we explain how we get to the result, and that's what the Law requires. But each of us has, also, a *special* audience located back in the places from which we come, that we feel we have to answer to, whether consciously or subconsciously.

When I write, inevitably, I think also of the Academy, and of the structure of the Law. I am concerned with whether people in the Academy will understand what I'm saying, even though there are things that I cannot say in the opinion. I hope they will understand what is going on in my mind. "How is the Academy going to deal with it?" is what all judges, whatever their ideologies, who come from the Academy, inevitably think about. It is what Judges as different as Bob Katzmann and Joe McLaughlin and Ralph Winter—judges of different ideologies who still have an academic side—think about. It affects how you write.

I had a wonderful recent conversation with Kenneth Abraham about the Zuchowcz case, which I will tell you about soon, and which he wrote an article about. Ken probably understands torts best in the country. I told him that there were some things that the opinion could not quite say yet, but which one could intuit actually moved the court. This conversation was between a judge who is also an academic, and an academic who is trying to understand the reasoning of a judge.

Delta v. Stagl taught me that you can and should write for your particular constituency, but not to the extent that it makes it difficult for other legal constituencies. Somebody like Jon Newman writes for "the Law," but also for district judges. He was a district judge and identifies with his many years of interacting with other district judges. When he writes an opinion, he always writes one that they can work with. That is what he and others who have the same background inevitably do. And so I was glad when Pierre Leval paid me a great compliment early on. He said, "You understand what district judges have to deal with." I thought it was wonderful, considering that I had never set foot in a district courtroom and I knew nothing about district judges.

Other Judges write for the Bar, maybe the prosecutorial Bar, or the defense Bar, or the corporate Bar, because they've been such lawyers themselves. "How will practitioners handle and react to our opinion?" What arguments will they be able to make in the next case? This is what judges like Amalya Kearse and Dennis Jacobs inevitably ask themselves.

When does a judge like me write more academically, as in *Taber v. Maine*, rather than as I did in *Stagl*? That's very complicated. It is always aggressive to do more than simply deciding the case. Whether one is doing so because it useful for the Academy, the lower courts, or the practicing bar, there are going to be judges who are activists and will take the language that is used in speaking to the Academy, etc., as if it were really part of the holding of the case. You wrote it to be informative and not to be authoritative—it was dicta—but they treat it as if it is a holding because they want to bind other people.

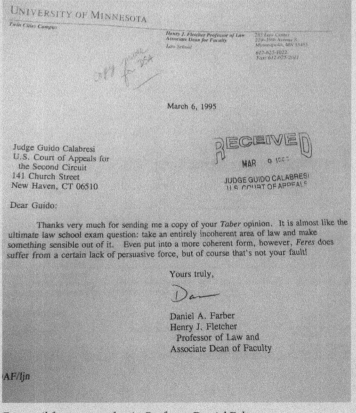

Fan mail from an academic: Professor Daniel Faber

This does not mean that there is not often a good reason to use dicta to write broadly; that is part of what speaking to your constituency is about; but one should be extremely careful not to call holding what is dicta. This is especially true when you are writing for a panel, because the only way a panel system—in which earlier panels bind later ones—can work, is if earlier panels are restrained. Making believe dicta is a holding is grabby. If some judges reach out to decide and bind later judges by writing aggressively in cases that can be decided narrowly, it will tend to make everyone do it.

That is a separate reason why making dicta into holding is dangerous. The reason that is most often and properly given is that when a court uses language which seems to decide a situation which is not yet before it, it may regret it when that situation actually occurs. It may want to reach a different result when "the rubber hits the road."

These two very separate reasons why dicta is dangerous help to explain why the Supreme Court can be much more loose in its use of "authoritative" dicta. It doesn't have the "panel problem," although it does have the other one—the danger of speaking about issues that are not fully in front of you. When it is a majority of the highest tribunal that speaks, it can give guidance and illuminate a problem in ways that are helpful to lower courts. This can be valuable. And it is also true when we are sitting as a Circuit Court *en banc*. We then very often will use dicta to guide people, even though it would not be technically binding. We may even make it sound like a holding, when it really is not, because we do not have the panel problem.

* * *

Even on panels, true dicta can be useful. It tells later courts who have to face an issue head-on, how other judges have felt about the issue. This can be very comforting to a judge. But there are times when using even clearly identified dicta would not be correct or even possible. In such situations, I have sometimes concurred in my own opinions. This allows the others on the panel to be quiet. They are not saying they disagree; they are not saying they agree. They are just being quiet. It becomes just you speaking, and you can go where you want to with your thoughts without imposing on others. Sometimes a judge is "more unique than rare" and has a duty to speak. A situation may occur where you are pretty much the only one who can speak to this subject with confidence, because of your own experience. And then you pretty well have to write more broadly. How you do it will depend on the panel. If others want to agree with you—as Judge Leval did in *Taber v. Maine*—it can become dicta that is part of the opinion. If others are not ready to join you it can be a separate concurring opinion by you alone.

It is hard to say when a judge should do it, but the temptation is always there. If you are writing a separate concurring opinion, you are free. You can do as much as you want. But even there, you have to decide. To what extent does one point out that the law we are enforcing is wrong, and yet I'm forced to go along with it? And do I do that broadly or narrowly? I can concur pointing out specific problems or I can write an opinion for history. And when you write to history, then you throw it all in! And oddly, you can do any of this when somebody else has written for the panel, but you can also do it when you are writing the opinion for the court.

These things are nuanced. Go through a whole lot of my cases and ask me, "Why did you do it here? Why did you not do it here? Why, in your footnote concurring in *United States v. Then*, did you talk about laws "heading towards unconstitutionality"? Why did you write a separate concurrence to your own opinion in *Restrepo v. McElroy*, or in *Ciraolo*? It might not have been necessary to decide those cases—but why was it important for you to do it?"

How do you become sufficiently self-conscious and self-restrained, so that you do not do it just for the fun of it? This is really *the essence* and, in a way, *the art*—of being a judge. One way to be careful is to train your clerks to stop you and to question you, when you are tempted to do it. Conversely, if they push you, because it is something they are interested in, you need to teach them to be careful.

* * *

Liriano v. Hobart is a wonderful, fascinating case. Liriano was a meat cutter at a supermarket, and he was given a machine that did not have a guard on it. The result was that he cut off his arm. He sued the maker of the machine, Hobart, because the employer, who had taken the guard off, covered him with workers' compensation. This meant that the damages Liriano could get from the employer were limited to workers' compensation benefits, which are quite low. Suing the manufacturer, in workers' compensation situations is what I call, in my torts class, "the common-law end run," a way around the fact that workers' compensation has gotten out of date and the recoveries are low. Some states barred the end run, but not many. Some states let it exist without saying anything about it. New York, interestingly, "statutorified" it. That is, they said, "Yes, it can be done where the injury is serious enough," which is not an unreasonable position.

> *You would think that when that happened, employers—whom the manufacturers, if they are held liable, then sue—and the manufacturers would say "Then bring up to date the workers' compensation law." Except that now unions sometimes oppose updating it because they like the idea of having both workers' compensation and the suit as a way around it. Unfortunately, torts laws are made by repeat players, among them plaintiffs' lawyers who kind of like this, because they can get a nice contingent fee percentage. And it probably is plaintiff's lawyers more than the unions—but one way or another, the old law remains.*

The problem with the *Liriano* case was, how can you say that the cutting machine was defective when originally it had been made with a guard? Well, there is a New York Court of Appeals case that says, "in such cases, the machine is not defective unless the guard is made in a way that it is easily taken off, is in effect, *made to be taken off*." But that was not the case here. The guard could be removed, but it took a fair amount of effort on the part of the employer to remove it.

Judge Jacob Fuchsberg had written a rather maddening dissent in an earlier New York case, saying that this was wrong, that there should be a products liability action against the manufacturer. But in his dissent, he also said, "This would keep the manufacturer from being liable, even if he failed to warn that the machine should be used with a guard."

> *Fuchsberg was an old plaintiff's lawyer who had defeated a very good judge on the New York Court of Appeals when its judges were elected. There had always been a tradition that no one would ever run against a sitting New York Court of Appeals judge, so in effect, it was an appointment system, though nominally it was an election. But Fuchsberg broke with tradition and he won. The leaders of the Bar then got it formally changed to an appointment system; that was the last time that there were judicial elections for the Court of Appeals.*

There was nothing in the majority opinion of that earlier case that said that. It made no sense! It was a typical overstatement in a dissent, which is one of the things that drives me mad: dissenters who undercut their own case by saying that what the majority did is even worse than it is—instead of pointing out what the majority did not decide! In fact, failing to include a warning might well be a question of negligence, and recovery would not be barred by the lack of strict products liability. But several appellate divisions in New York had followed the dissent and said, "no negligence actions for failing to warn."

***

Well, the *Liriano* case came up, and the other people on the panel were Jon Newman, who is a great judge but who does not care all that much about tort law. I do not know who taught him at Yale—it was not Jimmy James. And Judge Richard Cudahy, who was visiting from the Seventh Circuit, who was a very good judge—very liberal—and who understood meat cutting, because meatpacking was his family's business.

Both of them were ready to say, "The case should have been sent to a jury on the question of whether there was a reasonable warning or not." We all agreed that the district court had thrown it out on products liability correctly; it was clear that there was no strict product liability, because of this earlier New York case. But there was the question about whether it should have gone to a jury on the possible negligent failure by Hobart to warn.

I strongly believed that it should have gone to the jury and that this was the only sensible result; but I also thought that we could not just do it. It seemed to me it was a clear case for certification.

I thought that we should certify the case, and let the New York Court of Appeals face the issue. If they were stupid enough to go along with Fuchsberg's view of this, too bad. But that would be New York law, which bound us. If, instead, they viewed the matter as we did, then lower courts would no longer keep such warning questions from juries. There would be a clear statement by the New York Court of Appeals of what the law was.

So I wrote the opinion certifying the issue to the Court of Appeals, in what is now called *Liriano One*. We also asked if there was enough evidence of negligent lack of warning to go to a jury.

The New York Court of Appeals granted certification, and then it ruled correctly, saying that a cause of action *would* lie for negligently failing to warn. And saying that Fuchsberg was wrong about the meaning of the earlier case.

I felt very good.

They also said, "the question of warning depends on whether, in the particular circumstances, it was negligent not to warn." They added, "warning is not needed for obvious perils. That question remains, but we do not need to speak about it, because the law is clear."

They did their job perfectly, and didn't go any further.

At that point the defendants hired James Henderson and Aaron Twerski. They were the Reporters for the Third Restatement of Products Liability. I love Henderson; he was a very nice man and a dear friend. I think he is, however, quite wrong in his thinking about products liability. Like me, he received the Prosser Prize, and I think that is fine, and he was a wonderful teacher. Well, they wrote a brief which said, "It is perfectly obvious that to use a meat cutting machine is dangerous, so why ought one warn that it is dangerous? It isn't negligent to fail to warn of something that is commonly known."

> *Notice a nice torts distinction: the law is that where an individual knows of the risk, even if it is negligent not to warn, the failure to warn made no difference. The person knew the risk and so the failure to warn was not a cause of the harm. Here, these experts were arguing instead that if enough people know that cutting machines are dangerous, then a reasonable person does not need to warn, even though there may be somebody who does not know that the machines are dangerous. This argument goes back to Lorenzo v. Wirth, the Boston coal-hole case, where Holmes said that where there is a pile of coal and there was no other means of delivery, most people would know that there is a hole there; that is warning enough, even if the person who fell in came from Latin Amerca and had never seen coal delivered.*

It seemed like a powerful argument. The only problem is, that even if you do not need to warn that something is dangerous because it is obvious, that does not mean that the ordinary person knows that there is an alternative to facing the danger. You do not need to warn that it is dangerous to drive down a hill on an icy road. But if there is another way of getting where you want to go that does not bring you down a hill, then a reasonable person may need to tell you of that safer way around. A person who fails to do that may be negligent in not showing you the alternative.

It is perfectly obvious that a cutting machine is dangerous, but does the ordinary person know that guards exist? A person so warned could say to the employer, "Hey, I don't want to use it without a guard." And a reasonable manufacturer might well warn, by putting on the machine, "This machine should be used with a guard, and can be used with a guard. Do not use it without a guard." This does not warn of the danger, but it informs the user that there is a way around. The Henderson-Twerski brief did not mention this, which amused me, because in a very fine article Henderson and Twerski pointed out that a failure to warn about alternatives could be negligent even if a danger was obvious. I referred to their article in my opinion.

After our ruling they came back and said, "But this particular plaintiff actually worked in another company before. He used the machine with a guard, so he already knew of that specific alternative. And since he knew it, the failure to warn of the alternative could not have been the cause of his injury." What a powerful response!

Except, at that point, Jon Newman got mad. He said, "For heaven's sakes! If they knew that, they should have said that in the beginning, because then there was no causation issue and Liriano's whole case would fall apart." You know? On those facts, none of the issues we identified are there. Certifying the issue to the New York Court of Appeals about whether a cause of action for negligent warning existed would have been pointless because in this case the negligence—if there was negligence—wouldn't have caused the accident!

So Jon wrote a very fierce little summary order (I had written the earlier opinions). It said "YOU SHOULD HAVE TOLD US EARLIER. IT'S TOO LATE TO RAISE THAT NOW. GO AWAY."

End of case.

* * *

Liriano involved a "cause in fact" question: Was Liriano's injury caused by the failure to warn or by something else? And the same question came up in the next case I want to talk about, *Zuchowicz v. United States*. In dealing with cause in fact, it took a long time for courts to get over their concern with the "*post hoc/ propter hoc fallacy*," the mistaken notion that just because something followed an action, that action must be the cause of it. Situations arose, for example, where a tenant was found dead at the foot of the stairs, a landlord had violated a statute by not having lights at the top of the stairs, and the court said, "Yes, this *was* negligence per se'—but the tenant might have fallen anyway! What evidence of *cause* is there?"

Absurd! And yet this was one old way of looking at things. It certainly made it difficult for the plaintiffs to recover.

> *An unusual nineteenth century Louisiana case—and I quote the court—"of a corpulent lady," who was being helped to a train, began to relax the judicial concern about* post hoc *reasoning. There were no lights; she fell and hurt herself. The court said, "Why do you think we want lights? We want lights so that people won't fall." Showing a causal link, a causal tendency, the danger because of which we hold behavior to be wrong, was enough evidence of a but-for cause in that case.*

An important part of my torts teaching is helping students to judge whether circumstantial evidence satisfies the legal standard that is required. I get them to ask four questions about the fact situation. First, was there negligence? If there is direct evidence, that is easy, but even without direct evidence, the case can get to the jury through the doctrine of "*res ipsa loquitur.*" This doctrine allows cases to go to jury on the existence of negligence when the facts of the case by themselves suggest that negligence was there more probably than not.

Second question: Whose negligence is it? In the celebrated case of *Ybarra v. Spangard*, for example, a patient suffers an injury which everyone agrees must have been due to negligence. But we do not know which of several hospital employees acting at different times were the negligent ones. The court shifted the burden of proof to the employees to show that they weren't negligent.

Third question: Whose negligence was the cause? In a hunters' case, *Summers v. Tice,* for example, hunters who took shots at the same time both were negligent, but the plaintiff could not establish whose shot harmed him. So the court created alternative liability and again shifted the burden of proof, and required the negligent hunters to bring in evidence that their shot was not the injuring one.

And fourth: We know there was negligence; we know who was negligent; and we know that if negligence caused the harm, it was a given defendant's negligence. But was negligence the *cause* of the harm, or would it have happened anyway? This is the case of a tenant found dead at the foot of the stairs. You might think this question is the easiest. That is, you might think this because, if you think that fault is really important, you have identified the person who is at fault. So why not let the loss lie with that person?. But you do not have direct evidence that it was the negligent breach that *caused* the injury, and traditionally this was actually the hardest of these questions for courts to get right, the one that took the longest.

As to every one of these four questions, there are three key factors to consider: First, what is the strength of the circumstantial evidence that has been introduced (how likely is it that this accident would have happened without negligence; how likely was it that this defendant was negligent, etc.)? Second, which party can tell you more about what happened (does the defendant or the plaintiff know more about how the accident happened and who did what)? Third, if we make a mistake, are we indifferent to the direction in which we err (are we close enough to a strict liability situation so that we would prefer to make a mistake holding liable a non-negligent party than to err and fail to give liability when the defendant was in fact negligent; would we prefer to err and find that the defendant's negligence caused the harm, or to err and hold incorrectly that it did not, etc.)?

Two of my favorite cases about res ipsa demonstrate this. *Quinley v. Cocke* is about a patient who woke up with a fractured hip after receiving electric shock treatment. The patient said that the doctrine of *res ipsa loquitur* applied. The court said "it can happen without negligence." But not that often! As to knowledge, the defendant knew much more than the plaintiff, who was "out of it." What happened? Holding a doctor liable in the 1920s was more than disfavored, and the court said, "Gee, we do not really want to do it."

Compare this to the earlier case of *Judson v. Giant Powder Co.* in which a nitrogen-something factory blows up, and everyone around was killed. Do such explosions happen "more probably than not" without negligence? Who knows. Knowledge? The court says no one knows anything because everyone was sent "to the Four Winds and the Seven Seas." But this is a situation mighty close to blasting, and to liability regardless of fault, and so it is not surprising that the court applied res ipsa, and liability was found.

> *I mean, I punch you in the nose, and no one requires me to show more than that to allow a jury to find that* my punch *broke* your nose, *rather than that your nose just happened to break at that time. We act as if the link between the punch and the break is not "circumstantial evidence," but as Ken Abraham has written, of course it is also circumstantial—because the Almighty might have broken your nose without my punch!*

So why did it take so long? I do not think that causation is a constitutional requirement. We have some cases, like some early admiralty tort cases, that required a ship captain to pay for the care of his seamen regardless of what negligence caused their injuries. But the truth is, *anthropologically*, causation has very deep roots in tort law. While requiring that there must be fault is relatively a *parvenu*—a nineteenth-century invention, many say—you will see that proof of causation is required in the very earliest cases. Evidentally we have long been troubled by the "injustice" of holding somebody liable who was not the cause.

* * *

Causation was the issue in *Zuchowicz*, a case that has found its way into the torts casebooks. It involved a woman who had developed primary pulmonary hypertension, which at the time was an always-fatal disease. Sadly for Zuchowicz, it became curable, or treatable, but just a few years too late. There are various causes of this kind of hypertension, but in her case, every cause but one was excluded.

Expert testimony, including some by a professor of medicine at Yale, established that a particular medicinal that this woman was taking for another disease was occasionally causally linked to her disease. Significantly, her hospital doctors had, contrary to federal regulations, overdosed this medication.

In an ordinary products liability case we would analyze this as a matter of product defect. She was given this drug, perfectly properly, but this drug had this risk. The risk came about from the product, and there would be strict liability. Easy. None of the defenses like federal preemption or reasonableness of the product were even raised.

But the problem is that this was a United States Veterans Hospital, and, under the Federal Tort Claims Act, there can be no strict liability. There is an opinion by then Justice Rehnquist, *Laird v Nelms*, stating that there had been no waiver of sovereign immunity for strict liability. It is a terrible opinion, because it meant, for instance, that in all the asbestos cases, the injured parties went after poor asbestos manufacturers rather than the government, who had ordered people to use it. It systematically put the loss on the wrong party. But, there it is.

As a result, the question in *Zukowicz* was not whether the drug caused the hypertension, but whether the negligent overdose of the drug did. And on this there was darn little testimony. The plaintiff was alive, still she could not tell us anything about whether it was the dosage or the overdosage. But neither could the defendant hospital. Knowledge did not help us.

In the district court, Judge Eginton—a lovely judge—ruled that there was enough evidence of causation to go to a jury. He said there was evidence that the drug causd the harm and giving an overdose was clearly negligent, and he left it at that. They gave twice the dose allowed by the FDA. That was clearly wrongful, a breach of the FDA regulation, although not of a statute.

* * *

The question we faced was this: Did the wrongful giving of an overdose cause the harm—or was it simply giving the drug in a proper dose, that did it? In the opinion I said that giving an overdose, against administrative regulation, is causually linked to the harm. The reason we prohibit overdoses is because they are dangerous. And therefore violating the regulation against an overdose suffices as evidence that it was the overdose that in fact caused the harm. I cited a great opinion by Justice Cardozo in *Martin v. Herzog*, who said that when somebody drives at night without lights and an accident occurs, that is evidence enough, unless it is countered that it was the lack of lights that caused the harm.

Was there really that strong a causal link in *Zuchowicz*? Was it like punching somebody in the nose? Or even driving without lights? If you have a regulation limiting the amount of a drug you may give, that regulation is there because giving more of the drug increases the chances of all the possible harms of the drug. That is why it's there, and if you're negligent and disobey the regulation, you have increased the chances. So, it *is* "causally linked." I do not think there's any doubt that you have somewhat greater risk if you give more of the drug than is permitted.

But how much? There was no expert testimony about that. One statement that one might call "expert testimony" in *Zuchowicz* did not really stand up well enough to allow us to say that it was the excess of the medicinal that did it.

> *The great no-causal-link case is Berry v. Sugar Notch, where a trolley car is speeding, and because it is speeding, it travels under a tree at the moment it falls and hits it. And everybody said "no liability." They didn't explain quite why.*
>
> *I explained it in an article called* Concerning Cause and the Law of Torts: An Essay for Harry Kalven, Jr. *Certainly the speeding is a "but-for cause," and it's mighty close in time, space and so on. But, in fact, speeding diminishes the chances of a tree hitting it, because it's under the tree for less time. Not by much, but if anything, it diminishes, so it shouldn't be a cost of speeding.*
>
> *But suppose that you show that speeding increases vibrations, and so it increases the chances of rotten trees falling. By how much? Well, however little, the causal link is there. Was that enough to be the legal cause or not?*
>
> *And then you're in Zuchowicz. Then you would almost certainly hold for liability in the speeding trolley car case, because you say, after all, it is better to put liability on speeders than somebody who is hit. If a speeder wants to sue the person who did not maintain the tree; fine, let him do it.*

Professor Ken Abraham was writing a draft of an article called "Self-proving Causation, chiefly about this case. In his draft he wrote, "How can Calabresi say that the casual link was strong?" He talked about my three factors, and said none of the facts in *Zuchowicz* seemed to measure up.

I called Ken when I saw the draft of the article, which he had sent to me. He had been my student. I told him, "You have not really understood the third factor. It is not whether we *like* the plaintiff or the defendant. It is our view of whether or not this is close to strict liability. Which way we are more fearful of erring? In *Zuchowicz*, if it were not for the chance of this being in a U.S. Veterans Hosptial, there would be liability, clearly.

Why then did I call the causal link "strong"? There was causal link, but was it strong? Well, courts are wary of emphasizing the third factor—symmetry of error. I do not know why.

Some judges fear that it will be taken to suggest partiality, because they think, depending on the judge and the year, that this factor will favor plaintiffs or defendants. It is not that at all. Courts have always done it, as *Quinley v. Cocke* and *Judson v. Giant Power* illustrate. They both went in different directions on the third factor. Boiler explosions? Oh, we'll find negligence regardless of a weak link, because it's awfully close to blasting. Nevertheless, courts can be a little hesitant to say it.

My court was determined to give recovery in *Zuchowicz*. There was no question that it wanted to. There was some casual link that could be taken to show cause in fact. Perhaps I overemphasized that factor in what I wrote, but if you look at all these three factors, taken together, I think the opinion stands up pretty well, and now it is most Torts casebooks.

* * *

In 1995, a woman named Nelson worked as a ticket agent at a Metro-North Railroad station in Poughkeepsie. One of the railroad conductors harassed her, both verbally and physically, and she complained to Metro-North. According to Nelson, the railroad did not take her complaints seriously enough, and so she went to the police. They arrested the conductor and charged the conductor with sexual abuse.

Metro-North suspended the conductor, but when the suspension ended, he was kept on with Nelson at the same station, despite Nelson's wishes. Nelson sued Metro-North under the Federal Employers Liability Act, claiming that Metro-North negligently placed her in danger of further harassment and caused emotional distress.

Nelson v. Metro-North is interesting because the problem of emotional damages in torts—purely emotional damages— is one of the most intricate subjects, and in the opinion, I am really analyzing the issue of damages for emotional distress as a torts scholar. There really was not any *intentional* wrongdoing by Metro-North. The question therefore was this: Can Nelson proceed against Metro-North on a different theory? That's what allowed me to discuss purely negligent infliction of emotional distress.

* * *

The law does not usually award emotional damages without at least some physical injury from which the emotional damages flow. My view is that this is probably because we—*the polity*—in some way believe that emotional injury will likely be overcome in a short time unless the bringing of a lawsuit induces the parties to dwell on that nonphysical injury. So, for example, if you drive by an accident with blood and gore, caused by somebody negligently, you feel sick; but soon you get over it.

If we give you a cause of action for feeling sick, however, you will focus on it and feel the trauma more intensely and longer. I differ from others who say we deny purely emotional damages because it is easier to make a fraudulent claim when it does not derive from a physical injury. It is true that there are problems of distinguishing genuine from fraudulent assertions of emotional distress, but a fraudulent claimant can always make up a small physical injury, a pin prick from which the emotional damages flowed.

One of my students recently suggested, "If you are right and we are interested in discouraging injurers and yet in not inducing increased emotional costs, why can't we simply assess emotional damages on the defendant, but not give them to the plaintiff?" I said, "Brilliant. We are not accustomed to dividing things up that way in torts, but that would be an interesting way of doing it."

This is an indirect way of saying that, by denying pure emotional distress claims we reduce the sum of accident costs. We do increase callousness, but we reduce the amount of suffering. In effect, we say, "We do not let you get these damages, because we want to make you more callous about such events."

You might object to my position and say, if we want that, why then, do we generally give damages for pain and suffering? After all, the same thing happens when the emotional harm derives from the physical injury, as is the case in standard pain and suffering damages. I think the answer is, we give damages for pain in suffering which derives from physical injury because then there is another reason to give damages. We want a recovery for the negligently caused physical injury, and we want to make it possible for plaintiffs to be able to retain lawyers to get those damages. We do that, in America, by giving the lawyers contingent fees, and without pain and suffering damages, we would not be able to give injured plaintiffs full economic recovery and still allow them to pay their lawyers.

My perspective explains the exceptions to the "no emotional damages" rule, too. For instance, there has long been an exception where a parent sees their child being killed. The parent may feel the loss more if we give damages, but we give them nonetheless. We *do not want* people to become callous about *that*.

Another exceptional situation occurs when the defendant has done something intentional which is particularly bad. We pile damages on the defendants then because we want to penalize them enough really to discourage their behavior. That discouragement is more important to us—*to the polity*—than is the fact that it is achieved by allowing prolonged emotional suffering of plaintiffs. The total damages go up—but that is what we want.

Here are some classic cases of these exceptions. The case of the mother who sees the child being killed is Waube v. Warrington. *A case of a intentional tort is* Price v. Yellow Pine Paper Co., *concerning a man who is negligently injured and was all bloody. He told the injurer, "Don't take me home this way, my wife is pregnant." They take him home that way and she subsequently miscarried. Her physical reaction followed the emotional distress, rather than the reverse. The court said this was a wanton and willful, intentional wrong.*

There is also another set of situations where we might want to give emotional damages which do not derive from physical injury and are caused by negligence rather than willful misbehavior. These are situations where the injury is enormous; we know about it, but we know it might not happen for a considerable period of time, and before the physical injury, the plaintiff suffers significant emotional damages.

Clarence Thomas wrote the key opinion in federal FELA cases, in *Conrail v. Gottshall*, which I think deals with my last exception. He said "Some courts have said that you have to have physical injury leading to the emotional distress. But where somebody is in immediate risk of a physical injury, even if there is not physical injury, we can give emotional damages." What he was trying to do was to preserve the ability to go forward in some cases where we want to give only emotional damages.

The question is, what does "immediate risk of physical harm" mean? Let me give you two examples going in different directions. We might want to give damages to somebody who negligently is made to come in contact with asbestos and is in a panic that he will get mesothelioma or asbestosis, which may not show up for ten years or more. The misbehavior, and the need to deter that, is mighty great.

On the other side, while courts were tending to expand liability for emotional damages, there came the *Tylenol* scare. Somebody had tampered with *Tylenol* put poison in it, and any number of people who had taken *Tylenol* were in a panic, because they thought that they could die the next day. That is mighty immediate, in a temporal sense. Yet I do not think that is what "immediate risk of physical harm" meant to Justice Thomas and the Supreme Court in *Gottshall*.

If in the *Tylenol* case, because of the negligence of Tylenol in letting people tamper a huge number of people actually died, and any number of people were frightened, we might very well want to give damages for the fright. But that is not what happened. Somebody had tampered with the bottles—maybe Tylenol was negligent in letting them tamper—and there were only a few deaths. Although the scare was temporally immediate, courts were very clear that they did not want to give such damages.

* * *

What I tried to do in *Nelson v. Metro North* was to use a torts vocabulary to make "immediate risk of physical harm" apply only in those situations where purely emotional damages should be given. I tried to say, "immediate" means a combination of closeness in time and space, and the likelihood of the risk and other factors that will allow us to say in some cases (like the asbestos case) "yes," and in others (like the *Tylenol* scare) "no." On that basis, I ruled against the plaintiff in *Nelson v. Metro North*. Dennis Jacobs concurred. He claimed that "immediate" meant simply *temporal* and did not include these other factors. He concurred in the result and correctly pointed out that my discussion of these factors was dicta.

In a way, what I was doing in *Nelson* was to put a requirement on pure emotional damages, analogous to what the "proximate cause" requirement does in ordinary torts cases, but additional to it. "Proximate" sounds mighty temporal, and yet the requirement of proximity goes way beyond time—it includes many of the factors which affect whether the plaintiff defendant should bear the loss. Indeed, the Restatement 3rd of Torts suggests that we should substitute "scope of the risk" for "proximate cause."

A problem is that most of the factors under "proximate cause" are left to the jury. Cardozo in *Palsgraf* pulled one of these factors out, "category of defendant," and kept it for the court. In *Nelson*, I tried to do the same as to emotional damages by saying that the question of whether immediacy is there belongs to the court, not to the jury. I did this because I believe that juries would not be sympathetic to the need for callousness, and Courts, instead, would be pretty good at distinguishing between situations like the *Tylenol* one and the asbestos problems, which I think Justice Thomas and the Supreme Court may have had in mind.

* * *

Reactions to my opinion have been critical among some audiences. Some feminists in my class have criticized it because I came out against the plaintiff. They have said it sanctioned the railroad's policy of not separating harassers from their victims after harassment. That is fair enough. But one has to realize that on the law at the time, Mrs. Nelson had no chance of winning, which is why Dennis Jacobs could concur in the result without buying my expansive reading of the word "immediate." I could not help Mrs. Nelson. All I could try to do was to establish a rule which would make sense for emotional damages generally, in the future.

> *In a way, this too is analogous to what Cardozo did in* Palsgraf. *It is very sad that Mrs. Palsgraf did not win. But as a practical matter, she was not going to win under the law of that time because the railroad, in that case, was not negligent, whatever Cardozo chose to say. He used that case to establish a rule of law which may be right or may be wrong, but which, if we are realistic about it, did not affect the result.*

My theory may be right, or it may be wrong. But what I am saying is that *Nelson v. Metro North* is an opinion that could only be written by somebody who has taught and thought about torts for all his life.

* * *

I am always startled when I realize how much my "torts-nik" background—more than my background in law and economics or statistics—helps me to understand a case. We had, for example, the case of a person injured while riding a golf cart on a golf course. He had played the course a hundred times, but this time he ran onto a rock and went out of control. The district court found that he could not recover, because he had assumed the risk of his injury when he decided to play.

The panel I was on, with Dennis Jacobs and Debra Livingston, was, generally speaking, unsympathetic to plaintiffs in torts situations, and they were expecting me to disagree with them. I had to tell them, "Look, it is true that I'm much more sympathetic to plaintiffs in these cases than you are. But the fact is that New York, unlike Connecticut, in sports accidents has dramatically expanded the defense of assumption of the risk. New York now goes very far in saying that if you're injured in what is an ordinary risk of an athletic endeavor, you do not recover." I said, "Connecticut is very different. In Connecticut this would almost certainly get to a jury. But given the law of New York, our decision is right."

> *I keep up with torts cases, and to my surprise, a couple of days afterward I found a unanimous decision by the New York Appellate Division, Third Department in a golf cart case in which they said, "No assumption of risk." I immediately read it and found that the federal case and this one were completely consistent! In the state case, there was a factual dispute as to whether the golf cart had bald tires, which has nothing to do with golfing, hence, assumption of risk does not resolve the case.*

Knowing tort law can get you the right answer if you're honest about it. I am constantly struggling with judges who do not know tort law and who want the things to come out the way they want them to. Of course, there are some who are excellent tort lawyers. Dick Wesley is as good on these things as I am because he too is a "torts-nik"; he knows what you can do, and what you cannot do given the applicable law.

> *Of course, it sometimes happens that my torts knowledge interferes with my understanding a case correctly. If a case really involves bankruptcy or fiduciary obligation, I may think of it too much from a torts point of view when other areas of the law are more germane.*

Desiano v. Warner-Lambert is a products liability case in which my understanding of torts led me to get to the right result. It was originally brought in a Michigan state court, against the maker of a drug named *Rezulin*, which was designed to treat diabetes, but which caused liver damage. The federal district court dismissed the claims of victims because of a Michigan law that preempted their tort suit by protecting drug manufacturers from being sued at common law if their drugs had been approved by the Food and Drug Administration. There is an exception in the Michigan law, however, based on fraudulent marketing. But the district court held that a Food and Drug Administration regulation impliedly preempted and thereby eliminated that exception.

In the long history of tort law, regulations setting standards rarely gave the defendant a safe haven. But over the past few decades, the narrow situations where proof of compliance with FDA regulations will impliedly preempt state tort law claims have been expanded greatly. This expansion, which creates safe havens for defendants, flies in the face of the traditional view that regulatory requirements should be understood only as minimum requirements. That is, if you do not comply with the regulatory requirements, the defendants are effectively negligent per se. If a product violates an established safety standard and an injury has occurred, people can sue on that basis. But compliance with regulatory requirements did not mean that the defendant was free of negligence.

> *The classic tort law approach also holds that legislative requirements and not just administrative regulations are just minimum requirements unless they are explicitly stated to be maximum ones. Legislative acts do not give you a safe haven [from tort claims]. "The speed limit is 65 miles an hour." That doesn't mean if you are going 50 you cannot be negligent if road or weather conditions make faster driving dangerous.*

Drug companies have pushed very hard to defeat the traditional view. They prefer being subject to regulation to being subject both to regulation and to torts claims. This is in part because they feel they can control the regulators and in part because regulations give them more certainty. And they have argued successfully that federal regulations are different from state regulation because these regulations constitute federal law preempting and taking the place of state law.

* * *

From the drug companies' point of view this is what they want—and it is understandable. From the point of view of the Justices of the Supreme Court, however, enthusiasm for impliedly preempting common law tort claims is not so understandable. The conservatives on the Court, one would think, should be skeptical about any suggestion of federal law preempting state law that is not express. But they are not.

There are various reasons the Supreme Court has been leaning this way. Some justices, like Breyer, who taught administrative law, tend to prefer regulators and regulation to judges and juries. Others, frankly, just tend to do what big businesses want, even if it means federal dominance over state law. Not all the conservatives accept these preemption arguments. You do get people like Justice Thomas, who often demands express preemption for federalist reasons. But there are Justices who, like segments of the public, do not like the idea of jury verdicts; who do not like the idea of expensive tort judgments.

The result of all this lobbying by companies and the instincts of some of the Justices—is that the law about the preemption of tort claims by federal statutes and regulations has in recent cases become a total mess! Indeed, Justice Scalia acknowledged as much when he visited Yale Law School not long before he died.

* * *

The Court in fact is confusing different issues that should be evaluated separately. One consideration is whether reducing the cost of injuries and the cost of avoiding them is best accomplished nationally, with uniform national rules, or locally, with local ones. Traditionally in tort law, we have treated this objective as being best accomplished at a local level. That is not necessarily right. A second question is, regardless of whether we want rules that are national or local, is it best to deal with the problem by ex ante regulations or ex post damages and financial incentives? A third question to ask is whether our current system of tort law—rather than a system of ex post damages like workers' compensation, either at a national or a local level—is going to work best.

These are three completely different dimensions of the problem, and the Court—I guess understandably—has never sorted them out. And so some Justices have tended to find that they like a centralized ex ante regime which preempts common law tort actions, perhaps simply because some of them do not *like* tort law; do not *understand* it; or think it's *expensive*, or whatever!

> *Maybe, if public opinion really supports what business defendants have called "tort reform," we should try to understand why. Lord knows, I have criticized existing tort law all my life, but if we do not like unattractive parts of the tort system we should not, unnecessarily, throw the baby out with the bathwater. Perhaps the right answer could be either a national tort law with national standards—a national Worker's Compensation system, but one that is updated so it keeps up with inflation; or perhaps even as dramatic, a reform such as that which has been put in place in New Zealand. These retain* ex post *and incentive-based means of controlling harms, rather than replacing them with* ex ante *regulations.*
>
> *It may be, however, that people want the amount of damages to be paid to tort victims, at times, not to be set at "market value," but set above market. That, maybe, is why we allow large damages given by "runaway juries." I have recently written an article musing about that.*
>
> *In any event, I think it is wrong simply because there are aspects of tort law we do not like to go thoughtlessly to a regulatory regime whose problems, both in terms of capture by the regulated and in terms of capacity to see what worthwhile risks are, are all too obvious.*

The failure to analyze different relevant issues is the reason that law of preemption is such a mess—and the reason the cases have tended to depend much more on how awful what had happened was, and whether the Court thought that the companies were taking advantage of their power or not, rather than on the underlying policy questions.

* * *

Let me go back to *Desiano*. According to the Michigan statute that was at issue in *Desiano*, those who were injured by *Rezulin* were prevented from suing in tort unless they fit into a narrow exception to Michigan's statute which allowed them to sue only if the manufacturer had committed a fraud. When the question of whether even this local exception to a local minimum standards law survived federal preemption, analysis came to the Second Circuit in *Desiano*, everybody thought the Supreme Court would inevitably find that all but suits based on the most direct frauds on patients were preempted by federal regulations and barred. This was especially the general view because the Michigan statute and fraud exception had been interpreted extraordinarily narrowly—without asking Michigan—by the Sixth Circuit.

* * *

I thought that the entire approach was fundamentally wrong from a torts point of view. I convinced Wilfred Feinberg and Barrington Parker—my panel—that it was wrong. My view was based of my knowledge of torts law and of the contributions that tort law makes to our justice system which pure regulation does not. So in the panel's opinion, we distinguished between claims that might be based on the company's fraud against the FDA, which were likely preempted, and the traditional and preexisting common law claims—when patents were defrauded, which we said were not. On that basis, we upheld the possibility of a tort action, citing, among other things, the federalism-based presumption *against* preemption.

Everybody told me that we would be reversed by the Supreme Court, nine to nothing. As it happened, though, almost the reverse occurred. Justice Roberts did not take part, and the Supreme Court split, four to four. As a result, our decision was affirmed by an equally divided court, per curiam.

> *Did this tie happen in part because I wrote the opinion? Perhaps—it is hard to surmise. One person who might have paid attention to my opinion—a torts opinion written by me—is Justice Ginsburg, who understood tort principles and my knowledge of them. Another Justice, who usually is on the other side on these issues but might have had a special regard for my torts arguments, is Steve Breyer. And, you know, what the heck? If you split four-to-four, as in Desiano, you do not make new law.*

We decided *Desiano* in 2006; it was the first case to put a serious brake on the move to substitute completely ex ante federal regulation for ex post tort law. Up to then, the move against tort law had made enormous headway at the Supreme Court.

Interestingly, the next Supreme Court case addressing this question, which came up a few years later (and which I had nothing to do with) also came out against preemption. It was from Vermont, *Wyeth v. Levine*. The facts of that case were so horrible—involving someone whose gangrene was caused by an approved drug injected into her vein—that the Supreme Court couldn't bring itself to find preemption. I always wondered whether the fact that I had slowed them down in *Desiano* indirectly affected this case.

* * *

> My experience with *Desiano v. Warner Lambert* kind of amused me. On the one hand, it reinforced my belief in my ability, sometimes, to bring my colleagues and even the Supreme Court to my way of understanding tort law. On the other hand, it has led me to worry about what happens if you get federal courts at every level jumping into areas that they really do not understand, like common law torts and even common law contracts.
>
> If federal judges are picked primarily because they have done good work in U.S. Attorney's offices and do not know these fundamental areas of law, the situation can only get worse.

COMMENTARY

Chapter 27

Torts scholarship as preparation for jurisprudence. "From a standpoint as somebody who is a law professor, Guido is the most important figure in tort law in the 20th century," contends Professor Kenneth Abraham, the Harrison Professor of Law at the University of Virginia. "There is Prosser, the great treatise writer; there is Fleming James, Guido's teacher, the foremost proponent of enterprise liability—who saw enterprise liability as mainly serving the function of compensating victims; and there is Guido. Guido's contribution has been introducing 'category deterrence' to explain and justify imposing tort liability, and more generally, introducing his sort of economic thinking, into the Legal Academy."[1]

As we have seen, for decades before he joined the bench, Guido spread his thinking across the Academy—without any sort of "Calabresi on Torts" treatise or casebook. His ideas moved beyond his books, articles, and talks into the classrooms and the textbooks of others. His influence also spread directly through his teaching of Torts for more than sixty years to good law students—several of whom themselves became prominent torts teachers, scholars, and practitioners.[2]

Teaching as preparation for judging. Classroom interactions and scholarship left hardly any important American torts opinions unexamined. As a result, few have come to the bench with equivalent appreciation for the evolving common law of torts. Few had done nearly as much reflection about how to affect tort law development by unraveling difficult torts cases.

---

[1] Interview with Prof. Kenneth Abraham, June 24, 2015.
[2] See Chapter 16, "Teaching Aware."

An intended audience of appellate court judges? In his memoir, *Benched*, Newman mentions Guido telling him that while Guido wrote for the academy, Newman wrote for district judges. Newman wrote that Guido was "exactly right."[3]

Taber v. Maine. *Taber* permitted Guido—indeed required him at the very beginning of his judicial career—to invoke his scholarship about master-servant vicarious liability and introduce it into Second Circuit jurisprudence.[4] As described in the narrative, a Navy serviceman in Guam bought and consumed beer at his military base, continued to drink at social events, and became thoroughly inebriated. He drove off base, and on the way back caused the collision that injured Mr. Taber, who was an enlisted Navy construction worker.[5]

The trial court had rejected Taber's claims that the government should be held "vicariously" liable for his injuries on a theory of respondeat superior. On appeal, the Second Circuit needed to address the respondeat superior ruling and also an interpretation, adverse to Taber, of the Federal Tort Claims Act which flowed from the Supreme Court's *Feres* decision.[6]

Respondeat superior. Guido introduces one of his central economic approaches to assigning liability—"*What is a cost of what?*"—to Second Circuit jurisprudence. On these facts he decides that the toll taken by the accident is a cost of a large military enterprise.[7] The employee's "conduct [wa]s not so unusual or startling that it would seem unfair to include the loss resulting from it among other costs of the employer's business."[8] Given "the pervasive control that the military exercises over its personnel while they are on a base," the military could have deterred accidents by its employees more effectively. The court concludes that it was "totally in keeping with the doctrine of *respondeat superior* to allocate the costs of base operations to the government."[9] Guido borrows explicitly from his own article "Some Thoughts on Risk Distribution and the Law of Torts."[10]

The Feres doctrine. His elaborate discussion of the *Feres* doctrine first unpacks and then constrains the justification for barring tort recoveries on the basis of the availability of military benefits and the need to preserve military discipline. Guido observes that the injured Seabee in *Taber* was on liberty off the base and concludes "the link between Taber's activity when he was injured and his military status is too frail to support a *Feres* bar."[11]

Here again he explicitly incorporates insights from his scholarship. The recoveries provided in the Federal Tort Claims Act have become far less generous in relation to common law tort remedies that compensate others and deter accidents. It might

---

[3] JOHN NEWMAN, BENCHED, at 251.
[4] Taber v. Maine, 67 F.3d 1029 (1995).
[5] *Id.*
[6] Feres v. United States, 71 S. Ct. 153 (1950).
[7] 67 F.3d 1029.
[8] *Id.* at 1036.
[9] *Id.* at 1037.
[10] *Id.* at 1034; Guido Calabresi, *Some Thoughts on Risk Distributions and the Law of Torts*, 70 YALE L.J. 499 (1961).
[11] 67 F.3d at 1050.

be desirable, Guido contends, "for courts to invite legislatures to reconsider outdated statutes so that, unless the legislatures make clear their continued preference for disparate treatment, like cases may be treated alike."[12] Guido *the judge* refers to Guido *the professor's* work *A Common Law for the Age of Statutes*.[13]

Some colleagues, Guido reflects, were alienated by the academic tenor of Guido's decision; his application of California law rather than the law of Guam; and his diminution of the *Feres* bar to litigation.

Judge Pratt curtly concurred without offering any explanation of the basis for differing from the majority opinion and resigned from the bench before placing his name on the amended version.[14] Judge Ellsworth Van Graafeiland, whose daughter Anne represented the losing appellant, no doubt perceived Guido's exegesis of the common law as pedantic. Five years later he would complain that "[e]ver since Judge Calabresi moved to this Court from Yale Law School, ... [he has been pushing for certification, and ought to keep in mind that] "the pursuit of justice is not an academic exercise."[15] As Guido describes elsewhere, his relationship with Van Graafeiland improved in later years.[16]

Taber v. Maine has reshaped thinking about respondeat superior and the *Feres* doctrine. It has been cited in several hundred cases and secondary sources, only a handful of which distinguish *Taber*; and none of which undermines the logic of its argument in a significant way. After the case, it was reported that the Navy began taking steps to stop excessive drinking of Naval officers.[17]

The casebook written by Shulman, James, Fleming & Gray, which Guido uses to teach his first-year law students, excerpts the case to illuminate master-servant liability.[18] Students are also invited to explore the utility of using a deterrence approach through the presentation of an excerpt from "Some Thoughts on Risk Distribution and the Law of Torts."[19]

Stagl v. Delta Airlines. Guido follows the multi-faceted *Taber* opinion with this fairly straightforward case.[20] An unidentified man standing next to Eleanor Stagl at the Delta baggage terminal "reached across the conveyor belt, grabbed his satchel with great force, and unwittingly triggered a domino effect. His bag collided with another's suitcase, which, in turn, fell off the carousel, toppling Mrs. Eleanor Stagl," whose hip was broken.[21]

---

[12] *Id.* at 1039.
[13] *Id.* at 1039.
[14] Judge Pratt resigned on Jan. 31, 1995; the amended opinion was released on Oct. 5, 1995.
[15] Tunick v. Safir, 209 F.3d 67, 99 (2000) (Van Graafeiland, dissenting) (quoting Justice Douglas in Clay v. Sun Ins. Office, Ltd., 363 U.S. 207 (1960)).
[16] See Chapter 26, "Joining the Second Circuit."
[17] See Genevieve Ames & Carol Cunradi, Alcohol Use and Preventing Alcohol-Related Problems Among Young Adults in the Military, *Nat. Inst. on Alcohol Abuse & Alcoholism*, https://pubs.niaaa.nih.gov/publications/arh284/252-257.htm.
[18] HARRY SHULMAN, JAMES FLEMING, JR., & OSCAR GRAY, CASES AND MATERIALS ON THE LAW OF TORTS 114 (6th ed 2015).
[19] *Id.*
[20] Stagl v. Delta Airlines, 52 F.3d 463 (1995); Stagl v. Delta Air Lines, 117 F.3d 76 (1997).
[21] 52 F.3d at 466.

The case raised an apparently simple question: What duty does an airline owe a passenger in the baggage area of an airport terminal to prevent situations conducive to injuries from happening? In district court, Judge Manuel Real ruled that Delta owed no duty of care at all, including no duty to warn about possible negligent conduct by third persons within the terminal building.[22]

On appeal, Guido wrote that the district court had this wrong in most respects: Mrs. Stagl was injured in Delta's baggage terminal, over which Delta had full dominion, and under these circumstances, New York law would apply the traditional landowner's duty of reasonable care.[23] The presence of an unknown intervenor, furthermore—a passenger whose bag removal from the carousel allegedly led indirectly to Stagl's injury—did not, as a matter of law, break the chain of causation.[24] The appellate court sent the case back to the district court to determine whether Delta's behavior was a proximate cause of Stagl's broken hip.[25]

The district court judge might have been resentful of the remand. In any event, he conducted a jury trial, and at the end of Stagl's case-in-chief granted Delta's motion for a directed verdict.[26] He found insufficient evidence to support a jury determination that the accident was foreseeable by Delta, because no evidence had been presented that similar prior accidents had occurred. Mrs. Stagl appealed the judgment, and in 1997 the case came back to the Second Circuit.[27]

The second opinion reversed Judge Real once more. It held that evidence of negligence other than that of a similar prior accident had been presented and would be sufficient to survive a directed verdict. Accordingly, the trial judge abused its discretion by disregarding such evidence of other negligence and by excluding the testimony of expert witnesses.[28]

Guido says that his experiences in writing *Taber* and *Stagl* and his interaction with other judges in connection with these cases taught him virtues of stylistic simplicity and judicial economy. Comparing them both does reveal the more compact way Guido brought readers to understand standards of care by tracing the evolution of the common law.[29] As Guido says, *Stagl v. Delta* has found its way into torts casebooks because it neatly addresses legal causation by an institutional actor when there is an intervening cause.

Liriano v. Hobart. A seventeen-year-old recent immigrant to the United States, Luis Liriano, lost his hand in a Hobart meat grinding machine after only a week on the job at a supermarket. The machine had come with a guard attached, but the

---

[22] *Id.*
[23] *Id.* at 468.
[24] *Id.*
[25] *Id.* at 473–74.
[26] *Id.*; the trial court opinion is unpublished.
[27] Stagl v. Delta Air Lines, 117 F.3d 76 (1997).
[28] *Id.* at 81.
[29] *See, e.g.*, ROBERT E. KEETON ET AL., TORT AND ACCIDENT LAW: CASES AND MATERIALS 337 (2004); FOWLER VINCENT HARPER ET AL., HARPER, JAMES, AND GRAY ON TORTS 408 (2006); MARC A. FRANKLIN & ROBERT L. RABIN, TORT LAW AND ALTERNATIVES: CASES AND MATERIALS 72 (2001).

supermarket removed it, and the machine bore no warning to indicate that the grinder should be operated only with a safety guard.[30]

A jury ultimately decided to award damages to Liriano proportioned on comparative causation—5 percent against Hobart and 95 percent against the supermarket, for their failure to warn Liriano, who had neither been warned by the manufacturer or given instructions by the supermarket about how to use the meat grinder.[31] The district court then held a partial retrial limited to the issue of whether and to what extent Liriano was responsible for his own injury.[32] On that retrial, the jury assigned Liriano one-third of the fault.[33]

A vintage Hobart meat grinder

Writing his opinion in the appeal involved repairing unintentional damage inflicted by Judge Jacob Fuchsberg. Fuchsberg was a plaintiff-oriented New York Court of Appeals Judge who counterproductively dissented from a 1980 decision based on facts similar to *Liriano*, in *Robinson v. Reed Package*.[34] He observed that the majority opinion in that case *sub silentio* protected a manufacturer against liability not only for *defective design*, but also for *negligently failing to warn* of the danger of using a modified machine.[35] Judge Fuchsberg contended that there were circumstances in which negligent failure to warn *should* be actionable.[36] Ironically, his dissenting "hope" came to be recognized as the law of New York as a result of Guido's certification of *Liriano* to the New York Court of Appeals.[37]

Speaking for the court in *Liriano I,* Guido exposed the ambiguities in the state law jurisprudence and then certified to the New York Court of Appeals a question

---

[30] Liriano v. Hobart Corp., 170 F.3d 264, 266 (1999).
[31] *Id.*
[32] *Id.*
[33] *Id.*
[34] *Id.*; Robinson v. Reed-Prentice Div. of Package Mach. Co., 49 N.Y.2d 471, 481(1980) (Fuchsberg, dissenting).
[35] Robinson v. Reed-Prentice Div. of Package Mach. Co., 49 N.Y.2d 471, 481(1980) (Fuchsberg, dissenting).
[36] *Id.*
[37] *Id.* at 481–87.

asking whether in cases in which the "substantial modification defense" precluded liability under a design defect theory, manufacturer liability could nevertheless exist under a failure to warn theory.[38]

The New York Court of Appeals decided that holding a manufacturer liable for negligent failure to warn was possible.[39] The state's highest court did not decide the merits of the case, however; it left open the question of whether the danger was obvious and allowed the federal court to craft an opinion on this and returned the matter to the Second Circuit.[40]

In *Liriano III*, Guido explains the logical possibility that the giving of a warning—even of an obvious danger—may be needed when alternatives to encountering it are not obvious. He also holds that an injury may be presumptively caused by a failure to give such a warning. He acknowledges that meat grinders are widely known to be dangerous—but rejects the "obviousness defense" in situations where it would reduce the danger and prevent harm to alert a user to alternatives through the existence of mechanisms (like guards) to reduce its inherent danger:

> One who grinds meat, like one who drives on a steep road, can benefit not only from being told that his activity is dangerous but from being told of a safer way ... one can argue about whether the risk involved in grinding meat is sufficiently obvious that a responsible person would fail to warn of that risk ... Given that attaching guards is feasible, does reasonable care require that meat workers be informed that they need not accept the risks of using unguarded grinders?[41]

What had been dismissed or missed by jurists analyzing obvious dangers, as Guido would put it in a later opinion, was, "obviousness of what?"[42] A jury could have found that it was *not* obvious that safety guards were attachable; that guards actually *came as part of the grinders*, and that the grinders *should be used only with the guards*.[43] In Luis Liriano's situation—where the seventeen-year-old lost his hand in the unguarded machine—Hobart failed to warn of alternatives. Additionally, Guido, speaking for the court, established "a rebuttable inference ... that the lack of a warning about alternatives caused the injury."[44]

James A. Henderson, Jr., and Aaron Twerski. Professors Henderson and Twerski were already well-recognized torts experts when they defended the Hobart

---

[38] Liriano v. Hobart Corp., 132 F.3d 124 (1998) (Liriano I), certified question accepted, 91 N.Y.2d 885 (1998), and certified question answered, 92 N.Y.2d 232 (1998) (Liriano II).

[39] 91 N.Y.2d 885 (1998).

[40] *Id.*; Liriano v. Hobart Corp., 170 F.3d 264 (1999) (Liriano III). Judge Newman concurring (based on his view of jury discretion and addressing the possibility of disincentive created for manufacturers to install any guard at all in the future). *Id.* at 273.

[41] 170 F.3d at 270.

[42] Burke v. Spartanics Ltd., 252 F.3d 131, 137 (2001).

[43] Liriano III, 170 F.3d at 271.

[44] *Id.* When the case was remanded to the district court for determination of the failure-to-warn issue, a one-third deduction for the plaintiff's comparative negligence was upheld on appeal. Liriano v. Hobart Corp., 960 F. Supp. 43, 44 (S.D.N.Y. 1997).

company after the trial phase. Professor Henderson taught torts and products liability at Cornell Law School; Professor Twerski at Brooklyn Law School. Both were known for their work as co-reporters to the *Restatement of the Law Third, Torts: Products Liability*.[45] Both subsequently served as special masters in the 9/11 World Trade Center responder's litigation—among the most complex of American mass-tort cases. Professor Henderson died in 2019.[46]

Taking the fight to a different battlefield. After *Liriano*, the two professors pressed against Guido's treatment of obvious dangers on the ground that it imposes uncertain and excessive liability on manufacturers.[47] Unsuccessful at the bar, they asserted their views forcefully elsewhere.[48]

As the reporters for the *Restatement Third of Torts: Products Liability*, Henderson and Twerski inserted a comment asserting that the existing law left Guido as an outlier. Where a risk is "obvious or generally known," the Comment states, "the prospective addressee of a warning will or should already know of its existence [and therefore] Warning of an obvious or generally known risk in most instances will not provide an effective additional measure of safety."[49] The Comment does not, however, speak to Guido's concern that safer alternatives be warned about.

Henderson and Twerski published an article in the *Indiana Law Journal* arguing that the court's analysis should have found no liability for a failure to warn once it concluded that the meat grinder was obviously dangerous.[50] Twerski and others equated Guido's requirement that alternatives be shown to a "heeding presumption." They disputed the likelihood that a warning would have been heeded if it had been provided and challenged the wisdom of assuming as much. They asserted that it heralded a massive and unwise expansion of enterprise liability.[51] Whether or not requiring warnings about alternatives diminishes beneficial economic activity by producers is unknown, of course; as is whether or not warnings about alternatives minimize the overall social cost of accidents.

---

[45] RESTATEMENT (THIRD) OF TORTS: PRODS. LIAB. (1998).

[46] Remembering James A. Henderson Jr., https://www.lawschool.cornell.edu/spotlights/Remembering-James-A-Henderson-Jr.cfm.

[47] *See, e.g.*, James A. Henderson, Jr. & Aaron D. Twerski, *Doctrinal Collapse in Products Liability: The Empty Shell of Failure to Warn*, 65 N.Y.U. L. REV. 265 (1990).

[48] RESTATEMENT (THIRD) OF TORTS: PRODS. LIAB., CH. 1, § 2 cmt. j (1998). (Liability of Commercial Product Sellers Based on Product Defects at Time of Sale).

[49] *Id.*

[50] Aaron D. Twerski & James A. Jr. Henderson, *Fixing Failure to Warn*, 90 IND. L.J. 237 (2015); *see also* Hildy Bowbeer & David S. Killoran, *Liriano v. Hobart Corp.: Obvious Dangers, the Duty to Warn of Safer Alternatives, and the Heeding Presumption*, 65 BROOK. L. REV. 717, 728 (1999); Aaron D. Twerski & Neil Cohen, *Resolving The Dilemma Of Nonjusticiable Causation In Failure-To-Warn Litigation*, 84 S. CAL. L. REV. 125 (2010); Hildy Bowbeer & David S. Killoran, *Liriano v. Hobart Corp.: Obvious Dangers, the Duty to Warn of Safer Alternatives, and the Heeding Presumption*, 65 BROOK. L. REV. 717 (1999).

[51] James Henderson, *Echoes of Enterprise Liability in Product Design and Marketing Litigation*, 87 CORNELL L. REV. 958; Aaron D. Twerski & Neil B. Cohen, *Resolving the Dilemma of Nonjusticiable Causation in Failure-to-Warn Litigation*, 84 S. CAL. L. REV. 125, 136 (2010) (by endorsing "heeding presumption," courts have effectively applied enterprise liability to warning cases by shifting burden to rebut the plaintiff's prima facie case). But see Kenneth Abraham, *Self-Proving Causation*, 98 VA. L. REV. 1811, 1839 (2013) (Guido never speaks of burden shifting; rather he states that where the plaintiff is entitled to rely on self-proving causation, and the defendant does not rebut the plaintiff's prima facie case on causation, then that case is legally sufficient.).

The critical attacks on *Liriano* prompted counter-attacks, including discussions with political and philosophical overtones.[52] As a matter of political and social justice, the contest over warnings is part of a much older and broader fight to avoid the dangers of production and protect the welfare of workers.[53] The stakes raised by Guido—both monetary and ideological—are considerable, and the battle continues over what is the "best" or "optimal" legal rule.

Torts casebooks include the *Liriano* case to explore some of the "non-obvious dimensions of obviousness," and to consider the legal significance of the fact that warnings can inform users about safer alternatives.[54] As one text observes, "even if the danger of the grinder was obvious, informing users of the availability of guards and their benefits was additional information that a factfinder might determine was not obvious."[55] Students and seasoned attorneys are further challenged by the textbook question, "how could Hobart have a duty to warn about the dangers of operating its grinder without a guard, when Hobart had equipped it with a guard?"[56]

Guido, of course, had an answer for the question in his original opinion: a jury reasonably could have found Luis Liriano did not know that the grinder came with guards; and that Hobart had a duty to inform them that "safety guards exist; and that the grinder is meant to be used only with such guards."[57]

The opinion had another side to it, as well. He held that where a danger was sufficiently great, that very fact could constitute evidence of but-for causation. This approach to relaxing the requirement of but-for causation has been treated favorably in some other jurisdictions and refined in the Second Circuit.[58] Guido himself has had the opportunity to elaborate further on *Liriano*.[59]

Zuchowicz v. United States. Mrs. Patricia Zuchowicz, suffering from endometriosis, filled a doctor's prescription for the drug Danocrine at a Naval Hospital pharmacy in February 1989. Pharmacy personnel negligently instructed her to take 1,600

---

[52] *See, e.g.,* David Blankfein-Tabachnick & Kevin A. Kordana, *Kaplow and Shavell and the Priority of Income Taxation and Transfer*, 69 HASTINGS L.J. 1, 3 (2017) ("considered from the perspective of the least well-off, more cost might be borne by the manufacturer to protect workers, even the clumsy or illiterate); David W. Robertson, *Book Review: Metaphysical Truth vs. Workable Tort Law: Adverse Ambitions? Causation and Responsibility: An Essay in Law, Morals, and Metaphysics, by Michael Moore*, 88 TEX. L. REV. 1053, 1063 (2010)(Liriano discussed as a situation in which but-for-causation is appropriately relaxed). Robert L. Rabin, *Accommodating Tort Law: Alternative Remedies for Workplace Injuries*, 69 RUTGERS L. REV. 1119, 1127 n.43 (2017).

[53] *See generally* MORTON J. HORWITZ, THE TRANSFORMATION OF AMERICAN LAW, 1780–1860 (1977); HORWITZ, THE TRANSFORMATION OF AMERICAN LAW, 1870–1960 (1992).

[54] Horwitz, *supra* note 53 at 787.

[55] MARC A. FRANKLIN ET AL., TORT LAW & ALTERNATIVES 658 (10th ed. 2016).

[56] DAN B. DOBBS ET AL., TORTS & COMPENSATION: PERSONAL ACCOUNTABILITY AND SOCIAL RESPONSIBILITY FOR INJURY 787 (8th ed. 2017).

[57] 170 F.3d at 271.

[58] *See, e.g.,* Supriya v. Thermage, Inc., 2012 U.S. Dist. LEXIS 108631, 38 (2012); Cacciola v. Selco Balers, Inc., 127 F. Supp. 2d 175 (2001); Williams v. Utica College of Syracuse Univ., 453 F.3d 112 (2006); but *see* Castorina v. A.C. & S., 2017 NY Slip Op 27083, 55 Misc. 3d 968, 49 N.Y.S.3d 238 (Sup. Ct. 2017) (granting defendant summary judgment and refusing to charge a "heeding presumption," which would have presumed that the patient would have paid attention to a warning had there been one.)

[59] *See, e.g.,* Burke v. Spartanics Ltd., *supra* note 42.

milligrams of Danocrine per day, or twice the maximum recommended dosage; and for a month she took this overdosage until a doctor told her to cut that amount in half.[60]

By the time Mrs. Zuchowicz was told to stop taking the drug entirely, she was experiencing serious health problems—eventually she was diagnosed with primary pulmonary hypertension (PPH), a rare and fatal disease. She died in December, 1991, a month after giving birth to a son.[61] Patricia's estate sued the government.

Expert witnesses testified that Danocrine was safe and effective when administered properly at dosages not to exceed 800 mg/day.[62] The effects of the drug at higher doses had not been studied because "very, very few women have received doses this high in any setting."[63] The estate could not, therefore, definitively prove whether the overdosage proved fatal or the drug itself did, or some other medical intervention did.[64] A medical expert testified to his confidence "to a reasonable certainty" that the Danocrine caused the PPH, and, "when pressed," stated that he believed based on Zuchowicz's medical history that the overdose, rather than the ordinary dosage of the drug, was responsible.[65] The district court credited the testimony and awarded more than $1 million in damages to Patricia's estate.[66]

The central problem of causation in the appeal of *Zuchowicz* went "to the heart of the law of torts."[67] The uncontested fact of injury and of the wrongdoing by the pharmacy left, as the only issue, whether the defendant's wrongdoing was the *cause* of the plaintiff's death—in the legal sense of a "but-for cause."[68] This offered Guido the opportunity to speak about where the law about causation had been, and where it should be going:

> Over the centuries, courts have struggled to give meaning to this requirement—in the simplest of situations, who hit whom, and in the most complex ones, which polluter's emissions, if any, hurt which plaintiff. It is the question that we must seek to answer today in the context of modern medicine and a very rare disease.[69]

As he says in his narrative, earlier courts were overly concerned with the logical fallacy of *post hoc, ergo propter hoc* ("after this, therefore because of this") and placed a heavier burden than the one most plaintiffs could sustain by demanding direct evidence which connected the defendant's wrongdoing to the harm.[70]

---

[60] Zuchowicz v. United States, 140 F.3d 381 (1998).
[61] *Id.*
[62] *Id.*
[63] *Id.*
[64] *Id.*
[65] *Id.*
[66] Zuchowicz v. United States, 1996 U.S. Dist. LEXIS 20179 (1996).
[67] 140 F.3d at 383.
[68] *Id.*
[69] *Id.* at 383–84.
[70] *Id.*, citing Wolf v. Kaufmann, 237 N.Y.S. 550, 551(1929) (denying recovery where a decedent was found unconscious at foot of stairway which, in violation of a statute, was unlighted, because the plaintiff had offered no proof of "any causal connection between the accident and the absence of light").

Guido set out those "substantial factors" which the plaintiff needs to establish to build a prima facie case for compensation: the negligence of the wrongdoer must be the "but-for cause" of the injury; it must be the proximate cause of it; and must be causally linked to it—not merely part of a chain of events which led to the injury.[71]

The structure of his ruling about the sufficiency of evidence of but-for causation depended on a Legal Realist foundation—one that originally had been laid many years earlier by Chief Judge Cardozo in New York and Chief Justice Traynor in California. As Guido describes in the opinion, and as he has emphasized in countless torts classes, if a plaintiff can demonstrate a strong likelihood of but-for causation, it will trigger an obligation on the part of the defendant to refute but-for cause:

> if (a) a negligent act was deemed wrongful because that act increased the chances that a particular type of accident would occur, and (b) a mishap of that very sort did happen, this was enough to support a finding by the trier of fact that the negligent behavior caused the harm. Where such a strong causal link exists, it is up to the negligent party to bring in evidence denying but for cause and suggesting that in the actual case the wrongful conduct had not been a substantial factor.[72]

Guido says that the question he needs to face in *Zuchowicz* is twofold: whether it has been shown that prescribing Danocrine to her was "the source of her illness and death; and then that it was not just Danocrine, but its negligent overdose which led to her demise."[73] Invocation of the analytical lens used by Judges Cardozo and Traynor to address these questions leads him to find liability to Mrs. Zuchowicz. The concededly negligent act of the pharmacy in giving an overdose plainly increased the chances that harm would occur, and the federal regulation was designed to prevent a mishap of the sort that occurred.[74]

Zuchowicz is most often cited by courts for Guido's use of the "abuse of discretion" standard to review the district court's decision to exclude or admit expert testimony.[75] In the casebooks, however, *Zuchowicz* is a principal case for its discussion of legal causation, for its rationalization of the "substantial factor test," and for persuasively justifying a rebuttable presumption of causation.[76]

Rocking the torts landscape—Zuchowicz and Liriano. Guido received the William L. Prosser Award for "a lifetime of truly outstanding contributions to the world of torts," in 2011.[77] Bestowing it, Professor Catherine Sharkey, a former clerk to Guido, pointed out that the opinions in *Liriano* and *Zuchowicz* were both issued

---

[71] Zuchowicz v. United States, 140 F.3d 381, 390 (1998).
[72] *Id.* at 390–91.
[73] *Id.* at 389.
[74] *Id.*
[75] *See, e.g.,* U.S. v. Sterling, 763 Fed. Appx. 63, 66 (2019).
[76] FRANKLIN & RABIN, *supra* note 28, at 354–56.
[77] Catherine M. Sharkey, *AALS Torts and Compensation Systems Section William L. Prosser Award Bestowed Upon Guido Calabresi,* 8 IND. HEALTH L. REV. 331 (2011).

in a single term of the court (1997–1998). These two cases, Professor Sharkey said, "transformed the Torts landscape" and "entered the canon."[78]

The evolution of common law thinking about attributing causation. Guido speaks about five classic cases to illustrate the evolution of the judicial approaches.

1. *Assumptions about negligence—Ybarra v. Spangard.* Upon waking after a routine appendectomy procedure, Joseph Ybarra experienced pain and then paralysis and atrophy of his shoulder muscles.[79] The court relied on the theory of "*res ipsa loquitur*" (the thing speaks for itself) to say that a jury could find negligence in the defendants. Because the plaintiff was unconscious at the time of the incident, the court believed it would be "manifestly unreasonable" to require the plaintiff to point to a particular defendant as the cause of the injury.[80] It allowed the jury to burden all the defendants unless they established that their own particular role in the procedure was not the cause of plaintiff's injury.

2. *A multiplicity of possible causes—Summers v. Tice.* Guido cites *Summers* for its discussion of whose negligence caused the injury.[81] Members of a hunting party shot simultaneously in the same direction, injuring their guide Summers with birdshot. The Supreme Court of California affirmed the lower court in finding both defendants jointly liable and deeming the negligence of both to have caused the injury.[82] The Court also ruled that upon a finding that each defendant was negligent, it was up to the defendants to show that they were not individually the cause of the guide's injury.[83]

3. *Improbable—but possible—innocence—In Quinley v. Cocke. Quinley* the Supreme Court of Tennessee was unwilling to apply the doctrine of *res ipsa loquitur*.[84] It affirmed the lower court largely on the opinion of an expert who testified that the plaintiff's injury might possibly have happened non-negligently from administration of electro-shock therapy "even with every precaution used to prevent [it]."[85] As Guido mentions, the opinion reflects the reluctance at the time of courts to apply the doctrine of *res ipsa loquitor* in malpractice cases.[86]

4. *If it happened, a jury could find that it was caused by negligence*—Judson v. Giant Power Co. Guido cites *Judson,* which involved the handling of dynamite, as a contrast to the holding of *Quinley,* which was a malpractice action.[87]

---

[78] *Id.*
[79] Ybarra v. Spangard, 25 Cal. 2d 486 (1944).
[80] *Id.* at 492.
[81] Summers v. Tice, 33 Cal. 2d 80 (1948).
[82] *Id.* at 84.
[83] *Id.* at 88.
[84] Quinley v. Cocke, 192 S.W.2d 992 (Tenn. 1946).
[85] *Id.* at 997.
[86] *Id.* at 996.
[87] Judson v. Giant Powder Co., 107 Cal. 549 (1895).

Relying on several railway explosion cases, the *Judson* court applied *res ipsa loquitor* on the premise that "if dynamite is properly handled in the process of manufacture, explosions will not probably occur."[88]

5. *The plaintiff's contribution to his own injury was a condition, but not a cause—Berry v. Sugar Notch Borough.* While operating a trolley car at excessive speed in a violent wind-storm, Bryan Berry passed under an old chestnut tree. The tree was improperly close to the track, and in the wind, it blew down—crushing the roof of the car and causing Berry injury.[89] Was Berry's speeding a cause of the injury? No, said the judge, it was a not a cause. "That his speed brought him to the place of the accident at the moment of the accident was the merest chance, and a thing which no foresight could have predicted. The same thing might as readily have happened to a car running slowly. . ."[90] This case is indeed, as Guido says, perfectly wonderful for illustrating the difference between a causal red herring and a causal link.

Hahn v. Town of W. Haverstraw—the golf cart case. Mr. Minho Hahn alleged that the golf course was in such poor condition that it caused him to hit a rock and lose control of his golf cart, which led him to collide with a nearby tree, and therefore to sustain injuries to his knee and his leg.[91] The district court rejected Hahn's claim on the ground that the suit was barred by "the doctrine of primary assumption of risk."[92] Guido's opinion affirmed the district court's holding.[93]

Guido agreed that the plaintiff assumed the risk of the accident by voluntarily using the golf cart with prior knowledge of the golf course's conditions, including the steepness of the hill and the potential for small rocks on the path.[94] The opinion refers to other golf-related injury cases in which recovery was barred, confirming New York's expansive application of the assumption of risk defense in sports cases.[95] He mentions the case, of course, to demonstrate that his fidelity to clear common law precedents in state tort law will always dominate over his sympathy for injured parties.

The politics of preemption. When in 2001 President George W. Bush appointed Daniel Troy, a former PhRMA lobbyist, as general counsel to the FDA, many observers believed that it marked the initiation of a concerted "corporate friendly agenda at the federal agency."[96] Indeed, that was the year the FDA, in tandem with pharmaceutical industry, revved up a "preemption steamroller."[97]

---

[88] *Id.* at 561–62.
[89] Berry v. Sugar Notch Borough, 43 A. 240 (Pa. 1899).
[90] *Id.*
[91] 563 Fed. Appx. 75 (2014).
[92] *Id.*
[93] *Id.*
[94] *Id.*
[95] *See, e.g.,* Anand v. Kapoor, 942 N.E.2d 295, 296–97 (N.Y. 2010); Barbato v. Hallow Hills Country Club, 789 N.Y.S.2d 199, 200 (N.Y. App. Div. 2005); Egeth v. County of Westchester, 612 N.Y.S.2d 1763, 763–64 (App. Div. 1994).
[96] Jesse C. Vivian, *The Sorcerer's Apprentice*, 33 U.S. PHARM. 70, 70–74 (2008).
[97] *Id.*

Unprecedentedly, the FDA began siding with defendants in state drug product liability lawsuits, arguing in amicus briefs that common law tort judgments impermissibly interfered with the FDA's authority to regulate drugs.[98] It was an about-face: the previous general counsel maintained that FDA product approval and state tort liability were compatible, and that each offered "a significant, yet distinct, layer of consumer protection."[99] And in 2006, the FDA announced in proposed regulations that its labeling requirements preempted state law claims that imposed additional or different requirements, and that state drug product liability litigation was preempted by the FDA regulations.[100]

"Torts-niks," tobacco, and persuasiveness—an account by Judge Richard Wesley. Jeanette Bifolck died of lung cancer and her husband sued Philip Morris.[101] He wanted to use the recent determination of a District of Columbia court to preclude the tobacco company from denying in his case that it knew cigarettes were addictive and could manipulate addictiveness.[102]

The district court, however, employed a factor analysis to deny this "nonmutual offensive issue preclusion."[103] It ruled that the addictiveness findings were not "of necessity" to the final judgement; and that there was insufficient "identicality."[104]

On appeal, Judges Cabranes, Wesley, and Calabresi disagreed sharply—until Guido circulated an "extraordinary" memo to his colleagues."[105] Guido and his clerks went through the "monster record" in the District of Columbia case to demonstrate that Philip Morris knew about addictiveness, at least in general.[106] Although the district court judge had decided that the other court's finding was not necessary to its final judgment, Guido argued that the finding was at minimum necessary to impose the *remedy* it awarded. Wesley replied that this made sense; Guido promptly responded, "Let's remand. We can do a lot of good resolving the standard of review," expressing his view that Wesley should write the decision.

The near-impasse had been overcome—Guido had harmonized the panel so that differences of opinion or personal feeling no longer stood in the way of a resolution, while on remand the plaintiffs would have an easier time establishing preclusion. "It was brilliant… and so 'Guido.'"[107]

Desiano v. Warner Lambert. Caesar Desiano and other Michigan residents alleged that taking Rezulin caused their liver damage. They pursued common

---

[98] *Id.*
[99] *Id.*; *see* Leslie Kendrick, *FDA's Regulation of Prescription Drug Labeling*, 62 FOOD & DRUG L.J. 227 (2007).
[100] Vivian, *supra* note 97.
[101] Bifolck v. Philip Morris, No. 3:06-cv-01768 (PCD), 2010 U.S. Dist. LEXIS 158385 (D. Conn. 2010); Bifolck v. Philip Morris USA Inc., 936 F.3d 74 (2019).
[102] 2010 U.S. Lexis 158385; United States v. Philip Morris USA, Inc. 449 F. Supp. 2d 1, 27 (D.D.C. 2006).
[103] 2010 U.S. Dist. LEXIS 158385 (D. Conn. 2010).
[104] *Id.*
[105] Interview with Hon. Richard C. Wesley, Aug. 13, 2020.
[106] *Id.*
[107] *Id.*; After remand, however, in Bifolck v. Philip Morris USA Inc., No. 3:06-cv-1768 (SRU), 2020 U.S. Dist. LEXIS 83298 (D. Conn. May 12, 2020), Judge Stefan R. Underhill concluded, in favor of Philip Morris, that notwithstanding satisfying identicality and necessity, it would be *unfair* to apply nonmutual offensive issue preclusion. *Id.*

law claims that included breaches of implied and express warranties, negligence; fraud; defective product design; and defective manufacturing.[108] These were originally brought in disparate states, consolidated as multi-district litigation, and removed to federal court in the Second Circuit—applying Michigan law to the claims.[109]

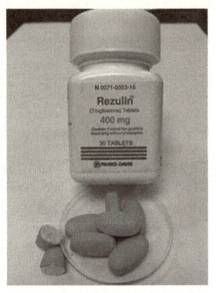

The diabetes drug Rezulin, manufactured by Warner Lambert

Warner-Lambert asserted that the Food, Drug and Cosmetic Act (FDCA), and the Medical Device Act (MDA) blocked all the state causes of action because Michigan had statutorily immunized drug makers from products liability claims whenever the Food and Drug Administration (FDA) had approved the allegedly injurious pharmaceuticals.[110] The drug company further asserted that a Michigan statute authorizing state law-suits for the exceptional category of claims premised on the company defrauding the FDA were also blocked under a unanimous Supreme Court decision, *Buckman Co. v. Plaintiff's Legal Comm.*[111]

The district court sided with Warner-Lambert.[112] It concluded that all of the common law claims failed in the face of the gist of the Michigan statute, and of the *Buckman* decision preempting the exception within it.[113]

---

[108] Desiano v. Warner-Lambert & Co., 467 F.3d 85 (2006).
[109] *Id.*
[110] 21 U.S.C. § 301, et seq.; 21 U.S.C. §§ 360e(b)(1)(A)–(B); *see* Amanda Melpolder, *A Tragic Blunder, Michigan's Drug Industry Immunity Law*, CENTER FOR JUSTICE & DEMOCRACY, Feb. 28, 2008, file:///C:/Users/HP%20USER/Downloads/Study_MIDrugImmunity_20080228F.pdf; Gillian E. Metzger, *Federalism and Federal Agency Reform*, 111 COLUM. L. REV. 1 (2011).
[111] Buckman Co. v. Plaintiffs' Legal Comm., 531 U.S. 341 (2001).
[112] See Desiano v. Warner-Lambert & Co., 467 F.3d 85, 88 (2006).
[113] The court also cited the Sixth Circuit case Garcia v. Wyeth-Ayerst Labs, 385 F.3d 961 (2004) (applying *Buckman*).

On appeal, however, Guido, on behalf of Judges Feinberg, Parker and himself, vacates the decision. He concludes that federal law neither preempts Michigan's "immunity exception" for suits involving fraud against the FDA, nor prevents other common law claims.[114]

Persuasiveness. In an earlier account, Guido says that when the panel first met to deliberate, "the other two judges on the panel were prepared to come out the opposite way from me," but Guido argued that tort law required his proposed result.[115] "The other judges on the panel warned me that the Supreme Court would reverse us 9-0. I told them, 'I don't give a blank,' and added, 'I think I can still tell them more about torts than any of them except possibly Ruth Bader Ginsburg and Clarence Thomas, the two members of that Court who know something about torts.'"[116] Guido believed that by the strength of his opinion he could convince them that they could not reverse "without doing harm to torts in a way that they may not fully appreciate."[117]

In the opinion Guido points out that this case does not need to drag the FDA into protracted litigation: it involves a controversy between a private party and a private pharmaceutical company; nor is it a claim brought against the federal government based on its duty or a manufacturer's duty to the government.[118]

The plaintiffs, Guido writes, are actually raising traditional state tort claims that implicate Warner-Lambert's fraud on the FDA, but do not depend on that alone; therefore, these tort claims enjoy the presumption of validity. That is, so long as there was fraud on the FDA, a traditional tort negligence claim survives under Michigan law.[119]

More than deciding against Warner Lambert, the opinion is a salvo against the forceful efforts being made by the Bush administration's FDA to preempt common law actions through regulation. Guido elevates the stakes in the case by placing the Circuit's position about preemption within as broad a frame as possible:

> Until and unless Congress states explicitly that it intends invalidation of state common law claims merely because issues of fraud may arise in the trial of such claims, we decline to read general statutes like the Federal Food, Drug, and Cosmetic Act as having that effect.... Because of its important role in state regulation of matters of health and safety, common law liability cannot be easily displaced in our federal system.[120]

---

[114] 467 F.3d at 86.
[115] *American Association of Law Schools Torts & Compensation Systems Panel: Civil Recourse Theory's Reductionism*, 88 IND. L.J. 449, 449–50 (2013).
[116] 385 F.3d 961.
[117] *Id.*
[118] *Id.*
[119] *Id.*
[120] 467 F.3d at 96, 98.

As a pharmacy industry journal observed, *Desiano v. Warner-Lambert* strikes "a blow to pro-preemption advocates."[121]

There ensued a concerted effort to have the case heard and overturned by the Supreme Court. Urging reversal, the Pharmaceutical Research and Manufacturers of America (PhRMA) supported Warner-Lambert with amicus briefs and a public relations campaign.[122] In legal circles, "smart money" was betting that a High Court decision in Warner-Lambert would put an end to nearly all drug product lawsuits by persons who claimed to be harmed by adverse effects.[123]

The case was recaptioned as *Warner-Lambert v. Kent* on appeal and argued on February 25, 2008. As Guido relates, Chief Justice Roberts recused himself because his financial disclosure statement revealed ownership of stock in Warner-Lambert worth between $10,000 and $50,000.[124]

The "smart money" turned out to be mistaken. The vote on the Court tied with four votes in favor, and four opposed. The tie upheld the Second Circuit ruling.[125] Beside Justice Roberts's recusal, a more fundamental reason for the affirmance is that—as Guido stated in *Desiano*—Congress never expressed any intent to preempt state drug-related tort actions over the better part of a century—notwithstanding the political and media effort to assert that approval by the FDA should inoculate drug makers against state tort claims.[126]

The "smart money" also may have overestimated the willingness of some conservatives on the Court to sacrifice federalism and the evolutionary nature of the common law tort system of justice to assist corporate defendants— Guido's *Warner-Lambert* opinion in fact cites recent Supreme Court precedents affirming the importance of ex ante access to courts in several Supreme Court opinions.[127]

The political significance of Warner-Lambert. Guido describes his opinion as "the first case to put a serious brake on the move to completely substitute *ex ante* federal regulation for *ex post* tort law," and offers the view that "[u]p to then, the move against tort law had made enormous headway at the Supreme Court." As indicated, this is an accurate claim—although it should be kept in mind that resistance to the Republican version of "tort reform" had been building up for more than a decade—in the Academy, the Torts Bar, and among the general public.[128]

---

[121] Warner-Lambert Co., LLC v. Kent, 552 U.S. 440 (2008); Linda Greenhouse, *Court Allows Suit Against Drug Maker*, N.Y. TIMES, Mar. 4, 2008; Jesse C. Vivian, Sorcerer's Apprentice, 33 US Pharm.70 (2008); Vivian, Recusal of Judges, 34 U.S. Pharm. 40, 40–42 (2009).

[122] See Vivan, Sorcerer's Apprentice, *supra*.

[123] *Id.*

[124] Vivian, *supra* note 122.

[125] Warner-Lambert Co., LLC v. Kent, 552 U.S. 440 (2008).

[126] *Id.*

[127] Citing Cipollone v. Liggett Grp., 505 U.S. 504 (1992); Medtronic, Inc. v. Lohr, 518 U.S. 470 (996).

[128] See David A. Kessler & David C. Vladek, *A Critical Examination of the FDA's Efforts to Preempt Failure-to-Warn Claims*, 96 GEO. L.J. 461 (2008); Douglas G. Smith, *Preemption After Wyeth v. Levine*, 70 OHIO ST. L.J. 1435 (2009).

As Guido says, *Desiano v. Warner-Lambert* turned out to be a precursor to *Wyeth v. Levine*, the case that more solidly determined that state-law suits were not totally preempted by FDA pharmaceutical regulation. As Justice Stevens explained the outcome in *Wyeth*, "If Congress thought state-law suits posed an obstacle to its objectives, it surely would have enacted an express preemption provision at some point during the FDCA's 70-year history."[129]

Guido's reasoning in *Warner-Lambert* is, today, referred to frequently—although as often to distinguish it or criticize it as to follow it.[130] The conflict over ex post access to the tort system continues.

Nelson v. Metro North Commuter RR—*negligent infliction of emotional distress.* Lisa Nelson worked as a ticket agent and Kregg Houle worked as a conductor.[131] Both were based at the Metro-North Commuter Railroad station in Poughkeepsie. Lisa experienced physical harassment by Houle and complained to the Affirmative Action Officer, who separated them but allowed them to continue to work at different parts of the same stationhouse pending a further resolution. Lisa obtained an order of protection after filing a criminal complaint as well.[132]

The Poughkeepsie Metro North Station waiting room

According to the testimony of her psychiatrist, the Railroad's negligent handling of the situation and her later occasional encounters with Houle led to post-traumatic stress disorder, including nightmares and flashbacks.[133] Nelson

---

[129] Wyeth v. Levine, 555 U.S. 555, 574 (2009) (Stevens, J.)
[130] Embraced in Warner-Lambert & Co. v. Kent, 128 S. Ct. 1168, 170 L. Ed. 2d 51 (2008); N.Y. State Rest. Ass'n v. N.Y.C. Bd. of Health, 556 F.3d 114, 123 (2d Cir. 2009); Meijer, Inc. v. Ranbaxy Inc., 2016 U.S. Dist. LEXIS 120780, 63 (D. Mass. June 16, 2016). Criticized or distinguished in Marsh v. Genentech, Inc., 693 F.3d 546, 551 n.6 (6th Cir. 2012); Lofton v. McNeil Consumer & Specialty Pharm., 672 F.3d 372, 380 (5th Cir. 2012); Guenther v. Novartis Pharm. Corp., 2013 U.S. Dist. LEXIS 43518, at *11 (M.D. Fla. Mar. 26, 2013); In re Aredia & Zometa Prods. Liab. Litig., No. 3:06-MDL-01760, 2007 U.S. Dist. LEXIS 98940, at *36 n.17 (M.D. Tenn. Feb. 2, 2007).
[131] Nelson v. Metro-North Commuter R.R., 235 F.3d 101 (2000).
[132] *Id.*
[133] *Id.*

sued for negligent infliction of emotional distress under the Federal Employers Liability Act.[134]

The district court granted judgment as a matter of law at the close of Nelson's case because Nelson failed to present evidence sufficient to meet the "*Gottshall* test" established by the Supreme Court.[135]

The Conrail v. Gottshall *test for negligent infliction of emotional distress.* Justice Thomas considered three ways to limit—but retain—the common law right to recover; he ultimately concluded that the "zone of danger of physical impact" test was most suitable.[136] Within the zone, a worker would be able to recover for emotional injury caused by an immediate risk of physical injury to himself.[137]

Justice Thomas did not define what constitutes "immediate risk of physical harm," which left the phrase open to judicial interpretation. The test requires establishing either a "sustained physical impact" or being placed "in immediate risk of physical harm" as a result of an employer's negligence.[138]

Guido's contribution. In the course of affirming the district court in *Metro-North*, Guido dissected the meaning of "*immediate risk of physical harm*" in *Gottshall*, with a deep dive into the relationship between space, time, and danger. He rejected the purely temporal meaning for "immediate" and also the purely minimalist test for "physical." Instead of conceptualizing the requirement as a necessity to meet a threshold, he proposed adopting an approach that evaluated degrees of temporality and the seriousness of the physical risk to uncover whether a minimal degree of gravity had been established.[139] As Guido mentions, Judge Jacobs disagreed with this innovation, and was content to affirm based solely on *Gottshall's* temporal factors.[140]

Guido's approach has been taken up in many other jurisdictions.[141] As Judge Otis Wright of the District Court for the Central District of California stated, "[a]lthough the *Gottshall* court did not supply guidance on how to analyze when a plaintiff is in immediate risk of physical harm, the Second Circuit has said that 'the risk of physical harm to plaintiff must be, at the very least, more than minimal.'"[142]

Why Guido concurs with himself. Guido mentions three instances from among many in which he has concurred with his own majority decision. In *Restrepo v. McElroy*, Guido, writing for Judges Katzmann and Parker in addition to himself,

---

[134] *Id.*
[135] *Id.*
[136] 512 U.S. 532 (1994).
[137] *Id.* at 556.
[138] *Id.*
[139] 235 F.3d at 113,/IBT>.
[140] *Id.* (Jacobs, concurring).
[141] Stampf v. Long Island R.R. Auth., No. CV-07-3349 (SMG), 2010 U.S. Dist. LEXIS 58551, at *17 (E.D.N.Y. June 14, 2010); Sloan v. United States, 603 F. Supp. 2d 798, 808 (E.D. Pa. Mar. 25, 2009); Waisonovitz v. Metro-North Commuter R.R., 550 F. Supp. 2d 293, 297 (D. Conn. 2008); Balance v. Energy Transp. Corp., No. 00 Civ. 9180 (LMM), 2001 U.S. Dist. LEXIS 16763, at *15–16 (S.D.N.Y. Oct. 17, 2001).
[142] Russo v. APL Marine Servs., Ltd., 135 F. Supp. 3d 1089, 1098 (C.D. Cal. 2015).

he unanimously vacated the district court's stay of a deportation order.[143] All three judges agreed that the stay improperly applied a statutory protection against retroactive enforcement of a criminal law; all agreed that the case should not be reversed but remanded to determine whether there was other ground for finding impermissible retroactivity.[144]

Guido concurred to advance a position of his—that holding a reasonable *expectation* of an opportunity to seek relief from deportation was possibly easier to establish than proving *reliance* on the ability to do so; and that on remand, a new review of facts by the district court might support its original position based on his expectation theory.[145] Because Guido concurred in his own majority opinion, his other colleagues were not forced to decide whether offering that approach for a remand was appropriate or not. Dicta in the opinion would have required them to choose, and so they were happy to allow Guido to proceed independently.

Ciraolo v. City of New York. Ms. Debra Ciraolo prevailed in a Section 1983 Civil Rights Law action, after her subjection to an unlawful strip search.[146] The City argued on appeal that punitive damages could not be upheld because municipalities were immune from suit under the Supreme Court's decision in *City of Newport v. Fact Concerts, Inc.*[147] For the whole Court, Guido sided with the City and reversed the decision.[148] He and Judge Robert Katzmann also concurred separately.[149]

Judge Katzmann concurred in order to separate himself from speculation about circumstances in which a municipality could be subject to punitive damages.[150] Guido did it, however, to state that although he was bound to reverse by Supreme Court precedent, he strongly regretted the obligation to do so, because the *Newport* rule fails to deter municipalities from violating the Fourth Amendment.[151] Guido further discusses *Ciraolo* and *Newport* later in his narrative.[152]

---

[143] Restrepo v. McElroy, 369 F.3d 627 (2004).
[144] *Id.*
[145] *Id.* at 645.
[146] Ciraolo v. City of New York, 216 F.3d 236, 242–50 (2000); 42 U.S.C. § 1983.
[147] City of Newport v. Fact Concerts, Inc., 453 U.S. 247 (1981).
[148] 216 F.3d at 242–50.
[149] *Id.*
[150] *Id.*
[151] *Id.* at 249–50.
[152] See Chapter 29, "The Analytical Reasoning of a Behavioral Economist."

28

The Anti-Discrimination Law Reasoning of an Outsider

Anti-discrimination law is grounded in the principle of equal treatment embedded in the Fourteenth Amendment and in the Civil Rights Act of 1964, which bans employment discrimination on the basis of race, color, religion, sex, or national origin. Originally applied to discrimination in the workplace and in places of public accommodation, restrictions on discrimination have expanded through executive orders and statutory regulations covering areas including housing, education, sports, and virtually all government-funded activities. The prohibited bases for discrimination originally covered only race, religion, and national origin. Gradually, impermissible grounds for discrimination expanded to include other personal attributes including age, marital status, gender, sex, and physical and mental disabilities. Landmark Supreme Court anti-discrimination decisions include Shelley v. Kramer (1948) *(invalidation of restrictive covenants);* Brown v. Board of Education (1954) *(elementary school desegregation);* Loving v. Virginia (1967) *(racial intermarriage);* Obergefell v. Hodges (2015) *(same-sex marriage);* and Bostock v. Clayton County (2020) *(sexual orientation).*

Because many civil rights cases of first impression have come before him, Guido has had the opportunity to contribute in important ways to anti-discrimination jurisprudence. Brown v. City of Oneonta *brought a new perspective to the problem of racial profiling;* Back v. Hastings on Hudson *created a new way of thinking about gender-based termination;* Holcomb v. Iona College *extended theories of discrimination based on association; and* U.S. v. Ingram *attacked disparities in sentencing that could be associated with cultural prejudices.*

I once reversed a very good district judge for "jury-mandering" in an explosive murder case, involving racial and religious conflict between the Black community and the Jewish community in Crown Heights, Brooklyn. With the agreement of the lawyers on both sides, the district court judge intentionally empaneled a racially and ethnically balanced jury. I said that this violated the Sixth Amendment requirement that juries be selected impartially, and also the Due Process Clause.

The district judge was quite upset, until I told him, "If I had been in your situation, I might very well have done what you did, in the heat of that case. But we have been given the job of sitting as a panel of the Court of Appeals, three of us, two years later. Everything is quieter, and we inevitably are looking at the case differently from the way you do. If you can explain to district judges that you are not saying that you are smarter than they are, but that you have been situated in a different place and time in order to look at a different set of things—the structural consequences of the decision, rather than simply the dispute that is before the district judge, then they can understand what you are doing, and perhaps, even why you may have reversed them. I feel that way about us and the Supreme Court.

* * *

As I have said, I have not been a district judge. In part because of my personality and my incapacity to see myself in that role, I may be at something of a disadvantage in understanding the reasons for a decision. But there are also judges who arrive at the Court of Appeals who *have* been district judges, but who have lost the trial court's perspective. Sometimes these judges can be harder and less sympathetic to those whose opinions they are reviewing than people who have never been first instance judges.

> *Just look at the way the Circuit reviewed the 'stop-and-frisk' activities of the New York police in 2013. A panel halted a district court order to change police department practices, and criticized Judge Shira Scheindlin for taking control of the case in the way she did and for giving interviews to the press. The panel condemned her in quite personal terms and removed her from the case before there was any need. What is striking is that this panel was made up entirely of former district judges and it behaved in a way which district judges really resented.*

Like some other judges on our Circuit, I come out of a different kind of background. One result is that I perhaps look at claims of discrimination and bias differently. These differences came out dramatically in *Brown v. City of Oneonta*.

Brown v. Oneonta grows out of the mugging of an elderly woman. She managed, in defending herself, to cut the attacker's arm. The description she gave to the police was that the mugger was "a young black man." Neither she nor the police went any further into what "black" meant.

To me, the use of "young" and "black" in this way serves as a racial/ethnic "connotator," that is, in addition to its literal meaning, a pejorative cultural stereotype. Neither the victim nor the police said—as did the pamphlets that used to go out to catch fugitive slaves before the Civil War—that the person was "yellow black" or "dark black," "tall" or "short," "heavy" or "thin," etc. They did not use the description as a way of making it easier to identify the perpetrator. This bare description of the mugger on the part of the victim may be understandable given the rush of events, but it is not helpful for the police to allow a description of the group of people the police should be questioning.

The police started looking and did not find anybody. They then went to a local college where they asked *every Black man* to show his arm. They questioned more than 200 Black men. Finding nobody, they started asking everybody in the street, including at least one woman. Still, they never found anybody.

Some of those who were stopped brought a lawsuit alleging, under Section 1983 and the Fourth Amendment, that their civil rights were violated. The suit was dismissed by the federal district court on the grounds that the facts presented could not possibly satisfy the requirements for success.

John Walker wrote the opinion of our Court, affirming. It was unanimous—which is kind of strange because the panel included Jim [James] Oakes, who often took a "liberal" position in civil rights cases. A public outcry then resulted over what seemed to many to be yet another instance of innocent Black people being suspected of wrongdoing and subjected to mistreatment without adequate justification. As you might expect, the outcry was particularly strong among my students. It was akin to the Black Lives Matter outcry.

I was very upset when I read *Oneonta*, because of my own feelings, and because I knew how upset my students were. I knew very well that how you stereotype, and what you describe, is a product of your time and its underlying prejudices. It is something that I knew from my own childhood experiences; from studying history; and from reading old cases. Indeed, I had always taught about it.

Why did some early cases describe a party as "a corpulent lady," but never the same about a man? Why did many of the newspaper accounts of the person trying to get on the train in Judge Cardozo's famous torts case, *Palsgraf v. Long Island Railroad*, say, "The people who were getting on the train were dark, swarthy, probably Italian." Today, that would never happen, although the papers might well say, "Hispanic." All these categorizations say something, usually unappealing, about the society, about us, and our basic prejudices.

* * *

I asked for the whole Circuit to reconsider the panel decision *en banc*. The strategic problem I faced is the question of whether objecting to a 12(b)(6) dismissal or a grant of summary judgment was given wrongly is not the sort of thing our court goes *en banc* to reconsider. It is too technical a question and one too much governed by the facts of a case. I could not, in trying to get the panel decision reviewed, simply say, "You made an error in deciding whether there was enough evidence alleged to get by a 12(b)(6) dismissal." So, in asking to go *en banc*, I emphasized—perhaps more than I probably should have— the impact that this "technical" decision was having on people, because it was based on stereotyping. I pretty well said that the public believed that we were upholding a racist practice.

By raising the ante and responding to the tremendous anger that there was among Black students and the whole law school, as well as elsewhere, I was probably tactically unwise. My asking for the *en banc* made John Walker, who had just become Chief Judge, very unhappy. Furious. He is a wonderful guy—but his skin is not thick. Like the rest of us, he can be blunt himself at times and not notice when other people feel hurt, and yet again, like the rest of us, he really takes it to heart if someone suggests that he has done something that he would not want to do. Walker got very upset because he believed that I had called him a racist—which, of course, I guess in a way I had! As I say, strategically, that probably was not wise; it made the panel and those on the court who were especially close to the people on the panel, become defensive. But I do not know if I could have found another way of conveying to my colleagues how very important the case was.

> *I wanted to have this sent back to the panel. My hope was that by reversing the panel, we might start a deeper conversation. I wanted a decision that included language which said, "Sometimes you can do this sort of dragnet; sometimes you can't." I wanted to make sure the police would ask, in a case like this, more than a stereotypical black/white description of the person they would be looking for. I did not want this to be the result of direct court rules, like the* Miranda *warning; rather, I wanted the New York legislature and Governor to come up with some appropriate regulations.*

Some judges, partly because they had been in the U.S. Attorney's Office, had a perspective that is very close to the police. They opposed my petition because they thought that this way of rounding up suspects is something that police had always done and have to be able to do. To me, they simply fail to understand the racial consequences of that position.

Other judges who rejected the petition were, frankly, silly. I wrote in a memo, "Since they searched a black woman when the description was of a black man, the police were clearly behaving in a racist manner," and one judge replied, "But, of course, somebody can fake their gender. The mugger might have been a *woman dressed as a man*." I responded, "Yes, and somebody can also fake whether he or she is *black* or not; the perpetrator in theory could have been a white person putting on blackface!" That particular judge is one that I am close to and we often speak bluntly to each other; so I felt comfortable saying that his position was the silliest I had ever heard of. That he could say what he did shows how much defensiveness there was at the time.

I converted several colleagues with a hypothetical in which I said, "Look, assume somebody attacks somebody, is identified ethnically, and also is wounded in some way. Assume that person goes into the bar next door, where there are six people of that ethnicity; and assume that the crime was a serious one. In these circumstances, it might be perfectly okay for the cops to start by looking at the six people with that ethnicity." I then said, "If somebody went swimming in the reservoir at Central Park naked, which was against the law, and somebody saw the person come out, and saw a large tattoo on the butt of that person, and identified the person on the basis of ethnicity, you certainly would not let the cops tell all the people of that ethnicity they ran into to drop their pants to see whether they had the tattoo." I argued that there has to be some kind of proportionality between the specificity of the ethnic identification, the number of people who could be suspected, and the severity of the offense. I wanted the Circuit to encourage the legislature to establish a set of considerations to be weighed when issues of racial profiling were involved.

In the end, lots of people went with me to ask for the *en banc*, including several people who are often fairly conservative where the rights of criminal defendants are concerned.

Still, I failed to get a review *en banc*. I came within one vote. The irony is that a very new judge who subsequently has turned out to be one of the strongest attackers of racial stereotypes voted against going *en banc*. New judges often go along with the Chief Judge when they first come on a court—and later regret it.

> *I criticized some of my friend Justice Souter's opinions which he wrote in his first year on the Supreme Court. At the time, I think he was a bit upset with me. Over the years, I believe he has come to agree that he may have been overly deferential and hence wrong in some of these cases.*

Having lost, I wrote a dissent to the denial of the rehearing, in which I proposed that if a wide sweep is based purely on a racial classification, it should be subject to strict scrutiny.

Judge John Walker wrote that this would never work; that my proposal would interfere with police methods and upset the balance in the Fourth Amendment by injecting Equal Protection standards into police investigations. But there *are* Equal Protection dimensions to a search! To Walker, the nature of the question was, is it all right to ask somebody to *drop his pants*, as against to *show his arms*? I thought he ignored the fact that the police are asking for the dropping of pants and showing of arms only of people *of a certain ethnicity*.

> *I didn't say this in the opinion, but suppose after the collapse of Lehman Brothers on Wall Street, the authorities had asked only Jewish financiers to show their bank accounts? It would be unacceptable beyond belief! Unacceptable beyond belief!*

As I think about it now, not only my being a teacher of students who felt personally threatened, but also personal history affected my position in *Oneonta*, undoubtedly, and my sensitivity to stereotyping more generally. I remember conversations in my family near when the Italian racial laws came in, and the Fascists published in newspapers pictures of ten people who were typically "Jewish." As it turned out, four of them were not of Jewish extraction at all! [Laughs] They had possibly Jewish sounding names. But you know, even in stereotypes, Italian and Jews often look very much alike.

And, of course, it was not lost on me that well after my immediate family had fled, in 1943, the Nazis went after everybody who they defined in some way as "a Jew."

In America today, stereotyping may still affect Italians more than Jews. Jews in America have been very good at making people be sensitive to any remarks that are anti-Semitic, or conceivably so. Yet the number of slurs and stereotypes that people will say about Polish people, about Italian people, etc., and not think it is anything at all, is quite remarkable.

Two of my fellow judges were talking about the television series The Sopranos *and what fun it was. I was there and not paying much attention. But I said, "Fun?" I said, "I've never watched it." They looked at me, and they said, "Why not?" I said, "Not interested." They said, "Why? Do you think it stereotypes?" I said, "Well, of course it does. But that doesn't bother <u>me</u> that much, although, I am sure it bothers many other Italians. I did not watch it, because I do not watch television. If I watched television, I certainly would not have watched that ... because of the stereotyping. They seemed surprised by my reaction.*

I think there is an insensitivity among many people, including liberals, who tell me, "You're too sensitive about certain ethnic things." Indeed, I am sensitive.

I am very comfortable with the arguments I made in *Oneonta* and am still disappointed with the response from some of my colleagues. John Walker and I are very good friends; we teach a course together. You should know that to this day, when the students ask, "What is the best opinion and the worst opinion you have written?," I always answer that each of us has written good and bad ones. If they press me about John Walker, I always say, "Well, *Brown v. Oneonta* is Walker's worst opinion. Just read the case. You'll see why."

And he looks kind of sheepish. We are friends, and I admire him very much, you know.

***

Deciding whether an employer has discriminated against an employee can also raise stereotyping problems, as happened in *Back v. Hastings on Hudson Union Free School District*. Elana Back was a school psychologist who was hired on a three-year tenure track basis, and near the end of her three years, she was denied tenure. In challenging the termination, she said the real reason for it was that the school believed that her childrearing would interfere with her work, and that she was told the job was "not for a mother." Her case required us to see whether stereotyping about the conflict between work and motherhood is a form of gender discrimination that violates Title VII of the Civil Rights Act.

The question raised in *Back* goes beyond whether there was employment discrimination based on gender alone. The Hastings on Hudson School District obviously hired and gave tenure to many women. The issue is whether anti-discrimination law also prohibits maltreatments based on stereotypical assumptions about a mother's future performance at work, assumptions which are associated with gender. If the administrators know she has children and they fire her because they think that looking after children will interfere with her professional work, does their action fit within the category of gender discrimination?

> *My former clerk, Noah Zatz, now a professor at UCLA, has written about the non-accommodation of groups that are protected under civil rights laws. It is no accident that he worked on the* Back *case with me. What is it that we are concerned with in these situations? Are some jobs deemed okay for women only so long as they behave like men?*

Our opinion said yes. Back had provided enough evidence that could allow a jury to hold that the real reason for her termination was a gender stereotype of this sort.

The principal of the school and the director of personnel there, who supervised Back, were both women. I am confident they met male-established terms for their own job performances. These women succeeded on male terms, but believed that Back wanted the job *on her own—female—terms.*

This raises the question, should people, in order to get equality, have to behave on the terms that characterize a previously dominant group, in this case men. Or should women, such as Back, be permitted to demand equality, to some extent, *on their own terms?*

> *My daughter Bianca came back to New York from teaching at Kenyon College, where she was about to get tenure, because she decided she wanted to have a child, and did. She went to teach at a place in New Jersey, at a second-rate place, well below her, but where they offered her tenure track.*
>
> *Because she had the child, she believed, they were discriminating against her—clearly, clearly. She left that New Jersey job, because she could, and took a job as a lecturer at Columbia. She could afford to do it and she, of course, did not sue.*
>
> *I thought of* Back v. Hudson, *and I could not help smiling and feeling that if it were not somebody who could say, 'The heck with you,' Bianca would have been protected by* Back. *She knew it, too, because people told her there is this case! She did not know I had written it.*

Taking equality on the terms instilled by the dominant group often will lead to discrimination even by people who are of the subordinate group. You get serious hostility from women who have gotten where they are by behaving like men. This is another example of "melting-pot" equality. The outsider will be given equality only if she or he melts into the behavior of the insider. Sometimes the outsider who has melted in will discriminate against the outsider who has not. How often do immigrants become "100 percent Americans?"

> There is a very strong feeling that I have that we are all in danger of being discriminators. We're all capable of, in certain situations, behaving very bravely, and very well, and we're all capable of behaving horribly. That comes from seeing what happened in Italy, a country of no history, really, of racial discrimination. Maybe religious, but basically none; but many people there have come to discriminate as circumstances in Italy change.
>
> This makes me start thinking about Holland, this country that we all think is wonderful. You take the Dutch and put them in South Africa, and then see what happens! Then I think of Israel. Here, you have a people whose tradition is: "Look to the stranger, because you were the stranger." Yet some find themselves in a new situation, and do the opposite.
>
> Then you think about the people who come to America. Being an immigrant, I see Italians who were treated terribly when they first came here, Irish who were treated terribly when they first came here, and some of them becoming the people who treat others terribly.
>
> Many years ago, we were at the Berenson villa in Florence, at a dinner, invited by a guy who had been married to a Rockefeller and was a "very good liberal." It happened that my daughter Bianca and her husband Jonathan were there with us.
>
> A very wealthy man from an old, okay Italian Jewish family that had suffered terribly during the war was there. In the middle of dinner, the question of gypsies— the Romany—came up, and he started saying all sorts of horrible things.
>
> Everybody was quiet, except Bianca; she politely, but firmly, let him know that what he was saying was unacceptable, and particularly bad from someone who had suffered from discrimination.
>
> This whole framework was behind me, in Back. We are all capable of being the discriminators, and we should read the laws with that firmly in mind. It is not that women cannot discriminate. It is not that Blacks can't discriminate. It is important to be very realistic about what the situations are when that happens.

I am not taking a position on whether "melting in" is appropriate. What I am saying is that if in such contexts there is a view of how people ought to behave, and that those who do not behave in that way are discriminated against, or inappropriately treated badly, that is discrimination, and where it affects women, it is gender discrimination.

The problem has arisen most in litigation in the context of women, because there has been a long-standing division in the Women's Rights Movement as to whether women should seek equality by behaving as men stereotypically do, or insist on equality while behaving in ways that they deem are appropriate for women. The great Pauli Murray tried to bridge that difference in her writings, but even she did not succeed.

> One does not, for the most part, see 'melting-pot' gay managers discriminating against gay employees who want to be themselves. In considerable part this is

because another former clerk of mine, Kenji Yoshino, has argued for a view that largely has won out; today there are not that many gays who are saying, "We will discriminate against gays who don't behave like heterosexuals."

The language of Section 1983 provides the right to sue those who have deprived others of their civil rights under the color of law. It has been applied to prohibit discrimination against gays; it has been applied to people who do not look like males even though they are not gay. It has already been applied in a variety of ways, and whether a court applies it to situations such as *Back*, depends on whether it sees this statute as a kind of organic statute that sets a context for common law development, or whether these broad statutes are viewed as very narrow, remedial statutes.

Needless to say, I think it is fair to read the combination of statutes in this area as being organic, and to allow for the common law development of what protected civil rights are. There is enough in what the Supreme Court has written about these statutes so that there is nothing wrong with reading it this way, and this is the spirit of *Back v. Hastings on Hudson.*

* * *

Another case that shows the importance of viewing these statutes as organic is *Holcomb v. Iona College*. I decided the case more than a decade ago and did not quite realize that the decision would be as influential or important as it later turned out to be.

Holcomb was a white assistant basketball coach who claimed that Iona College fired him because of his marriage to a Black woman. He claimed that there was a Civil Rights Act violation—not on the basis of a hostile work environment or of his race. He claimed he was discriminated against because of his relationship to someone else, his African American wife.

Title VII of the Civil Rights Act prohibits discriminating against an individual with respect to sex and race, and this language may not seem to cover Holcomb's situation. The facts raised the question, "Do you treat somebody as being in the category of "discriminated against" because they are married to somebody who is in the category? It was easy to say yes and to make this relational move, both because husband and wife have been treated as being one in marriage for many legal purposes and because pretty much everyone thought that the statute should prohibit that sort of discrimination. And so we held, for the first time, that an employer would violate Title VII if it fired an employee because of the employee's association with a person of another race. To construe the statute this way seemed sensible, and it was, at the time, not really a big deal.

Remember that the Yale of 1940 let my father know not to live in the Italian or the Jewish neighborhoods—perhaps because the University had the sense that we

> would be 'contaminated,' or that Yale would. Yale did not want to associate itself with 'them.'
>
> In my experience, discrimination was about nationality, and ethnicity, religion and citizenship. It still is today, but it is also race and sexuality.
>
> Is all this connected to Holcomb v. Iona College? Perhaps, but these encounters provide the sorts of lessons that everyone gets, one way or another. After all, the three of us on the panel— [Judge Robert D.] Bob Sack, John Walker and I—came from very different points of view, and we all agreed on the outcome.

But the relational move we made turned out to be extremely important, and *Holcomb* has shown up in more than a thousand cases since. It was especially useful to my Circuit in arriving at an outcome in *Zarda v. Altitude Express*—an important *en banc* decision which held that discrimination based on his sexual orientation violates the prohibition of discrimination based on sex in the Civil Rights Act. Since I was not on the original panel as a Senior Judge, I was not on the *en banc* court.

Judge Gerry Lynch wrote a dissenting opinion, joined by Judge Rena Raggi and Judge Deborah Livingston. Their dissent argued that applying the Civil Rights Statute to sexual orientation was stretching the clear language of the statute. They said, "The gay man involved was not discriminated against because of *his* gender." "Of course, the law should apply to protect sexual orientation," said Lynch, who by the way is genuinely progressive on gay rights; but he added, "Come on now! That ain't what they said and it ain't what they meant!" Lynch's dissent accepted various earlier "stretches" of the language in Title VII, including my stretch in *Iona v. Holcomb*. These earlier ones, Lynch said, were "close enough." But he would not include discrimination against sexual orientation, looking at the history at the time and the language of the statute, he repeatedly said, "That is stretching a statute too far."

* * *

My own view of all this as an academic is pretty clear. I have written that *interpreting* a statute is different from *construing* it; and construing a statute is not the same as the *updating* it. Interpretation is nothing but retrospective: one searches the text and relevant history to try to discover what the legislature meant to do at the time. But we all know that interpreting is not the only thing that courts do. Updating may be forbidden, but some situations require more from a court than interpretation; they require construction and so sometimes we *construe*.

We probably construe most often when we construe a statute to avoid constitutional problems. Although the Supreme Court has said, unanimously, that a court cannot *update* a statute, or *rewrite* a statute to avoid constitutional problems, it still often upholds decisions that avoid constitutional problems by construing statutes in ways that avoid the constitutional difficulties.

> *Interestingly, in his Zarda dissent, Judge Lynch says, "I'm all for doing something like this,"—he doesn't say "construing," but says "updating"—"when we are talking about the Constitution, but not statutes." But I think he has it wrong.*
>
> *Although courts sometimes must construe both constitutions and statutes, the dangers are greater when courts construe constitutions—because if they do it and they are wrong, they have created the "majoritarian problem"—the legislature is stuck with their constitutional construction. When courts do it with a statute, though, it is not the court saying, "We usurp your place," because the legislature need only overcome its own inertia and can come back and override the court.*
>
> *That inertia is great, but it is not the same as constitutionally imposed inertia.*

What then is the difference between construing and updating, or rewriting? By "construing," I mean using traditional canons of interpretation to determine a meaning when there is a reason to do more than look retrospectively at what was meant at the time of drafting. If there is a reason to avoid a constitutional problem, or if there are reasons to think the legislature today would weigh the interests balanced in a statute differently from when the statute was written, then it is appropriate to construe the statute.

But one may only do this with a statute if a traditional, relatively objective canon of interpretation will permit it. In other words, if you can understand what values the statute was designed to serve and can extrapolate to today, you can adopt those values as the ones that the statute was written to embody. But subject to a constraint: you can do this only if it can be done under one of the canons of interpretation under the theory of interpretation you subscribe to—linguistic, contextual, precedential, or otherwise. Construction is so limited.

Now, *when* you construe—and when is it overreaching to construe—is a much tougher problem. We certainly construe to avoid constitutional difficulties. We also construe statutes—for instance when a statute is sufficiently out of date for technological or value-change reasons, to leave it where it is would be a disaster.

Construing is what I did in *Holcomb v. Iona*; and no one objected. Indeed, even Judge Lynch in his dissent in *Zarda* cited *Iona* approvingly. But if the statute was properly construed as it was in *Iona*, then that precedent makes the statute apply directly to the situation in *Zarda*. *Zarda* was discriminated against because of his relationship to someone of a particular gender—another man. Had he been in a relationship with a woman, he would not have been discriminated against.

Verbally, the statute as it was read in *Iona* applied directly to *Zarda*, and so the *en banc* court held. The *en banc* court had any number of other reasons why they thought the statute could be so construed. It is not for me to comment on these; but its reliance on the relational theory as established by *Iona* was especially interesting to me.

Our Court is a very friendly court, and so knowing my views about construction, Dennis Jacobs, who had joined the mandate in Zarda, *sent me two limericks, one lamenting, the other delighting in being construed!*

The Statute's **Lament**

A statute that Guido "construed"
Complained that his treatment was rude:
"You did not rewrite me,
And I'm happy you cite me,
But construal has left me unglued."

The Statute's **Delight**

A statute that Guido "construed"
Was happy to be so renewed. "I had thought that the text
Explained I was sexed;
Now I'm LG-BTQ'd

I answered with a limerick which was quite crude:

> *The statute that you have construed,*
> *To use language that's terribly rude,*
> *Helps the plaintiff that's gay*
> *Assert the Wild Way,*
> *In which he was earlier screwed.*

I suppose one could have tried to limit *Iona* to its facts and said it applied only if the relationship was one of marriage. The coach in *Iona* was married to an African American woman. Would he be discriminated against if his relationship was not yet one of marriage? Applying it to gays, does the relational theory require discrimination of a *married* gay or to any persons who have relationships with people of their own sex?

After *Zarda* came down, I talked about this with Judge Bob Sack, who had been on the *Iona* panel with me, and he said, "I cannot imagine that it would not have applied if a person was discriminated against because his girlfriend was African American." I told him, "You know, Bob, when I was writing *Iona*, I did what one does when one talks about a relatively easy case. One always thinks about what you would do if it were more difficult." One of the things that I was thinking about when I was writing this was, What if it wasn't marriage? What if it was his girlfriend? Yes, or what if Holcomb was just "hanging out" with Black people? And of course, these cases would just have to come out the same way, ultimately, given the way the law works!

Of course, as I said earlier, my own view, as expressed in A Common Law for the Age of Statutes, is that courts ought to be given the power to update statutes openly, but with the strict limits that book suggests. But that authority has not been given to us and so we should not exercise it. Construing of statutes, though, with the constraints I have just described, is as old as the nation, and is what I did in Back *and* Iona.

Back *and* Iona are important on their own terms for what they say about the rights of women with children, and about discrimination against people because of whom they associate with, whether racially or as to gender. But they are also interesting because they both read Section 1983 as an organic statute which requires us to treat like cases alike in a broader sense. That is, the statute requires us to allow subordinated groups to behave in their own ways. It prohibits us from saying, "If such groups do not behave as we do, we can treat them badly."

That, it seems to me, is what discrimination is.

* * *

I am not much of a libertarian. I'm too much of a social democrat to say that government cannot do this or that. Government must be able to do things. For me, therefore, the most important question to ask is not, "Has your right to the due process of law been violated by a government rule? It is, "Does the law fail to do to me what it demands of you?" This springs not simply from anti-libertarianism but from my theory of Equality. I believe that any number of actions can be taken and be done by the police, or by the government more broadly speaking, if the state does them to everybody, and not just to some unfortunates.

As an example, I am not someone who has an expansive view of privacy as a judicial responsibility, but I do insist that if you invade privacy, you do it equally to everyone. For instance, if the state is concerned with the drug problem, then it must not search in public housing, but search everywhere; similarly, it must search everybody at airports, not just the people who 'look suspicious' for ethnic reasons. My feeling is that if we require that the whole public bears the cost of drug control, the public will decide whether this is worthwhile and court intervention will be less needed.

Brown v. Oneonta, the sweep case I started with, dramatically shows what happens if we do things to some which we are unwilling to have done to us. That is, if we are the "ins," we not do not need to worry about being stopped and searched, and it is absurd in a situation like *Oneonta* to suggest that we would in practice likely ever be in the position of the Black students who were stopped and searched.

Do you know who expressed the importance of equal protection to evaluating prohibited government behavior most dramatically? Ironically, it was Justice Scalia, in his concurrence in *Cruzan v. Missouri*, one of the right-to-life, right-to-death cases, which considered whether Missouri could override the wishes of a patient to refuse extraordinary measures that kept her alive. Scalia asked whether there are any limits the Constitution places on a state's demand for extraordinary measures. There *are* limits, he said, but not ones imposed by the Due Process Clause. He added, "Our salvation is the Equal Protection Clause, which requires the democratic majority to accept *for themselves and their loved ones what they impose on you and me*." Beautiful. His is still the best statement of this principle.

> *The opinion is funny because in it Scalia gives a catalog of 'horribles' which nonetheless can be done by the state if they are imposed on everybody. His list of horrible is amusing. They are things like the right to drive. I can think of things far more horrible than are on this list. But in the end that is beside the point, which is, whatever each of us thinks of as a horrible case can be kept from happening even without judicial intervention if everyone bears the burden.*

Justice Scalia, however, then kills "equality of burden" as a way of protecting us politically from state abuse. He does this by applying the Equal Protection Clause in a totally formalistic way. He says, "It does not violate equal protection to prohibit *everybody, male and female,* from having an abortion." Preposterous! It is the equivalent of saying that it does not offend equality to prohibit "*rich and poor alike from sleeping under bridges*," as Émile Zola said bitterly that the law does. You cannot use a formalistic approach to equality and then count on it to be your safeguard against an overreaching government.

Justice Scalia took a similar approach when he looked at searches and seizures. He said, "Don't look to a strong Fourth Amendment. Look to whether they can do it to me and to you." Fair enough; but one must ask, "Are these searches that *in fact* are done to me as well as to you?" He adopted the same perspective about criminal sentencing and was not concerned if a harsh drug sentencing rule was substantially targeted at a disfavored group, as long as the statute could be read as directed at everyone.

In fact, even a non-formal Equal Protection analysis will fail to do the job Justice Scalia assigned to it. This is because the Equal Protection Clause requires an *intent* to discriminate. Many of these cases instead do not involve a desire to discriminate. They simply want to achieve a goal … the elimination of drugs, the protection of fetuses. But that goal is only pursued when burden is on "the outsider" and not on "us." All this may well be what my next "academic" article is about.

* * *

This brings us to my concurring opinion in *United States v. Ingram*. It made Judge Reena Raggi angry; she wrote that I was "calling the law into disrepute." I replied, "Far from it." When you read the case, you will see why.

The panel's opinion affirms the sentence of a youngster which was below that recommended by the sentencing guidelines. It was still a *twelve-year* sentence for selling less than a gram of crack cocaine. The guidelines recommended a very high sentence because he was a career offender, subject to a "three-strikes" sentencing rule. He was a drug addict himself and he behaved very badly in jail. He got twelve years *instead of two years* because of sentencing enhancements that were contemplated in the sentencing guidelines.

It happens that Ingram, I believe, came from the family of a great actor, a kid who had been given all sorts of chances. He had support from his family and money, and he was able to argue his conviction and that his sentence was 'unreasonably high.' Although the overall disparity between the sentencing for crack-cocaine offenses and other forms of cocaine are a strong example of the equal protection problem I am talking about, Ingram's particular case was certainly not a case of the law being applied "to them" and not "to us."

The whole panel agreed that the sentence was not "unreasonably high"—in the sense that somebody else who had been given as many chances and violated them as he had done, would not receive the same sentence. There are crack-cocaine cases all the time which result in longer sentences. A per curiam opinion of our panel affirmed the district court's imposition of the sentence, unanimously. But Reena and I each also wrote separately.

What made my opinion unusual and set Judge Raggi off, was a footnote I included, which said that though the sentence was "not unreasonable, it was absurd." Being much more formalistic, Raggi said, "How can you say that?" I said, "It is easy. You do not think courts ought to write opinions that invite conversations with legislatures and other policymakers. I do."

My point was that as a court we are directed by the legislature to use certain tests to evaluate whether a lower court has arrived properly at a sentence. Within that context, I said, I do not see how any of us can say that this sentence was so out of line as to be unreasonable. The sentence here was a tough one, but one that would be imposed on rich and poor alike, and well within the guidelines by which the district court had been directed to be guided. In context, that is what "reasonable" and "unreasonable" mean.

But that is not the sum total of our job: a Court of Appeals is not restricted to deciding that question. As I had told the district judge in the "jury-mandering" case, our job is also to look at the way a decision will affect the system of justice for years to come. Viewed in that way, I believed that in *Ingram* we also had an obligation to examine both the narrow law and the broad policy it applied.

We would have been remiss not to encourage a conversation with the legislature about whether the relevant sentencing guidelines were sound! I suggested that we should be "stepping back from our labyrinthine and often draconian sentencing law," and that "there is nothing 'reasonable' about sending a man to prison for twelve years to punish him for a non-violent, $80 drug sale; it is absurd." Judge Gerry Lynch agreed with me about this in a prior decision called *United States v. Preacely*.

> Ingram's sentence had to be upheld; but it imposed unreasonable costs on society. Taxpayer money would be spent to house and feed Ingram; and such long sentences often disrupt the lives of children of defendants.
>
> I said a prison term of this length was not sensible. It was formally reasonable, but substantively, deeply disturbing. I added that, "A sentence of this length, for this crime, is *headed toward unreasonableness—and is, in fact, well along that road.*" My point was not primarily to lay down a marker for the judges who come after me who might understand the situation as I did, but mainly to alert legislators. It was yet again an example of my view about the role judges play by their dialogue with other institutions.

COMMENTARY

Chapter 28

U.S. v. Nelson—"jury-mandering." In August 1991, the Brooklyn neighborhood of Crown Heights was gripped by riots after the chauffer of a prominent rabbi struck two Black children, killing one.[1] During the riots, Yankel Rosenbaum, a Jewish man, was killed by a Black youth, Lemrick Nelson, Jr. His prosecution took many turns back and forth in state and federal courts.

In the trial that ultimately came under the scrutiny of Guido's panel through an appeal, the district judge, with the consent of counsel for both parties, took an unusual step when one juror had to excuse himself: "The district court did not simply replace this juror with the first alternate, who was white, but instead, *sua sponte*, removed a second (white) juror from the panel and filled the two spaces this created with an African–American juror and with ... [a] Jewish Juror."[2] The judge, with what Guido called "the best of intentions," had intended to create a racially and ethnically mixed jury, so that the public would "understand" and so that "nobody [could] complain whatever the result."[3] This agreement was not known until the defense raised the issue on appeal.[4] Guido, writing for the Second Circuit, dubbed the practice "jury-mandering," noting that it violated, or came close to violating, the Fourteenth Amendment's Equal Protection Clause.[5] On remand, Nelson was convicted of a lesser civil rights violation.[6]

---

[1] David Stout, *The Case That Rocked Crown Heights*, N.Y. TIMES, Aug. 15, 1996.
[2] U.S. v. Nelson, 277 F.3d 164, 172 (2000).
[3] *Id.*
[4] Devlin Barrett, *Judge Made Racial Deal on Crown Heights Jury*, N.Y. POST, May 4, 2000.
[5] *Nelson*, 277 F.3d at 208.
[6] Brian Bernbaum, *Conviction in Crown Heights Killing*, CBS NEWS, May 14, 2003.

A complete legal history of the Yankel Rosenbaum case would require a book and deserves one.[7] Guido later reflected that the many procedural maneuvers and delays appeared to tarnish the justice system—but that, with hindsight, the circuitous and time-consuming legal process allowed the heat and tensions in the community to dissipate enough to permit, finally, an appropriate result.

Brown v. City of Oneonta.[8] Fewer than three hundred African Americans lived in Oneonta, New York in 1992. In September of that year, a man in Oneonta attacked a seventy-seven-year-old woman in her friend's home. During the scuffle, the assailant suffered a cut to the arm. He then escaped before the authorities arrived. When police asked for a description of the attacker, the woman said only that the assailant was young, Black, and male; the police did not ask for more details.

The police obtained a list of seventy-eight Black male students from SUNY Oneonta—soon to be known as "the black list"—and proceeded to question all of them.[9] One student on the list, Jamel Champen, reported that a policeman shined a spotlight at him, asked him if he was stupid, and made him show his hands.[10] Later, another policeman told Champen that they had already interviewed "450 other black guys."[11]

The sweep soon spread to other African American residents in the small town, but the assailant was never found. Though the police professed to have no awareness of how their actions would be perceived, the racial dragnet soon created a national uproar.[12] The administrator who released the list was demoted; SUNY Oneonta suffered a drop in applications;[13] and the NAACP set up a local chapter.[14] Meanwhile, a group of students sued the school administrator who released the list,[15] while seeking certification of a larger class of individuals stopped by the police. Ultimately, all school officials were deemed to enjoy qualified immunity.[16] The initial suit against the police ended with the dismissal of equal protection claims and summary judgment for the defendants on numerous Fourth Amendment claims.

The first panel opinion and public reaction. A three-judge panel considered the case in 1999. Soon-to-be Chief Judge John M. Walker wrote the opinion, affirming most of the District Court's Fourth Amendment search and seizure judgments and, more notably, ruling against the plaintiffs on their equal protection claim. "We are

---

[7] There is a fine scholarly, historical account of events. *See* EDWARD SHAPIRO, CROWN HEIGHTS: BLACKS, JEWS, AND THE 1991 BROOKLYN RIOT (2006).

[8] Brown v. City of Oneonta, 911 F. Supp. 580 (N.D.N.Y. 1996); Brown v. City of Oneonta, 106 F.3d 1125 (1997); substituted opinion at 221 F.3d 329 (1999) [hereinafter Brown II]; rehearing and rehearing *en banc* denied, 235 F.3d 769 (2000) [hereinafter Brown III]; cert. denied, 534 U.S. 816 (2001).

[9] Dianne Jean Schemo, *College Town in Uproar Over "Black List" Search*, N.Y. TIMES, Sept. 27, 1992.

[10] First Amended Complaint, ¶¶ 109–10.

[11] *Id.* ¶ 112.

[12] "[New York State Police Maj. Robert] Farrand said the legal and racial issues of the case did not occur to him at the time. He has issued an apology for the racial dragnet his men used." Lynne Duke, *When Race Is Equated with Crime*, WASH. POST, Oct. 21, 1992.

[13] Associated Press, *Enrollment Dip Proves Costly for College*, N.Y. TIMES, July 22, 1993.

[14] Denise Richardson, *SUNY Oneonta Looks Past Black List*, DAILY STAR, Sept. 4, 2012.

[15] John T. McQuiston, *Black SUNY Students Lose Suit on List of Names Given to Police*, N.Y. TIMES, Feb. 16, 1997.

[16] *Id.*

not blind to the sense of frustration that was doubtlessly felt by those questioned by the police during this investigation," Walker wrote, but nevertheless indicated that this type of conduct was not merely constitutionally sound, but logistically sensible in areas with extremely skewed demographics, like Oneonta.[17]

Despite the measured tone of the opinion, its holding was inflammatory. As the *New York Times* put it, "a Federal appeals court ruled yesterday that police officers in Oneonta, N.Y., did not violate the Constitution when they tried to stop every black man in town in 1992 after a woman said she had been robbed in her home by a young black man." Columnist Bob Herbert emphasized the point. "Got that? Every black man in town," he wrote in disbelief. "With this ruling, cops are free to harass any and all black people as long as they have in hand a complaint that a black person has committed a crime."[18] "Everyone, regardless of his or her skin color, should shudder," a *New York Times* reader warned.[19] The decision "wounds me as a black man," wrote another.[20]

The practice of the racial profiling in Oneonta found its way into the 2000 presidential primary debates—Democratic candidates Al Gore and Bill Bradley both denounced the decision: they promised to issue executive orders banning racial profiling if they were elected.[21] Even state Attorney General Eliot Spitzer, who argued the case for the State of New York, had misgivings about the breadth of the circuit opinion. After the opinion was handed down, Spitzer was quoted as saying, "We won the case, but it makes your skin crawl."[22]

The amended opinion. Perhaps in response to widespread criticism and the possibility of an *en banc* hearing, the initial panel produced an amended opinion in August 2000, which hewed to the original equal protection reasoning, but reversed itself on several of the Fourth Amendment claims.[23] While the original opinion noted that "rudeness," which allegedly characterized Jamel Champen's encounter, did not amount to a seizure, for instance, the amended opinion found that "a reasonable person in Champen's circumstances would have considered the police officer's request to be compulsory."[24]

The plaintiffs petitioned for a rehearing *en banc* which was denied; to this denial Guido wrote a substantial dissenting opinion.[25] He sharply challenged the dismissal of the equal protection charges and argued that the amended opinion "still makes unnecessary, and inevitably hurtful, remarks about when following victims' descriptions involving race is constitutionally permissible."[26] Guido proposed

---

[17] "It may also be practicable for law enforcement to attempt to contact every black person, but quite impossible to contact every white person." Brown v. City of Oneonta, 195 F.3d 111, 120 (1999) [hereinafter Brown I].
[18] Bob Herbert, *In America: Breathing While Black*, N.Y. TIMES, Nov. 4, 1999.
[19] Sandy S. Head, *Stopping Blacks: A Chilling Decision*, N.Y. TIMES, Nov. 4, 1999.
[20] Eulas Boyd, *A Ruling on Race: A Blight on the Dream*, N.Y. TIMES, Nov. 7, 1999.
[21] THE 2000 CAMPAIGN; *Excerpts from Bradley-Gore Debate in Des Moines*, N.Y. TIMES, Jan. 18, 2000.
[22] Herbert, *supra* note 18.
[23] Brown II, 221 F.3d at 329.
[24] *Id.* at 340; Brown I, 195 F.3d at 122.
[25] Brown III, 235 F.3d at 789. The vote not to go *en banc* was 8-5. (Calabresi, J., dissenting; joined by Straub, and (in part) Parker and Sotomayor). Judge Kearse dissented separately without an opinion.
[26] *Id.*

that stops should be subject to equal protection strict scrutiny review when police ignored the nonracial components of a description and questioned persons who, the racial descriptor aside, did not fit the description.[27]

In chambers after hearing oral argument, 2015

His approach was ferociously attacked by both Judges Walker and Jacobs. Reacting to Guido's inference that the police had stopped numerous Black *women*, Walker replied that "[h]is math is speculative and ends up presenting at most another insufficiently particularized allegation."[28] Guido's proposal was "flawed and unworkable," and would "upset [the] carefully crafted balance" between "individual rights and the necessities of effective law enforcement."[29] "For better or worse, it is a fact of life in our diverse culture that race is used on a daily basis as a shorthand for physical appearance," Judge Walker wrote in his concurrence in the denial of rehearing *en banc*. "This is as true in police work as anywhere else."[30]

Judge Jacobs was harsher: "If Judge Calabresi's prescription is bad, the side effects are worse." In his view, the more stringent equal protection principles that Guido advanced would lead to the decline of policing in minority communities. "No doubt, some people will think that is a good idea, he wrote, "but no community has yet elected to rely on police protection furnished by a corps of federal judges."[31]

The plaintiffs filed a petition for certiorari with the Supreme Court in May 2001, but this was denied without comment later in the year.[32] One of the plaintiffs,

---

[27] *Id.*
[28] Brown III, 235 F.3d at 773 (Walker, J., concurring).
[29] *Id.* at 775.
[30] *Id.* at 769.
[31] *Id.* at 778 (Jacobs, J., concurring).
[32] Linda Greenhouse, *Supreme Court Roundup; In a New Term's Somber First Day, Justices Hear Arguments on Inmate Rights*, N.Y. TIMES, Oct. 2, 2001.

however—a Black woman admissions counselor at the University who had been required to show her identification to a state trooper before being allowed to board a bus to visit her sick grandmother—eventually did recover on state constitutional equal protection and seizure claims.[33]

Guido's *en banc* dissent in *Brown v. Oneonta* has been cited in case law, along with the concurrences, more than a thousand times.[34] In the secondary academic literature, the division between Guido and his colleagues in the course of the denial of the *en banc* hearing is a point of departure for nearly all discussions of racial profiling and stop and frisk.[35]

Stop-and-frisk redux. Some thirteen years after the *Brown v. Oneonta* cases, the long-standing controversy over New York's "stop-and-frisk" policy came to a new boil. The policy was closely associated with the mayoral tenure of Michael Bloomberg, who fiercely resisted any allegations that the program was racist in its execution. In August 2013, federal district court judge Shira Scheindlin issued an injunction against the policy; the following week, Mayor Michael Bloomberg labeled her "an ideologically driven federal judge who has a history of ruling against the police."[36] The Second Circuit issued a stay on Scheindlin's ruling and removed her from the case.[37] Mayor Bloomberg's successor, Bill de Blasio, dropped the city's appeal; during his mayoral campaign he had promised to curtail the policy; indications were that he did.[38] In 2020, Mayor Bloomberg, in advance of a presidential bid, acknowledged the disproportionate racial impact of "stop-and-frisk," and he apologized.[39]

Racial stereotyping and the exclusionary rule— another opinion of Guido's concerning racial stereotyping. Three Syracuse police officers thought suspicious a Black man walking on the street in a poor neighborhood who stared at them for too long. When the man drove off in a car, they tailed him and pulled him over, for the offense

---

[33] Brown v. State of N.Y., 814 N.Y.S.2d 492 (Ct. Cl. 2006); Michael Cooper, *Judge Sides with Woman in Oneonta Profiling Case*, N.Y. TIMES, Oct. 29, 2005.

[34] A Lexis-Nexis search in 2020 found 1,371 case law references to the Calabresi dissent.

[35] *See, e.g.*, Reva Siegel, *From Colorblindness to Antibalkanization: An Emerging Ground of Decision in Race Equality Cases*, 120 YALE L.J. 1278 (2011); Stephen Menendian, *What Constitutes a "Racial Classification"?: Equal Protection Doctrine Scrutinized*, 24 TEMP. POL. & CIV. RTS. L. REV. 81 (2014); Barry Friedman & Cynthia Benon Stein, *Redefining What's "Reasonable": The Protections for Policing*, 84 GEO. WASH. L. REV., 331 (2016).

[36] *See* Floyd v. City of N.Y., 283 F.R.D. 153 (S.D.N.Y. 2012); Michael Bloomberg, *"Stop and Frisk" Keeps New York Safe*, WASH. POST, Aug. 18, 2013.

[37] Ligon v. City of New York, 538 Fed. Appx. 101 (2013) (retaining mandate with the appellate panel); In re Reassignment of Cases, 736 F.3d 118, 124 (2013) (per curiam, finding that "conduct while on the bench... in conjunction with her statements to the media... might cause a reasonable observer to question her impartiality."); Joseph Goldstein, *Court Blocks Stop-and-Frisk Changes for New York Police*, N.Y. TIMES, Oct. 31, 2013.

[38] Jennifer Fermino, *Mayoral Candidate Bill de Blasio's Son Goes to and 'Fro in a New TV Campaign Ad*, N.Y. DAILY NEWS, Aug. 8, 2013; Azi Paybarah et al., *De Blasio on Stop and Frisk: "We changed it intensely,"* POLITICO, Dec. 08, 2016.

[39] "They just keep saying, 'Oh, it's a disproportionate percentage of a particular ethnic group," Mr. Bloomberg said, dismissively. "That may be, but it's not a disproportionate percentage of those who witnesses and victims describe as committing the murder." Colin Campbell, *Mayor Bloomberg on Stop-and-Frisk: "We Disproportionately Stop Whites Too Much and Minorities Too Little,"* N.Y. OBSERVER, June 28, 2013; Shane Goldmacher, *Michael Bloomberg Pushed "Stop-and-Frisk" Policing. Now He's Apologizing*, N.Y. TIMES, Nov. 17, 2019.

of failing to indicate a left turn sufficiently ahead of a stop sign. They conducted a pat-down frisk, during which an illegal firearm was discovered.[40] The district court denied Weaver's effort to suppress the evidence of the firearm as an unconstitutional search; but Judges Pooler and Calabresi reversed the district court.[41] Chief Judge Livingston dissented, writing that her colleagues had forgotten the lessons of the Warren Court.[42] "The ordinary person, looking at these facts," she wrote, "would, I believe, readily say: The officers wanted to search Weaver, they found a way, and hey, they were right. He was a felon with a gun and cocaine."[43] Moreover the facts appeared close to *States v. Padilla* where the Circuit denied a defendant's Forth Amendment claim in.[44] Acknowledging that the case was "not that many steps beyond *Padilla*, which itself was only a step or two from the prior precedent," Guido nonetheless declared that "these are steps we must not take."[45] He drew attention to an alternative he had proposed to the exclusionary rule to indicate his shared dissatisfactions with it, but insisted that a further dilution would be "absurd if the constitutional mandate against unreasonable searches and seizures is to have any meaning."[46]

Back v. Hastings on Hudson.[47] The Hillside Elementary School hired Elana Back as a school psychologist on a three-year tenure track. When she came up for review, she was denied tenure and her probationary period was terminated. She sought damages and injunctive relief under 42 U.S.C. § 1983, alleging the violation of her constitutional right to the equal protection of the laws. The school contended that Back was fired because she lacked organizational and interpersonal skills.

Back asserted that the real reason she was let go was that the defendants presumed that she, as a young mother, would not continue to demonstrate the necessary devotion to her job, and indeed, that she could not maintain such devotion while at the same time being a good mother. Writing for the Court, Guido stated "it takes no special training to discern stereotyping in the view that a woman cannot 'be a good mother' and have a job that requires long hours, or in the statement that a mother who received tenure 'would not show the same level of commitment [she] had shown because [she] had little ones at home.' These are not the kind of 'innocuous words' that we have previously held to be insufficient, as a matter of law, to provide evidence of discriminatory intent."[48]

---

[40] United States v. Weaver, 2020 U.S. App. LEXIS 29187 (2020).
[41] United States v. Padilla, 548 F.3d 179 (2008).
[42] Weaver, 2020 U.S. App. LEXIS 29187 (2020).
[43] *Id.*
[44] *Id.*
[45] *Id.*
[46] *Id.*; citing Calabresi, *The Exclusionary Rule*, 26 HARV. J. L. & PUB. POL'Y 111 (2003) (proposing that immediately at the conclusion of a trial, assertions as to the propriety of evidence should be entertained and possibly factored into sentencing and penalties against police).
[47] Back v. Hastings on Hudson Union Free Sch. Dist., 365 F.3d 107 (2004).
[48] *Id.* at 117 (citing Weinstock v. Columbia Univ. 224 F.3d 33, 45 (2000)).

The Supreme Court had first recognized—without mentioning the term—what became a "sex plus" doctrine in 1971 in *Phillips v. Martin Marietta Corp.*[49] Amy Kapczynski, a clerk to Guido at the time of *Back*, observed that *Back* has been remarkably influential in articulating the breadth of "sex-plus," and the ways in which "stereotyping can be used to understand discrimination."[50] Numerous casebooks, more than five hundred secondary sources, and nearly a thousand other cases have referred to or discussed the *Back* opinion to assist in interpreting and debating the usefulness of the "sex-plus" reasoning.[51]

Holcomb v. Iona. At a first glance, Holcomb seems to be a garden-variety antidiscrimination case: a basketball coach sues his former employer under Title VII, claiming that his termination was racially motivated.[52] An unusual detail of the case, however, is that Holcomb himself was white: the theory of the suit was that the employer discriminated against the plaintiff due to his marriage to a Black woman.

Title VII prohibits discrimination "because of such individual's race."[53] Reading the statute's text to preclude application to the race of a person's relations, the district court granted summary judgment in favor of the defendant University. Thus, the central question on appeal before the Second Circuit was whether Title VII could properly be applied to discrimination on the basis of a person's relationships.

In a matter of first impression, the panel found that Title VII did apply in this broader way. The panel's reasoning was "simple," in Guido's words, but compelling: it held that discrimination that focused, as in Holcomb's situation, on a plaintiff's relationship, *was* discrimination because of the plaintiff's race. After all, if the plaintiff had been of a different race, his relationship might no longer be an interracial one; if the relationship's interracial nature was the target of discrimination, then that kind of discrimination straightforwardly depends on the plaintiff's own race.

Though the panel did not dispositively conclude that Holcomb's termination was racially motivated, it found that the plaintiff had made a successful prima facie Title VII case, and that there was sufficient evidence in the record to permit a jury to conclude that the termination was based, at least in part, on racial discrimination. It remanded to the district court for further resolution of the disputed question of material fact.

Holcomb's influence. The decision was significant in its own right; it attracted news coverage from law blogs to ESPN. But it also laid substantial groundwork for subsequent cases to find Title VII protection for sexual orientation, deploying

---

[49] 400 U.S. 542 (1971) (per curiam) (upholding a Title VII violation where an employer discriminated against a subclass of women because of their sex plus another characteristic).

[50] Correspondence by email, Jan. 28, 2013.

[51] *See, e.g.,* KATHARINE T. BARTLETT ET AL., GENDER AND THE LAW: THEORY, DOCTRINE, COMMENTARY (2016); BETH ANNE WOLFSON ET AL., THE LAW OF SEX DISCRIMINATION (2010); Suzanne B. Goldberg, Discrimination by Comparison, 120 YALE L.J. 728 (2011); Noah Zatz, *Disparate Treatment and the Unity of Equality Law*, 97 B.U. L. REV. 1357 (2017); Kate Sablosky Elengold, *Clustered Bias*, 96 N.C.L. REV. 457, 497–98 (2018); Marc Chase McAllister, *Sexual Orientation Discrimination as a Form of Sex-Plus Discrimination*, 67 BUFF. L. REV. 1007 (2019).

[52] Holcomb v. Iona College, 521 F.3d 130 (2006).

[53] 42 U.S.C. § 2000e–2(a).

an "associational theory" of discrimination—that a person may be discriminated against on the basis of his associations—originating in *Holcomb*.

Despite the fact that by 2020 about half the states had passed anti-discrimination statutes that protect against sexual orientation discrimination, the U.S. Supreme Court had not recognized sexual orientation status as a class subject to heightened scrutiny; nor had legislative attempts to pass federal discrimination protections for LGBT individuals had yet been successful. In 2017, however, the Seventh Circuit became the first federal circuit to hold, in *Hively v. Ivy Tech Community College*, that Title VII's sex discrimination prohibition extends to sexual orientation discrimination, setting an important precedent for national employment sexual orientation discrimination protection.

The *Hively* court, in its majority opinion and with a concurrence by Judge Posner, explicitly referred to the holding in *Holcomb*, reasoning, on analogy with Guido's "simple" argument, that "it is actually impossible to discriminate on the basis of sexual orientation without discriminating on the basis of sex."[54] Judge Posner, instead, concurred on broader "updating" grounds that could themselves be described as having a Calabresian, COMMON LAW FOR THE AGE OF STATUTES, basis.

Zarda v. Altitude Express, Inc. The affirmation of Title VII protection to sexual orientation by *Hively* created a split among the circuits. Not long afterward, the Second Circuit produced a ruling similar to *Hively* with an *en banc* holding in *Zarda v. Altitude Express, Inc.*[55] There, the Court found, in an opinion by Chief Judge Katzmann, that sexual orientation discrimination is "motivated, at least in part" by sex, and therefore is a subset of sex discrimination that is barred by Title VII. The Court followed the "associational discrimination" theory of *Hively* and also cited directly back to *Hively's* use of *Holcomb*, to find that "sexual orientation discrimination, which is based on an employer's opposition to association between particular sexes... thereby discriminates against an employee based on their own sex," and is barred by Title VII.[56] *Holcomb* and its employment in subsequent cases has been cited and praised in secondary literature by proponents attempting to extend civil rights protection further.[57]

The Statute's Lament. Judge Jacobs elaborated to me that the premise for his two limericks was that his concurring opinion about *Zarda* in the en banc proceeding flowed from Guido's opinion in *Iona v. Holcomb*, which "may have been dubious, but was precedent."[58] Jacobs wrote that he expressed his disagreement with "[t]he rest of the majority analysis [, which] I dubbed woke dicta."[59] The second of his

---

[54] Hively v. Ivy Tech Cmty. Coll. of Indiana, 853 F.3d 339, 346, 357 (7th Cir. 2017).

[55] Zarda v. Altitude Express, Inc., 883 F.3d 100, 128 (2018), cert. granted sub nom. Altitude Exp., Inc. v. Zarda, 139 S. Ct. 1599, 203 L. Ed. 2d 754 (2019).

[56] Zarda, 883 F.3d at 128.

[57] References are made to *Holcomb* in over 1,500 cases and nearly 70 law review articles. One representative author expresses hope that the kind of reasoning in Holcomb, as adopted and deployed in *Hively* and *Zarda*, may "perhaps pav[e] the way for national employment discrimination protection for LGBT individuals." Devon Sherrell, *"A Fresh Look": Title VII's New Promise for LGBT Discrimination Protection Post-Hively*, 68 EMORY L.J. 1101 (2019).

[58] Email from Judge Jacobs, Sept. 22, 2021.

[59] Id.

limericks, he stated, "is satirical, depicting the statute as happy to discover, against all odds, that it is saying more than it itself thought. The way to read it is to distrust the narrator (i.e., the statute). In that way, it is Conradian."[60]

Zarda, Bostock, and the updating of statutes. When *Zarda* reached the Supreme Court, it was consolidated with *Bostock v. Clayton County*, a case that also required the Court to interpret the meaning of "because of ... sex" under Title VII of the Civil Rights Act of 1964.[61] Writing for the majority, Justice Gorsuch affirmed *Zarda* and held that sexual orientation is included within that phrase, and therefore is protected under Title VII. Gorsuch concluded that "it is impossible to discriminate against a person for being homosexual or transgender without discriminating against that individual based on sex."[62]

Along the way, Justice Gorsuch distanced himself from a Calabresian approach to "updating" the Civil Rights Act. He denied that the Court was "updating" the statute, arguing instead that although sexual orientation is distinct from sex, "discrimination based on homosexuality or transgender status necessarily entails discrimination based on sex; the first cannot happen without the second."[63]

Justice Gorsuch did not employ Guido's "simple," but highly influential argument in *Holcomb*—perhaps because the principle in *Holcomb* would not address transgender discrimination. Justice Alito, however, took on *Holcomb* directly. Dissenting, he asserted that it is a logical error to analogize discrimination on the basis of sexual orientation to discrimination on the basis of race. Sexual orientation, he argued, "cannot be regarded as a form of sex discrimination on the ground that applies in race cases since discrimination because of sexual orientation is not historically tied to a project that aims to subjugate either men or women."[64] Of course this argument is reductive if, as Justice Gorsuch suggests, the project of Title VII historically anticipated the proscription of the imposition of a particular sexual orientation.

United States v. Ingram: racially discriminatory disparities in sentencing for drug offenses.[65] Following "an extraordinarily hasty and truncated legislative process," and spurred on by the high-profile overdose of college basketball star Len Bias, Congress passed the 1986 Controlled Substances Act to impose sentences for crack cocaine that were one hundred times tougher than those for powder cocaine.[66] In ensuing decades, the disparity was challenged as racially discriminatory and unjustifiable.

In one notable challenge, a U.S. district court judge in Missouri declined to impose the then-mandatory minimum sentence for Edward Clary, who had pled guilty to

---

[60] Email from Judge Jacobs, Sept. 22, 2021.
[61] Bostock v. Clayton Cty., 207 L. Ed. 2d 218 (2020).
[62] *Id.* at 234.
[63] *Id.* at 240 (without referring to A COMMON LAW FOR THE AGE OF STATUTES).
[64] *Id.* at 261 (Alito, J., dissenting).
[65] United States v. Ingram, 721 F.3d 35 (2013).
[66] Deborah J. Vagins & Jesselyn McCurdy, *Cracks in the System: Twenty Years of the Unjust Federal Crack Cocaine Law*, AM. CIVIL LIBERTIES UNION, Oct. 2006, at i.

possession with intent to distribute crack cocaine.[67] Noting the role that anti-Chinese sentiment played in the passage of the 1909 Smoking Opium Exclusion Act and the anti-Black "hysteria" that led to laws against marijuana, the judge found that "unconscious racism" had guided Congress's imposition of the crack-cocaine differential.[68] The Eighth Circuit reversed this decision on appeal.[69] It held that the district court's discussion of unconscious racism did not suffice to establish that Congress had acted with a discriminatory purpose.[70]

In 2010, Congress passed the Fair Sentencing Act,[71] which amended the law so that crack cocaine was treated only eighteen times as severely as cocaine powder. However, the continued existence of a gap was criticized by observers.[72]

"Heading Towards Unreasonableness." Guido wrote in his concurrence to *U.S. v. Ingram* that, "To be clear, I am not saying that Ingram's sentence is substantively unreasonable, [because] [w]ere I to do so, this would be a dissent, not a concurring opinion. But I don't hesitate to say that a sentence of this length, for this crime, is headed towards unreasonableness—and is, in fact, well along that road."[73] In a footnote, Guido elaborated on this idea, suggesting that Ingram's sentence might be compared to "laws which, due to changed circumstances, can be described as 'heading toward unconstitutionality.'" He referred to his earlier concurrence in *U.S. v. Then*, where he made the identical point. When faced with the objection that the United States is the "mother" of judicial review, Guido replied that American judges should take a lesson from European approaches when facing difficult constitutional issues, saying that, "Wise parents do not hesitate to learn from their children."[74]

The application of Guido's earlier scholarship to this problem is evident: as an academic he had been deeply interested in the options available to courts when statutes became out of date.[75] Decades earlier, in *A Common Law for the Age of Statutes*, he had explained that constitutional adjudication had at times been used as a means for updating the law, and that in West Germany, courts not uncommonly told legislatures that "as of the time of decision the law is valid since its justification retains some rational basis [but] it is moving toward unconstitutionality."[76] Guido also pointed to American precedents that dealt differently, but analogously, to the same problem—as an example, he mentioned a U.S. Supreme Court decision which considered a social security law that allowed widows to obtain benefits automatically while on the other hand widowers had to show proof of dependency. Justice

---

[67] U.S. v. Clary, 846 F. Supp. 768, 769–70 (E.D. Mo. 1994).
[68] *Id.* at 779.
[69] United States v. Clary, 34 F.3d 709 (8th Cir. 1994).
[70] *Id.* at 713.
[71] Public Law 111-220, 124 Stat. 2372.
[72] "Because crack and powder cocaine are two forms of the same drug, there should not be any disparity in sentencing between crack and powder cocaine offenses—the only truly fair ratio is 1:1." Fair Sentencing Act, *Am. Civil Liberties Union*, https://www.aclu.org/issues/criminal-law-reform/drug-law-reform/fair-sentencing-act.
[73] United States v. Ingram, 721 F.3d 35, 44 (2014) (Calabresi, J., concurring).
[74] United States v. Then, 56 F.3d 464, 469 (1995).
[75] See Chapter 17, "Judicial Sunset."
[76] GUDIO CALABRESI, A COMMON LAW FOR THE AGE OF STATUTES 192–93 (1985).

Stevens found that the distinction might be constitutional, but nevertheless struck the statute down and advised the legislature to work toward re-enacting a statute that more accurately reflected modern working conditions.[77]

Apart from theoretical questions about doubtful lawfulness, Raggi objected to Guido's terminology. "[T]he suggestion that a sentence can be both substantively reasonable and absurd risks calling the law into disrepute," she wrote.[78] She also took issue with Guido's suggestion of dialogue, and in a footnote denied the appropriateness of judges telling Congress that its choices were "mistaken, even absurd."[79]

Kenji Yoshino. Yoshino clerked for Guido from 1996 to 1997 after earning a J.D. from Yale Law School. He went on, immediately, into academia, joining the Yale faculty. Guido mentored him on the path to tenure; he became the Guido Calabresi Professor of Law. Professor Yoshino introduced the law to the issue of "covering," by which individuals "pla[y] down their outside identities to fit into the mainstream."[80] His books include *Speak Now*, an account of the litigation that overturned California's Proposition 8, which would have mandated that "only marriage between a man and a woman is valid or recognized in California."[81] Guido officiated at Yoshino's marriage ceremony, which was among the first same-sex marriages in Connecticut.[82]

Zatz clerked for Guido from 2000 to 2001 and also went on to become a law professor. His scholarship focuses on employment and labor law with special attention to the intersection of disparate impact, disparate treatment, and "non-accommodation." Non-accommodation differs from disparate impact in that no discriminatory intent is required for a successful claim. The paradigmatic example is that of a worker who cannot use a tool because of a disability: "The employer does not care why the worker cannot use the tool; any worker who cannot use the tool is excluded."[83] In these claims, as Professor Zatz has explained, the "refusal to provide reasonable 'accommodation' for many employees amounts to 'discrimination.'"[84] Elsewhere, Zatz has written about the anomalous appearance of non-accommodation liability under Title VII.[85]

The Sopranos and Italian American stereotypes. David Chase's television series *The Sopranos* attracted widespread acclaim from the moment of its debut.[86]

---

[77] *Id.* at 10 (discussing Califano v. Goldfarb, 430 U.S. 199 (1977)).
[78] *Ingram*, 721 F.3d at 51.
[79] *Id.*
[80] Kenji Yoshino, *The Pressure to Cover*, N.Y. TIMES, Jan. 15, 2006; Kenji Yoshino, *The New Equal Protection*, 124 HARV. L. REV. 1747 (2011).
[81] Perry v. Schwarzenegger, 704 F. Supp. 2d 921 (N.D. Cal. 2010).
[82] Kenji Yoshino, *Book Excerpt: Kenji Yoshino, Speak Now: Marriage Equality on Trial*, 40 N.Y.U. REV. L. & SOC. CHANGE (2015).
[83] Noah D. Zatz, *The Many Meanings of "Because Of": A Comment on Inclusive Communities Project*, 68 STAN. L. REV. 68, 74 (2015).
[84] William N. Eskridge, Jr., & John A. Ferejohn, A REPUBLIC OF STATUTES: THE NEW AMERICAN CONSTITUTION 59 (2010).
[85] Noah D. Zatz, *Managing the Macaw: Third-Party Harassers, Accommodation, and the Disaggregation of Discriminatory Intent*, 109 COLUM. L. REV. 1357 (2009).
[86] A 2000 *New York Times* article dubbed the Sopranos "[t]he only series in years to become a critical hit and a pop-cult phenomenon." Caryn James, *The Ziti's in the Oven and the Matriarch's Still Not Dead*, N.Y. TIMES, Jan. 14, 2000.

Nevertheless, Italian Americans found much to criticize in the criminal exploits of Tony Soprano and his family. "Images of Italians as gun-toting psychopaths inexplicably continue to flourish—and, more inexplicably yet, earn reams of critical praise, even awards," Bill Dal Cerro wrote in the *Los Angeles Times*.[87] Frank Guarini, the chairman of the National Italian American Foundation, was determined to "get 'The Sopranos' off the air." According to Chase, certain cities in New Jersey told him they did not want the series filming there.[88]

Much of the criticism came from public officials. Congresswoman Marge Roukema, a Republican from New Jersey, dubbed the show "ethnic profiling" and introduced a congressional resolution to condemn it.[89] In 2001, Andrew Cuomo stated that he didn't watch *The Sopranos* and didn't think he "would find it particularly entertaining."[90] Justice Samuel Alito criticized the show during an event at Rutgers University, decrying the "insidious connection popular culture often makes between being a gangster and being Italian."[91]

There were also prominent contrarians, particularly among right-wing officials, who disparaged "political correctness." Then-mayor Rudy Giuliani defended and praised the series as an illustration of "the human drama."[92]

---

[87] Bill Dal Cerro, *Why No Outrage Over the Offensive Stereotypes on "Sopranos"?*, L.A. TIMES, July 26, 1999.
[88] Duncan Campbell, *You looking at Us? Italian-Americans Object to Sopranos*, GUARDIAN, May 21, 2001.
[89] Raymond Hernandez, *Congresswoman Takes a Whack at "The Sopranos" Stereotype*, N.Y. TIMES, May 24, 2001.
[90] Maureen Dowd, *Cuomos vs. Sopranos*, N.Y. TIMES, Apr. 22, 2001.
[91] Debra Cassens Weiss, *Justice Alito Criticizes "Sopranos" Stereotypes*, ABA J., Feb. 8, 2008; Clyde Haberman, *As "Sopranos" Returns, Art Irritates Life*, N.Y. TIMES, Mar. 10, 2006.
[92] George Rush et al., *Rudy Sings Praises of "Sopranos,"* N.Y. DAILY NEWS, Feb. 23, 2001.

29

The Analytical Reasoning of a Behavioral Economist

> *More than forty years ago, without the benefit of later research in behavioral and cognitive sciences, Guido explored the relevance of behavioral realities especially in the books* Tragic Choices *(1978) and also in* Ideals, Beliefs, and the Law *(1985). He returned to this theme in* The Future of Law and Economics: Essays in Reform and Recollection *(2016), arguing for the treatment of unconventional forms of wealth as objects of human aspiration for which "commodification" and market allocations have proven unsatisfactory, including "merit" goods, altruism, tastes, and values.*
>
> *In neither Guido's newer book nor his prior scholarly writings, however, did Guido reflect on the interconnectedness of his theories with his judicial opinions. In this chapter, Guido considers illustrative cases in which his academic theories about law and economics have informed his judicial decisions.*

After I concurred in the case about the absurd crack-cocaine sentence—the *Ingram* case— the late Jack Weinstein, an outstanding federal judge, quoted the passage in it where I said that "[W]e judges have a right—a duty even—to express criticism of legislative judgments that require us to uphold results we think are wrong." He referred to that not only for the merits of what I was saying about sentencing but for the broader proposition that this is what judges ought to do. I think the two of us are not alone among judges in subscribing to the theory that judges should be conversation makers and should foster positive changes in the law by those who have the authority to make those changes, whether they are legislators, administrators, or the Executive.

I also raised an issue which rested on our growing awareness of behavioral economics and psychology. I wrote about anchoring, that is, where one starts—in sentencing, for example—often affects where one ends up. A judge may say that a sentence is the appropriate one regardless of the guidelines, but the existence of the guidelines as a psychological starting point will often affect where the judge comes out—what that judge believes is an appropriate sentence. One of my clerks, Brian Soucek, called my attention to the fact that this applied in *Ingram*.

> *Harry Wellington used to tell the story of a guy who gets out of a car and goes into a diner where he is told by the counter man, "We have three kinds of*

sandwiches: cheese, turkey, and a hotdog." He goes back to the car and asks the person sitting there what he wants, and the person says, "I'll have a hot dog." He goes back inside, and the counter man says, "Oh, I forgot to tell you, we also have peanut butter and jelly." He goes back to the car and says to the person, "Oh, they also have peanut butter and jelly, and a hotdog, and cheese, and turkey." And the person says, "Well, in that case, I'll have cheese." [laughter] A starting point affects where you go. It's amazing how blind people can be to this fact.

It is a phenomenon that comes up in all kinds of cases, and yet it is quite amazing to see how this concept, which is one of the easiest concepts to understand intuitively, so often gets ignored. And why should not a judge raise the question of an anchoring bias sua sponte? In *Ingram*, although the parties did not call attention to that, I did.

I also think about the way my law school faculty hires. In the last few years, when there is a workshop of somebody who might be appointed to the faculty, the head of the appointments committee has sent out, after the workshop, a questionnaire which simply says, "What did you think of the workshop?," which is catastrophic [fatal to an unbiased hiring process], because the workshop might go well, or it might go badly, depending on whether somebody asks a hard question or whether somebody asks a nice question. The answer I have gotten [when I criticize this method] is that it doesn't matter because the appointments committee reads everything that the person has published. I have said, "Yes, but if you think about anchoring, you would realize that you read it one way if you know there are ten people who have already told you this guy is no good, or ten people who have told you this guy is great; and the person might be neither." So, if that [sort of anchoring bias] affects even a highly sophisticated faculty, think of the effect among judges.

The assumption that people behave in ways consistent with what economists define as rational was often useful to me when I was a student of economics, but it never occurred to me that that kind of economically rational actor exists. There are many things that are occasionally convenient to assume but which are not valid in many situations.

I have made this point clear again and again in my books. For example, I point out that it is often useful in economic theory to make the assumption that markets are costless, but of course that is not true. On one hand, it is often useful to make the assumption that there are no costs to convincing people that a different organization, structure, or point of view is better, and of course that is not true either. On the other hand, you do not need to take everything into account all of the time when you analyze a problem. People who say that economics is useless because it depends on the assumption that actors are rational are being simplistic. Still, there are any number of problems in the world which you can only deal with effectively if you realize that people are *not* going to be rational in this economic sense.

* * *

I was teaching about one of the chapters in my book *Ideals, Beliefs and the Law* called "The Gift of the Evil Deity." I talked about whether it is irrational to spend more money to save only one person who is rowing across the Atlantic than to save twenty people who will, if we do not spend money on safety measures, die in mining accidents. Saving the guy in the rowboat is not rational in the classic economic sense. But saving the guy may be perfectly rational in the sense that it upholds a value. It says, "I want life to be valued by Society as a "pearl beyond price." Spending that money often is a very cheap way of asserting that position. And it does so more dramatically than spending money to save unknown people who are statistically certain to die because we have not spent more on safety.

The logic behind seemingly illogical behavior is why I find the use of the term "irrational behavior" unfortunate. That suggests that the behavior does not have a good reason. It *has* a good reason—one which is rational, but not in the narrow sense of what expenditure will in fact save more lives. And of course, furthering the idea that life is "a pearl beyond price."

Can you say, rationally, that a twelve-year sentence for selling an ounce of cocaine is both reasonable and absurd? Yes. These are two different conclusions about substantive fairness and formal correctness: two distinct inquiries. This is an illustration of what has always been my chief problem with economic analysis of the law: not that it divides problems into small pieces and focuses on one of them; but that it then assumes that the discrete small piece is the *only* one. Apart from the fact that it bespeaks a narrow and categorical way to understand the world, it is bizarre to suppose that that particular purpose—or any single purpose—is the function of any given law.

* * *

Being a judge and being an academic who works in Economics and in Torts has convinced me that judgments have *many* different functions—including, in torts, compensatory ones, deterrent ones, spreading ones, and expressive ones. Let me give you an example from the summary order in a case, *Hollon v. Merck*. This was originally a huge, multi-district litigation between Merck Pharmaceuticals and victims of a drug for osteoporosis that Merck was selling.

In the particular case, the district judge instructed the jury that punitive damages could not be considered by the jury under Florida law. The instruction was appropriate since the evidence did not support any finding of intentional wrong but did support a finding of a negligent product defect, requiring compensation.

The Jury in *Hollon* came back with a verdict of $8 million in compensatory damages. The judge then ordered a remittitur reducing the judgment to

$1.5 million. There were going to be all sorts of appeals from this result. At that point, almost all of the case was settled.

What did remain? The judge had sanctioned the plaintiff's lawyer, who was a highly respected lawyer who had never been sanctioned before. He had been a good trial lawyer. The judge sanctioned him $2,500, —which, in a way, was a trivial amount—for injecting in his summation what the judge believed was an appeal to the jury to impose punitive damages notwithstanding that punitive damages had been removed from consideration by the judge.

Leave aside whether the judge warned him; leave aside whether the lawyer believed there had been intentional behavior that might have supported punitive damages. What got the lawyer in trouble was his statement that Merck's behavior was "reprehensible." The lawyer viewed the use of this term as one that was fair to apply to any selling of dangerous pharmaceuticals. In the eyes of the judge, however, the lawyer's sin was that in his summation, he was saying, "Send a message to Merck. Say, 'No.'"

In other words, the lawyer was trying to convince the jury to use tort law in an expressive sense. Merck objected to sending such a message, of course.

When one says to a jury "Send pharmaceutical companies a message" and the jury is charged with fixing only compensatory damages, is one in context suggesting punitive damages? To me this seems wrong. Allowing, across the board, tort verdicts to send a message may well be an appropriate aim of that field of law. One scholar has said that the function of tort law is to be expressionistic. As "*the*" function of torts that is unduly narrow; but it certainly is *one* function.

* * *

Another case I wrote, *Ciraolo v. City of New York*, also involves an economic analysis of compensatory and punitive damages. A woman was strip searched by the police in the course of an arrest for a misdemeanor, in clear violation of what our circuit permitted. The district court—I think it was Judge Robert Patterson—allowed punitive damages to be given because the violation was so clear. We reviewed an award of $19,000 in compensatory damages and $5,000,000 in punitive damages.

We had to deny the punitive award because an opinion of the Supreme Court called *Newport v. Fact Concerts* written by Justice Blackmun does not allow punitive damages against a municipality for the actions of their employees unless the municipality itself, somehow, is responsible, unless the People themselves are responsible. The reasoning, or lack thereof, is, simply, "why should taxpayers pay for punitives?"

> The opinion by Blackmun is illogical because if you charge a municipality for doing wrong things, you will deter it from doing them. I also do not know

what he was thinking of with his exception about the People themselves being responsible. He must have meant that if there was a public referendum that validated a clear violation, or something of that sort, then punitives would be allowed.

Not long before I wrote the opinion in *Ciraolo*, Dick Posner wrote an opinion in *Kemezy v. Peters*, in which he took issue with the position of Justice Blackmun. He said: "This is not punishing; this is charging appropriately," and he discusses the "multiplier," observing that one of the reasons one gives punitive damages in these cases is because not everybody who is injured will bring or win a case and if the proper cost is to be put on the wrongdoer, we must multiply the compensation damages by the number of times they should have been but were not awarded. He did this as part of his holding.

Judge Richard Posner

In my holding, I adhered to precedent and said, "This isn't what Blackmun is allowing," and so we reversed. But I concurred separately in my own opinion to say that extra-compensatory damages, call them punitive if you want, were appropriate for the same multiplier reason that Posner gave in his opinion. I wrote that such socially compensatory damages are an appropriate aspect of damages, because they are calculated to deter actors from future wrongdoing—they cause such actors to bear the cost of their activities.

I got very annoyed when the plaintiff's lawyer made the argument that we could give punitive damages where, under the Supreme Court ruling, we clearly could not—as much as we wanted to. I said to him, "Isn't there a possibility here that the jury, because they thought they could give punitive damages, gave lower compensatory damages than were appropriate?" I had in mind a First Circuit case which reversed the punitive damages but remanded so that the jury could determine compensatory damage in the absence of punitive damages. The lawyer said,

"Oh, no, no, no. The jury knew exactly what it was doing." I do not know what the lawyer was thinking. Perhaps he thought that because this case was so awful, the liberal panel might do what the district court did and ignore the law. Whatever moved him, I could not do anything about it once he said that, and we had to reverse, period. This poor woman got nineteen thousand instead of perhaps thirty-five or fifty thousand dollars. I was very annoyed about the lawyers' capacity, and perhaps, even, his ethics.

I like to give my Torts students both my opinion in *Ciraolo* and Posner's opinion in *Kemezy*, to see how similar they are conceptually, but how differently the Law gets treated by a judge like me who engages more in dialogue, and one who says, "This is the way it is."

* * *

Loreley Financing v. Wells Fargo Securities is another case that involves economics and people's behavior. This was a case, like so many, that involved the sale and purchase of securities which plunged after the stock market crashed in 2008. Untold numbers of investors bought securities that declined or even became worthless.

One of the issues in *Loreley* was the old tort issue of whether an alleged misrepresentation, which plausibly was the but-for cause of the purchaser buying the securities, had anything to do with the loss. In other words, was there loss causation, or what I have called "causal link" or "causal tendency"? Was the misrepresentation in any way linked to the decline in the stock value?

What makes *Loreley* interesting is that here the issue arises in a way that involves pleading questions, and it also says something about individuals' behavior. Is it the plaintiff's responsibility to plead loss causation or causal link? Or is it up to the defendant to raise its lack as an affirmative defense?

But apart from pleading, whose burden is it to bring in evidence one way or the other? What *Loreley* suggests, but does not need to decide, is that these pleading issues depend on the circumstances involved, and what one expects of people's behavior in these circumstances.

If I sell you a house telling you that Chief Justice Marshall lived in it, which is a lie; and you buy it because you believe me; and you show that had I not lied you would have bought a house in another part of town; and an earthquake destroys the house you bought, but not the one you would have bought, then it pretty clearly is up to you, the plaintiff, to show that the earthquake was more likely to hit the house you bought than the other. On the face of it, an earthquake is as likely to hit one house as the other in the same town, and so the lack of a causal link between the misrepresentation and the loss speaks for itself; it is up to the plaintiff to show otherwise.

But assume instead that my misrepresentation was that the house was extraordinarily well built, when in fact it was not; and that an earthquake hits it and destroys it. It may well be that even the best-built house would have been destroyed by the earthquake—but maybe not, and in that case it may be more appropriate to put the burden on the defendant to show that the strength of the earthquake was such that even a well-built house would have been destroyed.

Sometimes the distinction between my first hypothetical, and the second is clear enough so that both the duty to plead in a complaint and the duty to bring in evidence lies on the same party; but there may be situations in which the question of loss causation seems obvious in one direction until the other party raises it, and the very pleading of it should be enough to shift the burden of bringing evidence onto the other party. In other words, it is possible that the burden of pleading (subject to a "Rule 12 (b)(6) dismissal") and the burden of bringing in evidence (subject to a motion for summary judgment) should be placed on different parties.

All this lies behind *Loreley* and many cases of misrepresentation involving securities. The market takes a deep dive and so do the securities that were sold. Under what circumstances is it enough for the plaintiff to say, "the defendant misrepresented the goodness of the securities, and it is up to the defendant to plead and bring in evidence that the securities would have fallen just as much, regardless of the misrepresentation." And under what circumstances do we want the plaintiff definitively to show the link between the representation and the decline in the securities. Just as in *Ciraolo*, I raised a question which involves complicated law, economics, and behavior questions, and gave some hints of my views on them. So in *Loreley*, I raised these loss causation questions for later judges to decide in cases that turn on them, or for legislators to do so abstractly—but I did not need actually to decide them given the issues in *Loreley*, where we held that the pleadings were sufficient.

In a way, *Loreley* is a case made to order for me because it benefited from my background as a torts scholar, and my knowledge of economics. It also revealed my general judicial philosophy that judges should act more as a part of many lawmaking institutions rather than see their role as charged to impose a view and make it the law.

COMMENTARY

Chapter 29

Loreley Financing v. Wells Fargo Securities. *Loreley* is most often cited for its extended discussion of when a district judge may dismiss a securities fraud complaint with prejudice.[1] Guido's approach to entertaining allegations of fraudulent statements that are made by a group has, until recently, received less attention in the courts.

---

[1] Loreley Fin. (Jersey) No. 3 Ltd. v. Wells Fargo Sec., LLC, 797 F.3d 160 (2015). *See, e.g.*, Nat'l Credit Union Admin. Bd. v. U.S. Bank Nat'l Ass'n., 898 F.3d 243, 258 (2018); Abdul-Mumit v. Alexandria-Hyundai, LLC, 896 F.3d 278, 292 (4th Cir. 2018).

Noting that Second Circuit precedent permitted group pleading, Guido forgives "excusable mislabeling" of the defendants because "the costs of such mislabeling are better borne in this situation by those who authored the offering documents."[2]

This creative move effectively adopts the rationale for "penalty default rules ... to remedy asymmetric information in litigation," developed by professors Ian Ayres and Robert Gertner to address an analogous problem that can arise during the formation of a contract. Ayres and Gertner's theory, simply stated, is that unspecified terms in a contract should revert not to standard practices but be "purposefully set at what the parties would not want—in order to encourage the parties to reveal information to each other or to third parties (especially the courts)."[3] Interestingly, in 2005, Professor Eric Posner at the University of Chicago had diminished the value in the proposal by Ayres and Gertner, asserting that there were no penalty default rules in contract law.[4]

"Classic Guido": Sentencing and deterrence. When a convicted gun smuggler received a sentence exceeding the guidelines because the judge sought to deter arms shipments into New York City, the authority of a judge to impose the varying sentence was considered en banc.[5] Chief Judge Katzmann extolled Guido's decision for the tribunal:

> He looks at the sentencing guidelines. He looks at the case law. [He provides] a rich background of context in which to understand the role that appellate courts, in his view, should play in reviewing a sentence. He does that in the context of Supreme Court decisions which he may or may not wholly agree with. He talks about the degree of deference that a district court should be owed [and states general principles, and goes on to say that his broad statements] "require more specificity both as substantive and procedural reasonableness review if they are to guide us in particular cases, including the one before us ... [And he gets] to this: "Accordingly, we will continue to patrol the boundaries of reasonableness, while heeding Supreme Court's renewed message that responsibility for sentencing is placed largely in the prescience of the district court."[6]

Guido grounded the affirmance on the salience of deterrence. He cited economic studies and Judge Posner's textbook ("A person commits a crime because the expected benefits of the crime to him exceed the expected costs.").[7] The opinion concluded that the district court reasonably found "that the existence and enforcement of strict local gun laws in a particular jurisdiction is likely

---

[2] 797 F.3d 160, 173 (citing Luce v. Edelstein, 802 F.2d 49 (1986)).
[3] Ian Ayres & Robert Gertner, *Filling Gaps in Incomplete Contracts: An Economic Theory of Default Rules*, 99 YALE L.J. 87, 91 (1989).
[4] Eric Posner, *There Are No Penalty Default Rules in Contract Law*, JOHN M. OLIN PROGRAM IN L. & ECON., Working Paper No. 237 (2005).
[5] United States v. Cavera, 550 F.3d 180 (2008).
[6] Interview with Chief Judge Robert A. Katzmann, Dec. 17, 2014.
[7] United States v. Cavera, *supra* note 5, at 196.

to make the cost of getting a gun in that jurisdiction higher than in a jurisdiction with lax anti-gun laws."[8] Katzman referred to Guido's ability to convince so many of his colleagues of his view—including its language about the relevance of deterrence—in an en banc setting as the emblematic talent of a great judge.[9]

Chief Judge Robert Katzmann

Behavioral Economists. In 2012, after receiving the Ronald H. Coase medal, Guido suggested—as had some others, that *Tragic Choices* (1984) should be counted as among "the grandfathers of behavioral economics."[10] He explained that while scholars before him probed "the psychological and emotional complexities of rational decision at the individual level," that book had broken new ground by dwelling "at the societal level" about certain goods that were not often allocated by, or chosen through, unregulated markets.[11] Several who have pursued behavioral studies in the law, including former Northeastern Law School Dean James Hackney, credited Guido's "creative use of economic analysis with realist insights" with foreshadowing the "trend towards a more behavioral approach to law and economics."[12]

In 2016, in *The Future of Law and Economics*, Guido expanded on such earlier examples as the sale of body parts and the military draft, and added newer ones, developing his ideas more elaborately, with a more contemporary vocabulary.[13] He embraced behavioral economics, as he had done before, noting that his thinking

---

[8] *Id.*

[9] Interview with Robert A. Katzmann, *supra* note 6.

[10] Guido Calabresi, *Of Tastes and Values*, 16 AM. LAW AND ECON. REV. 313, 321 (2014); See Cati, Matteo Maria, *"Law and . . ." an Opened Door to a New World of Knowledge* (June 18, 2018) http://dx.doi.org/10.2139/ssrn.3274290; Michael Faure, *Calabresi and Behavioural Tort Law and Economics*, 1 Erasmus L. Rev. 76 (2008) (crediting the insights of THE COST OF ACCIDENTS as behavioral in nature).

[11] *Id.* at 321 n. 9.

[12] James R. Hackney, Jr., *Guido Calabresi and the Construction of Contemporary American Legal Theory*, 77 L. & CONT. PROB. 45, 63 (2014);; Michael Faure, *Calabresi and Behavioural Tort Law* at 93. (2008).

[13] CALABRESI, THE FUTURE OF LAW & ECONOMICS: ESSAYS IN REFORM AND RECOLLECTION (2016).

derived from a variety of sources, "but it has much in common with, and indeed can be viewed as an especially important example of, the kind of analysis I am here discussing," and contending that "if one looks again and with a slightly different eye at *Tragic Choices* . . . one finds analysis there of much the same sort."[14] He introduced his own theory of "merit goods," defined in two ways—as about being about values beyond pricing, or else as goods that large portions of society believed should not be allocated through bidding wars in the ordinary marketplace.[15] Interestingly, although he had been a judge for more than two decades and speaks here of cases involving "pearls beyond price," in the whole book he referred only to two of his decisions addressing merit goods.[16]

Conservative law and economics scholar Eric Posner, and the more progressive scholar Cass Sunstein, asserted that Guido's earlier book and his new one did not sufficiently define "merit goods," or justify allocating them outside the market. "The weakness of this book is that Calabresi advocates modeling choices without demonstrating that they are fruitful," Posner wrote.[17] Sunstein, too, critiqued Guido's discussion of merit goods, charging that "most of his examples do not seem to work."[18]

Reading this, Guido laughed and said "their problem is that they would like to see a theory of what ought to be merit goods. That is as unlikely as a theory of *why* some like caviar and others pizza. I am concerned with less—with dealing intelligently with what a given society treats as merit goods."

Anchoring in the Ingram *case.* Guido was not the first judge to raise a concern that the sentencing guidelines could have an unintended "anchoring" effect, as he did in *Ingram*. In a 2006 article, Judge Nancy Gertner of the District of Massachusetts noted that despite initial hostility to the guidelines, their influence remained strong even after the Court, in *United States v. Booker*, held that they should be advisory, and not mandatory.[19] Gertner posited that "the 300-odd page Guideline Manual provides ready-made anchors" and credited this cognitive bias for "the slide towards 'mandatoriness'" that ensued after *Booker*.[20]

In *Ingram*, Guido referred to Gertner's article, along with works by pioneering behavioral economists Amos Tversky and Daniel Kahneman; as well as a student note in the *Yale Law Journal* exploring the sentencing guidelines' effect on framing; and

---

[14] *Id.* at 5.

[15] *Id.* at 28.

[16] Guido cited his concurrence in Ognibene v. Parkes, 671 F3d 174 (2011), discussed infra, Chapter 32, "An Egalitarian Believer's First Amendment"; see also his concurrence in Landell v. Sorrell, 406 F.3d 159, 161 (2005, concurring) (upholding the constitutionality of a Vermont campaign expenditure limitation, in part, because "a large contribution by a person of great means may influence an election enormously, and yet may represent a far lesser intensity of desire than a pittance given by a poor person.").

[17] Eric Posner, *Book Review (reviewing Guido Calabresi, The Future of Law and Economics: Essays in Reform and Recollection)*, 54 J. OF ECON. LIT. 600, 601 (2016).

[18] Cass Sunstein, *Listen, Economists!*, N.Y. REV. OF BOOKS, Nov. 10, 2016

[19] United States. v. Booker, 125 S. Ct. 738 (2005).

[20] Nancy Gertner, *What Yogi Berra Teaches About Post-Booker Sentencing*, 115 YALE L.J. POCKET PART 137, 138 (2006).

a study of German judges showing that the roll of a die could affect their sentencing decisions.[21]

In response to Guido's contention—which cited, among other things, the German study—that judges may be unconsciously "anchored" by any initial guideline set, even when those guidelines are "randomly" drawn, Judge Raggi sardonically acknowledged that her "familiarity with the administration of criminal justice east of the Rhine is limited," but that her experience as a judge spanned more than three decades and—although hardly responsive to Guido's main point—she knew of no judges who allowed themselves to be influenced by randomly generated recommendations.[22] She found Guido's reliance on hypotheticals unconvincing. "As any judge with sentencing experience knows, a wide chasm separates the making of decisions that really deprive another person of liberty from the making of hypothetical decisions that do not, rendering analogies suspect," she wrote.[23]

Guido's discussion of anchoring in the concurrence in *Ingram* has been cited in sentencing cases decided by the Seventh Circuit[24] and by Judge William G. Young of the District of Massachusetts.[25] His opinion has also had an impact outside of the criminal sentencing world. In 2018, Jesse Furman of the Southern District in New York declined to use class counsel's proposed figure as a starting point in an antitrust settlement, noting that "it is well established that an initial numerical reference, whether or not it is reasonable, can have an 'anchoring' effect on a person's subsequent judgments." For that proposition, he cited Kahneman and *Ingram*.[26]

Ciraolo v. City of New York and Punitive Damages. Writing for a unanimous panel in *Ciraolo*, Guido invalidated a punitive damage award against the city due to an unlawful strip search.[27] He did it, as he says, because it violated Supreme Court precedent—particularly *Newport v. Fact Concerts*—which prevents the award of punitive damages against municipalities.[28] Guido concurred with his own opinion—illuminating the functions of punitive awards and urging the Supreme Court to reconsider its ruling in *Newport*.[29] He pointed to consequent inconsistencies and inefficiencies—noting, for example, that punitive damages could properly assessed against individual defendants in § 1983 actions and that to the extent that municipalities indemnify their officials against such awards of punitive damages, the distinction drawn by the Newport Court between cities and individual city officials" inevitably collapses."[30]

---

[21] United States v. Ingram, 721 F.3d 35, 37, 40 n.1 (2013) (Calabresi, J., concurring); see critique by Raggi, 721 F.3d at 29 (Raggi, J., concurring). See commentary in Chapter 28, "The Anti-Discrimination Law Reasoning of an Outsider."
[22] Ingram, 721 F.3d at 49 n. 7 (Raggi, J., concurring).
[23] *Id*. See further discussion in Chapter 29, "The Analytical Reasoning of a Behavioral Economist."
[24] United States v. Navarro, 817 F.3d 494, 502 (7th Cir. 2015).
[25] United States v. Moore, No. 00-cr-10247, 2018 WL 5982017 at *3 (D. Mass. Nov. 14, 2018).
[26] Alaska Electrical Pension Fund v. Bank of America Corp., No. 14-cv-7126, 2018 WL 6250657 at 2 (S.D.N.Y. Nov. 29, 2018).
[27] Ciraolo v. City of N.Y., 216 F.3d 236, 242 (2000) (Calabresi, concurring).
[28] *Id*.
[29] *Id*.
[30] *Id*. at n. 11.

The lawyer who would not take a hint. Courts take litigants, their attorneys, and their arguments as they hear them. Guido's pique over Ciraolo's attorney's rigidity or stupidity under questioning at oral argument is evident—it constrained Guido from crafting an opinion in this case that was at once fair to the plaintiff; loyal to precedent; consistent with the best torts jurisprudence; and in conformance with his view of the desirability of inter-court dialogue. Except for the overconfident response of Ciraolo's attorney, Guido might have been able to reach all of these goals at once.

Kemezy v. Peters. Kemezy is an appeal of a § 1983 suit brought against a policeman; it did not expressly consider whether the taxpayers of Muncie, Indiana, should be subject to punitive damages for the tortious behavior of one of the city's policemen.[31] It turned on whether the defendant's net worth was relevant to the jury's award of punitive damages.[32] Judge Posner referred to the Supreme Court jurisprudence in the area as "cryptic," citing *One View of the Cathedral*, among other sources, to emphasize the importance of deterrence. He allowed punitive damages against a municipality without explicitly tackling the precedent in *Newport v. Fact Concerts*. The Seventh Circuit opinion declared that it was unnecessary to introduce evidence of a plaintiff's net worth when seeking an award of punitive damages.[33]

To support the relevance of net worth in his concurrence in *Ciraolo*, Guido had referred to *Kemezy*'s "explicit" endorsement of the "multiplier" function of punitive damages. Judge Posner, however, offered no less than seven alternative rationales for them, ranging from "reliev[ing] the pressures on the criminal justice system" to "express[ing] the community's abhorrence at the defendant's act."[34] In another, later case, Judge Posner offered explicit reasoning to explain how a defendant's high net worth could justify uncapped punitive damages.[35]

---

[31] Kemezy v. Peters, 79 F.3d 33 (7th Cir. 1996).

[32] *Id.*

[33] Newport v. Fact Concerts, 453 U.S. 247, (1981) (municipalities immune from punitive damages); Kemezy, 79 F.3d at 37.

[34] Kemezy, 79 F.3d at 35.

[35] *Id.* at 34; A wealthy defendant might "mount an extremely aggressive defense against suits such as this and by doing so to make litigating against it very costly, which in turn may make it difficult for the plaintiffs to find a lawyer willing to handle their case." This counseled in favor of uncapped punitive damages, since "if the total stakes in the case were capped at $50,000 .. the plaintiffs might well have had difficulty financing this lawsuit." *Kemezy, supra* note 33.

30

Calabresian Complexities and the Value of Dialogue

> *Guido's embrace of dialogue, even when his position of authority has not required it, surely reflects more than an ingrained preference for courtesy. This penchant for seeking common ground and provoking discourse among decision makers and affected parties is also based on finding better solutions, reinforcing legitimacy, and getting at truth.*
>
> *An important dimension of his intricate approach is the willingness—and often enthusiasm—to refer to state courts for answers to discrete legal questions about state law which other federal judges would rather reserve to themselves. Becoming an early champion of this sort of judicial federalism, Guido added meaning to "comity" and in doing so elevated the stature, quality, and legal influence of state courts. Others paved the way for dialogue, but as New York's former Chief Judge, Judith Kaye, said, "a major change in state-federal relations was effected by certification ... Guido actually did it. He 'walked the walk.'"*
>
> *This chapter considers cases that have been important to the development of inter-judicial and inter-branch dialogue:* Quill v. Vacco, *regarding assisted suicide;* McCarthy v. Olin, *regarding the tort liability of bullet manufacturers; and* Tunick v. Safir, *regarding freedom of expression.*

Quill v. Vacco was brought by several physicians and terminally ill people who challenged a New York law making it a felony to help another person commit suicide or attempt it. This came up during the second year after I joined the Court.

One would have thought that the panel hearing the case was quite conservative. There was Judge Milton Pollack, who was in his nineties—a very powerful district judge who had been appointed by Eisenhower. Pollack was a very good judge: conservative, extremely wealthy, and a man who still rode the subways. The other was Judge Roger Miner, who had been seriously considered by President Reagan for the Supreme Court as a replacement for Robert Bork. I was the third judge.

It turned out that Roger thought that the laws on assisted suicide were wrong; and the strength of his feeling surprised me. Interestingly, later, during the High Holy Days, he had had a heart attack that could have left him in a terrible state, but luckily, he was surrounded by doctors who got him going again.

Roger and I were friendly. We wondered how Judge Milton Pollack would feel about it, and Roger said somewhat jokingly that, given his age, the question was whether Milton would be more afraid of doctors and nurses who would keep him alive, or the doctors and nurses who would kill him!

I was the youngest of the three, and not that young. Our age undoubtedly caused us all a certain amount of, say, "titubation."

When he was nearly 100, Milton developed cancer. Given his age, it probably would not have gone anywhere, but he did not want to be limited in his capacity; and so he had it operated on. Sadly, during the recovery period in the hospital he got a hospital infection, which did him in.

The background of the assisted suicide law was interesting. It was a very old New York law which, as far as I could make out, had never been interpreted. The law was passed at a time when suicide was a crime, so that on its own terms, it simply made "aiding and abetting" suicide a crime. Perfectly sensible. Then, around the end of the nineteenth century, suicide was decriminalized, because, you know, how could you punish somebody who had killed themselves? And you did not want to take away a person's property from his family, and so forth, as had once been done.

So they decriminalized it. But at the same time they called it a "grave moral wrong"; and the part that punished "aiding" suicide was kept on the books. Given the "grave moral wrong" language in the suicide provision, retaining this part was, again, quite understandable.

In the 1970s, the New York Legislature removed the clause about suicide being a "grave moral wrong," and soon there came to be an increasing number of decisions which spoke about a person's *right* to commit suicide. But the assisted suicide part was ignored; it was not altered even though the whole attitude towards suicide had changed.

The people who were trying to get the law struck down, were very aggressive, both in their public discussions and in their filings. They were extremely sure that they were right, and they reacted to anything which might be less than a total victory as, "You people just don't understand right and wrong." On the other side, the State defended the law particularly well.

At conference, I learned that the other two wanted to strike the law down, not under the Due Process Clause, but as a matter of Equal Protection. Using the Due Process Clause would have meant holding that "people have a right to kill themselves and that they have a right to get somebody else to kill them; and this right is fundamental. That's the end of it. Let's go home." This is what the Ninth Circuit had just done in a similar case.

The power that courts have to decide that a piece of law is unconstitutional because it violates the Due Process Clause is kind of like the power to drop a hydrogen bomb. When you have a power that great, you may have it, but boy, you should be reluctant to use it!

I use another analogy, to the Catholic Church. When the Pope speaks ex cathedra, *he is infallible. When has the Pope actually spoken* ex cathedra *since the nineteenth century when this power was asserted? He used it for the Immaculate Conception doctrine, which is powerful dogma but which cannot be proven one way or another. And for the Assumption of the Virgin Mary; which unless somebody—most unlikely—finds a grave somewhere marked "Virgin Mary," and finds a body there, it is not going to be disproved, either. Speaking* ex cathedra *is so powerful that it is too dangerous to use in practical situations—in these situations the Pope uses less absolute assertions of authority.*

The same thing applies to law. Given the force of a Due Process constitutional determination, it is something courts should be reluctant to use. It is better to use other doctrines.

Finding an Equal Protection violation, however, allows a legislature to come back and remedy the inequality. You ask, how do you strike down a prohibition on assisted suicide on an Equal Protection ground? The reasoning was that if people who are able to kill themselves are allowed to do it, and it is considered okay, aren't you treating 'handicapped people"—people who are unable to take their lives by themselves—unequally. They are discriminated against because they are not allowed to do what others can.

In effect, our Court used the Equal Protection Clause and said to the New York Legislature, "If you really think suicide is wrong, then you can still outlaw it and do what you can to prohibit the able from killing themselves. But don't split the difference to the disadvantage of the disabled." That is the way the Court went, though it did not say it quite as clearly as I just have.

Neal Katyal was my clerk that year and was pushing me to go as far—and maybe further—than the majority. I decided instead that this was a good occasion to be really explicit about my 'second look' ideas and my ideas about statutes that head toward unconstitutionality. As you know, I had been developing these from the time I was a student of Alex Bickel in law school, and while I was Justice Black's law clerk. And, you know, I developed them further in my own writing.

I decided to write a concurring opinion, in which I expressly talked about "second look." I wrote that I did not need to reach the issue of inequality that moved the majority. This law was passed with certain goals specifically in mind—to deter "grave moral wrongs." These reasons and their whole moral underpinning did not seem to apply in New York any longer.

The Supreme Court decisions about assisted suicide before our case had come very close to holding that prohibiting it was unconstitutional. This is why the Ninth Circuit could go as far as it did, calling the prohibition a Due Process violation. That closeness undoubtedly affected a majority of my court when it found a violation of Equal Protection.

Most of the time, statutes don't need to explain their reason and remain in effect even when their original motives have faded. This is unlike the common law. When the reason for a common law rule fades the rule fades, too; but that has never been so of statutes. A statute remains in effect, even if the reason for it is no longer clearly discernable. I suggest in Common Law for the Age of Statutes *that it might be a good idea for statutes that have lost their logic to fade, too. But I say that courts do not have power to extinguish them. They might be given the power by legislatures, and they may have that power when the statute raises significant constitutional questions, for then using a 'second look' is more deferential than striking it down.*

I said that we had no obligation to decide whether assisted suicide was constitutional or not, unless we knew that New York still wanted to prohibit it. So, as a starting point I said that we should invalidate the law prohibiting assisted suicide, but we should tell the New York Legislature that if it came back and said, "we want it," then it could re-enact the law—only then we could decide if the new law violated Equal Protection, or perhaps, even, Due Process.

What I wrote is probably the most express statement of "second look" doctrine that you can find, although Jon Newman's opinion concurring in the striking down of Connecticut's anti-abortion law, before *Roe v. Wade*, comes very close, if not as explicitly.

There is something significant, though, that I want to add. Going back, as we have been doing, to these early decisions, I realize now that I was not only embracing "second look," but also that in *Quill* the seeds of my interest in dialogue and conversation are all there, and hence, my interest in the importance of certification to judicial federalism.

I now realize that my analysis in my concurrence in *Quill* should not have started with "second look." The first step should have been finding out what this assisted suicide language meant, rather than declaring the law unconstitutional and saying that while it was not valid, they could re-pass it. I should have asked for certification. In *Quill* I jumped a step and went right to "second look."

This law had never been interpreted since 1818. The appropriate thing would actually have been to ask the New York Court of Appeals what was actually prohibited by the law. If that law did not prohibit what was sought in the case before us, we had no case or controversy. What is assisted suicide? Is giving extra-large doses of morphine to somebody who is already practically dead, assisting suicide? Does the statute prohibit actions by a doctor? What does it bar? All these things were totally open for interpretation. Some of the amici, non-parties who were attacking the law were saying—the doctors for instance—"Well, if you let us just give more morphine when somebody's already pretty well dead, then we have no problem with the law." By certifying, we would have let New York say, if they wanted to, that the law meant something very different from what at least a lot of people were objecting to.

> The constitutional question, and even the need for a second look, might then have looked very different. It would have been the New York courts, not the New York legislature, that would have been in conversation with us. Both the holding under Equal Protection and 'second look' spoke to the legislature. Certification would ask the New York Courts what is wanted in New York. Both conversations have their place. But in some ways, asking the New York of Appeals to interpret the law is a conversation that comes first.

So, why didn't I do that and argue the case for certification? I did not do it because it was still early in my thinking about it. And perhaps I thought that if our case was reconsidered *en banc*, another judge might ask for an interpretation from the New York Courts, while no one else but me was likely to present the "second look" option.

Another reason might have been that had I asked to send it to the New York Court of Appeals, I would have had to dissent. And that, in so hot a case, might not have been desirable.

It is important to realize that if we had certified we would not have told the New York Court of Appeals, "interpret the law this far, and we will uphold it." We would not have been giving them an advisory opinion. That is what we do when we interpret a law and then say, "So interpreted, it is constitutional." I believe this is undesirable because it states abstractly where the constitutional line is, rather than setting that line in response to what a legislature wants. Certifying says, "You tell us what you want to do. We'll tell you whether it's over the boundary or not." Interpreting the law ourselves says, "you can go all the way to this and we'll uphold it," even though New York might not want to go that far.

> The New York Court of Appeals might have said, "No, we don't want to take the question from you." Then we would have had either to interpret it ourselves, or send it back for a 'second look', or decide its constitutional validity under the Equal Protection or Due Process Clauses.

I had expected that the case would be reconsidered by our whole Court, *en banc*. It is the kind of case well worthy of such review, even in our court, which rarely goes *en banc*. The parties did not ask for such review, but this did not mean that we could not go *en banc*—we can go *en banc* whether the parties ask for it or not. We were considering that, when the U.S. Supreme Court granted certiorari, and so the possibility of an *en banc* review became moot. In retrospect I think this was too bad, because had we been *en banc*, we might have decided to ask the

New York Court of Appeals to interpret the law, and the whole anguishing case might have disappeared.

So *Quill v. Vacco* went right to the Supreme Court, which delivered an opinion by Chief Justice Rehnquist, distinguishing assisted suicide from withdrawal of life support. There were many conflicting concurrences. The opinion itself is so muddy that it is hard to say what the Court held. Some people say that what it said was, "In any number of contexts people do have a right to assisted suicide. In other contexts, they do not. We are not really going to tell you one way or another." It might have been better if the Supreme Court had simply reversed the Ninth Circuit case which relied on the Due Process Clause, with language saying that a Due Process holding did not give the legislatures enough of a second chance as an equal protection or "second look" approach would have done. But some might say that "muddiness" on the part of the Supreme Court in cases like this one is a good thing.

I do think that my concurring opinion in *Quill* pointed to a new direction for judicial review of legislation, which I had first charted in *A Common Law for the Age of Statutes*. It is no accident that Charles Krauthammer, on the Right, wrote a piece giving me "the prize for judicial presumption," because I would have struck down the statute unless the legislature reenacted it. He was smart enough to see that in some ways my approach was a dangerous perspective precisely because it was restrained.

> *Interestingly, a significant part of Gerald Gunther's original criticism of Alex Bickel's first writings, headed the same way as Krauthammer's criticism of me. Not without some validity. Think again about how active the Canadian Supreme Court has been because the Canadian Charter's non obstante clause gives ultimate power to the legislatures.*

Being restrained, these approaches conferred power to judges to do things which they might not have done, had they needed to go all the way.

* * *

The Olin Corporation made hollow-point bullets. They were called "Black Talon" bullets, and they were designed to expand as they went into a person and hence to make their injuries worse. These bullets were fired from a semi-automatic gun by Colin Ferguson, a mentally unbalanced person, to murder passengers on a Long Island Railroad Train, in New York. McCarthy was the wife and mother of victims. She sued Olin Corporation claiming basically that Olin Corporation could foresee that the bullets would reach people who would attempt to use them for mass killing and have tort claims. Her tort claims were based on negligence and strict liability. *McCarthy v. Olin Corporation* was not a question of guns, but of these bullets, whose function was only to make injuries worse—and which had no use for hunting, or any use except to maim. The issue was whether the bullets were marketed by Olin in ways that could reasonably be expected to reach dangerous people.

Now *McCarthy* could not be handled easily as an ordinary tort case because it involved a very strange problem in New York tort law, one that happened because of a quirk. Classically, the problem of assigning responsibility to a person who allows somebody else to get hold of something and then injure someone with it, was a question of foreseeability—was it foreseeable that somebody else, a third-party intervenor, would get hold of it? And if so, was there a duty not to let that happen?

This came up classically, in "keys-in-the-car" cases, in which somebody left a key in a car, and the car was stolen and injured other people. *Ross v. Hartman* in District of Columbia found liability on the truck owner for leaving a truck unlocked. Some other courts—a Pennsylvania case—said no liability. There is also a much older English case along the same lines in which liability was found. It deals with somebody leaving a wagon somewhere, and somebody else trying to steal the wagon, and ramming it into a window and breaking the window.

In most jurisdictions, these problems solved themselves at common law with decisions turning on whether you could foresee that the intervenor would injure a third party enough so that there would be a duty on the part of the enabler. And the issue would get resolved, almost always, in "keys-in-the-car" cases.

New York did not resolve the general issue that way, for a strange reason. In New York, a statute was passed which specifically made people liable to third parties for leaving their keys in cars. This meant that the issue which normally would have come up in a common law way did not come up, and so had not been resolved as a general matter. There are New York cases that say that where a product is defective, the maker of the defective product is liable to anybody who can reasonably be injured—foreseeability is the only limitation. But in negligence cases where a product is not defective, but where it may be dangerous if misused by a third party, and a criminal intervenor takes the product and injures somebody with it, there is no case that tells us that there is liability. So oddly, the result is that the liability of a negligent person on account of a third-party criminal intervenor may be less broad in a negligence than in a strict liability setting. That may seem queer; and it may or may not be. It depends on how New York would rule if the negligence case were clearly brought to the highest New York court.

I believed that that was the issue in McCarthy—that the New York law was open and underdeveloped. I could think of various ways that New York courts might handle the situation, and I thought that we should certify the case to the New York Court of Appeals, specifically raising the question of when and to what degree negligent parties were liable to people injured by third-party criminal intervenors.

This was in 1997, early on in my thinking about certification, and our Court had not yet gotten into the habit of certifying easily. I found myself with a panel of two others—Thomas Meskill and José Cabranes—who were not comfortable with certification. I think they also were uncomfortable with holding gun companies liable or putting them in a position akin to that.

The situation was fairly unusual: I wanted to certify, and a majority would not let me. I said to them, "I know that there is no obligation to certify. However, this case is only in our court because of diversity jurisdiction. These people have a right to be governed by the law of their state. *Erie v. Tompkins* says that is the governing law. Why would you not try to find out what that law is, by getting a statement by those who determine what that law is, the New York Court of Appeals? Is not that what you should do for the parties? And isn't this especially so, if you have situations which are unlikely ever to come up in state courts, because there is almost always diversity jurisdiction, so that federal courts end up pretty much always telling the state what its law is?"

I kept saying to them, "All you are doing is letting New York decide what it wants to do. If you are so sure that you are right, would you not want the New York Court of Appeals to say so, because then you have got the law clearly on your side? If instead you do not certify and you turn out to be wrong, well then it should not have been decided that way, and you would be depriving the parties of the law of their jurisdiction."

> *Prior to the time certification has become common there were any number of cases in copyright and other things, where the law of New York was almost always decided by the Second Circuit, because they never came up in New York state courts. This is one of the reasons why Chief Judge Judith Kaye and the New York Court of Appeals became so pleased with certification. It allowed them to do their job and tell us what New York law was.*
>
> *I emphasized these points in 2018 when I concurred to a per curiam opinion in* Tapia v. BLCH 3rd Ave. *A restaurant worker was not paid minimum wages or overtime by the employer and the panel disallowed cumulative liquidated damages under the Fair Labor Standards Act and New York labor law. Here in labor law is another example of a New York law question that would not come to New York courts; and yet rather than certify the case the Circuit interpreted New York law on its own.*

I could not make any headway with the panel. You had Judge Meskill; he was very old fashioned ... an older judge, who had not grown up with and was not comfortable with certifying. The other judge, José Cabranes, is not a judge who is inclined to let other people decide if he can help it. He is very able. He knows it and likes to hold into issues. He is not the sort of judge who is going to be comfortable with certification.

Whether the fact that bullets and guns were involved made the panel more anxious to decide, I don't know. The result was that the panel majority declined to certify, and it wrote a decision determining that the bullets were not defectively designed; and that Olin Corporation had no duty to prevent the criminal misuse of its bullets.

McCarthy is one of the truly bad decisions of our court. Here was the kind of a case where a federal court of appeals, talking about state law, ought to be very, very, very sure of what that law is, because it has no decision by the highest court to rely on. *McCarthy* is also a bad decision because Black Talons were being marketed in a way that might have caused the New York Court of Appeals to define its law with respect to negligence liability to third parties, in a way which would be quite interesting. By deciding the issue ourselves, we kept the New York Court of Appeals from focusing on that question.

My support for certification never depends on whether on the merits of a case I am in the minority on a panel. When we talked about the injury to the meat cutter in the Liriano *case, as I said earlier, the rest of my panel wanted to come out the way I would have come out, but I thought New York law was uncertain and insisted on certification nonetheless.*

The other side of my respect for state court lawmaking is that, for the same reasons, I wish when it is a matter of federal law, Congress and the Supreme Court did not tell us that we had to defer to what the states say is federal law. We are required to uphold what the state courts have done even if it is wrong if their holding is not unreasonable. But if it is federal law, which we know more about than state courts, there should be nothing insulting about allowing us to define that law.

There are judges who are reluctant to certify and say, as Dick Posner said to me "Oh, the states are offended by certification because we give them so much to do ... Indiana does not like certification." That is ridiculous! It all depends on how you certify. Indiana was offended because he had a case in which he said, "I think this law is absurd, but I think it is the law of Indiana!" I said, "Why didn't you certify?" "Oh, they do not like it, he said!" But I cannot imagine that they would have been offended if the Seventh Circuit had said, "If you *want*, take this case and help us out. If you don't, we'll do the best we can."

Much more controversial is the question of certification raisonné, *in which we say, "It's up to you, but here's how we would do it." This has the advantage, in a way, of making us look more like the intermediate appellate court, because after all, the appellate division decides a case, and says what it would do, and the Court of Appeals can take it and reverse it or decline to take it and leave it. When we certify and say, "Here's what we would do if you do not take it and certify," we're putting ourselves more in that situation. Some people say it's more aggressive. In a way, it is, because it tells the state what we think the law ought to be. I think you know me well enough to know that I think that is a good idea, so long as the state court*

> has the last say. Indeed, it makes it easier for them to say, "That's fine for now," and decline certification.

I was at conference where Judges Steve [Stephen] Reinhart, Dick [Richard] Posner, and Mike [Michael] Boudin were. All of them were telling me I was wrong on certification, and I was telling them that they were all wrong! I think it was because Steve and Dick wanted—very much like José—to be the ones who decide. Mike, instead, just likes to settle cases—even, to some extent, regardless of how. As I said earlier, my view differs from either of these, which is another reason I kept saying "It's our job to get it right," and that means letting the state court decide.

> There are situations where time matters and certification does not make sense. We had a Connecticut case in which the question was whether an 86-year-old man got a pension. Connecticut law was uncertain. If we didn't certify, we would decide in favor of the 86-year-old man. If we did certify? Connecticut was not fast in deciding such cases. "I am sorry, you probably won't hear until after you are dead!" Well, in that situation, we have to do the best you can, and decide ourselves. The same may be true where the cost of certification is out of proportion to the amount involved in the case.

It is also fascinating to see how often both parties in a case before us oppose certification. They say, "No, no, decide it my way. It's perfectly obvious." But rather than losing, they prefer it!

A few years after we decided *McCarthy*, a case named *Hamilton v. Beretta*, that was about the negligent marketing of guns, went to the New York Court of Appeals. Dick [Judge Richard] Wesley, who was then on that Court, said "Tort law is ever changing; it is a reflection of the complexity and vitality of daily life. Although plaintiffs have presented us with a novel theory—negligent marketing of a potentially lethal yet legal product, based upon the acts... of an industry—we are unconvinced that, on the record before us, the duty plaintiffs wish to impose is either reasonable or circumscribed... Whether, in a different case, a duty may arise remains a question for the future." It is a very limited, very careful opinion, not only limited to guns, but limited even as to guns, to that moment in time; and in any event it shows that I was right that the question in McCarthy was and is an open one in New York Law.

Dick Wesley left the New York Court of Appeals and joined the Second Circuit, where we have talked a lot about *Beretta* and *McCarthy*. Dick has been thinking and rethinking his position in *Beretta* since the horrifying shootings at the elementary school in Newtown, Connecticut. I said, "But you said, 'tort law is constantly evolving.' You left room for the evolution of your own position." And he said, "You're the only one who knows that." I don't know, but I think today he might well come out differently on facts like those in *Beretta*. He is a wonderfully careful judge and that is why we are such good friends; as I say, we are both "Torts-niks."

* * *

Spencer Tunick is a photographer who loves to photograph nude people by the hundreds, by the thousands, all over the world, in odd places. He's photographed them under the Eiffel Tower; in Saint Peter's Square; in Manchester, and Vienna, and Mexico City. He has staged what he calls "mass sculptures" all over. If you look at the photographs, when you have that many people, there are even some people in the crowd who are more than just naked, but tumescent, as you might expect. It is a mass of things of naked humanity!

Tunick v. Safir came up because he wanted to take photographs of naked people in New York City. He was totally willing to have the city name the time, place, and manner. It could be on a Sunday morning at four o'clock, or five o'clock, somewhere where nobody else would be up. It could be anywhere of that sort. But Mayor Giuliani, I suspect for political reasons, said, "Absolutely not. Nowhere. It can't be done." He was remarkable about the things he got worked up about. Giuliani prohibited the photography, anywhere, any time.

The law of the state of New York prohibits public nudity, unless a town or city permits it under the terms of that town. And New York, obviously, permits such nudity. You would have half of Broadway going dark! There is an ordinance authorized by the statute, permitting nudity in connection with an artistic performance. So the question in *Tunick* was, "is this an artistic performance?" At oral argument, I asked, "Why isn't it?"

New York City, parroting what Giuliani wanted, said, "No, it's not." "Well, why not? New York answered, "An artistic performance has to be indoors." And I said— this is literally what I said at the bench, "You mean you could have a naked *Hamlet* performed inside Grand Central Station at rush hour, and that would be alright under the statute; but you can't have this guy photograph some people naked on the street in New York at 5:30 am in the morning on a Sunday or at some other time, place, and manner which is all right?" The lawyer for the City said, "Yes." I said, "Well, it seems to me, One, that that's a very odd interpretation of the statute; and Two, if that statute were read that way, it would probably be unconstitutional under the New York Constitution, as *irrational*, and I would not even need to reach whether it would be unconstitutional under the Federal Constitution."

So, what do we do? The panelists were Bob Sack and the celebrated Judge Ellsworth Van Graafeiland. Van Graafeiland was obsessed with nontraditional sex, an obsession that is apparent in a variety of other cases.

There was a case that I wasn't involved in, with ALK (Amalya L Kearse) and BDP (Barrington Danny Parker) about a person who committed suicide unintentionally—who killed himself unintentionally—who hanged himself for

> *auto-erotic purposes and accidentally died as a result. The insurance company denied the family's claim, saying that this was "intentionally inflicted" suicide. The panel originally, two to one, went along with Van Graafeiland, with ALK dissenting, and she was going to take it en banc. I talked to Danny and helped change his mind. I said, "Look, are you going to say when somebody dies when they are smoking, which is much more likely to kill them than somebody doing that, they do not collect insurance?" Whether because of my conversation or because of Amalya Kearse's elegant arguments, Danny changed his mind. Van Graafeiland wrote a fierce dissent at the time—I think it was because he was unable to handle unusual sexuality or nudity.*

Okay, in *Tunick*, Van thought that the refusal to give a permit for a nude photo shoot was perfectly fine. He thought it was sufficient to deny the permit that it might attract voyeurs. Bob Sack, being an old First Amendment guy, wanted to come straight out and say this is unconstitutional, period. That the position of New York City was absurd.

I told Bob, look, if I'm pushed, I'd come out the same way, but I really think this is, first, a question of interpretation of the New York statute. Second, it leads to an interpretation of the statute that might call for interpretation of the New York Constitution, and we ought to certify this question. Bob grudgingly went along, because he had to deal with Van Graafeiland. He wrote a separate opinion which said, "I don't think we need to do this," but I will vote to certify.

So we had the two votes necessary to certify to the New York Court of Appeals. But we said, "Take this case only if you can act quickly. The photographer needs these pictures for an exhibition in the spring, and winter is coming. And you are not going to get many naked people out in New York when it is freezing!" I wrote a lengthy explanation of the value of certification as a general matter and discussed why it was the best course of action here. I did not, of course, give the Court of Appeals a deadline, but I did say, "We really would like you to take it, but be aware that time is of the essence, for these and these reasons."

The New York Court of Appeals, acting very intelligently, answered, "This is a very important and interesting case. We cannot deal with it quickly enough. So, we decline certification. You do what you think is right." This allowed us to interpret the statute and the artistic exemption, something that otherwise could not properly do. Now that they told us, "We don't take it," we were perfectly free to interpret the statute. We could say in a per <u>curiam</u> opinion, "This is covered by the exception in the New York statute, and the nude shoot can be done in a proper place and time."

We then await a dissent from Van Graafeiland. He did not write it. He went off to California to sit with the Ninth Circuit. And we had just told the New York of Appeals that time was of the essence! Van does not bring his hearing aids with him! No one can get to him! We finally do get to him and send him things; he just does not do anything!

We are in an impossible situation. It was already getting into winter, so in some ways it was already too late for the photography. The delay was just becoming an embarrassment and an injustice. I asked the Chief Judge, who then was Ralph Winter, what we should do. Ralph said, "try yet again, and if doesn't get you something within a week, then write the opinion noting that "dissent will be forthcoming." Which we did.

The Van Graafeiland dissent, when it came [sighs]—I do not know, you can read it, but it seems to me not worth reading. It is one series of insults after the other, and they are directed at me in particular. If it were written by anybody but Van Graafeiland, who was known to be a very peculiar fellow, it would have bothered me or anyone else. As it was, I don't think anybody ever paid any attention to it. But it is there, and it is absolutely fierce!

In any event, the story between me and Van, as I told you, has a happy ending. Not long afterwards, he had a heart attack, and I made a real effort to cheer him and let him know that I respected him, and it ended up, before he died, with him saying all sorts of lovely things about me. After two decades the personality clashes have faded.

Jurisprudentially, you know, *Tunick v. Safir* provoked an interesting professional clash over how judges should view their responsibility in a federal system. That clash never goes away.

COMMENTARY

Chapter 30

The incorporation of certification into New York judicial practice. Judge Jon Newman initiated the practice of certifying cases from the Second Circuit to the New York Court of Appeals. In January 1987, he issued a brief opinion interpreting an obscure provision of New York's Social Services Law.[1] Writing for the court, he cited no canons of statutory interpretation and no prior case law—instead, he explained that, under a newly enacted certification procedure, his court had relied on the New York Court of Appeals to interpret state law. It had presented the state law question to the Court of Appeals, which then answered about four months later. Reflecting on the process, Newman wrote that the procedure was "a valuable device for securing prompt and authoritative resolution of unsettled questions of state law, especially those that seem likely to recur and to have significance beyond the interests of the parties in a particular lawsuit."[2]

---

[1] Kidney by Kidney v. Kolmar Laboratories, Inc., 808 F. 2d 955 (2d Cir. 1997).
[2] *Id.* at 957.

The mechanism for allowing certification had begun to unfold decades earlier, in concepts of "abstention" and "cooperative federalism."[3] Commentators have observed that certification complements or potentially supplants what is known as *Pullman* abstention—the process by which federal courts simply refrain from deciding state law issues. Former Second Circuit Chief Judge John Walker observed that "[w]here the circumstances of a case would support *Pullman* abstention, certification serves the same purpose more efficiently."[4] In 1960, the Supreme Court praised the Florida legislature's foresight in enacting (although it did not actually make use of) a certification procedure.[5] Support for the approach was not unanimous, however. "Perhaps state courts take no more pleasure than do federal courts in deciding cases piecemeal on certificates," Justice Black surmised in a skeptical dissent.[6]

Still, the Uniform Law Commission promulgated a Uniform Certification of Questions of Law Act in 1967, and thirty-eight states had adopted a certification procedure by 1992.[7] But criticism flourished. Third Circuit Judge Dolores K. Sloviter observed that certification "generates cost and delay" and presented "at best an incomplete solution to the problem of state law decision making by the federal courts."[8] In 1995, First Circuit Judge Bruce M. Selya declared that experiments with certification demonstrated fundamental flaws: "[a]fter three decades of experience ... the practice has not lived up to its promise: neither federalism nor efficiency nor fairness sufficiently justifies the knee-jerk popularity that certification has acquired..."[9] "Knee-jerk popularity," was clearly an overstatement however—in the first five years that New York had a certification statute, the Court of Appeals only received seven certified questions.[10] And despite these critiques, the Supreme Court reaffirmed its endorsement: in 1996, Justice Ginsburg found that certification "allows a federal court ... to put the question directly to the State's highest court, reducing the delay, cutting the cost, and increasing the assurance of gaining an authoritative response."[11] The litigation before her had consumed almost a decade; Ginsburg suggested that "the complexity might have been avoided had the District Court ... accepted the certification suggestion made by Arizona's Attorney General."[12]

---

[3] *See* Philip Kurland, *Toward a Co-operative Judicial Federalism: The Federal Court Abstention Doctrine*, 24 FED. RULES DIG. 481 (1959).

[4] Allstate Ins. Co. v. Serio, 261 F. 3d 143, 155 (2d Cir. 2001) (Walker, J., concurring). *See also* Arizonans for Official English v. Arizona, 520 U.S. 43, 75 (1997) ("Certification today covers territory once dominated by a deferral device called 'Pullman abstention[.]' ").

[5] FLA. STAT. ANN. § 25.031 (1957); Clay v. Sun Ins. Office Limited, 363 U.S. 207, 212 (1960).

[6] 363 U.S. at 227 (Black, J., joined by Earl Warren and William O. Douglas, dissenting).

[7] Uniform Law Commission, Certification of Questions of Law (1995) Summary, available at http://www.uniformlaws.org/ActSummary.aspx?title = Certification%20Of%20Questions%20of%20Law%20(1995); Dolores K. Sloviter, *A Federal Judge View Diversity Jurisdiction Through the Lens of Federalism*, 78 VA. L. REV. 1671, 1684 (1992).

[8] Sloviter, *supra* note 7 at 1686.

[9] Bruce M. Selya, *Certified Madness: Ask a Silly Question ...*, 29 SUFFOLK U. L. REV. 677, 678 (1995)

[10] Judith Kaye & Kenneth I. Weissman, *Interactive Judicial Federalism: Certified Questions in New York*, 69 FORDHAM L. REV. 373, 404 n. 201 (2000).

[11] 520 U.S. at 76.

[12] *Id.* at 79.

Undaunted by the critics, including those who disparaged state court adjudication, Guido became an outspoken champion of certification. "My long-suffering colleagues know what *my* answer [to the problems of diversity jurisdiction] is, and that is certify, certify, certify," he joked in 2002.[13] In his Circuit, Guido was determined that New York, Vermont, or Connecticut courts would come to realize that the federal appellate court was "an intermediate court in their system, subject to them," and not the other way around.[14]

Some colleagues, as Guido recounts, were not on board. In his notably bitter dissent in *Tunick*, Judge Van Graafeiland complained that "[e]ver since Judge Calabresi moved to this Court from Yale Law School, he has verbosely crusaded for more extensive use of the certification process."[15] Van Graafeiland, as Judge Richard Wesley put it, epitomized "an old curmudgeon judge," and "frankly did not like Guido—there was animosity that *Tunick v. Safir* sharpened."[16] Several less vitriolic colleagues were hostile to certification in many situations as equivalent to a voluntary concession of federal authority.

He has, however, gained the widespread admiration of many federal judges and many state court judges for championing certification, and sits among a veritable pantheon of those who have made the greatest contributions to judicial federalism.[17] In 2014, Chief Judge Kaye gave her opinion concisely: Guido is, she said, a "certified, and certifying, genius."[18]

Vacco v. Quill and the "right to die" litigation. Unsurprisingly, the right-to-die litigation generated an enormous amount of controversy; shortly before the Supreme Court heard arguments in *Washington v. Glucksberg* and *Vacco v. Quill*, *New York Times* reporter Linda Greenhouse observed that the briefs and amicus briefs were marked by "a fervor rarely seen at the Court."[19] Even advocates who were working for the same outcome quarreled bitterly over strategies and principles; the Reverend Ralph Mero, a Unitarian Universalist minister and co-founder of Compassion in Dying, characterized the notorious Dr. Jack Kevorkian as "an unfortunate spokesman for a good cause" who "appears reckless, unrestrained, flagrant."[20]

The Supreme Court reversed both the Second and Ninth Circuits.[21] Before it did, however, both *Quill v. Vacco and Compassion in Dying v. Washington*[22] were the subject of intense debate. In the *Harvard Law Review*, Cass Sunstein concluded the

---

[13] Guido Calabresi, *Federal and State Courts: Restoring a Workable Balance*, 78 N.Y.U. L. REV. 1293, 1301 (2003).

[14] *Id.* at 1302.

[15] *Tunick*, 209 F.3d at 99 (von Graafeiland, J., dissenting).

[16] Interview with Hon. Richard C. Wesley, Aug. 13, 2020.

[17] Kaye & Weissman, *supra* note 10.

[18] Judith Kaye, *Tribute to Judge Guido Calabresi*, 70 N.Y.U. ANN. SURV. AM. LAW 33, 33 (2014); interview with Judith Kaye, June 14, 2011.

[19] Linda Greenhouse, *Before the Court, the Sanctity of Life and of Death*, N.Y. TIMES, Jan. 5, 1997; Vacco v. Quill, 80 F.3d 716, 731 (1996); 521 U.S. 793 (1997).

[20] Lisa Belkin, *There's No Simple Suicide*, N.Y. TIMES MAG., Nov. 14, 1993.

[21] Vacco v. Quill, 521 U.S. 793 (1997); Washington v. Glucksberg, 521 U.S. 702 (1997).

[22] Compassion in Dying v. Washington, 79 F.3d 790 (9th Cir. 1996), rev'd, Washington v. Glucksberg, 521 U.S. 702 (1997).

Ninth Circuit opinion exemplified "judicial hubris." He reasoned that courts lacked "the necessary fact finding expertise and policymaking competence" to decide the right-to-die question.[23] At the same time, however, Sunstein commended Guido's "inventive" solution to the problem: striking down the statute but inviting legislative re-articulation of its rationale.[24] Guido's "second look" approach, of course, drew heavily on the logical argumentation he developed at great length in *A Common Law for the Age of Statutes*.[25]

The Second and Ninth circuit opinions were assaulted by critics, including columnist Charles Blow who castigated Stephen Reinhardt for writing a "manifesto longer than the Unabomber's" in *Compassion in Dying*. With respect to the Second Circuit opinion, commentators pointed out, as does Guido here, that the position taken in his concurrence permitted, potentially, a great expansion of judicial power. Conservative columnist Charles Krauthammer reserved special disdain for the concurrence, asserting that judges were obligated to "rule on the constitutionality of laws, not their currency."[26]

Remarkably, despite the reversal of *Quill v. Vacco* by the Supreme Court, Guido's concurring opinion has continued to be cited for its discourse on the relationship between courts and legislatures.[27]

McCarthy v. Olin Corp. On December 7, 1993, Colin Ferguson killed five people and injured nineteen others on a Long Island Railroad commuter train from New York City. A sixth individual died from her injuries a few months later.[28] Ferguson's criminal trial drew substantially more media coverage than otherwise it might have due to Ferguson's decision to fire his lawyers and represent himself; his former attorneys, William Kunstler and Ron Kuby, warned that he was not mentally competent to stand trial. Ferguson was sentenced by a jury to a minimum of 315 years in prison. Writing in the *New York Times*, McCarthy defended the court's disposition and its orderliness, asserting that Ferguson's questioning of his victims was "as adversarial as our system allows."[29]

The tragedy spurred action and grassroots advocacy to curtail the availability of lethal firearms. Various victims filed suit against manufacturers in New York state court based on the distribution for domestic sale of unreasonably dangerous firearms.[30] These suits were dismissed—the New York Supreme Court, Appellate Division

---

[23] Cass R. Sunstein, *Foreword: Leaving Things Undecided*, 110 HARV. L. REV. 4, 93 (1996).

[24] *Id.* at 94.

[25] See Chapter 17, "The Judicial Sunset."

[26] Charles Krauthammer, *Physician-Assisted Suicides Should be Decided by Public, Not Courts*, CHICAGO TRIBUNE, Apr. 15, 1996.

[27] *See, e.g.,* Landell v. Sorrell, 382 F.3d 91, 209 (2d Cir. 2004) (Winter, J., dissenting) (a constitutional ruling "would leave the Vermont legislature in a position to deliberate on the full ramifications of its actions in considering new legislation but still free to pursue it"); *see also* Arnold's Wines, Inc. v. Boyle, 571 F.3d 185, 199 (2d Cir. 2009) (Calabresi, concurring) (noting interpretive difficulties when it is apparent that "a legal provision is 'born in another age'").

[28] Woman Becomes Sixth Victim to Die from N.Y. Commuter Train Shooting, WASH. POST, Dec. 12, 1993.

[29] Op-ed, Carolyn McCarthy, *Order in the Court*, N.Y. TIMES, Jan. 12, 1998.

[30] *See, e.g.,* John T. McQuiston, *Victims Sue Arms Makers in Shooting on L.I.R.R.*, N.Y. TIMES, Oct. 27, 1994.

concluded that "New York does not impose a duty upon a manufacturer to refrain from the lawful distribution of a non-defective product."[31]

During Eliot Spitzer's tenure as New York Attorney General, the state also brought suit against several gun manufacturers, on a public nuisance theory.[32] Its complaint was dismissed in the trial court. In affirming that dismissal, the intermediate appellate court held that it was "legally inappropriate, impractical and unrealistic" to impose "unspecified measures urged by plaintiff in order to abate the conceded availability and criminal uses of illegal handguns."[33]

The motivation to challenge gun manufacturers was especially great on Long Island, where the shooting occurred. Robert Vilensky, a New York personal injury attorney, wrote in the *New York State Bar Journal* that "[t]he Long Island Railroad tragedy might provide the vehicle for a court to rise to the occasion and bring some justice to the victims."[34] Carolyn McCarthy was the wife of a man killed on the train, and the mother of a son who was severely injured. A Long Island resident, she contended that along with Ferguson, weapons manufacturers should be held liable in connection with their criminal use. McCarthy became the named plaintiff in *McCarthy v. Olin Corp.*[35] As Guido discusses, *McCarthy* was addressed principally to whether the bullets Olin manufactured were defectively designed or unreasonably dangerous, and it did not succeed.[36]

More successful, at least initially, was the action in *Hamilton v. Accu-Tek*, a lawsuit brought by family members of people killed by illegally obtained handguns. Presided over by Judge Jack Weinstein of the Eastern District of New York, a jury returned a verdict for the plaintiffs,[37] however with Judge Weinstein referring to the issues as "novel" and "not easily resolved using well-established state substantive and procedural law."[38]

After the appeal, the Second Circuit certified several unsettled questions of state law, and in response, the New York Court of Appeals rejected the plaintiffs' theory of liability.[39] In an opinion by Judge Richard Wesley mentioned by Guido (then on the New York Court of Appeals and later a judge on the Second Circuit), the state court rejected the plaintiffs' theory of liability while commending the approach, observing that "[t]ort law is ever changing; it is a reflection of the complexity and vitality of daily life."[40] In a footnote, the Court of Appeals opinion ventured that it

---

[31] Forni v. Ferguson, 648 N.Y.S. 2d 73, 74 (1996).
[32] People ex rel. Spitzer v. Sturm, Ruger & Co., Inc., 761 N.Y.S. 2d 192, 204 (2003).
[33] *Id.*
[34] Robert Vilensky, *Should Gun Manufacturers Be Liable for the Long Island Railroad Tragedy*, 67 N.Y. ST. B.J. 16, 18 (1995). In hindsight, it seems remarkable that federal action to limit the availability of firearms was not stopped by gun rights advocates. Ferguson had used a Ruger P-89 semiautomatic assault pistol to carry out the killing. Nine months later, President Bill Clinton signed a federal assault weapons ban. See Tom Brune, *Today's gun debate has echoes of the LIRR shootings era*, Newsday, May 19, 2018.
[35] 119 F.3d 148 (1997). McCarthy also won election to the House of Representatives as a Democrat in 1996. See Rick Hampson, "Gun Lady" Carolyn McCarthy Finally Going Home, USA Today, Jan. 2, 2015.
[36] 119 F.3d 148.
[37] Hamilton v. Accu-Tek, 62 F. Supp. 2d 802 (E.D.N.Y. 1999), judgment vacated by Hamilton v. Beretta U.S.A. Corp., 264 F.3d 21 (2d Cir. 2001).
[38] Hamilton v. Accu-tek, 935 F. Supp. 1307, 1314 (E.D.N.Y. 1996).
[39] Hamilton v. Beretta U.S.A. Corp., 222 F.3d 36 (2d Cir. 2000).
[40] Hamilton v. Beretta U.S.A. Corp., 96 N.Y.2d 222, 242 (2001).

might "well be that a core group of corrupt Federal Firearms Licensees will emerge at some future time," which could "alter the duty equation."[41]

Guido's dissent in *McCarthy* has been cited in other jurisdictions to address the advantages of certification in limiting forum shopping and other harms.[42] In opinions where Guido himself has urged certification, he has cited *McCarthy*; he also has done so in cases in which he has found certification unwarranted.[43] Perhaps surprisingly, although *McCarthy v. Olin Corp.* is a dissent, it is also has been cited as an authoritative statement of products liability law—no doubt because Guido is a torts law authority.[44]

Judith S. Kaye. Judith Kaye grew up in the foothills of the Catskills, the child of Jewish immigrants from Poland who lived on a small farm and later opened a clothing store. She graduated from Barnard College and while working in journalism attended New York University at night. She was the first woman named to the highest court in New York, appointed by Governor Mario Cuomo in 1983, after practicing as a commercial litigator for Sullivan and Cromwell—where she met and married her husband, Stephen Rackow Kaye—and for IBM. When she retired from the bench to resume practice at Sullivan & Cromwell, she had served longer as Chief Judge than any other. Among a great many significant opinions are those voiding New York's mandatory death penalty and dissenting from an opinion denying a constitutional right to marry to same-sex couples. She also played a major institutional role in restructuring the New York State judicial system to include specialized courts. Judith Kaye died at age seventy-seven in 2016.

Chief Judge Kaye and certification. Kaye, as we have seen, credited Guido with increasing the flow of certified questions to the Court of Appeals' docket, noting that he "immediately saw the wisdom of the [statutory] reform, and was quick to make it an everyday reality."[45] She observed that certification is especially valuable in New York, in the areas of products liability, contracts (particularly insurance contracts), and state statutory interpretation.[46] In the latter category, Kaye had the

---

[41] *Id.* at 237 n. 5.

[42] *See, e.g.*, Reddington v. Staten Island University Hosp., 511 F.3d 126, 136 (2d Cir. 2007) (certifying question); Falise v. American Tobacco Corp., 94 F. Supp. 2d 316, 356 (E.D.N.Y. 2000) (asserting "excessive determination of state law by federal judges"); Cyprus Plateau Min. Corp. v. Commonwealth Ins. Co., 972 F. Supp. 1379, 1383 n. 1 (D. Utah 1997) (quoting Guido's dissent at length, describing the arguments as "interesting" but that Tenth Circuit precedent would not permit certification to the extent that Guido urged.)

[43] *See, e.g.*, Gutierrez v. Smith, 702 F.3d 103, 117 (2012); Benjamin v. Jacobson, 172 F.3d 144, 191 n.32 (1999); Messner Vetere Berger McNamee Schmetterer Euro RSCG, Inc. v. Aegis Group PLC, 150 F.3d 194, 201 n.11 (1998); Liriano v. Hobart Corp., 132 F.3d 124, 132 (1998).

[44] Kovalesky v. Carpenter, No. 95-cv-03700, 1997 WL 630144 (1997); Nelson v. Ranger, Inc., No. 05-cv-00093, 2009 WL 3851622; (N.D.N.Y. 2009); Maxwell v. Howmedica Osteonics Corp., 713 F. Supp. 2d 84, 90 (N.D.N.Y. 2010); Richards v. Johnson & Johnson, Inc., No. 17-cv-00178, 2018 WL 2976002 (N.D.N.Y. 2018). Coincidentally, Judge Jack Weinstein relied on Guido's McCarthy dissent to elucidate a point of New York law during the Hamilton gun litigation: "in a design defect case there is almost no difference between a prima facie case in negligence and one in strict liability." *Hamilton*, 62 F. Supp. 2d at 823.

[45] Judith S. Kaye & Kenneth I. Weissman, *Certified Questions in New York*, 69 FORDHAM L. REV. 373, 422 (2000); Judith S. Kaye, *Tribute to Judge Guido Calabresi*, 70 N.Y.U. ANN. SURV. AM. L. 34 (2014); interview with Judith Kaye, June 14, 2011.

[46] Kaye & Weissman, *supra* note 10, at 399–403. Guido has published a considerable amount of scholarship about certification. *See Federal and State Courts: Restoring A Workable Balance*, 78 N.Y.U. L. REV. 1293, 1300 (2003); *see also Statutory Interpretation as "Interbranch Dialogue"?*, 66 UCLA L. REV. 346 (2019); Judith S. Kaye,

opportunity to clarify the requirements for removing a child from a mother's custody in *Nicholson v. Scoppetta*.[47] According to *City Limits*, Kaye's decision "led to steep declines in the practice of simply removing kids at will" and "g[ave] families a chance at mediation ... before a case goes before the judge."[48]

Chief Judge Judith Kaye, 2015

Tapia v. BLCH 3rd Ave. The members of the Second Circuit panel unanimously found that two overlapping labor law statutes—one federal and one state—did not permit a double recovery for a violation. Guido however concurred, to add that a state court's reading of the state statute would be more authoritative than the federal one—and that "if there is any new reason to doubt an earlier federal court's decision as to state law, the state's highest court should be given the opportunity to weigh in."[49] There were possible policy justifications to permit double recoveries, and Guido suggested that it would have been more appropriate to extend a type of "second look" opportunity to the state's highest court, to review the Circuit's interpretative prediction.[50]

Tunick v. Safir, cultural background. Tunick brought two elements of political theater into the courtroom: the ongoing "culture war" between contemporary art and conventional morality; and the political machinations inflicted on New Yorkers by the city's ambitious mayor. Rudolph Giuliani's position in *Tunick* effectively aligned him with other social and religious conservatives, nationally, and as critics

---

State Courts at the Dawn of a New Century: Common Law Courts Reading Statutes and Constitutions, 70 N.Y.U. L. REV. 1, 23–24 (1995).

[47] 820 N.E. 2d 840 (N.Y. 2004); Robert Weisberg, *The Calabresian Judicial Artist: Statutes and the New Legal Process*, 35 STAN. L. REV. 213, 241–49, 256–57 (1983); Vittoria Barsotti, *A Scholar on The Bench: A Conversation with Guido Calabresi*, 70 N.Y.U. ANN. SURV. AM. L. 101 (2014).
[48] Helen Zelon, *React, Reform, Repeat: A Round of Changes Faces Family Court*, CITY LIMITS, June 1, 2012.
[49] 1999 U.S. Dist. LEXIS 10902; 906 F.3d</IBT< 58, 65 (2018) (Calabresi, concurring).
[50] *Id.*

observed, set him in opposition to much of secular modernity and liberality—against "television, movies, books, museums and music" that assertedly exposed young people "to unsavory [evils such as] abortion and lust."[51]

Spencer Tunick, Pink Tenderness (diptych, 1999)

The catalytic national moment occurred in 1989, when a photograph by Andres Serrano titled "Piss Christ," of a crucifix inside a tub of urine, motivated Senators Al D'Amato and Jesse Helms to threaten the National Endowment for the Arts.[52] In the same year, the Corcoran Gallery of Art, which received federal funding, had canceled an exhibition of Robert Mapplethorpe's photography in fear of a similar response.[53]

Giuliani not only displayed hostility to profanity and nudity in art on many occasions, but he took a cramped view of First Amendment expressive freedoms. In *Tunick,* Guido cites a remarkable sixteen cases where the city's actions were blocked on First Amendment grounds.[54] In 1997, Giuliani forced the Metropolitan Transit Authority to take down advertisements for *New York Magazine,* which chose to promote itself as "Possibly the only good thing in New York Rudy hasn't taken credit for." Bringing suit in federal court, the magazine quickly won a preliminary injunction.[55] In 1999, the Brooklyn Museum hosted "Sensation," a controversial British exhibition including a portrait of the Virgin Mary made from elephant dung.[56] Giuliani threatened to pull $7 million worth of funds from the museum, calling the exhibit "sick."[57] The museum, represented by civil libertarian Floyd Abrams, ended up with a settlement that gave them $5.8 million for building improvements.[58]

---

[51] Wesley Morris, *The Morality Wars,* N.Y. TIMES MAGAZINE, Oct. 3, 2018.
[52] William H. Honan, *Artist Who Outraged Congress Lives Amid Christian Symbols,* N.Y. Times, Aug. 16, 1989; Barbara Gamarekian, *Corcoran, to Foil Dispute, Drops Mapplethorpe Show,* N.Y. TIMES, June 14, 1989.
[53] Gamarekian, *supra* note 52.
[54] 209 F.3d 67 at 85.
[55] New York Magazine, Div. of Primedia Magazines, Inc. v. Metropolitan Transit Authority, 987 F. Supp. 254 (S.D.N.Y. 1997), *aff'd in part, vacat'd in part,* 136 F.2d 123 (2d Cir. 1998), *cert. denied* 525 U.S. 824 (1998). *See also* Benjamin Weiser, *Judge Rejects Giuliani's Attempt to Kill Bus Ads Using His Name,* N.Y. TIMES, Dec. 2, 1997; *Between the Lines: Credit Where It's Due,* N.Y. MAG., Dec. 15, 1997.
[56] Gersh Kuntzman, *City Goes to Court to Have Museum Evicted,* N.Y. POST, Oct. 1, 1999.
[57] Maggie Haberman, *Rudy Shouts It Out with Radio Caller Over Museum Flap,* N.Y. POST, Oct. 9, 1999.
[58] Robert Hardt, Jr., *Rudy Drops Legal Battle with "Dung Art" Museum,* N.Y. POST, Mar. 28, 2000.

As Guido says, *Tunick* began in federal district court as a successful effort by the photographer to stay Police Commissioner Safir from interfering with a photographic shoot after the city refused to issue a permit tolerating naked models; the stay was granted and appealed.

Tunick v. Safir, *certification rejected*. Guido's panel invited the New York Court of Appeals to weigh in and was spurned. Richard C. Wesley, who was at the time on the New York Court of Appeals and would join the Second Circuit in 2003, recalled how the *Tunick* certification potentially threatened the wonderful relationship which had been developing between the New York Court of Appeals and the Second Circuit—particularly between Guido and Chief Judge Kaye.[59] A key difficulty was that Guido not only wanted the Court of Appeals to determine whether Tunick was exempt from criminal prosecution under the statute, but he also added an unbriefed state constitutional argument. Guido's certification also contained the unusual proviso that if it took too long for an answer, the Circuit might prefer for New York to decline the certification—it would "lift the stay of the district court's injunction should the delay entailed by certification lead to conditions that would justify immediate adjudication of the right asserted."[60]

Judge Richard C. Wesley

The New York Court of Appeals therefore delicately approached whether and how to respond to the certification request. Judge Wesley had a "most wonderful memory" of sitting with Judge Howard Levine and Judith Kaye in her chambers:

Judith was bereft, because she knew that we really did not want to answer, for a number of reasons: one, the fact that Guido was going to pull it back if we did not get it done on time; two, there was a very shortened schedule for the answer and

---

[59] Interview with Judge Richard C. Wesley, *supra* note 16.
[60] *Id.*

this was issued late in our court calendar; and lastly, Guido had injected this constitutional argument the parties hadn't briefed, and so the briefs were going to be useless to us. We loved being asked, and we wanted certification to continue; but we knew we did not want to take the case; we didn't know how to say it without the Second Circuit being offended by our saying no. I think that in our response we were able to do that.

Coming as it did early into Guido's judicial career, *Tunick* offers a snapshot of Guido allowing "his academic nature and inquisitiveness to run a little amok."[61] The Court of Appeals declined to answer the certified question. It was an event which was "extraordinarily unusual in this really wonderful relationship between Guido and the Court of Appeals."[62]

Tunick v. Safir *and the construction of legal doctrine.* The *Tunick* case resumed in the Second Circuit, where the stay was dissolved.[63] On its merits, the initial opinion in *Tunick v. Safir* was cited merely weeks after its issuance, when yet another district court judge granted an injunction against the Giuliani administration on First Amendment grounds.[64] Other circuits too refer to *Tunick* when considering overbreadth challenges to municipal ordinances, or in discussing First Amendment protection generally.[65] On certification procedure, *Tunick* has been cited often by the Second Circuit when deciding whether or not to certify.[66]

---

[61] *Id.*
[62] *Id.*
[63] Tunick v. Safir, 209 F.3d. 67 (1999); 94 N.Y.S. 2d 709 (2000); 228 F.3d 135, 136 (2d Cir. 2000) (Calabresi, concurring).
[64] Housing Works, Inc. v. Safir, 101 F. Supp. 2d 163, 164 (S.D.N.Y. 2000) (invalidating a rule limiting the size of groups conducting expressive activity on the steps of City Hall or of groups assembling, quoting Guido's observation that the mayor had catalyzed a "a relentless onslaught of First Amendment litigation").
[65] Schultz v. City of Cumberland, 228 F.3d 831, 849-50 (7th Cir. 2000) (noting that unlike the law in *Tunick*, the challenged ordinance "contains no explicit exception for expression that ... possesses serious artistic, social, or political value"); Entertainment Productions v. Shelby County, 588 F.3d 372, 379 (6th Cir. 2009) (citing *Schultz & Tunick*); Nuxoll ex rel. Nuxoll v. Indian Prairie School Dist. #20, 523 F.3d 668, 669 (7th Cir. 2008) (supporting proposition that loss of First Amendment freedoms, for even minimal periods of time, constitutes irreparable injury).
[66] See Schoenfeld v. New York, 748 F.3d 464, 469-70 (2014) (certifying question to New York Court of Appeals); CFCU Community Credit Union v. Hayward, 552 F.3d 253, 265-66 (2009) (declining to certify); Burlington v. Indemnity Ins. Co. of North America, 346 F.3d 70, 74 n .4 (2003) (discussing reasons a state court may decline certification); Allstate Ins. Co. v. Serio, 261 F.3d 143, 154 (2001) (certifying questions to New York Court of Appeals). City of Goodlett v. Kalishek, 223 F.3d 32, 40-41 (2000) (Feinberg, J., dissenting) (citing *Tunick* to show that state courts are free to decline a certified question should they so choose).

31

The Immigration Law Decisions of an Immigrant

During the 2000s, the immigration law jurisprudence of the U.S. Court of Appeals for the Second Circuit was relatively sympathetic toward immigrants with respect to asylum denials and deportation orders. Statistics about the denial of asylum claims by hearing examiners at the INS in the jurisdiction of the Second Circuit were also more favorable to asylum applicants than in many other places. In later years, asylum denials and deportation orders rose, in both absolute and relative terms, in the Second Circuit and nationwide.

In the Circuit, Guido's jurisprudence—again, generally—encouraged a broader scope for appellate review of denials and called for more stringent standards of evaluation by agencies and lower courts when they rejected claims. In Jin Shui Qiu v. Ashcroft *(2003) (rev'd on other grounds), for instance, Guido raised the standard of evidence necessary for an immigration judge above "clear error." As he reminded others in* Ming Shi Xue v. Bd. of Immigration Appeals, *"[E]ach time we wrongly deny a meritorious asylum application ... we risk condemning an individual to persecution ... [W]e must always remember the toll that is paid if and when we err."*

The most important part of my education, I have said before, is that I am a refugee and an immigrant. One thing this means is that I may look at immigration cases differently from some other judges—because I know some things.

I reject the view that if you lie about one thing, you must be treated as having lied about everything. I have seen people coming from Germany or Italy who were asked, "Were you a Fascist?" Or, "were you a Nazi?" They said, "No," when in fact they had signed or joined one of those groups, because, as a practical matter, *they had to* in order to hold a job. Was that a lie? In a way it was. But does that mean that *they were liars*? Unless they did something more positively Fascist or Nazi, I have tended not to give such evidence of dishonesty much weight.

Something else I know is that when people who have sought refuge go back home to the place that they claim maltreated them terribly, this does not necessarily mean that they are lying about how people had maltreated them there. As I said earlier when we talked about my childhood, my mother's father, who was still in

Fascist Italy, would not let anyone tell my mother that he was dying of cancer because he knew perfectly well that if she had known, she would have taken the first ship and gone back to Italy and might well have been trapped there.

Having lived through certain experiences inevitably informs one's approach to legal situations. In my case, it causes me to appreciate the ways immigrants think and behave.

I know as well that immigrants—along with prisoners—are among those groups needing courts most, because they do not vote, and their rights are often subordinated to other interest groups that legislators care more about. During the time they are not citizens, immigrants cannot vote, and afterward, when they become citizens, they often—for unclear reasons—do not vote. This means that courts should be solicitous when they decide cases that would put immigrants in jeopardy. People who are not represented or were underrepresented when the laws affecting them were made, need courts to protect them— as I explained when I talked about some discrimination law cases.

* * *

The fate of those who are trying to stay in this country will sometimes depend on whether they are so unfortunate as to have their cases decided in a circuit whose law is more hostile than others to them. Soon after I came onto the Court I heard the case of a permanent resident of the United States, named Michael, who had come from Guyana. He served ninety days in prison for a weapons offense, and upon his release, the INS started to deport him.

The case was originally brought in our Circuit because Michael was living here, and at that time—the middle 1990s—one could, as a resident alien, ask for a waiver of one's deportation where you resided. But what the government was doing was transferring people from our Circuit to detention in Louisiana, so that the law that applied to them would be the law of the Fifth Circuit, and not our law.

The claim for a waiver that Michael was making was an open question in the Second Circuit: it had not been decided one way or the other. It was a closed question in the Fifth Circuit. If he was tried by Fifth Circuit law, he would have lost automatically. In the Second Circuit, he stood a good chance of losing, ultimately, but the question was one that was fairly complicated and still open.

When the case came before us, I proposed that we use the All Writs Act of 1789 to prevent the case from being transferred to the Fifth Circuit. We could issue the writ, I said, in aid of our jurisdiction, which is one of the bases for invoking the "All Writs" Act: to protect the jurisdiction of the court. If it went to the Fifth Circuit, we would not have jurisdiction and we could not hear the argument that was being brought before us and was of the first impression in our Circuit.

Dennis Jacobs was on the panel in *Michael* and was absolutely opposed to the idea of using the All Writs statute. The third member of the panel was Fred Parker, who was a new judge, as was I. He was inclined to come out my way, but he was very worried about it, because he was unsure about my proposed resolution.

* * *

Memos flew back and forth between Dennis and me, and they were getting more and more heated. We love each other—and our memos to each other are often very funny, but they can get quite hot, because we are both people who do not mind litigating. We just went after each other and after each other! My problem was that I could find no case whatsoever that had done what I wanted to do. Dennis kept emphasizing this and Fred was worrying about it. I got increasingly worried about it, too, because I knew that I was now a judge. I was not acting as an academic. I thought, "This is right, but if there are no cases, am I really right?"

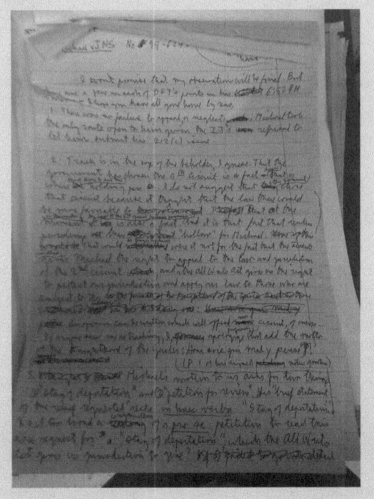

A page from Guido's thoughts on his opinion in Michael v. INS.

Then I found dicta in an opinion by Judge Ed Becker, who was a year ahead of me in law school. He was a moderately conservative, very good Republican appointed judge on the Third Circuit. His was a case that hinged on other issues, in which he ruled against an alien, but in it he said, *If it should ever happen that something like this would come up*—that is, a case where the government was moving the case because the law was more certain in another jurisdiction—*there is the "All Writs" Statute, which we could use to preserve our jurisdiction....* He did not need to employ the All Writs in his case, but if a situation like ours arose, he said, he could do it.

Becker was persuasive on this point, and I was reassured that I was right in my case. This also convinced Fred Parker. Becker's comment was not binding—it was dicta in another jurisdiction—but it told later judges, including us, that an earlier judge who had worried about this problem was inclined to come out the same way as we wanted to. In other words, we should take heart! This is what we did and that is how the case came out.

> *Dennis Jacobs dissented very strongly, but interestingly, later the same year, Jacobs had a strange securities case where the same problem came up. He relied on the majority opinion in* Michael *to use the All Writs statute. And once he had some distance from the* Michael *case, he saw the issue in a different context and he thought, "Hey, you know, that may make sense."*

Michael was one of the earliest cases I heard as a judge, and Becker's dicta shaped the approach I took in many later cases. Congress tightened up the All Writs statute after *Michael*, and any number of things have changed, so that today, this case could not have been decided as it was. But this was an early introduction to the importance of the dicta of a judge who is respected, and the effect that it later can have on you; on a later panel; and ultimately on the law.

* * *

Not long after the attack on the Twin Towers in 2001, President George W. Bush pressed for accelerated resolution of INS deportation proceedings. John Ashcroft became the Attorney General and he announced that the pace at which Immigration Judges were deciding cases, and the resulting backlog in cases, was a disgrace. He told the Board of Immigration Appeals, "If you don't decide these quickly, I will fire you at the BIA. I will also administratively say that you can review decisions of the IJs below as a one-judge review panel, rather than with three judges. I want you to get these cases out now!"

In this new accelerated system, the Board decided most cases summarily, without issuing precedential opinions or setting up rules that would apply to future cases. It just decided individual cases ad hoc. At the hearing level, the IJs were overwhelmed by the amount of work they were given, and some were not particularly able in the first place. Able or not, they made any number of mistakes. Their decisions were appealed in great number to the BIA, which no longer was able to review them with care. Then, they were appealed to us. We were—and are—supposed to pay deference to the findings made by the IJ and BIA, but the BIA was just stamping out decisions. The result was that we were deluged with five thousand immigration asylum cases. The Ninth Circuit was deluged also.

> *Now some people might say, "Why did the cases all come to us?" Politically stupid people said, "Oh, because you are liberal circuits." But in fact, the Seventh Circuit was far more "liberal" in such cases than we were (Posner was being his usual aggressive self, and here on a liberal side.) The reason for the deluge in the Ninth and Second Circuit was quite plain, if you bothered to look a little bit: The IJs in the Second Circuit were considerably more responsive to asylum claims. Applicants looking for asylum would obviously try to get venue there. You might come into the U.S. at New Orleans, but you would find some reason why you had to be tried out in New York or San Francisco, where the more sympathetic IJs were. Applicants hope to win immediately and are not concerned with what might happen in a second round of appeals. That's why we got so many of them.*

Now there were zillions of cases coming from the BIA to which we were supposed to pay deference, even though many of these cases were decided quickly in ways that made deference dubious.

* * *

A number of the immigration opinions I wrote were reviews of Board of Immigration Appeals rulings that had been issued through this process. For instance, without setting up rules governing whether and when delays or continuances should be granted, the BIA would affirm an Immigration Judge's denial of such requests. This would occur, for example, where a citizen had put in a petition to allow a spouse to remain pending investigation of the genuineness of the marriage, or where an alien requested a delay in a deportation to obtain a certification of employment from the Department of Labor. The BIA would affirm the Immigration Judge's decision to deny the request for a continuance summarily, even though other IJs would allow continuances in similar situations.

Another set of cases were those in which an asylum application was deemed sufficiently false so that the applicant would be found to have done something totally improper. The application would then not only be denied, but the person would be prohibited from reapplying for any helpful immigration status of any sort for ten or fifteen years. Some immigration judges were deciding this sort of case harshly; others more leniently. The BIA was affirming them summarily whichever way they came out.

Problems also arose when the question was what to do when an alien's actions in this country would lead to a change in their treatment in their home country.

Somebody would become a Christian while in America, while at the same time, the treatment of Christians in China was becoming much worse than it had been when that person had left. Again, different immigration judges decided such cases differently, and the BIA affirmed inconsistent results, summarily.

The position I took was not to reverse the BIA, but to remand such cases. I did not say, "The continuance should be granted because this is a case which is pretty awful, and here is the better rule." Nor did I say, "This person was pretty dishonest, and we therefore affirm the BIA decision barring him from future immigration benefits." I ruled that we should send these back to the BIA and ask it to think about the issues fully and in a precedential way.

Rather than saying what the result should be and trying to set the standards immediately ourselves, I wanted the BIA, at least in the first instance, to consider the question and set the standard. Except in the most extreme of cases, I wanted the administrators, *in conversation with us*, to make a principled decision (there have not been many extreme cases, by the way, and when they occur, I have diminished their precedential value by saying that they were very extreme cases). Of course, once the BIA had made a precedential opinion, we would get another chance to consider whether that decision was legally correct. There would be a conversation, back and forth.

When I first started using this approach, some colleagues on the bench who were not particularly favorable to asylum claims were saying, "Oh, what the BIA did in a particular case was alright. Why send it back? Just affirm." Conversely, the colleagues who *were* very much pro-immigrants tended to say, "No. What the BIA did was wrong. Reverse it. Write an opinion that will make a better rule, because if we send it back to the BIA, they will come up with standards that are bad."

I instead said, "No, the BIA should be the one that is given the opportunity to set the standards." Maybe I am unduly optimistic, but I think there is a difference when the BIA is acting summarily as one judge under the gun to get things through, and therefore affirming the IJs inconsistently; and when they actually sit down and think about the issues as a three-judge precedential body trying to set standards.

In taking this position, I took advantage of the fact that the Supreme Court had reversed the Ninth Circuit in a couple of cases where that Court had tried to make its own standards rather than remanding to the BIA. As a result, we sent several of these cases back.

Of course, when we did remand, we could, and did, say what our concerns were. In continuance cases, we for instance asked, "Why shouldn't a person have a right to more time?" In this way we got the BIA thinking about it. Conversation is more than just remanding; it is indicating to the other body what is troubling about the situation.

And, you know, the standards the BIA came up with have not been bad! They have been *more* than not bad regarding what is a frivolous claim that would exclude somebody forever. Their standards on continuances have been okay. The standards they have come up with might not be the ones that I would have imposed, but they have been quite reasonable!

On the whole my approach won out—in a very quiet way. It is not something that anybody I know has explored in any depth, but more judges are doing it. I believe that this is just another way of common law judging—dialogue, conversation even—with this, to many, very unpopular agency.

* * *

Dialogue between courts and other institutions flows in two directions. To be productive, it needs to be between parties who show respect for each other. Tell somebody they are a grown-up, and you can talk to them effectively. That is true with respect to the BIA. If you treat the BIA—or any administrative agency—as jerks, which is what Ashcroft in a way did by making their jobs miserable, speeding them up, and threatening them with firing if they moved too slowly, then people are going to behave at a low level and with resentment. Instead, say to them, "Give some thought to these things," or "Consider what are really frivolous applications and what are not, you who see an awful lot of them." The BIA judges might be convinced that most of the appeals are not good; but they are not going to exclude people for fifteen or twenty years because they brought them in their desperation to remain here. If you tell them to think seriously about these questions, they're very likely to do it.

Whether this is an attitude I have of treating other parts of the lawmaking community with respect, or it is a recognition that the one case that gets to the circuit court is the tip of the iceberg, and that many other cases will be decided badly at the agency level unless the agency is encouraged to think systematically about them; or whether apart from the Law, it is just a matter of what is a decent human behavior, it strikes me as the right way for us to conduct ourselves.

There are judges who feel that our job is primarily just settling disputes; that the legal rule that comes out of a dispute is really of little importance. There is an argument between parties. We settle it; and that is it. That is something of a caricature of as distinguished a judge as Michael Boudin. There are other judges for whom the dispute is essentially an excuse for making law, and that making law is what we should do. That is something of a caricature of great judges, like Dick Posner and Steve Reinhardt. If instead you recognize the role of courts like mine, as just being a part of multiple lawmaking institutions, and are always conscious that you are only part of the game, then you understand your job differently from either of the caricatures.

The odd thing is that understanding the job in this way was almost automatic when courts were primarily deciding common law cases. Common law courts decided the case but knew that they were talking to other courts and other agencies—sometimes, but rarely, legislatures—and together with these, slowly making law.

The world has changed, but still, that approach to continually revising the rules step by step and slowly to meet modern needs is one of the things judges are good at; it was not by accident that judges traditionally were selected to do that job. We are still good at it, if we will do it. But we have to recognize whom we talk to, whom we give respect to, whom we ask our respect back from.

* * *

The Right and the Left very rarely look at immigration asylum issues in the same way—but that happened with respect to abortion in China. Both ends of the ideological spectrum agreed that compelled abortion was persecution, and so, in 1994, Congress revised a statute (8 U.S.C. § 1101(a)(42)) providing that forced abortions are per se persecution, which triggered asylum eligibility.

There is a lot to be said for that position. But the practical problem with it was that, on its face, it would grant asylum to almost half the population of China—all the women there who were facing or compelled to have abortions. And in practice, this was not something that was in fact going to be tolerated, politically.

There were a few judges on our court who I think treated the Chinese forced abortion cases differently from others. They were not particularly interested, because for them, abortion was not a real problem, and so they tended to accept any technicalities barring asylum. When it was instead a case of someone who had been or was likely to be tortured for political reasons, they treated the asylum requests far more sympathetically.

This led the INS to develop all kinds of legalistic and technical barriers to the new persecution claims that were being made by Chinese asylum seekers. It also led to investigations to show that these abortion claims were fakes.

The only fact that kept the United States from being completely overwhelmed was that by and large, in societies like China, women do not migrate for economic reasons as frequently as men. That meant that the numbers of women who came claiming abortion protection was more limited, and so the system did not entirely break down.

What is faking? What is not? One of the ways you find faking—when you are looking hard to find it—is to look for inconsistencies, small or large. In the early days, there were cases in which an inconsistency was the date of birth of the children that this applicant already had, because of which abortion had been required. Why? Because in China, or certain parts of China, all children are dated from the first of the year. They come here, and they are told, "No, no, no, that's not the right date. Tell the *real* birth date." So, in a later document, they tell a different date, and ignorant INS people—who did not know about Chinese dating practices—think it is an inconsistency.

This was a mess made worse by the fact that these people had either no lawyers, or worse, horrible lawyers, who were untrained, lying in many cases, cheating in some cases, and missing arguments. These cases were madness—but the madness got worse!

At a certain point, a male made an argument before the BIA that where his wife was to be aborted or sterilized, *he* was persecuted. It is not irrational. Again, both Left and Right seemed to agree, and no one argued against that position. It became the law, which meant that now, all of China could come here, and men do emigrate for economic reasons.

What is more, because of the way the asylum law worked, somebody who came and got asylum did not have to bring his spouse. It became perfectly possible for a bright young Chinese kid who wanted to get to America for economic reasons, to marry somebody, impregnate her twice, so she becomes subject to a forced abortion; take off for America, get asylum, and then divorce that wife, and live happily in Minneapolis, or San Francisco, or wherever, with a new wife. Things like this began to happen, with some regularity.

The Immigration Service then tried to figure out whether those making such forced spousal abortion claims were faking. And of course, it turned out that many were faking. Why? Because if you are a decent person who wants to emigrate, you make up the facts rather than marrying, impregnating, and virtually abandoning a woman.

Troubled by all this, our court asked for argument specifically on the question of whether to treat a husband as being automatically persecuted if his wife was forcibly aborted.

This presented a conflict for me. I tend to be in favor of immigration, but for me, abortion is a very serious issue and mandatory abortion is a manifest evil. In mandatory abortion, it is the state that is acting. Since China had a policy of compelling abortions, my moral view of that is the same as my view about the state imposing the death penalty. As a result, one part of me felt that it is appropriate to grant asylum to those—husband and wife—who suffered from a state policy of forcibly aborting fetuses.

One of the reasons I do not agree with the argument of some Catholics that if you oppose the death penalty, consistency requires that you also oppose allowing abortions, is that in the death penalty, it is the state that is killing people, whereas in abortion it is not. When do you prohibit people from doing things, and when, although you dislike what they are doing, do you not make these acts crimes?

Even apart from whether an abortion is a killing, the question of whether it makes sense to make it criminal is a very different issue. Recognizing that individuals in the United States have a right to abortions is simply not the same thing as state mandated abortions or capital punishment.

Notwithstanding my moral convictions, however, the approach of the statute and its expansion to husbands was counterproductive in every way. It was, in fact, leading to many people actually going out of their way to create abortion situations so that they could come to America. If you think abortion is a bad thing, you certainly wouldn't want to create incentives for people to be forced to have abortions. It was also creating incentives for perjury and placing enormous burdens on the Immigration Service. My conclusion was that there had been a series of mistaken steps in which people thought they were doing the right things, but which led to the creation of a policy that was wrong.

The majority of our Court became the first circuit to say—in the cases that were grouped together as *Shi Liang Lin v. United States DOJ*—"We will *not* follow this decision by the BIA stating that a man is *automatically* eligible for asylum because his spouse was subject to coercive abortion. We will require some actual showing of persecution of the man." The majority opinion went on to deny the petition of one of the asylum seekers who had not asserted in his papers that he himself had been subjected to "coercive family planning." I joined the majority in part but dissented from this conclusion.

I agreed that there was no automatic eligibility for asylum under the statute, but believed that a spouse defending his wife from an abortion might well be beaten up, or himself, be threatened with sterilization. I wanted it to be held specifically that the fact that the person did not argue originally that he was being persecuted directly did not mean that he forfeited this argument.

If you are a man whose wife was aborted, why would you make a claim of personal persecution and have to prove more difficult issues in which you could be found to be lying? The BIA rule was that you had a right to asylum without doing that. A good lawyer would have told you, "No, you are going to get asylum by virtue of her abortion. Don't say anything else." A really good lawyer might have said to his client, "Tell the INS, 'there are other things that happened to me, but I do not need to say them.'" But that wasn't necessary, and asylum seekers rarely have *really* good lawyers.

My partial dissent in *Lin* was not about objecting to the denial of automatic eligibility for asylum; I thought this was essential—and on the whole, this key part of the decision in *Lin* helped to sustain the overall viability of the asylum claims system.

* * *

I recently had a case in which the Immigration Service denied asylum to a person who said he was an anti-Communist in China and fled because of that. The record showed, however, that in China he was a *quiet* anti-Communist. A year after he came here, he became a *very active* anti-Communist. The Immigration Service held that he could not ask for asylum because his activism here was not a "new condition," that his condition had not changed. The Service was taking the position that passively resisting a political system is the same as coming forward and aggressively opposing it.

I said, in open court, "Government, what do you mean, nothing has changed? I can tell you the day, the event, at which my father went from being a quiet anti-Fascist to being somebody who was beaten up and taken to jail. That was a specific event that happened." The question of whether somebody can do something here, which changes their original eligibility, is an interesting question, but the BIA had not reached that question in the case. I said, "I am for sending it back for reconsideration to see whether what he says he did in the United States was true, and whether it would in fact lead to his persecution in China were he deported."

Because of my approach and my decisions, I am sometimes referred to as a judge who is very sympathetic to immigrants. I do not know. It is true that I am constantly drawing on my background, which leads me to listen to people who say they are persecuted in other countries, even though some judges may say that the conditions in those countries are endurable. And I strongly believe that our laws granting asylum to those who have been persecuted were initially passed as a reaction to how badly we sometimes acted in the 1930s when Jews were fleeing Germany.

COMMENTARY

Chapter 31

Michael v. INS. In *Michael*, a native of Guyana and legally a permanent U.S. resident, attempted to challenge a deportation order following a criminal weapons possession charge.[1]

The case was a procedural muddle when it arrived at the Second Circuit: it involved a parade of government bodies, including the Board of Immigration Appeals, the INS, and district courts in both New York (Michael's home state) and Louisiana (where he was transferred by the INS). It also saw several changes of venue and a crucial motion that was lost in the mail. As the case finally reached the Second Circuit, however, the central questions to be decided were straightforward: first, whether Michael could appeal the transfer of his case from New York to Louisiana; and, second, whether a federal appeals court had jurisdiction to grant a temporary stay of deportation while Michael awaited the BIA's decision on his pending motion to reopen deportation proceedings.

The main issue came down to jurisdiction, along two separate dimensions. The first was the basic question of whether the case was to be heard by a New York district court or one in Louisiana. The second was whether, assuming the transfer to Louisiana could not be appealed, the Second Circuit had jurisdiction to consider

---

[1] 48 F.3d 657 (2d Cir. 1995).

a question of a different order—whether Michael could secure a temporary stay of deportation while the proper situation of his case was being worked out—or whether that question itself had to be presented to the Fifth Circuit and not the Second.

Guido ruled that the Second Circuit did not have the power to hear Michael's appeal concerning the transfer from New York to Louisiana. But he ruled that his court *did* have the jurisdiction to stay his deportation—that is, that regardless of how the underlying appeal of his case would come out, Michael would enjoy at least a temporary stay of deportation until BIA ruled on his appeal.[2]

To secure jurisdiction for issuing the stay, Guido invoked the venerable All Writs Act, which, he held, could be used in "extraordinary cases" to preserve the jurisdiction of a court of appeals.[3] He describes in his narrative the path of discovery which led him to invoke the Act to anchor the holding, and the lasting importance of this search through other opinions for encouragement. His primary reference point in *Michael* became dicta in the opinion by Judge Becker in the Third Circuit, which, while obviously not even binding in its own jurisdiction, nevertheless convinced Guido that it would be proper to apply the Act to his case.[4]

Judge Jacobs, who wrote a forceful dissent, conceded that "it is possible that this Court has the raw power to issue this writ," though "every prudential consideration argues against" it. Jacobs regarded Guido's holding as, first and foremost, enablement of blatant forum shopping.[5]

Judge Dennis Jacobs

---

[2] 48 F.3d at 665–66.
[3] 28 U.S.C. § 1651 (originally adopted in 1789).
[4] Reid v. Immigration & Naturalization Serv., 766 F.2d 113 (3d Cir. 1985).
[5] *Id.* at 666 (Jacobs, J., dissenting).

Michael was subsequently cited for the proposition that, in certain circumstances, courts have the power to issue stays.[6] One commentator interpreted Guido's invocation of the All Writs Act favorably as "identifying a new source of jurisdiction" for courts.[7] The particular mechanics that Guido used to preserve the Second Circuit's jurisdiction in this case would likely no longer work; nonetheless, this case assumes importance for Guido because, early in his judicial career, it introduced him to the value of attentively studying "mere" dicta in other opinions and providing analogous discussions for others to reflect upon.[8]

Shi Liang Lin v. U.S. Dept. of Justice. *Shi Liang Lin* took place in the context of China's one-child policy: a thirty-year-long state-imposed population control plan. From its implementation in 1980 until its formal abolition in 2015, the policy used mandatory birth control and involuntary sterilization, forced abortions, and the imposition of heavy fines to prevent women from having more than one child.[9]

The United States law granted asylum to women who could prove that they had undergone forced sterilization or abortion. In *Shi Liang Lin*, the central question was the extent to which such protection would apply to these women's partners—in this particular case, the three petitioners were the boyfriends and fiancé of women victimized by China's family planning policies.

One might think that the policy considerations for including spouses under the scope of refugee protections were clear: forced abortion or sterilization seems, as then-Judge Sotomayor writes in her concurrence, to be a harm "directed as much at the husband as at the wife."[10] But as Guido points out, there was a significant, but less obvious, policy concern in the background: granting automatic refugee status eligibility to the partners of such persecuted women could lead to situations in which men deliberately impregnated, and then abandoned, their partners simply in order to gain asylum. A proper treatment of this issue would need to be sensitive to both sets of concerns.

---

[6] *See* Arevalo v. Ashcroft, 344 F.3d 1, 7 (1st Cir. 2003); Kyei v. I.N.S., 65 F.3d 279, 279 (2d Cir. 1995); Nancy Morawetz, *Detention Decisions and Access to Habeas Corpus for Immigrants Facing Deportation*, 25 B.C. THIRD WORLD L.J. 13, 33 (2005) (citing *Michael* to illustrate that "courts have recognized the power of courts to enter stays where necessary to preserve their jurisdiction.").

[7] Maurice A. Roberts, Immigration and Nationality Decisions in the Federal Courts: The Year in Review, 95–12 *Immigration Briefings* 1. Dec. 1995.

[8] Subsequent to the decision in *Michael*, Congress enacted the Illegal Immigration Reform and Immigrant Responsibility Act of 1996, and the REAL ID Act of 2005, depriving district courts of jurisdiction to hear claims relating to execution of removal orders. *See* Elizabeth Cronin, *When the Deluge Hits and You Never Saw the Storm: Asylum Overload and the Second Circuit*, 59 ADMIN. L. REV. 547, 555 (2007) (citing *Michael* to illustrate that "prior to the enactment of IIRIRA, stays of deportation were automatic," but noting that "this stay is no longer automatic."); De Souza v. Sessions, 2018 U.S. Dist. LEXIS 126462 (D. Conn. July 30, 2018).

[9] China to End One-Child Policy and Allow Two, *BBC* (Oct. 29, 2015), https://www.bbc.com/news/world-asia-34665539; Mara Hvistendahl, Analysis of China's One-Child Policy Sparks Uproar, *Science* (Oct. 18, 2017), http://www.sciencemag.org/news/2017/10/analysis-china-s-one-child-policy-sparks-uproar; Wang Feng et al., Population, Policy, and Politics: How Will History Judge China's One-Child Policy?, *The Population Council Inc.*, http://dragonreport.com/Dragon_Report/Challenges_files/Wang_pp115-129.pdf; Edward Wong, *Reports of Forced Abortions Fuel Push to End Chinese Law*, N.Y. TIMES, July 22, 2012; Why Is China Relaxing Its One-Child Policy?, *The Economist* (Dec. 10, 2013), https://www.economist.com/the-economist-explains/2013/12/10/why-is-china-relaxing-its-one-child-policy.

[10] Shi Liang Lin, 494 F.3d 296, 330 (Sotomayor, J., concurring).

When the case first came to the Second Circuit, the court remanded to the BIA, asking the agency to confirm the scope of refugee protection accorded to partners.[11] The agency's response seemed to suggest that spouses, though not unmarried partners, were to be granted per se presumption of persecution under § 601(a) of the Illegal Immigration Reform and Immigrant Responsibility Act of 1996.

In *Shi Liang Lin,* the majority rejected this position of the BIA, holding that § 601(a) clearly does *not* automatically grant eligibility for refugee status to spouses. Moreover, the majority precluded the possibility of the BIA extending automatic eligibility to spouses under a more general rule: § 1101(a)(42)(A). This was a highly significant decision, explicitly parting ways with ten years of clearly established precedent, and creating a circuit split as to the proper application of § 601(a).

Judges Sotomayor and Katzmann each wrote concurrences that strongly condemned the majority's position. They emphasized the forceful moral considerations against narrowly limiting refugee status to particular individuals, thereby ignoring the concrete harms that the persecution of individuals causes to their loved ones.

Guido's partial dissent, while echoing the moral considerations raised by Judges Sotomayor and Katzmann, parted company from both the majority and the concurrences.

He concluded that they all exceeded the Court's proper authority when it came to interpreting § 1101(a)(42)(A). Guido believed that the majority was correct in finding that § 601(a), as written, did not extend to spouses. But the majority, he wrote, overreached in its broader ruling that § 1101(a)(42)(A) *precludes* the inclusion of spouses.

He believed that the concurrences were right to reject, partially on moral grounds, the idea that § 1101(a)(42)(A) definitively bars extending protection to spouses—but they, too, overreached when they found that § 1101(a)(42)(A) definitively *allows* extending protection to spouses.

Guido maintained that both the majority and the concurrences were wrong to interpret § 1101(a)(42)(A) in the first place—*that was the BIA's job*. And since the BIA's ruling on the subject of § 1101(a)(42)(A) was unclear, the Second Circuit should have asked for further clarification. Instead, both the concurrences and the majority engaged in their own definitive interpretations rather than allowing "the agency [to think] deeply and fully about the matter."[12]

Guido's partial dissent is remarkable in reconciling three very different policy and interpretative concerns within one nuanced holding. By concurring with the majority's judgment in denying per se refugee status to these particular defendants, Guido addresses his concern about individuals deliberately impregnating and abandoning women in order to gain refugee status. At the same time, and unlike the majority, he firmly rejects a position that would definitively *bar* spouses and

---

[11] Shi Liang Lin v. United States DOJ, 416 F.3d 184 (2d Cir. 2005).
[12] *Id.* at 343 (Calabresi, J., dissenting).

other family members from automatic asylum status—here, he asks us to consider a "child who sees his parents tortured and murdered before him by a totalitarian government"; categorically denying eligibility to asylum in such a case would be "manifestly absurd."[13]

Finally, by insisting that the relevant question should have been remanded to the BIA, Guido abides by his essentially consistent interpretive method according to which a court should provide an opportunity, whenever possible, for the relevant expert agency to consider whether its previous ruling was reasoned and proper.

The *Shi Liang Lin* decision has been criticized in the secondary literature, mostly from the perspective that spouses should enjoy automatic asylum eligibility.[14]

Rajah v. Mukasey. This short opinion serves as a companion to *Shi Liang Lin* in revealing Guido's views about jurisdiction, agency competence, giving relevant expert agencies the time and space to make reasoned judgments.

Mohamed Rajah, a native of Morocco, petitioned for a review of an immigration judge's order of removal. The specifics of Rajah's case were knotty, but in brief: he had applied for labor certification that would allow him to remain in the country but did so a full six years after his initial tourist visa had expired. As a result, the processing of his labor certification proceeded in parallel with deportation proceedings initiated on the grounds of overstaying his tourist visa. Due to a variety of logistical complications—first waiting for one lawyer and then for another—Rajah's case before the immigration judge was postponed no less than six times. He thus had received a year and a half of extra granted time—and his labor certification was *still* pending—when the immigration judge finally refused to grant another extension. Rajah appealed to the Second Circuit to determine whether rejecting the continuance was proper.

In line with the judicial methodology he described in *Shi Liang Lin*—that is, encouraging agencies to "think seriously" about the matters in their purview, rather than trampling over their authority—Guido remanded the case to the BIA. On remand, the BIA ultimately ruled against Rajah, holding that "the pendency of a labor certification generally would not be sufficient to grant a continuance in the absence of additional persuasive factors." The case ended unfavorably for this particular defendant, but Guido's opinion in *Rajah* ensured that the decision to grant or deny an extension would issue from "the agency charged with this area of law," and not from an overreach by a higher court.

---

[13] *Id.* at 335.
[14] *See* Katherine F. Riordan, *Immigration Law-Withholding Automatic Asylum for Spouses or Partners of Victims of China's Coercive Family-Planning Policies-Shi Liang Lin v. U.S. Dep't of Justice, 494 F.3d 296 (2007)*, 41 SUFFOLK U. L. REV. 983, 989 (2008) for an interpretation of the case that strongly criticizes the majority opinion, claiming it "failed to recognize" that the relevant statutes were ambiguous, but claiming that the BIA should have "defer[ed] to the BIA's reasonable interpretation" of § 601(a), in contrast to Guido's position that the relevant BIA reading was of § 1101(a)(42)(A). *See* Tamika S. Laldee, *A Proposal for Change in Immigration Policy: Asylum for Traditionally Married Spouses*, 41 CASE W. RES. J. INT'L L. 149, 169 (2009) for a criticism of the *Shi Liang Lin* majority decision, in the context of a policy argument that automatic asylum eligibility should be extended to legally married or cohabitating couples.

Ashcroft's immigration "reforms." Guido describes John Ashcroft's approach to the Board of Immigration Appeals as "making their jobs miserable, speeding them up, and threatening them with firing if they moved too slowly." This succinctly and pithily sums up the Bush administration's stunning overhaul of immigration court procedure.

Arguing that extended delays "encouraged unscrupulous lawyers to file frivolous appeals," Ashcroft imposed strict time limits for the disposition of cases and expanded the number of cases which a single board member could decide. At the time the changes were proposed, Senator Ted Kennedy had described them as "drastic," and said that the proposal would "limi[t] an immigrant's opportunity to be heard."[15]

BIA decisions are appealable to federal circuit courts. Under a new "streamlining" regulation,[16] the BIA made more and more of its decisions without opinion—meaning federal appellate judges were soon swamped with immigration appeals with little understanding of their context. "At least write a couple of pages, three pages," pleaded Second Circuit judge Jon Newman.[17]

Guido does not emphasize another aspect of the "streamlining": Ashcroft also reshaped the political and ideological character of the BIA by reducing the size of the board to eleven members—ostensibly to "streamline," but in fact cashiering the Board members who were most sympathetic to immigrant rights.[18] A board member who was fired described the process as "hack[ing] off all the liberals." It was, in the opinion of immigrants' rights supporters, nothing less than a "purge."[19]

Deaf ears and closed minds? In the narrative, Guido defends his preference for dialogue with the BIA as compared to the direct assertion of the judicial power to reverse outcomes and redraw rules. He persisted notwithstanding the purge.[20] In addition to his general perspective about the proper role for courts, which he has elaborated throughout the narrative, Guido takes the position that the newly reshaped conservative ideological bent of the Board was not something that should have dissuaded him. He maintains that his position was based on a greater likelihood of compliance by the immigration bureaucracy if it was treated with respect; by the "second look" the Second Circuit would have at new BIA rules if they were not redrawn fairly; and by the relatively "not so bad" rules the BIA came up with when required to decide cases fully and with sufficient time.[21]

Critics were not persuaded that continued judicial solicitousness to BIA rulemaking was justified. They argued that the Bush administration had tampered

---

[15] Eric Schmitt, *Justice Dept. Seeks to Change Rules for Deportation Appeals*, N.Y. TIMES, Feb. 1, 2002.

[16] "The BIA's streamlining regulation allows a single member of the BIA to affirm an IJ's decision without opinion. 8 C.F.R. § 1003.1(e)(4)(ii)." Recinos De Leon v. Gonzales, 400 F.3d 1185, 1188 (9th Cir. 2005).

[17] Adam Liptak, *Courts Criticize Judges' Handling of Asylum Cases*, N.Y. TIMES, Dec. 26, 2005.

[18] Attorney General Issues Final Rule Reforming Board of Immigration Appeals Procedures, U.S. Department of Justice, Aug. 23, 2002, available at https://www.justice.gov/archive/opa/pr/2002/August/02_eoir_489.htm.

[19] Ricardo Alonso-Zaldivar & Jonathan Peterson, *5 on Immigration Board Asked to Leave; Critics Call It a "Purge,"* L.A. TIMES, Mar. 12, 2003.

[20] Alonso-Zaldivar & Peterson, *supra* note 19.

[21] See Chapter 30, "Calabresian Complexities and the Value of Dialogue."

with the objectivity and legitimacy of the BIA, a subordinate administrative body, rendering it a revanchist body partially deaf to pro-immigrant voices.[22] As a result, the value of prioritizing dialogue above discipline could be questioned.

Judge Posner's judicial monologues. Given his endorsement of the Bush administration's approach to national security and tight borders, it was not immediately clear that Seventh Circuit judge Richard Posner would be the one to challenge the administration. Indeed, in a critical review of Posner's *Not a Suicide Pact*,[23] law professor David Cole noted that Posner would allow "virtually all of the Bush administration's counterterrorism measures, including coercive interrogation, incommunicado detention, warrantless wiretapping, and ethnic profiling."[24] But Guido is correct that in immigration matters, Posner was harshly critical of the aggressive approach pioneered by Bush and Ashcroft.

Unlike Guido, Judge Posner did not invite conversation. In one opinion, he referenced "the continuing difficulty that the Board [of Immigration Appeals] and the immigration judges are having in giving reasoned explanations for their decisions to deny asylum,"[25] and in another, he identified a "gaping hole in the reasoning of the board and the immigration judge."[26] The sharp tone of these opinions sprang from what he identified as the life-or-death stakes of the proceedings. "The Immigration Court is not small-claims court," Posner wrote forcefully in one dissent. "[M]istaken rejection of an asylum claim can doom the claimant, literally."[27]

Guido believes his efforts to engage the Board of Immigration Appeals in a conversation, rather than overrule it, were bolstered by a series of Supreme Court decisions summarily reversing the Ninth Circuit. Of particular note is *INS v. Ventura*, where the Court chastised the Ninth Circuit for not remanding a decision to the agency and accused the appeals court of "seriously disregard[ing]" the agency's legally mandated role and "independently creat[ing] potentially far-reaching legal precedent."[28]

The plight of immigration judges. During the Trump administration, efforts from the executive branch to influence the immigration court system drew even sharper criticism than before. In 2018, Attorney General Jeff Sessions imposed a quota of seven hundred cases per year on immigration judges, telling them "volume is critical."[29] Sessions also made aggressive use of his authority to reverse decisions of the Board of Immigration Appeals, virtually ensuring that domestic abuse or gang violence could no longer serve as grounds for asylum.[30]

---

[22] Alonso-Zaldivar & Peterson, *supra* note 19.
[23] RICHARD POSNER, NOT A SUICIDE PACT: THE CONSTITUTION IN A TIME OF NATIONAL EMERGENCY (2006).
[24] David Cole, *How to Skip the Constitution*, N.Y. REV. OF BOOKS, Nov. 16, 2006.
[25] Guchshenkov v. Ashcroft, 366 F.3d 554, 556 (7th Cir. 2004).
[26] Kourski v. Ashcroft, 355 F.3d 1038, 1039 (7th Cir. 2004).
[27] Apouviepseakoda v. Gonzales, 474 F.3d 881, 894 (7th Cir. 2007) (Posner, J., dissenting).
[28] INS v. Orlando Ventura 537 U.S. 12, 17 (2002).
[29] Katie Benner, *Immigration Judges Express Fear That Sessions's Policies Will Impede Their Work*, N.Y. TIMES, June 12, 2018.
[30] Matter of A—B—, 27 I&N Dec. 316 (A.G. 2018). *See also* Katie Benner & Caitlin Dickerson, *Sessions Says Domestic and Gang Violence are Not Grounds for Asylum*, N.Y. TIMES, June 11, 2018.

In early 2019, news sources reported that many immigration judges had begun to resign en masse.³¹ One judge told a news source that his retirement was a "direct result of the draconian policies of the Trump Administration, the relegation of [judges] to the status of 'action officers' who deport as many people as possible as soon as possible with only token due process, and blaming [judges] for the immigration crisis caused by decades of neglect and underfunding of the Immigration Courts."³²

Notwithstanding Trump administration pressure on the BIA to diminish the availability of asylum, Guido continued to support having the Bureau express its position in a reasoned way even while identifying and vacating erroneous determinations. *In De Artiga v. Barr*, for example, Guido vacated a BIA decision affirming the denial of protection to a Salvadoran woman who faced terrifying threats to her and her children's lives by a notorious gang.³³ Although Patricia Martinez "testified credibly concerning serious, individualized threats against her and her children"—including an episode in which gang members threatened to kill her pregnant daughter and "cut her child out of her body"—the Immigration Judge denied all forms of relief, citing the absence of physical injuries, and that she fled the country after the first time she had been threatened. The BIA affirmed the IJ's decision.³⁴

Remanding the case for the majority, Guido held that it was an error of law to require waiting "until [the applicants] suffered physical harm or until the threats recurred before they fled."³⁵ Still, Guido emphasized aspects of the case that properly fell under BIA's authority. For instance, he explicitly declined to address whether, for purposes of asylum, families are a cognizable social group; or whether opposition to gangs was a cognizable political opinion.³⁶ Instead, citing that BIA's and his own Court's approaches to these issues are "in a state of flux," Guido deemed it "advisable to forgo any discussions at this time," leaving these issues to BIA.³⁷

---

³¹ Hamed Aleaziz, *Being an Immigration Judge Was Their Dream. Under Trump, it Became Untenable*, BuzzFeed News (Feb. 13, 2019), https://www.buzzfeednews.com/article/hamedaleaziz/immigration-policy-judge-resign-trump.
³² *Id.*
³³ De Artiga v. Barr, 961 F.3d 586 (2020).
³⁴ *Id.* at 589.
³⁵ *Id.* at 591.
³⁶ *Id.*
³⁷ *Id.* at 593.

32

An Egalitarian Believer's First Amendment

Jurists and academics advance competing interpretive frameworks for determining how the First Amendment should be applied to cases. Many of these are clause-specific explorations of the constitutional text, which, for example, prohibit Congress from establishing religion, or abridging freedom of speech. So it is that Justice Holmes reasoned the design of the Free Speech clause was to protect the search for truth through a "competition of ideas"; Alexander Meiklejohn contended that the clause should be more absolute but understood to protect only speech that advances the political process. John Hart Ely prioritized maintaining the integrity of the Constitution's representative system of government. Robert Post emphasized that the clause is about encouraging "discursive democracy."

*The First Amendment also bears holistic consideration. Some believe that regardless of any benefit to society, at the heart of the Amendment is regard for self-realization and individual autonomy. Others—as Professor Frederick Schauer has said it, argue that "the first amendment is a commitment to future generations not to place too much of **their** welfare under **our** control." As Guido has discussed, Justice Black adopted an "absolutist" position, believing that the Amendment's first words, "Congress shall make **no** law . . ." empowered courts to be aggressive in protecting the Amendment's underlying values.*

Guido has not taught or written widely in constitutional law nor offered a unitary view of the First Amendment. In several of his opinions and public addresses, however, he has taken positions about important first amendment questions, such as whether hate speech limits free speech; how to handle conflicts between self-realization and the imperatives of security; what power governments have to restrict the amplification of political power by the expenditure of money; and about how far local governments can go to identify themselves with particular religious traditions. His further reflections on these problems and the common threads in his thinking about them are offered in this chapter.

Very early in my judgeship there was a case, *Giano v. Senkowski*, which involved the First Amendment rights of a prisoner. The prison had a rule that inmates could not get from their wives or girlfriends pictures in which the wife or girlfriend was partly naked. Prison rules, however, did not prohibit the prisoners from getting the scummiest sort of publications. They could get *Hustler*, *Playboy*, etc. When Mr. Giano challenged the rule, the district judge said, "This is a matter of prison discipline, and we're not going to interfere. We must defer."

My problem with this was that I didn't see any link, or any argument even being made, connecting the policy to maintaining prison discipline. I could see that it might help prison discipline if the question was, could this person get this picture and *put it up in his cell*, where another prisoner might comment on it or laugh at it and then there might be a fight over it. I could see that. But the government didn't make this argument. Because the prisoners were allowed to get sexually explicit magazines, the prison could not argue, either, that it did not want these people to become sexually aroused when they could not have ordinary sex. Prisoners' mail was routinely opened and no reason was given why, when a letter with explicit photos came in, they did not tell the prisoner, "Come and look at the photo we have received. You cannot put it up, but you can look and see what your girl has sent you."

I wanted to send the case back down. I did not want to reverse it, because I did not want to take a chance on doing something that might hurt prison discipline. I was conscious of the danger to people who run prisons and aware that I did not know as much as they about disciplinary needs, but I thought that we should ask for more than an ipse dixit. I wanted to say, "Send it back and tell the government to explain to us what the link between the rule and prison discipline was." I wanted for equality reasons to protect the First Amendment rights of those who cannot vote. I wanted, as I always do in First Amendment cases, to look at the facts before deferring to the government.

There is nothing in my dissenting opinion in Giano that sounds as if I was expressing a preference for dialogue. And I was not explicitly thinking in those terms at the time. But if you think about it, I wanted to talk to jailers and say, "Explain to me what your reasoning is that I should defer to."

I wrote to Judges McLaughlin and Jacobs, my colleagues on the panel, saying, "After all, these people are all eventually getting out of prison, and, it is better if they are able to reconnect with their wives or their girlfriends." Why should we do things that take them sexually in a different direction—allowing them to see scurrilous magazines—but not connect to sexuality with their loved ones? It is furthering family values, in a way."

Neither McLaughlin nor Jacobs saw it that way. Joe McLaughlin wrote this funny little opinion in which he talked about romantic *cartes de visite* that soldiers received during the Civil War which, he said, were sufficient for soldiers to "keep green the memory of their beloved."

In our memos back and forth it was Dennis who had come up with this bit of history. I wrote back, "DJ, have you never heard of where the word 'hooker' comes from? That word for prostitute came about because there were so many prostitutes hanging around General Hooker's Union troops during the Civil War! These nice little billets from spouses and girlfriends—that did not show them naked—did not do very much for family values!

There was one aspect of my dissenting opinion that I think irritated them. I said that courts make their most serious mistakes when they take the government's word at face values in situations where if the government's facts are correct, courts must defer. I said that in such cases, they should *not* take the government's word for it, that it is our job to ask the government to explain and only defer if that explanation is believable. And I cited *Korematsu*, and the *Pentagon Papers* case for my position that deference requires courts to ask that those to whom we are deferring put on the table the facts to which we should defer. You know, that is what went wrong in *Korematsu*—Black, and Rutledge, and Frankfurter, and all of the majority—deferred to facts that were fake or nonexistent. Roberts, instead, had it right and asked the right questions.

All of that was perfectly fine. But just as you do not call somebody Hitler every time somebody discriminates, *Korematsu* is such an upsetting case to courts that a judge should not cite it except in a "big deal" case! That is a difference between the Academy and the courts: to the Academy, when you have the best case that stands for a principle, you cite the case. If I had shown my dissent to someone I felt comfortable sharing with, like Jon Newman, for example, before circulating it to my panel, he might very well have said, "Oh, Guido, don't cite that case. You just don't do it. Find another one."

Giano also had something of a political side effect. My dissent was picked up by Senator Orin Hatch during his senatorial campaign, who used it to emphasize the need for Republicans like him to win so that conservative judges could be appointed. He described the case as one in which a dangerous Clinton-appointed judge wanted pornography sent to prisoners. I believe the origin of the attack came about when Hatch asked one of the people on his staff, John Yoo, to look for ways to criticize "liberal judges," and Yoo came up with this case and completely misstated it.

I find it amusing that at the same time, Senator Hatch was apparently saying to Bill Clinton that if there were a vacancy on the Supreme Court, he would be inclined to support me. Another member of Hatch's staff, who was a former student of mine, Mike O'Neill, convinced him that it would be rather nice if Clinton chose somebody like me. He convinced the Senator that "Guido is old, and basically a moderate. He isn't a person you would appoint, but he's better than most that Clinton would choose."

I didn't care about Yoo and the Hatch attack then, but I cared a lot later when Yoo opposed his Boalt Hall colleague, William Fletcher, for a seat on the Ninth Circuit in a way that was indecently wrong.

But apart from all that, *Giano* does reflect the fact that, like it or not, the First Amendment today not only goes beyond Meiklejohn's views and protects not only the free expression of political views, but also intimate personal expressions. It also stands for the proposition that, to an egalitarian, these rights do not evaporate behind the walls of a prison.

* * *

Personal experience has also taught me something about what is perhaps the hardest of First Amendment issues: hate speech. Speaking freely is the essence of being "yourself." But some speech, especially racist and ethnic hate-mongering which appears to represent the views of the State, can make a country uncivilized and lead those who think the State is speaking to fear it. I told you earlier that as children, Paul and I refused to march in a Fascist parade and I got a failing grade in "fascist behavior" as a result. Did others who just watched the parade fear what the State was saying?

At a Labor Day parade in 1998, some firefighters and a police officer from a white section of New York put on Blackface and Afro wigs and rode on a float, which demeaned Black people and what the community would be like if it were to become integrated. The float was called "Black to the Future," and it was decorated with buckets of Kentucky Fried Chicken and had riders, including some of the defendants, tossing pieces of watermelon. Even more outrageously, at least one of the firefighters recreated the dragging death of a Black man who had been murdered not long before in Texas.

This episode became notorious after there was much press coverage, and after a hearing, the two firefighters and a police officer named Locurto were fired. The district court reversed on First Amendment grounds and the city appealed. In the case, *Locurto v. Giuliani*, Locurto claimed that the district court was correct, and that the parade activities were protected free speech. [Sighs]

I wrote the opinion with Jamal Greene—now a distinguished professor at Columbia, as my clerk. I said that the firefighters and police officer did not have a right to appear in Blackface; that they could be fired for doing this. I said the State may feel, and the City may feel, that these people perpetuated the perception of police officers and firefighters as racist, and by doing so, made it much more difficult for them to do the work that they have to do.

Hate speech is one of the hardest issues there is. When Justice Black first heard Hitler speak on the radio he, for a while, doubted the absoluteness of the First Amendment. Then he heard FDR's fireside chats and decided good speech against horrible speech was still the best answer. But it may not be quite that easy. At a seminar of Constitutional Court judges from around the world, at Yale, Aharon Barak, the great Chief Justice of Israel, was arguing that hate speech could not be prohibited. His friend, Dieter Grim of the German Constitutional Court, was taking the opposite position. They went back and forth, and finally Grim put his arm around Barak's shoulder, and said, "you are right from your point of view, but from where I stand, limits must be permitted." Perhaps, in this area, context is all.

An individual may well be able to make statements of belief that are horrible without punishment from the state. And yet, being able to express ones' self in such a way does not mean—and here I am echoing Justice Holmes' discredited dictum—that such a person has a constitutional right to be a policeman.

* * *

I said earlier that my general judicial philosophy is that judges should only rarely try to impose a particular view and make it the law. There was a case, however, in which I simply stated my views because under Supreme Court decisions, I had no power to do more, but in which, perhaps, if I could have, I would have made law. The case is *Ognibene v. Parkes*, which came down in 2011.

Ognibene involved New York laws controlling campaign financing in order to avoid corruption. Because to date the Supreme Court has allowed such laws, my court affirmed the lower court's upholding of the New York laws. But the deeper question was: could states ever control campaign funding even when corruption was *not* involved? And here, the Supreme Court has increasingly said, "No."

Justice Roberts in the *Arizona Free Enterprise* case and again in the *McCutcheon* case said—and was absolutely explicit about it—that a campaign finance law designed to equalize the spending of different candidates, or to "level the playing field," is not a valid ground for campaign finance regulation. He said derisively, "This is important. It's the First Amendment; it's not sports." He said that as a joke, but it is a ridiculous comment, as if the "level playing field" people were talking about was sports rather than something far more important, the democratic process!

What I tried to say in *Ognibene*—in a concurring opinion that maybe is more emotional than some of my other opinions—is that while the Supreme Court is correct that there is a First Amendment right to express political beliefs through money, this cannot mean that the states are prohibited from "leveling the playing field" as to contributions between the very rich and the very poor. This has gotten good reviews from quite a few judges, and other people, because in part, my concurrence says, "You are wrong, Supreme Court, and sooner or later, this view will win."

I had in the back of my mind Justice Black, who said to me, "Ultimately, bad as it was, it did not matter that Andrew Jackson said in Worcester v. Georgia, 'John Marshall has made his decision. Now let him enforce it.' Marshall was right on the law, and while it took a very long time, Marshall's view won out. Similarly, even though people are saying that they will refuse to follow Brown v. Board of Education, it will win out, because it is right. Likewise, the Supreme Court originally said, "Oh, we can't get into One Person, One Vote, later, in Reynolds v. Sims, it did, because it had to, because it was right."

My concurrence in *Ognibene* focuses on two different aspects of the Supreme Court's election law jurisprudence. First, the Supreme Court is correct that people have a First Amendment right to speak politically through money, or through time, or just plain talking. And second—and here is where the Court is wrong—that this right is not simply a right to speak; it is a right to make the intensity of one's political feelings known.

My concurrence begins—to some people shockingly, because some liberals questioned it—with the Gospel. I quote the Bible, where it says Jesus walks into the synagogue and he sees people putting money into the plate. He sees wealthy people putting in gold coins and he sees a widow lady putting in a little copper coin. He says, "Verily I say unto you, she has given much more because she has given from her poverty, while they have given from their excess."

Some people said, "How can you cite the Gospel?" Oddly, some of these are the same people who complain when others try to prohibit us from citing Sharia! Or citing foreign law! Or whatever. I believe a court can cite anything. It is ridiculous! Of course we can cite anything that gets the point across. We are not bound by it but can cite anything that helps get across what we are trying to say.

What is at stake in the First Amendment in campaign contributions, and in the First Amendment in general, is *intensity* of feeling. That is, the First Amendment, when it protects people's ability to speak, is concerned with people expressing their political views, and how strongly they feel.

That means, as I say in *Ognibene*, that I agree with the Supreme Court that spending is a way of expressing one's feeling. For some people, *spending* is the way to express; for other people, *speaking* is the way to express. For other people, time spent working on a campaign and passing papers around is. They are all First Amendment expressions. But what the First Amendment protects is the right, in a democracy, for everyone to express with equal weight equal political feeling.

When and how much a state steps in to protect this ideal is of course very complicated. We are nowhere near making such an equality a constitutional requirement, like One Person, One Vote, but it surely must be wrong to prohibit the states from furthering that ideal. And yet, that is just what the Supreme Court is up to.

When you have no controls on campaign spending, a person who has a billion dollars may care relatively little, and yet be able to drown out the person who cares passionately, because a person who cares passionately can throw everything in and still be drowned out. You can speak so loudly or have so strong a megaphone that I cannot be heard. This gives rise to a state interest—a compelling state interest—in controlling the loudness of a speaker.

Similarly, there is a state interest in making sure that people's intensity of feelings is given equal weight in the political process; that we give as much weight to the Gospel's widow lady wanting to contribute, as to the wealthy.

All this is related to something I have written about in law and economics terms. There are some "goods," and some "bads," in a society that we do not want people to buy on the basis of a prevailing wealth distribution. We call these "merit goods." They include such things as a minimum amount of education, of health, and perhaps, even the right to get transplants. Normally such special goods are limited in number. In wartime, however, when there is rationing, we recognize right away the truth of this and apply it very broadly. During the Second World War, some people could buy broccoli; other people could buy Cheerios, and they could trade off these things. A market was fine in these circumstances, but it was a market in which all started out with the same amount of money or "Green," rationing coupons.

The right to buy participation in the political process is, I believe, a merit good like minimal education and health that a state can further apart from wartime. In that sense, it is very much analogous to the right of "One Person, One Vote"; and that is what my concurring opinion in *Ognibene* says.

How do you extract from the First Amendment this principle, which says the state can keep me from drowning you out by speech or money; the state can aid people's strength of feeling to be expressed as near equally as possible—this "anti-distortion" notion? Here, I think, one comes back to the constitutional theories of John Ely, that the structure and language of the First Amendment and much of the Constitution that courts are there to enforce, is to aid democracy. The Constitution supports as much what I am saying as it supports the One Person, One Vote principle embodied in *Reynolds v. Sims*.

> *The One Person-One Vote principle suggests that there may be a constitutional imperative for this to be done. That is, a Supreme Court might one day take the view that states are not just free to control campaign financing if they wish, but that campaign financing in a democracy must be controlled so that people of wealth and people of poverty can speak with an equally leveled voice. That might become a constitutional requirement, rather than a constitutional permissibility. Wow, isn't that interesting?*

How could a state further the equality I am talking about in *Ognibene* without keeping people from speaking through financial contributions? They can level the playing field by taxing the wealthy contributor and by using some of that money to multiply the contributions of the poor. Thus, a state could say that when a Koch, or a Soros, or a Buffet, gives a million dollars, they are taxed five million. That five million is then given to match and more the contributions of the homeless. If you want to do it, there are a number of ways of doing it.

Ognibene may be one of the most important opinions that I have written. Because we are a constitutional democracy, I believe it will win out eventually. I am kind of glad that the Supreme Court has decided all of these cases on the basis of corruption, and has said, "leveling the playing field is not a goal," because I know that is wrong and I believe that one day, when a different Supreme Court is there, that Court is going to say, "All those old cases were decided on the basis of anti-corruption, because the Court did not think that anti-distortion was a goal. They were wrong, manifestly wrong, and therefore, we now must start all over."

* * *

Interpreting the meaning of the First Amendment with respect to the protection of freedom of religious belief requires a special degree of care. Many cases of this sort come to the Court of Appeals, and the Supreme Court would be wise to be careful about what cases it takes for review and what to say. Here, especially, the Court needs go no further than is needed, and to speak narrowly when it takes a case, and to decide only the particular issue before it. Too often the Supreme Court has taken multi-issue religious freedom cases with difficult facts and then waffled. It jumps in; the decision gets made, in recent years generally by Justice Kennedy, in a way that sounds extreme, but then provides a hatch-door way out. Such waffling is not really helpful.

Cases dealing with the Establishment Clause particularly have been handled in this way. There is no series of decisions, carefully drawn, that can lead you to a solution, which on the whole, works. It is not clear from the Court decisions why some practices are violations and others are not. Pronouncements have been made, using words like "coercion"—that then do not go anywhere or provide enough context or meaning so that lower courts can make sense of them.

In *Town of Greece v. Galloway*, a suit was brought asserting that the regular opening of town meetings by a Christian prayer violated the Establishment Clause. Until the suit was brought, the Town of Greece had uniformly Christian prayers, having asked only religious leaders in the town to do it—and the Town just had Christian churches in it. When the suit was brought, the Town, for a few months, asked a local Wicca and an atheist, and I think on two occasions, Jews, to lead off. Then they went back to their old way. Nonetheless, the district court sided with the Town. I was on the panel when the plaintiffs appealed.

We felt that it was clear enough from their arguments that the Town was trying to define itself as a Christian place. Their defense was odd. They said, "Look, we don't have Jews here. We don't have synagogues here. So why should we go look outside and have Jews lead prayers here?"

That raised the question of at what level is it important to people in a town to be able to identify themselves in a way that excludes others? I held that it depends on many things; even on the way the town describes itself. A neighborhood may be able to say as a neighborhood, "Most of us here are Satmar Hasidic Orthodox Jews. But anyone is welcome here." This announces a preference, but it does not overtly exclude others. But what about another neighborhood which says, "We are NOT a Satmar town." That may well be something that should not be permitted.

Waiting for an interview to start.

The problem we faced in *Galloway v. Town of Greece* was that the Supreme Court had held that there is nothing wrong with opening official government sessions with prayers. That is the law of the land. It is not surprising that they held that, because it has been so, pretty much, from the beginning of the Republic. There have been cases, however, mostly school settings, where the Court said, "You cannot conduct opening prayers, because they involve compulsion or some degree of compulsion."

The position that my panel took was that it was wrong to look to the substance of the prayers in order to decide the question, because doing that would involve courts too much in religion—except to prohibit any prayers that are actually insulting to outsiders. This position got lost in much of the public debate that followed our ruling. We also did not believe that the way out of the difficulty is by having non-denominational prayers, non-sectarian prayers. Judge Harvey Wilkinson had struck down a sectarian prayer in the Fourth Circuit, and said, "You have to have non-denominational prayers," and interestingly, no one really got mad about that. But our panel did not believe one could have truly non-sectarian prayers. My view was that, similar to an opinion by Justice Kennedy, that non-denominational, non-sectarian prayers are just as sectarian as expressly sectarian ones. That is, they are also an establishment of that group of "okay religions," that I call "banquet religions"—the sort that preachers use to open a public banquet. That is an establishment of a different sort—an establishment of what it is okay to say about religion.

The position we took was that a town cannot choose the prayer-giver and the structure of the prayers in a way that says, "This town, this state, this entity, is of a particular religion." The prayer cannot be said in a way that says to insiders and outsiders, "We are a Christian town." Or, "We are a Satmar Hasidic Jewish Town." Or, "We are Judeo-Christian," or "a Judeo-Christian-Muslim" town. What cannot be done is to define the town that way, because that is an establishment of religion.

What *can* a town do? We said it must go out and get enough prayer leaders so that the town does not define itself in one way or another. It is not enough to say, "We ask anybody who has a congregation in the town to do the prayer," because that means the town is defining itself. If a town has only churches and no synagogues, and if you ask only insiders, it defines the town as Christian. And the same is true in reverse if it has only synagogues.

We said that the town needs to make a statement that is inclusive if it is to have regular opening prayers; for instance, it needs to say, "We allow prayer. We allow non-prayer. We allow an atheist to say we should think about goodness apart from God." All of that. If a town does that, the town can also have plenty of Christian prayer leaders, so long as it does not do that in a way that defines the town as Christian or as any particular religion.

> *The answer we favored is like the New Haven Grove Street Cemetery, where in the nineteenth century the planners of the cemetery, wanting it to be open to everybody, made it in a motif that is Egyptian—because at that time, there being no Egyptians in New Haven, it did not define the city. And, just as important, it did not exclude anybody!*

My compromise was one that said, "You can have local establishments, locally defined identities, so long as you do it in a way that also states that your place is open to everybody." I did not say that explicitly, but that is certainly the model I gave them.

This drove the Christian Right crazy because that is specifically what they do not want. It also explains why I got any number of supportive letters from people who are very conservative, but in a sense, outsiders. Gerald Walpin, one of the founders of the Federalist Society, speaking for his conservative foundation, and many others, said this was great, because they did not want a town to define itself as Christian, and they also did not want "Satmar" to do the same.

Town of Greece was appealed to the Supreme Court. The Obama administration filed a brief and caved in. It took the position that prayers were acceptable as long as nonbelievers were not coerced. Stupid. Stupid. Stupid! Obama's Justice Department did not notice that this position meant that so long as there is no "coercion," this would allow towns to define themselves as being of an exclusive faith. This flies in the face of what we want a cohesive society to look like.

* * *

Justice Kennedy wrote the Supreme Court opinion, which reversed us by a vote of five to four. He wrote about an "unbroken tradition of opening sessions with prayer." He rejected the idea that legislative prayers needed to be non-sectarian to stay within that tradition. He said it could violate the Establishment Clause if the prayer insulted nonbelievers or "coerced" them. And in that way, the Supreme Court's opinion in *Town of Greece* continued the long pattern of muddled rulings about the Establishment Clause and set a very low bar for Establishment "coercion."

I do not believe the issue is whether the Town of Greece "coerced" people to hear Christian prayers at town meetings, which was the test that was applied. Coercion is of course forbidden, but it is not enough. I have told you that growing up in New Haven, I never felt *coerced*, but nevertheless, I did not like it when we recited the Lord's Prayer, *Protestant version*, in all these local elementary schools, which were loaded with Irish Catholic kids. The public-school teachers—themselves Irish Catholic—were using the Protestant version of the prayer. I did not feel coerced! It was not coercion—but still I thought, "What the heck is going on?" And I soon realized that what was going on, was saying what was true in those days, "New Haven is a Congregational town."

It is of course true, as Justice Kennedy says, that we have a tradition of opening sessions with prayer. And it is equally true that, at the Framing, it was perfectly acceptable for localities and even states to have an established religion. But the Court's opinion neglected to consider a crucially important historical fact: that the Reconstruction Amendments ended the period when states and localities could identify themselves in that way. Yes, at the Framing, James Madison lost out in his effort to prevent any unit of government from defining itself in religious terms. Religion, much more than anything else, was a controversial issue in the seventeenth and eighteenth centuries! Madison lost because of the profound controversies, and the First Amendment and Non-Establishment, as it was drawn, *did not apply to the states.*

But as in so many things, a majority of the Justices forget or do not understand fully the full consequence of the Civil War and the amendments that followed. What these amendments, and in a sense the War itself, did was to say that all sorts of things that previously only limited the national government, now controlled locally. Many people today forget the Civil War and what it must mean for us.

Actually, Doonesbury has! [laughter] He has focused on the fact that much of what is going on today is a refighting of the Civil War, of the pre-Civil War position. A Sunday cartoon from not long ago is marvelous. A man, who looks like a modern politician of an all-too identifiable sort, is saying, "We've got to stand up for our rights. We've got to stand up for what our nation stood for. We've got a man in Washington who is a dictator, and who is imposing Washington's will on us. We've gone too far. We've got to fight it." And the last cell of the cartoon is captioned, "1861," and a Confederate kid says, "I'm going to go out and fight for you, sir."

While our *Town of Greece* decision was being appealed to the Supreme Court, I gave a lecture at the Danforth Center on Religion and Politics at Washington University in which I went into more detail about this. From the beginning of the Nation, all religions have been treated by the First Amendment as alike under the Law: There are no "we" religions, no "they" religions. Of course, some religious belief systems have been excluded as cults, but almost all religions were protected.

At the beginning, furthermore, secularism was rare, and if anything, it was treated preferentially. There was something resembling "affirmative action" towards secularism because unlike a religion, it needed protection. Oddly, leftovers of that remain today in our much more secular world. For instance, there is a square in front of a courthouse in New York that is called "Tom Paine Square." If it were called "Aquinas Square," or "Maimonides Square," or "Calvin Square," there likely would be a fuss about having a name like that right in front of the courthouse.

As so often happens when you go to a place and teach, I was asked by the local university events office to do an interview. I did that, and talked about my upcoming lecture, with the understanding that the university magazine would publish it, but only at some later point. I am so antediluvian that it never occurred to me that these people would immediately post an edited version of the interview online! The result was that a fiercely partisan National Review *person—someone I know called him "a lizard"—wrote a story reporting that I said it would be too bad if the Supreme Court reversed Town of Greece and claimed that this violated the Canons of Judicial Ethics, because I talked about a case that was* sub judice *(under review).*

At the bottom of his story, the lizard barely noted the important exception for talking about cases that are sub judice for scholarly purposes or legal education; but the lizard said this could not plausibly apply here. Inevitably, some bloggers picked that up, and the whole thing got mentioned in the Washington Post.

People at Washington University called me and asked, "Should we pull it down from the website?" I said, "No, that would be admitting that there was something wrong. There was nothing wrong." I did ask them to state on the website that this interview was in conjunction with a lecture and a scholarly event. This they did.

All this reminds me about one of the frescoes in my family's house across the street from the University of Ferrara. The fresco of Prudence is holding a globe. This was painted a hundred years before Copernicus said that the world was round; and yet nobody got excited—because what was going on, clearly, was just a scholarly, in-house debate. It was when Copernicus went public that people got excited.

> *Today the relationship between the Academy and the World has changed; we blog everything immediately. Many scholars are public intellectuals who talk, right away, to the World. Once again, I am antediluvian. Despite the fact that I am a judge, I never have been a public intellectual. When I teach, I simply teach, and talk to students and other scholars.*

But today, secularism in society is at least as prevalent as religion, which helps to explain and, to some extent, to justify some of the recent decisions of the Court, which have held that you cannot favor secular over religious beliefs, expressions, and activities. Many religious zealots argue that this should be so because we are a "religious" country. They have it backwards! It should be so because we no longer are so totally a religious country that secularism needs special protection.

On the other hand, First Amendment religious values, though, do not give the Religious Right a constitutional right to discriminate. The notion or idea that individuals have a constitutional right to discriminate, which I think Chief Justice Rehnquist believed, has not won out generally; but it returned as a First Amendment right linked to religion: the government infringes on my right to exercise religion when it tells me that I cannot, in the name of religion, discriminate against gays, for instance.

But this does not recognize that the Fourteenth Amendment is subsequent to the First, and it modifies it. The Equal Protection Clause of the Fourteenth Amendment and the Fourteenth Amendment's empowerment of Congress in Section 5 to enforce the Amendment, apply even to the religious imperatives of the First Amendment. The First is so important that any laws limiting it in any way must be read narrowly and carefully—but the power to bar discrimination, and to do so even when that discrimination is based on religious grounds, is there!

* * *

It would be useful if the courts truly recognized that there is something unique about our freedom of faith and of worship; and that these should not be trivialized by loose decisions. Because these freedoms are unique, they can cause all sorts of problems in adjusting them to our other rights. If we are able and willing to face the dilemmas that arise squarely, we can find ways of dealing with the problems, which are workable. It is possible to express moderate views strongly and without being fuzzy or ambiguous.

> *Hugo Black spoke so strongly in one case that I said to him, "Judge, how can you be so sure you're right?" And the judge said, "I'm not sure. I could change my mind tomorrow." I said to him, "Then why are you speaking so strongly?" He said, "I wouldn't want the only people to speak strongly to be those who would never change their minds. I think we, who are open to other views, have to speak strongly about what we believe, and still be open to changing our point of view."*

> One of the funny things about me is I am deeply a liberal, in the sense that I think people can have very different points of view. I am, even more deeply, egalitarian, and I have very profound value commitments. I often make them known.
>
> I just saw a statement by Pope Francis saying that, "Speaking to people about God is not trying to impose a view. It is sharing your joy." What a wonderful statement! You are enjoying your belief.
>
> Is all of this consistent? I do not know. Perhaps it is another instance of what I wrote in *Tragic Choices*—that societies would handle their wrenching social conflicts through institutions that recognize that disagreements are always going to be present.

COMMENTARY

Chapter 32

Giano v. Senkowski. On First Amendment grounds, an incarcerated man challenged a prison policy that banned receipt of nude photographs sent by the inmates' partners; yet commercially produced pornography was accessible to the prisoners. The district court granted the government's motion for summary judgment, and Giano appealed to the Second Circuit. The decision was upheld based on the majority's conclusion that the prison's policy was "rationally related" to a legitimate institutional concern.[1]

Judge McLaughlin's majority opinion, joined by Judge Jacobs, held that a prisoner's First Amendment rights must be consistent "with the legitimate penological objectives of the corrections system"—in other words determined that a prison's institutional objectives impose a limit on a prisoner's constitutional rights. In evaluating whether particular objectives are legitimate, the majority called for "a policy of judicial restraint." It followed established law in adopting the relatively lax standard of "reasonableness" review and placed the burden on the plaintiff to prove that the disputed policy is *un*reasonable.

The majority rejected Giano's argument that there must be actual evidence of a link between the nude photos of partners and an increase in violence. Instead, and "[b]ecause there is ample case law," the court upheld the reasonableness of presuming such a connection, stating that there was no "need for extensive factual 'proof.'" Setting a framework favorable to the defendants, the court found that the government's explanation for the photo ban—that allowing nude photos

---

[1] Giano v. Senkowski, 54 F.3d 1050 (2d Cir. 1995).

of partners would increase the risk of fights among inmates—was "both valid and rational."[2]

In his dissent, Guido pointed to the broader implications of the majority's holding. He argued that the matter of allowing nude photographs in prisons raises broader and deeper questions regarding how to properly exercise deference to the State in evaluating whether a regulation violates the First Amendment.[3]

Guido accepts the well-established principle that the courts must defer to the government's "informed judgments" about how to best manage its institutions. But deference, he writes, should not "lead us automatically to accept unsubstantiated assertions that a prison regulation is 'reasonable.'"[4] In other words, Guido insists that proper deference to the State's judgment requires an actual showing of what that judgment is based on: bald assertions of "reasonableness" are not enough.

Overkill? Giano did raise significant constitutional concerns, but it raised them in circumstances where the injury could be characterized as marginal or de minimis—deprivation of photographs engendering emotional distress—in comparison to the preexisting legal deprivations by the state of the prisoners' physical liberty. Viewed in this light, Guido's references to the momentous, nationally consequential outcomes in the *Pentagon Papers* and *Korematsu* were—although apposite—out of place.

Guido was new as a judge, as he recalls, and—to use a different metaphor—he employed a judicial bazooka when pistols might have been more likely to hit their target. The majority believed it was a simple case resolvable by common sense. It dismissed Guido's reference to *Korematsu* as a "lyric leap."[5] Guido acknowledges that he knew he was taking a risk at the time.

Guido's concerns about undue deference found a more amenable setting later: he addressed them thoroughly in a law review article in the *University of Pennsylvania Journal of Constitutional Law*.[6] There Guido amplifies his position in *Giano*, stating that deference to the State nonetheless requires an adequate judicial inquiry into the reasonableness of an administrative judgment as becoming of an independent judge.[7] As Guido sees it, the *Giano* decision has further political significance: it feeds an accelerating decline of judicial independence. In accepting the government's assessment of "reasonableness" on the basis of a bald assertion, the majority effectively "move[d] the decision from somebody who makes it independently to someone who may have reasons for pleasing the then-majority or the then-power structure in making the rule."[8]

---

[2] *Id.* at 1054.
[3] *Id.* at 1057.
[4] *Id.* at 1057.
[5] *Id.*
[6] Guido Calabresi, *The Current, Subtle—And Not So Subtle—Rejection of an Independent Judiciary*, 4 U. PA. J. CONST. L. 637 (2002).
[7] *Id.*
[8] *Id.*

Senator Orrin Grant Hatch (R-Utah). Hatch targeted Guido as part of his campaign to portray judges appointed by Democrats as "soft on crime." He criticized six Clinton appointees, including Guido, whose judicial records Hatch described to the Senate as, "putting criminals back on the street."[9] Commenting on the *Giano* case in particular, Hatch observed that "Convicted criminals are in prison for a reason: punishment. Sometimes activist judges forget this simple fact."[10] The *Deseret News* reported that Senator Hatch "said Second Circuit Court of Appeals Judge Guido Calabresi argued that prison inmates had a right to possess sexually explicit photos of spouses and girlfriends—but was outvoted by Republican [judicial] appointees."[11]

Hatch's criticism of liberal appointees did not prevent many appointments, but with such criticism, he proved effective in shaping the acceptable pool of nominees, especially nominees to the Supreme Court. "Arguably more than any other senator, Orrin Hatch has helped shape the Supreme Court for decades," said Professor Jonathan Turley of George Washington University—by offering advice about nominees he considered unpalatable or acceptable. Hatch went so far as to lend support to the Supreme Court appointments of both Justice Ginsburg and Justice Breyer, whom he regarded as "highly honest and capable jurists [whose] confirmation would not embarrass the president."[12]

Perhaps Guido's reputation as a dean, his conduct during the Bork and Thomas nominations, or maybe his age, led Hatch to view Guido's temperament favorably notwithstanding his liberal position on criminal justice. At least some of these factors no doubt account for Hatch's subsequent favorable inclination toward Guido as a potential democratic Supreme Court nominee, as Guido describes.

Locurto v. Giuliani. The plaintiffs were a New York City police officer and two firemen who were fired from their jobs for participating in a parade float while wearing Blackface and engaging in mocking stereotypes of Black Americans.[13] Their subsequent lawsuit attracted strange political bedfellows and considerable public attention, due in part to the involvement of Mayor Rudy Giuliani as a defendant.

---

[9] *See* Lee Davidson, Demo Appointees Soft on Crime, Hatch Says, *Deseret News* (Mar. 27, 1996), https://www.deseretnews.com/article/479883/DEMO-APPOINTEES-SOFT-ON-CRIME-HATCH-SAYS.html; Eric Schmitt, *Senator Renews Attack on Clinton's Judges*, N.Y. TIMES, Mar. 26, 1996.

[10] Davidson, *supra* note 9; Schmitt, *supra* note 9.

[11] Davidson, *supra* note 9.

[12] Thomas Burr, Sen. Orrin Hatch's Impact on the Supreme Court, *Salt Lake Tribune* (July 29, 2018), https://www.sltrib.com/news/politics/2018/07/29/sen-orrin-hatchs-impact.

[13] Locurto v. Giuliani, 269 F. Supp. 2d 368 (2d Cir. 2003).

Float re-enacting the dragging death of a Black man, Labor Day, 1998, in Broad Channel, Queens.

Following the parade, Giuliani was strident in calling for the termination of any participating officers, telling the *New York Times* that "any police officer, firefighter or other city employee involved in this disgusting display of racism should be removed from positions of responsibility immediately.... They will be fired."[14]

Giuliani's involvement was perceived by some as opportunistic and political. The African American civil rights advocate and news personality, Rev. Al Sharpton, testified for the white plaintiffs, suggesting that Giuliani was using the incident to ameliorate criticism that had arisen from mishandling a recent "Million Youth March." Norman Siegel, director of the New York Civil Liberties Union and frequent critic of both Giuliani and the NYPD, was Locurto's lead defense attorney. The court's decision was intently anticipated and widely covered in the press.[15]

The plaintiffs argued that their termination constituted retaliation, and unlawfully infringed on their First Amendment rights.[16] The New York District Court held that the firings were retaliatory and political, rather than based on "reasonable concern" for the operation of the police and fire departments.[17]

The Second Circuit reversed.[18] In a majority opinion by Guido, the Court held that the City was acting out of reasonable concern for disruption when it fired the plaintiffs; in particular, that "expressive activities that instantiate or perpetuate a widespread public perception of police officers and firefighters as racist" are disruptive in and of themselves, even if they don't lead to further disruptive acts.[19]

---

[14] Kit R. Roane, *City Suspends Three Workers in Racial Float*, N.Y. TIMES, Sept. 12, 1998.
[15] *Id.*; John Lehmann, *Judge Rips Rudy—Fumes at Firing of Blackface Paraders*, N.Y. POST, Mar. 28, 2003.
[16] Locurto v. Giuliani, *supra* note 13.
[17] *Id.*; Firefighters, Policeman Fired in Racist Float Incident Awarded Back Pay, *Firehouse* (Nov. 30, 2004), https://www.firehouse.com/home/news/10513797/firefighters-policeman-fired-in-racist-float-incident-awarded-back-pay.
[18] Locurto v. Giuliani, 447 F.3d 159 (2d Cir. 2006).
[19] *Id.*

Guido was careful to acknowledge that the plaintiffs' expressive interests in this case were "not insubstantial": no matter how objectionable or offensive the speech in question may be, it falls under the scope of the First Amendment. He identifies commentary about race as "within the core protections of the First Amendment." At its bottom, the case required a fact-dependent balancing of interests between the police and fire department's interests in maintaining the public's trust on one hand, and the plaintiffs' expressive interests on the other.[20] The crucial importance of public trust to a functional police and fire department dictated that the government's interests should prevail: "an individual police officer's or firefighter's right to express his personal opinions must yield to the public good."[21]

Locurto, Guido, and Justice Holmes. Guido concludes the Locurto opinion by reprising Justice Holmes's "widely discredited dictum" that one has "a constitutional right to talk politics, but ... has no constitutional right to be a policeman."[22] The dictum comes from *McAuliffe v. Mayor of New Bedford*, in which the Court limited public employees' First Amendment rights.[23] It held that a "city may impose any reasonable condition upon holding offices within its control," including those that suspend an employee's constitutional right of free speech.[24] *McAuliffe* governed First Amendment doctrine for over half a century, but when the Court entered a phase of expanding due process rights during the 1960s, the "*McAuliffe* gap" of First Amendment protection was closed. In *Pickering v. Board of Education*,[25] the Court officially established that public workers retain considerable First Amendment protection.

Guido points out that the constitutional protections established in *Pickering* are not unconditional. He writes: "One does, of course, have a First Amendment right not to be terminated from public employment in retaliation for engaging in protected speech. But one's right to be a police officer or firefighter who publicly ridicules those he is commissioned to protect and serve is far from absolute. Rather, it is tempered by the reasonable judgment of his employer."[26]

Guido then—and despite referring to Holmes's *McAuliffe* dictum as "discredited"—extracts from the dictum an important component: it isn't that one has no constitutional right to be a policeman, but that one has no constitutional right to be an openly *racist* policeman. In that light, the reader can understand why it is precisely with an echo of Justice Holmes's "discredited dictum" that Guido concludes his commentary on this case.

---

[20] Guido applies the balancing analysis as part of the two-step Pickering test governing the application of the First Amendment to government employees. The test asks, first, whether the employee's speech in question was a "matter of public concern." In this case, the racial speech, repugnant though it may be, was undoubtedly a matter of public concern. The second part of the test balances the employee's interest in expressing a matter of public concern against the government's interest in providing a public service.
[21] *Locurto*, 447 F.3d at 183.
[22] *Id.*
[23] 29 N.E. 517 (Mass. 1892).
[24] *Id.* at 518.
[25] 391 US 563 (1968).
[26] *Locurto*, 447 F.3d at 183.

Jamal Greene. Greene graduated from Harvard in 1999 and Yale Law School in 2005. After clerking for Guido and then Justice John Paul Stevens, he entered the Academy and became the Dwight Professor of Law at Columbia University. His academic scholarship has centered on the nature of constitutional adjudication and, in particular, intentionalist and originalist theories of interpretation.[27]

Ognibene v. Parkes continued. Guido mentioned *Ognibene* in his discussion of behavioral economics in an earlier chapter, but in the context of economic analysis rather than free expression.[28] The plaintiffs challenged a New York City "pay-to-play" rule regulating campaign finance, principally on First Amendment grounds.[29] The law limited contributions from individuals and groups who did business with the City, excluded these contributions from matching with public funds, and prohibited contributions from certain kinds of corporations. Among other claims, the plaintiffs argued that *Citizens United* prohibited "all contribution limits" based on the contributor's identity.

The Second Circuit upheld the District Court's dismissal of the suit. To begin with, it distinguished *Citizens United* as applying only to prevent the regulation of "independent expenditures" based on corporate identity, and not to limit the ability to cap campaign contributions. So while *Citizens United* found restrictions on independent expenditures to violate contributors' right to free speech, that limitation had "no impact on the issues" in *Ognibene,* which concerned only direct campaign contributions.[30]

With that distinction made, the court held that the proper standard for evaluating restrictions on campaign contributions is that they be "closely drawn to address a sufficiently important state interest."[31] The heart of the decision lay in the *kind* of state interest that the court emphasized: namely, "the prevention of actual and perceived corruption." The bulk of the opinion elaborated on how New York City had ample cause to act on its anti-corruption interest, discussing both actual and perceived instances of corruption connected with campaign contributions.

Guido's concurrence. As Guido says, he prefaced his concurrence with a biblical parable, known as "The Widow's Offering." It reads:

> As Jesus looked up, he saw the rich putting their gifts into the temple treasury. He also saw a poor widow put in two very small copper coins. "Truly I tell you," he said, "this poor widow has put in more than all the others. All these people gave their gifts out of their wealth; but she out of her poverty put in all she had to live on."[32]

---

[27] *See, e.g.,* Jamal Greene, *The Supreme Court as a Constitutional Court,* 128 HARV. L. REV. 124 (2016); Jamal Greene, *On the Origins of Originalism,* 88 TEXAS L. REV. 1 (2009).
[28] Ognibene v. Parkes, 671 F.3d 174 (2d Cir. 2011); see Guido's narrative and the commentary in Chapter 29, "The Analytical Reasoning of a Behavioral Economist."
[29] *Ognibene,* 671 F.3d at 179.
[30] *Id.* at 183.
[31] *Id.*
[32] Luke 21:1–4 (New International Version).

Professors Klick and Parisi, who write about law and economics, observe that "there is a great deal of economic intuition in many of the parables," and relate that in this particular one, Jesus recommended measuring generosity according to a scale which values gifts subjectively and relatively.[33] Guido, not dissimilarly, interprets this as a statement about the importance of hearing truth by paying attention to—and making it possible to pay attention to—the relative intensity of expression.[34]

Attacking Supreme Court Doctrine. Guido's concurrence to his own opinion is notable for its explicitly aspirational and idealistic posture. It is not the clarity or the logical consistency of the Supreme Court precedent that Guido condemns; it is the *jurisprudence itself.* The jurisprudence has established, in a series of decisions beginning in 1976 with *Buckley v. Valeo,* that a "level playing field" or "anti-distortion" interest is not a constitutional justification for contribution limits.[35] That is, the Court has had no use for the idea that campaign contributions may be limited for the purpose of curbing significant inequalities in ability to influence political outcome.

Guido makes a moving argument for leveling the playing field because doing so serves two essential First Amendment values. Every individual has a right to make his voice heard, and the right to be heard includes the right to convey the intensity of one's feeling. These interests, he argues, are not served by the Court's recognition of an "anti-corruption" value, which is currently the only acceptable basis for regulating campaign finances. The result, Guido says, amounts to an impoverished understanding of core First Amendment values.[36] Coming from Guido, this rather passionate, resolute condemnation of established Supreme Court jurisprudence—spoken in his capacity as a judge and not as a professor—is remarkable for making it perfectly clear that he thinks the Court has gone off course, and that he knows where it should be headed. The anti-distortion and intensity-leveling principle is "so fundamental that sooner or later it is going to be recognized. Whether this will happen through a constitutional amendment or through changes in Supreme Court doctrine, I do not know. But it will happen."[37] The intrepid prediction is more prophecy than dialogue.

And the prophecy thus far has not come to pass. Subsequent to Guido's concurrence in *Ognibene,* the Supreme Court entrenched its position against the leveling interest in campaign finance regulations. In 2014, it held in *McCutcheon v. FEC* that such limits may only be enacted to prevent "a direct exchange of an official act for money."[38] *McCutcheon* makes clear that Congress may not "regulate contributions

---

[33] Jonathan Klick & Francesco Parisi, *Wealth, Utility, and the Human Dimension,* 1 NYU J.L. & LIBERTY 590, 607–08 (2005).

[34] *Id.*

[35] Buckley v. Valeo, 424 U.S. 1 (1976).

[36] In a similar vein, First Amendment scholar Robert Post argues that "the concept of "corruption" in judicial opinions has now become a "bankrupt construct" and that courts need to develop a new and theoretically defensible framework of analysis." See https://www.scotusblog.com/2014/08/ask-the-author-robert-post-citizens-divided.

[37] Ognibene, 671 F.3d at 201.

[38] 572 U.S. 185.

simply to reduce the amount of money in politics, or to restrict the political participation of some in order to enhance the relative influence of others."[39]

How does one make sense out of all this optimism about the future? Perhaps he takes heart from close votes on the High Court, and academic, political, and popular criticism. The key holdings, including *Buckley*, *Citizens United*, and *McCutcheon*, were each decided by a 5-4 vote and included lengthy and passionate dissents. Justice Ginsburg has stated publicly that if she could pick one case to undo, it would be *Citizens United*.[40]

It should be noted too that in 2016, when Guido recorded his feelings, it seemed as though the tide would turn: presidential candidate Hillary Clinton announced that she would only nominate to the Supreme Court judges who rejected *Citizens United*, and would introduce a constitutional amendment to overturn the decision within her first thirty days in office.[41]

But a conservative Court further entrenched a conservative doctrine of campaign finance. Justice Brett Kavanaugh remarked that "one of the most important sentences in First Amendment history" is *Buckley*'s central rejection of the level playing-field value: "the concept that government may restrict the speech of some elements of our society in order to enhance the relative voice of others is wholly foreign to the First Amendment."[42] It seems unlikely that Guido's prediction will happen anytime soon. But then again, Guido said only that the change *will happen*—not that it will happen soon.[43]

Galloway v. Town of Greece. Guido's holding in *Town of Greece* was based on a holistic analysis of the circumstances of the case, rather than an application of any clearly defined set of tests or rules. "[O]ur inquiry cannot look solely to whether the town's legislative prayer practice contained sectarian references. We must ask, instead, whether the town's practice, viewed in its totality by an ordinary, reasonable observer, conveyed the view that the town favored or disfavored certain religious beliefs."[44] On the basis of this highly fact-specific inquiry, the panel held that the town's prayer practice "must be viewed as an endorsement of a particular religious viewpoint": Christianity.[45] Guido's inquiry centered on whether a particular religion was being favored or disfavored.

---

[39] *Id.* at 185; *see also* Kate Andrias, *Separations of Wealth: Inequality and the Erosion of Checks and Balances*, 18 U. PA. J. CONST. L. 419, 439 (2015); Samuel Issacharoff, *On Political Corruption*, 124 HARV. L. REV. 118, 125–26 (2010).

[40] Amanda Holpuch, Ruth Bader Ginsburg: I Would Overturn Supreme Court's Citizens United Ruling, Guardian (Feb 4., 2015), https://www.theguardian.com/law/2015/feb/04/ruth-bader-ginsburg-supreme-court-citizens-united.

[41] Lawrence Norden, *The U.S. Supreme Court Can Still Take Big Money Out of Politics*, *Atlantic* (Jan. 13, 2016), https://www.theatlantic.com/politics/archive/2016/01/campaign-finance-supreme-court/423567.

[42] Adam Liptak, *How to Tell Where Brett Kavanaugh Stands on Citizens United*, N.Y. TIMES, July 23, 2018.

[43] Reviewing his transcript, Guido later told me that this flaw in the constitutional fabric reminded him of what Justice Black had said to him about the end of racism in America. "He said 'It will not happen until it is as easy for blacks and whites to marry each other as it is now for the Irish and Italians to marry.' He added, 'Guy, It will not happen in my lifetime, and not in yours. But it must and it will happen!'"

[44] Galloway v. Town of Greece, 681 F.3d 20, 29 (2d Cir. 2012).

[45] *Id.* at 30.

The Supreme Court, however, adopted a different line of analysis. It set out "to determine whether the prayer practice in the town of Greece fits within the tradition long followed in Congress and the state legislatures." In addition to this historical aspect of its inquiry, the Court also emphasized the question of coercion: Does the prayer practice "coerce participation by non-adherents"? Finding that the practice in Greece was both consistent with tradition and not coercive, the Supreme Court held that it does not violate the First Amendment and reversed.[46]

Trouble in St. Louis. In the *Religion and Politics* interview that Guido refers to, he made a remarkably accurate prediction of what would happen when the case reached the Court. To begin with, he said that he "would not be surprised if the Supreme Court reversed us."[47] He predicted that *Town of Greece* would be a "hard case for them," and ventured that the Court may be "prepared to hold that self-definition doesn't matter so long as the state action doesn't coerce—which is a position one could take: it doesn't matter if a town defines itself as of this, that, or the other religion, so long as it doesn't coerce."[48] In other words, Guido predicted that the Supreme Court "may go on a coercion/non coercion ground"—exactly the position that the Supreme Court ultimately took. Finally, Guido correctly guessed that Justice Breyer would be "closest to our point of view." In fact, Breyer began his dissent by stating that the opinion's "conclusion and ... reasoning are convincing."[49]

An additional remarkable aspect of *Town of Greece* is its foreshadow of First Amendment issues that would soon loom large. Guido articulates these central questions clearly in the interview:

> After all, while the nation may not define itself as Judeo-Christian, and a state may not any longer define itself as Congregational, an individual or a church certainly has the right to define itself in [that] way. But, to what extent can an organization: an individual, a church itself, a church-related corporation or a corporation which is owned by individuals ... define itself in ways that exclude others, that—in effect—discriminate against them?[50]

The ability of an individual or corporation to self-define in a way that excludes or discriminates—particularly on religious grounds—would come up dramatically in a different First Amendment context: the free speech *Masterpiece Cakeshop* decision, in which the Supreme Court held that it is constitutional for a baker to refuse to bake a wedding cake for a gay couple.[51]

---

[46] Marie Griffith, The Establishment Clause: An Interview with Judge Guido Calabresi, *Religion & Pol.* (Mar. 27, 2014), https://religionandpolitics.org/2014/03/27/the-establishment-clause-an-interview-with-judge-guido-calabresi/.
[47] *Id.*
[48] *Id.*
[49] Town of Greece v. Galloway, 572 U.S. 565, 611 (2014) (Breyer, J., dissenting).
[50] Griffith, *supra* note 46.
[51] Masterpiece Cakeshop, Ltd. v. Colo. Civil Rights Comm'n, 138 S. Ct. 1719 (2018).

Speaking at the Danforth Center for Religion and Politics at Washington University in St. Louis.

Attacked in the National Review. Guido's *Religion and Politics* interview appeared in the *National Review* under the title, "Judge Calabresi's Flagrant Ethical Violation." The article argued that Guido violated the Code of Conduct for United States Judges, according to which "A judge should not make public comment on the merits of a matter pending or impending in any court."[52]

> Despite the fact that the case remains pending, Second Circuit judge Guido Calabresi, who wrote the opinion under review, has somehow seen fit to offer extensive public comments—in the form of an edited interview—about the case. Among other things, Calabresi seeks to defend his ruling (including by emphasizing the ideological diversity of the panel), saying that it "would be too bad" if the Court reverses it, identifies what he thinks is the "closest question in our case," and rejects the notion of a "non-sectarian prayer."[53]

The *National Review* article finished with a brief disclaimer, marked off by an asterisk, noting that there is an exception to the rule for "scholarly presentations made for purposes of legal education." Indeed, and in fact, the published *Religion and Politics* interview had explicitly stated that "The lecture and interview were part of the academic program of the John C. Danforth Center, and were both made for purposes of legal education."[54] But the author of the piece claimed not to see "any

---

[52] Ed Whelan, Judge Calabresi's Flagrant Ethical Violation, *Nat'l Rev.* (Mar. 31, 2014), https://www.nationalreview.com/bench-memos/judge-calabresis-flagrant-ethical-violation-ed-whelan.
[53] *Id.*
[54] Griffith, *supra* note 46.

plausible argument" that Guido's interview fell within any of these exceptions.[55] The story was eventually picked up in the *Washington Post* where his comments were deemed a violation, but a "relatively minor" one.[56]

The Doonesbury cartoon Guido refers to, revealing the enduring appeal of *antebellum* Confederate arguments in support of bigotry, appeared in many newspapers.[57]

"Time to Take a Stand," *Doonesbury*, Nov. 10, 2013.

---

[55] Whelan, *supra* note 52.
[56] Jonathan H. Adler, *Did Judge Calabresi Violate the Judicial Code of Conduct?*, WASH. POST, Apr. 3, 2014.
[57] Sunday's Doonesbury—Dark Days, Democratic Underground (Nov. 10, 2013), https://www.democratic underground.com/10024010269.

33

Craft, Independence, and Ideology

Guido's craft is the natural outgrowth of education in norms of his profession and a career in the Academy studying opinions good and bad. His attention to precedent and minor details of the legal process reflects a generational response to clashes between the Legal Realists, the Formalists, and the Process Scholars—where craft could mediate between formalist intellectuality, procedural neutrality, and realist subjectivity.

His generation appreciated Karl Llewellyn's 1960 book The Common Law Tradition, *which extolled appellate craftspersonship as a judicial responsibility and hallmark of common law adjudication.*

Professor Anthony Kronman echoed Lewellyn, writing more recently that "no matter how many choices the rules leave open, a judge ... will be guided in his deliberations by what might be called the ethos of his office, by a certain ideal ... and by the habits that a devotion to this ideal and long experience in attempting to achieve it tend to instill."

A related view relies on craft to constrain activism and guarantee prudence, while others have concentrated on craft as the mark of success at a trade. Professor Brett Scharff, for example, claims that adjudication "is neither an art nor a science. It is a craft like carpentry, pottery, angling, or quilt making..."

For Guido craft is generally crucial, not as an imposition of judicial restraint nor an end in itself, but as an essential part of finding and palatably delivering the right result—to colleagues, to the professional bar, to superior courts, and to the Academy. A well crafted opinion—especially one faithful to procedure and precedent—can make inevitably tragic choices tolerable and are the best way to frame dialogue.

These perspectives unfold as he illustrates his craft in cases that required understanding of procedural rules, ethical responsibilities, and the difference between ideology and judicial duty. He also offers a perspective about judicial independence and the perception of nonpartisanship. Craftsmanship can fall down even in the biggest cases and notwithstanding the work of hundreds of capable lawyers from the best law firms spending years and sparing no time or expense. Blunders can happen, and one did in Squibb v. Accident Ins. et. al.

Squibb is a very large case that was brought against makers of diethylstilbestrol by grandchildren of the pregnant women who took it. Taking DES, tragically, resulted in cancer in their daughters, and also in their daughters' offspring, their grandchildren.

Cases arising from the sale of DES formed the basis for a California court creating, for the first time in the United States, "statistical causation." Plaintiffs, instead of having to prove "more probably than not" that a particular defendant was the cause—which in this case they couldn't possibly do, since the drug had been sold by varying producers to their long-gone parents—were allowed to recover from manufacturers according to their share of the market. This was relatively easy to prove, because 100 percent of these cancers were due to this drug. What does one do when it is 80 percent, 90 percent, or whatever, or even when the plaintiff's own behavior is partly responsible? That is harder, but all these complications came afterwards. In the original case, *Sindell*, California said that market share was all plaintiffs needed to show.

> *The California Supreme Court did not know—although I did—that in an amazing pollution case, Japan had, about ten years before, done the same thing. I learned this while I was lecturing in Japan. I had said that it seemed to me that in the future, we might have situations where we should permit a showing of statistical causation rather than of individual causation.*
>
> *A man named Morishima—who later became my student—was listening to my talk and got all excited. He came up to me and said, "We have a case. It's going to come down tomorrow, and I have been arguing it. It is a horrible case, in which lots of people died because of pollution by various companies. No one knows which one did it, and so we argued that they had to go to statistical cause." I said, "How do you know it's going to come down tomorrow?" He said, "Because the judge, a very distinguished trial judge, has been holding the case, and he retires tomorrow evening. Obviously, he's going to issue his decision before he retires."*
>
> *Indeed, the next day the case came down, establishing statistical causation in the face of a statute which required proof of individual causation more probably than not. I said to Morishima, "That's a wonderful opinion. Of course, the defendants will appeal it because it flies in the face of the statute." He looked at me and said, "No. Here is a tragic occurrence in which people have died. A great judge waits until he retires to issue an opinion, and does this, which is obviously pushing the envelope, but Just. They couldn't appeal. They'd lose face."*
>
> *I said, "Really?" But they didn't appeal, and Japan changed the law to allow, in limited circumstances, what this judge did!*

So, California, on its own, though, established statistical causation. Many other jurisdictions followed it.

At the point the *Squibb* case reached me, liability to the plaintiffs had been established. The fight was essentially among insurance companies—any number of them. They had been litigating among themselves as to who owed what for something like eighteen years. In other words, the appeal was a fight among the insurance companies over which of them was liable, to whom, for what, and up to which amount.

One of the insurance companies was *Lloyd's of London*. And *Lloyd's* was not, at this time, a true "company." It was, and perhaps still is, a series of individual underwriters. Originally, those underwriters were almost exclusively wealthy citizens of the United Kingdom.

The beginning of Lloyd's was something like this. Somebody in a bar, pub or whatever would announce—often in writing, "A ship is going out. I am insuring them. Which of you want to join me in doing that?" They would draw a line under the advertisement, and people would write their name below that line. That is where the term "underwriters" came from.

During the 1980s *Lloyd's* did not behave well, and it got into terrible financial trouble. Some of the underwriters lost everything. To stay in business, what the *Lloyd's* people, at one point, did, was to expand and to invite people from the United States to be underwriters.

Well, what that meant in the *Squibb* insurance litigation was, that some U.S. underwriters from Lloyd's were citizens of the same states as their adversaries. As a result, it could not be said that there was total diversity between the plaintiffs and defendants. And yet, the case could be and was tried in federal court only because of diversity jurisdiction—and that required *total* diversity.

What had happened was that the original [case] was transferred from the District of Columbia, and the very good Southern District judge, [Broderick], when the case came on—remember that this case had been going on for years and years—assumed that all jurisdictional issues had been decided by the first judge, as is normally done. Accordingly, he assumed that diversity jurisdiction had been established. The case went back and forth in litigation, Judge Broderick died, another Judge, Martin, took it over, and finally it came to my panel.

I looked at the record and said, "We have a real problem of jurisdiction, because I don't think diversity has been established." The presiding judge, Dennis Jacobs, agreed with me that we should ask the parties to argue jurisdiction, and that is what we did.

You have never seen so many angry lawyers!

I mean, so many of the top Boston, Washington, and New York firms, representing different insurance companies, were there; and not a one of them had focused on this. They were fit to be tied! I remember that they kept saying, "But we've been in litigation for eighteen years!" What they were *not* saying was, "Our *clients* will be fit to be tied, because there has been a judgment on liability and now it looks as though the question will have to be re-litigated from the bottom up." They would have had to start the suit again in state court, from the beginning in a state court! It would have been at an administrative cost of gigantic proportions!

They said to us, "All of us agreed that there should be jurisdiction." I said, "I know all of you agree—but you know perfectly well that that is not enough. We are bound to see for ourselves if there is diversity jurisdiction. Your agreement is beside the point." What I did not say was, "What you're really angry about is that your clients will say, 'Well, why didn't you spot this? We've been paying you huge amounts of money for nearly two decades! Why didn't you see that and avoid having to go back and start the whole litigation again?'"

This army of lawyers came up with an assortment of theories to save jurisdiction which just did not work. One—which was plausible though not very strong, and which could have gone their way—unfortunately had been rejected by Judge Easterbrook in an analogous case in the Seventh Circuit. When they presented this proposal, I remember saying to them, "This, of all the theories that you have proposed, *is* plausible, and one is tempted to find a way of having jurisdiction. But... do you really want us to do something that is going to create a conflict with another Circuit? The case will go up to the Supreme Court, after which you might have to start all over again, Lord knows how many years from now."

Then I came up with a way to help them. I suggested sending it back to the district court but in a way that might avoid starting from scratch. I said, "As of now, we cannot say that there is jurisdiction. But if the district court permits you to drop all but one of the *Lloyd's* parties and retain one Lloyd's underwriter who is diverse—if there is such a person—then there would be diversity jurisdiction. For this we would have to send it back to the district court to find out if there is such a person.

They said, "But what happens to *Lloyd's* liability as a whole? Because you know, all of Lloyd's underwriters have to be liable." I said, "There is a contract, is there not, among all the *Lloyd's* people that they will contribute to anyone who is held responsible. One person cannot possibly bear all of Lloyd's' share. Doing it the way I have suggested would mean that the district court might find that the other *Lloyd's* underwriters were not, because of this agreement, necessary parties. The fact that there may be people liable by contract does not defeat diversity; so, it may be that you can go back and create diversity. Then you can go back and create diversity, *nunc pro tunc* ("now for then"). We are allowed to establish diversity jurisdiction retroactively." I had found a Supreme Court case which allowed us to do that. I said, finally, "It might just work."

Discussing *E.R. Squibb & Sons*

When they saw that there was a way, they calmed down. And that is essentially what took place. We sent the case back down, where the district court judge, a lovely judge, Judge Martin, said, "I understand what is needed. I have a roadmap." [laughter]

The case came back to us not that long after that. We were then able to decide, on the merits, which insurance companies were required to pay what part of the claims. I was happy to remain on the case because the ultimate merits did interest me a great deal. And we were justified in retaining it because before we had found the jurisdictional problem, we had done a huge amount of work sorting out the merits. As a matter of time-saving and judicial administration for other judges, it made sense for us to keep it. Where a case must be sent back and the panel that sent it back has not invested that much time, though, I think it is "grabby" to keep a case simply because one likes it.

* * *

There are other times when you simply cannot stay on a case, as much as you might want to. In 2000 there was a case, *In Re Holocaust Victim Assets Litigation, Weisshaus v. Swiss Bankers Association*, which had involved as one of the defendants a great Italian insurance company named *Assicurazioni Generali*, a company which originally had been owned primarily by Italian Jews. Among the people who were very much involved in that insurance company in a high management position was a man named *Orefice*: which in English would be "Goldsmith" and in German, "Goldschmidt." Mr. Orefice came from a fine Venetian Jewish family, probably Ashkenazi. I told you before about Mr. Orefice and his family.

After the Italian Racial Laws were passed, this insurance company *Assicurazioni Generali* was taken over by the Fascists. The Jewish owners and with them the Orefices were kicked out. But the company continued to have as insureds many Jewish clients primarily in Eastern Europe, where any number of Jews had taken out policies because of its Jewish ownership.

Associcurazioni Generali building, Trieste

Now, more than half a century later, the claim by the large group of plaintiffs was that the Fascists who had taken it over then did not pay insurance benefits to survivors after insured Jewish people were taken away to the camps, to their deaths or had simply fled and subsequently died. The legal issues were extraordinarily interesting.

I did not believe that my family was ever involved with the *Generali* company because none of us was ever in the insurance business. Nor did I believe that my family had insured with *Generali*. When I had read the record, I did notice that among the people who were claimants were actually Marina and Paola, the daughters of "Madame Orefice" whom I have told you about. They had been friends, but this was not enough in itself for me to recuse myself from the litigation.

At the argument, however, it appeared that among the people whom the plaintiffs were claiming to represent were many Italian Jews and Italian anti-Fascists who had in some ways been injured by the defendant companies' non-payments. I asked from the bench, "Are you saying that the group of injured people includes any Italian Jews and anti-fascists who had insurance policies with *Generali*?" They said "Yes."

When I had originally read the papers, there seemed to be no need for me to recuse myself. The plaintiffs seemed to be mainly Eastern Europeans and a few specified Italians. But once it was stated that Italian anti-Fascists and Italian Jews were also involved, it was different. I did not know for sure that no members of my family had a claim, and the link between this suit and my own family had become strong enough that it just did not seem right to me to rule on the case.

I abruptly said, "I am recused," and immediately walked off the bench. Both sides looked at me and toward the bench, as if to ask, "What's going on?"

I remember that I sort of made a gesture of regret as I left the courtroom. It was fairly dramatic. But what else was one to do?

This left two judges, Judges Cabranes and Pooler, to decide the case as a two-judge panel. Two-judge panels happen, actually, not that infrequently. One gets close to argument and finds that some party one did not know of actually has links to you, and you step down. For that reason, there is a provision in the rules that allows you to decide it as a two-judge court. It is always unpleasant. If it really happens at the last minute, then it is probably better to go on, and have two judges decide it if they are on the same page. If they disagree then there has to be a re-argument, and if the two remaining judges have a sense that that might happen, it is better to put the case off.

This can happen when a judge dies. Then if that judge had written the opinion the two remaining judges will often publish it as a "per curiam," but say that it had really been written by their deceased colleague. More cheerfully, something like it happened when Sonia Sotomayor went to the Supreme Court. There were any number of cases that she had sat on which ultimately were decided by just two judges.

Recusals are complicated matters. When one has a financial interest in a case, recusal is mandatory. But there are other situations where recusal is not required and yet a judge feels that it would just not look right if he or she heard the case. I recused myself in a case in which I had some financial dealings with one of the lawyers; and in another case, which involved the constitutionality of the "Don't Ask, Don't Tell" rule that then governed the status of gays in the military. I did this because when I was dean I had co-signed, with many other deans, a letter stating that a previous rule, barring gays from the military altogether, was unconstitutional. In neither case was recusal required, and some of my colleagues told me that I was wrong in recusing myself, while others said I was correct. Their views on recusal had nothing to do with whether they agreed with me or not on the likely merits of the cases.

* * *

More interesting is the question of whether a judge ought to recuse because people have criticized the judge's handling of analogous situations, or even have threatened to impeach the judge because of such prior cases. These raise directly the question of judicial independence.

This happened to judge Harold Baer, who decided a case against the police which led to enormous criticism and seemingly serious threats of impeachment. At a later stage, the case returned to Judge Baer, and the defense moved for the judge to recuse himself, saying, "since this guy was threatened with impeachment when he decided in my favor, how can he decide this case fairly, now?"

Justice Baer did not recuse himself and did rule against the defendant. On appeal of the recusal motion to the U.S. Court of Appeals, I wrote an opinion which said that he did not need to recuse himself. It discussed independence, recusal, and the danger of allowing attacks on a judge to create pressure for recusal. Requiring recusal, I wrote, would invite people to attack judges simply to get them to recuse themselves. Again, the line between when a judge chooses to recuse is a fine one.

It is not pleasant to be insulted [by the public or your peers]. In general, if we are attacked, there's nothing we can do about it. We cannot fight back and say some things [in our defense]. It used to be that the organized bar would just regularly step in and say, "Don't do that. Don't do that, Senator. If you do that, you're—" They don't do that anymore. I don't know why.

Being insulted may affect us. On the other hand, it may affect a judge in the opposite way, as it did the southern segregationist judges that President Kennedy put in when the far segregationist Right attacked them for not doing more to block integration. (They were doing all they legally could.) They got mad and became more like the judges they should have been.

US v. Bayless led to my thinking more about judicial independence, and about the freedom of judges to exercise their craft. It gave rise to a lecture that I gave at the University of Pennsylvania, which became an important article about these topics. In it, I recalled a conversation I had with Justice Black during my clerkship about an article William Rehnquist had written in *U.S. News & World Report*, in 1957. The article—which he had written shortly after he clerked, and disowned parts of later when he was a judge—said that clerks were dangerous left-wing influences on the Court and should be confirmed by the Senate.

I said to the Judge, "Judge, what do you think of that?" The Judge looked at me, twinkled and said, "Oh, no. Oh, no. I'd never—I'd never allow that. I'd never allow that. I was a Senator! I know the kind of questions we would ask! Why, we'd ask young men [*sic*] about their sex lives. Oh, no."

I said, "But Judge, what would you do?" He looked at me and said, "Well, I guess I would have to do without law clerks!" [laughter] Then Black smiled and said, "My opinions would be less learned, but they surely would be shorter." [laughter]

I felt, of course, awful, just stupid, because I knew this guy could do everything on his own. Black then turned serious and said, "Guy, there's actually something very important here. The reason that judges, like me, are independent, does not have anything to do with the fact that we are here for life. We could be here for fourteen years, or nineteen years, the way administrative agency people are." Which is interesting, in view of the current discussion by people like Akhil Amar and Steven Calabresi about not having judges be there for life.

"It isn't being here for life that matters," he said. "What it is, is that I can do my job without relying on anybody else *financially*. If they closed down the Court, I could hold court on the mall. If they closed down the library, I could use the library of any law school." Today, of course, with computers, even more so. "My salary is fixed. It is protected by the Constitution. I am independent."

"Contrast that with administrative agencies, where to do the job they must do, they need large staffs and finance. That makes them automatically dependent on Congress. They need to deal with the Senate, with the Senate committee that deals with them, and not just the majority chairman, but the ranking minority member, in order to do their job. Now, this may be good or bad if you want people to be dependent; but it is the difference between judges who can just do what they want, what they think right under the law; and agencies which must be politically responsive."

He then said, "Beware of anyone who, supposedly wanting to make life easier for judges, starts to give judges all sorts of help—benefits, extra things, which can be taken away and so on, because that will undercut independence."

For this reason, I worry about what Chief Justice Warren Burger and others have done in building up the Administrative Office of the Court. Supposedly it helps judges, but it tends to make us more financially dependent than we otherwise would be. In that way, Burger was being anything but conservative. He thought of himself as conservative, but he didn't know what he was conserving.

Basically, we federal judges are still independent, financially. The recent decision that our judicial salaries now must keep up with inflation will help this, because low salaries were becoming a serious disincentive, for some, to continue in a federal judgeship.

But concerns about money still can affect us perniciously. Soon after I came on the court, I wrote an opinion in which I used a phrase that was unnecessarily rude to Congress— something nasty, snotty, in describing what Congress had done. A senior judge, a judge who had been there a long time, quite properly said to me, "Guido, don't put that in. It's the kind of thing an academic does in discussing other academics, or Congress, but there's no reason for judges to do anything like that. We really shouldn't." And he was quite right.

But then he went on, and said, "And besides, they hold the purse strings." I took the phrase out because it shouldn't have been there, but not because of any financial concern. I did it because this had been me still writing as an academic, and not writing as a judge. But the fact that the other Judge was conscious of financial concerns suggested some real danger to me. I heard Justice Black's voice then and I hear it now.

What about the danger of impeachment of a federal judge because of his politics? In the lecture I gave at the University of Pennsylvania, I said that nobody should worry seriously about that. It's just too difficult. Ever since the early 1800s when Judge Samuel Chase, after an impeachment trial, was not removed, notwithstanding his obnoxious manner, his drinking and his political biases, impeachment for this kind of thing is not really a danger. People will bray about it, but it is not a real threat.

What is instead a very significant limitation on judicial independence today is the tendency increasingly and systematically to promote people—to take Magistrate Judges and make them District Judges; to take District Judges and make them Court of Appeal judges; to take Court of Appeals judges and put them on the Supreme Court. Because while people may not worry about being kicked out, they do like the idea of being advanced. There are advantages in having some promotions of this sort, but it should not be the dominant way in which these positions are filled.

A system of promotions is very dangerous if it becomes routine because you will see people who want to go to the next, higher level perhaps being motivated to decide cases in ways that might help get them there.

Do you remember Father Drinan, the Jesuit congressman who then had to leave Congress because the then Pope required Priests to leave politics? I was telling him about my concern. He smiled at me, and he said, putting on a fake Irish accent, "Sure'n we have the same thing in the Church. We call it 'scarlet fever,' the desire to become a cardinal, who wears scarlet!" [Laughs] Dangerous.

This goes even beyond appointments with the lower courts. While it is absurd for people to worry about going to the Supreme Court, given the improbability and the countless variables involved, I have seen too many people, very good judges, who, when some journalist somewhere, says, 'Ah, that person might go to the Supreme Court,' start to dance. There is a notable number of people who do and did. Then, when they were no longer really in contention, became better judges for it. I hope I never did.

Not everybody. Sonia, to her credit, never paid any attention to that. It is one of the things that makes Sonia so remarkable. She did what she wanted to do, what she thought was right, and that's it. It's greatly to her credit that she never trimmed her sails. One cannot say the same of all appointments.

To me, however, the greatest danger to judicial independence is something else. As I wrote in the *Pennsylvania* piece, it is the tendency to remove things from independent decision makers and give them to dependent decision makers. Now, in each case that this is done, there are good substantive reasons for doing it. The Supreme Court in *Chevron v. N.R.D.C.* required courts to give deference to administrative agencies because these had "superior expertise," et cetera, et cetera. But note the effect. The administrative agency then becomes the *dominant* decision maker, notwithstanding that the administrative agency, for the reasons

Justice Black said, is much more dependent than courts on the Legislative and Executive branches. And this is so even if the agency is nominally an "independent" one.

Similarly, the Prison Litigation Reform Act requires prisoners to exhaust grievances before they can go to court. The argument is that we ought to give the prison system the chance to address certain things before courts do. Okay, but the effect is that basically dependent agencies end up deciding these matters almost exclusively, and courts do not play their constitutionally assigned role.

One of the most important areas where federal court deference is most troubling has been our required deference to state courts when they are deciding federal questions. As to this, my attitude is the reverse of that which I have about the certification of state law questions, where I think, as I have told you, we should not just defer, but actually yield decisions to the states. Conversely, when it is an issue of federal law, it is we federal judges who know more.

But apart from whether the question of deference is justified given who knows more, and apart from whether doing this is a matter of respect to the sovereign states who are co-sovereigns, which it certainly is, there is a deeper problem with deference. If you look across the country, most state courts are elected, and so deference is to a politically dependent decision maker. So, deference to a states' constitution by a federal court removes the decision from an independent body and gives it to a dependent decision maker. This move away from judicial independence is not a Right or Left matter; you can see it in death penalty cases in one direction, and in torts, often in the other.

I have compared the diminution in the scope of what federal courts decide to our failure to safeguard our architectural history. In 1900 New Haven, for example, there were more 18th-century houses than any city in the United States except Charleston, South Carolina. But most of them were not important enough to be worth saving. They were not that fancy and there was always a reason for tearing a particular house down. We now have three 18th century houses left, and that's all.

My point is that there is always a good reason to move to dependent decision makers. No one of these areas of independence is all that important. But if we are not careful, we will have independent decision making relegated to the equivalent of just three houses.

It's funny. The Bayless case dealt with judicial recusals. It got me thinking about that, judicial independence, and what Justice Black had told me. That led to a lecture, and an article grew from it. As so often with me, there was an odd combination of so many thoughts—as an academic, as a law clerk, and as a judge.

* * *

I try always to be polite on the bench, but sometimes I fail. When a party has a strong case but tries to go beyond what is needed to win and makes arguments that go to a broader cause rather than what is in the real interest of a lawyers' own clients, I don't like it. There are times, of course, when a client is interested in a cause rather than the case. But where this is not so, I don't like it.

I decided a case in which there had been some terrible sexual abuses. It happened to have been in a yeshiva, many years ago. The district court, Judge Koeltl, a very good judge, had found that the statute of limitations had run. The lawyer for the schools, instead of just relying on Judge Koeltl's opinion, was arguing that whenever *anybody* is injured, *even if they don't know by whom, or anything else*, the statute of limitations starts to run. Of course, this is much too broad. Parties need to know enough at least so that they are meaningfully prompted to investigate further. This lawyer was doing what he did because that would obviously help him in *other cases* and was doing it despite a strong court opinion which had held, "Here, in this case, in this situation, the plaintiffs knew enough so that the statute started to run." The lawyer, a fancy lawyer from a fancy firm, kept going on and on.

I thought he was intentionally misreading the lower court ruling in order to set up the law so that he could win other cases of this sort. This is always unpleasant, but it is particularly dangerous when the lawyer is doing this in a case where the court would love to decide against you and your client, because the equities are the other way. By playing for a broader victory, that lawyer was actually endangering his client, which is inexcusable!

I said, "Now, look. You are arguing for a position that is very broad and hard to buy. This is a case where all the equities seem to be against your client. You have a very good *narrow* case. Why are you doing this?" I was strong, but polite. At which point he said, "Oh, this is what Judge Koeltl *held*," which of course was nonsense. Judge Koeltl, a very good judge, had been very careful.

When the lawyer said that, I got angry and I said, "Judge Koeltl knew what he was doing. Do *you* know what *you* are doing?" All the judges were disturbed at what the lawyer was doing, but I guess I was the one who spoke up about it.

We then wrote a short per curiam opinion affirming the district court, but on the narrow grounds that are appropriate, because the district court was right about the law. The newspapers picked up my remarks. They picked them up because the equities in the case were so clear.

This case does suggest the sort of situations in which I have gotten angry on the bench. I try not to, because I do not think one should. I get angry when I think that a lawyer is looking after his or her own interest rather than the clients'.

Or when the government is forgetting, in the words of Pierre Leval, who often asks U.S. Attorneys, "Who are you working for?" They kind of hesitate, and Pierre says, "No, who are you working for?" and finally the lawyer will say the Department of Justice. Leval will say, "Yes, the Department of Justice, not the Department of Public Prosecutions."

* * *

Craft involves more than protecting judicial independence, and more than making sure that lawyers do the job of defending their clients, and more even than writing carefully, solidly researched decisions. It sometimes involves judgment about when and how far to go in a particular case.

There was a case about the secrecy of the grand jury that came up late in the 1990s. A doctoral candidate was writing a dissertation about Harry Dexter White, a government employee who was accused of having been a communist spy in the late 1940s and was called to appear before a grand jury to answer the charges against him. The grand jury minutes were secret, and the district court declined to let them be released.

Harry Dexter White on the cover of Time magazine, Nov. 23, 1953.

The student wanted access to them because he said that this was the only way to understand White's position on the charges—and that there was a significant public interest in knowing historical truth. The government took the position that unless the government okays it, no grand jury minutes can *ever* be opened. An organization of historians filed amicus briefs saying that is a terrible rule.

I asked the government, "Are you saying the rule is that if John Wilkes Booth had not been killed, but had been before a grand jury, we couldn't now see what he said there? Or Aaron Burr?" They said, "Absolutely."

I wrote an opinion which said, "That is nonsense. In due course, history must have its due, and grand jury minutes must be opened. I indicated some factors that a district court could use to balance the importance of secrecy with the public interest and said that it was entirely possible that historical or public interest *alone* would justify the release of grand jury information. Thus, if the John Wilkes Booth conspiracy had led to grand jury investigations, historical interest would by now overwhelm any continued need for secrecy. In the particular case, however, with people still alive, I read the district court to have exercised its discretion not to open, because it was too soon.

Why did I come down this way? I stretched a bit to say what the district court had held—I articulated justifications for still keeping the minutes sealed which the district court had not really expressed. What I was doing was moving the law in the direction that the historians wanted, and more importantly made sense, but I did it in a way that—since the government had won in the actual case—prevented it from taking it to the Supreme Court. Since then, several other circuits came out my way, and it is going to be harder for the Supreme Court to take an absolutist position and go in the other direction, against the interest of History.

I think circuit judges are very much aware of what can happen if an issue goes to the Supreme Court too soon. Considerations of this sort are very much a traditional part of the inner workings of courts of appeals. I do not think it makes us "political."

* * *

A statement that judges are "only politicians in black robes" is much too strong. There are plenty of cases where that is not so—even at the Supreme Court, which, in the last few decades, has had many more cases than in the lower courts where politics did seem to have a direct effect. *Bush v. Gore* seems to me to have been one of them. In *Bush v. Gore*, the Court made a political decision, and then, four years later, George W. Bush got re-elected, which in a sense ratified its power to do so. I believed then, and believe now, that *Bush v. Gore* is a political decision, a non-principled decision. It was a case where the Court felt it had to—and so it could—make a non-principled decision.

> *Sandra Day O'Connor thought it was a political decision and regretted it afterwards; Justice Souter said that if he had a few more days, he believed he would have been able to talk one or another Justice out of it.*

The majority, a plurality of the Court, determined the outcome of the national election for President in a situation where it wasn't absolutely essential. It wasn't *Bush v. Hitler*, after all.

Now, there are some people who took *Bush v. Gore* consistently, relatively, with their legal philosophy. That is, I do not think there was anything strange about

Justice Scalia wanting to take that case, because he was a person for whom, if the legislature has used certain words, you must follow those words—up to the point where it is complete nonsense! That is, he goes much further in that direction than others. *Bush v. Gore* is a case where Scalia could strengthen his philosophy of: "I do not care what they meant; it's what they said." So, I do not think you can accuse him of having been political in taking the case. Nor could I blame Justice Thomas in this case, either, because he's even more—he's more consistent about that approach than Scalia.

But in their willingness, in *Bush v. Gore*, to decide that case to serve political ends, some of the Justices furthered a mindset. Others have come on the Court since and joined that mindset. The politics of the moment have come to have more influence than formerly; more than is appropriate; more than one would hope for on the highest court. The result is that since *Bush v. Gore* there have been more cases than previously that look like non-principled, political decisions.

Even an opinion that many have praised—Chief Justice Roberts' opinion about Obamacare, National Federation of Independent Business v. Sebelius *(2012), seems to me a terrible decision. Striking down Obamacare would probably have helped President Obama in the coming election, and perhaps that is why Justice Roberts came out the way he did; the Chief Justice is politically savvier than many people on the Court, and perhaps that is why he upheld the law.*

How did he uphold the law? Along with four others, he was interested in trimming the Commerce Clause, and so he joined them in holding that the Commerce Clause cannot justify a mandate to buy insurance because those who do not buy it are not in commerce. I think that is nonsense, just plain nonsense, for the reasons that Judge Sutton gave in his Sixth Circuit opinion upholding the law. But if you take that position, you cannot save the law on the basis used by the Chief Justice.

Here was a law that was close to the Constitutional line as far as the Commerce Clause was concerned—over it, for five Justices of the Court—being upheld on the basis of a power the Legislative and Executive branches claimed they were not using and which it would have been politically unpopular for them to have relied upon.

A fully principled opinion either would have upheld the law under the Commerce Power—as I believe it should have—or struck it down.

Moreover, Justice Roberts actually got Justices Kagan and Breyer to go along with the position, for the first time ever—that where the federal government pays the states to do something, this may be an unconstitutional infringement on the states if the amount of payment is too much.

But what is too much, and what is too little? That has been left completely open, which is very dangerous, for it is a huge opening to the exercise of power by the Court over Congress. That part of the opinion is not unprincipled, it is just extremely dangerous.

You say, "Isn't it strange that a court made up so much of Court of Appeals judges should become that political?" I don't think so. Politicians or people from practice often know the danger of politics better than appellate judges. Judges elevated from Courts of Appeals who rarely acted in political ways may well think, "well, we are now in a very different position on the highest Court, where we have to do some judicial policymaking." And then, anything goes. Good politicians traditionally have known that pushing for the results you want can go just so far before it becomes improper.

> *This is also why academics in government can be so dangerous. Even Erwin Griswold, that most righteous person and Dean of Harvard Law School, did things as Solicitor General in working with the Attorney General, Mitchell, who went to jail, that many have criticized as beyond the pale.*

So, the short of it is, I don't like this Supreme Court, and, I don't like it in part because it has a tendency to behave more politically than is needed, even for the highest court And I fear that an inclination to make politically motivated decisions will naturally seep down to the lower courts.

There are inevitably cases where the pull of ideology is so strong that it is determinative. Often, however, even if a case *is* linked to ideology, it is more closely related to general theories about what is appropriate in difficult situations.

To give an illustration of what I mean, let me focus on what is the biggest difference in deciding cases between my wonderful colleague Dennis Jacobs and me. There are many situations in which cases come up where, if a party wins, there is a possibility that people on the same side will abuse that and will bring "strike" suits which will win them settlements that they should not get. In such cases, Dennis tries, if possible, to close the door to such a suit, altogether—even though there will be people who have real rights that will be lost if the door is closed. I, on the other hand, will always try to find a way of saving the right in question, but hemming it in with restrictions that make the strike suit, the judicial blackmail, less likely. That may be because of our background. He was a practicing lawyer who defended clients who had to settle. I am an academic who wants the law to be "right."

Is his position, or mine, ideological? It is not fair to describe either of our positions just that way. It is a point of view—about how you treat injured people and how you feel about people who are wrongly accused of injuring others. It is about generalization and particularization. At some point, each of us would say that the other is right. Dennis would not say "bar every anti-discrimination suit because a few can abuse it." I would not say "you had better grant most people's anti-discrimination suits because sometimes discrimination is real." Our instincts on where to draw the line differ—but neither of us would allow such instincts to overwhelm our common sense and our judicial responsibilities.

COMMENTARY

Chapter 33

E.R. Squibb & Sons v. Accident & Casualty Ins. Co. The Squibb Corporation sued its insurers in 1982 on claims for costs resulting from litigation over the injurious consequences of using its product diethylstilbestrol ("DES").[1] The case was brought in federal court based on the geographic diversity of the parties, and it chugged along for years. As Guido describes, the parties and the court were indifferent or oblivious to an unrelated admiralty case decided in the Second Circuit in 1998 which declared that the structure of Lloyd's of London, one of the largest insurance marketplaces in the world, did not permit confidence in complete diversity jurisdiction when there was a "representative suit" by a "lead" underwriter against a New York party.[2]

On remand, the presiding district court judge, judge John Martin, Jr., observed that the court's inattention to the jurisdictional defect occurred because the case "progressed... without any party... asserting that this Court lacked jurisdiction over the matter that was consuming so much of its time and that of the parties."[3] The judge further explained that he did not address the question on his own because he relied on the stipulations of the parties, as well as language in the insurance contracts at issue which obligated them to "comply with all requirements necessary to give such Court jurisdiction."[4]

As Guido says, his panel did address the matter on its own. His decision held that all the subscribing Lloyd's underwriters are "real parties in interest" when the lead underwriter is suing in a representative capacity; and that when, as here, a suit is filed against a lead underwriter, each and every name whom the lead underwriter represented needed to be diverse with respect to an adversary. Guido reveals breathtaking self-assurance while throwing a procedural spoke into the flywheel of a substantive, multimillion-dollar, multi-year, multi-party settlement.

On the other hand, his offer of a "way out" of the mess diminished the fury of the lawyers and the litigants. Without mentioning Guido by name, a leading insurance law journal conceded that the opinion did offer the way out: "if the Lead Underwriter were sued only in his individual capacity, and not his representative

---

[1] E.R. Squibb & Sons, Inc. v. Accident & Cas. Ins. Co., 160 F.3d 925 (2d Cir. 1998). The recoveries were awarded under different approaches to calculating the apportionment of damages; *see, e.g.*, Sindell v. Abbott Laboratories, 26 Cal. 3d 588 (1980); Collins v. Eli Lilly & Co., 116 Wis. 2d 166 (1984); Sindell v. Hymowitz v. Eli Lilly, 539 N.E.2d 1069 (N.Y. 1989).

[2] Advani Enters. v. Underwriters at Lloyds, 140 F.3d 157 (2d Cir. 1998) (declining to accept jurisdiction on the grounds of diversity but accepting the case because admiralty jurisdiction sufficed to support jurisdiction over the lawsuit).

[3] E.R. Squibb & Sons, Inc. v. Accident & Cas. Ins. Co., 1999 U.S. Dist. LEXIS 8333, at *31 (1999).

[4] *Id.*

capacity, only his residence and amount-in-controversy need be analyzed, and not that of all other Names on the Lloyd's policies at issue..."[5]

His solution worked in the immediate case, but the insurance bar was not convinced it would work to allow most litigation against Lloyd's to proceed in federal courts any longer.[6] Indeed, after *Squibb* and other decisions in other circuits, the general rule when filing a lawsuit against Lloyd's has become that suits against the insurer be filed in state court, listing the insurer as "Certain Underwriters at Lloyd's."[7]

His willingness to review stringently bland assertions of diversity, finally, accords with his general perspective about federalism, the quality of state courts, and the respect due to state court judicial systems. Why not trust state courts to decide complex insurance cases? Perhaps Guido has never countered arguments that state courts are truly inferior because to do so—at least with reference to state courts in New York, Connecticut or Vermont (his circuit)—would be inaccurate as well as insulting.

United States v. Bayless. Judge Harold Baer suppressed evidence that Carol Bayless ran duffel bags full of cocaine and heroin into Washington Heights, New York.[8] The evidence against her included a videotaped confession in which she admitted her role and that of her son and his associates.[9] In her confession, she also detailed her involvement in twenty other similar transactions.[10]

Judge Baer also suppressed testimony from two New York City police officers who said they observed her double-park her car in the neighborhood and flee when she caught sight of the police.[11] In suppressing the confession and testimony, Judge Baer wrote that it was not unusual for citizens to run from the police in Washington Heights, where, he said, police were viewed as "corrupt, abusive and violent."[12]

---

[5] *See* John M. Sylvester and Roberta D. Anderson, *Is it Still Possible to Litigate Against Lloyd's in Federal Court*, 34 TORT & INSURANCE L.J. 1065 (1999).

[6] *Id.* at 1078.

[7] Chip Merlin, Lawsuits Against "Lloyd's of London" are Often Wrongly "Named," *Prop. Ins. Co. L. Blog*, Aug. 13, 2010, https://www.propertyinsurancecoveragelaw.com/2010/08/articles/insurance/lawsuits-against-lloyds-of-london-are-often-wrongly-named; *See* Underwriters at Lloyd's, London v. Osting-Schwinn, 613 F.3d 1079 (11th Cir. 2010).

[8] United States v. Bayless, 913 F. Supp. 232 (S.D.N.Y. 1996).

[9] *Id.*

[10] *Id.*

[11] Dan van Natta, Jr., *Under Pressure, Federal Judge Reverses Decision in Drug Case*, N.Y. TIMES, Apr. 2, 1996.

[12] 913 F. Supp. at 242.

Judge Harold Baer, Jr., in 1996

The court's *Bayless* opinion became a flashpoint for the simmering national debate about whether courts were "hamstringing" police in their efforts to control the flow of illicit drugs.[13] Governor Pataki, Mayor Giuliani, and Police Commissioner Bratton attacked Baer and defended the truthfulness of the police.[14] An aide to President Clinton told the media that Baer should resign if he did not change the decision.[15] There were calls for the judge to be impeached.[16]

The trial proceedings continued after the decision to suppress, with Judge Baer presiding. As Guido says, the defendants moved for recusal in light of the extreme pressure on him caused by the political storm and the harsh public glare. Nonetheless, Judge Baer denied the motion for him to recuse himself in an oral ruling, for three reasons:

> First, to be swayed by outside influence would run counter to the central theme of judicial independence.... The second thought was that ... it would simply be passing the buck to another jurist. That did not seem appropriate or fair ... And, lastly, it seemed to me that it would be a significant waste of judicial time to have someone else have to go through any part of what I had done already.[17]

---

[13] Michael A. McCall, *William Rehnquist: Leadership & Influence from the Conservative Wing*, in THE REHNQUIST COURT AND CRIMINAL JUSTICE 91 (Christopher E. Smith, Christina DeJong, Michael McCall ED. 2011).

[14] Don van Natta, Jr., *supra* note 11.

[15] CNN-Time Daily, Apr. 2, 1996, https://www.cnn.com/ALLPOLITICS/1996/news/9604/02/judge.reverses/index.shtml

[16] United States v. Bayless, 201 F.3d 116, 126 (2d Cir. 2000); *see also* Jon O. Newman, *The Judge Baer Controversy*, 80 JUDICATURE 156 (1997).

[17] 201 F.3d 116 at 125.

Baer subsequently, and without making any direct reference to the political storm, vacated his earlier suppression order and allowed in additional testimony. He expressed regret for the remarks in his original decision that had prompted the greatest outrage.[18] Afterward, he removed himself from the case and was replaced by Judge Robert Patterson. Carol Bayless was convicted of possessing and distributing cocaine.[19]

Guido, speaking for his panel, upheld Baer's decision not to recuse himself or reconsider his decision. The judge's decision was not "plain error."[20] Baer's behavior met the standards of reasonableness, as Guido determined, by considering it from the viewpoint of an "objective, disinterested observer" at the time the decision was made and privy to full knowledge of the surrounding circumstances.[21] Concerns about the appearance of impropriety were to be determined "not by considering what a straw poll of the only partly informed man-in-the street would show[,] but by examining the record facts and the law, and then deciding whether a reasonable person knowing and understanding all the relevant facts would recuse the judge."[22]

As Guido points out in the narrative, however, his thinking had a more strategic basis—although the opinion barely mentions judicial independence, it was at the heart of his concerns.

In Re Holocaust Victim Assets Litigation, Weisshaus v. Swiss Bankers Association. When it came to recusing himself and not ruling on the recusal decisions of others, Guido defined his obligation strictly.

The *Swiss Bankers* case arose from an appeal by several Polish individuals and the Polish American Defense Committee, who wanted ethnic Poles included in the settlement of four worldwide class actions that were brought by victims of Nazi crimes and their heirs, against a group of Swiss banks.[23]

The $1.25 billion settlement resolved a complaint alleging that Swiss banks knowingly participated in Nazi crimes; that they failed to account for money which was deposited in somewhere between 21,000 and 4.1 million accounts of persons who feared that they would become the targets of persecution and did perish in death camps. The banks also allegedly served as vehicles for the disposal of Nazi plunder looted from victims; and allegedly financed the construction of Nazi slave labor camps and provided a safe haven for profits the Nazis obtained through the use of slave labor.[24]

The Polish intervenors objected to the settlement. They asserted that the original complaint encompassed a broader class of victims than the ultimate settlement, and

---

[18] *Id.*
[19] *Id.*
[20] *Id.*
[21] 201 F.3d at 126.
[22] *Id.*
[23] Weisshaus v. Swiss Bankers Ass'n (In re Holocaust Victim Assets Litig.), 225 F.3d 191 (2000) (Cabranes, J.).
[24] *Id.*

that because the settlement was made "on behalf of the worldwide classes delineated in the complaints" and would provide "complete and total releases" for defendants for the claims, it should include *all ethnic Poles*.[25] In a broad sense, the intervenors were really trying to assault the "historically incorrect view" that ethnic Poles were not victims of Nazi persecution.[26]

The district court turned down these motions to intervene as untimely, and the Second Circuit affirmed. Carving a smaller group from a larger class of victims was not improper, the court decided, and that the would-be intervenors' ability to pursue claims was not foreclosed. Polish Jews, Polish homosexuals, Polish disabled persons, Polish Romani, and others of Polish ethnicity, further, were among those covered by the settlement.[27] And the court emphasized that the court did not want its ruling to be misinterpreted: nothing in the decision addressed the suffering of the non-Jewish people of Poland under Nazi attack and occupation.[28]

Guido's decision to recuse himself. Congress and Second Circuit case law make it clear that as Guido announced in the *Bayless* case, judges should apply an objective standard to determine whether to disqualify themselves.[29] When making a decision about recusal Judges are to ask whether their impartiality might be questioned from the perspective of a "reasonable person."[30] Second Circuit cases provide judges much latitude when ruling on their own recusal obligation: recusal is not required "when the alleged interest or bias on the part of the judge or his spouse is 'not direct, but remote, contingent, or speculative.' "[31]

What about this case? Guido says he principally was motivated to recuse himself by learning in the middle of oral argument that the settlement class included Jews and anti-Fascists who had insurance policies with *Generali* insurance organization and were injured by the non-payments of death benefits. Could a reasonable person, aware of the relevant facts, possibly have believed that Guido's father's connection to anti-Fascists should have led Guido to leave a panel deciding whether Polish individuals and Polish groups were entitled to intervene in a settlement in order to have ethnic Poles included?

It seems highly unlikely that there was any legally sufficient basis for objecting had Guido remained on the panel. The specific question of intervention would

---

[25] *Id.* at 194.
[26] *Id.* at 202.
[27] *Id.* at 191.
[28] *Id.*; *see* CHARLES GARDNER GEYH, JUDICIAL DISQUALIFICATION: AN ANALYSIS OF FEDERAL LAW (2d ed. 2010).
[29] Statutory provisions pertaining to judicial recusal are contained at 28 U.S.C. § 455; 28 U.S.C. § 144, "Disqualification of justice, judge or magistrate judge" and "Bias or prejudice of judge."
[30] Judicial codes also pertain: MODEL CODE OF JUDICIAL CONDUCT R. 2.11(A) (2007) (... "in any proceeding in which the judge's impartiality might reasonably be questioned, ...); CODE OF CONDUCT FOR UNITED STATES JUDGES Canon 3C(1) (2011) ((1) " ... in a proceeding in which the judge's impartiality might reasonably be questioned ... ").
[31] United States v. Arena, 180 F.3d 380 (1999).

not have had an obvious effect on the overall settlement. Guido, however, considered that an ordinary observer might well think it wrong for a judge to decide any aspect of a case in the final merit of which that judge had a possible financial interest.

Guido extended his view of recusal further, suggesting in a later conversation that for district court judges, recusal for almost any reason should be virtually automatic, and nearly as much for membership on a panel where, after all, the fact that a particular judge is on that panel is just a matter of chance and that judge can readily be replaced. He thinks recusal, when the court is sitting *en banc*—and the judge cannot be replaced by another judge—is a totally different matter. The same applies in his view, to the Supreme Court—but even there, where there is a direct interest, recusal is appropriate.

Study in contrasts. Guido adopted a rather extreme view of his recusal obligation in *Holocaust Assets*; some judges occupy the other extreme. For example, Justice Scalia declined to recuse himself when the Sierra Club asked him not to participate in a pending case it had brought against a longtime friend of his Vice President Cheney. Justice Scalia went duck hunting with Cheney, in fact, while the case was still pending.

Newspaper editorials called his impartiality into question.[32] Legal ethicists concluded that there were surely reasonable grounds for questioning the Justice's objectivity and that his memo rationalizing his decision misapplied the Federal Disqualification Statute.[33] Nonetheless, Scalia insisted, the "reasonable observer" must be "informed of all the surrounding facts and circumstances."[34] And in Scalia's view, the editorials in question were factually inaccurate.[35] Justice Scalia declined to recuse.

The Yeshiva High School case. Former students at the Marsha Stern Talmudical Academy-Yeshiva High School for boys sued their secondary school for sexual abuse by teachers, abuse which allegedly had taken place two decades before or earlier.[36] They brought suit under civil rights provisions in the Education Law.[37]

The district court dismissed the suit as untimely; the Second Circuit issued a per curiam opinion affirming the lower court.[38] The students had been aware of their injuries; they knew the abuser's identities; and they knew about the continued employment of the teachers.[39] Judges Calabresi, Raggi, and Chin agreed that this was

---

[32] Steve Twomey, *Scalia Angrily Defends His Duck Hunt With Cheney*, N.Y. TIMES, Mar. 18, 2004; Cheney v. United States District Court for the District of Columbia, 541 U.S. 913 (2004) (mem.) (Scalia, J.).
[33] *See* Monroe H. Freedman, *Duck-Blind Justice: Justice Scalia's Memorandum in the Cheney Case*, 18 GEO. J. LEGAL ETHICS 229 (2004), 235.
[34] Cheney v. United States District Court, *supra* note 32.
[35] *Id.* at 924.
[36] Twersky v. Yeshiva Univ., 579 F. App'x 7 (2014); cert. denied 2014 U.S. App. LEXIS 25041 (2014).
[37] 20 U.S.C. § 1681 et seq.
[38] *Id.*
[39] *Id.*

"sufficient to put them on at least inquiry notice as to the school's awareness of and indifference to the abusive conduct by its teachers."[40]

As Guido relates, this was not the broad and definitive sort of ruling that the school's counsel appeared to be maneuvering to elicit. When the attorney's maneuvering became apparent, Guido, angry, rebuked the school's counsel for overstating the lower court's holding.

An attorney who falsely asserts that a lower court issued a much broader ruling than it did might be sanctioned under Rule 3.3 of the Rules of Professional Responsibility, a comment which notes that "although a lawyer in an adversary proceeding is not required to present an impartial exposition of the law … the lawyer must not allow the tribunal to be misled by false statements of law or fact or evidence that the lawyer knows to be false."[41] Judges and their clerks should be held responsible for seeing through the skillful but fallacious argumentation of litigants—but how far does freedom to stretch the meaning of a holding extend?

The rule on representing clients in different suits over related matters simultaneously would also be relevant.[42] It prohibits the representation of multiple clients when serving the interests of one will damage the interests of another. Guido here asserts that distorting a holding, even for the sake of *future* clients, is not a proper justification for an intentional misstatement of what a court held. From Guido's perspective, the lawyer had a very good case for his present client, but he had declined to make that case, for the sake of possible future clients. As Guido told me, he was "fighting the cause, not the case."

The Harry Dexter White case, and grand jury secrecy. Searching through records at the National Archives in the course of writing a doctoral thesis entitled *Treasonable Doubt: The Harry Dexter White, 1948–1963*, Bruce Craig learned about a transcript of White's grand jury testimony relating to allegations of communist subversion made in 1948.[43] This testimony could reveal whether or not White passed secret documents to the American Communist Party, illuminating the Party's infiltration of the government during the postwar period.

A court order, however, would be necessary in order to obtain sealed grand jury transcripts. Obtaining an order would require defeating a firm rule against disclosure that makes no exception for the imperatives of scholarship.[44] The Public Citizen Litigation Group took up Craig's case, pro bono, to try to promote inquiries into historical truth.[45]

---

[40] *Id.*

[41] New York Rules of Professional Conduct, Rule 3.3, cmt. 2, Candor Toward the Tribunal-comment.

[42] Model Rules Prof Conduct R 1.7(a) provides that "… a lawyer shall not represent a client if a reasonable lawyer would conclude that either: (1) the representation will involve the lawyer in representing differing interests; or (2) there is a significant risk that the lawyer's professional judgment on behalf of a client will be adversely affected by the lawyer's own financial, business, property or other personal interests."

[43] Bruce Craig, *Unsealing Federal Grand Jury Records: The Case of the Harry Dexter White Transcript*, 20 THE PUBLIC HISTORIAN 45 (1998)(Linda Sikes, esq. representing Mr. Craig).

[44] See it Fed. R. Crim. P. 6E.

[45] Linda Sikes represented Craig; amici in support of the litigation included the American Historical Association, the Organization of American Historians, the National Council on Public History, and the Society of American Archivists.

District court judge Sara Scheindlin, in line with precedent, concluded that Craig's petition did not justify the release of the secret grand jury material.[46] She recited the leading Second Circuit case:

> No matter how much, or how legitimately, the public may want to know whether a candidate for high public office has invoked the privilege against self-incrimination before a grand jury, or has lied about having done so, that interest must generally yield to the larger one of preserving the salutary rule of law embodied in Rule 6(e) of the Federal Rules of Criminal Procedure.[47]

Judge Scheindlin concluded her decision with the statement that a public interest exception to serve scholarship "would swallow the general rule of secrecy," and denied the petition.[48]

The judges "listened intently" at oral argument, with Guido in particular "[finding] the case interesting and ask[ing] penetrating questions."[49] "In a legal atmosphere where all too often the cases that come before the appellate court focus on technical legalese surrounding the intricacies of dry corporate cases," non-lawyer Craig wrote, the morning's exchange of arguments "appeared to have been a welcome relief to the judge."[50]

Guido's remarkable creativity is on display in his decision: the opinion discovers openings in the Second Circuit *Biaggi* precedent and openings in Judge Scheindlin's *Craig* district court opinion which prove sufficient to craft a new exception to grand jury record secrecy—in the very process of denying victory to the plaintiff in front of the court.[51]

First, he embraces Judge Scheindlin's outcome and reasoning, but asserts that it has left open a public interest exception to the nondisclosure rule. This is deft considering that Judge Scheindlin concludes her opinion by rejecting a public interest exception, because she believes it would swallow up the general statutory mandate for secrecy.

He accomplishes it through minimization. "The district court's comment that public interest, without more, cannot permit disclosure," he writes, "must be read simply as the commonplace observation that the 'special circumstances' test cannot be satisfied by a blanket assertion that the public has an interest in the information contained in the grand jury transcripts."[52]

Then, a second step: he broadens the restrictive "special circumstances" test imposed to confine testimony disclosure that is contained in the *Biaggi* decision.

---

[46] In re Petition of Craig, 942 F. Supp. 881, 882–83 (1996).
[47] In re Biaggi, 478 F.2d 489, 492–93 (1973) (allowing disclosure based on the waiver exception).
[48] 942 F. Supp. 881 at 883.
[49] Craig, *supra* note 43, at 57.
[50] *Id.*
[51] Craig v. United States (In re Craig), 131 F.3d 99 (1997).
[52] *Id.* at 105.

He does so by crediting the test itself as a recognition that *some type of multi-factor analysis* ought to be conducted to determine whether or not an exception to the nondisclosure would be made:

> Lest there be any doubt in the matter ... we today hold that there is nothing in *In re Biaggi's* "special circumstances" test—despite some dictum that can be read to the contrary—that prohibits historical interest, on its own, from justifying release of grand jury material in an appropriate case.[53]

Guido states that without undermining anything in the *Biaggi* approach it is "entirely conceivable" that "historical or public interest alone" would warrant disclosure. He offers the compelling example which he mentions in the narrative:

> To the extent that the John Wilkes Booth or Aaron Burr conspiracies, for example, led to grand jury investigations, historical interest might by now overwhelm any continued need for secrecy.[54]

And at last, having expanded the opportunity for supplementing *Biaggi*, he presents a "non-exhaustive list of factors" that are relevant to the assertion of a public interest for a court to consider.[55]

Had the decision favored Mr. Craig, it might have created an uproar and been appealed. But it did not upset the judicial system at the time, because it affirmed Justice Scheindlin's decision and denied Mr. Craig the chance to read grand jury minutes which might cast the history of Cold War espionage in a new light. Why? Because the instant case is said not to satisfy the Court's new set of factors since there appeared to be living parties whose assurances of secrecy deserved protection.[56]

In this subtle way, a new exception emerges from the ashes of the plaintiff's defeat, and Mr. Craig acknowledged as much. "In the end," he later wrote, "although the battle to seek the immediate release of the White grand jury records was lost, the war to clarify the legitimacy of the historian's task in seeking to disclose grand jury records on the basis of history alone was won."[57]

---

[53] *Id.*
[54] *Id.*
[55] The enumerated factors to be considered are (i) the identity of the party seeking disclosure; (ii) whether the defendant to the grand jury proceeding or the government opposes the disclosure; (iii) why disclosure is being sought in the particular case; (iv) what specific information is being sought for disclosure; (v) how long ago the grand jury proceedings took place; (vi) the current status of the principals of the grand jury proceedings and that of their families; (vii) the extent to which the desired material—either permissibly or impermissibly—has been previously made public; (viii) whether witnesses to the grand jury proceedings who might be affected by disclosure are still alive; and (ix) the additional need for maintaining secrecy in the particular case in question. *Id.* at 106.
[56] *Id.* at 107. According to Mr. Craig, however, the parties, any who might have been mentioned in the transcript, were dead. *Id.* at 59.
[57] *Id.*

Craig has proven muscular in prying open historical truths: it has been adopted in other circuits and been useful to many district courts.[58] Courts weighing the imperatives of history according to the *Craig* factors have helped historians and journalists to illuminate mysteries large and small.[59]

---

[58] Nonetheless, other circuits have adhered to a "plain meaning" construction of the statute, holding that it does not grant district courts the power to graft a public interest exception. See Pitch v. United States 275 F.Supp.3d 1373 (2017), 915 F.3d 704 (2019) (vacating a circuit court decision releasing records pertaining to the Moore's Ford Lynching in Georgia and reversing after a rehearing *en banc*).

[59] *See* Lepore v. United States, 2020 U.S. Dist. LEXIS 30533 (release of redacted transcripts pertaining to Daniel Ellsberg's dissemination of the Pentagon Papers); In re Unseal Dockets Related to the Independent Counsel's 1998 Investigation of President Clinton, 308 F. Supp. 3d 314 (2018)(release of many transcripts in the Starr Investigation of Bill Clinton); Carlson v. United States, 109 F. Supp. 3d 1025 (2015) (release of transcripts related to government knowledge of Japanese attacks on Pearl Harbor); In re Nichter, 949 F. Supp. 2d 205 (2013) (release of some material from the Watergate investigation); In re Kutler, 800 F. Supp. 2d 42 (2011) (release of some Nixon grand jury testimony in Watergate investigation); In re Tabac, 2009 U.S. Dist. LEXIS 123229 (release of some transcripts pertaining to the disappearance of James Hoffa).

34
Giustizia e Liberta' Recollected: Bad Laws and Injustices

Many reasons may lead Judges to find that a case is particularly hard to decide. When an outcome is not dictated by precedents or statutes, or when no remedy appears adequate, practical guides and philosophical approaches to discretion will lead to different possible resolutions. Novel cases may also be hard because, as Ronald Dworkin suggested, a judge "feels an obligation to be unoriginal."

Sometimes cases are hard because clear statutes and precedents direct a judge to conclusions running against the value system of the judge. It may also be hard to determine whether to decide a case on the basis of welfare policy for the collective; or on the basis of the rights of a particular party—a problem Guido addressed extensively in The Cost of Accidents and elsewhere. And on multi-judge panels or tribunals, even simple cases can be hard ones. Reaching a majority requires dialogue with other judges to reach an agreement.

Some cases present legal, moral, and practical questions of unusual complexity that call for something more than a complete grounding in the law—they also require an additional degree of creativity, resourcefulness, and a moral perception of the tension, sometimes, between justice and law.

Judge Learned Hand famously described a meeting between himself and Justice Oliver Wendell Holmes, where as Holmes walked off Hand bid him, "Well, sir, goodbye. Do justice!" Holmes turned sharply and retorted, "That is not my job. My job is to play the game according to the rules." Guido's view about the better of these responses emerges clearly in the cases below. Each centers, at its base, on a personal story: a judge must decide how to reconcile the individual stakes—often maximally high—with practical constraints and ethical values.

All the cases share a unifying theme: In them, Guido draws from an arsenal of legal tools, including academic insights, historical knowledge, and professional experience, to reach what he views as a just result which is also legally justifiable.

Do you know *Grabois v. Commissioners*? This is the case of a pro se litigant, Kay Jones, who was married for many years, or so she thought, to a man named "Junior." Junior had a good job as a carpenter. They were both African Americans. Kay looked after him, and she brought up his daughters. Junior received a decent union pension and was eligible for Social Security and Disability payments. Kay started to collect his Social Security benefits, because he was disabled and had reached a certain age.

Finally, Junior dies. Kay is collecting Social Security benefits on his account when his *first* wife shows up, and says, "We were married and there was no divorce. I am the legal wife. I have a right to his pension and Social Security benefits in the future, and I also have the right to get back what was paid to this other woman before."

The insurance company, represented by a twerpy guy, says to the court, "Well, tell us whom we're supposed to pay . . . We think we should pay the first wife." So, that's it.

The case goes before Judge Griesa, who was by then old and tired. The matter seems open and shut to him. He gives the woman short shrift, because the law in New York seems really very clear: if there is no divorce, then the first wife inherits. The legal "first" wife has the rights to his pension and benefits.

Comes the appeal and I am presiding, with two senior judges. One is Frank Altimari; the other is Tom Meskill. In preparation for the oral argument, I already have prepared a "Disposition without an Opinion," affirming the district court summarily, because the law of New York seemed perfectly clear.

And then this elderly lady comes in to make her oral argument. Under our procedures you can argue pro se. She starts to argue. She starts to talk about her longtime life with Junior, but then almost collapses because she is so old and weak; she is really unable to go on. One of her daughters asks if she can continue arguing. This is not proper because as a pro se, you are not permitted to let somebody else who is not a lawyer represent you. Nonetheless, I decide to allow it, and to let the daughter argue.

The daughter tells the Court that this old woman was the mother who brought her up, and who should have these rights. Some of the things she said led me to think she was the child of the first wife. She said, "I was a child brought up by this woman." I do not know it for a fact, but I know that at that time, I thought that this "daughter" was not genetically a daughter of the elderly woman before us.

We go back into conference, and I say, "I just can't affirm. This just seems too wrong. I would like you to give me some time to look into it and see if the law really is so clear. The insurance company said it was clear. Everything seemed that way. But you know, this case bothers me."

We had not really taken any deep look into it. Judge Meskill does not much want to look further. Frank Altimari says, "Of course, take all the time that you want." Altimari was the more ferocious person, in some ways, but he was a person of emotions and of feeling. Meskill was more constrained. Finally, he said, "Okay, it is just before Christmas. Let's not take it away from her now. You have got the Christmas holidays to look this up."

I start looking at all sorts of possibilities that might help the "second" wife. I look at whether there's such a thing as a common law *divorce*. There's common law marriage in New York. Is there anything can amount to a common law divorce? No.

I look, and I look, and I look, but there is nothing. I start to say to myself, "You know, Guido, maybe what you think is so so wrong *is not* so wrong, because you cannot find any cases. "I have the doubt that judges should have when the legal topography runs totally against them."

Finally, I find a couple of cases that make me think that there were some other people who did not like this absolute rule that favors the first wife. A couple of Social Security opinions by Jim Oakes, a judge I greatly admired, and by Irving R. Kaufman, a more controversial judge, put a strong burden on the first wife to show that there had been no divorce and that this second marriage is not a valid marriage. This did not *change* the rule, but it made it more difficult for the first wife, and it suggested an underlying concern with protecting the good faith reliance of the second wife.

Then, I find a *wonderful* opinion—which the others on the panel would not let me cite. It is written by the great Lord Devlin, who lived to be a hundred. He was a legendary, very opinionated jurist—an activist, you know. In the best sense of the word, an *English* judge of the old school.

Devlin had the case of Farmer Jones, I believe was his name, who had died intestate, so that his wife of many, many years, expected to inherit. But then a "first" wife shows up and claims that there had never been a divorce; that the second marriage was invalid, and that she has a right to all of his property. Lord Devlin says in his opinion that the law is clear, that where there is no divorce, the first wife takes by intestacy, and that a so-called second-wife does not. No question.

However ... before the intestate estate is determined, the estate must pay its debts, and its debts include debts by contract. "It seems to me," Lord Devlin said, "that Farmer Jones violated a contract to his second wife when he agreed to marry her and could not. She has a contractual cause of action against him. And if you tell me that the statute of limitations has run, I will tell you that Farmer Jones violated that contract every day and every night of his life until he died." The opinion is so *English-y*!

> *They wouldn't let me cite Lord Devlin's case, because it is an English case, and this is Judge Thomas Meskill, the same judge who, as I mentioned earlier, would not let me talk about laws heading towards unconstitutionality. There was no point in getting into an argument with Meskill in this case.*

All this convinced me that it is not just me feeling bad about this; but that there have been others, distinguished judges, who saw an underlying problem.

What could I do about it when there was seemingly no law at all in New York, going my way? I decided that what I could do about it was to certify the case to the New York Court of Appeals by using a gambit based on federalism. I used the fact that ERISA, a federal reform of pension law, had been passed, and that Junior's pension was subject to the ERISA law. The interpretation of who has what rights under ERISA is partly a matter of state law; but the policies of ERISA also influence it.

Essentially I asked whether the New York rule about first wives holds totally firm in the face of the policies of ERISA. I implied that the Social Security cases suggest placing a heavy burden on the alleged "first wife," and ERISA may have the same policy. What does New York say of its law in the light of that policy?

The New York Court of Appeals turns down certification. It says in effect, "This an interesting and complicated issue; and while we could perfectly well say what we think, we would rather have *your* opinion about what our law requires, given the strength of what is, after all, a federal policy."

Notice what the New York Court of Appeals did. Very smart people, they in effect said, "This is a terrible case. We don't know if we are ready to change New York law about first and second spouses. If you, Second Circuit, say New York law has changed, you do not do any final harm to New York law. That leaves us free to do what we want in the future. So be our guests. We would rather this case be decided by you, our "appellate division for federal cases."

That is what I think our court is in such situations.

Well, Meskill is furious! He did not think we should have certified in the first place. Judge Altimari is amused; he was perfectly happy to have me certify and he thought the district court's result was unfortunate—unjust, even.

You would think that at this point I would decide, okay, the second wife wins—and interpret the interplay between ERISA and New York State law that way. But I do not do that, because there are two things that come into play. First, I'm not really anxious to interpret New York law, even though it is too strict, too brittle.

But more important, what moved me was the fact that although when I heard the case I thought the law was morally wrong, when I thought about it at this point I also realized that I did not know anything about the "first" wife. You know? I did not know what her situation really was. She was not before me. Perhaps the first wife might be in a terrible financial situation. Perhaps Junior had abandoned her; I did not know anything about it. For me to stretch to protect the "second" wife would be one thing; but for me to stretch and say that somebody not before me was not entitled to anything would be wrong.

So, I said to my colleagues, "Hey, you know, New York has said this is a very difficult issue. There's a lot of money here." The pension and the Social Security were sizable and are probably enough to take care of both of them. I think we should send it back to the district judge, Judge Grisea, and say, "This is a difficult issue of New York law, as New York has told us. We would rather you decide it first."

Now Judge Meskill is perfectly willing to go along with Altimari and me, because previously he had thought we were stretching and now, clearly, we were not. We were not doing anything! But what we were doing, certainly, was sending Grisea plenty of signals.

I originally wrote a footnote which said, "And if the district judge finds that because of the difficulty of this issue, the parties choose to settle, so much the better." I do not now see this in the opinion; I had thought it was in but it was not. Probably one of the other judges said, "Don't put it in. Too far."

Judge Grisea was old and tired, but he was a smart guy. And as soon as he saw what was going on, I have no doubt that he knew what to do. And the parties probably did, too.

The case never came back to us.

It is less rare than you would think that a Court of Appeals sees it as appropriate to induce a settlement rather than to declare the law. But, apart from that, I came away feeling how important it is to let pro se litigants argue. One really could not have known what was at stake from the briefs alone.

In the end, no law was mangled, and justice was probably done. Moreover, I had learned about another way in which certification could be helpful.

* * *

United States v. Martinez is an amazing case about the raid of a drug house in the Bronx. What happens is the police arrest somebody who is there and charge him with dealing—not just with buying drugs to consume them. The difference in the penalty for dealing is enormous, and the defendant is convicted of that. He appeals, and his problem is essentially that the evidence is that he was there, and it is perfectly obvious that some of those who were in the room were dealers. But what evidence is there that Martinez is a dealer and not a buyer?

As the case comes up, Jon Newman, John Walker, and I are on the panel. I look at the facts. They were all sitting around eating pizza when the raid happened. I see no evidence at all that this person Martinez is a drug dealer. And if there is no evidence at all, then even if somebody in that room was a drug dealer, the conviction has to flip! Jon Newman agrees that Martinez is "not guilty beyond a reasonable doubt," in part because Jon had quite a wonderful view of what "beyond a reasonable doubt" should be. Rather than deciding, "Is there evidence on the basis of which a jury can decide on guilt?" Jon thought that there should be an independent judgment on the part of the court as to what is *not* reasonable doubt.

This had been a position of Jon's for years. He had lost out on it, but it was still the position he favored, and he still wanted to try to get it back. I hadn't quite realized that, at the time. I think, it is probably a right position—but it just doesn't happen to be the law of the Second Circuit.

Jon believed that the appellate court has to decide for itself whether, when there was evidence running both ways, whether there was a reasonable doubt of guilt; and on that basis Jon too has doubts about Martinez being a dealer.

John Walker, looking at it much more from his experience in the U.S. Attorney's Office, believes that there is much more evidence that could have been introduced; he thinks that the police were just lazy—which it is clear that they were. He believes the police and prosecutors could have shown all sorts of things in the trial but did not. But still he thinks enough evidence has been proffered.

So, two to one, we vote to reverse the conviction, and Martinez is released.

Walker writes a very strong dissent. He really is worried about letting these drug dealers out when "we all know" they are guilty. Although the government does not do so, he asks for the case to be taken up *en banc*. The exchange of memos between us at that point is quite interesting; among other things it illuminates the difference between a newcomer on the bench and a well-established Judge. I did not really understand, at the time, completely, that as a kid on the Court I should have been more deferential, and so my memos are very strong, while Jon's memos on Martinez are, conversely, "I have this view, and that's it."

As the *en banc* proceeds I find myself in the forefront of defending the panel opinion. People are saying: "there is *this* evidence, and *this* evidence, and *this* evidence, and *this* evidence." I answer them, saying, "This evidence is *zero*. The next piece of evidence is *zero*, and the one after that is *zero*." And I write a memo which says "Listen, *zero* plus *zero* plus zero plus *zero* equals *zero*! So, do not tell me that there is some evidence, and that is enough."

People started voting. And while they are voting, something happens. I change my mind.

Why? What happened was that while most of these memos say nothing to me—Fred Parker's memo does. His memo is different.

Fred often said to me that he admired how fast I was and regretted how slow he was. I would tell him, "Yes, Fred, you are slow, and I am fast. And it is no use my trying to be slow and no use your trying to be fast. Because you are slow—and very good—you see some things that I do not see." I told Fred Parker many times that he was the one who changed my mind more often than anyone else.

Fred wrote a memo about where an easily accessible gun was in the apartment. He convinced me that dealers would not let a buyer who could easily get hold of a gun in their apartment when they were buying drugs. That would be too dangerous for the dealers. As a result, a gun left in a place where the defendant could readily get it was evidence on which a jury could say, "No, they were all in it together." I said to myself, "You know, this is evidence."

> *There was also evidence that Martinez also had a small scale with him, and the police saw him throw a gun out of a window, but that would not have had the same effect in showing that he was a dealer because there was no evidence that others knew he had a gun.*

What is more, once you have *some* evidence, all the other facts started to have some weight. They started to have some meaning. One finding affects the other. And if you do not accept Jon Newman's notion that it is up to the appellate court to decide how much weight to give once there is some evidence, then you think that it is up to the jury to say, "This convinces me, beyond a reasonable doubt, of guilt."

Keep in mind, too, that this is 1995, and I am a new judge. It matters to me that somebody who is as thoughtful as Parker is, and has as much experience as a district judge as Parker does, says to me "Look, the presence of the gun does make a difference, and it should be persuasive to you, because reasonable people know that when you have a drug-selling operation, you do not leave weapons around so that the buyers who are hooked can get them, and shoot you up, and go away with the whole drug inventory. Each of the dealers might have guns, but what they certainly do not do is leave weapons lying around."

So I flipped, and it was very dramatic, because Martinez, poor fellow, did not know that his case might be considered *en banc*, had not fled, and so he ended up back in jail. John Walker said, "If I had been him, I would have gotten out of town so fast!"

That I changed my mind was criticized on the court—and elsewhere. Some judges just assumed—I think because they were themselves more result-oriented—that "Guido flipped because he doesn't want to be reversed *en banc*." All sorts of people started to say, "Guido thought he was going to lose the *en banc*, and therefore he shifted sides."

That was baloney. I have shifted at an *en banc* because other judges persuaded me on several occasions. For example, I wrote an opinion with a visiting judge, and Amalya Kearse dissented. She asked for an *en banc*, and everybody voted to go *en banc*. I had written the opinion with a visiting judge. Jon Newman said to me, "Don't worry, Guido. Early on, I was taken *en banc*, and I was reversed twelve to one. You will probably do better." As it turned out, I changed my mind in that case also—and so I was reversed thirteen to nothing!

In *Martinez*, I would have loved to be reversed *en banc* with me and Jon Newman dissenting, maybe picking up two or three others! That would have been very nice. Being in a minority allows you to speak broadly. But after Parker's memo, I just did not think the panel decision was right, and so I changed my mind.

In the Academy, you know, people change their minds all the time; you kind of laugh at people who are not capable of changing their minds.

> *Many academics laugh somewhat nervously at Saint John Fisher, who was executed by Henry VIII, as was Saint Thomas More. Thomas More tried to avoid martyrdom, but he sincerely believed that the King was improperly divorcing. John Fisher, it is said, was not equally devout, but he had written a scholarly—academic—opinion that Henry's first marriage, with Catherine of Aragon, was valid. He could not support the King's position that the marriage to Ann Boleyn was valid without taking back his earlier Academic position that Henry was already properly married. The story is that he was willing to get his head cut off, rather than admit that he has made an academic error! There are academics who treat him as an object lesson, and say, "No, as an academic, you have to be able to admit you're wrong."*

On a court, I certainly think you should change your mind if it lets somebody out—if a conviction was improperly upheld. But then, shouldn't you change your mind the other way as well? You should not worry terribly much about what people say about you.

Of course it is easier to admit mistakes in the distant past. I have seen Jon Newman do it this way. In an oral argument, someone will cite an opinion of his from twenty years earlier. John smiled, and said, "But you know, I may have been wrong. What makes you think that I have learned nothing in twenty years?"

> *Judges do change their mind, even before too much time has passed. Justice Black admitted—soon afterward—that he was wrong about his vote permitting state double jeopardy in* Palko v. Connecticut. *And any number of Justices admitted having been wrong in the first of the* Flag Salute Cases, *which caused them to flip on essentially the same facts within a year.*

What happened in *Martinez* was unusual, but only because I changed my mind about my own opinion in the very same case, and with no new evidence.

* * *

Martin Tankleff was a seventeen-year-old who was accused of killing his parents in 1988. Police arrested him and questioned him for hours and hours. They used all sorts of deceptive tactics, saying his father, before dying, had said it was Martin, and other things, which were just not true. They thought that he looked as though he was in a daze. So they convinced him that he may have done it while in a daze without knowing he had done it. He confessed; but he immediately after took the confession back and just said, "no."

At the trial the prosecution developed some theory about his being mad because the parents would not let him drive the family's fancy car. He was convicted and was sentenced to life in prison. The conviction was affirmed, in the face of this somewhat dubious confession and in the face of all sorts of other things that had happened in the trial that were really troublesome. He filed a habeas petition which reached our court, and all that transpired was sufficiently troublesome that it seemed to me to be a truly unusual habeas case—one of the odd few in which I really thought that there was a significant chance that the petitioner was innocent.

The problem with habeas cases is that in many of them the court is basically pretty confident that the person is guilty of the crime charged, and yet there are significant possibilities that violations of the person's constitutional rights occurred. The habeas judge is then torn between releasing a criminal and ignoring constitutional rights.

> *Justice Scalia said in one of his early talks, that we should stop looking for constitutional violations in habeas cases and instead should focus on habeas as a way of letting only the innocent out. Many liberals said this was outrageous, and in a way it is.*

Because courts who found constitutional errors did let some guilty people out, Congress put in a huge number of trivial—but very difficult—procedural impediments to the bringing of federal habeas. For example, you cannot bring it more than once; you must file within a year of the end of the direct appeal. You also must defer to the state determinations, even if they are wrong, if they are not "unreasonable." At the same time, Justice Rehnquist started to say that innocence did not really matter, that for habeas to be granted there had to be a separate constitutional violation.

The result of the liberal opposition to Justice Scalia's position has in a way been the worst of both worlds. Some people who meet the technical requirements are still released even though they are guilty, and the technical impediments together with decisions that say being innocent may not be enough to allow habeas mean that some innocent people are denied the "Great Writ."

Martin Tankleff's habeas petition case comes up to my Court. I see that the prosecution did any number of things which were wrong. I am willing to say that these things were bad enough, and we should grant habeas—primarily because I think there is something smelly about the whole case. This leads me to want to have a new trial where some of the dirty things that were done at trial, some of the things that were said, some of the mistakes that were made, would not happen, so that the jury will be able to view the whole case in a different way. I tried to convince my colleagues on the panel that there was something about this case that was deeply troubling. The other two judges agreed that this was a case where there is some serious question about possible innocence, but told me, "You cannot grant the habeas petition. There just isn't enough wrong here."

These were both former district court judges, and they said, "there are mistakes and the prosecution overstepped here or there; but not enough to say that the state courts, in upholding the conviction, were unreasonable."

Such mistakes happen in any number of other trials. If we had written an opinion saying, "There are enough issues here so that we should reverse," that would probably make too many other trials flip where the person was pretty manifestly guilty. The panel contained two experienced trial judges who were saying to me, "What you want to do would screw up any number of trials and you want to do it for something—this guy's possible innocence—which is only a bare possibility."

I was not, at that time, convinced that this guy was innocent. I can't say that. But all I could say, and I think they saw it, too, was that this was a case in which, had we been on a jury, we might have said, as jurors, "I have a reasonable doubt."

It's that level. I do not mean that we knew for certain that Tankleff was innocent. No, I cannot say that. But there was enough going on so that one had the feeling this may be a case where there is innocence.

I was sufficiently upset that I thought about dissenting. But if I dissented, what would have happened? Tankleff would have stayed in jail, and the opinion affirming the conviction would have approved of many of the objectionable tactics the prosecution used. If, on the other hand, I wrote the opinion, I could say these behaviors were bad even if insufficient to justify a reversal. I decided not to dissent.

I said to my colleagues, "Look, I'll write the opinion affirming, but sending it back to find out if there was serious racial bias in the way the jury was chosen—to have them do a '*Batson* reconstruction.'" I did not think prosecutors would be able to reconstruct the voir dire because the trial was already quite a few years back. I thought that if this meant that a new trial would be required, it was fine with me. The others agreed. That was the narrow way we chose to write, affirming but remanding for a *Batson* hearing.

It seemed like a sensible kind of compromise—except that it was a compromise that did not say that we had doubts about Tankleff's guilt. To my surprise, hearings were held on remand, a *Batson* reconstruction was done, and the court ruled that there had been no exclusion of jurors on racial grounds. How they did that I do not really know, but the result was that Tankleff's conviction stood, and he remained in jail.

My opinion in Tankleff has since gotten cited a lot for the proposition that we do not reverse the prosecution for certain types of trial error. This is technically correct but because of the peculiarities of the Tankleff case, I hate to see myself cited that way.

Years go by. More and more evidence emerges that Tankleff is really innocent; that the murderer or the one who arranged it was likely to be his father's partner, who it was already known had taken off. As more evidence comes in, Tankleff goes to state court—but the state court says no! It is very hard to overturn a conviction of that sort.

I start to think that Tankleff really is innocent, and yet the state courts are doing nothing. This bothers me greatly and it becomes something I talk about with my clerks; something that is part of our mutual education. I ask them whether one should dissent even though it does not seem to do any good, or else join the others to make an opinion that is less damaging. I say with regret to the clerks, "If I had dissented and had pointed out all the reasons I thought this person might be innocent, and then emphasized all the terrible things that I thought the prosecution and the police had done, it might have made it easier for a state court now to flip." But I also say, "Keep in mind that if I had written that kind of dissent, the majority opinion would have said, "Everything that happened was okay." This is the bind you are in, in such a situation.

As time goes by, I get more and more upset with myself and with my part in all this. The injustice of the situation haunts me. I am troubled enough about it to ask Jon Newman whether I can write a letter to the state judge that says, "Look, I wrote the opinion affirming, but I did that because of the limits that are put on habeas, and because of comity; but I was convinced at the time, and am more convinced now, that there is real, real doubt about guilt." I want to try to influence the state court judge that way. Jon said I cannot do it, but that the panel as a whole can. Unfortunately, one of the judges on the panel had by now died, and the other is not inclined to do it.

More time goes by—until in 2006, when one of my clerks, Roberto Gonzalez, is working at the D.C. office of the WilmerHale firm, which was one of several firms working pro bono to free Tankleff. Roberto jumps on it. He knows the story well because it had been part of our discussions in my chambers.

Tankleff's legal team found enough new evidence, so that finally—seventeen years or so after this guy had gone to jail!—the state court orders Martin Tankleff released.

Not long after his release, Martin Tankleff is asked by Roberto, who has been working with him as his lawyer, "Would you like to meet Guido?" Martin says, "Absolutely!" I meet him.

We talk about his case. I tell him the whole story. He is remarkably understanding.

Since then he has written to me from time to time. He went back to college. He finished college. He entered Touro Law School. He became involved in the moot court program there and I judged the moot court, because he asked me to do it. He graduated. He got married and adopted a child. Recently, when he was admitted to the New York bar, I wrote a letter and appeared in his behalf. We are still in touch, and he is now doing some teaching at Georgetown and elsewhere about unjust convictions in general.

He received several million dollars from New York for his wrongful conviction, and millions more from Suffolk County to settle a suit against those who were involved in the deplorable stuff that went on in the DA's office there, stuff that had been responsible for sending him to prison. It is hardly a surprise that he has devoted his life to undoing wrongful convictions.

Luckily, he was young enough so that despite seventeen years in jail, he still has a life. In that way, the story has a happy ending. And yet seventeen years wrongly in jail is mighty awful.

* * *

Have you heard of "penile plethysmography"? It is a horrible technique that supposedly measures blood flow to the penis. Some people in Czechoslovakia invented it and used it supposedly to screen out homosexuals from the military. Some courts and parole offices have used it as well. A "plethysmograph" is attached to a penis and later the person has been told to masturbate, supposedly to calibrate the machine. And then the person must look at pornography, while the machine measures the size of the person's erection. The purpose is not altogether clear. Some parole boards have had the discretion to compel sex offenders to undergo this before they can be released.

In the case before us, *United States v. McLaurin*, McLaurin was a convicted sex offender who had served his prison term. As a condition for his release, he was required by the court to comply with a probation officer's program of sex offender evaluation and treatment. This program included plethysmograph examinations.

[Barrington D.] Danny Parker and I together wrote the opinion, which reversed this order. We each wanted to write because we each felt so strongly about it. José Cabranes was presiding; he was quite willing to write but he let us do it.

We all agreed that plethysmography is "junk science" which has no reasonable relation to sentencing or supervising probation. But we went further than that, and we said that at least in this context, using plethysmography violated *substantive* Due Process, and might well do so even if it were not junk science. We noted that even if convicted of a crime, a person retains humanity and a right to substantive due process, and we wanted to say that this kind of thing is just not acceptable.

This was a highly unusual position for me to take, for it said that at least on the facts of this case this was a violation of substantive Due Process. Substantive Due Process places a court in the position of holding that the law cannot treat a person a certain way even if procedural protections are present, even if there is no discrimination involved, and even if protection from this action is not mentioned in the US Constitution. It is holdings of this sort that got the Court in terrible trouble with the New Deal.

There are many possible ways we might have decided *McLaurin* without finding such a Due Process violation. The procedure is debasing and humiliating to sex offenders, which might give rise to a perfectly good Eighth Amendment argument—that it is cruel and unusual punishment to humiliate them with a "Scarlet Letter." But penile plethysmography is not torture. If it were, this would clearly be a violation of the Eighth Amendment.

Calling it an unacceptable privacy invasion would have been another way to decide this case. There are any number of ways in which you can hold that penile plethysmography violates the Fourth Amendment. It certainly forces a person to disclose some of the most intimate and personal aspects of behavior, but some probation and release requirements that demand highly intimate or private revelations have been permitted. More to the point, what is most deeply troubling about this to me was not this particular invasion of privacy. What I could not get away from was the horror that the law demanded a person to become a sexual guinea pig to pseudoscience.

It is interesting is that while I had this reaction, perhaps as someone of Jewish heritage, it was also the reaction that Danny Parker, an African American, also had, and José Cabranes, a Puerto Rican.

We all condemned this use of "science," and I wonder whether, in each of us, this plethysmography did not pull each of us back to the dark period of eugenics; to Justice Holmes and his decision in Buck v. Bell, which upheld compulsory sterilization; and to the horrific experimentations that took place in Nazi hospitals and concentration camps during the Second World War. All this history united the whole panel. Germans were perfectly willing to experiment on Jews and others they considered to be an inferior race. There was much the same sentiment in our own country with respect to Blacks in the Tuskegee syphilis experiments. And it was not very different when birth control devices were tested on poor Puerto Rican women in the 1950s.

This led all of us to agree that if there is anything that is not to be accepted, it is the compulsory subjection of a particularly disfavored group to "scientific" experimentation.

Of course, the singling out of a particular group could have led us to call this a violation of the Equal Protection Clause. We might. But in our case, plethysmography was compelled with *no basis whatever*, because it was based on pseudoscience; and this meant that it would be wrong regardless of whom it was imposed on. That also meant that we could have held it a violation of procedural Due Process, because procedurally it had no basis. But that would have left open that someone could come up with a procedurally acceptable way of using it.

In other words, there were any number of ways in which this case could have been decided without reaching the rather drastic conclusion that "This is so shocking that it can't be done." But we didn't want to suggest that it might be acceptable in a really terrible situation but it cannot be used in a probation situation.

> *Are there other procedures that are so unacceptable that they cannot be used? The problem of the death penalty sits there in the background. Is it acceptable if it is applied only in "the most horrible cases," which are identified through the use of strict procedural Due Process?*

* * *

Jed Rakoff, a judge in the District Court in New York, held that the death penalty is unconstitutional. Why? Rakoff said, in *United States v. Quinones*, that recently there have been many cases in which, because of new DNA testing and other scientific advances, a person was found to be innocent, and was released from jail. He wrote that people who are executed are in practice deprived of the opportunity to show their innocence later. He held that that was a violation of the Due Process Clause. He did this before Quinones' trial began.

Rakoff obviously wanted to hold the death penalty unconstitutional; but he was unable to do it in more direct ways given previous rulings by the Supreme Court. So he came up with this rather ingenious theory. His case went to a panel of our Circuit.

José Cabranes wrote the opinion reversing him, on the ground, ultimately, that there is no way that one can say that Due Process is violated. Similarly, it is not violated because sometime in the future one might be able to exonerate one's self. For better or for worse, I think José applied the precedents correctly. Although the holding that the death penalty was unconstitutional was reversed, the jury ultimately did not impose the death penalty in *Quinones*.

> *In* Quinones *Judge Cabranes also relied on dicta from an opinion by Justice Rehnquist, mentioned earlier, which suggested that innocence, without a constitutional flaw, is not enough to get habeas. José goes out of his way to note that this is dictum. Perhaps this was because if he had that as part of his holding, there is a substantial chance that other judges might have taken it en banc.*
>
> *After all, some justices have said that "innocence may be enough" in a capital case. It would be extraordinary to hold that someone who demonstrated true innocence could be executed, unless a separate constitutional violation were shown.*

The cases in our Circuit about the death penalty are relatively few, but they are complicated, and they make a judge's choices very difficult. There was the situation involving Michael Ross. He was on death row for years and years and years, for sexually assaulting, kidnapping and murdering quite a few young women. Finally, Ross decided that he was not going to appeal any longer. He decided that he had had it. He wanted to die.

The question was this: Was he sane? His own lawyer refused to ask for a hearing on the man's sanity and said, "The guy wants to die, and that is it." I do not know for sure why the lawyer did it, for if it turned out that the Ross was insane, he could not legally give up his rights to appeal even if he wanted to. His family asked for a hearing on his sanity; but the state prosecutor opposed it. The Connecticut Supreme Court denied a hearing and certiorari was denied.

Subsequently, Judge Chatigny, in the Connecticut District Court granted a stay to a public defender who stood in as a "friend," and a panel of our Circuit declined to vacate it. Connecticut then appealed to the U.S. Supreme Court, which vacated the stay in a perfunctory sentence. It essentially reversed us without giving any reasons, five-to-four. This was, to put it mildly, offensive. While it is possible that neither the parents nor a friend who had long been his lawyer has standing to ask for an insanity hearing, and that *only* he, that is, the prisoner through his current lawyer, can ask for it, still there is something very peculiar about a situation in which the only one who can ask is the current lawyer who can refuse to do so even though it might save his client's life. One might expect the Supreme Court at least to talk about the issue.

What happened then was that the Judge Chatigny, a wonderful district judge—a former clerk of José's and Jon Newman's and very close to Senator Dodd—arranged a conference call with the prosecutor, the defense lawyer, and all concerned. Using language which was probably too strong, he said to the defense lawyer something like "Look, if it turns out that this guy is executed, and then we find evidence that he was insane, I will have you before the Bar." The lawyer then did what he should have done all along—he asked for a hearing on sanity, which was held. At the hearing, the conclusion of some psychiatric professionals rather than others was accepted, and the guy was found to be sane. He was subsequently executed.

> *Demanding the sanity hearing is probably the reason Chatigny is not on our court. He was nominated by Senator Dodd. The prosecutor, who had never forgiven him, brought charges against him to our Court for browbeating the lawyer. A panel headed by Judge Walker said, "Nonsense! He did exactly what should have done." But that did not stop Senator Sessions and other Southern senators, who were also mad at Dodd, who was leaving office, from using this episode to block him.*

I was not directly involved in either *Ross* or *Quinones*, but these cases brought home how emotionally and legally difficult capital cases are.

* * *

Now jump to *United States v. Fell*, where I became involved. It is a kidnapping-murder case out of Vermont, which does not have the death penalty. Because of the kidnapping it could be brought federally; but it was, essentially, a straight state murder case. Why was it brought federally? Because the Justice Department under Attorney General Ashcroft believed that it was unjust that somebody who would be executed in some states would not be executed in Vermont.

> *I believe this sentiment demonstrates a fundamental misunderstanding of what federalism is about. There are some who feel that the death penalty is unconstitutional across the country, and that the "Cruel and Unusual Punishment" clause does that. There are others who feel that it is justified and that all states should impose it.*
>
> *But if federalism stands for anything, it is that often I must be willing to accept your immorality in exchange for your accepting mine. The question of what is national and what can be decided locally is the deepest of the questions in a federalism. We have gone both ways on many issues and continue to do so. Think of slavery; segregation; abortion; the right to die; and the death penalty.*
>
> *As to the latter, the Supreme Court has made it clear that this is not a national, but a local issue, and it federalism stands for anything, it means that as to non-national issues, I must be willing to accept your immorality if you're willing to accept mine. It never has been said that every state has to have the death penalty because some do. Still the temptation is very great for the death penalty proponents to say, "Oh, this person is really nasty, so we will try him federally, because then we can get him on the death penalty," when the state doesn't have it.*

They tried him federally and they got a death penalty—the jury came out for death. There was an appeal to the Second Circuit. The *Fell* panel—Judges Cabranes, Walker, and Danny Parker upheld it—after a long period of time. They found that there were no problems. This was the death penalty panel which had reversed the federal district court in Vermont, when Judge Sessions, in the same case, held that the Federal Death Penalty Act violated the Fifth Amendment and Sixth Amendment because it ignored the rules of evidence when it considered information about the defendant's eligibility for the death penalty.

The *Fell* panel took a very long time to issue its decision. My instinct is that this was because there was a conflict about what language should be there about the desirability or undesirability of the death penalty in general. Ultimately, Danny Parker wrote a moderate opinion which upheld Judge Sessions's very careful rulings about all sorts of questions that had arisen in the case. Judge Sessions, perhaps because he had been overruled in his broader death penalty holding, had not done what Judge Jack Weinstein had done in some other cases: you know, make it virtually impossible for a jury to come back with a death penalty. There it was; the death penalty was upheld.

I asked the Chief Judge to request an *en banc* vote, based on two arguments that were literally, "unusual." One, that in a state like Vermont, which has no death penalty, it is extraordinarily unusual for a jury to come in with a federal death penalty. Such cases seeking the death penalty are rarely brought in federal court, and when they are brought it is very unusual for the jury to impose the death penalty.

> *The most dramatic example of this is New York. When New York did have the death penalty, New York juries came in fairly regularly with death penalties. But the death penalty was abolished in New York—thanks to Chief Judge Judith Kaye's procedural gimmicking—and since then I think New York juries have imposed the death penalty in a federal case involving essentially a state crime only once, and this one was flipped by a panel presided over by Dennis Jacobs because there was something wrong with what the prosecutor did. After many backs and forths, the defendant ended up with a life sentence.*

The death penalty is cruel, no question about that; but is it *unusual*? I said that the Circuit should get briefing on whether it is unconstitutional because it is "unusual," as well as "cruel" punishment. I thought I could demonstrate that it is rarer for jurors in a non-death penalty state to impose the death penalty in a federal case than it was in death penalty states to execute minors or the insane—and the Supreme Court has held the latter to be unconstitutionally cruel and *unusual*.

I believe that the reason executions of minors and the insane were so rare was because of values associated with the treatment of minors and the insane. The value that is behind the infrequency of federal death penalties in non-death penalty states is *federalism*, which is as important a value as any. Federal juries in such states are in effect saying, "our state has decided against the death penalty. We don't like the federal government attempt to override our state's judgment by bringing this case federally." It seems to me that when something is unusual because it undermines the federal system by trumping federally a state attitude toward the death penalty, that should be enough to make it "cruel and unusual" for purposes of the federal Constitution.

In my request for *en banc* I made a second point as well. I suggested that prospective jurors, and jurors after they are chosen, ought to be able to be informed that Vermont does not have a death penalty, in cases like the one before them. This is a subsidiary federalism argument. It says, "okay, even if you do not want to say it is cruel and unusual, the jury ought still to be a jury 'of one's peers,'" meaning a Vermont jury informed about Vermont's attitude toward the death penalty.

That is what my request to go *en banc* was about.

I lost the vote on it overwhelmingly. Only Judges Robert Sack and Rosemary Pooler joined me. You would have thought that that would have been the end of it. But Judge Reena Raggi wrote a very strong opinion concurring in the denial of the *en banc*. She took on both of my arguments, and this made me write more in answer to her. Our two opinions got quite heated. What is interesting about them, and I think upset Reena, was that I wrote, "You do not understand federalism. You understand the rules, but you do not understand what federalism is really about."

> *Discussions of federalism need to talk about not just economic federalism and political federalism, but juridical federalism. Our federal court system is a Madisonian compromise of what is state, and what is federal. The jury, even in federal cases, is always a jury of the locality. While a federal jury is nationally named it is essentially a locally sitting body. Federal district judges are, in many ways, representative judges—judges that are selected with significant local influence, sitting with juries that are from the state. That is all part of our federal structure.*

Reena, whom I greatly like and admire, is a wonderfully bright product of Harvard of that time. I think she was taught, "these are the rules," without looking to the reasons and structure behind the rules. Her argument was based on the fact that these murders can be brought federally under the Constitution, which should end all concerns about federalism. I was talking instead about what the structure of federalism is, and how it allows people with different values to coexist in the same country. I was talking about what the whole system is about. It is not surprising that under the circumstances, two able people should disagree. The disagreement here is, intellectually, not that different from the one Reena and I had over whether one could say a rule was reasonable and yet absurd, about which I spoke earlier. And these are less ideological differences than differences in approach.

Interestingly, the *Fell* case ultimately flipped. It did so because Louis Liman—a very good Yale Law School graduate and now a federal district judge—took the case pro bono and discovered improprieties in the jury behavior. This led to the overturn of the conviction, and so here too, after many, many backs and forths, the government accepted a plea of guilt followed by a life sentence. What was already highly "unusual" in our circuit has become rarer still.

And this brings us to the recent decision of our Court in *United States v. Aquart*. *Aquart* was tried federally in Connecticut for a murder that was subject to two federal laws. Shortly before he was tried, when Connecticut had the death penalty, a jury had handed it down, in a particularly gruesome and much publicized home invasion case. Soon afterward the Connecticut Legislature voted to abolish the death penalty prospectively—that is, in all future cases. Subsequently, and after the *Aquart* case trial, the Connecticut Supreme Court, in a closely decided opinion, held that under those circumstances, the death penalty could not be imposed on those previously convicted and sentenced to death. This would be "cruel and unusual" under the Connecticut Constitution, with considerable emphasis on "unusual."

But the *Aquart* case had been brought federally, and so the state court decision did not directly affect it. The district judge in the case, Janet Bond Arterton, happens to be a very good judge and a good friend of mine and Anne's. I don't know her views on capital punishment, but I expect that she was extremely careful not to let any possible personal opposition to capital punishment affect her rulings. In any event, the jury imposed the death penalty on Aquart, one of several people—probably the leader—of those involved in what, like so many murders, was brutal.

I was selected to be a member of the Death Penalty Appeals Panel. Because under our procedure such panels hear everything that has to do with a case, including any eventual habeas petitions, until the case is concluded—and this will inevitably take many years—Senior Judges can decline to serve. I decided that it was my obligation to take it on.

I dislike the death penalty intensely and think the Supreme Court should have held it unconstitutional; but I have also stated that being a judge, if it is properly imposed, I will concur, perhaps with a strong criticism of the Supreme Court's holdings but upholding it. On the other hand, because of my view I am apt to look more probingly for any errors in its imposition in the particular case and for any reasons why it violates the Constitution in ways not precluded by the Supreme Court in the particular context.

That is what I did in *Fell*.

The other members of the panel were Reena Raggi and Dick [Richard] Wesley. Dick describes himself as the most conservative judge in Upstate New York. Whether that is true or not, it is the case that, to date, we have never dissented from each other on a panel, although we have disagreed on *en banc* questions. And, of course, he did not join my request for an *en banc* in *Fell*.

The *Aquart* appeal was argued to us, and after argument, at my request, the parties were asked to brief whether the death penalty was "cruel and unusual" because in cases of this sort it had almost never been carried out in the relevant jurisdiction.

The suggestion we asked them to look into was whether a jurisdiction could do something to the very few, which they were not willing to do to the many. That would mean that a state that has the death penalty but never exercises it, or does so only once in fifty years, cannot do it, but that Georgia and Florida can, because in them it is commonly applied. We asked whether the federal government could apply it given that the federal government had only executed one person in the last fifty years for murders of the sort involved in the *Aquart* case. There have been a few federal executions—not that many. But virtually all of them involved terrorism, or military or similar conduct like spying in wartime. The death penalty might in this sense be "unusual" in many jurisdictions that nominally have it, but not in others.

This view of "unusual" in one sense can be said to represent an original understanding—one that both reflects the situation in England at the time of our founding, and also the demands of federalism.

> *The history is interesting. In England, at the time the words "cruel and unusual" were first used, it was impossible to do what the Supreme Court has done in capital cases—look to how many or how few states impose a punishment in particular circumstances. England had no states. This meant that "unusual" had to mean either "among cognate countries"—something the Supreme Court has excluded—or "unusual" within that particular jurisdiction.*
>
> *Because the words "cruel and unusual" derive from language used in England in 1689, following the Glorious Revolution, in a document that was highly influential in our Framing, this view may well reflect an original understanding of those words. More historical research needs to be done, and in particular about other constitutional prohibitions, including ex post facto and attainder that were also used to prohibit punishments that were "unusual" in this sense.*

I cannot say that the parties in their briefing understood this possible argument. They made a series of other arguments linked to what they believed was the original understanding of the Framers. In any event, because of this, and other reasons which usually indicate strong disagreements and the need for extended discussion among those on a panel, the *Aquart* case remained undecided for a very long time—almost three years. In the end, the panel unanimously vacated the death sentence and remanded the case for further proceedings.

We were unanimous in upholding the conviction in *Aquart*; we had different views on whether the death penalty could be constitutionally applied in a situation like this. The majority said "yes," although it did not deal fully with the "unusuality" argument. In concurring I said that under the circumstances we did not need to discuss most of the arguments concerning the constitutionality of the death penalty that had been made to us.

We could discuss in short order the constitutionality arguments that *Aquart* made before the district court and on appeal. But these could be dealt with briefly because they had already been foreclosed by the Supreme Court. I said that the additional arguments that were made partly in response to our request for more briefing were not made to the district court and did not need to be considered since we were vacating and remanding; they could be raised before the district court and considered there in the first instance should the death penalty be reimposed, and there was no reason for us to decide them, or even to discuss them.

But we all agreed on the crucial point—that the sentence of death had to be vacated because of instances of improper conduct by the prosecution, and the district court's inadequate reaction to them.

I think I can properly say that it was the hard work of my chambers and me that made the result convincing to all of us. We found cases that had not been cited to us. As originally presented, a finding that the errors which all of us admitted were there, warranted reversal, would have been problematical. But digging deeper and harder, we came up with what, on the law was ultimately convincing to every one of us.

It reminded me of when I had been a clerk in Justice Black's chambers and he had made me look harder and deeper than I thought could possibly be justified—even to the point of seeking out the original of a Tudor statute. I did that and the result was that the death penalty was not applied to Aquart.

* * *

New York has a law that prevents someone who has been convicted of a felony from being able to vote while they are in prison. The overwhelming effect of felon disenfranchisement was racial discrimination, given the disproportionate numbers of Black people who are in prison, and in 1996, when Jon Newman was the Chief Judge, the issue was considered by our Court in *Baker v. Pataki*. The language of the section in the Voting Rights Act, that no voting qualification can be imposed if it "*results* in a denial or abridgement of the right to vote on account of race," seems to be as clear as language can be; but the district court had said, "The Voting Rights Act is not violated by prohibiting felons from voting."

There were fifteen judges of our Court who had the right to vote on *Baker* when it first came up *en banc*. Rather astonishingly, though, one-third of us were recused. The argument was brought by the Yale Clinic, which meant that Judges Winter, Cabranes, and I were recused.

This was a practice of our Court at the time. Many other judges in other circuits, for instance Richard Posner in the Seventh Circuit, did not recuse themselves. More recently judges Winter and Cabranes stopped recusing themselves merely because the Yale Clinic is involved. And I am reconsidering.

Pierre Leval was recused—and this is kind of odd—because his clerk had been the one at the Yale Clinic who had brought the whole thing. Normally, you are not recused if a clerk is involved in something, but this was so much his clerk's case that Pierre thought that he should take himself out of it. Another judge was recused for another reason.

I do not know whether, if the people who were recused had been in it, it would have made a difference, given who they were. The other ten split, five-to-five, and the Court in *Baker* issued a per curiam opinion affirming the district court by an equally divided court.

Judge Mahoney wrote an opinion supporting the affirmance and saying that the Voting Rights Act was not violated. Wilfred Feinberg and Chief Judge

Newman both wrote also, explaining why they believed it was a violation. This was unusual, for normally no one would write any opinion if there were a five-to-five split. One would just say, "Affirmed by an equally divided court." But both sides wanted very much to write, and they wrote quite powerful opinions. I jokingly sent around a memo saying that I thought Ralph Winter, as the senior judge among the five who were recused, should write an opinion for the five judges who were recused, because it was such an unusual kind of situation!

Because of the way it had been decided, we all knew that felon disenfranchisement was going to come back up, and it did in *Hayden v. Pataki* and a related case. The Circuit was deeply divided again. There was a majority for saying, "The Voting Right Act is not violated." The majority opinion did not seem very satisfactory to me, even just in terms of how it read the statute. The statute prohibits any voting qualification that results in abridging the right of any citizen to vote on account of race or color; and the Supreme Court had held under the statute it clearly did not matter whether the impact is intentional or unintentional. As a result, there were real problems with the Majority reading.

Apart from the question of statutory interpretation, there is a whole other dimension—political and financial—to these cases. These people who cannot vote are nonetheless counted in the Census, which determines representation in legislatures and the allocation of state and federal funds. New York State law allocates the population to the places where the prison is. The prisoners cannot vote, but where they *are imprisoned* results in more money and higher representation being given to white, rural, poor parts of New York, rather than in predominantly Black, urban, and also poor parts of the state. All this reminds me of the constitutional provision that counted slaves as "three-fifths of a person" for representation in the early days of the Republic. This issue was completely ducked by the majority.

There is also an even deeper issue involved. It is one that John Ely wrote about, going to the fundamental question of who is allowed to speak in a democracy; and who, by being able to vote, can protect their interests. To me, this set of cases is akin to those which laid down the principle of "one person, one vote." Its importance is akin also to what I wrote about campaign financing in *Ognibene*; and to cases like *Harper v. Virginia*, which struck down poll taxes; and to the gerrymandering and the voter suppression cases that have come up recently in the courts. These are some of the most important issues affecting our democracy/non-democracy. Upholding restrictions and suppressions of voting limits the vote to certain categories—to the "haves," which is an old game.

> *Before 1832, very few people in England voted. The Reform Act of 1832 helped expand suffrage, and after the reform of 1867, you got a predominantly democratic system in England. That changed everything there about what courts needed to do and did. In the United States, we moved fairly early to a broad suffrage—except*

for women and Blacks. But there have been any number of attempts here over the years by particular groups to give themselves an advantage by playing with the voting system. "One person—'one man'—one vote," was a dramatic attempt to break that. As you would expect, courts have been deciding any number of cases that allege efforts to diminish participation by "have-nots."

The Voting Rights Act is just barely the tip of the iceberg of what is going on in these cases. It is interesting to me that states which one would think are pro-voting, such as New York, have not yet done something legislatively to make sure that these votes count *where* and *how* they should. Other states have tried to level the field do it in campaign financing and the Supreme Court said "No." And yet New York has not even attempted to do it in these felon franchise cases.

I am all for getting to the point where we are a much more universal democracy, where everyone can vote; where it is easy for everyone to vote; and where everyone's ability to vote and to speak before voting is equal. But we are a very long way from getting to a point where wealth and power cannot structure the voting system, and I am enough of a student of history to know that even if we have gotten there, the wealthy and powerful will employ other ways to keep their power. This may be done by selling the ideology of unregulated capitalism and promoting trickle-down economic theories as a way of promoting economic well-being. One should recognize that it is not impossible that such an unregulated capitalist system will in the long run make everyone better off than regulations that protect the economic interests of the poor in the short term.

More dangerous than pushing these claims is the attempt of the wealthy and powerful to maintain their position in the face of full-voting democracy through modern versions of "Tory Radicalism." This was something thought up by my maybe-relative, Benjamin Disraeli.

Disraeli's family came from the Low Countries to Italy and spent several hundred years in the small town of Cento, near Ferrara. He proudly recounted that there they intermarried with ancient Italian Jewish families who were Italim—Jews who were in Italy from Roman times. Cento is a very small town and yet three branches of my family—two precisely of such Italim extraction and one noble Catholic—came from Cento. It is inconceivable that on the right side or the wrong side of the bed I am not related to him.

As I said earlier, the passage of the Reform Act of 1867 brought about nearly total enfranchisement in England. As a Tory, he saw the need to convince the poor to vote against their immediate economic interest and for his party. How? By emphasizing the Empire, the Queen, and the Church.

It was not, in its time, totally noxious. Yes, it did lead to killing some people here and there in the British Empire! But it was not systematically catastrophic.

It is a small step, however—when you don't have Empire or the Church—to go from that to promoting race hatred, or to ginning up homophobia, or to berating the "Theys." It is a tried and true technique for allowing the wealthy and powerful to stay in power. Today we call it an appeal to populism.

You see it in the South, before and after *Brown v. Board of Education*. You see it today in America, dramatically, throughout the country, when the emphasis is very much on: "You have to vote against 'them.'" Immigrants. Muslims. Gays. Or for some religious imperatives.

Who backed Hitler, and why? Who backed Mussolini, and why? First Mussolini fosters dreams of an Empire; and then, even though some people said he began as a semitophile, he becomes viciously anti-Semitic.

Why is it that in Israel you get some people talking about reclaiming "Biblical Palestine," saying, "We have a right to all of it because God gave it to us." No doubt some may really believe it, but the effect of it is, "don't worry about your immediate economic interest; vote for us because we're going to do that holy thing." You see this all over. I have these views. For me they go to the heart of what is going on in *Hayden v. Pataki*, and my dissent.

How much of this can you say in a dissent in a case like *Hayden*? You cannot say much. You can give some hints about what the underlying issues are. They are not fully spelled out, because that really is not the province of an appellate court judge. Accordingly, my dissent in *Hayden* was limited. I emphasized the fact, as the majority's correctly insists, that race-neutral felon disenfranchisement is lawful, is irrelevant to whether *racially discriminatory* felon disenfranchisement is clearly prohibited by the statutory language. Maybe a Supreme Court Justice could go much further. It is certainly something that academics should speak to.

Even as I limited my dissent, I could not convince my colleagues to see things my way. There were several reasons for this. First, the underlying issue of where the people who could not vote were counted for representation, etc., was not decided in the case. The majority ducked. They said it was not really argued; that what was argued was only the narrower question of whether the Voting Rights Act was violated. They sent back the prisoner location issue and it has never really come back to us yet. I think in New York this issue may ultimately get solved politically, because it is New York. It was not wrong, in a way, for the majority to say that deciding that issue was not necessary to decide the case before us.

> By the way, people like me were not necessarily unhappy because there was then a very conservative majority in our court, and I am not sure that we would have decided the issue correctly had we dealt with it.

The location issue will come back to us, though. There is no question that you can constitutionally exclude felons from voting under the Fourteenth Amendment. The constitutional question that is open and must return is: When you exclude them, do you count them for Census purposes where they are incarcerated, or where they lived before going to jail?

Why others viewed the Voting Rights Act in the way they did is speculative. I think there were probably some judges who worried about adopting a disparate impact thesis in this area, and with respect to felons. They were concerned with what that would have meant for other cases involving felons. These judges were, in a sense, updating the language of the statute in order to reach a result that they were comfortable with.

But there were also some people on our court who were afraid that if the Voting Rights Act were read to cover felons, the Voting Rights Act would be weakened by Congress. This is ironical given the way the Supreme Court has gutted it subsequently, but at the time, they were not afraid that it would be gutted. Now here, my "A Common Law for the Age of Statutes" take is, that if you read the statute as it says, and declare that felon disenfranchisement violates the Voting Rights Act, then Congress will come back and debate it. If you read the statute the other way, it would not.

There is a part of *A Common Law for the Age of Statutes* that says something like, "A judge should consider the asymmetry of legislative reaction when deciding which way to come out and make a decision that encourages legislative reform." Unless you are afraid of legislatures, you would not object to such a debate. I don't know that what Congress would say would be that good or will be bad. It might well be that the compromise reached would be "Yes, you can keep them from voting, with certain conditions."

Of course, as I also say in *A Common Law for the Age of Statutes*, there are some problems that are best decided by courts rather than legislatures. We assume too readily that things are always best decided by legislatures. There are other things that are best handled slowly, in a common law way. And when that is true courts should consider the asymmetry of legislative reaction and decide in a way that leads the legislature to stay out of it.

* * *

One of the few cases in which I wrote a strongly emotional dissenting opinion is *Arar v. Ashcroft*. I began by writing that "when the history of this distinguished court is written," the majority decision will be remembered regretfully" I said that I was writing "more in sorrow than in anger." I then added that wise people would ask how such able judges could have reached so dreadful a result.

After the oral argument, *en banc*, people mentioned to me that it was rather shocking that the judges on our Court could be so acrimonious and quarrelsome toward each other. How would we ever be able to speak with each other, following such an argument? And wise elders like Jon Newman, who did not sit on the *en banc* court, certainly tried to cool things down. But many of us thought that rarely—but once in a while—one had to speak fiercely, and that judges have to be mature enough to know that such cases will come up, that strong things will be said, and that after, one can remain friends.

Arar involved a dual citizen of Canada and Syria who was flying from Switzerland back to Canada. The Canadian Secret Service had reason to believe—incorrectly, as it turned out—that he was connected with terrorists. It told American security people of this, and the result was that when the plane landed from Switzerland at JFK Airport, where Arar was for no other reason than to change planes and take another plane to Canada—he was hauled off, questioned, and not allowed to get to a lawyer.

Whether he was beaten up in the United States is not clear. Although he alleged he was beaten up here we assumed he was not, because there was not enough evidence. But he certainly was not allowed a lawyer. He asked to go on to Canada and was told: "No." Nor was he sent back to Switzerland. Rather, he got put in a plane back to Syria, where he was held for a very long time, and where, clearly, he was tortured. I find it ironic, given the current situation in Syria, that we were using Syria as a place for doing interrogations that we wanted done but did not want to do ourselves.

Ultimately, the Syrians released him because they decided he was not a terrorist, and so he got to Canada. The equivalent of a Royal Commission was appointed to look into the matter. It found that Arar was innocent; that he had been brutally treated, and that the Canadian Secret Service had made a terrible mistake. The Commission recommended, and the Conservative Canadian government made a payment to him of many millions of dollars. Arar brought suit in the United States against the federal agents who he claimed mishandled him and sent him to Syria to be tortured, in a "*Bivens*" action, to obtain compensation for the deprivation of his constitutional rights.

The opinion of the panel of our Court which denied him relief seemed to me—I'll be very blunt—to be ridiculous. It said, "This guy was an immigrant, and there are procedures for immigration complaints he did not follow. But Arar was in no sense an immigrant! Yes, technically, he was in the country, and the panel relied on language from statutes dealing with immigration. But immigration had nothing to do with this case of a person who was only here to change planes from one foreign country to another!

Bob Sack dissented from the panel in what I thought was a beautiful opinion, He then asked that the case be reviewed *en banc*, and a majority of all of the active judges on our Court supported his motion. And so we did what is unusual for us: we went *en banc*.

What is one to say about what happened *en banc*? On the one hand, you have got to say that we did one thing right. We vacated the panel opinion, which would have been a terrible precedent that nobody could have lived with. In other words, the case did not turn at all on immigration issues.

Having vacated the panel opinion, we might have sent it back for consideration as to whether a civil suit such as this could be brought notwithstanding the possible difficulties presented by the Government Secret Act and the government secrets doctrine if there were government secrets involved.

En banc hearing, Arar v. Ashcroft, Apr. 8, 2011
(Guido is seated at far left)

I suggested that it be done this way. The governments secrets doctrine, which bars some plaintiff suits, is a not-very-salubrious doctrine. But there would have been an advantage in doing it that way. If a suit is blocked because, although it may be valid it cannot go forward because of government secrets, two things will happen. First, there will be pressure to review the government secrets doctrine, which needs serious review. Second, if the Court in effect says, "This might be a valid suit, but there are government secrets involved, because of which somebody who ought, perhaps, to get compensation cannot, for national security reasons," the Court invites an extrajudicial settlement of it. That, after all, is what happened in Canada, and is often a very good way of handling such situations. By saying, "There are national security problems with allowing this suit, but this person may have rights," you invite the kind of extrajudicial review that makes sense.

What happened *en banc*, instead, is that judges who have been hostile to *Bivens* actions, and perhaps even hostile to 1983 civil rights actions, because they think that they are used often as blackmail—which may from time to time be the case—were joined by judges reacting to a national security issue. A majority said, in effect, "A *Bivens* action cannot lie in situations of national security."

After the Civil War, Congress passed a very broad statute, Section 1983, to allow individuals who were deprived of their statutory or Constitutional rights by state actors, to bring a federal suit to recover damages from these actors. No equivalent statute applies to federal actors. But in Bivens v. Six Unknown Federal Narcotics

Agents, the Supreme Court held that some violations of rights by federal actors are sufficiently grievous that the Constitution itself commands that a suit for damages be allowed. Because this is entirely a judicially created right, courts have applied it narrowly.

Now, that is a very indiscriminate holding. It is perfectly fair to say, "If there is another way of suing, then a *Bivens* action doesn't lie." And there are many reasons why *Bivens* should be limited in other ways. But to say that it cannot lie where there is a "national-security interest," when there is already a government secrets doctrine, is unfortunate. Saying that no *Bivens* action lies in such situations dismisses the suit before the Court can determine that there are government secrets involving national security in the particular case. The holding of the court *en banc*—though logically and legally plausible in a way that the original panel's opinion was not—is also, in some way, worse.

It was nevertheless right to go en banc. *Now at least we were talking about an issue where I think the Court was wrong but reflects a position that is both clear and that one can hold. I hope that the Supreme Court at some point, in some case, will say, "No, no, no. The fact that national security may be involved does not per se' limit* Bivens *actions." That said, the* en banc *majority decision in* Arar v. Ashcroft *is still a very bad decision.*

But what lies underneath the whole case—and the reason that it really graveled me—is deeper. It is not so much my strong disagreement as to what are or are not the appropriate limits on *Bivens*. I would hope that some Congress someday will pass the equivalent of Section 1983 of the Civil Rights Act covering federal employees. At that point, *Bivens*, as a judicially created direct constitutional action, will remain only as an interesting historical background. That is the appropriate solution, and someday we will get there. All that can happen.

I was not most troubled by the lost opportunity to cause a rethinking of the government secrets doctrine, either. Someday, courts and legislatures will go back and will reconsider it. Together they can think about situations in which a lawsuit, open to the public, is so undesirable, that the government should act in an extrajudicial fashion, as Canada has, to remedy a wrong that was done. All that can also happen.

The judicial secrets doctrine is a court-made doctrine. The Government Secrets Act, designed to protect government secrets, is a statute. As such, this is an area eminently suited for the kind of judicial-legislative dialogue that I have discussed earlier. Courts might very well push legislatures to act by suggesting that judicial action is possible, but not desirable, and if the legislatures do not act, serious constitutional problems may arise. It is an interesting analog to the problem of statutes heading toward unconstitutionality.

No, what really gravels me about this case—and the reason I wrote in such an emotional way—is the fact that it reminds one of the all-too-human frailties that characterized the *Dreyfus* affair, I am not talking about the original conviction of Alfred Dreyfus for selling military secrets. I am talking about what moved the judges who reconvicted Dreyfus after it was clear that he was innocent. I fear that some of the same motives may have moved my beloved colleagues in the majority in *Arar*.

I feel strongly, morally, that if one makes a mistake and knows it, one should admit it and go out of one's way to compensate for it. I have always felt that way. It may be because I was brought up on the *Dreyfus* case. Or it may be that I read the *Dreyfus* case that way because I already felt that people, human beings, make mistakes, and that when they do, they should admit them and let the person who is maltreated say, in one way or another, "Screw you!"

As a professor, as dean, as former dean, I always take the position: If we make a mistake and do not appoint somebody whom we know later we should have appointed, we should go out and make that person an offer, even though we know that person is not going to accept it any longer, and let that person throw it in our face! But we have done the right thing when we say, "we made a mistake, and we own up to it, and there it is." And it is right, regardless of that person's reaction.

Too often, instead, when people make a mistake, they seek to hide it, which causes them to behave in an appalling fashion. That was *Dreyfus*. A mistake was made. Maybe at the time it was an honest mistake. Maybe at the time it was a dishonest mistake. Nevertheless, by the time of the famous letter written by Zola came out, *J'accuse . . .*, it was clear that his first conviction by a court-martial was wrong. When Dreyfus was retried, the judges knew there had been a mistake; and yet at the second trial they fought desperately to deny and hide the previous error, so they reconvicted him.

This—or something like it—is what happened in *Arar*. Everyone on the *en banc* Court knew that a mistake had been made, and that Arar had been terribly mistreated. Yet allowing a *Bivens* action would have made that manifest to all—and so they averted their eyes.

I say in my dissent that I am not going to get into whether, when a man is a terrorist, rendition for probable torture in Syria is lawful. Here I will say that I do not think it is lawful to treat even a terrorist that way. Sending terrorists off to be tortured is wrong! But even assuming that it would be all right to do to a terrorist what was done to Arar, in this case, it was a complete mistake, because he was innocent.

It is *that* which really, really, graveled me about the case: the unwillingness to say, "Gee, we've made a mistake." It was the perfectly human, common failing, which leads people to act as if no mistake was really made. If we have executed an innocent man, or if we have sent someone to jail wrongly, we should stand up and say so!! We should do the best we can to admit our error and to compensate for it. Trying to compensate is what justice in torts is all about, and it applies both whether the wrong originally was fault-based, or whether it was not but nevertheless gives rise to strict liability.

Admitting a past wrong to an injured party and to the world, is an essential aspect of justice and compensation, in my view. Sometimes, in other parts of the world, this has happened through "truth and reconciliation" proceedings. But something comparable can and should occur in the American system, through explanations about wrongdoings and compensations that are given through court decisions.

Looking at it from this perspective, *Arar* is a beautiful *en banc* case because the dissenting opinions are each one better than the other in exposing the wrong. You have Judge Robert Sack writing a perfectly straight opinion on the legal consequences of depriving Arar of a *Bivens* remedy simply because national security is involved; you have Judge Danny [Barrington] Parker magnificently focusing on the impact that the decision will have on executive overreaching; and Rosemary Pooler, interpreting the Torture Victims Protection Act. And you have my anguished dissent.

It is also the case that in terms of the willingness of judges to stand up and be counted, in a court that is by and large collegial, the *Arar* dissenters contributed something at a time when an unchecked executive power in the areas of national security has become a deep, deep problem. The dissenters sent up a flare, set down a marker. And did it while acknowledging past errors.

Nevertheless, in terms of result, it was a sad day for the court. There is no doubt in my mind that there is a parallel between *Arar v. Ashcroft* and *Koramatsu v. United States*—and, indeed, to other cases, particularly in wartime, where fundamental rights have been sacrificed because courts were unwilling to stand up.

I have frequently, and to the great annoyance of some of my colleagues, cited *Koramatsu* in situations that are similar in principle, even if not in gravity—in cases like the prison photo case I discussed earlier, in which courts, rather than doing their jobs and seeing what is really going on, accept facts and descriptions given to them by politically pressured parties. When this happens, courts are at their worst.

There are other times, as in the *Pentagon Papers* case, when courts resist. When this happens, they are at their best.

COMMENTARY

Chapter 34

Grabois v. Jones. Kay was a pro se litigant challenging summary judgment in a case that seemed straightforwardly decided by the relevant statute. When she appealed to the Second Circuit, her chances of prevailing were small. But the Second Circuit is the only circuit which hears pro se appeals as a matter of right (except for those incarcerated) and it heard her appeal, and the case took a number of surprising turns.[1]

Guido certified to the New York Court of Appeals a question that the district court did not seem to have considered: whether a spouse whose marriage is concededly void, but was undertaken in good faith and continued until her husband's death, is nevertheless entitled to some benefits given the existence of the federal pension statute, ERISA. The New York Court of Appeals declined to answer, explaining that, because the question implicates a federal statute—the Employee Retirement Income Security Act, or ERISA—it would prefer the matter to be resolved by the federal courts. The case returned to the Second Circuit. This time, relying in part on the indeterminacy left open by the refusal of the Court of Appeals to accept certification, Guido, writing for the Court, held that there was an insufficient factual basis to grant summary judgment.[2]

The case was remanded to the district court and ultimately settled before a judgment was reached. In the end, as Guido says, a sympathetic pro se litigant whose case initially seemed to have no recourse in law was able to avoid walking away empty-handed.

Later cases have cited *Grabois* for the proposition that it is "well established in New York law that when a court is confronted with the claim that a formal second marriage is invalid because of the existence of a valid first marriage, a strong presumption of validity attaches to the second marriage."[3] The certification process in *Grabois* is discussed in Judith S. Kaye and Kenneth I. Weissman, *Interactive Judicial Federalism: Certified Questions in New York.*[4]

Hayden v. Pataki. In *Hayden*, Black and Latino inmates and parolees challenged a New York statute preventing incarcerated and paroled individuals from voting in local, state, or federal elections.[5] The plaintiffs claimed that the statute violated the Voting Rights Act, which, among other things, places restrictions on the right to vote that are based on race. In an opinion by Judge Cabranes, the Second Circuit

---

[1] 89 F.3d 97 (2d Cir. 1996).
[2] *Id.*
[3] Poulos v. Poulos, 169 Vt. 607, 737 A.2d 885, 887 (1999; De George v. Am. Airlines, Inc., 338 F. App'x 15, 18 (2d Cir. 2009).
[4] 69 *Ford. L. Rev.* 373, 410 (2000).
[5] 449 F.3d 305 (2006).

held that the Voting Rights Act does not apply to the disenfranchisement of current and former prisoners.

The case comes down to a matter of statutory interpretation; in his dissent, Guido insists that the majority opinion reflects a basic misunderstanding of the plaintiff's position and is therefore "almost totally irrelevant to the question presented in this case."[6] The majority illustrates at length that Congress did not intend the Voting Rights Act to prohibit *all* felon disenfranchisement. But Guido argues that the majority does not give "a single reason to suggest" that Congress meant not to prohibit a *specific kind* of felon disenfranchisement—namely that based on race. Guido argues that the plain language of the law, together with "all of the canonical indicators of legislative intent," indicates that such disenfranchisement was meant to be prohibited.[7]

The first half of the dissent reads as a lesson in logic. Yes, Guido patiently explains, the majority demonstrates through legislative history that Congress blocked an amendment that would prohibit disenfranchisement of felons whose offense was not related to voting. And yes, this implies that Congress didn't mean to prohibit *all* felon disenfranchisement.[8] But it does not imply that Congress intended to protect *racially motivated* felon disenfranchisement. And again: "Nor do subsequent enactments that presuppose the validity of felon disenfranchisement laws ... suggest in the slightest that Congress understands *discriminatory* felon disenfranchisement to be consistent with the Voting Rights Act."[9]

Guido writes that the majority opinion constitutes a "remarkable decision to buck text, context, and legislative history"—one might have added "basic logic" to this list—"in order to insulate a particular racially discriminatory practice."[10]

In the narrative, Guido extends his remarks about the reasons why. He surmises—notwithstanding protestations to the contrary by colleagues—that the underlying reason for misinterpretation is depending on what the *current* Congress would intend, rather than what the Congress that passed the Voting Rights Act would intend.[11] Of course Guido is well aware of the arguments in favor of a genre of statutory interpretation which employs the lens of contemporary values: he literally wrote the book about the problem of the obsolescence of reasonable justifications for an old statute, and about the consequent reasonableness of assessing current legislative sentiment.[12] Guido has spoken for the view that when legislative change is

---

[6] *Id.* at 362 (Calabresi, J., dissenting).

[7] *Id.* at 364.

[8] Guido's emphasis on the difference between universal prohibitions on felon disenfranchisement and those based specifically on discrimination has been widely cited in disenfranchisement scholarship; *see, e.g.*, Jonathan Sgro, *Intentional Discrimination in Farrakhan v. Gregoire: The Ninth Circuit's Voting Rights Act Standard "Results in" the New Jim Crow*, 57 VILL. L. REV. 139, 176 (2012); Michael A. Wahlander, *Constitutional Coexistence: Preserving Felon Disenfranchisement Litigation Under Section Two of the Voting Rights Act*, 48 SANTA CLARA L. REV. 181, 212 (2008); Thomas G. Varnum, *Let's Not Jump to Conclusions: Approaching Felon Disenfranchisement Challenges Under the Voting Rights Act*, 14 MICH. J. RACE & L. 109, 142 (2008).

[9] 449 F.3d at 365.

[10] *Id.*

[11] *Id.* at 337 (Sack, J., concurring in part and in judgment) (expressly rejecting Guido's surmise).

[12] See Chapter 17, "Judicial Sunset."

likely to be slow and hard-won, interpreting statutes according to current congressional intent can help to avoid cementing outdated and antimajoritarian results.[13]

Nevertheless, in this context he maintains that this argument fails to apply. That is because—consistent with his other "second look" jurisprudence, the Voting Rights Act would be up before Congress the following year for reauthorization: if Congress wanted to update the Act to explicitly allow even racially discriminatory felon disenfranchisement, it would have a clear opportunity to do so without any judicial meddling.[14] Guido concentrates his dissent on correcting the majority's *mis*interpretation of the statute and undermining any justification it might have.

Here, Guido emphasizes broader historical patterns that have colored his thinking: the "old game" of attempting to limit the vote to certain racial, social, and political categories, and, more broadly, the ways in which "wealth and power ... structure the voting system to protect its wealth and power."[15]

U.S. v. McLaurin. One of the conditions of McLaurin's release after being convicted for failing to register as a sex offender was the necessity to participate in a program of sex offender treatment. The treatment included a "plethysmograph" examination—a two- to three-hour procedure that "involves placing a pressure-sensitive device around a man's penis, presenting him with an array of sexually stimulating images, and determining his level of sexual attraction by measuring minute changes in his erectile responses."[16]

In a joint opinion written with Judge Parker, Guido held that a plethysmography examination "involves a greater deprivation of liberty than is reasonably necessary

---

[13] CALABRESI, A COMMON LAW FOR THE AGE OF STATUTES (1982).

[14] The point Guido makes in his dissent about the questionable propriety of interpreting legislative intent with respect to current legislative bodies rather than the drafting ones has been cited in scholarship; *see, e.g.*, Eric A. Johnson, *Dynamic Incorporation of the General Part: Criminal Law's Missing (Hyper) Link*, 48 U.C. DAVIS L. REV. 1891, 1894 (2015); and by Guido himself in a subsequent case, Harrington v. Atl. Sounding Co., 602 F.3d 113, 133 (2d Cir. 2010).

[15] For a general discussion of the history of felon disenfranchisement laws, *see* George Brooks, *Felon Disenfranchisement: Law, History, Policy, and Politics*, 32 Fordham Urb. L.J. 851 (2005); JEFF MANZA & CHRISTOPHER UGGEN, LOCKED OUT: FELON DISENFRANCHISEMENT AND AMERICAN DEMOCRACY (2008). For specific discussions of the role of racism in felon disenfranchisement, *see* Lauren Latterell Powell, *Concealed Motives: Rethinking Fourteenth Amendment and Voting Rights Challenges to Felon Disenfranchisement*, 22 MICH. J. RACE & L. 383 (2017) (discussing *Hayden* at 393); Erin Kelley, Racism and Felony Disenfranchisement: An Intertwined History, The Brennan Center for Justice at New York University School of Law, available at https://www.brennancenter.org/sites/default/files/publications/Disenfranchisement_History.pdf, and Brent Staples, opinion, *The Racist Origins of Felon Disenfranchisement*, N.Y. TIMES, Nov. 18, 2014.

[16] 731 F.3d 258, 260. A plethysmograph, in general, is any instrument that measures changes in volume within an organ resulting from fluctuations in either the amount of air or blood it contains—for instance, lung plethysmography is widely used to study respiration. The particular use of penile plethysmography to measure sexual response was developed in the 1950s by Kurt Freund, a Czech physician, who was initially looking for a test to identify pedophilic tendencies. K. Freund, *Reflections on the Development of the Phallometric Method of Assessing Sexual Preference*, 4 ANNALS OF SEX RESEARCH 221 (1991). The test was subsequently used to attempt to distinguish homosexual and heterosexual males in the Czechoslovakian army. *See* W. O'Donohue & E Letourneau, *The Psychometric Properties of The Penile Tumescence Assessment Of Child Molesters*, 14 J. PSYCHOPATHOL. BEHAV. ASSESS. 123 (1992). Today, penile plethysmography is still "commonly used" to assess sexual arousal, but the practice suffers from "a lack of standardization." Lisa Murphy et al., *Standardization of Penile Plethysmography Testing in Assessment of Problematic Sexual Interests*, 12 J. SEX MED. 1853–61 (2015).

to serve any ... statutory goals," and that therefore, on substantive due process grounds, it could not be imposed on McLaurin.[17]

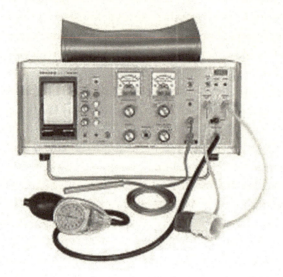

A penile plethysmograph

Some of the circumstances in McLaurin's case are fairly unusual. For instance, the court notes that since McLaurin's only "substantively sexual" crime occurred over ten years ago, and that his current case concerns no more than a failure to submit paperwork, the reasonableness of subjecting this particular defendant to "the government-mandated measurement of his penis" is diminished.[18] These and other aspects of the case might have been deemed dispositive of the outcome.

Nevertheless the court goes beyond them to rest its holding on the condemnation of plethysmography as a whole and to provide a generalized critique of plethysmography.[19] The court finds it "odd that, to deter a person from committing sexual crimes, the Government would use a procedure designed to arouse and excite a person with depictions of sexual conduct closely related to the sexual crime of conviction."[20] It finds no convincing connection "between fluctuating penis size and public protection—certainly none strong enough to survive the careful scrutiny that we give to unusual or severe conditions of supervised release."[21]

Finally, while the relevant factor in this particular case is the government's failure to make a *showing* of the technique's accuracy or efficacy, the court reveals doubt that any such a showing possibly could be made. The opinion cites a Ninth Circuit statement that "the accuracy and reliability of penile plethysmograph testing have

---

[17] 731 F.3d 258 (2013).
[18] 731 F.3d 258, 264 (2013).
[19] Id.
[20] Id.
[21] Id.

been severely questioned," and expresses "serious doubts" about the basic psychological and physiological assumptions underlying the practice.[22]

Guido's narrative reveals a panel that is determined to anticipate attempts to escape the reach of its holding—to frame its decision to thwart future moves by the state to force or coerce vulnerable members of the population into being test subjects for pseudoscience. Among the resonances driving such a determination are experimentation in German death camps during World War II, the Tuskegee syphilis experiments on Black males, and the testing of birth control devices on poor Puerto Rican women in the 1950s.[23]

Such associations do not rise to the surface of the opinion itself—but they shed light on Guido's feeling about the personal significance that each panel member— Guido, of Jewish heritage; Parker, an African American; and Cabranes, a Puerto Rican—may have found in this case.[24] And so, although the case sounded in substantive due process, significant egalitarian concerns may have motivated the panel.

Guido amplified his concern about the "branding and shaming" of sex offenders in 2020.[25] When Salvador Diaz defended his failure to register as a sex offender by challenging the underlying conviction for rape and indecent acts, the panel unanimously rejected the challenge but Guido concurred, criticizing statutes which "made it difficult if not impossible for [sex offenders] to reintegrate into society."[26] Guido put on the table a compelling viewpoint: it was "a fundamental mistake to treat as nonpenal, and perhaps civil, any number of laws the effects of which exceed in severity those of many quite severe criminal laws."[27] He cited civil deportation statutes, limitations on habeas relief, and some limitations on punitive damages as cases in point.[28] The Supreme Court had applied his reasoning to restrain penalties against large corporations, and he wished similar logic would apply "to situations in which those bearing the punitive effects were not large corporations but individuals without similar means.[29]

---

[22] *Id.* at 263.

[23] *See, e.g.,* JAMES H. JONES, BAD BLOOD: THE TUSKEGEE SYPHILIS EXPERIMENT (1981); VIVIAN SPITZ, DOCTORS FROM HELL: THE HORRIFIC ACCOUNT OF NAZI EXPERIMENTS ON HUMANS (2005); The American Experience, *The Puerto Rico Pill Trials*, https://www.pbs.org/wgbh/americanexperience/features/pill-puerto-rico-pill-trials.

[24] *McLaurin* enjoyed a substantial amount of news coverage, much of it focused on the case's more salacious aspects. *See* Erin Fuchs, *JUDGES: Bizarre Penis Monitoring Device for Sex Offenders Is "Extraordinarily Invasive,"* BUSINESS INSIDER, Oct. 3, 2013, https://www.businessinsider.in/JUDGES-Bizarre-Penis-Stimulation-Device-For-Sex-Offenders-Is-Extraordinarily-Invasive/articleshow/23478206.cms; David Lat, Second Circuit to Feds: Don't Touch His Junk, *Above the Law*, Oct. 4, 2013, https://abovethelaw.com/2013/10/second-circuit-to-feds-dont-touch-his-junk/2/; Joseph Ax, NY Court Finds "Invasive" Penile Stimulation Test Unjustified, *Reuters*, Oct. 3, 2013, https://www.reuters.com/article/us-usa-crime-penile-idUSBRE99214I20131003. But it has also been cited in scholarly work examining the legality of penile plethysmography: *see, e.g.,* Lindsay Blumberg, *The Hard Truth About the Penile Plethysmograph: Gender Disparity and the Untenable Standard in the Fourth Circuit*, 24 WM. & MARY J. WOMEN & L. 593, 595 (2018).

[25] United States v. Diaz, 967 F.3d 107 (2020) (Calabresi, concurring).

[26] *Id.* (citing Doe v. Pataki, 940 F. Supp. 603, 628 (S.D.N.Y. 1996), rev'd, 120 F.3d 1263 (1997)).

[27] *Id.*

[28] *Id.*

[29] *Id.*

Reena Raggi. Judge Raggi graduated from Wellesley and received her law degree from Harvard in 1976. After private practice she became an Assistant United States Attorney for the Eastern District of New York where she was the first woman to head both the Eastern District of New York's narcotics unit and its corruption unit, She became a District Judge for the Eastern District of New York in 1987 and joined the Second Circuit in 2002.

An academic analysis of her opinions in 2012 confirmed a generally conservative approach to statutory interpretation, particularly in to criminal matters where she revealed "great deference to trial court convictions" and much reluctance to overturn a conviction or a sentence on appeal. She exhibits "respect [for] court precedent, and [is] hesitant to stray from existing decisions."[30]

United States v. Fell. Donald Fell, twenty years old, stabbed to death his mother and her partner in their home in Vermont in November 2000.[31] The next morning, while attempting to flee the state, Fell and his accomplice carjacked and kidnapped fifty-three-year-old Teresca King, a convenience store employee who they came across in the store's parking lot. After driving with King into New York State, Fell and his accomplice forced her out of the car and beat her to death.[32]

Because King's murder originated with kidnapping across state lines, it qualified as a federal crime; Fell was indicted by a federal grand jury sitting in the District of Vermont. In June 2005, a federal petit jury in Vermont found Fell guilty and unanimously voted for the death penalty. Fell challenged the death sentence, claiming error in jury selection.

A panel of Judges Walker, Cabranes, and Parker rejected the challenge and affirmed Fell's conviction. Guido, as was his privilege, called for a rehearing *en banc*. This was denied, and so the death penalty conviction stood.

Why was it brought federally? Although technically this was an interstate kidnapping, it was fundamentally a "straight state murder case," as Guido says. He insists that this was deliberately done in order to pursue the death penalty: "It was brought federally because [President Bush's Attorney General] Ashcroft actually said, 'It's unjust that somebody who would be executed in Georgia would not be executed in Vermont.'"[33]

Setting aside any general doubts Guido may have had about the constitutionality of capital punishment, Guido saw a procedural defect that was simpler, and ideologically bipartisan, and more specific: Ashcroft's position was a straightforward misunderstanding of federalism, and a misunderstanding that belied the proper resolution of an important and undertheorized matter: how to handle federal capital cases in states that have abolished the death penalty.

---

[30] Michael C. Tedesco, Conservatism In The Second Circuit: An Analysis Of The Dissenting Opinions Of Judge Debra Livingston & Judge Reena Raggi, 75 *Albany L.Rev.* 1205 (2012) 1221.
[31] U.S. v. Fell, 571 F.3d 264 (2009).
[32] *Id.*
[33] *Id.*; Benjamin Weiser, *Ashcroft's Death Penalty Edict Could Backfire in New York, Lawyers Say*, N.Y. TIMES, Feb. 9, 2003 (spokesperson for Ashcroft).

Calling for a capital sentence in Vermont on the grounds that one would have been given in Georgia is, for Guido, a profound misunderstanding of basic constitutional principle. Vermont had abolished capital punishment by legislative action—a strong indication that the people of Vermont have themselves decided against it. And in this federal case, the jury's judgment was "constitutionally required to reflect the values of the people of Vermont."[34]

Guido asks to go *en banc* on two grounds: first, that in states that have no death penalty, for a federal jury to nevertheless call for the death penalty is, quite literally, as Guido says in the narrative, "extraordinarily unusual." Second, he argues that a federal jury deciding a capital case should be informed by—and informed *of*—the values, with respect to capital punishment, of the citizens of the state in which the case is being decided.

Guido raised the possibility that a juror in the case was excluded on the basis of her negative stance toward the death penalty and should not have been so long as she was prepared to follow the law; and also the possibility that the jury should have been informed that the *local* U.S. Attorneys handling the case were willing to pursue a life sentence rather than capital punishment. Animating both of these objections was the central theme in his dissent: the significance of respect for variations in the moral and choices embraced by localities—"as important a value as any."

The Second Circuit rejected Guido's call for an *en banc* hearing. Lewis Liman, an attorney at Cleary Gottlieb Steen & Hamilton, took on Fell's case and demonstrated that one of the jurors had badly misbehaved. The conviction as well as the death sentence failed, and after substantial negotiations, Fell pled guilty but without the death penalty. Liman was subsequently appointed to the federal bench by President Trump.

In a heated opinion, Judge Reena Raggi deemed Guido's federalism' concerns "more imaginary than real."[35] She denied that the juror with anti-death penalty sentiments was improperly removed and insisted that federalism concerns only trench on the "distribution of *power*" between the nation and the states, not issues of "local ideology."[36]

Guido responds that Raggi "completely misunderstands" the nature of federalism; that while her technical and formal analysis accurately reflects certain limited *aspects* of federalism, it fails to grasp the significance of this case and important purposes of federalism. He ends with a broad appeal to the values left unaddressed by Raggi's formalist approach. Federalism is meant to mediate "profoundly different values," to help the nation "remain united and yet responsive to significant difference..."[37]

---

[34] United States v. Fell, 571 F.3d 264 (2d Cir. 2009).
[35] United States v. Fell, 571 F.3d 264 (2d Cir. 2009).
[36] *Id.* at 269.
[37] *Id.* at 292; Guido Calabresi & Eric Fish, *Federalism and Moral Disagreement*, 101 MINN. L. REV. 1 (2016).

Here is another instance of Guido's capacity for methodological "ju-jitsu."[38] Appeals to federalism are associated historically with the political and judicial Right of Center; as props for the defense of slavery, and as code for Jim Crow policies in the 1950s.[39] Progressives have, instinctively, been wary of calling for a bigger role for states in the federalist system.[40]

He is among the earlier of the modern judges who have turned federalist theories toward progressive ends.[41] Subsequently a newer school of scholarship has formed; in 2018, for example, the *Yale Law Journal* published a symposium on the "new school" of federalism as "the new nationalism:" that is, as a tool for "improving national politics, strengthening a national polity, bettering national policymaking," and generally "ensuring our national democracy thrives."[42] Guido's position in *Fell* anticipated these newer adaptations which would unfold more fully a decade later.

United States v. Quinones. Quinones was charged, among other things, with murder in the aid of racketeering. He moved, unsuccessfully, to strike death penalty notices which were filed by the government.[43] Judge Rakoff raised,—*sua sponte*, and at a preliminary hearing—the issue of the constitutionality of the Federal Death Penalty Act (FDPA). He indicated, innovatively, that in light of evidence raised by recent advances in DNA testing, arguments against the constitutionality of the death penalty based on the inability of the justice system to rectify a deprivation of life are "neither a hypothetical nor so remote."[44] Judge Rakoff granted motions to strike all death penalty aspects from the case and held the FDPA to be unconstitutional for violating due process.[45]

As the text describes, Judge Rakoff was reversed on appeal, but the jury ultimately did not impose the death sentence.

In connection with his discussion of *Quinones*, Guido looks at an interesting political dynamic shaping the law around habeas review. He attributes to Justice Scalia the position, made public in an early talk, that the purpose of habeas corpus review is *not* fundamentally to address procedural violations during trial, but instead to "let the innocent out."[46] According to Guido, the predictable liberal response to this

---

[38] In his academic work he self-consciously turned law and economics toward progressive ends. See, e.g., Chapter14, "Deep Structures in the Law" ("The impulse that drove me [in writing THE COST OF ACCIDENTS and which then influenced others, was, "Why should Milton Friedman have all the good music?").

[39] *See, e.g.,* DAVID BRIAN ROBERTSON, FEDERALISM AND THE MAKING OF AMERICA (2018) 71.

[40] Interview with Dean Heather Gerken, May 28, 2014; Michael Jonas, *Progressive Politics from the Ground Up*, COMMONWEALTH, July 11, 2017.

[41] *See* Ilya Somin, *Heather Gerken on the Future of Progressive Federalism*, WASH. POST, July 15, 2017; Ilya Somin, *The New Liberal "Nationalist" Case for Federalism*, WASH. POST, Apr. 16, 2014; Emily Bazelon, *States' Rights Are for Liberals*, THE ATLANTIC, July/Aug. 2013.

[42] Heather K. Gerken, *Federalism as the New Nationalism: An Overview*, 123 YALE L.J. 1626. The other contributions to the symposium were by Abbe R. Gluck, Our [National] Federalism, Alison L. LaCroix, The Shadow Powers of Article I), Cristina M. Rodriguez, Negotiating Conflict Through Federalism: Institutional and Popular Perspectives, and Jessica Bulman-Pozen (*From Sovereignty and Process to Administration and Politics: The Afterlife of American Federalism*).

[43] 313 F.3d 49 (2002)

[44] *Id.*

[45] United States v. Quinones, 205 F. Supp. 2d 256 (2002).

[46] In Herrera v. Collins, 506 U.S. 390, 427 (1993), Justice Scalia, concurring, found "no basis in text, tradition, or even in contemporary practice for . . . a right to demand judicial consideration of newly discovered evidence of innocence brought forward after conviction." *Id.* at 427. The talk Guido references cannot be

assertion was outrage, and an insistence on the role of habeas as a tool in preventing procedural violations.[47]

But the end result of the outrage was, in Guido's eyes, "the worst of both worlds." On one hand, Congress and the courts continued the use of habeas in cases of procedural violations but adopted a set of extremely demanding technical criteria for when such a case could be made. So while the practice was superficially in line with the liberal agenda—ensuring that habeas is used to right genuine procedural violations—the practical result was that it became extremely difficult to actually secure habeas review.

Thus—in Guido's estimation—the liberal insistence on procedural propriety threatened, ironically, to significantly undermine the successful use of habeas in actual cases. To make matter worse, the political dynamics surrounding the question may have emboldened Justice Rehnquist to articulate just the opposite position: that actual innocence is insufficient ground for habeas review, so long as there is no constitutional violation![48]

Azibo Aquart's sentencing and remorse. The Trump Justice Department decided not to try to impose the death penalty in a retrial, in Guido's estimation "probably because they did not think the principal witness to Aquart's brutality—a collaborator who was sentenced to only thirteen years because he testified for the government—would now come on as hard."

Aquart was sentenced to life in prison. At the sentencing, he made a statement of repentance and determination to be a better person. The Judge in the case—the same one that Guido's court reversed—was moved by the beauty of the statement to send it on to Guido, with a note telling him that as a result of it she was glad the Circuit had found reversible error in her decision! It was, Guido said, a remarkable end to a difficult case.[49]

Arar v. Ashcroft. In September 2002, Arar, a dual citizen of Syria and Canada, was detained at a New York airport on his way home to Ottawa from a vacation abroad.[50] He was fingerprinted, searched, and interviewed by the FBI and INS, who

---

located, but it is evident that in fuller context, Scalia argued that "once a person had been fairly convicted and sentenced in court, and had exhausted all his possible avenues of appeal, a last-minute claim of innocence was not by itself sufficient grounds for further delaying the carrying out of the sentence," because it would impose an unmanageable burden on courts. Kim Lacapria, Antonin Scalia Death Penalty Quote, Feb. 13, 2016, Snopes.com. But see Lee Kovarsky, *Justice Scalia's Innocence Tetralogy*, 101 U. MINN. L. REV. 94, 105 (2016) (characterizing Justice Scalia's habeas jurisprudence from 1993 on as "strongly proceduralist" and concluding that in In re Davis, 557 U.S. 952 (2009), "Justice Scalia began to use actual innocence cases to explain that the Constitution permitted systematic criminal punishment in the face of some imperfection," leading many to view him as a "candid realist.").

[47] For a comprehensive discussion of habeas policy history from the Burger to the Rehnquist Courts, see William R. Thomas & Stephen E. Sussman, *The Rehnquist Court and Judicial Activism: The Development of Conservative Habeas Corpus Policy*, 23 S.E. POL. REV. 498 (1995).

[48] The case is Herrera v. Collins, *supra* note 46, in which Justice Rehnquist, writing for the majority, suggested that a claim of innocence does not entitle a petitioner to federal habeas corpus relief. See supra note 46.

[49] Edmund H. Mahony, The last federal inmate on death row from Connecticut is spared execution, sentenced instead to life in prison for a horrifying, triple murder, Hartford Courant, Oct. 21, 2021. United States v. Aquart 2021 U.S. Dist. LEXIS 199845 (D. Conn. Oct. 18, 2021) (Arterton, J.).

[50] 585 F.3d 559 (2009).

questioned him about his alleged terrorist associations. Arar admitted to knowing at least one individual from a list of suspected terrorists but denied being a member of any terrorist group.[51]

At one point during his interrogation, Arar was offered a voluntary return to Syria. He refused, saying he feared torture; he asked to go to Canada instead, or to be sent back to Switzerland. Nevertheless, the INS eventually ordered his removal to Syria and barred him from the United States for five years, on the grounds of his association with terrorist groups. Upon his forced return to Syria, he endured a brutal twelve-day interrogation, during which he was beaten with an electric cable and by his interrogator's bare hands; he was imprisoned for the next ten months in a cramped underground cell. Arar was never charged with any crime.[52]

In November 2003, Arar was released home to Canada. In addition to his claims against the Canadian government, which resulted in legislative compensation, he filed a complaint in the Eastern District of New York seeking damages against the United States. He sought relief under the *Bivens* doctrine, based on a violation of the Torture Victim Protection Act and Fifth Amendment, as well as a declaratory judgment that the government's conduct violated his "constitutional, civil, and human rights." His action was dismissed by the Eastern District of New York for failure to state a claim on which relief might be granted.[53] That court dismissed all four of Arar's counts, concluding that he lacked standing to bring a claim for declaratory relief.

On appeal, the Second Circuit found that Arar indeed had *personal jurisdiction* over the defendants, but had no *standing to seek declaratory relief*, and affirmed the dismissal of his claims. The stated rationale behind the majority opinion was that granting relief to Arar would be equivalent to creating a "new cause of action" against the federal government. It held that a remedy in damages for harms suffered in rendition must be created by Congress, because the court lacked the "institutional competence" to establish such relief.

The Second Circuit affirmed in an *en banc* rehearing, holding that *Bivens* actions—which might be brought to hold federal agents responsible for civil rights violations—did not apply to the circumstances of this case. Four judges filed vigorous individual and joint dissents.

Arar's detention and rendition to Syria occurred almost exactly one year after the September 11, 2001, attacks on the World Trade Center, during a time when national security concerns were running extraordinarily high; the United States had launched one war in Afghanistan and was on the eve of another in Iraq. At the time *Arar* reached the Second Circuit, the courts were still struggling to define their role with respect to the other branches of government in a post-9/11 environment. Matters such as extraordinary rendition, interrogation techniques, the

---

[51] Id.
[52] Id.
[53] Id.

scope of international law, and targeting killings became urgent—and significantly open—questions.[54]

In this context, the *Arar* holding, which denied the foreign defendant's *Bivens* claim, has been regarded as contributing to the general weakening of the *Bivens* doctrine and as an instance of judicial deference to the Executive and Legislative branches post 9/11.[55]

This case is remarkable for its extensive and impassioned dissents. Guido, Pooler, Sack, and Parker each wrote a separate dissent, emphasizing particular aspects of the case, and they joined fully in the dissents of each of the others. Together, they developed a comprehensive and interdependent series of objections that, at fifty-four pages, more than doubled the length of the majority opinion.[56]

Guido's dissent. Echoing his colleagues' criticisms of the various "distorted," "unrealistic," and "wrong" aspects of the majority opinion, Guido focused on the particular question of "judicial willfulness": the majority reached out "to decide an issue that should not have been resolved at this stage of Arar's case."[57] Courts "ought not to pass on questions of constitutionality... unless such adjudication is unavoidable," a proposition, Guido's dissent reminds us, that is "axiomatic."[58] But here the majority went "out of its way" to decide on *Bivens* grounds a question that ought to have been resolved without implicating constitutional questions.

Guido draws attention to substantive mistakes in the majority's holding. In particular, the majority invokes graymail using privileged information and government indemnity as two key factors in its limitation of the *Bivens* remedy. But Guido points out that both worries—graymail and government indemnity—are present in virtually *every* tort suit against a government agent; to say that *Bivens* actions are inappropriate in those contexts would amount to a declaration that "*Bivens* actions are *always* inappropriate."[59]

His dissent works in two dimensions. It argues that the majority's *Bivens* analysis is substantively wrong, and "errs in its use and abuse of other fields of law." His larger objection is that, regardless of outcome, a *Bivens* analysis was improper in the first place: the majority's central mistake was to engage in that analysis at all, thus committing an overreach "of a particularly dangerous sort."[60] The asserted conflict

---

[54] *War, Terror, and the Federal Courts, Ten Years After 9/11*, 61 AM. U. L. REV. 1253, 1255 (2012).

[55] For a discussion of the role of federal courts post-9/11, including the significance of *Arar*, *see id.* For a general discussion of the role of *Arar* in shaping post-9/11 *Bivens* doctrine, *see* Stephen I. Vladeck, *The New National Security Canon*, 61 AM. U. L. REV. 1295, 1301–25 (2012); Alexander Steven Zbrozek, *Square Pegs and Round Holes: Moving Beyond Bivens in National Security Cases*, 47 COLUM. J.L. & SOC. PROBS. 485, 498–505 (2014); and Peter Margulies, *Noncitizens' Remedies Lost? Accountability for Overreaching in Immigration Enforcement*, 6 FIU L. REV. 319, 332 (2011).

[56] In addition, seven retired federal judges submitted amicus briefs in favor of Arar, arguing that dismissing defendant's *Bivens's* claim would undermine the Judiciary's role as a check on Executive conduct. *Arar v. Ashcroft (Amicus Brief)*, Brennan Center for Justice, https://www.brennancenter.org/legal-work/arar-v-ashcroft-amicus-brief

[57] 585 F.3d 559, 630 (Calabresi, J., dissenting).

[58] *Id.*

[59] *Id.* at 636.

[60] *Id.* at 633.

between national security and precedent turns out, after all, Guido argues, illusory: national security interests could have been upheld in this case without "dangerous overreach."

Reading his narrative reinforces the view that the national security rationale is disingenuous. Rather, Guido sees a wholly innocent man subjected to terrible abuse resulting from an obvious mistake in the application of the U.S. rendition policy—even granting the acceptability of the policy itself.[61] Guido expresses his position in no uncertain terms: "a civilized polity, when it errs, admits it and seeks to give redress."[62] In the United States, as Guido relates, the mechanism of such redress is typically the courts—it is the job of courts to "facilitate the giving of compensation, at least to innocent victims."[63]

What seems principally to motivate his upset—a feeling that he all but explicitly articulates toward the end of his emotional dissent—is that the Circuit *en banc* did not face its own failings. Instead, the majority engaged in an implausible and strictly improper overreach into constitutional issues precisely in order to avoid acknowledging fault.

Tankleff v. Senkowski. In September 1988, Martin Tankleff, a seventeen-year-old boy, called the police to his house, shouting that his parents had been murdered. When detectives arrived, they found the couple stabbed and bludgeoned.[64] While questioning him police found seeming inconsistencies in Tankleff's story, and he was taken into custody.

---

[61] The government's mistake might have appeared all the more stark in light of the $9 million settlement awarded to Arar by Canada. Ian Austen, *Canada Reaches Settlement with Torture Victim*, N.Y TIMES, Jan. 26, 2007, https://www.nytimes.com/2007/01/26/world/americas/26cnd-canada.html.
[62] *Id.* at 638.
[63] *Id.*
[64] 135 F.3d 235 (2nd Cir. 1998).

At the police station, Tankleff was subjected to increasingly aggressive interrogation, much of it occurring before he was read his *Miranda* rights. Eventually Tankleff confessed to the murders, saying "I need psychiatric help." The police did not vigorously pursue other likely suspects.[65] Tankleff was convicted after a jury trial and sentenced to two consecutive terms of twenty-five years to life.

After the New York Court of Appeals affirmed his conviction on appeal, Tankleff filed an unsuccessful habeas corpus petition with the Eastern District of New York. Tankleff appealed to the Second Circuit, which rejected all of his claims but one, and remanded the case to the District Court.

Guido's *Tankleff* opinion proceeds through a detailed examination of each of the defendant's habeas claims. His discussion of each claim follows a similar pattern: after a painstaking presentation of a litany of prosecutorial, police, and judicial misdeeds, Guido finds that all things considered the mistakes were harmless, and the claim is dismissed.

Consider the question of the alleged mishandling of Tankleff's confession: Tankleff claimed that because his initial confession was produced as a result of aggressive questioning *before* he was read his *Miranda* rights, the confession should have been suppressed. Guido found that because Tankleff was not read his *Miranda* rights at the beginning of his questioning, any inculpatory statements he made at that point should have been suppressed. More generally, Guido is clear that the existing policy surrounding *Miranda* laws does not furnish "a license for police to neglect the *Miranda* warning in order more easily to obtain a confession."[66] And in determining whether Tankleff's subsequent statements should also have been suppressed, Guido emphasizes that the relevant policy issue is the "goal of deterring unlawful police conduct," in addition to "assuring the receipt of trustworthy evidence."[67]

He temporizes, however, falling back on the procedural rule that tolerates "harmless error." Having clearly condemned the relevant police misconduct, both in the case's particulars and as a general policy matter, Guido nevertheless concludes that, though the issue is a close one, Tankleff's subsequent confession is *legitimate*, and the trial court's failure to suppress his original confession was harmless error.[68]

Guido takes a similar stance with respect to Tankleff's claim that the prosecutor improperly mentioned his sister's absence as a witness. Guido finds that statements made by the prosecutor in Tankleff's trial were "clearly improper" and "particularly

---

[65] Martin identified the likely suspect, at the time of his arrest, as his father's bagel-store partner, who "owed his father half a million dollars, had recently violently threatened his parents, and who was the last guest to leave the Tankleff home the night before." And "as Marty's father lay unconscious in the hospital, the business partner would fake his own death, disguise himself and flee to California under an alias." Martin Tankleff, The True Story of a False Confession, https://www.martytankleff.org/the-story; RICHARD FIRSTMAN & JAY SALPETER, A CRIMINAL INJUSTICE: A TRUE CRIME, A FALSE CONFESSION, AND THE FIGHT TO FREE MARTY TANKLEFF (2008).

[66] 135 F.3d 235, 245 (1998).

[67] *Id.*

[68] *Id.*, citing, e.g., Arizona v. Fulminante, 499 111 S. Ct. 1246 (1991) (applying harmless error analysis even to a coerced confession).

troubling," and quotes them at length—his intention seems to be to convey just how improper they were. He also confirms that the district court insufficiently remedied the prosecutor's improper statements after they had been made. Nevertheless, he concludes that Tankleff "has not met his burden of showing that he was substantially prejudiced by these, admittedly improper, comments," and dismisses the claim.[69]

The only claim Guido upholds is Tankleff's *Batson* challenge: Tankleff claims that he was prejudiced by the government's striking of three Black jurors. Guido confirms, first, that a party can make a *Batson* challenge regardless of his own race, and second, that an error relating to jury selection is *structural*, and therefore a "harmless error" defense can never apply.

From hindsight—knowing that Tankleff was an innocent man convicted corruptly and incarcerated wrongly, Guido's approach of emphasizing the existence of various prosecutorial, police, and judicial misconduct, and then ultimately dismissing those errors as harmless—is depressing. His narrative renders the approach he decided to take intelligible and defensible as a "Hobson's choice," within the context of the immediate dynamics on the tribunal, and also a fundamental intellectual quarrel with progressives and conservatives alike on the proper implementation of habeas corpus relief.

From the court record, Guido could see that the prosecution acted badly in the original trial—that it did "wrong" and "dirty things." And he had misgivings. Even then, he suspected Tankleff's possible innocence. But he faced a dilemma in presenting these problems to his colleagues on the bench. The rest of the panel may also have had qualms about Tankleff's guilt. But Guido recounts that the other members of the panel, both former district court judges, worried that granting habeas would set an impossible precedent for trial courts.

So Guido reasoned that if he dissented, Tankleff would stay in jail, and the case would be cited for the proposition that any number of prosecutorial errors are ultimately sanctioned by the majority. But if Guido *himself* wrote the opinion, he could castigate, shame, and lay bare various procedural mistakes, even ones that would not ultimately suffice to secure a reversal.

When Guido's decision issued, prisoner Martin Tankleff received a phone call from his lawyer:

> It was one of those phone calls: "Well, we've got good news and bad news.' [The Second Circuit says] the case is remanded for a hearing; the decision says the state courts have violated your constitutional rights.' I said, "okay... so I shouldn't be in jail, so why am I in jail? What's the bad news? And he said, "the court has acknowledged that there's a legal issue here, but [until we litigate it further] you're still stuck in prison."[70]

---

[69] *Id.* at 253.
[70] Interview with Martin Tankleff, Apr. 8, 2021.

Unfortunately for Martin—as Guido recounts—when the case was sent back based on the basis of the *Batson* challenge, the trial court concluded that the jury strikes were legitimate after all. Tankleff stayed in jail. And much to Guido's chagrin and dismay, the unfortunate actual result of the tactic was for him to have written an opinion that would later be cited for the unsavory proposition that even the most serious of mistakes may be insufficient to reverse or remand a case.[71]

A remarkable turn. Many years later, as Guido recounts, one of Guido's former clerks, Roberto Gonzalez, joined others who were working on Tankleff's case. With renewed attention and resources, the team found decisive evidence of Tankleff's innocence. After seventeen years in prison, Tankleff was eventually acquitted.[72]

A happy ending "in a way." There could be no truly happy ending for Martin Tankleff; nor does Guido suggest as much.[73] The corrupt Suffolk County law enforcement and malfunctioning court system which accused him and convicted and punished him wrongly compounded the suffering that the murder of his parents ordained.

Tankleff was convicted in 1990, incarcerated, and finally exonerated in 2008.

On his release, Martin thanked friends and supporters, including his attorneys Laura Taichman and Stephen Braga, who had known and supported him for a very long time, and Guido's former clerk Roberto Gonzalez, who had come later. He told a reporter not long after his release that he was finding happiness in small things, like waking early, watching the sun rise, and appreciating good coffee. He said his days were "mostly days of joy" except for the moments when he stood in a cemetery and mourned at the grave sites of his parents, Seymour and Arlene Tankleff."[74]

An exceptional relationship. When Roberto Gonzalez let Martin know that Guido would like to talk to him following his release, Martin remembered he had no idea what to expect. He recalled somewhat nervously "driving up to New Haven [and] going through the security [at] this grandiose building," When they met, he found that "there was no tension, which shocked me a bit, because I would have thought there would be."[75] Guido did something remarkable:

---

[71] Cited, e.g., Mojica-Rivera v. United States, 2010 U.S. Dist. LEXIS 40726, 16 (2010) (proposition that "Federal habeas corpus review of prosecutorial misconduct claims is 'quite limited.'"); Moore v. Conway, 476 Fed. Appx. 928, 930 (2012) (proposition that "In order to grant relief, we would have to find that the prosecutor's comments constituted more than mere trial error, and were instead so egregious as to violate the defendant's due process rights."); Alvarez v. Kirkpatrick, 2019 U.S. Dist. LEXIS 34282, 31 (2019) (proposition that "To establish prosecutorial misconduct, a petitioner must show that the prosecutor's comments were "so egregious as to violate the [petitioner's] due process rights.").

[72] Martin Tankleff, The True Story of a False Confession, https://www.martytankleff.org/the-story/; RICHARD FIRSTMAN & JAY SALPETER, A CRIMINAL INJUSTICE: A TRUE CRIME, A FALSE CONFESSION, AND THE FIGHT TO FREE MARTY TANKLEFF (2008).

[73] See narrative *supra*; *see also* Calabresi, *A Failure Redeemed in Part*, in Bill Felstiner, WHAT LAWYERS DO (2018) 31, 35.

[74] Anahad O'Connor & Colin Moynihan, *Tankleff Says He Relishes Freedom*, N.Y. TIMES, Jan. 3, 2008.

[75] *Id.*

He actually asked for my forgiveness for—I don't want to say for writing a decision that kept me in prison—[but for] not being able to do more. It was one of those moments where there was a bond. I remember sitting there talking to him for a decent amount of time ... It was a once in a lifetime meeting."[76]

They saw more of each other at other meetings and events. Martin applied to colleges; Guido wrote him with a letter of recommendation. And when he applied to law school, Guido wrote a strong letter of support. After telling Tankleff's story, Guido concluded that Martin would make an exceptional law student:

> The next step in this amazing journey will be law school. Marty has the brains to be a very good law student and will, even in that traditional way, contribute to whatever school he attends. But he has so much more. His awful experience [gives] Marty a degree of knowledge that none of the rest of us can possibly have. This will make him a law student who will contribute immensely. The school to which he goes will indeed be fortunate. And I recommend him to you with great enthusiasm.[77]

After graduation, Martin applied for admission to the New York Bar. The Committee on Character and Fitness, gave him "a very difficult time," and scheduled a day-long hearing. Along with other distinguished members of the Bar, Guido prepared to testify. Years later Martin was also admitted to the New York Court of Appeals, and Guido wanted to swear him in, so that there would be "another full circle."[78]

There are a small number of judges who would personally apologize for prolonging the incarceration of a defendant freed from prison. Smaller still is the number who would make special effort to help get that person into college, go to law school, and gain admission to the Bar.

Martin's perspective is also extraordinary:

> People say to me, "how do you have this level of admiration for Guido and this relationship with him when he kept you in prison?" I say that it is hard to explain. They think, "Oh my God, here's this judge that ruled against you!" I have said to them, "I understand and respect [his decision]. As a human being, I'm angry [about it], but as somebody who understands the law and the concept behind it, I understand [it].[79]

As Guido relates, Martin moved on with his life and made the best of his circumstances. He married, won a settlement from Suffolk County, and became the

---

[76] Interview with Martin Tankleff, *supra* note 68.
[77] Letter of Recommendation, Mar. 11, 2010 (provided by Martin Tankleff, copy on file with the author).
[78] Interview with Martin Tankleff, *supra* note 68.
[79] *Id.*

teacher at Georgetown of a course called "Making an Exoneree," in which students re-examine the cases of imprisoned men.[80]

United States v. Martinez. The path of Ramon Martinez through the court system was a tortuous one. After police apprehended him and found on his person a variety of drug paraphernalia—an eighth of an ounce of cocaine, half an ounce of cut, a handheld scale, and a gun—Martinez was convicted in the District Court for the Southern District of New York of possession of cocaine with intent to distribute.[81] Much was at stake in the distinction between a conviction for mere possession and one for intent to distribute—the latter carried a sentence that was up to fifteen times as severe.[82]

Martinez appealed to the Second Circuit, before a panel of Chief Judge Newman, Judge Calabresi, and Judge Walker. The majority opinion by Judge Newman, with Judge Calabresi concurring and Judge Walker dissenting, held that although the question was a close one, the evidence was insufficient to permit a finding of "intent to distribute." The court vacated Martinez's intent-to-distribute conviction, reducing it to one for simple possession, and remanded the case for resentencing.

This decision did not sit well with everyone, however, and a poll was conducted to hold a rehearing *en banc*.

But before the vote on a hearing *en banc* was completed, Guido reconsidered his earlier position: now he held that there *was* sufficient evidence to find intent to distribute. And the original decision of the Second Circuit was, itself, vacated.[83] This time Judge Walker, the original dissenter, wrote for the majority, with Judge Calabresi explaining his reversal in a concurring opinion. Judge Newman, standing by his original opinion, now found himself in the dissent.[84]

In the end, Martinez was convicted in accordance with the original judgment of the district court, and sentenced to seventy-eight months in prison.

Guido's change of mind. His opinion takes the reader on a path—suspenseful because told in something like real time, with a couple of dead ends along the way—of the steps leading to his change of mind. The first error that Guido identifies in his original reasoning concerns the significance of the government's framing of the case: Guido originally thought that the Second Circuit was constrained to examine the case as the government made it. Because the government didn't deny that Martinez was a user, Guido believed that the Second Circuit was also constrained to take that possibility as given.

But this was wrong: the Second Circuit in fact must consider the entirety of the trial evidence, and not just the government's framing of it. So the court was obliged to consider a significant piece of evidence that the government

---

[80] Maggie Astor, *Man Wrongly Convicted of Murdering Parents to Get $10 Million*, N.Y. TIMES, Apr. 20, 2018.
[81] United States v. Martinez, 44 F.3d 148, 153 (2d Cir.) [hereafter *Martinez I*], opinion vacated and superseded, 54 F.3d 1040 (2d Cir. 1995) [hereafter *Martinez II*].
[82] *Martinez I*.
[83] *Martinez II*.
[84] *Martinez II*.

underplayed: Martinez's own statement that he is *not* a user. The significance of this statement is clear: if it could be established that Martinez is not a user, then the other elements—gun, cut, and scale—would no longer be in equipoise, but would instead point definitively in favor of his being a seller.

But Guido emphasizes that if an element is—as it would be here—a "cornerstone" of the case, it isn't enough to establish it *more probably* than not: it needs to be established *beyond a reasonable doubt*.[85] And one might feel that the evidence presented at trial doesn't meet this standard: all we have is Martinez's own statement that he is not a user. So even after Guido corrects his initial mistake, and considers the entirety of the trial evidence, one might think that there still is not enough to establish beyond a reasonable doubt that Martinez is not a user, and therefore that there is not enough to establish an intent to distribute. But whether the evidence is enough to meet the standard of "beyond a reasonable doubt" is for the jury to decide—not for the court. And so, back to the drawing board.

Significance of the gun. Guido explains that conversations with his colleagues drew his attention to an aspect of the case that he had previously underappreciated: the particular circumstances of Martinez's gun possession. Once the context is properly taken into account—Martinez was the only person with a gun in an apartment used for drug sales—the fact of gun possession turns out to supply clear evidence for being a seller. The fact of gun possession, even duly appreciated in context, may well not *in itself* prove intent to distribute beyond a reasonable doubt. But because it is a significant piece of evidence in favor of being a seller, and not just a user, this piece of evidence has a kind of ricochet effect on the *other* elements of the case.

Once the gun is properly appreciated, the case no longer stands or falls just with the question of whether Martinez is a user—that question just becomes one among a variety of elements. And if it's not a cornerstone of the case, the jury need not be convinced beyond a reasonable doubt that he was not a user. It merely needs to believe this *more probably than not* and, with respect to this new, lower threshold, Martinez's statement that he is not a user *is* sufficient.

And now, the final move: once it is established, more probably than not, that Martinez is not a user, the remaining elements—scale, narcotics, and cut—all clearly become evidence, also on the more-probably-than-not standard, for his being a seller. The original equipoise is disturbed: the other elements of proof are no longer valued as "zeroes," but instead they are small *positive* values that together can be summed to meet the reasonable doubt standard. Properly considering the significance of the gun thus triggers a kind of chain reaction, swinging the other elements of the case into a new configuration, and allowing a jury to conclude, beyond a reasonable doubt, that Martinez had an intent to distribute!

Guido opened himself to personal criticism and to the questioning of his motives—some of his colleagues seemed to assume that he was changing his mind in anticipation of being reversed. And changing his mind, in this case, seemed

---

[85] Here he cites Smith v. United States, 348 U.S. 147, 75 S. Ct. 194, 99 L. Ed. 192 (1954).

contrary to Guido's empathetic tendencies: it meant that a man who had already been freed would be returned to prison, this time facing a far harsher sentence.

More than twenty years later, the lingering sting of disapproval by a large part of the Circuit resurfaced in a limerick he passed to one of his colleagues who had been similarly bruised:

We vote to rehear you en banc,
I read and my heart deeply sank
Twas a clear implication
And a loud proclamation
That my views on the case grossly stank.
The vote to rehear the appeal
Tolled my bell and led me to kneel
For enbanc-cification
Felt as bad as castration
Or breaking my bones on the wheel.
The vote to en banc got all twelfth.
Opposed, with a guest, just myself.
My position's clear wrong
Was established ere long
In Fed 3d on the library shelf.

In the narrative Guido says his reversal was "broadly criticized." Beyond vacating his decision, however, criticism apparently did not find its way into print.

CODA

35
Explanations in *The Garden*

Literary critics count The Garden of the Finzi-Contini[s], written by Giorgio Bassani in 1962, among the great works of twentieth-century Italian fiction. The Garden bears interpretation at many levels, including as a personal and arresting love story; as an allegory about the price of decadence, detachment, and self-absorption; as a story about the effect of class and religious insularity on happiness and well-being; and as a cautionary tale about the perils of cultural assimilation. It is also a historical treatment of Ferrara, of Italian Jews, the Fascist racial laws, and of the decimation of the Italian Jewish community. It is one of several stories by Bassani featuring the commune of Ferrara.

The personal drama centers on a young boy and girl who grow up with mutual affection. Over time, as the boy's love for the girl deepens, she begins to pull away and ultimately rejects him. At the same time, he is telling this story, Bassani is also telling another story about rejection—of the Jewish community by the Italian community. Fascist anti-Semitic cruelty steadily crushes the vitality, ambition, and security of the Jewish Italian families, until, at the end, in his novel, only a few survive deportations to concentration camps and the genocide of the Holocaust or Shoah.

The novel was adapted into a successful film of almost the same name, directed by Vittorio De Sica. The Garden of the Finzi-Contini (Il Giardino Dei Finzi Contini) won the Academy Award for Best Foreign Film in 1972.

Given its title, readers reasonably might assume that the novel provides a fictionalized account of Guido's mother's family, the notable Finzi-Contini. In addition, there are also resemblances to the Del Vecchios, and to members of Guido's father's family, particularly the Minerbi. Guido and his family have spent decades decoding these artistic works for themselves and others, and disentangling fact from historically grounded fiction.

We have been talking about opinions that I have written as a judge. These involve such subjects as law and economics, torts, how injured people are treated, the position of immigrants, and the right of people to speak and be heard in a democracy. Where do my attitudes about justice, and righting wrongs, and correcting mistakes, and prejudice, come from?

Many times I have told you that the fact that I am an immigrant, a refugee, an outsider (who seems to most people to be the epitome of an insider and somebody who has made it) is certainly relevant.

I have also told you before that I have been married for almost sixty years to an amazing woman, who is as independent-minded as anyone can be, but who also carries the luggage of descending from the very first people to come from England to settle New England and New Haven. I have three children, who are all hard-working, successful, and just plain good. I have told you about them and the rest of my background, and how all this background connects to these judicial attitudes. A lot of it has been pretty much private, as you would expect.

But there is more. There is one aspect of my Italian past which, through a novel that came out in English in 1965 and was made into a movie that was released in 1970, and became, for many years, part of common American culture.

The book is still read today by almost every schoolchild in Italy. Great numbers of American moviegoers and readers of fiction in the 1960s and 1970s read the book or saw the movie. Today it is not very widely known among younger generations in the United States, but it still gets studied and admired in literature and film classes.

And so the accuracy of the book, and its connection to my life, requires more discussion. In a way, talking about the book also explains a lot about who I am and where my perspectives have come from. The book that became a movie is *The Garden of the Finzi-Contini* written by Giorgio Bassani. The family name "*Finzi-Contini*" became well known because of Bassani's novel.

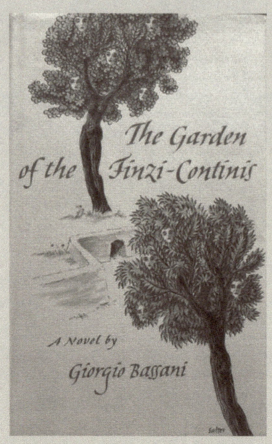

First American edition of The Garden of the Finzi-Continis

The Garden is a sad book, really, in which Bassani plays out his notion of these great Italian Jewish families being decadent, and having no sense of life, and essentially letting themselves be killed in the Holocaust. Some people have said that this view is anti-Semitic. But it is not an anti-Semitic view—it is just Bassani's non-aristocratic feeling toward these aristocratic characters.

> *A very, very, distant cousin, Sergio Minerbi, who lived in Israel and was a distinguished Israeli diplomat, wrote a book about the Minerbi family in which he said that in some ways Bassani was anti-Semitic, because he pictured these great Jewish families as having decayed.*

Bassani was very close to my father's cousin, Beppe Minerbi. He dedicated one of his other novels, *The Heron*, to him. At the time Bassani was writing *The Garden*, during the later 1950s, Beppe was Bassani's patron; *The Garden* was written in the library of my father's family's house in Ferrara. Part of that house is now a museum dedicated to his papers.

Bassani was the outsider, looking in. Looking at these old families, and he had any number of things to say. He picked the name "Finzi-Contini" because he wanted to connote something which my family's name suggested—a prominent, aristocratic, and in his view decadent Italian Jewish family with roots that were many centuries old. I think he thought of the name in connection with the house, which was especially evocative in those days, when it was entirely owned by us, with its courtyards and fourteenth-century frescoes.

Even though the house did not look like the one in the movie, that is not what Bassani thought about or what the great houses in Ferrara were. But it all— the house and the family name—gave the sense of a special world that Bassani wanted. If he was going to write a book which talked about elegance, and decadence, and other things, to the audience to whom he was speaking, this name "Finzi-Contini" was "just right."

Remember that he was starting to write—he was not writing to the world yet. He was writing to people for whom this would say something. There were names of certain Jewish families that connected, that said something, and ours was one of them.

> *My parents, of course, had brought the Minerbi and Finzi-Contini together when they married in 1929. And the two families were brought together again when my mother's brother, Bruno Finzi-Contini, married Beppe's sister, Fernanda Minerbi in 1931. So these two marriages brought the families together; and through the Minerbi connection, Bassani knew the Finzi-Contini family, and he decided to use the name Finzi-Contini in his novel. I have learned there is a letter Bassani wrote to Beppe's brother-in-law, my uncle Bruno Finzi-Contini, asking for approval to use it.*

Although the name on the cover of the book was *Finzi-Contini*, the story was inspired by any number of people beyond just this one family. Some who were not even related to us, like the *Finzi-Magrini*.

The garden, the villa, and the tennis court he describes in the novel are features that Bassani gathered from several different locations. The house and the description of it have nothing to do with the Finzi-Contini; for instance, the place where the kids went to study, when they were kicked out of schools, was modeled after the fantastic library of some people named Bonfiglioli. That house is now the most elegant hotel—quite overdone—in Ferrara. The choice of the name, like the setting of various events, does not derive from particular details, but from the ambiance, the feelings of "place."

It *is* a novel, but I know that a few of the things that happened in it refer to us. And I also know where many of the events happened, and to whom they happened when it was not us. There are some things that are there that involved my family, but no more us than anybody else.

Still, I believe that my great-uncle, Alberto Minerbi, may well have been in part the inspiration for Bassani's old professor, Ermano, in the novel. Beppe was Bassani's patron, and Alberto Minerbi was Beppe's father. Alberto was the wealthiest man in Ferrara, and with his black Malacca cane, he was elegance personified.

It's also interesting that when they made the movie, Bassani wanted his patron, Beppe, to play the old professor. Thank goodness they did not use him, because Beppe could never have acted!

Like the head of the Finzi-Contini family in *The Garden,* Alberto would not hide from the Germans in 1943. I do not know if at the back of Bassani's mind was this knowledge about Alberto—that he was the one person in my family who did not hide from the Nazis and he was taken away, and then, through his chauffeur, rescued. Even if he knew about this, Bassani could not know whether Alberto did not hide because he thought it would help his family if he did not hide, or as Professor Ermanno is portrayed in the *Garden of the Finzi-Contini*, because it was beneath him. Who knows what the truth is? Alberto and Bassani each had unknowable reasons.

Vittorio de Sica made the movie a decade later, and Bassani was a script consultant for the film for a while; but in the middle of making the movie, Bassani broke with de Sica, and decided not to participate any further. He did not like the changes de Sica made to the ending.

In the book, the apolitical Finzi-Contini are taken away, having lost their will to resist. Their decadence, and their insularity and their indifference doomed them. But the person who represents the father of Giorgio—and Giorgio Bassani's name, too—who was also of course Jewish, plays footsie with the Fascists, and escapes. Why? Because people who are not so aristocratic, somehow retain the capacity to survive. Would Bassani say that they are "more Jewish?" I do not know. But for Bassani it is some greater strength that they have. These others are doomed, doomed by the catastrophe and their own passivity.

In the movie, instead, the vision of Vittorio de Sica is a different one. In his movie, they *all* get taken away to the camps, because De Sica wants to say something different—to say something about the impossibility of escape by Jews of any class or political belief. All this elegance, all this beauty, this whole aesthetically wonderful world, gets swept away in madness. Everyone who is even slightly connected with it gets swept up in it and taken away. In a way, it was a paean to this way of life.

Promotional still, Vittorio De Sica film.

De Sica, the movie maker, says that this catastrophe is something so horrible that it sweeps everybody in, including the figure of Bassani's father. This, for Bassani, is the last straw. In the movie, they are all sitting in their old schoolhouse and they are all under arrest. And there is Giorgio's father being taken away, too. To Bassani, that was a complete rejection of his work—and after he saw that ending, he would have nothing to do with the movie, because it was not his vision. The ending made Bassani furious.

* * *

My family are much more book people than movie people; and the big reaction to the book was primarily in Italy. The impact in the United States came later, but in Italy it was very quick, and the feeling in the family was, on the whole, negative.

My mother was not pleased. She resented this sense that Bassani gave of the Finzi-Continis being too aristocratic and too decadent to fight back. She was very proud of the way she and her brothers in Italy *had all managed to survive*, and to do that in spite of some aristocratic sense of invulnerability or initial indifference.

When push came to shove, my mother felt, the real Finzi-Contini were perfectly adaptable, and they had plenty of life force; that, when put to it, whatever might have been, whatever kind of ethereal sensibility might have been an apt description of them before, when the time came, we *survived*. She—*we*—made it to America. All her relatives in Italy survived. The real Finzi-Contini were not about to roll over and play dead.

My mother might have thought this could be an apt description of her husband's mother's family—Minerbi—and some other families she knew; but that it wasn't really us. So hers was a reaction of, "Yes, we go back to Roman times, and all of that, but do not think that we have lost our capacity to survive." That would be true both of the people who were actually Finzi-Contini, and of the Cavalieri and of the Del Vecchios on her mother's side, the oldest of all on her side.

And I think she was right. I mean, for families like mine, survival strategies came naturally; you do not worry about it, because it is who you are. Your history makes you somebody who survives. It is a quality that made both my brother and me, without thinking about it, try to rebuild, and re-create. This is what everybody in our family has tended to do.

＊＊＊

My father, too, disliked the book because it invaded our privacy. He resented people treating us as more than good, bourgeois, middle-class citizens. And of course, he also disliked its theme—repeated again and again in Bassani—that these great Italian Jewish families had become so aristocratic that they were decadent, missing the spirit of life, missing the capacity to survive. This idea runs through many of Bassani's other writings as well. For my father, the entire tone that Bassani struck was offensive.

My mother also found that the use of her name, her family name, was a great invasion of privacy. You know, these were a very private kind of people and she was a private person. She did not like the idea of our name and us being in the public square.

After the book was a success, a nephew of my mother's walked into a bar in Italy. He heard somebody order the drink that the girl in the story—Micol—liked, which had come to be called a "Finzi-Contini." It was some sort of drink made with grenadine and something. You know the way these things happen—for a while it was a fad. The nephew got very angry—so offended, in fact, that he said he wanted to sue.

My mother forbade him from doing it. She was the eldest at the time, and for a variety of reasons she was the head of that family. She told him: "You will not sue. You will not sue, because suing just puts us in public all the more and the thing we object to *most* is just this sort of invasion of privacy."

"But in addition," she said, "you will not sue because you, and I, are Catholic. There will be some people who inevitably, if you do sue, will say that you are doing it because you did not like the Jewish connection being made so much of. And that would be the height of irony, because we have been so proud of this connection, and we remain proud of it. It is what we are, whatever our religion is. I will not have people thinking that." My mother was proud of the Jewish connection. She would not have people say that the Finzi-Contini objected to the book because of something which,—in so far as that book had made the Jewishness of the family central—we were proud of. But inevitably, she believed, some people, somewhere, would say that.

And of course the kid did not sue. That was the end of the thing. I mean, he had just gotten mad. It was a silly reaction; he understood, when my mother said it, and that was that. But having laid down the law to her nephew, my mother was upset, because she was not a person who liked to tell people—to take that role, and say to people, "You will not do this." This was very much in the nature of my mother, this person who, when she got older said, "I'm becoming ever more Catholic, and ever more Jewish."

*　*　*

In 1974 Anne and I were in Florence on sabbatical. My parents had come to see us there. My father's cousin Beppe happened to speak to Bassani about something or other. Bassani was in Rome—and Beppe told him that my father Massimo was in Florence visiting us. As was typical of that side of the family, which was so patrilineal—regarding where money went and everything else—Beppe did not say anything about my *mother* being there.

So Bassani said, "I haven't seen Massimo in a hundred years." Bassani got our number from Beppe and called us up. He said that he was driving from Rome to Ferrara, and he wondered if he could stop by to see my father. I put my hand over the phone and said, "Mother, it's Bassani. He's heard Papa´ is here and he wants to come by. Should I invite him?" My mother said, "By all means. Tell him to come to tea." She was thinking of the travel time from Rome. So, I said to him, "Fine, could you come to tea?" And Bassani said, "Perfect."

Around 4:00, 4:30 in the afternoon, the doorbell rings, and my mother said, "Let me answer." So she goes to the door, opens it, and says, "*Buona sera*, vieni, vieni." Good evening, come in. "*Sono Bianca Finzi-Contini.*"

Now he, of course, knew perfectly well who she was; but he was not expecting to see her. And he was not expecting this somewhat assertive statement of my mother.

My mother would not normally have opened the door. She would have let me, or Anne open the door and even if she had opened it, she would not have introduced herself as she did.

> *You know, in Italy, women retain their names. I mean, usually you use your married name, but technically your name remains your name and you're Bianca Finzi-Contini in Calabresi, "in marriage to Calabresi." Then when your husband dies, very often people go back to their pre-marriage name, socially, as well. So it was perfectly okay, but a bit stylized, and assertive, to introduce herself as she did.*

Bassani jumps backwards. He understands immediately her implicit criticism of his use of her name. And then, quickly, says this clever fellow, "*SIGNORA: the only thing that matters about a book is its quality as Literature.*" He knew perfectly well that literature was my mother's field. My mother characteristically reacted by saying "That's right. And I have some views about that, too. *Parliamo*." Let's talk.

So in they go, and spend an hour talking to each other. They come out perfectly happily, because—after all—it was a good book. I wasn't privy to the discussion, but it must have been about the literary value of doing this, that, and the other. I assume he understood and accepted my mother's criticisms. After all, it was a discussion between a good literary scholar and a good author.

I tell the story because in many ways it reflects our family's attitude about the whole thing. I mean, it is a good book and Bassani is a good writer.

* * *

But you asked me about what *The Garden of the Finzi-Contini* meant to *me*. I started thinking about it and thinking about my reaction to it when it was published, and why, in an odd way, I was kind of pleased. Everything I had said before about the family losing privacy and the suggestions of "decadence" and everything else was true—but your question makes me realize that I actually *was* kind of pleased, and that now I understand the reason why.

In order to tell you, I want to go back to when my brother Paul married Celia, who was, on her mother's side, from an old New Haven family. Not that fancy. Old New Haven, but not that fancy. They were engaged while I was at college, and then they were married in 1954 when I was at Oxford.

When Paul and Celia became engaged, and the news got out, one of my roommates said to me, sort of laughing, that his *parents* were very pleased that Paul was engaged to her! Well, his parents were from New Haven; they were business types. And I said, "What? Why on earth should *your parents* care?" The roommate said, "because when people ask, "Who is this Italian, 'Guy Calabresi,' your son rooms with,' implying that WASPS did not associate with Italians—my parents now will say something like, "Oh, he must be okay, his brother is part of an old New Haven family." And that made me laugh! Because you know, we always thought *we* were better than anybody!

But I think this explains part of my reaction to *The Garden of the Finzi-Contini*. When the movie appeared, I saw the things my parents disliked about it, and I understood my parents' negative reaction—that they were who they were and did not need to explain to others who they were, and where they came from. But I was the next generation, and the notion of not having to explain who I am was appealing—the notion that people no longer needed to identify me with reference to my brothers' wife's family, or my own wife's family. That they would say, "Oh, he's a Finzi-Contini," was something that *The Garden* helped with.

So I am afraid that I do not mind, when people say, "Oh, you know, his mother's a Finzi-Contini. You've seen the movie."

It just saves an awful lot of the work of explaining me.

In his chambers in New Haven

COMMENTARY

Chapter 35

Coda

Giorgio Bassani. Giorgio Bassani was born in 1916 and raised in a middle-class Jewish family in Ferrara. In 1938 he began to teach literature at the Jewish School there, to write, and also to engage in anti-Fascist activities in the Resistance. In the spring of 1943 he was arrested as a Resistance member and spent three months in prison. After the War he settled in Rome, where his writing career blossomed; he continued, however, to maintain a home in Ferrara.

Early in the 1950s Bassani began writing *Le cinque storie di Ferrara* (The Five Stories of Ferrara) (1956). *Il giardino dei Finzi-Contini* appeared in 1962. Bassani revised his

Ferrara-centered stories and novels three times, culminating in *Il Romanzo di Ferrara* (The "Romance" or "Novel" or "Fantasy" of Ferrara) (1978). In addition to writing novels, poetry, screenplays, and essays, he edited literary journals. A bibliography of writing about his work published in 2010 contains more than 6,600 entries.[1]

Bassani belonged to a branch of the Minerbi family remotely related to Guido's: the writer's maternal grandfather was Cesare Minerbi, born in 1856, a Jewish doctor, professor of medicine, researcher, and head of the main hospital in Ferrara, the Arcispedale Sant'Anna. Giorgio's mother was Dora Minerbi, who studied singing before she married Giorgio's father, Angelo Enrico, a nonpracticing doctor.[2]

The Garden of the Finzi-Continis was translated by Isabel Quigly from the Italian, *Il Giardino dei Finzi-Contini* (1962); it appeared in English in 1965. In the *New York Times* review, Bassani indicated that he pulled his characters from personal experience. "'The characters of Professor Ermano and signora Olga or others who lived or like me spent time at the house in Corso Ercole I d'Este' were ones that Bassani said that he had been wanting to write about for years."[3]

Fictional Characterizations. Bassani embraced a complicated view of fidelity to historical truth through fictional representation. "My aim is to realise an art which does not expect any precedence over life, an art which is simply a mimesis of life," he wrote.[4] One scholar explains this "merging of fiction and reality" by stating that Bassani's characters are "fictionalized realities, arisen from his private universe," and suggests, as an example, that "the Finzi-Continis and the blond, attractive Micòl have some superficial analogies with the Ferrarese family of the Finzi-Magrinis and their daughter Giuliana."[5] And although Bassani describes the location of Il Giardino precisely, the place does not exist.[6]

Guido Fink, who grew up contemporaneously in Ferrara, wrote that the publication of *Il Giardino* bruised the feelings of some people who felt they were identifiable and misrepresented in the novel; some who felt they had been omitted; and some who felt they were underrepresented—"some people did recognize themselves in the characters of the book, or did not and were disappointed, or did recognize themselves but not enough."[7]

Bassani's use of the name "Finzi-Contini." Bassani sought and received permission from Guido's uncle, Bruno Finzi-Contini, (who was married to Beppe's sister) to use the name—or so Guido was told by Bruno's granddaughter, who said she saw a letter

---

[1] PORTIA PEBYS, LA MEMORIA CRITICA SU GIORGIO BASSANI (2010).

[2] See http://www.giorgiobassani.it/Biographical%20Notes.htm; http://www.giorgiobassani.it/cronological.htm; Obituary, Jonathan Keates, Giorgio Bassani, *The Guardian*, Apr. 14, 2000.http://www.theguardian.com/news/2000/apr/14/guardianobituaries1; *see also* GUIA RISARI, THE DOCUMENT WITHIN THE WALLS, THE ROMANCE OF BASSANI (1999) 1.

[3] *See* Mitgang, *A World of Its Own*, N.Y. TIMES, Aug. 1, 1965; Mitgang, *Giorgio Bassani, Man of Letters*, N.Y. TIMES, Oct. 1, 1972.

[4] F. Camon: Il mestiere di scrittore (The skill of the writer), Garzanti, Milano, 1973, 66 (quoted in Risari, *The Document Within the Walls*, 5.).

[5] RISARI, *supra* note 2 at 5.

[6] *Id.*

[7] *See* Guido Fink, *Growing Up Jewish in Ferrara: The Fiction of Giorgio Bassani, a Personal Recollection*, JUDAISM (Summer-Fall, 2004), accessed on BNET, http://findarticles.com.

to that effect. Beppe, moreover, told Guido that one afternoon in the courtyard of Casa Minerbi, Bassani said to him "I am writing a novel and I'm calling it 'The Garden of the Finzi-Contini.'"

The earlier chapter *Finzi-Contini* provides a discussion of the etymology of Guido's family name.[8] Why Bassani chose the same name Finzi-Contini, however, has been the subject of speculation. In 2005, in the *New York Review of Books* at the time of a new edition of *The Garden* introduced by the writer Tim Parks, Ms. Anna Saxon-Forti commented on Parks's "blunder" in asserting that the name suggested "absurd pretensions to nobility," based on Parks's view that the name Finzi-Contini "in Italian actually suggests 'fake little counts.'"[9]

Ms. Saxon-Forti ventured that "Evidently, Mr. Parks doesn't know the difference between the Italian word *finti* (fake, phony) and the name of a prominent Italian Jewish family, the Finzi, whose origins can be traced back to the fourteenth century: a name that has no particular meaning in Italian (and was probably derived from the biblical Pineas)." Parks replied that "Finzi is, of course ... the name of a well-known family [as is] Contini [but placing] the names together... is suggestive. 'Finzi' can well evoke *finzione*, 'a made-up story,' and is very near to *finto*, 'fake,' of which the plural is *finti*. Contini does literally mean "little counts." In Bassani's novel the narrator's father accuses the Finzi-Contini of aping the Italian aristocracy..."[10]

Bassani alluded to his personal experience and to the cultural resonance of the real Finzi-Contini family, and "decadence" as a source for his characters; but as far as can be discovered, he never fully explained his reasons for the choice of the name and certainly never intimated "fakeness." His daughter, Paola Bassani, recollected that her father had multilayered reasoning for his choice.[11]

The Bonacossi tennis court in Ferrara. At the core of the plot of *The Garden* is a tennis court in a large stone-walled garden, where young Jewish students go because the Fascist government of Mussolini has declared the ordinary tennis clubs off limits for Italian Jews. The Contini-Bonacossi (see the chapters on *Finzi-Contini* and *During the War*), kept a grand home in Ferrara, which included a large garden and tennis court. The tennis club in Ferrara was built in a "vast garden that had once united the Palazzina Marfisi with the adjacent structures of the Orange Lodge and the Palazzo Bonacossi."[12] In 1929, after

---

[8] See Chapter 3, "Conviction, Conversion, and Assimilation: Finzi-Contini."

[9] Tim Parks, *On 'The Garden of the Finzi Continis'*, NEW YORK REVIEW OF BOOKS, July 2005. http://www.nybooks.com/articles/2005/07/14/on-the-garden-of-the-finzi-continis/.

[10] *See* Tim Parks, Bassani's Father, Author's Reply, *N.Y. Rev. Books*, Oct. 20, 2005, http://www.nybooks.com/articles/archives/2005/oct/20/bassanis-father/

[11] A letter from Paola Bassani to Matteo Cati Finzi (the great grandson of the sister of Guido's grandfather on the Finzi-Contini side), shared in relevant part with Guido, expresses general agreement with the view that Guido expresses but adds that her father had friends and family called only 'Finzi,' and others called only 'Contini,' and that combining them "contributed to create a sort of foundation, of ambience, of grandeur," which "pushed my father to choose precisely such a family name." The choice of the combined names, she said, was "absolutely of his own, lucid and free, a choice dictated essentially from his aesthetic taste and from his imagination." Giorgio felt that the hyphenated name was indispensable to emphasize the aristocratic nature of the characters, she recalled, and he was quite satisfied by his choice, even "amused" by it. "Of this I am a witness. He did tell me about it, full of satisfaction and laughing…" Email relayed from Matte Cati Finzi, Mar. 22, 2020.

[12] See http://www.tennisclubmarfisa.it/la-storia.

receiving permission from the city government, a group of aficionados restored the old tennis courts in the garden, and in 1937 they opened the courts to the public as the Lawn Tennis Club Marfisa.[13] Among the members in that first year was Giorgio Bassani, who was expelled along with all other Jews just a year later, with the racial laws of 1938.[14]

Beppe was Bassani's patron. Among the frequent visitors to Beppe's home, Casa Minerbi-Del Sale (*see the chapter Post-War Convolutions*), was Giorgio Bassani. Bassani was a decade younger than Beppe, and connected to the Minerbi through his mother, Dora, the daughter of Cesare Minerbi, a physician born in Ferrara in 1856.[15] The author's frequent visits from Rome helped to encouraged its salon culture still further, making the house "the very essence of cultural life in Ferrara." In 1960, Beppe exchanged letters with Bassani asking for his help in writing a dedicatory inscription for a plaque he planned to place in front of the house.[16]

The friendship between Beppe and Bassani was cemented by their mutual membership in the Action Party (see comment in chapter *Anti-Fascist Jews in Dark Times*) and their shared "anticlerical culture and values." Later, he would dedicate to Beppe his last highly acclaimed novel, *The Heron*. The friendship between Beppe and Bassani spanned decades and continued until late in life.[17] With the completion of the Casa Minerbi-Del Sale's current renovations, part of it has become home to the *Centro Studi Bassaniani di Ferrara*, a museum and archive devoted to the author's work.[18]

Renovated exterior, Casa Minerbi-Del Sale

---

[13] *Id.*
[14] *Id.*
[15] See http://www.giorgiobassani.it/Ferrara%20Cimitero/Ferrara004.html.
[16] See http://rivista.fondazionecarife.it/it/2004/20/item/111-casa-minerbi-a-ferrara.
[17] See, e.g., http://www.giorgiobassani.it/1989%20foto/indice.html.
[18] See http://www.artecultura.fe.it/1920/presentazione-di-gianni-venturi; see also the Finzi-Contini Family chapters.

Did Bassani write Il Giardino at Casa Minerbi-Del Sale? As mentioned before, a modern creation of a center for the study of Bassani's work is located at Casa Minerbi-Del Sale—justified by Bassani's close connection to the place and his relationship to Beppe Minerbi.[19] Early sections of what would be the novel appeared in various literary magazines during the 1950s, including *The Coffee Political and Literary Magazine* (1955) and *The Palatine* (1961), in which Bassani noted that his piece had its origin in 1942 "under the emotion of a true story": the death of a friend, Alberto."[20]

Micòl's favorite drink. Bassani describes the drink in detail in the novel:

Skiwasser: a thirst-quenching drink, this—composed, in equal parts, of water and raspberry syrup, with a slice of lemon added and a few grapes—which Micòl preferred above all else, and in which she displayed a special pride ... Micòl often gulped down an entire glass of her dear "beverage," constantly urging us also to take some ... and though Skiwasser, as its name indicated, was a winter drink, and thus should be served boiling hot, still, in Austria too, there were people who continued to drink it in summer, in the iced version and without the lemon slice; and they called it Himbeerwasser, in this case.[21]

One scholar has written that "in a chapter both decadent and prophetic," Bassani has Micòl wax on at so much length about this drink, which she and her brother discovered on an Austrian skiing trip, in order "to depict the pretensions and contradictions of an elegant and privileged Jewish world on the brink of catastrophe."[22]

Suggestions of anti-Semitism. Apart from the contention of Guido's distant relation, the critical literature does not suggest that either Bassani or his book manifest anti-Semitism, although a distinction between Bassani and others on the subject of Jewish identity and secularism among Jews during the Fascist period has been noted. Natalia Ginzburg, for example, argues that although both Bassani and the autobiographical writer Primo Levi were searching to understand the nature of Jewish identity in the period between 1938 and 1945 as "not a denial of Italianness, but a conscious attempt to retrieve a Jewish past," for Bassani, "Jewishness remained in the past, held within the walls of his city; the exclusion suffered was irreparable, and the loss of the Jewish presence could never be restored."[23]

---

[19] See Gianni Venturi, Presentation, Centro Studi Bassaniani Ferrara, https://translate.google.com/translate?hl = en&sl = it&u = http://www.artecultura.fe.it/1920/presentazione-di-gianni-venturi&prev = search

[20] See Bassani's works, http://fondazionegiorgiobassani.it/opere.htm; 1942, in "The Palatine," year V, no. 20, October, December 1961, pp. 5–8. In a short note following the text, Bassani states that this is the beginnings of a story written in 1942 "under the emotion of a true story": the death of a friend, Alberto. This is "arguably the first attempt to write The Garden of the Finzi-Continis." THE GARDEN OF THE FINZI-CONTINIS (1962).

[21] THE GARDEN OF THE FINZI-CONTINIS, 59–60.

[22] LUCIENNE KROHA, THE DRAMA OF THE ASSIMILATED JEW: GIORGIO BASSANI'S ROMANZO DI FERRARA 133 (2014).

[23] NATALIA GINZBURG, JEWISHNESS AS MORAL IDENTITY 108 (2010).

Bianca's cold shoulder. Guido told essentially the same story of his mother's encounter with Bassani to Chiara Beria di Argentine in 2011.[24] To Bianca, Guido said, the characters in the novel were nothing like her family. What most disturbed her "was that the real Finzi-Contini, in spite of everything, never gave up. They all survived.'"[25]

Bianca's granddaughter and namesake Bianca witnessed the episode in the doorway. A nine-year-old child at the time, she remembered, many decades later, tension in the air and a coldness in her grandmother she had not seen her reveal before.[26]

Giovanni Finzi-Contini's novel. Although it is an imagined account, Alberto Minerbi and the Minerbi are the focal prism for understanding the traumas brought by Fascism and Naziism in Giovanni's novel *Il più lungo viaggio di A.M.* (Giuntina, Firenze, 1990), translated into English by Brian Moloney as "*A.M.'s Longest Journey*" (2002).[27] The book portrays the Minerbi as a Jewish family that became deeply connected to Ferrarese agrarian values after the opening of the ghetto in 1859; was damaged fundamentally by its need to navigate the 1938 racial laws; and was subjected to the terrors and horrors of persecution in the events of 1943. One reviewer wrote that whereas writers including "Primo Levi, Natalia Ginzburg [and] Bassani himself [have] ... movingly recorded the impact of state anti-Semitism and genocide on an assimilated urban Jewish middle class," Giovanni's characters endure the same travail, although sharing "the age-old preoccupations and skills of an agrarian class from which Italy's Jews had always been excluded ..." The novel's hero, A.M., is "essentially apolitical,"[28] but connected to anti-Fascist values in ways that belie Bassani's *Finzi-Contini*." Giovanni Finzi-Contini's novel is a "rebuke" to Bassani's "troubled and inward-focused characters who live in an extremity of bourgeois decadence, entirely walled off from the world around them."[29]

Vittorio De Sica. De Sica, who today is recognized as a master of Italian and world cinema, directed the movie version of *The Garden*.[30] He began his career as a successful comedic actor during the 1930s and during the 1940s began to direct low-budget films with social and political themes. De Sica's major films—*The Children Are Watching Us* (1944), *Shoeshine* (1946), *Miracle in Milan* (1951), *Umberto D.* (1952), and *The Bicycle Thief* (1948)—"are preoccupied with urgent social and political topics facing postwar Italy—poverty and the hardscrabble life of the streets, intergenerational estrangement, and the sense of general moral decay and vacuity cast by the dark shadow of the Fascist regime," and are described as the beginning of "neorealism" in cinema.[31]

---

[24] See Chiara Beria di Argentine, *Di Profilo* at 154–55 (Mondadori, Milano 2011) (quoting an interview with Guido Calabresi).
[25] *Id.*
[26] Interview with Bianca Finzi-Contini Calabresi, Sept. 27, 2020.
[27] GIOVANNI FINZI-CONTINI, A.M.'S LONGEST JOURNEY (transl. Brian Moloney, 2002).
[28] *Id.*
[29] *See* Brian Moloney, *Finzi-Contini, Giovanni Alberto Armando*, *in* ENCYCLOPEDIA OF MODERN JEWISH CULTURE 270 (Glenda Abramson ed. 2004).
[30] Bert Cardullo, *Vittorio De Sica: Actor, Director, Auteur* (2009).
[31] *Id.*; Harvard Film Archive, Vittorio De Sica, http://hcl.harvard.edu/hfa/films/2010aprjun/de_sica.html

De Sica's films after the 1950s were less favorably received than his earlier efforts—until the comeback he accomplished through *The Garden of the Finzi-Continis*, which premiered in American theaters, with subtitles, on December 14, 1970. It starred Dominique Sanda as Micòl Finzi-Contini; Helmut Berger as Alberto; Fabio Testi as Malnate; and Camillo Angelini-Rota as Prof. Ermanno Finzi-Contini, Micòl's father. It was widely acclaimed. Critic Roger Ebert wrote that it did not owe much to Di Sica's earlier work: "It is not neorealism; it is not a comic mixture of bawdiness and sophistication; it is most of all not the dreamy banality of his previous few films. In telling of the disintegration of the Jewish community in one smallish Italian town, De Sica merges his symbols with his story so that they evoke the meaning of the time."[32] *Il Giardino* won the Oscar for best foreign language film in 1971, and it has been recognized as a masterpiece.

Conflict over the ending. De Sica told an interviewer that he had taken on the project "because I intimately feel the Jewish problem. I myself feel shame because we are all guilty of the death of millions of Jews.... I wanted out of conscience to make this film and I am glad I made it."[33]

The producers hired Bassani as a script consultant, but Bassani quit, in a dispute about the treatment of his father and the ending in the final version. Herbert Mitgang reported that "One of the main reasons Bassani disavowed the film version of "Finzi-Continis" is that the character of Giorgio is devoid of moral stature in the face of anti-Semitic persecution. 'To have used my house in Ferrara for filming, attributing incidents there that did not involve me, and then to claim that I seemed capable of toying with the life of my beloved father, added up to outrageous abuses of power,' Bassani thundered. 'Had I suffered these without protesting, I would not be a writer, much less a man.'"[34] De Sica explained his perspective to a different interviewer: Bassani had renounced the film "because of the character of the father, which has been minimized in the film; but I think the character is well treated." Bassani litigated to remove his name from the credits; as a result of their disagreement the title of the film was slightly changed to distinguish it from the novel.[35]

Who is this Italian, "Guy" Calabresi? Guido was "Guido" from his birth in Milan in 1932, and the name came across the ocean to America with him. He kept it, un-Americanized, from elementary school until his last years at Hopkins School.

Then, in his late adolescence, he listed himself as "Guy" in the high school yearbook and allowed himself to be known as "Guy" by some who were outside his circle of family and close friends. As a result, a fair number of his college classmates knew him as "Guy." Arriving at the Law School, he completed a form noting his

---

[32] Roger Ebert, *The Garden of the Finzi-Continis*, CHICAGO SUN-TIMES, Jan. 1, 1971, http://www.rogerebert.com/reviews/the-garden-of-the-finzi-continis-1971.
[33] Millicent Marcus, *De Sica's Garden of the Finzi Contini*, *in* VITTORIO DE SICA: CONTEMPORARY PERSPECTIVES 271 (Snyder & Curle eds. 2000).
[34] Mitgang, *A World of Its Own*, *supra* note 3.
[35] "Vittorio De Sica in the Garden of the Finzi-Continis," POSCRITTO A GIORGIO BASSANI: SAGGI IN MEMORIA DEL DECIMO ANNIVERSARIO DELLA MORTE 499–516 (Roberta Antognini & Rodica Diaconescu ed. 2011). The hyphen in Finzi-Contini was removed for the Italian release of the film.

"occasional use of the nickname 'Guy,' 1946–1953."[36] As Guido mentions, Dean Rostow and Justice Black also referred to him as "Guy."

Guido struggled with acquiescing in the use of "Guy." He did not find anything especially wrong, because his "Italian-ness" was indelible: *he* knew who he was. Nothing could have obscured his roots and his identity, even if he wanted to do it, especially considering his surname. Choosing "Guy," he told me, had been an intuitive, adolescent decision.

Like the American coat which his brother Paolo had wrapped around himself when he first came to America, this did not necessarily fit him—but it signaled an effort at assimilation and may have deterred some discrimination, which was important.[37]

By the time that *The Garden of the Finzi-Contini* appeared, Guido had reestablished the exclusive use of his given Italian first name. Perhaps because *The Garden* helped to explain his identity, he not long afterward reduced the social distance between himself and the rest of the world: everyone should call him and know him, he urged, just as "Guido."

Which is what everyone did.[38]

END

Guido Calabresi and Norman I. Silber

---

[36] Yale Law School Registrar Student Record file.
[37] See Chapter 4, "Departure and Arrival."
[38] Except in court, of course, where parties address Judges by their surnames.

Image Acknowledgments

Chapter 1

1.1 Guido Calabresi.
1.2 Centro Primo Levi.
1.3 Norman I. Silber.
1.4 Guido Calabresi.
1.5 Guido Calabresi.
1.6 Centro Primo Levi.
1.7 *LaStampa*

Chapter 2

2.1 NYC Dept. Finance.
2.2 Wikipedia.

Chapter 3

3.1 Ariel Toaff, Collegio Rabbinico Italiano, Annuario Di Studi Ebraici 1980-1984 (1984) (Yale Library photograph).
3.2 Guido Calebresi.
3.3 Guido Calabresi
3.4 Guido Calabresi.
3.5 Guido Calabresi.
3.6 Ariel Toaff, Collegio Rabbinico Italiano, Annuario Di Studi Ebraici 1980-1984 (1984) (Yale Library photograph).
3.7 Guido Calabresi.
3.8 Guido Calabresi.
3.9 Ariel Toaff, Collegio Rabbinico Italiano, Annuario Di Studi Ebraici 1980-1984 (1984) (Yale Library photograph).
3.10 Guido Calabresi.
3.11 Guido Calabresi.
3.12 Wikipedia.
3.13 Guido Calabresi.
3.14 Norman I. Silber

Chapter 4

4.1 Guido Calabresi.
4.2 Guido Calabresi.
4.3 Guido Calabresi.
4.4 Norman I. Silber.
4.5 Guido Calabresi.
4.6 Norman I. Silber.
4.7 Casa Minerbi-Del Sale.
4.8 FloodMap.net.
4.9 Ariel Toaff, Collegio Rabbinico Italiano, Annuario Di Studi Ebraici 1980-1984 (1984)(Yale Library photograph).
4.10 Museo Ferrara

Chapter 5

5.1 Guido Calabresi.
5.2 New Haven Museum.
5.3 Manuscripts and Archives, Yale University.
5.4 New Haven Register, New Haven Museum Collection

Chapter 6

6.1 Guido Calabresi.
6.2 Guido Calabresi.
6.3 Guido Calabresi.
6.4 World War II Database *(https://ww2db.com/image.php?image_id=17422)*

Chapter 7

7.1 Salone Casa Minerbi - Del Sale.
7.2 Guido Calabresi.
7.3 Guido Calabresi.
7.4 Wikipedia.
7.5 Guido Calabresi

Chapter 8

8.1 New Haven Museum.
8.2 Guido Calabresi.

8.3 Yale Daily News Publishing Co.
8.4 Norman I. Silber.
8.5 Mark Wickham, *Sir John Hicks*, All Souls College, University of Oxford.
8.6 New Haven Museum.
8.7 Special Collections Library, University of Virginia.
8.8 Wikimedia.
8.9 Terrence Spencer, Time & Life, Getty.

Chapter 9

9.1 Vintage Press.
9.2 Oxford University Catholic Chaplaincy.
9.3 Westminster Cathedral blogspot.com.

Chapter 10

10.1 Manuscripts and Archives, Yale University.
10.2 Manuscripts and Archives, Yale University.
10.3 Manuscripts and Archives, Yale University.
10.4 Federal Judicial Center.
10.5 Yale Law Report
10.6 Yale Law Journal.
10.7 Yale digital commons.
10.8 Guido Calabresi.
10.9 Yale Law School

Chapter 11

11.1 Guido Calabresi.
11.2 Wikipedia.

Chapter 12

12.1 Wikipedia.
12.2 Norman I. Silber.
12.3 University of Chicago Photographic Archive, Special Collections Research Center, University of Chicago Library.
12.4 University of Chicago Photographic Archive, Special Collections Research Center, University of Chicago Library.
12.5 Harvard Law School Library, Historical & Special Collections

12.6 Chicago Sun-Times file.
12.7 Norman I. Silber

Chapter 13

13.1 Guido Calabresi.
13.2 Guido Calabresi.
13.3 Thomas S. LaFarge, *The Tyler Children*, Anne Calabresi.
13.4 Guido Calabresi.
13.5 Guido Calabresi.
13.6 Norman I. Silber.
13.7 Guido Calabresi

Chapter 14

14.1 Harvard Law School.
14.2 Douglas Melamed

Chapter 15

15.1 Philip C. Bobbitt.
15.2 Symposium Publicity Photograph, Calabresi collection

Chapter 16

16.1 Heino Prahl, Donald M. Lerner, *Yale Law Report*
16.2 Norman I. Silber.
16.3 Norman I. Silber.
16.4 Norman I. Silber.
16.5 Norman I. Silber
16.5 Yale Law School

Chapter 17

17.1 Yale Center for Corporate Law.
17.2 *Yale Bulletin and Calendar*.
17.2 Norman I. Silber.

IMAGE ACKNOWLEDGMENTS   443

Chapter 18

18.1 Yale Law School.
18.2 Manuscripts and Archives, Yale University.
18.3 William K. Sacco, Yale University

Chapter 19

19.1 Yale Law School.
19.2 Yale Law School.
19.3 Yale Law School.
19.4 Yale Law School.
19.5 Yale Law School.
19.6 Yale Law School.
19.7 Yale Law School.
19.8 Yale Law School.
19.9 Yale Law School

Chapter 20

20.1 Yale Economics Department
20.2 PBS, *Charlie Rose Show*, Sept. 11, 1992.

Chapter 21

21.1 Manuscripts and Archives, Yale University.
21.2 Yale Law School.
21.3 Manuscripts and Archives, Yale University.
21.4 Manuscripts and Archives, Yale University.
21.5 Yale University.
21.6 David Ottenstein, *Yale Alumni Magazine*.
21.7 Yale University.
21.8 Yale University

Chapter 22

22.1 1970 Yale Law Reporter
22.2 pastdaily.com
22.3 AP Photo/Charles Tasnadi,

Chapter 23

23.1 Yale Law School.
23.2 Yale Law School.
23.3 Yale Law School.
23.4 Norman I. Silber.
23.5 *Yale Daily News* Publishing Co.
23.6 Yale Law School

Chapter 24

24.1 C-SPAN.
24.2 Wikipedia
24.3 Obama White House Archives.
24.4 Yale Law School.
24.5 Yale Law School.

Chapter 25

25.1 Manuscripts and Archives, Yale University.
25.2 C-SPAN.
25.3 Norman I. Silber.
25.4 Yale Law School.
25.5 Norman I. Silber.
25.6 Elliott Banfield, *New York Times*.

Chapter 26

26.1 Guido Calabresi

Chapter 27

27.1 Guido Calabresi.
27.2 ebay.com.
27.3 Wikipedia.
27.4 Wikipedia

Chapter 28

28.1 Norman I. Silber

Chapter 29

29.1 Wikiquote.
29.2 Norman I. Silber

Chapter 30

30.1 Norman I. Silber.
30.2 Spencer Tunick, *Pink Tenderness* (diptych, 1999).
30.3 Norman I. Silber

Chapter 31

31.1 Guido Calabresi.
31.1 Fordham University.

Chapter 32

32.1 Norman I. Silber.
32.2 *Houston Chronicle.*
32.3 Washington University.
32.4 *Garry Trudeau, Doonesbury, Andrews McMeel Syndication.*

Chapter 33

33.1 Norman I. Silber.
33.2 Johan Jaritz, *Times of Israel.*
33.3 *Time Magazine*, Nov. 23, 1953.
33.4 Associated Press.

Chapter 34

34.1 C-SPAN.

34.2 Ninth Circuit Blog
34.3 Norman I. Silber

Chapter 35

35.1 Atheneum Press.
35.2 Ronald Grant, Promotional photograph.
35.3 Norman I. Silber.
35.4 Norman I. Silber.

Index

For the benefit of digital users, indexed terms that span two pages (e.g., 52–53) may, on occasion, appear on only one of those pages.

Abbate v. United States, Vol 1:273, 280–81
Abel, Richard, Vol 2:397
abortion, Vol 1:345–54; Vol 2:166, 169–70, 185
abortion in China, Vol 2:310–12, 315–17
Abraham, Kenneth, Vol 1:305, 375–64; Vol 2:202, 210, 212, 221
Abrams, Floyd, Vol 2:300
Abramson, Jill, Vol 2:146–47
abstention concept, Vol 2:294
abuse of discretion standard, Vol 2:230
Acheson, Dean, Vol 1:177–78, 202, 248–49
Ackerman, Bruce
    Balkin and, Vol 2:52–53
    career moves, Vol 1:377–78
    on Guido's Deanship, Vol 2:147–48
    as Guido learning from, Vol 1:359, 367
    on Guido's writings, Vol 1:395–96
    hiring of, Vol 2:50–51, 53, 389
    on Pollak's dismissals, Vol 2:399
    on social/individual values, Vol 1:346
    Torts classes, Vol 1:224
Act Up, Vol 2:116
addictiveness of tobacco, Vol 2:233
affirmative action, Vol 1:103, 104, 271, 344; Vol 2:93, 167
Age of Anxiety, The (Gilmore), Vol 1:243–44
Ages of American Law, The (Gilmore), Vol 1:399
Albert, Lee, Vol 2:397
Alexander v. Yale, Vol 2:146
Alfred M. Rankin Professorship, Vol 2:67
Alito, Samuel, Vol 2:267
All Writs Act of 1789, Vol 2:304–5, 306, 314, 315
Altimari, Frank, Vol 2:178, 179, 181, 372, 374–75
Amar, Akhil, Vol 1:380; Vol 2:53, 124, 147, 352
Amendola, Giovanni, Vol 1:10–11, 19, 20
America First agenda, Vol 1:105
American President Lines, Vol 1:29–30, 36–37
Amici Israel, Vol 1:59
A.M.'s Longest Journey (Finzi-Contini), Vol 2:436
Angell, James Rowland, Vol 1:105, 120–21, 224; Vol 2:76
anti-conformity, Vol 1:33, 103, 149

anti-discrimination law
    associational discrimination, Vol 2:250–51, 262–64
    background, Vol 2:241
    gender-based termination, Vol 2:241, 246–49, 261–62
    racial intermarriage, Vol 2:241, 249–53, 262–63
    racial profiling, Vol 2:241, 242–46, 253, 257–61
    same-sex marriage, Vol 2:241
    sentencing disparities/cultural prejudices, Vol 2:241, 254–56, 264–67, 269, 278–79
    sexual orientation, Vol 2:27–264
Antitrust Paradox, The (Bork), Vol 1:298
Arar v. Ashcroft, Vol 2:395–400, 409–12
Arch of Titus, Vol 1:64
Arizona Free Enterprise case, Vol 2:325
Arnold, Richard S., Vol 2:169–70
arrival in United States, Vol 1:30–31, 37–38
Arterton, Janet Bond, Vol 2:389
Aryanization, Vol 1:17, 58–59
Asbestos Hazards Compensation Act, Vol 1:339–40
Ascoli, Marion Rosenwald, Vol 1:137–38
Ascoli, Max, Vol 1:40–41, 131–32, 137–38
Ashcroft, John, Vol 2:306, 309, 318, 385–86
Assicurazioni Generali, Vol 2:349–51, 365
assisted suicide/euthanasia, Vol 2:192–93, 281–86, 295–96
associational discrimination, Vol 2:250–51, 263–64
assumption of risk, Vol 2:216–17
Assumption of the Virgin Mary, Vol 2:283
Atiyah, Patrick, Vol 1:327, 338
Atropos, Vol 1:353
Audubon, John J., Vol 1:320
autonomy. *See* finance/fundraising
Ayres, Ian, Vol 1:300; Vol 2:50, 53, 55, 276

Babb, James, Vol 2:80
Babbitt, Bruce, Vol 2:169
Back v. Hastings on Hudson, Vol 2:241, 246–49, 261–62
Badoglio, Pietro, Vol 1:138–39
Baer, Harold, Vol 2:351, 362–64
Baker, James, Vol 2:175

Baker, Robert C., Vol 2:88
Baker v. Carr (1962), Vol 1:276–77
Baker v. Pataki, Vol 2:391
Bakke, E. Wight, Vol 1:168–69, 191, 195–96
Bakke decision, Vol 1:274; Vol 2:167
Balance of Payments, The (Mead), Vol 1:298
Balbo, Italo, Vol 1:16
Balkin, Jack, Vol 2:45–46, 52–53
banking trade, Vol 1:52–53, 65–66, 67, 69–70
Barak, Aharon, Vol 2:324–25
Baraldi, Lucrezia Neri, Vol 1:45–46
Barenblatt v. U.S., Vol 1:269, 270–71, 280
Barr, Tom, Vol 2:33
Bartkus v. Illinois, Vol 1:273, 280–81
Bassani, Giorgio, Vol 1:78, 87, 144–45; Vol 2:425, 429–30, 431–32, 434–35
Basseches, Bob, Vol 1:235
Batson reconstruction, Vol 2:380, 414, 415
Bayne-Jones, S., Vol 1:35, 118
Bazelon, David L., Vol 1:252
Becker, Edward, Vol 2:306, 314
behavioral realities
   anchoring/starting points, Vol 2:269–70, 278–79
   deterrence, Vol 2:276–77
   functions of judgments, Vol 2:271–72
   misrepresentation, Vol 2:274–76
   punitive damages, Vol 2:271–74, 279–80
   rational actors, Vol 2:270–71
   transaction costs, Vol 2:271
   writings on, Vol 2:269, 277–78
Benedict XIV, Vol 1:53, 67
Beneduce, Alberto, Vol 1:28
Berlin, Isaiah, Vol 1:187
Berry v. Sugar Notch Borough, Vol 2:212, 232
beyond a reasonable doubt, Vol 2:375–78, 417–19
Biaggi precedent, Vol 2:368–69
Bickel, Alexander M.
   aspirations as Dean, Vol 2:384
   background, Vol 1:254–56
   Bork and, Vol 2:92
   death of, Vol 2:96
   delegation theory, Vol 1:270
   Guido's clerkship and, Vol 1:239
   Holmes Lectures, Vol 1:383
   legislature updating in Canada, Vol 1:389
   teaching style, Vol 1:233
bicycling, Vol 1:99, 102, 106–7
Biddle, Francis, Vol 1:130
Biden, Joseph, Vol 1:352; Vol 2:104, 131, 141
Bishop, Joe, Vol 1:256
Bittker, Boris, Vol 1:224, 225, 231–32, 247–32; Vol 2:396
Bivens actions, Vol 2:396, 397–99, 410–12
Black, Charles, Vol 1:256, 268–69, 279, 342, 383–84, 392, 394; Vol 2:37, 92, 96

Black, Hugo
   absolutionism/originalism, Vol 1:267–69, 277–78, 282–61; Vol 2:321, 324–25
   allocated power/abuse of power, Vol 1:263, 264, 270–71
   appointment to Supreme Court, Vol 1:261
   backwards incorporation, Vol 1:266–68, 273
   Barenblatt dissent, Vol 1:270–71, 280
   Bill of Rights application to state governments, Vol 1:272–73
   clerkships, Vol 1:235, 236–37, 257–58
   Court of Star Chamber, Vol 1:274–75, 281–82
   decisions generally, Vol 1:261
   on diversity of Court, Vol 1:271–72
   on doing right, Vol 1:268–69
   double jeopardy, Vol 1:263, 272–75, 280–81
   drumhead trials, Vol 1:274, 281
   dual sovereignty double jeopardy cases, Vol 1:273–75, 280–81
   Equal Protection/Due Process provisions, Vol 1:266–68, 273
   on federal court deference, Vol 2:354–55
   Federal Judges and press ethics, Vol 1:265–66, 276–77, 278–79
   First Amendment legacy, Vol 1:282
   on First Amendment rights, Vol 2:324–25
   Frankfurter and, Vol 1:264–66
   on Guido's career, Vol 1:285
   Guido's clerkship for, Vol 1:237–40, 258–59, 261
   improper delegation, Vol 1:269–70, 279–80
   incentives, Vol 1:263
   on judicial independence, Vol 2:352–53
   judicial philosophy, Vol 1:263–65, 273–74
   Korematsu decision, Vol 1:266–63; Vol 2:323
   Ku Klux Klan involvement, Vol 1:261–62, 276
   "Law" writ large, Vol 1:275
   Lewis on, Vol 1:277
   no-fault liability, Vol 1:384–85
   Privileges and Immunities Clause, Vol 1:272
   search and seizure decisions, Vol 1:263–64, 278
   Second Look doctrine, Vol 1:269–70, 280
   segregated schools in DC, Vol 1:266–68
   strict scrutiny, Vol 1:268–69, 279
   on Sturges, Vol 1:252
   undue delegation, Vol 1:269
   use of torture, Vol 1:268–69, 279
   voter redistricting, Vol 1:276–77
Blackmun, Harry, Vol 1:345; Vol 2:170, 272–73
Black Talon bullets, Vol 2:286–91, 296–98
Blake, Francis G., Vol 1:35
Bloomberg, Michael, Vol 2:260
Blow, Charles, Vol 2:296
Blum, Walter, Vol 1:290, 291, 292, 301–3
Bobbitt, Philip, Vol 1:341–44, 351–53, 355–56
Bogan, Samuel, Vol 1:113–14

Bolling v. Sharpe, Vol 1:266–68
Bologna, Italy, Vol 1:46, 53, 57, 62, 80, 139, 141
Book of the Law, Vol 1:64
Borchard, Edwin Montefiore, Vol 1:117–18
Boren, David, Vol 2:155
Bork, Mary Ellen, Vol 2:104–5
Bork, Robert
    anti-trust scholarship, Vol 2:91, 92, 100
    appointment of, Vol 1:222; Vol 2:91–92
    on Bowman, Vol 1:298
    civil rights legislation, Vol 2:101
    Clinton's opposition to, Vol 2:103–4
    dismissal of, Vol 1:255
    on Dworkin, Vol 1:208
    faculty lounge conversations, Vol 2:93
    family/marriages, Vol 2:92–93, 104–5
    Guido on nomination of, Vol 2:96–97, 102–3
    Guido relationship with, Vol 2:165, 167
    homophobia, Vol 2:93–94, 99, 100–1
    judicial philosophy, Vol 2:97, 99–100, 102–3
    Judiciary Committee attacks on, Vol 2:98–99, 105
    legal writings, Vol 1:298
    nomination aftermath, Vol 2:99, 105–6
    nomination/confirmation, Vol 2:67, 91, 96–99
    Saturday Night Massacre, Vol 2:94–96, 101–2
    sense of humor, Vol 2:92, 104
    as Solicitor General, Vol 2:94
    teaching, Vol 1:371–59; Vol 2:91–93
    work ethic, Vol 2:93, 98
Bostock v. Clayton County (2020), Vol 2:241, 264
Bottai, Giuseppe, Vol 1:124
Bottoni, Piero, Vol 1:155–56
Boudin, Michael, Vol 2:290, 309
Bowman, Cathy, Vol 2:122
Bowman, Ward, Vol 1:256, 288–89, 298, 340
Bradley, William, Vol 2:258
Braga, Stephen, Vol 2:415
Bread and Chocolate, Vol 2: 26, 393
Breaking the Vicious Circle (Breyer), Vol 1:353–54
Brennan, William J. Jr., Vol 1:261, 271, 280–81, 400
Brewster, Kingman, Vol 1:105, 222; Vol 2:38–39, 384–85, 390, 391–92, 396, 400, 401–2
Breyer, Stephen, Vol 1:345, 353–54; Vol 2:170–71, 218, 336, 342, 359
Brillmayer, Lea, Vol 2:389
Brinkley, Stuart, Vol 1:167
Broderick, William, Vol 2:120
Brouwer, Dirk, Vol 1:111
Brouwer, Jimmy, Vol 1:99, 111
Brown, Ralph, Vol 1:224–25, 230–31; Vol 2:38–39
Brown, Ralph Sharp, Vol 1:377
Brown University Medical School, Vol 1:189
Brown v. Board of Education, Vol 1:223, 245, 261; Vol 2:241, 325–26, 394

Brown v. City of Oneonta, Vol 2:181, 241, 242–46, 253, 257–60
Brown v. Maryland, Vol 1:246
Bruce, Lenny, Vol 1:302
Brudney, Jim, Vol 2:132
Buchanan, James M., Vol 1:194, 286, 297–98
Buckley, William F., Vol 1:168–69, 172–73, 191–93, 215–16; Vol 2:192
Buckley v. Valeo, Vol 2:188, 341
Buckman Co. v. Plaintiff's Legal Comm, Vol 2:234
Buck v. Bell, Vol 2:383
building renovations. *See* Sterling Law Building renovation
bullet manufacturers tort liability, Vol 2:281, 284–85, 286–91, 296–98
Bundy, Harvey Hollister, Vol 1:177–78
Bundy, McGeorge, Vol 1:192
Burchardt, F. A., Vol 1:182–84, 204–5
Burger, Warren, Vol 2:353
Burns, James (Jimmy), Vol 1:261
Burr, Ralph, Vol 2:39–40, 41
Burt, Robert "Bo," Vol 1:214; Vol 2:24, 389
Burton, Harold, Vol 1:261
Bush, George H. W., Vol 1:174; Vol 2:105, 127, 186
Bush, George W., Vol 1:19; Vol 2:232, 306, 358
Bushey v. U. S., Vol 2:198
Bush v. Gore, Vol 2:189–90, 358–59
but-for causation. *See* causation
Butler, Nicholas Murray, Vol 1:105
Buzzoni, Andrea/Michele, Vol 1:154–55

Cabranes, José
    appointment to Court of Appeals, Vol 2:155, 162–63
    background, Vol 2:175–76, 187–88
    on certification, Vol 2:287–88
    characterization, Vol 2:288
    confirmation, Vol 2:163
    death penalty cases, Vol 2:384, 386
    discussions of Second Circuit with, Vol 2:174
    on felon disenfranchisement, Vol 2:401–2
    Guido's Presidency and, Vol 2:155, 156
    judicial philosophy, Vol 2:188
    penile plethysmography case, Vol 2:382, 383, 405
    Philip Morris case, Vol 2:233
    recusals, Vol 2:391
    relationship with Guido, Vol 2:175–76, 180, 351
Cahn, Edmond, Vol 1:237
Calabresi, Amadio, Vol 1:82–83, 91–92
Calabresi, Anne Gordon
    background, Vol 1:11, 161, 175–76, 317, 319
    building a family/buying a home, Vol 1:323–25
    children, Vol 1:325–26
    early education, Vol 1:314
    early memories of Guido, Vol 1:314

Calabresi, Anne Gordon (*cont.*)
  engagement, Vol 1:318–19
  faculty children's dances, Vol 1:314–15
  family picture, Vol 1:321
  father's side, Vol 1:319–20
  Guido's impressions of, Vol 1:316
  Harkness and, Vol 2:76–77
  home as security/repose, Vol 1:321
  marriage to Guido, Vol 1:313, 322–23
  Masters School, Vol 1:321–22
  meeting Guido, Vol 1:313–14, 316–17
  mother's side, Vol 1:320–21
  other suitors, Vol 1:322
  relationship development, Vol 1:315, 317–18, 322
  sixtieth anniversary photo, Vol 1:326
  "the Assemblies" dance, Vol 1:315
Calabresi, Armando, Vol 1:84–85, 93–95, 209
Calabresi, Bianca (née Finzi-Contini)
  arrival in United States, Vol 1:37–38
  dislike of *The Garden,* Vol 2:428–30, 436
  emigration from Italy, Vol 1:29–30
  fate of relatives, Vol 1:133–34
  father's death, Vol 1:108, 127
  Finzi-Contini family history, Vol 1:43–50
  hybrid identity of, Vol 1:122
  Knight/Italian Republic, Vol 1:107
  marriage/family life, Vol 1:13, 58, 78; Vol 2:425
  religiosity/conversion of, Vol 1:48, 50, 59, 102, 209
  returning to Italy permanently, Vol 1:148–50
  social teas in New Haven, Vol 1:107, 112, 122
  university teaching post, Vol 1:130–31
  US citizenship, Vol 1:147
Calabresi, Cecilia, Vol 1:9, 19, 106, 147, 148
Calabresi, Cesare, Vol 1:83
Calabresi, Enrica, Vol 1:91
Calabresi, Ettore
  anti-Fascist views, Vol 1:16–17, 27
  background, Vol 1:7–9; Vol 2:58–59
  corporate activities, Vol 1:16
  death of, Vol 1:27
  departure from Ferrara, Vol 1:7, 16
  fascist restrictions on, Vol 1:85
  as Freemason, Vol 1:83, 93
  knighthood, Vol 1:84, 93
  nationalism of, Vol 1:92
  personal history, Vol 1:82–84
  philanthropic activity supporting veterans, Vol 1:92–93
  vulnerability to creditors of tomato company, Vol 1:56, 72–73
Calabresi, Massimo
  anti-Fascist views, Vol 1:11–12, 14–16
  arrests/beatings by fascists, Vol 1:12, 19–20
  arrival in United States, Vol 1:30–31, 37–38
  assistance to FBI by, Vol 1:130
  background, Vol 1:9–10
  birth/parentage, Vol 1:78
  dislike of *The Garden,* Vol 2:428
  emigration from Italy, Vol 1:27–31
  Fedele a Giustizia e Libertà, Vol 1:13
  immigrant visas/exit permits, Vol 1:28–29, 38
  loyalty oath, Vol 1:15, 22
  marriage/family life, Vol 1:13–14, 78; Vol 2:425
  medical licensure exams, Vol 1:33–34, 39–40
  as non-entity, Vol 1:15, 25
  non-religiosity of, Vol 1:48–49, 102, 121, 209
  opinions on conversions, Vol 1:49
  returning to Italy permanently, Vol 1:148–50
  US citizenship, Vol 1:147
  Yale fellowship, Vol 1:27, 28, 29, 30, 33–36, 97, 118
Calabresi, Olga, Vol 1:8–9
Calabresi, Paolo, Vol 1:13, 14, 37–38, 102, 106–7, 121, 161, 165–67, 173–74, 182, 189, 210–12; Vol 2:324, 430–31
Calabresi, Pellegrina (née Pisa), Vol 1:82–83
Calabresi, Renata, Vol 1:8–9, 19, 22, 40–41, 83, 84, 147
Calabresi, Renato, Vol 1:83, 134
Calabresi, Steven, Vol 1:189–72; Vol 2:103, 167–68, 180, 352
Calabresi family history, Vol 1:79–85
Cameron, Edwin, Vol 1:329–30
Camp Adventure, Vol 1:101–2
campaign financing to avoid corruption, Vol 2:325–28, 339–41, 392
Camus, Albert, Vol 1:213, 216–17
Canham, Erwin D., Vol 1:203
cannabis, Vol 1:145
Cantoni, Marcello, Vol 1:139
capital cases. *See* death penalty
Caradossi, Umberto, Vol 1:124
Cardamone, Richard, Vol 2:178, 191
Cardozo, Benjamin, Vol 1:232, 245, 272, 351, 354–55, 391, 399; Vol 2:211, 230
Carducci, Giosuè, Vol 1:125
Carpenter v. United States, Vol 1:278
Carroll, Dick, Vol 2:34
Carter, James E., Vol 1:234; Vol 2:187–88
cartes de visite, Vol 2:322–23
Casa Minerbi-Del Sale, Vol 1:86; Vol 2:434
Casa Minerbi frescoes, Vol 1:145–46, 155–56
Casati, Father Innocence Maria, Vol 1:49, 60
Cases on Trials, Judgments and Appeals (James), Vol 1:243
Catholicism
  bullying incident, Vol 1:212
  conversion of Jews as protection, Vol 1:49–50, 59–61, 209–10
  in England, Vol 1:212–14
  Guido's belief in God, Vol 1:212–14

Jewishness and, Vol 1:214, 218–19
job market effects of, Vol 1:175
in New Haven, Vol 1:210
Old Palace, Vol 1:213–14, 217
religiosity/conversion in, Vol 1:48–50, 59, 78–79, 175
at Yale University, Vol 1:211–12
causation
chain of, Vol 2:201–3
common law attribution, Vol 2:231–32
Improbable but possible innocence, Vol 2:231
jury finding of negligence, Vol 2:231–32
Librarian, Vol 2:205–8, 224–26, 289
misrepresentation, Vol 2:274–76
multiplicity of possible causes, Vol 2:231
negligence assumptions, Vol 2:231
negligent overdose, Vol 2:27–230
plaintiff's contribution to injury condition not cause, Vol 2:232
reasonable warning, Vol 2:205–8, 224–26, 289
statistical causation, Vol 2:346–49, 361–62
Zuchowicz, Vol 2:27–230
Cavalieri family history, Vol 1:57–58, 72
Ceka, Vol 1:18
Celentano, William C., Vol 1:114
certification of cases
bullet manufacturers tort liability, Vol 2:284–85, 287–90, 296–98
first spouse pension rights, Vol 2:373–74, 375
forum shopping limitation, Vol 2:298
freedom of expression, Vol 2:291–93, 295, 299–302
incorporation of into judicial practice, Vol 2:281, 293–95
Kaye on, Vol 2:298–99
Cesa-Bianchi, Domenico, Vol 1:14–15, 24–25
chain of causation, Vol 2:201–3, 223–24
Charcot, Jean-Marie, Vol 1:61–62
Chase, Samuel, Vol 2:353–54
Chatigny, Robert N., Vol 2:385
Chevron v. N.R.D.C., Vol 2:354–55
child removal from mother's custody, Vol 2:298–99
choosing to stay in America, Vol 1:135, 148–50, 157–58
Christian Democratic Party, Vol 1:10, 151
Christian Science Monitor, Vol 1:176, 177, 203
Church of Santa Sabina, Vol 1:11
Ciraolo v. City of New York, Vol 2:205, 239, 272–73, 279–80
Circolo Italiano, Vol 1:107, 122
Citizens United, Vol 2:339, 341
City of Newport v. Fact Concerts, Inc, Vol 2:239
civil rights violations/suit for damages, Vol 2:395–400, 409–12
Civil War, Vol 2:331–32

Clark, Charles E., Vol 1:224, 232, 235–36, 240, 247–48; Vol 2:176, 177, 179, 180–81, 184, 189
Clark, David, Vol 1:237, 240, 257–58
Clark, Eli, Vol 2:110
Clark, Tom C., Vol 1:234, 261
Class of 1964 Auditorium, Vol 2:67–68
Class of 1964 Reading Room, Vol 2:68
Clay, Eric, Vol 2:130–31
clerical workers strike, Vol 2:24, 26, 119–20, 393–94
Clinton, Hillary, Vol 2:44–45, 127, 156, 165, 169–70, 341
Clinton, William J., Vol 1:176; Vol 2:44–45, 103–4, 127, 153, 156–57, 159–62, 165–66, 168–71, 186, 323, 363
Coase, Ronald
externalities, explaining to Chicago faculty, Vol 1:298–300
inalienability rules, Vol 1:340
Nobel Prize, Vol 1:286, 295, 299–300
popularity of works, Vol 1:331
Problem of Social Cost, Vol 1:288, 290–91, 292, 295
on social costs, Vol 1:288, 292
symmetrical causation, Vol 1:289
on transaction costs, Vol 1:170–71, 194–95, 286, 292, 293
coats of arms, Vol 1:44, 62, 81, 86, 89
Coberly, Jennifer, Vol 2:120–21
Cochetti, Anna Maria, Vol 1:137–38
Code of Conduct of United States Judges, Vol 1:278–79
Cohen v. California, Vol 1:282
Coleman, Jules, Vol 1:7–310, 361
collective responsibility for conspiracy doctrine, Vol 1:84
Common Law For the of Statutes, A (Calabresi)
basis of, Vol 1:225, 383, 389–84; Vol 2:173
comparative negligence, Vol 1:387–88, 398–99
constitutional right to updating, Vol 1:394
Constitution in updating, Vol 1:388–89
counter-majoritarian problem, Vol 1:394
equal protection, Vol 1:389
fading of illogical statutes, Vol 2:284
felon disenfranchisement, Vol 2:395
grant of certiorari, Vol 1:385–86, 400–1
Guido's perception of, Vol 1:396
judgmental sunset, Vol 1:392–93
judicial updating for inflation, Vol 1:392
judicial updating of statutes, Vol 1:388–86; Vol 2:199, 252–53, 265–66, 286
legal blackmail, Vol 1:385–86, 387–88
legislative delegation, Vol 1:393–94
majoritarian difficulty, Vol 1:391–92
no-fault liability, Vol 1:383–85
reception, Vol 1:396, 397
recommendations, Vol 1:396

Common Law For the of Statutes, A
    (Calabresi) *(cont.)*
  relational updating, Vol 1:386–88
  Restatements, Vol 1:390
  Second Look doctrine, Vol 2:295–96
  statutes/common law relationships,
    Vol 1:390–91
  statutory interpretation as field of study,
    Vol 1:401–2
  structure of, Vol 1:343, 395
  subterfuges, Vol 1:344, 351, 396
Common Law Tradition, The (Llewellyn), Vol
    2:345
Communist associations/McCarthyism, Vol
    1:269–70, 279–80
Communist Democracy, Vol 1:10–11
Communist Party cases, Vol 1:262
comparisons to Hitler/Hitlerian racism, Vol 2:67,
    111, 189–90, 323
Compassion in Dying (Reinhardt), Vol 2:296
Compassion in Dying v. Washington, Vol
    2:295–96
compensatory damages, Vol 2:271–74, 279–80
Competition Among the Few (Fellner), Vol 1:198
compulsory sterilization, Vol 2:383
Comstock, Ada, Vol 1:314
condotta, Vol 1:53, 67–69
confession coerced, Vol 2:378–82, 412–17
Conrail v. Gottshall, Vol 2:215, 238
Constitutional Fate (Bobbit), Vol 1:356
Contini, Bruno, Vol 1:44
Contini, Camillo, Vol 1:44–45
Contini, Paolo, Vol 1:30–31, 41
Contini-Bonacossi family, Vol 1:44–45
Contini-Bonacossi Palace, Vol 1:44–45, 61
Contini-Morava, Ellen, Vol 1:41
Contracts in Context (Mueller), Vol 1:222, 244
contributory negligence, Vol 1:399
Coolidge, Calvin, Vol 1:263
cooperative federalism concept, Vol 2:294
Corbin, Arthur, Vol 1:222–23; Vol 2:74–75
Cormier, Rufus, Vol 2:128Vol 2:–29
corporate finance theory, Vol 1:297–98
Corrupter of Railway Cars, Vol 1:8
Corwin, Robert N., Vol 1:117
Cost-Benefit Revolution, The (Sunstein),
    Vol 1:354
Cost of Accidents, The (Calabresi)
  cleanup costs responsibility allocation,
    Vol 2:165–66
  critiques of, Vol 1:306–7, 309–11, 338
  impacts of, Vol 1:285, 303–4, 309–11, 331,
    332
  law/economics approach, Vol 1:292, 305–6,
    310–11
  legal themes of, Vol 1:294–95
  master-servant doctrine, Vol 2:198–99

  neologisms in/translation of, Vol 1:307–9
  no-fault auto insurance, Vol 1:303
  publishing of, Vol 1:303–4
  reviews of, Vol 1:304
  structure of, Vol 1:395–96
  theorizing in, Vol 1:307
Cotes, Roger, Vol 1:190
Court of Appeals for the Second Circuit. *See*
    Second Circuit court characterization
Cover, Robert, Vol 2:108–9, 110, 121–22
COVID-19 pandemic, Vol 1:355
Cox, Archibald, Vol 1:387; Vol 2:94–95, 101–2
Cravath firm, Vol 1:228
Crosby, Franklin Muzzy, Vol 2:76
Crosby, Harriett Eugenie, Vol 1:313, 318, 320
Crosby, Sumner, Vol 1:317
Cross, Rupert, Vol 1:181
cruel and unusual application of law,
    Vol 2:388–91, 409
Cruel and Unusual Punishment clause, Vol
    2:386–87
Cruzan v. Missouri, Vol 2:253–54
Cudahy, Richard, Vol 2:206
Culvahouse, Arthur B., Vol 2:104
Cum nimis absurdum, Vol 1:90–91
cumulative liquidated damages, Vol 2:288
Cuomo, Andrew, Vol 2:267
Cuomo, Mario, Vol 2:165, 169
currency restrictions, Vol 1:30, 38–39
Curtis, Dennis, Vol 1:380–71; Vol 2:43–44
Cutler, Lloyd, Vol 2:170–71

Dahl, Robert, Vol 1:171, 199–200
Dalton, Harlon, Vol 2:124
Damaška, Mirjan, Vol 2:25, 47
D'Amato, Al, Vol 2:300
Dane, Perry, Vol 2:124
Danforth, John "Jack," Vol 2:127–29, 130, 132,
    136–37, 140, 141–42, 168
Danocrine, Vol 2:27–230
Dauer, Ed, Vol 2:33–34, 37
Davidson, Claire, Vol 2:92–93, 96, 104–5
Days, Drew, Vol 2:22, 44–45, 120, 153–54
D'Azeglio, Massimo, Vol 1:10
Dazian Foundation for Medical Research,
    Vol 1:34–35
Deanship
  acceptance of, Vol 2:393–94
  administration of, Vol 2:33–35, 42–43
  agenda generally, Vol 2:29, 58
  approaching Guido for, Vol 2:385
  approvals, Vol 2:37–38, 43
  attitude towards, Vol 2:383
  birthday wishes, Vol 2:47
  as calling, Vol 2:148
  candidacy, Vol 2:7, 23–25, 388–89, 392–93
  clinical programs, Vol 2:55

COAP (loan forgiveness program), Vol 2:29–31, 46
dean designate actions, Vol 2:394–95
Dean of Admissions, Vol 2:35–36, 44–45
Deputy Deans, Vol 2:7–56
    faculty hiring process, Vol 2:31–33, 48–50, 389–90, 399–400
    faculty perspectives on, Vol 2:43–44
    faculty selection committee, Vol 2:388–89, 392–93, 396
    finance/fundraising (*see* finance/fundraising)
    hiatus, Vol 2:55
    "Humanity and Excellence," Vol 2:48–49
    incentives, Vol 2:37–38
    legacy of, Vol 2:147–48
    letters of congratulations, Vol 2:396
    liberal approach to, Vol 2:35–37, 45–46
    listening to complaints, Vol 2:47–48
    nurturing excellence, Vol 2:54
    old/new integration, Vol 2:41–42
    other candidates, Vol 2:174–9, 384–85
    perspectives on, Vol 2:147
    persuasiveness/authenticity, Vol 2:25
    reappointments, Vol 2:124–25
    Registrar's Office, Vol 2:36–37
    return to faculty following, Vol 2:155–56, 158–59
    salary reforms, Vol 2:31–33, 39, 40, 64, 71
    serving out second term, Vol 2:153, 157, 158
    subterfuges/redemptive transparency, Vol 2:23, 24
    turning over of the maces, Vol 2:26–27, 395–96
    two-career families, Vol 2:33
De Artiga v. Barr, Vol 2:320
Death of Contract, The (Gilmore), Vol 1:243–44
death penalty, Vol 2:384–91, 406–9
de Blasio, William, Vol 2:260
"Decision for Accidents: An Approach to Nonfault Allocation of Costs, The," Vol 1:294–95
"Decision for Accidents, The," Vol 1:295
defective design, Vol 2:225
De Gaspari, Alcide, Vol 1:10, 144, 151
Dellinger, Walter, Vol 2:156–57
Del Sale family, Vol 1:86
Del Vecchio, Beatrice "Bice" (née Cavalieri), Vol 1:47, 52, 54, 55–58, 70–71, 73, 133
Del Vecchio, Cesare, Vol 1:54–55, 70
Del Vecchio, Giorgio, Vol 1:54, 59, 60–61, 71, 144, 153–54
Del Vecchio, Giulio, Vol 1:54, 55, 65, 71
Del Vecchio, Gustavo, Vol 1:22, 58, 73, 133, 143, 144, 151–54, 175, 183
Del Vecchio, Isacco, Vol 1:53, 57
Del Vecchio, Salomon David, Vol 1:69
Del Vecchio, Salvatore, Vol 1:53–54, 56, 70
Del Vecchio, Samuele (Shemuel) ben Mahalaleel, Vol 1:69
Del Vecchio *condotta*, Vol 1:68–69
Del Vecchio family history, Vol 1:47, 50–58, 63–73
Demsetz, Harold, Vol 1:292
Dershowitz, Alan, Vol 1:105, 124
Desiano v. Warner-Lambert, Vol 2:217, 219–21, 233–36
De Sica, Vittorio, Vol 2:423, 426, 427, 436–37
DeVane, Milton, Vol 1:259
dialogue, Vol 2:281
Diaz, Salvador, Vol 2:405
Dickenson, Alfred J., Vol 1:277–78
diethylstilbestrol (DES), Vol 2:346–49, 361–62
Dink Stover at Yale, Vol 1:173, 200–1
diphtheria, Vol 1:89
Director, Aaron, Vol 1:290–91, 298–99, 300–1
discrimination. *See* anti-discrimination law
discrimination based on association, Vol 2:241
discriminato/discriminazione, Vol 1:59
Disraeli, Benjamin, Vol 2:393
Ditta Salvatore Del Vecchio, Vol 1:70
doctrine of trusts, Vol 1:81
Dodd, Christopher, Vol 2:157, 162–63
Donnelly, Richard, Vol 1:223, 246
Donohue, John, Vol 2:50
"Don't Ask, Don't Tell" rule, Vol 2:351
Doonesbury, Vol 2:331–32, 344
double recovery, Vol 2:288, 299
Douglas, William O., Vol 1:225, 248–49, 253, 261, 271, 384–90; Vol 2:97
Do We Own Our Bodies? (Calabresi), Vol 2:166
Drayton, Bill, Vol 1:332
Dreyfus case, Vol 2:399
drug dealing *vs.* buying to consume, Vol 2:375–78, 417–19
dry goods trading, Vol 1:70
DuBois, W. E. B., Vol 1:157
Due Process Clause
    assisted suicide/euthanasia, Vol 2:282–84, 286
    death penalty, Vol 2:384
    judicial application to federal government, Vol 1:267, 273, 280
    jury-mandering, Vol 2:241, 256
    penile plethysmography, Vol 2:43–405
    prohibited government behavior, Vol 2:253–54
Dukakis, Michael, Vol 2:130
Duke, Steven, Vol 1:256
Dunne, James, Vol 1:152
duty of care, Vol 2:201–3, 223–24
Dworkin, Ronald
    appointment of, Vol 2:91
    characterization, Vol 1:344
    Guido and, Vol 1:178, 207–8
    Legal Realism/Legal Process group, Vol 1:256
    Magdalen studies, Vol 1:179–81

Dworkin, Ronald (*cont.*)
  moral underpinnings of constitutional law, Vol 1:208
  "non-viva'ed" First, Vol 1:186
  Rhodes interview, Vol 1:176, 177, 203–4
  tennis story, Vol 1:176
  Wellington and, Vol 1:233–34

E. R. Squibb v. Accident Ins. et. al., Vol 2:346–49, 361–62
Easterbrook, Frank, Vol 2:348
education in US. *See also* Yale Law School; Yale University
  classmates, Vol 1:161
  dormitory at Princeton, Vol 1:163
  early years, Vol 1:32–33, 102–3
  Foote School, Vol 1:104, 115, 161–62, 188–89
  Hopkins Grammar School, Vol 1:162–63
  Magdalen College/Oxford, Vol 1:178–88
  overview, Vol 1:161
  Princeton *vs.* Yale, Vol 1:163–64
  racism at Princeton, Vol 1:163–64
  Worthington Hooker school, Vol 1:102–3, 112–13
Eginton, Warren W., Vol 2:211
Einaudi, Luigi, Vol 1:144, 151, 152–53
Eisenhower, Dwight D., Vol 1:261, 342, 349; Vol 2:281
elementary school desegregation, Vol 1:223, 245, 261; Vol 2:241
Elia Cardinal Della Costa, Vol 1:134
Elishà, Shabatai Elhanan ben, Vol 1:69
Ellickson, Robert, Vol 1:357; Vol 2:24, 40–41, 50, 53, 55–56, 79, 89, 119–20
Ely, John Hart, Vol 2:321, 327, 387, 392, 397
Emerson, Tommy, Vol 2:128
emigration from Italy, Vol 1:27–31, 36–37, 50, 147–48
emotional harm, Vol 2:213–16, 237–39
Empirical Problems and Particular Goals (Lindblom), Vol 1:200
"Empty Cabinet of Dr. Calabresi, The," Vol 1:291–92
en banc cases
  applications of procedure, Vol 2:174, 182, 185, 204, 276–77
  Arar v. Ashcroft, Vol 2:395–400, 409–12
  Brown v. City of Oneonta, Vol 2:242–46, 257–61
  bullet manufacturers tort liability, Vol 2:284–85
  characterization, Vol 2:184–85
  death penalty, Vol 2:385–91, 406–9
  government secrets doctrine, Vol 2:395–400, 409–12
  Hayden v. Pataki, Vol 2:391–95, 401–3
  Holcomb v. Iona College, Vol 2:249–53

  intentionally inflicted suicide, Vol 2:291–92
  Pan Am case, Vol 2:177–79, 180
  Pentagon Papers, Vol 2:193–94
  Puddu v. Royal Netherlands Steamship Co., Vol 2:189
  Quill v. Vacco, Vol 2:281–86
  recusals, Vol 2:366, 391
  Taber v. Maine, Vol 2:197–201
  United States v. Aquart, Vol 2:388–91, 409
  United States v. Martinez, Vol 2:375–78, 417–19
  Zarda v. Altitude Express, Vol 2:250–51, 262–64
enterprise liability, Vol 2:221
Epstein, Richard, Vol 1:181, 298
Equal Protection Clause
  assisted suicide/euthanasia, Vol 2:282, 283–84, 286
  First Amendment religious imperatives, Vol 2:333
  gender-based termination, Vol 2:261–62
  judicial application to federal government, Vol 1:266–67
  jury-mandering, Vol 2:256
  penile plethysmography, Vol 2:43–405
  prohibited government behavior, Vol 2:253–54
  racial profiling, Vol 2:257–60
  search and seizure, Vol 2:245
  sentencing disparities, Vol 2:255
Erie v. Tompkins, Vol 2:288
ERISA, Vol 2:373–74, 401
Eskridge, William, Vol 1:401–398; Vol 2:42–43, 86–87
Este lands, Vol 1:66–67, 80, 90
ethnic profiling, Vol 2:246, 266–67
euthanasia, Vol 1:344–45
ex cathedra, Vol 2:283
excusable mislabeling, Vol 2:274–76
expert testimony, Vol 2:212, 229
Eyster, Rodney, Vol 1:316–17

Fair Labor Standards Act of 1938, Vol 1:121
family members, Vol 1:8–10
fascio di combattimento (band of combatants), Vol 1:7
fault-based system/auto insurance, Vol 1:301, 302–3
Fedders, John, Vol 2:104
Fedele a Giustizia e Libertà, Vol 1:13
Federal Death Penalty Act (FDPA), Vol 2:386, 408
Federal Employer's Liability Act (FELA), Vol 1:384–85, 400–2; Vol 2:213
federalism
  cooperative, Vol 2:294
  death penalty cases, Vol 2:385–86, 387–88, 406–8

ex ante access to courts, Vol 2:236
judicial, Vol 2:281, 284, 294, 362
preemption and, Vol 2:218, 220
spousal rights, Vol 2:373–74
subsidiary, Vol 2:387
symposia on, Vol 2:103
Wall postings, Vol 2:116
Federalist Society, Vol 2:103, 107, 159
Federal Rules of Civil Procedure, Vol 1:247–48
Federal Taxation of Income (Bittker), Vol 1:225
Feinberg, Wilfred, Vol 2:220, 391–92
Feinberg, William, Vol 2:181, 193–94
Feldman v. Allegheny Airlines, Inc., Vol 1:362, 378–79
Fellner, William, Vol 1:169, 170, 184, 186–87, 192, 197–98
felon disenfranchisement, Vol 2:391–95, 401–3
Fels Lectures, Vol 1:342, 352
Feltrinelli, Carlo, Vol 1:38–39
Feres doctrine, Vol 2:197, 199, 222–23
Fermi, Enrico, Vol 1:30
Ferrara, Italy
  Allied retaking of, Vol 1:141
  Bonacossi tennis court, Vol 2:426, 433–34
  Calabresi arrival in, Vol 1:79–80, 81–82
  Calabresi buried in, Vol 1:27
  Calabresi business interests in, Vol 1:82
  Casa Minerbi, Vol 1:86–90
  doctrine of trusts, Vol 1:81
  Ettore's departure from, Vol 1:7, 16–17
  farming in, Vol 1:145
  fragmentation of Minerbi estate, Vol 1:144, 145–46, 154–55
  ghettos, Vol 1:67, 80–81, 90–91
  hemp industry, Vol 1:76, 82, 91
  land reform/redistribution in, Vol 1:144–45, 155
  Minerbi arrival in, Vol 1:89
  Papal States and, Vol 1:67, 90
  property rights of Jews in, Vol 1:66–67, 80–81, 90–91, 154
  reclaiming land from the sea, Vol 1:88–89
  sugar beet refinery sale, Vol 1:56–57
  sugar refineries in, Vol 1:56–57, 89–90
Film Society, Vol 2:112, 120
finance/fundraising
  alumni communications, Vol 2:66–67
  Annual Fund, Vol 2:39–40, 41, 59, 60, 66
  autonomy from central administration, Vol 2:57–59
  building renovations, Vol 2:58, 61, 62, 70–71 (*see also* Sterling Law Building renovation)
  capital giving, Vol 2:59–61, 66–67
  captivation/embarrassment, Vol 2:67–68
  charges for University services, Vol 2:71
  endowments, Vol 2:43, 59, 62, 63–64, 70–71, 401
  every tub on its own bottom, Vol 2:57–58, 63–64
  fiscal neutrality, Vol 2:64
  Guido's management of, Vol 2:37–38, 39–40, 41–42, 46, 48–49, 54
  independence in hindsight, Vol 2:67, 69–70
  liquidated damages, Vol 2:62
  negotiations for independence, Vol 2:61–62, 63–64
  primary business model, Vol 2:57
  progressive admissions policies and, Vol 2:59–60, 65–66
  revenue-neutral independence, Vol 2:61–62, 64
  risks/benefits of independence, Vol 2:59–60, 62–63
  Yale Law School Fund, Vol 2:64
Finley, Lucinda, Vol 2:124
Finzi, Jacopo Amadio, Vol 1:43–44
Finzi-Contini, Armando, Vol 1:29, 46–47, 49–50, 61–62, 108
Finzi-Contini, Bianca. *See* Calabresi, Bianca (née Finzi-Contini)
Finzi-Contini, Bruno, Vol 1:78–79, 132; Vol 2:425
Finzi-Contini, Giovanni, Vol 1:109; Vol 2:436
Finzi-Contini, Leon Vita, Vol 1:44–45, 46
Finzi-Contini, Luisa (née Del Vecchio), Vol 1:29, 47, 49, 54, 133
Finzi-Contini, Sandro, Vol 1:50
Finzi-Contini, Zaccaria (Zachary), Vol 1:45–46
Finzi-Contini family history, Vol 1:43–50, 58–63
Finzi e Minerbi, Vol 1:89–90
First Amendment
  anti-distortion, Vol 2:327
  Black's legacy, Vol 1:282
  campaign financing to avoid corruption, Vol 2:325–28, 339–41, 392
  compelling state interest, Vol 2:326–27
  compulsion in legislative prayers, Vol 1:268; Vol 2:328–33, 341–42
  dialogue approach, Vol 2:322
  Establishment Clause, Vol 2:328
  freedom of religious belief, Vol 1:268; Vol 2:328–33, 341–42
  free expression, Vol 2:108, 109, 183–84
  hate speech, Vol 2:324–25, 336–38
  interpretive frameworks, Vol 2:321
  Kalven's application of, Vol 1:302
  merit goods, Vol 2:327
  military recruiting in Yale College, Vol 2:114
  prison discipline/pornography, Vol 2:321–24, 334–36
  public nudity, Vol 2:291–93, 299–302
  Scalia's jurisprudence, Vol 2:96
  sexualized conversation/pornography, Vol 2:143
  spending as free expression, Vol 2:325–28
first spouse pension rights, Vol 2:371–75, 401

Fisher, Irving, Vol 1:168
Fiss, Owen, Vol 1:252, 394; Vol 2:47–48, 50
Fleming, Alexander, Vol 1:95
Fletcher, William, Vol 2:323
Florence, Italy, Vol 1:7–8, 16, 27, 44–45, 134, 135
Florence Rogatz Professorship, Vol 2:67
forced spousal abortion in China, Vol 2:310–12, 315–17
Ford, Gerald, Vol 2:154
Ford Pinto case, Vol 1:297
Foreign Sovereign Immunities Act, Vol 1:242
foreseeability and liability, Vol 2:287
Forman, James, Vol 1:367
Fort Sumter/Pearl Harbor comparison, Vol 1:129, 136–37
forum shopping, Vol 2:298, 314
fragmentation of Minerbi estate, Vol 1:144, 145–46, 154–55
Francis I, Vol 2:334
Frank, Jerome, Vol 2:183, 184
Frank, John, Vol 1:236, 282
Frankfurter, Felix
    Bickel influenced by, Vol 1:255
    Black and, Vol 1:264–66
    civil liberties decisions, Vol 1:261
    clerkships, Vol 1:235, 236–37
    on double jeopardy, Vol 1:274
    Dworkin and, Vol 1:204
    grant of certiorari, Vol 1:385–86, 400–1
    on Guido's career, Vol 1:285
    Holmes the liberal myth, Vol 2:176
    judicial philosophy, Vol 1:267
    Korematsu decision, Vol 2:323
    Lewis on, Vol 1:277
    no-fault liability, Vol 1:384–85
    nomination of, Vol 1:261
    Shulman and, Vol 1:236–37, 248–49
    voter redistricting, Vol 1:276–77
freedom of expression, Vol 2:281, 291–93, 295, 299–302, 321–24
Freemasons, Vol 1:20, 72
free speech. *See* Wall/Wallsters
Frickey, Philip, Vol 1:401–2
Friedman, Milton, Vol 1:195, 291
Friendly, Henry J., Vol 2:184, 186, 198, 200
Fuchsberg, Jacob, Vol 2:225
Furman, Jesse, Vol 2:279
Future of Law and Economics, The (Calabresi), Vol 1:354
    behavioral realities in, Vol 2:269, 277

Gamble v. United States, Vol 1:281
Garden of the Finzi-Contini, The (Bassani)
    anti-Semitism in, Vol 2:435
    basis of, Vol 2:423, 425, 432–33
    Bassan/Bianca visit, Vol 2:429–30
    Bassani's background, Vol 2:425, 431–32
    Beppe as patron of Bassani, Vol 1:77; Vol 2:425, 426
    cover art, Vol 2:424
    fictional characterizations, Vol 2:432
    Guido's connection to, Vol 2:423–24, 437–38
    Guido's family's reaction to, Vol 2:428–30, 436
    Guido's reaction to, Vol 2:430–31
    impacts of, Vol 2:427–29
    inspiration for, Vol 2:426
    Micòl's favorite drink, Vol 2:428–29, 435
    movie, Vol 2:423, 426–27, 431, 436–37
    storyline, Vol 2:423, 426–27
    translation of, Vol 2:432, 436
Garibaldi monument, Vol 1:12
Geiger, Arthur, Vol 1:97, 111
gender-based termination, Vol 2:241, 246–49
Gerken, Heather, Vol 2:51–52
Gertner, Robert, Vol 2:276
Gesell, Gerhard, Vol 2:169–70
Giamatti, A. Bartlett "Bart," Vol 2:727–25, 38–39, 57, 59, 63–64, 391–94, 400–1
Giano v. Senkowski, Vol 2:321–24, 334–36
Gilmore, Grant
    background, Vol 1:243–44
    as constructive realist, Vol 1:231–32
    Death of Contract, The (Gilmore), Vol 1:243–44
    legacy, Vol 1:327
    legal philosophy, Vol 1:225, 243–44
    love of common law, Vol 1:390
    no-fault workers' compensation, Vol 1:383–84, 399–400
    on Sturges, Vol 1:252
    teaching methods, Vol 1:359–60, 373–74
Ginsburg, Douglas H., Vol 2:105, 135, 175
Ginsburg, Ruth Bader, Vol 2:160, 170, 235, 336, 341
Ginzburg, Natalia, Vol 1:28
Girard, Robert, Vol 1:237, 257–58
Giuliani, Rudolph, Vol 2:267, 291, 299–300, 336, 337
Giuoco del Pallone, Vol 1:145–46
Giustizia e Libertà (Justice and Liberty), Vol 1:12, 14, 21–22, 27
God and Man at Yale (Buckley), Vol 1:168, 191–93, 215
Goizueta, Roberto, Vol 1:165
Goldberg, John, Vol 1:310, 361
Goldman, Lillian, Vol 2:67
Goldstein, Abraham
    building renovations, Vol 2:58
    as candidate for Dean, Vol 2:384–85
    Cromwell Chair, Vol 1:228, 250–51
    on Guido's agenda as Dean, Vol 2:394–95
    Holmes Lectures, Vol 1:394
    Legal Realism/Legal Process synthesis, Vol 1:256

President selection procedure, Vol 2:155–56
slaughter of the innocents, Vol 2:124, 385–87, 397–99
Goldstein, Joseph, Vol 1:224, 231–32, 233, 251–52; Vol 2:93–94, 97
golf cart case, Vol 2:216–17, 232
Gonella, Guido, Vol 1:60, 153–54
Gonzalez, Roberto, Vol 2:381, 415
Gordon, Robert, Vol 2:50, 53
Gore, Al, Vol 2:258
Gorsuch, Neil, Vol 1:281; Vol 2:264
government overreach, Vol 2:253–54
Government Secrets Act, Vol 2:398–99
government secrets doctrine, Vol 2:395–400, 409–12
Grabois v. Jones, Vol 2:371–75, 401
grand jury minutes release, Vol 2:357–58, 367–70
Grand Sanhedrin, Vol 1:69
grave moral wrong, Vol 2:282
Greene, Jamal, Vol 2:324, 339
Greene v. McElroy, Vol 1:269–70, 279–80, 389
Green Fields of the Mind (Giamatti), Vol 2:400–1
Griesa, Thomas P., Vol 2:372, 375
Griffiths, John, Vol 2:397, 399
Grim, Dieter, Vol 2:324–25
Griswold, Erwin, Vol 2:131, 360
Griswold, Sally, Vol 1:161, 315
Griswold, Whitney, Vol 1:130, 192, 236, 313; Vol 2:85, 384, 391
Grossman, Gregory, Vol 1:199
Grutter v. Bollinger, Vol 1:271
Guarnieri, Patrizia, Vol 1:22
Gulliver, Ashbel Green, Vol 1:225–26, 248–49
gun manufacturer liability, Vol 2:290–91, 296–98
gun possession, Vol 2:376–77, 418
Gunther, Gerald, Vol 2:286
Guy nickname, Vol 2:437–38

habeas cases, Vol 2:378–82, 412–17
Hahn v. Town of W. Haverstraw, Vol 2:216–17, 232
Hallows, E. Harold, Vol 1:387–88
Hamilton v. Accu-Tek, Vol 2:297
Hamilton v. Beretta, Vol 2:290–91
Hand, Augustus Noble, Vol 2:183, 184, 189
Hand, Billings Learned, Vol 1:164; Vol 2:176, 179, 180–81, 183, 184, 186, 189, 371
hard cases, Vol 2:371
Harkness, Edward "Ned," Vol 2:75–77
Harlan, John Marshall, Vol 1:234–35, 236–37, 240, 261, 271, 273, 386–87, 401–396; Vol 2:184
Harper v. Virginia, Vol 2:392
Hart, Gary, Vol 1:327; Vol 2:127
Hart, H. L. A., Vol 1:327
Hatch, Brent, Vol 2:103
Hatch, Orrin, Vol 2:169, 323, 336

Havighurst, Robert, Vol 2:119
Hayden v. Pataki, Vol 2:391–95, 401–3
Hayek, Friederich von, Vol 1:300–1
Haynsworth, Clement, Vol 1:276
Hazard, Geoff, Vol 1:394
Healy, Kent, Vol 1:168–69
heckler's veto, Vol 1:302
heeding presumption, Vol 2:227
Helms, Jesse, Vol 2:156–57, 300
Henderson, James, Vol 2:27–228
Heron, The (Bassani), Vol 2:425
Heyman, Michael, Vol 1:240
Hicks, John, Vol 1:170, 183, 184, 187–88, 205, 286
Hill, Anita, Vol 2:127, 131, 132–36, 137–38, 139–40, 141–42, 145–47, 163, 165
Hiroshima, Vol 1:113–14
Hirschoff, Jon, Vol 1:339
Hitler, Adolf, Vol 1:15, 18, 19
Hively v. Ivy Tech Community College, Vol 2:263
Hogan, C. C. Crosby, Vol 1:317
Hohfeld, Wesley Newcomb, Vol 1:327
Holcomb v. Iona College, Vol 2:241, 249–53, 262–63
Hollon v. Merck, Vol 2:271–72
Holmes, Oliver Wendell, Vol 1:232, 387; Vol 2:176, 189, 338, 371, 383
Holmes Lectures, Vol 1:383, 394–95
Holocaust Victim Assets Litigation, Weisshaus v. Swiss Bankers Association, In Re, Vol 2:349–51, 364–66
Holy of Holies, Vol 1:64
Horton, Willie, Vol 2:130
Hospital de la Salpêtrière, Vol 1:62
Hotel Raleigh, Vol 1:31–32
house arrest, Vol 1:8
Hudec, Robert, Vol 2:397
Hughes, Charles Evans Sr., Vol 1:270, 280
Hundred Years' War, Vol 1:52
Hutchinson, William D., Vol 1:397
Hygienic Ice Company, Vol 1:99
Hylton, Keith, Vol 1:305–6

Ideals, Beliefs, Attitudes and the Law (Calabresi), Vol 1:354, 363, 380
behavioral realities in, Vol 2:269, 271
Il Conformista (The Conformist), Vol 1:14, 24
Il Duce. *See* Mussolini, Benito
Illegal Immigration Reform and Immigrant Responsibility Act of 1996, Vol 2:316
Il Quarto Stato, Vol 1:20–21
Il Resto del Carlino, Vol 1:57, 72
Il secolo d'Italia, Vol 1:154
Immaculate Conception doctrine, Vol 2:283
immediate risk of physical harm, Vol 2:215, 238
immigration law
Ascroft's reforms of BIA reviews, Vol 2:307, 318

immigration law (*cont.*)
  asylum requests, Vol 2:303, 307, 309, 319–20
  automatic eligibility for asylum, Vol 2:310–12, 315–17
  deportation waivers, Vol 2:304–6, 313–15, 317
  dialogue approach to, Vol 2:309–10, 318–19
  forced spousal abortion, Vol 2:310–12, 315–17
  Guido's jurisprudence, Vol 2:303–4, 316–17
  judge quota, Trump-era, Vol 2:319–20
  labor certification, Vol 2:317
  new conditions, Vol 2:307–8, 312–13
  persecution claims/asylum, Vol 2:310–12, 320
  post-9/11, Vol 2:306–7
  remanding of cases, Vol 2:308–9, 317, 320
  standard of evidence, Vol 2:303
independence of judiciary. *See* judicial independence
independence of Yale Law School. *See* finance/fundraising
Independent Counsel Law, Vol 2:102
infanticide, Vol 1:84, 94
Innocent III, Vol 1:66–67
insult (*ingiuria*), Vol 1:93–94
intentionally inflicted suicide, Vol 2:291–92
intervening wrong-doer, Vol 2:201–3, 223–24
In the matter of Jersey Central Power & Light Co., Vol 2:166
In the matter of Metropolitan Edison Co., Vol 2:166
Int'l Ass'n of Machinists v. Street, Vol 1:282
invalidation of restrictive covenants, Vol 2:241
Italian Diaspora, Vol 1:64–65
Italian rite, Vol 1:50–51, 63, 79–80
Italy. *See also* Ferrara, Italy
  anti-fascism in, Vol 1:7–9, 10–12
  anti-Semitism in, Vol 1:126–27
  as Axis power, Vol 1:107–10, 122–23
  Bologna, Vol 1:46, 53, 57, 62, 80, 139, 141
  end of Monarchy, Vol 1:151
  Este lands, Vol 1:66–67, 80, 90
  family wealth protection, Vol 1:144–46, 154
  fascism in generally, Vol 1:7–9, 10–12, 14–16
  Florence, Vol 1:7–8, 16, 27, 44–45, 134, 135
  Italian miracle, Vol 1:143–44, 152–53
  Milan, Vol 1:13–14
  property ownership, post-WWII, Vol 1:144–46, 154
  property rights of Jews in, Vol 1:80–81, 90–91, 154
  protection of Jews in, Vol 1:108–9, 134
  purging of Fascists, post-war end to, Vol 1:150–51
  racial laws in, Vol 1:15, 17, 18, 25, 27, 28, 38, 49, 58–59, 108–10, 116, 127, 139, 154
  reconciliation with Fascists, Vol 1:143–44, 150
Ives v. South Buffalo Railway, Vol 1:287

J. Skelly Wright Professorship, Vol 2:67
Jackson, Robert, Vol 1:261
Jacobs, Dennis, Vol 2:177, 180, 184–85, 186–87, 216, 259, 305, 306, 314, 322–23, 334, 347, 360, 387
James, Fleming (Jimmy), Vol 1:222, 224, 225, 227–28, 231–32, 235, 243, 247–49, 286, 287, 305, 340, 380; Vol 2:221
James A. Thomas Lecture, Vol 2:45
Janus v. ASCFME (2018), Vol 1:282
Japanese internment, Vol 1:266; Vol 2:400
Jaworski, Leon, Vol 2:95
Jefferson, Thomas, Vol 1:262
Jin Shui Qiu v. Ashcroft (2003), Vol 2:303
Johnson, Lyndon, Vol 1:343, 351, 352
Johnson, Virginia, Vol 2:143
Johnstone, Quintin, Vol 1:223, 224, 238–39, 241–42, 246; Vol 2:129
Jones, Frederick S., Vol 1:117
Jones Act, Vol 1:383–85, 399–400
"Judge Calabresi's Flagrant Ethical Violation," Vol 2:332, 343–44
judgeship
  acceptance by colleagues, Vol 2:181–82, 184–85, 189
  appointment to, Vol 1:388; Vol 2:156–57
  Attorney General *vs.*, Vol 2:154, 158, 161–62
  Cabranes relationship, Vol 2:175–76, 180, 351
  changing his mind, Vol 2:376–78
  clerks, Vol 2:194–95
  Clinton's approach to judicial appointments, Vol 2:156, 159–60
  concerns regarding Guido, Vol 2:175, 176–77, 180–81
  concurrences with own opinion, Vol 2:204–5, 238–39, 340
  confirmation hearings, Vol 1:351
  craftsmanship importance, Vol 2:345
  criticism of Guido, Vol 2:377, 418–19
  demeanor, Vol 2:112
  dicta *vs.* holding, Vol 2:203–5
  en banc cases (see *en banc* cases)
  Guido's qualifications for, Vol 2:173–74, 179, 242
  impatience/anger, Vol 2:356–57, 366–67
  initial tasks, Vol 2:174
  judicial career, Vol 2:171
  judicial philosophy, Vol 2:253, 269, 362
  limerick writing, Vol 2:177, 252, 263–64
  nomination for, Vol 2:153–56, 168–71
  public reactions, Vol 2:163–64
  recusals, Vol 2:349–52
  relevance of literature to judging, Vol 2:187
  sign-off message, Vol 2:167
  social faux pas as junior judge, Vol 2:177–80, 189–90
  Solicitor General *vs.*, Vol 2:153–54, 158, 166

statute interpretation *vs.* construal, Vol 2:250–53
Supreme Court, Vol 2:167–71
swearing in, Vol 2:157
torts approach to, Vol 2:200, 216–17, 221, 222–23
unusual ideas presented, Vol 2:182, 200
vetting inside White House, Vol 2:164–67
Winter relationship, Vol 2:175
judging people in context, Vol 1:261–62, 276
judicial independence
  Black on, Vol 2:352–53
  depth/breadth of proceedings, Vol 2:357–58
  federal court deference, Vol 2:354–55
  grand jury minutes release, Vol 2:357–58, 367–70
  impeachment of Federal judges, Vol 2:351, 353–54, 363
  political decision-making, Vol 2:358–60
  promotion of Federal judges, Vol 2:354
  recusals, Vol 2:349–52, 362–66, 391
judicial updating of statutes, Vol 1:388–86; Vol 2:199, 250–53, 263–64, 265–66, 286
Judson v. Giant Powder Co., Vol 2:210, 212, 231–32
jurisdiction/diversity jurisdiction, Vol 2:347–49, 361–62
jury-mandering, Vol 2:241–42, 255, 256–57
jus chazakà, Vol 1:90–91

Kafka, Alexandre, Vol 1:194
Kagan, Donald, Vol 2:108–9
Kagen, Elena, Vol 2:359
Kahn, Paul, Vol 2:53, 124
Kahneman, Daniel, Vol 2:278–79
Kalman, Laura, Vol 2:396
Kalven, Harry, Vol 1:290, 291, 292, 301–3
Kapczynski, Amy, Vol 2:262
Katyal, Neal, Vol 2:283
Katzmann, Robert, Vol 1:379–64; Vol 2:202, 238–39, 276–77, 316
Katz v. United States, Vol 1:278
Kauffman, Blair, Vol 2:54
Kaufman, Irving R., Vol 2:184, 373
Kavanaugh, Brett, Vol 2:341
Kaye, Judith
  background, Vol 2:298, 299
  on certification, Vol 2:288, 295, 298–99, 301
  death penalty rulings, Vol 2:387
  on dialogue, Vol 2:281
  Wesley and, Vol 2:301–2
Kearse, Amalya, Vol 2:175, 181, 188, 291–92
Kemezy v. Peters, Vol 2:273, 280
Kennedy, Anthony, Vol 2:105, 165, 175, 328, 331
Kennedy, Duncan, Vol 1:233–34
Kennedy, Edward, Vol 2:170–71
Kennedy, Raymond "Jungle Jim," Vol 1:211–12, 215–16

Kennedy, Ted, Vol 2:318
Kessel, Reuben, Vol 1:298–99
Kessler, Fritz, Vol 1:222, 244–45, 365, 366
Kevorkian, Jack, Vol 2:295
keys-in-the-car cases, Vol 2:287
King of Hearts, Vol 1:382
Kirkland, John T., Vol 2:63
Kirkpatrick, Ralph, Vol 1:317
Kissinger, Henry, Vol 1:202
Klagsbrunn Scholarship, Vol 2:67
Klein, Lawrence, Vol 1:15, 170, 184, 206
knee-jerk popularity, Vol 2:294
Knight, Frank, Vol 1:195
Knox, Ronald, Vol 1:214, 217
Koeltl, John G., Vol 2:356
Koh, Harold, Vol 1:381–66; Vol 2:53, 88, 124, 147, 393
Kone v. Holder, Vol 1:127
Korematsu v. United States, Vol 1:266–63; Vol 2:323, 400
Krauthammer, Charles, Vol 2:286, 296
Kronman, Anthony, Vol 1:357, 364; Vol 2:7–403

labor strikes, Vol 1:94
La Fondiaria Fire and Life Insurance companies, Vol 1:16–17
Laird v Nelms, Vol 2:211
Lamar, Harold, Vol 2:155
Lamar, Howard, Vol 2:83
L'amministrazione, Vol 1:145–46
Landes, Elisabeth, Vol 1:341
Landis, James, Vol 1:390
landowner's liability, Vol 1:388–89, 397–98
Langbein, John, Vol 1:357–56; Vol 2:51, 53, 84, 399
Langbein's Law, Vol 2:158–59
L'Aurora, Vol 1:16, 89–90
Law of Credit Transactions, The (Sturges), Vol 1:252
Lawrence v. Texas, Vol 1:208
Least Dangerous Branch (Bickel), Vol 1:270
Leff, Arthur, Vol 2:93, 390
legal doctrine construction, Vol 2:302
legal fictions, Vol 1:344–45
*Leggi Razziali (*Racial Laws*). See* racial laws in Italy
legisfuration, Vol 1:391
Lend Lease program, Vol 1:107–8, 123
Lessico Familiare (Family Stories/Ginzburg), Vol 1:28
Letters Venetian, Vol 1:82
Leval, Pierre, Vol 2:179, 200, 202–3, 204, 356–57, 391
Levi, Edward, Vol 1:290
Levi, Giuseppe "Pom," Vol 1:27–28
Levinson Auditorium, Vol 2:67–68
Levy, Edward, Vol 1:384–85; Vol 2:154

Levy, Mark, Vol 1:381
Lewellyn, Karl, Vol 1:327
Lewis, Anthony, Vol 1:265–66, 276–77
Libman, Emanuel, Vol 1:34–35
Liddy, G. Gordon, Vol 2:185
Lieberman, Joe, Vol 2:131, 133; Vol 2:157, 162–63
Lillian Goldman Library, Vol 2:68
Liman, Arthur, Vol 1:287
Liman, Lewis, Vol 2:388, 407
Linaweaver Scholarship, Vol 1:107
Lincoln, Abraham, Vol 1:136
Lindblom, Charles E., Vol 1:171–72, 193, 200
Lindsey, Bruce, Vol 2:160
Lipson, Leon, Vol 1:256, 334–35
Liriano v. Hobart, Vol 2:205–8, 224–26, 289
Liu, Goodwin, Vol 1:272
Livingston, Deborah, Vol 2:250, 260–61
Llewellyn, Karl, Vol 1:328–27; Vol 2:345
Lloyd's of London, Vol 2:347–48, 361–62
Locurto v. Giuliani, Vol 2:324–25, 336–38
Lodge, John Davis, Vol 1:148
Lombroso, Nora, Vol 1:72
Long, Barbara, Vol 1:315
Long, Chip, Vol 2:38–39, 61–62
Lord's Prayer, Vol 1:114–15
Loreley Financing v. Wells Fargo Securities, Vol 2:274–76
Lorenzo v. Wirth, Vol 2:207
Loving v. Virginia (1967), Vol 2:241
Lowell, A. Lawrence, Vol 2:76
Loyalty and Security (Brown), Vol 1:247
loyalty oaths, Vol 1:15–16, 22, 184
Luciano, Charles "Lucky," Vol 1:135, 138–39
Luconi, Stefano, Vol 1:123–24
Lugo di Romagna, Italy, Vol 1:52–53, 66, 70–71
Lynch, Gerry, Vol 2:250, 251, 255

Machiavelli and the World He Made (Bobbit), Vol 1:344, 356–57
MacKinnon, Catherine, Vol 2:124, 134, 145, 146
Macmillan, Harold, Vol 1:184–85
Madison, James, Vol 2:331
Magazzini R. Finzi, C. Miccio e C. Napoli, Vol 1:16
Magdalen College/Oxford
  Bachelor of Arts degree, Vol 1:182
  characterization, Vol 1:178–79
  figuring things out, Vol 1:181–82
  Institute of Statistics, Vol 1:184
  law major, Vol 1:179–80
  leaving, Vol 1:188
  Old Palace, Vol 1:212–14, 217
  philosophy/political theory, Vol 1:185, 186
  Presidential Collection, Vol 1:185–86
  Schools (exams), Vol 1:186–88, 206–7
  social status importance in, Vol 1:184–85
  taking chances, Vol 1:185–86
  tutorials/tutors, Vol 1:182–84
  US *vs.* English law, Vol 1:181
  viva voce (oral exam), Vol 1:186–87
Mahoney, J. Daniel, Vol 2:180–81, 192, 391–92
Manifesto della razza, Vol 1:18
Manning, Bayless, Vol 1:256
Manning, Henry, Vol 1:214
Manton, Martin Thomas, Vol 1:232, 253
Manzoni, Domenico, Vol 1:16
Marconi, Guglielmo, Vol 1:14
Margolick, David, Vol 2:163–64
Marks, Jonathan, Vol 1:331
Marshall, Burke, Vol 2:97
Marshall, John, Vol 2:325–26
Marshall, Thurgood, Vol 2:129–30, 184
Marshall Plan, Vol 1:152
Martin, John Jr., Vol 2:361
Martin v. Herzog, Vol 2:211
Mashaw, Jerry, Vol 1:332
Masonic membership, Vol 1:16
Masterpiece Cakeshop decision, Vol 2:342
Masters, William, Vol 2:143
master-servant doctrine, Vol 2:189, 197–201, 222, 223
Matteotti, Giacomo, Vol 1:10, 12, 18–19, 20
Max Planck Institute, Vol 1:331, 339
McAuliffe v. Mayor of New Bedford, Vol 2:338
McCarthy loyalty oath, Vol 1:15, 184
McCarthy v. Olin, Vol 2:281, 286–91, 296–98
McCutcheon v. FEC, Vol 2:325, 340–41
McDougal, Myres, Vol 1:244, 246, 247
McKellar, Kenneth, Vol 1:237
McLaughlin, Joseph, Vol 2:202, 322–23, 334
McReynolds, James Clark, Vol 1:384
Meade, James E., Vol 1:297–98
medical experimentation, Vol 2:383
Meese, Edwin, Vol 2:175
Meiklejohn, Alexander, Vol 2:321
Melamed, Douglas, Vol 1:171–72, 327–28, 336–37
Mendel, Lafayette B., Vol 1:117–18
Mendenhall, Tom, Vol 1:175–76, 318
Menger, Carl, Vol 1:193
Menorah, Vol 1:64
Mero, Ralph, Vol 2:295
Meskill, Thomas, Vol 2:174, 179, 181, 193, 287–88, 372, 373, 374–75
Mi-Beth El *(de Sinagoga)*, Vol 1:65
Michael v. INS, Vol 2:304–6, 313–15
Michelman, Frank, Vol 1:171–72, 304, 328, 338
Milan, Italy, Vol 1:13–14
Miller, John Perry, Vol 1:168–69, 192–93
Miller, Merton H., Vol 1:286, 297–98

Miner, Roger, Vol 2:180–81, 192–93, 281–82
Minerbi, Alberto, Vol 1:76–77, 78–79, 146; Vol 2:426, 435
Minerbi, Beatrice (née Tosi), Vol 1:154–55
Minerbi, Ebe, Vol 1:75–76
Minerbi, Fernanda, Vol 1:78; Vol 2:425
Minerbi, Ginevra, Vol 1:75–76, 77, 139
Minerbi, Giulio, Vol 1:77, 78, 144, 145, 146, 154–55
Minerbi, Giuseppe "Beppe," Vol 1:75, 77–78, 81, 86–87, 143, 144–46, 154–55; Vol 2:425, 426, 434–35
Minerbi, Olga, Vol 1:75, 77, 83, 92, 147–48, 155–56
Minerbi, Sergio, Vol 2:425
Minerbi, Settimo, Vol 1:76, 78, 89–90
Minerbi family history, Vol 1:75–79, 86–90
Ming Shi Xue v. Bd. of Immigration Appeals, Vol 2:303
Min ha-Adummim *(de Rossi)*, Vol 1:65
Min-ha Anawim *(delli Mansi)*, Vol 1:65
Min ha-Dayyanim *(del Giudice)*, Vol 1:65
Min ha-Ne'arim *(dei Fanciulli)*, Vol 1:65
Min ha-Tappuhim *(de Pomis)*, Vol 1:65
Min ha-Zekenim *(del Vecchio)*, Vol 1:65
misrepresentation, Vol 2:274–76
Mit Brennender Sorge (With Burning Sorrow), Vol 1:15
Mitchell, John N., Vol 2:193
Modigliani, Franco, Vol 1:286, 297–98
Moisè, Salomone (Shlomo) David di, Vol 1:69
Monopoly, Vol 1:259
Moore, J. W., Vol 1:99, 111, 233
Moore, Underhill, Vol 1:360
Moravia, Alberto, Vol 1:14
Morris, John H. C., Vol 1:180, 204
Mount Sinai Hospital, Vol 1:34–35
Moynihan, Patrick, Vol 2:163
Mueller, Addison, Vol 1:222–23, 244
Mueller, Robert, Vol 2:102
Mulligan, William Hughes, Vol 2:191
Murphy, Frank, Vol 1:261
Murphy, John, Vol 1:114
Murray, Pauli, Vol 2:248
Musgrave, Richard, Vol 1:336
Mussolini, Benito, Vol 1:7, 8, 10, 15, 17, 36, 49, 71, 119–20, 124, 125, 135, 138–39; Vol 2:189–90, 394
Myrdal, Gunnar, Vol 1:157
Myth of Sisyphus, The (Camus), Vol 1:213, 216–17

National Fascist Syndicate of Journalists, Vol 1:20
National Federation of Independent Business v. Sebelius (2012), Vol 2:359
National Origins Act in 1924, Vol 1:111
National Review, Vol 2:192, 332, 343–44
"Nature of the Firm, The," Vol 1:292
Nature of the Judicial Process, The (Cardozo), Vol 1:354–55
negligently failing to warn, Vol 2:225
negligent overdose, Vol 2:27–230
Nelson, Lemrick Jr., Vol 2:256
Nelson v. Metro-North, Vol 2:213–16, 237–39
Neppi, Gino, Vol 1:132, 139–40
New Deal justices, Vol 1:261
New Haven, Connecticut. *See also* education in US
    anti-Fascist sentiment in, Vol 1:105, 123–24
    anti-Italian sentiment in, Vol 1:114, 119–20, 130–31
    arrival in, Vol 1:97–99
    assimilation into, Vol 1:103–5, 106
    Bishop Street house, Vol 1:106–7
    Boy Scouts, Vol 1:102, 113–14
    Catholicism in, Vol 1:101–2, 112, 210
    connection, Vol 1:100–2, 107
    driving, Vol 1:97, 102
    education in, Vol 1:102–3, 104
    election of 1940, Vol 1:105, 108, 123
    ethnic/racial segregation in, Vol 1:97–98, 110–5; Vol 2:249–50
    family livelihood in, Vol 1:104, 106, 116
    Fascism/anti-Semitism in, Vol 1:105–6
    importance of profession, Vol 1:104
    Italian Consulate, Vol 1:105, 123–24
    misconceptions/misunderstandings, Vol 1:99–100
    newspapers/stoking coal, Vol 1:106–7, 121
    racial injustices in, Vol 1:149, 157
    religious divisions in, Vol 1:101–2, 114
    social teas in, Vol 1:107, 112
    Willow St house, Vol 1:98–99
    YMCA camp/proselytization, Vol 1:101–2, 112
New Haven Grove Street Cemetery, Vol 2:330
New Haven State Teacher's College, Vol 1:130
Newman, John H., Vol 1:214, 227–28, 235; Vol 2:132
Newman, Jon O., Vol 2:174, 175, 181, 182, 184–85, 201–3, 206, 208, 293, 375–76, 378, 381, 391–92, 417
Newport v. Fact Concerts, Vol 2:272–73, 279
New School, Vol 1:40–41
New York, Vol 1:30–31, 37–38, 100
New York Central/Penn Central Railroad matter, Vol 1:229, 250
Niagara Falls, Vol 1:99
Nicholson v. Scoppetta, Vol 2:298–99
Nido Cavour, Vol 1:92–93

Nixon, Richard M., Vol 1:196, 202, 362, 379–63; Vol 2:95, 101, 193
Nobel Prize competitors, Vol 1:72
no-fault auto insurance, Vol 1:303
Non Mollare (Don't Give Up), Vol 1:12, 20
nonmutual offensive issue preclusion, Vol 2:233
Nordhaus, William Dawbney, Vol 2:61–62, 65, 82–83
Norton, Robert C., Vol 1:191–92
Not a Suicide Pact (Posner), Vol 2:319
Notestein, Ada Comstock, Vol 1:175–76
Notestein, Wallace, Vol 1:82
novel cases, Vol 2:371
Nussbaum, Bernard, Vol 2:153, 160, 161, 163, 168–69, 170
Nutter, G. Warren, Vol 1:167–68, 171, 184, 191, 193–94

Oakes, James L., Vol 2:174, 181, 193, 243, 373
Obama, Barack, Vol 1:269, 272; Vol 2:159, 359
Obamacare, Vol 2:359
Obergefell v. Hodges (2015), Vol 2:241
O'Brien, Father, Vol 1:211–12
O'Connor, Sandra Day, Vol 2:358
Ognibene v. Parkes, Vol 2:325–28, 339–41, 392
Oklahoma Press Pub. Co. v. Walling, Vol 1:278
Olds, Irving, Vol 1:192
one-child policy in China, Vol 2:310–12, 315–17
O'Neill, Michael, Vol 2:323
One Person, One Vote, Vol 2:326–27, 339–41
One View of the Cathedral (Calabresi)
   All of the Law, Vol 1:332–33
   applications of, Vol 1:333–34, 336; Vol 2:280
   cheapest cost avoider, Vol 1:307, 332, 339
   eminent domain, Vol 1:329, 330
   'entitlements' language, Vol 1:333
   fourth rule, Vol 1:328–29, 338
   Guido's originality/knowledge/impacts, Vol 1:340
   inalienability rules, Vol 1:330
   incentives, Vol 1:331–32
   inspiration for, Vol 1:338
   language of rights, Vol 1:335
   last responsible employer, Vol 1:339–40
   legal entitlement modeling, Vol 1:171–72, 327, 337
   legal liability rule, Vol 1:171–72
   legal rules setting, Vol 1:334
   liability rules/entitlements structure, Vol 1:327–28
   nuisance, Vol 1:327–30, 336, 338–39
   ownership/shifts of ownership, Vol 1:332–33
   payment of damages, Vol 1:329
   publishing of, Vol 1:330–31
   shifting of entitlements, Vol 1:330
   structure of, Vol 1:333
   title significance, Vol 1:332
   torts/contracts, Vol 1:334–35
   writing of, Vol 1:327
Orefice family, Vol 1:101–2, 104; Vol 2:349–50
"O Sole Mio," Vol 1:103, 112–13
Otanelli, Fraser, Vol 1:123–24

Palko v. Connecticut, Vol 1:272, 280
Palsgraf v. Long Island Railroad Co., Vol 2:216, 243
Pan Am case, Vol 2:177–79, 180, 191–92
Pareto efficient, Vol 1:170
Parker, Daniel B., Vol 1:272; Vol 2:220, 238–39, 291–92, 382, 383, 386, 403–4, 405, 411
Parker, Fred I., Vol 2:174, 179, 186, 305, 306, 376–77
Partito d'Azione (Action Party), Vol 1:13
Partito Liberale Italiano, Vol 1:19
Patterson, Robert, Vol 2:272, 364
Paul IV, Vol 1:90–91
Paul VI, Vol 1:133
penicillin, Vol 1:95
penile plethysmography, Vol 2:43–405
pension rights, Vol 2:371–75, 401
Pentagon Papers case, Vol 1:238; Vol 2:193–94, 323, 400
periodicals licensing in Italy, Vol 1:20
Perlitz, Charlie, Vol 1:212, 213
Petacci, Clara, Vol 1:15
Peters, Ellen, Vol 1:224; Vol 2:155
Petit Cercle Française, Vol 1:107, 122
Philip Morris, Vol 2:233
Phillips v. Martin Marietta Corp, Vol 2:262
Pickering v. Board of Education, Vol 2:338
Pirani, Costanza Levi, Vol 1:78
Pisa, Benvenuta, Vol 1:45
Pisani, Larry, Vol 1:102
"Piss Christ," Vol 2:300
Pius IX, Vol 1:80
Pius XI, Vol 1:15, 24–25
Pius XII, Vol 1:15, 134
Planned Parenthood v. Casey, Vol 1:208
Politics, Economics, and Welfare (Lindblom/Dahl), Vol 1:200
Pollak, Louis H., Vol 2:38–39, 384–85, 396–97
Pollack, Milton, Vol 2:281–82
Pollak, Louis Heilprin, Vol 1:223, 245–46, 252, 256
poll taxes, Vol 2:392
Pooler, Rosemary S., Vol 2:351, 387–88, 411
pornography
   as anti-feminist, Vol 2:145
   First Amendment on, Vol 2:143
   prison discipline, Vol 2:321–24, 334–36

Thomas's interest in, Vol 2:134, 139, 142–43, 144
    on the Wall, Vol 2:108, 112–13, 120–21
Posner, Eric, Vol 2:278
Posner, Richard
    on certification, Vol 2:289, 290
    commonalities with Guido, Vol 1:357–58
    evaluation of Guido's writings, Vol 1:306–7, 339
    free baby market proposal, Vol 1:341, 357
    immigration law jurisprudence, Vol 2:307, 319
    intemperance, Vol 2:190–91
    judicial philosophy, Vol 2:309
    penalty default rules in contract law, Vol 2:276
    photo, Vol 2:273
    on punitive damages, Vol 2:273, 280
    reception in Seventh Circuit, Vol 2:176–77, 180–81, 189
Post, Robert, Vol 2:69–71, 88
post hoc, ergo propter hoc, Vol 2:229
Powell, Lewis, Vol 2:91, 103
Pratt, George C., Vol 2:200, 223
preemption, Vol 2:218–20, 232–36
President Monroe, Vol 1:29–30
Prezzolini, Giuseppe, Vol 1:125
Price v. Yellow Pine Paper Co., Vol 2:214
Priest, George, Vol 1:340–33; Vol 2:389
primogeniture, Vol 1:76, 89, 144
prisoner rights litigation, Vol 2:185
Prison Litigation Reform Act, Vol 2:355
privacy rights, Vol 2:166, 253–54
Problem of Social Cost, The (Coase), Vol 1:288, 290–91, 292, 295
procedural violations, Vol 2:384, 408–9
products liability, Vol 2:217, 219–20, 233–36, 287
property rights of Jews in Italy, Vol 1:80–81, 90–91, 154
"Property Rules, Liability Rules, and Inalienability: One View of the Cathedral" (1972), Vol 1:285
Prosser, William Lloyd, Vol 1:305; Vol 2:221
proximate cause requirement, Vol 2:215–16
Public Law Perspectives on a Private Law Problem (Blum/Kalven), Vol 1:291
public nudity, Vol 2:291–93, 299–302
public nuisance theory, Vol 2:297
public sector unions, Vol 2:188
Puddu v. Royal Netherlands Steamship Co., Vol 2:189
Pullman abstention, Vol 2:294
punitive damages, Vol 2:271–74, 279–80
Purcell, Edward, Vol 2:173
Pye, A. Kenneth, Vol 2:87

Quill v. Vacco, Vol 2:281–86, 295–96
Quine, Willard, Vol 1:181, 187
Quinley v. Cocke, Vol 2:210, 212, 231

racial intermarriage, Vol 2:241, 249–53, 262–63
racial laws in Italy, Vol 1:15, 17, 18, 25, 27, 28, 38, 49, 58–59, 108–10, 116, 127, 139, 154
racial profiling, Vol 2:241, 242–46, 253, 257–61
radians, Vol 1:162, 190
Raggi, Rena, Vol 2:250, 254, 255, 266, 279, 387–88, 389, 406, 407
raisonné, Vol 2:289–90
Rajah v. Mukasey, Vol 2:317
Rakoff, Jack, Vol 2:384, 408
Ramsdell, Charles, Vol 1:136
Randall, Kenneth C., Vol 2:66
Reagan, Ronald, Vol 2:91, 96, 105, 175, 191, 192, 281
Real, Manuel, Vol 2:224
reasonable doubt, Vol 2:378–82, 412–17
reasonable warning, Vol 2:205–8, 289
Reconstruction Amendments, Vol 2:331–32
Reed, Stanley, Vol 1:261
Reform Act of 1832, Vol 2:392–93
Reform Act of 1867, Vol 2:393
regulatory requirements, Vol 2:217–19
Rehnquist, William, Vol 2:286, 333, 352, 379, 384
Reich, Charles, Vol 1:256, 257
Reichman, Jerome, Vol 1:238–39, 253
Reinhardt, Stephen, Vol 2:290, 296, 309
Reisman, Michael, Vol 2:397
rendition policy, Vol 2:395–400, 409–12
Reno, Janet, Vol 2:154, 160
Reporter, The, Vol 1:138
res ipsa loquitor, Vol 2:209–10, 231–32
respondeat superior, Vol 2:222 Vol 2:222
Responsibility Centered Management (RCM), Vol 2:57–58, 63–64
Restrepo v. McElroy, Vol 2:205, 238–39
returning to Italy permanently, Vol 1:135, 148–50, 157–58
Rex, Vol 1:30, 36–38
Reynolds, Lloyd, Vol 1:192
Reynolds v. Sims, Vol 2:325–26, 327
Rezulin, Vol 2:217, 219–20, 233–36
Rhodes scholarship committee, Vol 1:84
Richard Nixon, Esq., on Automobile Liability (Nixon), Vol 1:362, 379–80
Richardson, Elliot, Vol 2:94–95, 101–2
Riggs, T. Lawrason, Vol 1:211, 215
right to commit suicide. *See* assisted suicide/euthanasia
Riley, Richard, Vol 2:169
Roberts, John, Vol 2:220, 325, 359
Robinson, William Callyhan, Vol 1:117–18
Robinson v. Reed Package, Vol 2:225
Rodell, Fred, Vol 1:238, 239, 252, 253

Roe v. Wade, Vol 1:343; Vol 2:128, 166, 185
Rogers, Henry Wade, Vol 2:386
Rogers, James Gamble, Vol 2:75, 76–77
Rogers v. Missouri Pac. R. Co., Vol 1:400
Romano, Roberta, Vol 2:50, 389
Rome, bringing of Jewish slaves to, Vol 1:51, 64–65
Ronald H. Coase medal, Vol 2:277
Roosevelt, Franklin D., Vol 1:107–8, 122–23, 136–37, 247–48, 261
Rose, Carol, Vol 2:53
Rose-Ackerman, Susan, Vol 1:330–34; Vol 2:50–51, 53, 390
Rosen, Jeffrey, Vol 2:109
Rosenbaum, Yankel, Vol 2:256
Ross, Michael, Vol 2:384–85
Rosselli, Amelia/Rosselli family, Vol 1:131–32, 137
Rosselli, Carlo/Nello, Vol 1:12, 14, 19, 20–21, 23–24, 27, 137
Rossi, Bruno, Vol 1:72
Ross v. Hartman, Vol 2:287
Rostow, Eugene
   antitrust classes, Vol 1:232–33
   appointments, Vol 2:91, 393
   approaching Guido as dean, Vol 2:385
   background, Vol 1:241–42
   Bowman and, Vol 1:298
   Cambridge sabbatical, Vol 2:80
   clerkship, personal, Vol 1:228
   as Dean, Vol 2:383
   as example to Guido, Vol 2:383
   generosity, Vol 2:32
   on Guido attending law school, Vol 1:182
   Guido's clerkship, Vol 1:7–240, 258–59
   handling of Guido's education, Vol 1:222
   handling of Guido's teaching career, Vol 1:369
   hiring of, Vol 2:389
   Legal Realism/Legal Process group, Vol 1:256
   letter of recommendation, Vol 1:7–259
   student clerkships, Vol 1:234–36
   teaching style, Vol 1:232–33
   Tyler family and, Vol 1:316
Rostow, Walt Whitman, Vol 1:242
Roukema, Marge, Vol 2:267
Rowland v. Christian, Vol 1:388–89, 397–98
Rubenfeld, Jed, Vol 2:53
Ruckleshaus, William, Vol 2:94–95, 101–2
Ruebhausen, Oscar M., Vol 2:67
running the Court, Vol 2:182
Rutledge, Wiley Blount Jr., Vol 1:223, 245, 263; Vol 2:323
Rylands v. Fletcher, Vol 1:181

Sacco, Luigi, Vol 1:10
Sacco, Nicola, Vol 1:106, 119–20
Sachs, Albert, Vol 1:395

Sack, Robert, Vol 2:250, 252, 291–92, 387–88, 396, 400, 411
Safriet, Barbara, Vol 2:115
Salvemini, Gaetano, Vol 1:12, 20
Salve Regina v. Russell, Vol 2:200–1
same-sex marriage, Vol 2:241
sanity hearings, Vol 2:384–85
Sarfatti, Margherita, Vol 1:17–18
Sargent, Agnes, Vol 1:107
Sargent, Ziegler, Vol 1:106–7, 121
Saturday Evening Post, Vol 1:106–7
Savoy Monarchy, Vol 1:10–11
Saxon-Forti, Anna, Vol 2:433
Say's Law, Vol 1:170–71, 293
Scalia, Antonin, Vol 1:105, 278–79; Vol 2:190–91, 253–54, 358–59, 366, 379, 408–9
Scalia, Salvatore Eugene, Vol 1:105, 124–2; Vol 2:96, 98
Scharff, Brett, Vol 2:345
Schauer, Frederick, Vol 2:321
Scheindlin, Sara, Vol 2:368
Scheindlin, Shira, Vol 2:242, 260
Schmidt, Benno, Vol 2:30, 59, 64, 68–69, 82–83, 110, 114, 118, 155
Schuck, Peter, Vol 2:40–41, 43–44, 112, 117, 122–23, 399–400
Schultz, Vicki, Vol 2:53, 122
Schuster, Alfredo Ildefonso, Vol 1:49, 59
Schwartz, Alan, Vol 1:376–63; Vol 2:7–51, 53
scope of the risk requirement, Vol 2:215–16
Scorpions, The (Feldman), Vol 1:264–65, 276, 278
search and seizure, Vol 2:253–54
Second Circuit court characterization, Vol 2:173, 183–84, 185–86. *See also* judgeship
Second Look doctrine, Vol 1:264, 269–70; Vol 2:283, 284–85, 286, 295–96, 403
Second Temple, Vol 1:50, 51, 63
secularism, Vol 2:332–33
securities fraud, Vol 2:274–76
Selya, Bruce M., Vol 2:294
"Sensation," Vol 2:300
sentencing disparities/cultural prejudices, Vol 2:241, 254–56, 264–67, 269, 276–77
Sephardim, Vol 1:80
Serrano, Andres, Vol 2:300
Sessions, Jeff, Vol 2:319
Sessions, William K. III, Vol 2:386
settlement inducing, Vol 2:371–75, 401
Sewall, Richard, Vol 1:173
Seward, Paul S., Vol 1:191–92
Sex and the Yale Student, Vol 2:143
sex offender evaluation/treatment, Vol 2:43–405
sex plus doctrine, Vol 2:262
Sexton, John, Vol 2:149–50
sexual abuse by priests, Vol 2:199
sexual harassment, Vol 2:131, 132–36, 139–40
sexual orientation, Vol 2:27–264

Seymour, Charles, Vol 1:105
Seymour, Whitney North Sr., Vol 1:229, 250
Shaffer, Zina, Vol 2:37
Shapiro, Fred, Vol 1:339
Sharkey, Catherine, Vol 2:230-31
Sharpton, Al, Vol 2:337
Shelley v. Kramer (1948), Vol 2:241
Shi Liang Lin v. United States DOJ, Vol 2:310-12, 315-17
Shugerman, Jed, Vol 1:281
Shulman, Harry, Vol 1:223, 225, 235, 239, 241, 243, 248-49
Shulman, Steve, Vol 1:101, 224, 230, 235, 240
Siegel, Norman, Vol 2:337
Simon, John, Vol 1:227; Vol 2:35, 40, 55-56, 91, 177
Simon, Larry, Vol 2:397
Simons, Henry, Vol 1:195
Simpson Thacher law firm, Vol 1:228-30, 249
Skull and Bones Society, Vol 1:190
Slovik, Eddie, Vol 1:349, 356
Smoking Opium Exclusion Act of 1909, Vol 2:264-65
Sneed, Joe, Vol 1:391-92
Some Thoughts on Risk Distribution (Calabresi)
   impacts of, Vol 1:285, 289-91, 303, 331, 332, 339
   law/economics approach, Vol 1:292, 303
   publishing date, Vol 1:303
   symmetrical causation, Vol 1:288-302; Vol 2:189
   writing of, Vol 1:227-28
Sopranos, The, Vol 2:246, 266-67
Sotomayor, Sonia, Vol 2:184, 315, 316, 354
Souter, David, Vol 2:105, 131, 165, 171, 245
special circumstances test, Vol 2:368-69
Spector, Arlen, Vol 2:132
Spitzer, Eliot, Vol 2:258, 297
Spur v. Del E. Webb, Vol 1:329, 338-39
Squatrito, Dominic, Vol 2:35-36
Stagl v. Delta Airlines, Vol 2:201-3, 223-24
Stalin, Joseph, Vol 1:10-11
States v. Padilla, Vol 2:260-61
statistical causation, Vol 2:346-49, 361-62
statute interpretation *vs.* construal, Vol 2:250-53
Statute's Lament, Vol 2:252, 263-64
statutorification, Vol 1:391
stereotyping
   exclusionary rule, Vol 2:260-61
   gender-based termination, Vol 2:241, 246-49, 261
   racial profiling, Vol 2:241, 242-46, 253, 257-61
Sterling Law Building renovation
   accreditation as negotiation tool, Vol 2:57, 61, 87
   administrative/faculty offices, Vol 2:77-78
   background, Vol 2:73
   Beinecke Rare Book Library, Vol 2:80-81
   building codes/standards, Vol 2:79, 82-83, 88
   classes simultaneous with, Vol 2:79
   classrooms, Vol 2:77
   clinical program, Vol 2:78-79
   design, Vol 2:75, 77-79
   draws as loans, Vol 2:70-71
   expansion/spatial limitations, Vol 2:80-81, 88
   financing, Vol 2:58, 61, 62, 70-71, 75-76, 85
   First Floor central hall, Vol 2:75
   Guido's hopes for, Vol 2:83
   Guido's motivations, Vol 2:73-74, 85, 86-87
   handicapped accessibility, Vol 2:75
   library, Vol 2:74-75, 79, 85, 86, 89
   location of, Vol 2:85
   moving/symbolism of University, Vol 2:83-85, 88-89
   power plant, Vol 2:82-83, 86-87
   problems with building, Vol 2:74-75
   Second Floor, Vol 2:75, 78
   seminar rooms, Vol 2:77
   student housing, Vol 2:79-80, 81-82, 86, 88
   Tower Parkway, Vol 2:82, 86-87
Sterling Trust, Vol 2:38
Stevens, Carroll, Vol 2:39-40, 41, 42, 43
Stevens, John Paul, Vol 2:265-66
Stevens, Robert, Vol 1:256
Stevenson, Adlai, Vol 1:202
Stevenson, Anne, Vol 1:161, 212
Stewart, Potter, Vol 1:105, 261, 271
Stigler, George, Vol 1:195, 292, 298-99
Stiles, Ezra, Vol 2:84
Stille, Alexander, Vol 1:27
Stith, Kate, Vol 2:124, 155, 162, 187-88
stop-and-frisk, Vol 2:242-46, 253, 257-61
Storrs Lectures, Vol 1:351, 354-55, 383
struzionismo, Vol 1:109, 126
Studley, Steve/Jamie, Vol 2:35-36, 39
Sturges, Wesley, Vol 1:225, 226, 230-32, 241, 252, 257
Sturges v. Bridgman, Vol 1:298-99
Sturley, Winifred, Vol 1:115
Sturzo, Luigi, Vol 1:10
subterfuges
   allocation and, Vol 1:347-48
   Common Law discussion of, Vol 1:344, 351, 396
   mechanisms, Vol 1:346-47
   reasons for using, Vol 1:345-46
   redemptive transparency and, Vol 2:23-24
   Tragic Choices discussion of, Vol 1:296-97, 344-45, 354-55, 363-64
Sullivan & Cromwell, Vol 1:228, 250-51
Summers, Clyde, Vol 1:256
Summers v. Tice, Vol 2:209, 231
Sumner, William Graham, Vol 2:84

Sunstein, Cass, Vol 1:345, 353–48; Vol 2:278, 295–96
suppression of confession and testimony, Vol 2:352–53, 355, 362–64
Swan, Thomas Walter, Vol 2:189
Swiss Bankers case, Vol 2:364

Taber v. Maine, Vol 2:180, 197–201, 204, 222, 223
Table of the Showbread, Vol 1:64
Taichman, Laura, Vol 2:415
Tankleff v. Senkowski, Vol 2:378–82, 412–17
Tapia v. BLCH 3rd Ave, Vol 2:288, 299
Tate, Jack, Vol 1:222, 242–43; Vol 2:36
Tate Letter, Vol 1:242
Tate Letter in International Law, The (Tate), Vol 2:36
taxation reform, Vol 1:301
teacher misconduct, Vol 2:356, 366–67
teaching
    accidents/medical experiments, Vol 1:295–96
    alternatives foregone, Vol 1:296
    on bias, Vol 1:362–63
    brains and character, Vol 1:362
    comparative law, Vol 1:285–86
    context, Vol 1:361–62
    correspondence/compassion, Vol 1:381
    course vision/rationale, Vol 1:368
    differences in classes/people, Vol 1:364–66
    doing good *vs.* doing well, Vol 1:365–66
    Econ 10, Vol 1:221, 222–23
    economic analysis of civil liability, Vol 1:305–6
    externalities/torts, Vol 1:286, 297–300
    final exams, Vol 1:361–62, 376–77
    foolery, Vol 1:381–82
    Gilmore's methods, Vol 1:359–60, 373–74
    Guido as example, Vol 1:372
    Guido's love of, Vol 1:360
    Guido's methods, Vol 1:360–63, 374–75
    interplay between facts and law, Vol 1:368, 370–71
    law/economics approach, Vol 1:291–94, 331–32
    learning from students, Vol 1:367
    leitmotif, Vol 1:369–70
    no negligence defense, Vol 1:296–97
    nonfault allocation of costs, Vol 1:294–95, 303, 306–7
    previous torts scholarship, Vol 1:305
    reasonable person standard, Vol 1:363
    respondeat superior liability, Vol 1:286–87
    selection as career, Vol 1:285–86
    self-consciousness, Vol 1:372–73
    slowing people down, Vol 1:365
    Socratic method, Vol 1:244–45, 252, 374–75
    student discussions, Vol 1:366–67
    student feedback, Vol 1:367, 380–81
    subterfuges, Vol 1:296–97, 363–64
    symmetrical causation, Vol 1:288–90
    techniques, Vol 1:375
    torts paradigm, Vol 1:305–6
    transaction costs, Vol 1:287, 288–89, 292–93, 296–97, 298–300
    transaction costs (Evil Deity), Vol 1:363, 380–60; Vol 2:271
    women's issues, Vol 1:363
    wrongful death, Vol 1:362
Tedeschi, Guido (John)/family, Vol 1:22, 52, 103–4, 116, 127
Testa, Maria, Vol 2:120
"*The hand that held the dagger,*" Vol 1:107, 122–23
"*The Heron,*" Vol 1:144–45, 156
"*The Widow's Offering,*" Vol 2:326, 339–40
Thomas, Clarence
    common law right to recover, Vol 2:238
    conservatism, Vol 2:129–31, 137
    crudity/interest in pornography, Vol 2:134, 139, 142–43, 144
    Danforth relationship with, Vol 2:127–29
    Guido relationship with, Vol 2:165, 167
    Guido's opinion statement, Vol 2:132–33, 139–40
    Guido's testimony, Vol 2:129, 136–37, 138–39, 141–42, 163
    Guido's theory of the case, Vol 2:133–38, 141–42
    immediate risk of physical harm, Vol 2:215
    Johnstone relationship, Vol 2:129
    judicial legacy of, Vol 2:147
    nomination of, Vol 2:105, 127, 129–30, 138–39
    opportunism, Vol 2:130
    political decision-making by, Vol 2:358–59
    portrayals as dumb, Vol 2:129–30, 131, 138
    preemption, Vol 2:218
    remarriage, Vol 2:131
    sexual harassment allegations, Vol 2:131, 132–36, 139–40
    torts expertise, Vol 2:235
    Yale alumni support of, Vol 2:132
    Yale culture 1970s, Vol 2:133–34, 142–44
    Yale student career, Vol 2:143–44
Thomas, James A., Vol 2:35–36, 44–45
Thompson, Mike, Vol 2:25, 46–47, 89
Three Mile Island, Vol 2:165–66
Tinker v. Des Moines Independent Community School District, Vol 1:282
Tite, Kenneth, Vol 1:185
Titus (Emperor), Vol 1:51, 64–65
Tobin, James, Vol 1:169, 170–71, 184, 192, 196–97
Torts: Cases and Materials (James/Shulman), Vol 1:243

Torture Memos, Vol 1:279
Town of Greece v. Galloway, Vol 1:268; Vol 2:328–33, 341–42
Tragic Choices (Calabresi)
   on absolutism, Vol 1:279
   academics role, Vol 1:350
   behavioral realities in, Vol 2:269, 277–78
   in cognate societies, Vol 1:348
   Coleman's review of, Vol 1:207
   collaboration with Bobbitt, Vol 1:341–44, 353
   cost/benefit analyses, Vol 1:345–46, 353–54
   critiques of, Vol 2:277–78
   distributional values, Vol 1:346, 350, 357
   Guido's motivations for writing, Vol 1:335, 348–49
   impacts of, Vol 1:285
   individual choice, Vol 1:346–47
   language/structure of, Vol 1:342–43
   "life-or-death" situations, Vol 1:341
   pearl beyond price, Vol 1:345, 353–54
   privileges/obligations allocation, Vol 1:341, 347
   publishing of, Vol 1:341
   resource allocation, Vol 1:347–48, 355–56
   sacrificing the worthiest, Vol 1:349–50
   structure of, Vol 1:395–96
   subterfuges, Vol 1:296–97, 344–45, 354–55, 363–64
   subterfuges, mechanisms, Vol 1:346–47
   subterfuges, reasons for using, Vol 1:345–46
   subterfuges and allocation, Vol 1:347–48
   transaction costs, Vol 1:296–97, 349–50
transaction costs
   behavioral realities, Vol 2:271
   characterization, Vol 1:287, 288–89, 292–93, 296–97, 298–300
   Coase on, Vol 1:170–71, 194–95, 286, 292, 293
   Evil Deity scenario, Vol 1:363, 380–60; Vol 2:271
   Tragic Choices discussion of, Vol 1:296–97, 349–50
"Transaction Costs, Resource Allocation and Liability Rules," Vol 1:292–93
Traynor, Roger J., Vol 1:391; Vol 2:230
Tremaine, James G., Vol 1:191–92
Treves, Guido, Vol 1:7–8, 16–17
Tribe, Larry, Vol 2:387
Trieste, Italy, Vol 1:57
Triffin, Robert, Vol 1:169, 192
Trillin, Calvin, Vol 1:190
Troy, Daniel, Vol 2:232
Trubek, David, Vol 2:50, 397, 399–400
Trubek, Louise, Vol 2:399–400
Truitt, Max O'Rell, Vol 1:240
Truman, Harry S., Vol 1:202, 261

Trump, Donald, Vol 1:272; Vol 2:102, 159, 407
Tullock, Gordon, Vol 1:194
Tunick v. Safir, Vol 2:281, 291–93, 295, 299–302
Turley, Jonathan, Vol 2:336
Tushnet, Mark, Vol 2:398–99
Tuskegee syphilis experiments, Vol 2:383
tutors/Roman nobility, Vol 1:51, 65
Tversky, Amos, Vol 2:278–79
Twerski, Aaron, Vol 2:27–228
Two Jewish Justices (Burt), Vol 1:219
two-judge panels, Vol 2:351
Tylenol case, Vol 2:215
Tyler, Morris F., Vol 1:319, 320

Umberto I, Vol 1:85, 95
"Uneasy Case for Progressive Taxation, The," Vol 1:301
Uniform Certification of Questions of Law Act of 1967, Vol 2:294
Unions and the Cities, The (Winter/Wellington), Vol 1:254
United States v. Aquart, Vol 2:388–91, 409
United States v. Bayless, Vol 2:352–53, 355, 362–64
United States v. Fell, Vol 2:385–88, 406–8
United States v. Ingram, Vol 2:241, 254–56, 264–67, 269, 278–79
United States v. Martinez, Vol 2:375–78, 417–19
United States v. McLaurin, Vol 2:43–405
United States v. Nelson, Vol 2:241–42, 255, 256–57
United States v. Preacely, Vol 2:255
United States v. Quinones, Vol 2:384, 408–9
United States v. Then, Vol 2:205, 265
University of Bologna, Vol 1:67
University of Michigan, Vol 1:285–86
unjust convictions, Vol 2:378–82, 412–17

Vance, Cyrus, Vol 1:228, 229, 249–50
Van Graafeiland, Ellsworth, Vol 2:178–79, 182, 191–92, 200, 223, 291–93, 295
Van Voorhis, John, Vol 2:178
Vanzetti, Bartolomeo, Vol 1:106, 119–20
Varano, Vincenzo, Vol 1:308
Varet, Elizabeth (née Rosenwald), Vol 1:137–38
Vaughan v. Menlove, Vol 1:375
Victor Emmanuel II, Vol 1:85
Victor Emmanuel III, Vol 1:10, 19, 138–39
Vietnam War, Vol 1:242, 343–44; Vol 2:110, 115
Vilensky, Robert, Vol 2:297
Vincent v. Lake Erie, Vol 1:368
Vincent v. Pabst Brewing Co., Vol 1:387–88, 398–99
Viner, Jacob, Vol 1:195
Vogel, Louis, Vol 1:397
voting rights of felons, Vol 2:391–95, 401–3

Walker, John M., Vol 2:177, 243–44, 245, 246, 250, 257–58, 259, 294, 375, 376, 386, 417
Wallich, Henry, Vol 1:169, 192, 196
Wall/Wallsters
  civility/respect necessity, Vol 2:117–18
  employee upset with content, Vol 2:117
  free speech expression upon, Vol 2:107–8, 109–10, 118
  incitements to violence, Vol 2:108
  military recruitment, Vol 2:114
  motivations for protesting, Vol 2:115–16
  motivations for student inclusion, Vol 2:116–17
  offensive speech, Vol 2:110–11
  penis on the wall affair, Vol 2:116–17, 119, 122–23
  pornography, Vol 2:108, 112–13, 120–21
  racism/stereotyping, Vol 2:27–123
  signing requirement, Vol 2:108–9
  tape on, Vol 2:123–24
  teachable moments, Vol 2:110–11, 113–14, 115, 117, 119–20, 124–25
Walpin, Gerald, Vol 2:330
Wanda Whips Wall Street, Vol 2:112–13, 120–21
Warner-Lambert v. Kent, Vol 2:236
Warren, Earl, Vol 1:237–38, 272; Vol 2:68, 185
Washington, George Thomas, Vol 2:185
Washington v. Glucksberg, Vol 2:295
Waube v. Warrington, Vol 2:214
Wechsler, Herbert, Vol 1:327
Weicker, Lowell, Vol 2:154
Weinberg, Bob, Vol 1:173
Weinrib, Ernest, Vol 1:309–10
Weinstein, Jack, Vol 2:269, 297, 386
Weiss, Paul, Vol 1:117–18
Wellington, Harry
  agenda as Dean, Vol 2:29, 42–43, 389–90, 402
  appointments, Vol 1:394
  background, Vol 1:254
  Bork and, Vol 2:92
  Cabranes support by, Vol 2:157
  fundraising, Vol 2:31, 38–39
  influence on Guido's writings, Vol 1:331
  Legal Realism/Legal Process synthesis, Vol 1:256
  professional life, Vol 1:402
  public sector unions position, Vol 2:188
  Registrar's Office, Vol 2:37
  Rostow and, Vol 1:241–42
  Second Look jurisprudence and, Vol 1:280
  selection as Dean, Vol 2:388–89, 401–2
  on starting points, Vol 2:269–70
  teaching style, Vol 1:233–34
  Woodward Committee Report, Vol 2:110

Wesley, Richard C., Vol 2:184–85, 217, 233, 290–91, 295, 297–98, 301–2, 389
"When Does the Rule of Liability Matter?," Vol 1:293
White, Byron, Vol 2:168
White, Harry D., Vol 2:357, 367–70
Whiteman, Hal, Vol 1:164–65
Whitney, Eli, Vol 1:122
Whittaker, Charles, Vol 1:261, 272
Who Governs? Democracy and Power in an American City (Dahl), Vol 1:199–200
Wiggin, Fritz, Vol 2:34
Wilkerson v. McCarthy (1949), Vol 1:385–86, 400
Wilkinson, Harvey, Vol 2:329
Wilkinson, John, Vol 2:111, 119
William L. Prosser Award, Vol 2:230–31
Willkie, Wendell, Vol 1:105, 107–8, 123
Wilson, James, Vol 1:391
Wilson, Woodrow, Vol 1:105
Wimsatt, William Kurtz Jr., Vol 1:117–18
Winter, Ralph, Vol 1:224, 233–34, 254; Vol 2:93, 103, 175, 181, 188, 202, 293, 391–92
Winternitz, Milton, Vol 1:117–18
Wise, Stephen, Vol 1:140
Witt, John F., Vol 2:173, 184
wives' dowries/husbands' debts, Vol 1:52, 66
wives' unhappiness, Vol 1:229–30
Woe Unto You, Lawyers! (Rodell), Vol 1:253
Wolf, Elsa, Vol 2:36–37
women's liberation, Vol 2:134, 142–43
Women's Rights Movement, Vol 2:248
"Wonderful World of Blum and Kalven The," Vol 1:291
Woodward, C. Vann, Vol 2:110
Woodward Committee Report, Vol 2:110
Worcester v. Georgia, Vol 2:325–26
World War II
  anti-Italian sentiment, Vol 1:130–31
  deportation of Jews, Vol 1:139–40
  Exclusion Program, Vol 1:137
  fate of relatives, Vol 1:132–36
  Final Solution, Vol 1:140
  on home front, Vol 1:129–31
  Italians as enemy aliens, Vol 1:130, 137
  Nazi extermination camps, Vol 1:134, 139, 140–41
  Pearl Harbor bombing, Vol 1:129, 136–37
  Sicily assault, Vol 1:135, 138–39, 141
  VE Day, Vol 1:135
  visiting old friends, Vol 1:131–32
Worswick, G. D. N., Vol 1:182, 184, 186–88, 205
Wright, Charles A., Vol 1:253
writ of habeus corpus, Vol 2:378–82, 412–17
wrongful convictions, Vol 2:378–82, 412–17
Wyeth v. Levine, Vol 2:220, 237

Wylie, Karen, Vol 1:161, 188
Wylie, Philip, Vol 1:161

Yale Daily News, Vol 1:173, 190, 192, 215, 216; Vol 2:69, 120–21, 123
Yale Journal of Law and Feminism, Vol 2:43–44
Yale Law Journal, Vol 1:227–28, 230, 238, 249, 287–95; Vol 2:38, 86–87, 278–79, 408
Yale Law School. *See also* Deanship; teaching
  administration of, Vol 2:391–92
  Administrative Law, Vol 1:233
  Advanced Contracts, Vol 1:233–34
  Antitrust, Vol 1:232–33
  Appointments Committee, Vol 2:386
  Arbitration, Vol 1:230–32
  board games/bias, Vol 1:259
  Business Units—Corporations, Vol 1:224
  class ranking, Vol 1:227
  clerkships, Vol 1:234–36, 257–58
  Constitutional Law, Vol 1:223
  Contracts, Vol 1:222
  Corporate Tax, Vol 1:225
  Criminal Law, Vol 1:223
  Cromwell chair, Vol 1:228, 250–51
  Dark Ages, Vol 2:396, 397
  debt as control, Vol 2:38–40, 58
  Debtor's Estates/bankruptcy, Vol 1:233
  earnings, Vol 1:221
  Estate and Gift Tax, Vol 1:225, 370–65; Vol 2:36
  exam results, Vol 1:226
  faculty hiring process, Vol 2:31–33, 48–50, 270, 389–90, 399–400
  first year curriculum/teachers, Vol 1:222–25
  functionalism, Vol 1:231
  Future Interests, Vol 1:225–26
  heraldic symbol, Vol 1:256
  hiring prejudices, Vol 1:228, 250–51
  Income Tax, Vol 1:225
  legal realism, Vol 1:7–252
  legal realism/legal process synthesis, Vol 1:256–57
  Negotiable Instruments, Vol 1:225, 360
  overview, Vol 1:221
  President selection procedure, Vol 2:155–56
  Procedure, Vol 1:222
  Procedure Two, Vol 1:224
  Property, Vol 1:223, 224, 238, 369
  Real Estate Investments, Vol 1:369–70
  removal of significant records from, Vol 2:176
  Rostow's letter of recommendation, Vol 1:7–259
  second year curriculum/teachers, Vol 1:225–28
  seminar requirement, Vol 1:230–31
  slaughter of the innocents, Vol 2:124, 385–87, 397–99
  Sterling Law Buildings, Vol 2:38
  summer associate experience, Vol 1:228–30, 249
  teaching Econ 10, Vol 1:221, 222–23
  tenure, Vol 2:27–125, 386–87, 397–99
  third year curriculum/teachers, Vol 1:230–34
  Torts, Vol 1:222, 225, 286
  University of Chicago attitudes towards, Vol 1:357
Yale Law Women, Vol 2:120–21, 143–44
Yale University
  Analytical Economics major, Vol 1:169–70
  banking as career, Vol 1:175
  barracks as dormitories, Vol 1:164–65, 190
  cases and facts emphasis, Vol 1:171–72
  Catholic Chapel, Vol 1:211–12
  Chicago School of economics, Vol 1:167–68, 170, 194, 195
  command economics, Vol 1:161, 199
  Dean Acheson gambit, Vol 1:177–78, 202
  Economics Department as leftists, Vol 1:168–69
  Economics Department reconstruction, Vol 1:169, 192–93
  economics/Econ 10, Vol 1:167–68, 191–93
  Elizabethan Club, Vol 1:174, 182, 201
  exclusion policies, Vol 1:105–6, 117–19
  gay culture, Vol 1:174
  Graduate Records Exam, Vol 1:180
  Guido's political identity, Vol 1:172–73
  Guido's priorities, Vol 1:173–74
  influences on Guido, Vol 1:170–72
  Law School Aptitude Test, Vol 1:180
  most loved courses, Vol 1:167
  Pigouvian strain of economics, Vol 1:170, 198–99, 288, 298–99
  Rhodes scholarship, Vol 1:167, 174, 175–78, 201
  Rhodes selection committee/Guido, Vol 1:177, 352, 364
  Russell Henry Chittenden Prize, Vol 1:169, 200
  "Semi-micro Qualitative Analysis," Vol 1:166
  sibling rivalry, Vol 1:165–67, 189
  Timothy Dwight College, Vol 1:174
  Vienna School of economics, Vol 1:193
  Virginia School of economics, Vol 1:167–68, 193–94
Yandle, Stephen, Vol 2:37–38, 39, 43, 54
Ybarra v. Spangard, Vol 2:209, 231
Yeshiva High School case, Vol 2:356, 366–67
Yoo, John, Vol 2:323
Yoshino, Kenji, Vol 2:248–49, 266
Young, William G., Vol 2:279

Zamorani, Amilcare, Vol 1:72
Zamorani, Eva, Vol 1:57, 72

Zarda v. Altitude Express, Vol 2:250–51, 263–64
Zatz, Noah, Vol 2:247, 266
zekenim, Vol 1:51, 175
Zevi, Tulia Calabi, Vol 1:100
Zipursky, Ben, Vol 1:310
Zuccherificio Agricolo Ferrarese, Vol 1:89–90
Zuccherificio di Sermide, Vol 1:16
Zuchowicz v. United States, Vol 2:202, 208–13, 228–30
Zweigert, Konrad, Vol 1:339